D1728553

Public Transport in Developing Countries

Related books

ELVIK & VAA	Handbook of Road Safety Measures
BREWER, BUTTON & HENSHER	Handbook of Logistics & Supply-Chain Management
BUTTON & HENSHER	Handbook of Transport Systems and Traffic Control
BUTTON & HENSHER	Handbook of Transport Strategy, Policy and Institutions
HENSHER & BUTTON	Handbook of Transport and Environment
HENSHER & BUTTON	Handbook of Transport Modelling
HENSHER, BUTTON, HAYNES & STOPHER	Handbook of Transport Geography and Spatial Systems

Related journals

Transport Policy
Editor: M. Ben-Akiva

Transportation Research Part A: Policy and Practice
Editor: P. Goodwin

Cities
Editor: A. Kirby

For details of all Elsevier transportation titles please go to:
www.elseviersocialsciences.com/transportation

PUBLIC TRANSPORT IN DEVELOPING COUNTRIES

Richard Iles

2005

ELSEVIER

Amsterdam – Boston – Heidelberg – London – New York – Oxford
Paris – San Diego – San Francisco – Singapore – Sydney – Tokyo

ELSEVIER B.V.
Radarweg 29
P.O. Box 211
1000 AE Amsterdam
The Netherlands

ELSEVIER Inc.
525 B Street, Suite 1900
San Diego
CA 92101-4495
USA

ELSEVIER Ltd
The Boulevard, Langford
Lane, Kidlington
Oxford OX5 1GB
UK

ELSEVIER Ltd
84 Theobalds Road
London
WC1X 8RR
UK

First edition 2005

Library of Congress Cataloging in Publication Data
A catalog record is available from the Library of Congress.

British Library Cataloguing in Publication Data
A catalogue record is available from the British Library.

ISBN: 0-08-044558-6

♾ The paper used in this publication meets the requirements of ANSI/NISO Z39.48-1992 (Permanence of Paper).
Printed in The Netherlands.

CONTENTS

PREFACE

SCOPE AND PURPOSE OF THIS BOOK

Transport problems in both developed and developing countries, and the planning and management of transport systems in developed countries, have been the subject of numerous books. However, while many of the characteristics of public transport are common throughout the world, there are others which are unique, or of greater significance, to developing countries. In addition, with a higher proportion of the population dependent on public transport in these countries, the problems tend to be much more critical. Thus there is a need for a book which addresses the issues of planning, regulation, and management of public transport specifically in developing countries.

This book aims to meet that requirement. It examines and explains the problems and characteristics of public transport systems in developing countries, and discusses the alternative modes, management methods, and forms of ownership, control, regulation and funding, in the context of different stages of development, operating environments and cultural backgrounds. While it deals with urban, rural and long distance transport services, a significant part of the content is devoted to road-based public transport systems in urban areas: this emphasis reflects the magnitude of the urban transport problem, and the predominance of road transport in most developing countries. However, in the planning or operation of any public transport system, it is necessary at all times to consider the alternatives, as well as the complementarity of the different modes. Other forms of transport, including light rail transit, suburban and long-distance rail, are therefore also covered in this book, albeit in much less depth than the principal road transport modes. The planning of bus services, particularly in urban areas, is covered in some detail, since this is often an area of considerable weakness. Similarly, the management of transport services and the maintenance of vehicles, including vehicle design and transport fleet planning, are also dealt with at length.

There is no clear definition of a "developing country". The term tends to be used loosely, as it is in this book, and applies mainly to the poorer countries of the world, principally those in Asia, Africa and South America. Every country in the world is developing to some extent, although the rate of development varies significantly; some countries, which may still be regarded as developing, have reached a much more advanced level of development than others. Some are in fact becoming poorer: populations are increasing rapidly, but economic growth is slow or even negative, so that purchasing power is diminishing, and achievable standards, including those of transport services, are falling as a result.

There are a number of important differences between the operation of public transport in developing and developed countries. Income levels are lower in developing countries, resulting in low car ownership and hence a strong demand for public transport, and a supply of relatively cheap labour; low incomes also lead to problems of affordability of fares. There is often a lack of skills, at various levels: skilled drivers and mechanics, as well as skilled managers, may be scarce. In the poorer countries shortage of funds is a major problem, while political instability, poor enforcement of laws and regulations, and corruption may have a significant effect on the management of a transport system. Road conditions tend to be difficult, with poor road surfaces on inter-city and rural routes, and severe traffic congestion in urban areas, while climate is often more of a problem in developing than in developed countries. Standards of safety, comfort, punctuality, reliability and air and noise pollution, and users' expectations, are often far lower than those in developed countries; for example, people in some countries do not expect buses to run to schedule, and are prepared to endure long waiting times, and to travel in conditions which would be unacceptable elsewhere.

While the developing countries have many characteristics in common with one another, there are also very significant differences between them, particularly in terms of culture, geography, expertise and stage of development. No two countries or cities are alike, and each has different problems. Many of the problems discussed are not encountered in every country, while others may vary considerably in severity between one country and another. Similarly, although in broad terms the potential solutions are often similar, and some measures are applicable in most situations, the differences must be recognised and taken into account. What may be appropriate in one case may not be workable or acceptable in another, and solutions need to be tailored so that they can work within the prevailing environment. In addition, while the highest possible standards should be aimed for, it is important to be realistic with regard to what can and cannot be achieved. The objective of this book is therefore not to prescribe universal or "ideal" solutions to the problems, but to show how the various options for future development may be identified, and how to determine which are most appropriate in the circumstances.

Several of the countries mentioned in this book may be regarded as developed in many respects, although their transport problems may be similar to those in much less developed countries. In any case, much of the content of the book will apply equally to developed countries, and examples from developed countries have been included where these are considered to be useful or relevant. Since the pace of development in some countries is rapid, many of the specific examples given in this book may be out of date; this does not, however, detract from their relevance or validity.

THE AUTHOR

Richard Iles began his career in transport in the United Kingdom in 1964, but has spent most of his working life in developing countries. He was born in England in 1945, and was interested in transport from an early age, choosing to study economics at the University of Newcastle-upon-Tyne with a view to eventually working in the transport industry. At that time there were few degree courses with a significant transport content, and his course was no exception, but as an undergraduate he submitted a dissertation on the economic problems of rural transport. After receiving an Honours Degree he spent a further two years at Newcastle as a postgraduate carrying out research into economic aspects of the co-ordination of transport. As a student he worked during the vacations for Scottish Omnibuses Ltd. in Edinburgh, as a bus driver and in various administrative capacities; on leaving university he joined another major Scottish bus company, the Central S.M.T. Company, as a junior manager.

After a few years with Central he decided to broaden his transport experience and moved into the logistics field as a distribution depot manager for a food company. This was followed by a spell as manager of a London coach company, operating long distance and tourist services. He then entered the consultancy profession, in which he was involved in a variety of projects in passenger and freight transport and distribution, both in the United Kingdom and overseas. Finding overseas work interesting and stimulating, in 1977 he joined United Transport Overseas, which later became United Transport International (UTI), a holding company with subsidiaries in road passenger and freight transport in many parts of the world.

With UTI he worked first as a consultant on assignments in several countries, and later in the management of some of its subsidiaries in Africa. In Kenya, he was involved in the management of urban and long-distance bus services, a large tourist operation and a passenger and vehicle ferry service. For six years he was Managing Director of United Transport Malawi Ltd, which was jointly owned by the Malawi Government and UTI, and operated passenger transport services throughout Malawi and into neighbouring countries, as well as freight and car hire operations. Following UTI's decision to withdraw from transport operation in developing countries, he started a small consultancy business, IBIS Transport Management Services, in 1990, but has been operating as an independent transport consultant since 1996. In this capacity he has worked in more than twenty different countries in Africa, Asia, the Middle East and the Caribbean. As well as advising on passenger transport, he has worked on other road transport projects including several involving the management of government vehicle fleets in various African countries.

1

PROBLEMS AND CHARACTERISTICS OF PUBLIC TRANSPORT IN DEVELOPING COUNTRIES

AN ILLUSTRATION

It is late afternoon on a weekday in a large city in the tropics. The weather is hot and humid, and the heat reflects from the road surface and from the broken concrete of the footpaths. Some shade is provided by the concrete spans of an elevated highway, its supporting columns scarred by frequent assaults by badly driven vehicles. The traffic, both at street level and on the highway, is congested and slow moving; for long periods it does not move at all. Vehicles are illegally parked along both sides of the street; it is difficult to walk along the footpaths because these, too, are used as additional parking space by the owners and customers of the adjacent shops. The air is filled with exhaust fumes and the sound of motor horns; when the traffic does move, the noise level increases with the sound of badly tuned engines and defective silencers.

Private cars, many carrying only the driver, some chauffeur-driven with a single passenger in the rear seat, and others carrying more than they were designed to, are interspersed with taxis whose drivers are particularly aggressive in their attempts to maximise their earnings; all taxis seem to be occupied, and potential passengers peer anxiously at each in the hope of finding one available for hire.

Drivers are irritable and impatient, and have little consideration for one another or for pedestrians; some have had to park long distances from their places of work, and have struggled along crowded pavements to find their cars; some were obstructed by other inconsiderate drivers who had double-parked, requiring much use of the horn before the offending vehicles were moved. Motor cycles weave noisily between the cars, intimidating pedestrians who are attempting to cross the road.

There are long, undisciplined queues at the bus stops. There are two kinds of bus: large single-deckers with two doors, and smaller "minibuses" with about twelve seats. All are disreputable, old, shabby, badly maintained, and unreliable. All are crowded: the larger buses have over 100 passengers on board, mostly standing, and several clinging precariously to handrails in the doorways. The minibuses have up to twenty passengers crushed into their twelve seats, and some passengers crouching between the seats: there is insufficient headroom to stand upright. The passengers at the bus stops rush at each bus as it approaches, and some manage to squeeze aboard, often gaining only a toehold on the step and a finger-hold on the handrail. The majority must wait for the next bus to arrive; there is no means of knowing when that will be, or whether it will have room for them.

It will be several hours before all passengers reach their homes, and many will have to walk for thirty minutes or more after leaving the bus. Passengers complain bitterly about the irregular bus service and about the buses themselves. They grumble that the bus owners have no consideration for passengers' safety, comfort or convenience, and charge excessive fares, which they can barely afford. Bus drivers drive dangerously, and race each other to the stops for passengers. The conductors are rude and unhelpful, and cheat the passengers whenever they can; some of them refuse to let schoolchildren board their buses, since they pay lower fares than adults. Many passengers have to transfer more than once from one bus to another during the course of their journeys, suffering yet another long wait and another scramble for a place. The buses frequently break down, but there is rarely a relief vehicle, and the stranded passengers must wait for another bus with the capacity to take them; fares are rarely refunded in these circumstances. Passengers are vulnerable to pickpockets, and may even occasionally experience armed robbery. They certainly do not feel they are getting value for their money; but this is the way things are, and the majority have long been resigned to the situation.

This illustration may seem over-dramatised to those unfamiliar with the problems of developing countries. But it is typical of large cities in many parts of the world. It is depressing; but even more depressing is the fact that in many cities these problems are worsening by the day. More cars are appearing on the road, increasing congestion further. There are increasing numbers of bus passengers requiring transport, but the supply of buses does not keep up: in fact the number of buses in service is declining in many cases, as vehicles wear out and insufficient funds are available for their replacement. As city populations increase, so does the size of the cities, and people have to travel even greater distances from home to work.

Not all of the problems described are experienced in every city, but many of them are common to all. Different, but often equally unpalatable problems, are experienced by long-distance and rural travellers. It is difficult to quantify them all; but it is a fact that this kind of situation hinders development and contributes to a poor quality of life. However, as this book sets out to demonstrate, measures can be taken to improve matters, within the financial capabilities of most developing countries, provided there is commitment on the part of everybody concerned.

THE ROLE OF PUBLIC TRANSPORT IN DEVELOPING COUNTRIES

Civilised life depends on transport, for the movement of goods from where they are produced to where they are needed, and for the movement of people from their places of residence to where they must go to pursue all the activities of life, such as work, education, shopping and leisure activities. A good transport system is vital to a country's development; at the same time the factors affecting the development of a country play an important part in determining the way in which its transport system evolves. Ensuring that the transport system develops in the way which is most conducive to the overall development of the country can have far-reaching benefits, and conversely, failing to do so will have an adverse effect on development.

Passenger transport is required to move people from one place to another, and requirements vary considerably between different places and between different social groups. In some areas people travel in large numbers at the same time; in others there are few people, who travel infrequently. There are people who travel daily to and from their places of employment, and there are those who use public transport less frequently, for example as a means of carrying their produce to market. There are some people who can afford cars, and at the other end of the scale there are those who can barely afford the most basic form of transport.

Populations in most developing countries are increasing much faster than car ownership levels, and therefore an increasing proportion of the population is dependent on public transport except for very short journeys. In most countries, walking is the most common mode of travel for distances of up to one or two kilometres in urban areas, and much farther in rural areas; those who own bicycles tend to use them for journeys of up to about eight kilometres, beyond which public transport is the preferred mode. Public transport also provides an alternative to those who have private transport, but are sometimes deterred from using it by traffic congestion, parking difficulties or problems in accessing certain streets, although in practice it is relatively unusual, particularly in developing countries, for car owners to use public transport to any significant extent. However, in many developing countries families tend to be large, so that even if there is a car belonging to a household, most members of the family are still likely to use public transport for at least some of their travel.

Public transport is therefore vital for the vast majority without access to private transport. There is need for personal mobility, in particular for access to employment opportunities, but with low income levels affordability is a common problem, while the services provided are often regarded as inadequate.

Most of the transport problems experienced in developing countries are similar to those found everywhere in the world, although there may be significant differences in magnitude, while some are peculiar to developing countries. In most western countries, demand for public transport, and therefore the level of service provided, have declined as car ownership has increased; by contrast, public transport services in many developing countries have also deteriorated, but in the face of rapidly increasing demand.

As discussed in more detail later, the main contributory factors to the public transport problems of most developing countries are rapid growth in population, particularly in the urban areas; low standards of efficiency, reliability and safety; poor enforcement of regulations; and shortage of money. A special characteristic of most developing countries is the speed at which they are developing, and in certain respects some are developing very quickly indeed: in less than a hundred years some have achieved what has taken the present developed countries many centuries to achieve. In particular, the rate of population growth in most developing countries is very high, and it is not unusual for population to double within a generation. Rapid growth of cities is a major problem; in many developing countries, the rate of urbanisation is so great that even in countries which were predominantly agricultural in the past, the population living in urban areas now exceeds that living in rural areas, and the disparity is increasing steadily.

The pace of change brings its own problems, since developments in some fields are inevitably faster than in others, particularly in urban areas, where the transport systems and infrastructure have often failed to keep pace with the rapid growth; formal transport operators have been unable to cope, and have been largely replaced by informal systems, which do not provide the same quality of service. In nearly every case, public transport is lacking in both capacity and quality. In addition, despite relatively low levels of car ownership, there is chronic traffic congestion in many cities which is attributable to private transport and often also to a scarcity of road space.

Inadequate public transport services have a detrimental effect on the economy, and there would be far-reaching benefits if the demand for public transport could be satisfied in order to enable people to go about their business without unnecessary hindrance. Improved public transport services, particularly in urban areas, would help to reduce the tendency for passengers to upgrade to private transport as soon as they can afford to, and the alternatives between investment in urban road infrastructure and improvements in public transport should therefore always be carefully assessed. In many cases, if expenditure on urban road improvements were instead invested sensibly in appropriate public transport measures, the benefits would be far greater. Yet in virtually every case, public transport services in developing countries are far from satisfactory. The root causes of the problem are complex and inter-related. For example, bus services may be unreliable because of lack of maintenance of the vehicles; this in turn may be due to lack of funds, which itself may be attributable to the form of regulation arising from inappropriate political decisions.

OPERATING ENVIRONMENT

The public transport operating environment is determined by various geographic, climatic, demographic, political, institutional, economic, environmental and cultural factors, as discussed below.

Geographic and Climatic Factors

The principal geographic factors which affect the provision of transport services are the size of a country, and its location, topography and climate. Size will affect the requirement for long distance services, and in a very large country this may entail journeys of more than one day's travelling. The shape of a country also sometimes causes problems; for example, the direct route between the eastern and western parts of Mozambique is through Malawi, involving two border crossings, and the alternative route without leaving the country is much longer.

The most relevant aspects of location are distance from the coast, and the number of countries en route to the coast. Direct access to sea ports is a major advantage for any country, and creates demand for international freight transport. Landlocked countries are at a disadvantage, since all imports and exports, except those which are received by air, must be transported through neighbouring countries; as a result, the costs of imported essential items for the operation of a transport service, such as fuel, tyres, spare parts and the vehicles themselves may be increased significantly, while there are also increased delays in deliveries which may create serious problems.

Geography also influences population distribution: mountains, lakes and rivers, and soil types determine where crops can be grown and hence population distribution and density. Topography affects the facility with which passengers and goods can be transported within the country. Difficult terrain impedes communication and makes the construction of roads and railways costly: some countries, such as Indonesia and the Philippines which comprise large numbers of islands, are heavily dependent on air and water transport; a mountainous country may depend almost entirely on road transport, while in a very flat country rail transport has greater potential.

Although not strictly a geographic factor, urban layout affects transport provision. In several former British colonies, such as Zimbabwe and Zambia, and particularly in South Africa, indigenous population was traditionally housed in townships, which were often a considerable distance from city centres; this pattern necessitated relatively long urban bus routes, with the majority of passengers travelling for the full length of the route. In other cities, land use is more mixed, with residential, commercial and industrial activities in close proximity, resulting in generally shorter travelling distances, and different bus route patterns.

Climatic conditions affect the demand for both freight and passenger transport services, and their operation, in a number of ways. As well as making transport operation more difficult, problems attributable to climatic factors can result in significant increases in costs, and must be taken into consideration in the design of vehicles and infrastructure, and in the planning and scheduling of services.

Climate affects agricultural activity, which in turn influences the seasonality of transport demand, particularly for long distance services, and also affects road conditions. The intense heat and heavy rain which are characteristic of tropical climates can damage road surfaces, particularly unsurfaced roads which are often impassable during rainy seasons, making some rural areas inaccessible to motor vehicles at these times, while on surfaced roads, if minor damage is not repaired expeditiously, the rate of deterioration will accelerate rapidly during periods of heavy rainfall. Extremely cold climates also cause problems: roads may become dangerous or impassable due to snow or ice, while buses may suffer from cold-start problems. Finally, periodic climatic disasters such as heavy rainfall or floods, washing away roads and bridges or blocking roads with landslides, are also more prevalent in developing countries, and can cause major disruption of transport services.

Demographic Factors

Population density, distribution and growth are three very important factors in determining a country's passenger transport needs. A densely populated country obviously has a greater need for transport services than one of similar size which is sparsely populated; a scattered population may result in greater demand for long-distance transport than a more concentrated population; and rapid population growth creates additional demand which in many cases is not satisfied.

A serious demographic problem in many countries is the steady shift of population from the rural areas to the cities, resulting in rapid, and often totally uncontrolled growth in urban areas. To some extent this is a direct result of national population growth. As the number of people living in a rural area reaches the point where there are too many to work on the available land, and subsistence farming can no longer support everybody, people tend to move to the towns and cities in search of employment. In some countries the problem is exacerbated by inappropriate farming practices which are reducing agricultural yields. Thus in many parts of the world there are massive urban population explosions. Even if there are insufficient jobs in the city for everybody, many still migrate in the hope of finding some employment, congregating in the sprawling shanty towns which surround many cities.

This places a considerable strain on urban transport services, in three ways: first the increased population results in demand for an increased number of passenger trips; second, because of the increasing sizes of the cities the average length of journey is increasing; and third, increasing traffic congestion results in reduced productivity of road transport vehicles. There is a strong relationship between the size of a city and the average length of passenger journey: in general terms, the larger the city, the longer the length of journey. The exact relationship depends on factors such as population density, the nature of the road network, and the pattern of land use, and therefore varies considerably from one city to another. In a city of one million population, a typical average public transport journey length is between four and six kilometres; this increases as the city grows and therefore the number of public transport vehicles required increases even faster, proportionally, than the size of the population.

The impact of the urban population explosion tends to be worse in the poorer countries, where money for investment is scarce: while the demand for bus services is increasing, there is insufficient money to finance fleet expansion. In general terms, the greater the size of an urban area, the more difficult it becomes to provide a satisfactory, well co-ordinated public transport system; at the same time, the need for such a system increases with the size of the city.

The age distribution of the population is also significant. Because of the rapid population growth, and medical advances which have reduced the rate of infant mortality, age distribution is becoming increasingly biased towards younger people than in developed countries, where the average age is tending to increase. Thus while in developed countries there is increasing concern regarding the requirements of older passengers, a large proportion of whom are likely to suffer from physical disabilities, a major concern in developing countries is the requirements of schoolchildren and students.

Economic Factors

Also of significance is the effect which demographic factors have on the economy. There is a limit to the number of people which a country can support: if a country cannot grow sufficient food to sustain its population, and cannot generate sufficient foreign exchange from exports to enable it to import the shortfall in food production, it is a poor country, and if its people are not to starve it will be heavily dependent on foreign aid. Many developing countries are in this situation, which has arisen through rapid population growth; this in turn has, ironically, been strengthened by improved medical services which have reduced the mortality rate. In countries where this situation exists, especially where the population is still increasing, development is retarded severely and shortage of money for essentials such as food has an impact on all aspects of the economy, including transport.

Other economic factors which affect the operation of public transport services in developing countries include low levels of GNP per capita, and the resulting poor purchasing power of the majority of the population; uneven distribution of income, both demographically and geographically; fluctuations in world commodity prices; and poor availability of foreign exchange. High rates of inflation are common in developing countries, and this is inevitably accompanied by deteriorating rates of exchange, with an adverse effect on the cost of providing services such as transport, particularly when a significant proportion of costs is in respect of inputs which must be imported. Foreign exchange shortages, or the total lack of foreign exchange, severely limit the scope for investment in transport facilities; this is a common problem in many developing countries, particularly in Africa, and one which, unfortunately, is increasing. Thus although a good transport system is essential for development, the funds available for transport are often grossly inadequate.

Many developing countries depend to a large extent on exports of natural resources such as minerals, or agricultural produce, in order to be able to import commodities which cannot be produced locally. Fluctuations in world commodity prices, or failure of crops, can therefore have a very serious impact on a country's economic circumstances and in turn this can affect the transport operator, both directly in terms of the availability of foreign exchange to purchase inputs, and indirectly in terms of the demand for its services.

Because of the dependence of many developing countries on imports for essential items such as oil and transport equipment, the availability of foreign currency is vital, and fluctuations in exchange rates can have a serious effect on operating costs. There may be periodic shortages of foreign exchange, which often result in an inability to import vehicle spare parts, or new vehicles for fleet replacement and expansion. Sometimes foreign exchange is allocated by government, based on various priorities which may or may not be appropriate; in most cases, such controls lead to long bureaucratic delays in importing essential items. Many countries have removed foreign exchange controls in recent years, allowing their currencies to float. This has led to other problems for transport operators: although imported items such as vehicles, fuel and spare parts may be more readily available, they are much more expensive than before. In some countries the cost of imported spare parts and replacement vehicles has increased at a rate far beyond the internal rate of inflation; if the costs of these items are to be recovered, fares increases may be necessary which passengers are unable to afford. In the absence of such fares increases, the operators' ability to maintain or replace vehicles in the fleet will be reduced, with the inevitable result that fleet ages will increase, and maintenance standards, and hence vehicle availability and reliability, and ultimately standards of service, will fall. This historically has been a major contributory factor in the decline in the level and quality of public transport service in many developing countries, and while the services currently provided may be considered to be poor, it is often all that the majority of passengers can afford.

A characteristic of most developing countries is a highly skewed distribution of income, with a large majority of the population receiving extremely low incomes, and a small minority earning very high incomes: the range of incomes is normally much greater than in most developed countries. This has significant implications for transport. In particular, private transport is beyond the reach of the majority of the population, who are able to afford only a very basic standard of public transport.

In geographic terms also, wealth tends to be very unevenly distributed, with a strong bias to urban areas; one significant effect of this is that car ownership levels in cities are usually many times higher than for the country as a whole, and may be up to five times more. Even if only 10% of the population of a country lives in cities, as many as 50% of the country's cars, and even more in some cases, may be based in the cities.

Political and Institutional Factors

Public transport is inextricably linked with politics, and since it affects virtually everybody, is often manipulated by politicians in an attempt to win the support of potential voters. Politicians are also often inclined to rely on advice from people who are not qualified to give it, or to rely too heavily on their own judgement without a full understanding of what is involved. Many of the decisions made by politicians relating to transport, even if well-intentioned, are misguided or inappropriate, and while they may sometimes result in short-term benefits, they often make the problems even worse in the longer term: a typical example is the control of bus fares, through which, for political reasons, fares are often restricted to a level which is insufficient to sustain the service. Politicians frequently use their influence to persuade transport companies to provide unprofitable services to their own constituencies; the more powerful the politician, the greater the problem for the transport operators, although the constituents may benefit substantially at their expense, and at the expense of transport users on less favoured routes.

A common example of the way in which political decisions can harm an organisation is in the area of employment. Many labour laws have been passed for political reasons with little concern for the effect they will ultimately have on commercial activity. There have been cases where, in an attempt to reduce unemployment, governments have decreed that all companies over a certain size, including those in the private sector, should employ additional staff whether they are needed or not; this results in increased costs and reduced efficiency, and puts larger operators at a disadvantage. State-controlled industries are often at a competitive disadvantage where they, but not private sector companies, are subject to rules regarding employment which result in excessive staff levels. A very common problem for state-owned undertakings is the appointment, for political reasons, of unqualified and unsuitable officers to senior management positions, invariably to the serious detriment of the organisation.

Major political change, for example from socialism to capitalism, or from a one-party state to full democracy or vice versa, is more likely in developing countries than in developed countries, and can have a significant effect on the transport industry. In the countries of the former Soviet Union, for example, state-controlled organisations have been subject to wholesale privatisation, leading to major changes in the structure of the transport industry. There has also been a trend towards a less regulated approach in many countries, and this too has had a major impact on the provision of transport services.

Political instability, which often leads to civil unrest, is a significant problem in some countries, and can discourage investment in large projects such as fleets of buses. Buses seem to be a popular target in many parts of the world for rioters demonstrating their dissatisfaction with the government, but of greater significance is the fact that in an atmosphere of civil unrest it is difficult for any industry or public utility to function efficiently, especially in those areas where government has an involvement. Unrest tends to be closely linked to the population problems affecting many developing countries: people become dissatisfied, understandably, with deteriorating living conditions, and this frequently develops into major civil upheaval.

The way in which the transport industry works, and its efficiency, is influenced to a large extent by its structure and ownership. There is a wide range of alternatives: at one extreme is the planning and operation of all services by a single authority; at the other is a totally unregulated system. Both have advantages and disadvantages, and the most appropriate structure, which will vary according to circumstances, usually lies somewhere between the two. In most developing countries the transport industry is highly fragmented, resulting in poor standards of service; there is a tendency for large operators to decline, and although there are some notable exceptions, many of those which still exist are inefficient and unprofitable.

Problems may also arise from the manner in which transport services are planned and regulated. There is often very little planning of transport systems, and where plans have been made many are based on inadequate information and inappropriate principles, and may also suffer from a lack of expertise amongst the planners. A poorly planned system is an inefficient one: unsuitable route structures, for example, can add to traffic congestion, and reduce the capacity of the public transport system. The regulations applicable to the operation of public transport services are frequently inappropriate to today's conditions, and in some cases have been a primary cause of many of the problems. Even where the regulatory framework is appropriate, a major contributory factor to the transport problems of many countries is weakness in the enforcement of the relevant laws and regulations; this may be due to inadequate resources or ineffectiveness of the enforcement agencies, while corruption in the police or other law enforcement agencies is often a serious problem. In a large number of cases, measures introduced to solve transport problems have failed purely for this reason.

Transport operators are directly affected by poor enforcement of regulations applicable to road traffic generally, such as speed and parking restrictions, and those affecting the operation of public transport services, such as route licensing regulations. One effect is to undermine responsible transport operators, and encourage those who do not respect the law, resulting in poor quality services, overcharging of passengers, and the operation of unroadworthy vehicles, driven in a dangerous manner. In a wider sense, poor law enforcement generally also creates problems for transport operators: theft of vehicles, fuel, parts, passengers' belongings, or fare revenue is common in many countries where crime is not well controlled, and in some countries there are major public order problems, resulting in buses being damaged or destroyed in riots.

Cultural Factors

Cultural and related factors, such as work ethic, honesty, manners, traditions, religion and education, all have a significant bearing on passengers' requirements and the way in which transport systems operate. An understanding of the relevant factors, and the extent to which they may be catered for without creating problems, is essential; foreign advisers or expatriate managers frequently fail to recognise their importance, and as a result make recommendations or take decisions which are wholly inappropriate.

Of particular significance is the work ethic. In some cultures, people enjoy and take pride in their work; productivity is high within the constraints of the available technology, and disciplinary and work standards are usually good, both when working for an employer and when self-employed. Small businesses tend to thrive in this atmosphere, and large organisations, if appropriately structured and managed, can also operate successfully. On the other hand, there are countries where the work ethic is such that productivity is low, and staff do not work well except under close supervision. Large organisations are difficult to manage efficiently under these circumstances, and small family-based businesses tend to be more successful. Discipline is an aspect of the work ethic which is particularly important in transport operation, where much of the work carried out is on the road and largely unsupervised: poor standards of discipline have an adverse effect on many aspects of an operation, in particular on safety and reliability.

Standards of honesty also influence the nature of the services provided. Where stealing of fare money by conductors is rife, revenue will be seriously depleted and service standards will suffer as a result; revenue integrity considerations therefore often determine the way in which services are operated, the fare structure, and fare collection methods. Dishonesty on the part of passengers requires far more rigorous control procedures than would be the case if people were basically honest: in some countries it is possible to rely on passengers to pay their fares into unmanned machines with minimal inspection, while in others such a system would result in virtually no fare revenue being received at all. Standards of honesty determine the extent of corruption, and hence the effectiveness of enforcement of regulations.

Behaviour standards vary considerably from country to country. An obvious manifestation in the transport context is the way in which passengers queue at bus stops. In some countries passengers form orderly queues, and board buses in the sequence in which they arrived; in others, passengers form unruly crowds at bus stops, and push and jostle for a place on the bus when it arrives. Passenger behaviour can therefore affect vehicle design requirements, bus stop and terminal design, and crowd control and safety procedures.

Traditions and customs often affect the way in which businesses operate, including the provision and use of transport services, although in many countries serious attempts are being made to eliminate some of the problems which arise. A strong tradition in many countries, particularly in Africa, is the extended family. This often results in distorted recruitment and promotion policies, with preference being given to relatives of existing employees or influential members of management, rather than selection on the basis of merit. Tribalism has a similar effect in many countries, with preference sometimes being given to members of particular tribes or ethnic groups: in extreme cases members of some tribes are excluded altogether from certain occupations or organisations. In some cultures, great deference is shown to position of the chief or its equivalent, and senior managers may be shown the same deference to the extent that they may abuse their positions with impunity. In some countries, it is widely recognised that personal interests may take priority, and many managers spend a considerable proportion of their working time on their own personal business affairs. Even what may be regarded by some as a clear conflict of interest, such as the employed manager of a bus company operating his own vehicles in direct competition, is perfectly acceptable in certain cultures.

Religion can have important implications, and in countries where there are several different religions the operation of public transport services can become complicated. An obvious effect of religion on public transport is the demand for travel during religious festivals: the huge transport operation required in Saudi Arabia to transport pilgrims to and from Mecca during the Hajj is a classic example. More far-reaching, however, are the customs and traditions associated with each religion. For example, in some Muslim countries segregation of men and women is customary on buses, necessitating the provision of separate compartments or even separate buses for men and women. It may be customary for drivers to stop their vehicles to pray at certain times, or to have religious icons or even small shrines on board their vehicles. In some religions it is considered that the inevitability of fate may absolve the driver from any responsibility for safety, with the result that driving standards may be dangerous.

Status is regarded as important in some societies, and private transport is often regarded as a status symbol, while the use of public transport is seen almost as a stigma. Everybody aspires to ownership of their own car or motorcycle, and as per capita incomes rise, so does the level of ownership of private transport. Therefore even where public transport services are of a high standard, the majority of people will travel by private transport if they can afford to do so: they are often happy to sit in stationary cars in traffic jams for long periods, and cannot easily be persuaded not to use their cars, even if the alternative public transport service would enable them to make their journey more quickly, more cheaply, or both. Similarly, members of car-owning families tend usually to use taxis or other forms of individual public transport, rather than bus or paratransit services, when the car is in use by another family member.

In some developing countries there is also a strong consciousness of class or social status, to the extent that members of higher social groups are unwilling to travel on the same vehicle as people whom they regard as inferior.

Finally, although rapid progress is being made in some areas, standards of education in developing countries tend to be low, resulting in a shortage of skills, sometimes necessitating the employment of expatriates for certain posts, and imposing serious constraints on the standards which can be achieved.

Road and Traffic Conditions

Road conditions in developing countries vary widely, and often create major problems for transport operators. There are some excellent roads, many funded by overseas aid; but many are in poor condition. Maintenance is often very poor, so that even good roads deteriorate in a very short time, while urban growth, and the corresponding increase in the length of the urban road system, puts an increasing strain on road building and maintenance resources in the cities. In addition, climatic factors, as discussed earlier, can cause serious damage to roads. Poor road conditions have a detrimental effect on all vehicles using the road, accelerating wear and tear, increasing operating costs, and in extreme cases, preventing their operation altogether. Road conditions also influence vehicle design: for example, buses must be built with adequate ground clearance and suspension systems in order to be operated safely and economically on rough roads, and the types of "passenger-friendly" urban buses becoming common in most western cities are not practical in many developing countries.

Traffic congestion in urban areas is often more serious in developing countries than in developed countries, despite lower car ownership levels. This is due to various factors, including inadequate road system capacity, poor traffic discipline, in particular a high level of illegal parking, the use of road space by vendors, and slow moving non-motorised traffic. There is a common tendency for car users to assume that they have the right to travel, and to park, wherever they wish. Since car owners, and often motor traders, represent a powerful lobby, this assumed right is tacitly accepted; few, if any, measures are taken to control the misuse of road and footpath space by private car users. There are special traffic problems in some of the older city centres, where narrow streets may be unsuitable for normal motorised traffic. Increasing commercial and industrial activity also leads to increasing volumes of freight traffic, which adds to congestion, particularly on routes leading to and from ports and industrial areas. Public transport costs are increased by the slower speeds resulting from congestion: increased journey times result in reduced bus productivity and therefore reduced revenue, and increased vehicle requirements and time-based costs per kilometre.

Some of these problems may be eased by increasing the capacity of the road system through road construction, but such measures are often less successful than anticipated due to the additional traffic which is invariably generated by road improvements; moreover, they are usually very costly, and may detract from the quality of the urban environment. Alternative measures, which are often much more cost-effective, include traffic management schemes, enabling better use to be made of existing road capacity, and demand management measures, such as road pricing, to reduce the overall volume of traffic. Bus priority measures can be particularly effective in reducing the effects of traffic congestion on public transport services, although the success of any such schemes is heavily dependent on the effectiveness of enforcement.

In some countries the standards of road construction and maintenance is high, even in rural areas; in others, however, away from the main roads between towns, there may be no major roads which are suitable throughout their length for the operation of maximum-sized buses; even the main routes may have stretches where because of poor alignment or bad surface conditions the drivers of large vehicles must proceed with extreme caution. On some routes, on which full-sized buses are used, carriageway widths and alignment on some sections are not conducive to the safe operation of such vehicles. Road conditions on some minor bus routes may be very bad indeed, and may be dangerous for even the smallest vehicles.

ALTERNATIVE PUBLIC TRANSPORT MODES

There are several different modes of public transport, and while this book is concerned primarily with public transport by road, it is important to understand the roles of the other modes, and the ways in which they complement and compete with one another. Alternatives to road-based modes are heavy and light rail systems, including metro and tram systems; water transport, which is sometimes an option both for long and short distance transport; and air transport for longer journeys.

Road Transport

Road-based public transport modes include conventional buses, informal paratransit vehicles, taxis, and human and animal powered vehicles. It is useful to distinguish between the mass public transport modes (MPT) and individual public transport modes (IPT). MPT may be defined as those forms of public transport which are available to multiple passengers travelling independently of one another, usually operating on fixed or flexible routes; IPT covers those forms of public transport which are used by individuals, or small groups of individuals travelling together, who select the route. There is a range of vehicle types used for mass public transport, from mass-produced minibuses carrying about ten passengers to high-capacity double-deck buses carrying 100 or more, or articulated single-deckers which may carry over 270. Vehicles used for individual public transport are naturally smaller, ranging from saloon cars downwards to motorcycles and human-powered vehicles. While most road-based public transport shares road space with other traffic, exclusive rights of way, such as bus lanes or busways, may also be provided.

Conventional bus services are the most flexible form of mass transport for urban, long-distance and rural operation. A bus can operate along virtually any road or city street where it is required, with minimal special infrastructure requirements. It may also operate on dedicated rights of way, or "busways", as described in Chapter 3. Naturally there may be some constraints on size: some large buses may not be able to negotiate narrow streets in some parts of a city or some rural roads, or double decked buses may not be suitable due to low bridge heights or overhead cables, but because of the range of bus sizes which is available such constraints are rarely a major problem.

Buses are also flexible in terms of route capacity, which can be varied by changing the frequency of operation, by varying the capacity of the vehicles used, or both. Moreover, a new bus route can be introduced with minimum of investment, unlike a rail system which first requires the track. In most urban areas, the bus is the most effective form of transport for the vast majority of travellers; other modes have their role, but are generally complementary to the bus. As a general rule, most cities in developing countries will require approximately one full sized conventional bus per two thousand population if this is the sole means of public transport, but the exact requirement will vary substantially according to the geographical size of city, income and car ownership levels, levels of traffic congestion and therefore operating speeds. In practice there are normally far fewer buses than this, because of the large market share attributable to other modes, particularly paratransit.

An important advantage of the bus is its versatility in meeting a wide range of passengers' requirements. For example, those on very low incomes will require, and be able to afford, only a very basic standard of service; while a relatively highly paid traveller will demand a higher standard of service, and will be prepared to pay a higher fare. On many main line rail systems this range of requirements may be catered for by the provision of various classes of accommodation on the same train, although on commuter rail services this is not normally practical. Light rail usually offers only a single class of service, but this is often too expensive for the majority of travellers, who therefore use alternative, perhaps less convenient modes. With buses, however, it is possible to provide several different standards of service by using different vehicles, built to varying specifications and perhaps of different sizes; sometimes several standards will be available on the same route, but usually the routes will vary, since people travelling from different residential areas will tend to be from different income groups, and require different standards. Two or more standards of accommodation may be offered on the same bus, but such differentiation is very unusual.

Bus services may be categorised in various ways. The distinctions between urban, long-distance and rural services are self-evident. Services are also sometimes categorised as "stage" or "express" services. The former are those which stop frequently to pick up and set down passengers, while the latter stop much less frequently; in practice, stage services are usually relatively short-distance services, while express services tend to cover longer distances, but this need not necessarily be so. In the United Kingdom, the difference between a stage and an express service was officially defined by the minimum fare charged on the route, which was higher for an express service.

A conventional urban bus service is typically provided by an operator with a fleet of buses, providing scheduled services along recognised routes. Such operators often provide a network of routes in an area, and these may be operated in accordance with published timetables. The size of the bus fleet can vary. Some operators, who otherwise have most of the characteristics of a conventional operator, have only one bus; others have several thousand. Traditional city bus operators in developing countries normally have fleets ranging from about thirty to one thousand vehicles; the majority of fleets probably consist of between 300 and 600 buses. In some cities there is a single operator of conventional bus services; in others there are many.

"Paratransit", also described as "informal", "intermediate" or "unconventional" public transport, is becoming increasingly significant as a form of urban and rural transport in developing countries. It usually operates in direct competition with conventional bus services, but in many towns and cities it is the only form of mass public transport. The characteristics of this form of transport vary considerably, but it is generally operated on a much less formal basis than a conventional bus service, usually, but not always, with smaller vehicles, and often by owner-drivers or small fleet owners. Paratransit is a somewhat loose term, and is not always used consistently. It is sometimes used to include a range of public transport modes, from pedestrian or cycle-powered rickshaws to full sized buses operated in an informal manner. In this book, the term is used to refer to all informal types of mass public transport by road.

Over time, paratransit has become more accepted, invariably because it has become a significant component of the public transport system. In the majority of cases paratransit commenced as an illegal operation, which gradually became legalised and formalised. In Bangkok, for example, more than 100 public transport routes are now operated under franchises by paratransit vehicles which initially were operated illegally.

Paratransit has flourished for a number of reasons. The vehicles normally used are relatively easy to purchase, operate and maintain; the capital investment is low; a minibus requires relatively little special skill to drive compared to a full-sized bus, and often no special driving licence is required, so that drivers are more readily available, and cannot usually demand high salaries; most paratransit vehicles are based on mass-produced models which are familiar to many mechanics, and for which spare parts are easily obtainable; while even if there are regulations governing the operation of paratransit vehicles these tend to be relatively ineffective. It is sometimes argued that paratransit services are more appropriate than conventional bus services in developing countries. They are often seen by passengers as being quicker, more convenient and more comfortable; they can provide flexibility, and a wider coverage than ordinary buses, although fares are usually higher. Paratransit is usually highly competitive, and up to a point, the laws of competition ensure that the service provided is matched to passengers' needs. Finally, where unemployment is at a high level, paratransit has the added attraction of providing jobs.

In reality, there are often roles for both paratransit and conventional bus services. In small towns, local public transport services operated by conventional buses are not normally viable, except on the main roads through the town, where long-distance buses passing through may also carry short-distance local passengers. Smaller vehicles operated on an informal basis are normally the most effective form of public transport. The size of town above which a more formalised bus service of transport becomes viable cannot be precisely defined: it depends on factors such as population density, income levels, road network, and cultural attitudes towards public transport. In most developing countries, the critical size lies somewhere between 250,000 and 500,000. As discussed in Chapter 20, when a city's population increases to the point where a more formalised system is desirable, there are often practical difficulties in bringing about the change.

In many cases paratransit routes are flexible, and may be varied to meet the requirements of individual passengers; usually the vehicles will stop anywhere as requested by passengers. This type of operation may be referred to as "personalised mass transit" (PMT) or "demand-responsive transport" (DRT). A typical example is the "shared taxi" or "route taxi". This, as its name implies, is a taxi used by several individuals, who are likely to be strangers to one another, travelling between the same two points, or along the same route; each pays an individual fare. In some cases it is customary for shared taxis to deviate from the direct route in order to drop passengers close to their destinations.

Shared taxis are sometimes regarded as a superior form of paratransit service, and usually charge higher fares. Often, however, the only difference between the shared taxi and other forms of paratransit is the type of vehicle used: shared taxis are normally saloon cars (or estate cars and, more recently, "multi-purpose vehicles" with up to eight seats) while other paratransit vehicles are usually larger. In some cases a vehicle may be used to provide different forms of transport during the course of the day: for example it may operate as a conventional taxi during most of the day, but as a shared taxi during peak periods.

In some countries it is common for car or truck drivers employed by commercial or government organisations to use their employers' vehicles, usually without their knowledge or consent, to operate informal shared taxi or minibus services at peak times. Even ambulances are sometimes used for this purpose.

Individual public transport (IPT) services represent an important public transport mode in most towns and cities, and their importance is not always taken into account in urban transport studies. IPT, typified by the taxi, is a form of public transport which is available for the use of individual travellers, or small groups travelling together between the same two points. There are several other forms of IPT in addition to the conventional taxi, such as motorised and human-powered rickshaws, and motorcycles. These operate in a similar manner to taxis, but are generally cheaper and slower, and are used for shorter journeys. Regular taxis may be supplemented, usually illegally, by car and van owners who carry passengers for payment when commuting to and from work.

In addition to providing a faster and more convenient alternative to mass public transport services, IPT can fill gaps in the public transport service at times or in places where demand does not justify a regular mass transport service, and can meet the requirements of market sectors which are not catered for by these modes. It has an important role in areas of low population density, between points where there is insufficient demand to justify a through bus service, or at times of the day or night when demand does not justify bus operation. They are also useful as an alternative to private transport where parking is restricted. While taxis have no advantage over private cars in terms of road space used per passenger, the fact that they are moving for a greater proportion of the time, and each vehicle is used by a large number of people during the course of the day, means that the requirement for parking space per traveller is significantly less; in most cities this is an important advantage. Encouraging the development of a good IPT service can also slow growth in private transport usage, with beneficial results.

Where labour costs are low, IPT can be relatively cheap, and can often provide a viable alternative to private transport. The demand for IPT is influenced to a large extent by the availability and cost of alternatives. Taxis also tend to be used a great deal by visitors to a city, particularly businessmen and tourists, who do not have time to become familiar with alternative forms of public transport. In many Asian countries taxis and other forms of IPT such as rickshaws are also used by middle income families for taking their children to and from school, and by women who prefer not to use the more crowded buses or minibuses.

The importance of taxi services is increasing in both developing countries, as the number of people who can afford them increases, and in developed countries, where bus services generally are in decline. Most IPT users in developing countries are people with higher incomes than typical bus passengers, but who do not have access to private transport, although some car owners use taxis in preference to their cars for certain journeys, often where there are serious parking difficulties. On the other hand, some IPT users would prefer to use a cheaper form of transport if such were available: for example, there is often a considerable gap in terms of service quality between the basic bus service and the taxi, and if a "premium" bus service were to be offered, many taxi users would prefer to use it.

In many cities, especially the larger ones, there are different standards of taxi service: for example taxis may be available with and without air conditioning. Often there are taxis offering higher standards of comfort for passengers with higher incomes, as well as for tourists and other visitors. In some cities only one form of IPT is available: in Kingston, Jamaica, saloon cars were the only option, although even here there were two standards, namely the basic taxis, and more expensive taxis operated by members of the tour operators' associations, offering slightly greater comfort and aimed at tourists and foreign businessmen. In others, for example Jakarta, virtually the full range is available, from air-conditioned and standard taxis to three-wheeled bajajs, motorcycles and human-powered becaks, as described later. The fare scales for the different types of vehicle can vary considerably, with "upmarket" services for tourists and other visitors using hotels of international standard often costing many times more than the basic services used by the majority of residents.

Rail Transport

Rail passenger transport systems range from heavy rail systems, comprising full sized trains running on main line tracks, to street tramways, using rolling stock of suitable dimensions for operation in the same road space as ordinary traffic.

Heavy rail transport is normally best suited to moving large volumes of passengers and freight over comparatively long distances, and most developing countries have systems for this purpose. The quality and extent of these systems vary considerably; those in Asian countries are generally more highly developed, while with the exception of the South African system, those in most countries in sub-Saharan Africa are least developed, with slow and infrequent services which do not compete effectively with road transport.

Many national rail systems also provide commuter services in large urban areas, and new urban rail systems are being developed in several major cities, in both developed and developing countries around the world. Some heavy rail lines are provided solely for the use of suburban passenger trains; in other cases suburban trains are operated only on main lines, which they share with long distance passenger and freight traffic. The characteristics of heavy rail are such that stations tend to be widely spaced (typically at least two or three kilometres apart in urban areas, and very much farther apart elsewhere) and trains relatively infrequent, though there are exceptions to this. In large cities underground or elevated heavy rail systems, sometimes referred to as "metro" systems, can provide a fast form of mass transit which is not affected by surface traffic.

A heavy rail system can be an effective form of mass public transport in large cities, although the infrastructure is expensive, and it is rarely possible to justify the construction of a new heavy rail line purely for the use of urban passengers on economic grounds alone. However, where lines are already in existence, and money has been sunk into the system, it is often economically justifiable to continue with the operation. It is more likely that a suburban service sharing a main line with other traffic will be viable, but even this is uncertain in view of the cost of the requisite rolling stock, and its usually relatively low level of utilisation. Moreover, because of low network densities, the share of passenger traffic carried by urban rail systems tends to be a very low proportion of the total public transport traffic in a city, although several systems enjoy a comparatively large market share on the corridors in which they operate.

Because of limitations of track capacity and signalling systems most heavy rail systems cannot cater for high-frequency services, and often the only practical means of increasing capacity is to increase the length of the trains; however, even this may not be possible if station infrastructure, in particular platform lengths, cannot be increased to accommodate longer trains. Conflict between fast long-distance and slow local trains may also create problems of capacity and control, and a relatively small increase in long-distance services may have a disproportionately adverse effect on the level of local service which may be provided. Therefore unless a separate network of lines is available for local traffic, the potential for heavy rail as an urban transport mode is limited in most developing countries.

Light rail transit (LRT) systems, including monorail and other less conventional systems, are generally constructed solely for the operation of passenger trains providing relatively high frequency urban and suburban services. They have many of the characteristics of heavy rail systems but are constructed to cater for vehicles of lower weight and usually to smaller dimensions. As a result they can be significantly cheaper in terms of both capital and operating costs, although capacity is also lower.

Street tramway systems are LRT systems which operate on city streets alongside other traffic, and as such have much in common with conventional bus services: they do not require special infrastructure at stopping places, which may be spaced as closely as every 300 metres, or even less. A disadvantage shared with buses is that they can be obstructed by other road traffic. Some tramway systems operate entirely on streets; however, many incorporate lengths of dedicated track, which may be above or below street level, on which the trams are fully segregated from other traffic. Away from city centres, it is often practical to provide dedicated track alongside or away from the main highway; sometimes the central median strip of a dual carriageway may be used for this purpose.

LRT and street tramway systems are efficient movers of large volumes of passenger traffic. On most systems the vehicles may operate as single units or as short trains of two or three vehicles. This makes efficient use of road space, and the facility to add extra vehicles makes it relatively easy to increase capacity at peak periods without requiring additional staff. Crew productivity is substantially higher than for buses, although this is less of an issue in developing countries where wage costs are generally low, than in developed countries where labour costs are usually significant.

The capital cost of a tram or LRT vehicle is typically three times that of a large conventional double deck bus, but it will have a life approximately twice as long, while its carrying capacity may be up to 50% more. Direct operating costs for LRT and street trams are lower than those for buses, but the fixed costs of infrastructure and rolling stock are much higher; therefore the overall cost per passenger by rail is lower than by bus only where there are high volumes of traffic.

Trams are common in many European countries. In the United Kingdom nearly every major town and city had a tramway system, but during the 1950s and 1960s these were progressively replaced by bus systems with the exception of only one town, Blackpool; however, the advantages of tramways are again being realised, and they have already been reintroduced in Manchester, Sheffield, Nottingham, the West Midlands and Croydon, with other systems proposed. In most other European countries, street tramway systems have been retained; many have been extended and modernised over the years, and constitute a major component of the public transport system. They are relatively uncommon in developing countries; there is still an extensive system in Cairo, for example, but systems in other countries, such as Indonesia and Thailand, were abandoned many years ago.

Most urban heavy rail systems, and virtually all LRT and street tramway systems, are powered by electricity; diesel power is used in some cities, particularly where demand is low, and in some cases where suburban services are operated on non-electrified main lines. Long distance services are more commonly diesel powered except where the volume of traffic is very high, when electric power may be a viable alternative. Steam locomotives are still employed in some countries but are becoming increasingly rare. Some LRT systems, such as the Docklands Light Railway system in London or the PUTRA system in Kuala Lumpur, are fully automatic, in that they can be operated without drivers.

Rail systems have several advantages over other public transport modes where there is sufficient traffic to justify the investment in infrastructure and rolling stock. Heavy rail is advantageous over long distances, and light rail for intensive urban services. In addition to its efficiency in moving large volumes of traffic, another perceived benefit of a rail system is its stability: a bus service may be withdrawn at short notice, but a substantial investment in a rail system indicates greater long term commitment to the provision of a service. On the other hand a fixed transport system may become obsolete if demand patterns change significantly, whereas a bus service has much greater flexibility to adapt to changes.

However, rail systems are appropriate only where the volume of demand along a route corridor is very high. The actual volume required for viability depends on a number of factors, including capital and operating costs and the level of fares which passengers are able to afford. As a rough guide, an average of approximately 10,000 passengers per hour in each direction over the working day is the minimum required to justify an urban LRT or street tramway system, and up to three times this volume for a heavy rail system. Traffic volumes of these magnitudes may be achieved towards the central area of a city, but demand will normally be less towards the outer terminals of each route, while if routes diverge towards outlying areas, the traffic volumes on each branch may be too low to justify the high infrastructure costs, limiting the extent to which suburban areas may be served.

An urban rail system may therefore be viable only if a dense network of relatively short routes is provided in the central area, fed by bus services with convenient interchange points. In practice there are comparatively few systems, in developed or developing countries, which are able to cover fully all costs, including the investment in track and other infrastructure, from passenger fare revenue. Some systems are able to make operating profits, but do not cover the cost of capital, or depreciation of infrastructure or even rolling stock.

Many recent LRT schemes have been justified on the basis of over-optimistic forecasts of demand and revenue. Some LRT lines competing with bus services perform worse than predicted because it had been incorrectly assumed that most passengers would transfer to them from buses: because LRT systems are expensive to construct, the fares charged are usually high compared with alternative modes for the equivalent journey. In some cases an attempt has been made to boost LRT patronage by withdrawing or restricting parallel bus services, and operating feeder bus services into the LRT system instead. This strategy is rarely successful: passengers are usually required to pay considerably more for their journeys than they would if they made the entire journey by bus, and may resent the inconvenience of having to change from one mode of transport to another. In such circumstances, it is common for informal road transport operators, often operating illegally, to carry most of the traffic instead. A well planned through ticketing system, and efficient interchange facilities, may be effective in encouraging passengers to use bus and LRT as part of an integrated system, but until now such systems have been largely confined to developed countries.

Other problems frequently encountered in the development of rail systems, in both developing and developed countries, are significant underestimates of construction costs and the time required for construction and commissioning. Construction costs in particular have exceeded the initial estimates by several hundred percent in some cases, and some projects have not been completed. Several early schemes involving private sector investment have failed to provide the returns anticipated, and investors are tending to become less willing to take on as great a share of the risk as governments would like.

Therefore while there are frequent proposals for new light and heavy rail schemes for cities around the world, many of these will never materialise, while those which do are unlikely to meet expectations. In the United Kingdom, the government published a ten year transport plan in 2001 which included a target of 25 new LRT systems; by 2004, however, in the light of experience of recently introduced systems this target had been recognised as unachievable, and several proposals for new systems, or extensions for existing systems which had already received government approval, were abandoned.

Nevertheless, in most of those schemes which have been implemented, patronage is slowly but steadily rising, and for their users, they have invariably resulted in an improvement in travelling conditions. The elevated LRT system introduced in Bangkok in 1999, for example, is a far pleasanter way of travelling than the alternatives; unfortunately, it is a very limited system, which is of use to a relatively small proportion of travellers in the city.

As a general rule, an all-bus system is usually the only economically viable option for an urban public transport system, except in exceptional circumstances. However, if an investment has already been made in an LRT or street tramway system, it is usually appropriate to maintain it.

Rapid Transit

In discussion of urban public transport in particular, reference is often made to "rapid transit", or "mass rapid transit", and sometimes "bus rapid transit". Rapid transit is not a transport mode as such, but, as its name implies, is a means of mass transportation offering a faster service than the alternatives which are available, typically with average operating speeds of 50 kph or more; this generally requires exclusive rights of way. Rapid transit services are usually provided by light rail, but certain heavy rail systems fall into this category, as do bus, guided bus or trolleybus services which operate on dedicated rights-of-way and which are therefore faster than those sharing road space with other traffic.

Rapid transit systems are often more attractive to higher income groups who value their time more than those with lower incomes, who may be unable to afford the higher fares which may be charged for these services. Nevertheless, if high load factors can be achieved, rapid transit systems can be commercially advantageous on corridors where demand is high due to the better utilisation of vehicles which can be achieved by virtue of the higher operating speeds.

Water Transport

Where there are navigable waterways, public transport by water can be a viable option. Although high-speed craft are available, transport by water is generally slow but relatively cheap, and journey times can be lower than by road when the route by water is significantly shorter, such as between two towns on opposite sides of a lake or estuary, or when city streets are heavily congested. Ferries are important where there are major water crossings, and where there are many rivers or islands.

As a form of long distance transport where roads are poor water transport can be very attractive. Vessel size can range from small "water taxis" to very large passenger ferries, depending not only on demand but also on the depth of water available and landing facilities. Infrastructure, particularly for large vessels, may be costly to construct and maintain, and "track costs" may be substantial where regular dredging is required to maintain the necessary depth. Very small vessels, on the other hand, require minimal infrastructure.

Water transport is relatively uncommon as a form of urban public transport, but is significant in some cases, where urban areas are built on islands or there are major rivers or canal networks, as for example in Hong Kong, Bangkok, Cairo, Abidjan and Mombasa.

Air Transport

Air transport services are often available between major towns and cities, over distances of about 200 kilometres or more. There is a considerable range of aircraft types and capacities, from light aircraft and helicopters carrying fewer than ten passengers to high capacity aircraft carrying 400 or more; the type of aircraft used on a particular route will be influenced by the level of demand and the availability of airport facilities. In some countries, particularly where surface transport is hindered by poor road conditions or unbridged water crossings, considerable use is made of light aircraft, requiring only basic runway facilities, for relatively short journeys, or for longer journeys where demand is low. In a few cases helicopters, requiring minimal ground facilities, are used.

Air transport is relatively expensive in terms of cost per passenger-kilometre, and requires expensive infrastructure if large aircraft are used. However, other than terminal and air traffic control costs, there are no track costs as with road and rail. This can be an advantage where difficult terrain makes the construction of roads or railways expensive.

Air transport is often considerably faster, even taking into account airport processing times, although a common disadvantage of air transport is the travelling time between airports and city centres: in many cases, because of the requirement for large areas of level land, airports must be located a considerable distance from the city centre, and, particularly if the journey to and from the airport must be made on a congested road system, journey times may be significant. The longer these times are, the greater the distance before total journey times using air transport become shorter than the alternative. In most developing countries the number of passengers travelling by air as a proportion of the total is very low, and as an alternative to road or rail transport it is of minor significance.

PUBLIC TRANSPORT MARKET SECTORS

The market for public transport services is highly diversified, and can conveniently be divided into three main sectors: urban, long-distance, and rural transport. There are also certain categories of user, with special requirements, of which two significant groups are students and tourists. While the broad principles of transport operation apply in all sectors and to all user categories, there are some fundamental differences, as discussed below.

Urban Transport

The provision of public transport in urban areas has become a major problem in most developing countries, in some respects more so than in developed countries. A major cause is rapid urban population growth, resulting in increased demand with which many transport systems are unable to cope adequately, compounded by low levels of income, inadequate road infrastructure, uncontrolled use of private transport, severe traffic congestion, and inadequate and inefficient public transport systems. Increasing car ownership is also having an effect on the layout of cities, with greater decentralisation of commercial activities and dispersal of residential areas. This has implications for transport provision: public transport is relatively inefficient in serving areas of low population or employment density. The urban transport problem, in both developed and developing countries, has been well documented: this book does not set out to re-examine the problem, but instead examines the role of public transport in meeting urban transport requirements, and discusses the specific problems involved in providing public transport services in cities in developing countries.

All but the smallest towns usually have some form of local public transport service, ranging from those in which conventional and formal public transport services predominate, to those which are heavily or totally dependent on informal public transport modes. Typically the majority of urban passenger journeys in developing countries are by public transport. The greatest demand for transport is from residents of the city, travelling as commuters to work or school, on business, or for social and leisure purposes, together with visitors including business travellers and tourists. The proportions of these categories of user vary widely from city to city, as do their requirements.

Urban traffic patterns are determined by the layout of the city, and the relative locations of residential, commercial and industrial areas, but usually the main traffic flows are between the outer districts and the centre, with less movement between outlying areas or between intermediate points on the radial routes. There are some extreme cases: in some cities, almost all bus passengers travel to or from the central area, with very little intermediate traffic; in others, there is a high turnover of passengers along each bus route due to a high proportion of short-distance intermediate traffic. Where different land uses are well segregated, distinct traffic flows are usually discernible; where land uses are mixed, however, traffic patterns are much more complex. In addition to the public transport services operating wholly within an urban area, there is usually also a requirement for peri-urban services, linking points outside the main urban area with the city centre. Some peri-urban bus services stop short of the central area, so that there is no through service from the outlying point to the city centre, requiring passengers to change buses; alternatively, such services may be arranged to connect with LRT services, providing a quick journey into town. In some larger cities, peri-urban transport services are provided by light or heavy rail systems; there may be feeder bus services at the outer ends of the rail routes to provide broader service coverage.

The rate of urban population growth in the majority of developing countries is very high, with natural population growth compounded by migration from rural to urban areas. In many countries, therefore, the urban population is increasing at a much faster rate than the national population as a whole. The volume of passenger movements increases due not only to population growth but also, in many cases, to increasing mobility resulting from growth in GDP. Moreover, as the city population grows, so does the size of the city itself in terms of area; some people therefore have to travel longer distances from home to work as residential areas spread outwards at the city boundaries, and for many commuters walking ceases to be an option. Average commuting distances increase, so that the rate of increase in passenger kilometres is often substantially greater than the increase in the number of journeys. However, growth in the level of public transport provision tends to lag behind the increase in demand.

Road capacity requirements increase with the size of the city, and as with public transport services, new road construction seldom keeps pace. Traffic congestion, due principally to increasing car ownership, is becoming a serious problem in most towns and cities, restricting economic activity, detracting from the quality of life generally, and resulting in pollution which is damaging to both health and the environment. It is generally recognised that increasing road capacity tends to result in the generation of additional traffic, and therefore that simply building more roads is not always the solution; nevertheless, vast amounts of money continue to be invested in major road construction schemes.

Public transport can make a positive contribution to overcoming these problems by providing a more efficient alternative to the private car, although in reality the provision of a public transport service which by itself has effectively reduced traffic congestion has rarely, if ever, been achieved. There are various reasons for this: apart from the fact that many public transport services are inadequate and inefficient, there is usually inadequate control over the use of private transport, and unless effective bus priorities are in force, public transport suffers from the same congestion as private transport.

The most appropriate mix of the various public transport modes to meet the requirements of any particular urban area varies considerably, depending on the size, layout and other characteristics of the area. In particular, the size of the town or city will have a bearing on the type of transport system which is most appropriate. As cities grow, the appropriate mix of modes is likely to change: for a small town, a system based on small vehicles is normally most suitable, but this is not usually adequate for a larger town or city, which is likely to require a system using at least a proportion of larger vehicles. However, without external influence the industry structure is unlikely to change accordingly, and problems arise when a city grows in size so that its transport system is no longer suitable. With the rapid urban growth in developing countries, there are many cities which have outgrown their transport systems: where the system has been based on paratransit vehicles, the number of operators has tended to increase, but in many cases no formal transport operation has developed to cater for high demand on the main route corridors, even though this is what is usually required.

Inter-urban and Long-distance Transport Services

Inter-urban and long-distance transport services cater for people travelling between one town or city and another, and between rural districts and the towns. Passengers include business travellers and others travelling to the towns to visit markets, often carrying large quantities of freight with them, and people travelling to and from their places of employment. The requirement for long distance public transport in most developing countries is substantial. It is closely linked to the degree of urbanisation: in a country where large numbers of people have migrated to the cities and have found employment there, there is a constant demand for travel back to home areas, usually with considerable peaks at holiday times.

In many developing countries, where distances are great, car ownership low, railways slow and infrequent, and air travel expensive, long-distance passenger transport by road, linking the larger towns and intermediate villages on the main routes, is a lucrative business. It is also often highly competitive, with numerous small operators, and in some cases several large ones, all operating on the same routes. To cater for the different types of traffic, standards of service range from basic bus services to those using highly specified luxury coaches. Full-sized buses are normally used for this type of service, although in certain countries long-distance services are also provided by minibuses or shared taxis, generally to a higher standard than those operated on urban services. Routes of up to 1,000 kilometres in length, and sometimes considerably longer, are common in larger countries; on main routes frequencies are usually high, with most buses operating at or near full capacity. Since the traffic is profitable, service standards are usually good. In most countries, long-distance buses are operated both by day and by night. Passengers travelling long distances often prefer overnight travel; it can save time, reduces the need for overnight accommodation, and in tropical climates is cooler.

Inter-urban bus services are also used, to a limited but increasing extent in some countries, by tourists. In Africa in particular, there is also a considerable amount of international passenger traffic; many people have tribal ties in other countries, and there is frequent migration across borders. There are sometimes problems where smuggling operations are carried out by passengers or bus crews, which can further compound the long delays at borders which are a common problem on international services.

Demand for long distance passenger transport is growing rapidly in many developing countries, as a result of population increase and the continuing migration from rural to urban areas. The expansion and improvement of the road network, which facilitates long-distance travel, also generates demand. Demand for many long distance services is subject to pronounced seasonal fluctuations, while seasonal climatic factors often affect the operation of long-distance services, especially where these are operated on unsurfaced roads, which may become impassable during prolonged periods of rain.

Rural Public Transport

Rural public transport may be conveniently considered under two headings: purely rural, and rural-urban transport. Purely rural transport consists of movement wholly within rural areas, to and from work and transporting goods for domestic use. Rural-urban travel is between rural locations and, usually, the nearest market town, and demand often fluctuates considerably according to the incidence of market days. The main purposes of rural-urban travel are normally business-related, principally taking goods to and from market. At this level, many journeys are a combination of passenger travel and freight transport: much of the traffic could be classified as "accompanied freight". Apart from limited use of water transport where this is an option, or rail in those areas near a railway line, virtually all rural travel is by road. There is often little or no formal public transport for purely rural transport, except in areas near major highways.

Rural services are usually less attractive to the transport operator than urban or long-distance routes. Demand is more variable since it is more seriously affected by factors such as seasonal changes, crop cycles, and road conditions; in many cases incomes are lower in the rural areas so that passengers' ability to pay is limited, and revenue potential is often insufficient to justify the operation of conventional buses.

Rural services tend to be provided by small local operators, with various types of vehicle depending on the circumstances. They may be operated using old buses bought cheaply from a large operator; in this case the capital cost is low but running costs are high due to the age of the vehicle, and reliability is often very poor. More common than the full-sized bus is the minibus, or converted pick-up, again often bought second-hand and often unreliable. Also common are "truck-buses", or lorries, usually in the range of three to five tons capacity, constructed to carry freight but adapted, typically with bench seats along each side, to carry passengers also.

Where smaller vehicles are used, there are usually several operators, each with a single vehicle, running on the same route. Therefore if one vehicle is out of service due to mechanical failure, there are alternatives; on routes with only one operator there is not usually a replacement vehicle, so that the service ceases to run until the bus is back on the road. In any case, the service provided is nearly always irregular and travellers are never sure when transport will be available. Provision of passenger transport in rural areas is therefore a problem in many countries, and services in the majority of cases are very limited.

Transport for Schoolchildren and Students

Transport for schoolchildren and students is a major issue in many developing countries. As populations increase, the number of children of school age increases both in absolute terms and as a proportion of the total population. At the same time, improvements in educational facilities in many countries, with a higher proportion of children attending school and many of them continuing their education for longer, are resulting in the number of children travelling to and from school increasing at a much faster rate than population growth.

As urban areas increase in size, the construction of new schools often fails to keep pace with population growth in each residential area, while in some countries parental choice of school is encouraged, often resulting in children attending schools which are not those nearest to their homes; there is also a tendency towards centralisation of education, with larger schools catering for pupils from wider catchment areas. Distances between homes and schools therefore also tend to increase, sometimes considerably. In some countries the universities account for a significant element of student travel, particularly where many students live at home rather than on campus: some students have to travel long distances daily, since by their nature universities are usually large and centralised.

The primary transport requirement for schoolchildren is for the journey between home and school, but there may also be requirements for transport for other purposes such as sports, educational visits and to events such as national celebrations. There are various means by which these requirements may be met, including public transport, chartered buses and dedicated buses operated by the education authority or by the schools themselves. Although this book deals mainly with public transport, it is relevant to consider the alternatives to public transport for schoolchildren, since this is an important element of the overall passenger transport demand, and policy in this regard can have a significant impact on public transport requirements. Even where dedicated transport is provided for some children, such as those living significant distances from school, the majority are likely to use public transport except those who walk, and therefore the specific public transport requirements for schoolchildren and students must be addressed in any case.

In most developing countries children tend to walk long distances to and from school, particularly in rural areas. Distances of ten kilometres are relatively common, while some children walk considerably farther, because of inadequate transport facilities, or because parents are unable to afford the fares. Walking to and from school becomes less practical as the distance increases, and there are increasing concerns about the safety of young children travelling on foot in crowded and congested streets, while many children who must walk long distances are unable to attend school every day. Some education authorities, through the provision of subsidised transport, aim to eliminate such problems, and specify maximum acceptable walking distances: these vary considerably from one country to another, and even between different authorities within the same country. Where children use public transport, long distances combined with poor transport links often result in very long journey times, and therefore long days away from home; over ten hours is relatively common. Therefore as well as specifying maximum walking distances, there is also a case for setting limits to the duration of journeys, in order to avoid excessive hours of travel and total time away from home.

It is generally recognised that the provision of dedicated buses, solely for the use of schoolchildren, is the most satisfactory means of meeting their travelling requirements. The school or education authority has control of the services provided. In addition, it is easier to supervise children when boarding and leaving vehicles, and they are protected from possible interference from strangers; these are often significant safety issues. Vehicles used for this purpose may be owned by schools or education authorities, or hired from transport operators. The cost of owning and operating dedicated school transport is high, especially if purpose-built vehicles are purchased new. If high quality vehicles are hired from transport operators, the costs may be even higher, since, if the buses are used at peak periods, their utilisation is likely to be low, and the cost of providing drivers relatively high. In many cases, where buses are hired, tenders are awarded to the lowest-cost operator, which often means that the quality of vehicles and service is poor.

Dedicated school transport is costly to provide and therefore relatively uncommon; the main exception tends to be in respect of the more expensive private sector schools, which often own one or more buses in order to provide home-to-school transport and for other purposes during the school day. In some countries it is common for parents to contribute directly to the provision of dedicated vehicles: in Sri Lanka, for example, there are numerous "school vans", which are minibuses carrying approximately ten children each, paid for by parents on a contract basis. In several Asian countries, individual public transport modes, particularly rickshaws but to a lesser extent auto-rickshaws and taxis, are also used for carrying children to and from school by middle-income families.

The use of private transport for taking children to and from school, which is becoming widespread in developed countries, is much less common in developing countries where car ownership levels are generally low. Even so, the number of children from higher income families who are driven to school by car is already resulting in a significant contribution to traffic congestion in many countries. Bicycles are commonly used by schoolchildren in some countries, but this mode of travel is expensive for low-income families and may be dangerous, particularly in urban areas. However, the encouragement of cycling, where it is safe, may be appropriate in some cases.

It is customary in many countries for schoolchildren to travel at concessionary fares; sometimes the concession is funded by government but in most cases the transport operators are expected to bear the cost themselves. Very often, transport operators, particularly those in the private sector, are unwilling to carry children at peak periods at concessionary fares, since this will mean turning away adult passengers who would pay the full fare. Where no concessionary fares are available for students on public transport, travel can be expensive; parents of large families often find it difficult to meet the cost of the concessionary fares, let alone the full fare. In general, the larger conventional bus operators are more willing to carry schoolchildren at concessionary fares without compensation, but in cities where the public transport services previously provided by a conventional bus operator have been replaced by paratransit services, the situation has been deteriorating over the years. Although in some countries public transport operators are legally required to carry schoolchildren at concessionary fares, in practice the authorities often have little power to ensure that operators comply with any requirements in this respect.

Where school hours are similar to business hours, as is often the case, particularly in the mornings, problems of peak demand are accentuated; this increases the cost of transporting school children, and is an argument frequently used as a reason for charging full fares for schoolchildren and students. A potential solution is to stagger school hours, both between different schools, and between schools and other organisations, but in practice this can be difficult to implement; in any case, where distances and travel times are considerable, the peaks tend to be extended, thus reducing the scope for staggering of hours. Alternatively it may be used as an argument in favour of subsidising transport for schoolchildren. In Ethiopia, for example, the state-owned bus operator in Addis Ababa receives a subsidy to compensate for schoolchildren's concessionary fares, although not to the extent necessary to fund the concession in full. However, there are relatively few developing countries where such subsidies are paid.

Regular public transport services are often unsatisfactory in terms of meeting the requirements of school children. Buses are invariably overcrowded in the cities and services are usually inadequate in rural areas to cater for the home-to-school travel of the majority of students. Schools are often located away from the major commercial centres so that bus routes designed to meet the requirements of commuters are unsuitable for schoolchildren, who may be required to walk long distances between the bus route and their schools. Despite the disadvantages, however, in most cases public transport is the only practical option for the transport of schoolchildren and students. It is therefore important to ensure that measures are taken to ensure that the service provided for schoolchildren is the best possible within the various constraints.

Tourist Transport Services

Tourism is an important and growing industry in many developing countries. In some of the larger countries, such as Indonesia or China, there are significant numbers of domestic tourists, usually the more affluent members of society. However, in most countries the majority of tourists come from overseas, so that tourism is usually a valuable source of foreign exchange. While the transport of tourists might not be regarded as public transport in the true sense, many public transport operators are involved to some extent in the provision of services to the tourism industry; in addition, many tourists make extensive use of regular public transport services, and a good, reliable and safe public transport system will help to attract tourists to a country.

The transport requirements for tourist services are diverse, and include transfers between airports and hotels, various kinds of day and extended tours, game drives or safaris, and bus services between tourist resorts and major tourist attractions. Some services for tourists are operated on a scheduled basis, and are used by individuals paying separate fares; others are operated for tourists travelling in large groups, often as part of package holiday arrangements. Tourist transport is usually catered for by specialist operators; it is uncommon for operators of ordinary bus services to become involved except as providers of vehicles to tour operators under charter arrangements. Some tourist operations are carried out by local operators as franchisees of international tour operators: for example, the US-based Gray Line operates through local franchisees in tourist areas throughout the world. Many tour operators provide not only transport services, but also related services such as travel agencies or hotels.

In some countries tourism services, while provided by numerous small operators, are co-ordinated by a tourist authority or an association of tour operators. In Jamaica, for example, the Jamaica Union of Travelers Association (JUTA) acts as a travel agent to obtain work for its members, and negotiates prices for new vehicles, insurance premiums and finance charges on behalf of its members.

The tourism business in most countries follows a highly seasonal pattern, which varies between regions: the high tourist season is generally when the weather tends to be most favourable, often with a short "summer" season in July-August, which is the traditional holiday period in many western countries, where a large proportion of tourists originate. This results in uneven utilisation of vehicles, hotels, and employees in the industry, with a significant proportion of idle time for vehicles and other assets, which must be reflected in the charges. Over a full year, all costs must be covered if an operator is to remain in business, so that costs incurred whilst vehicles are standing idle must be recovered from revenue earned at other times. This necessitates complex charging systems, usually with a range of charges reflecting demand at different times of the year.

SUSTAINABILITY AND ENVIRONMENTAL CONSIDERATIONS

All of the principal transport modes consume non-renewable resources, principally oil, and produce pollutants which cause permanent environmental damage. In urban areas, an increasing proportion of the land area is being consumed by roads, which are often congested with traffic for most of the day, detracting seriously from the quality of life, while major inter-city highways often cause environmental damage in rural areas. The provision of transport is therefore having a serious impact on the environment all over the world. The problem is becoming progressively more serious. More people are consuming more and travelling more, requiring more freight and passenger transport. Those countries which are consuming non-renewable resources at the highest rate, and causing the most pollution, are those with the highest levels of transport use, namely the developed countries: the USA heads the league in both respects. However, rates of consumption and levels of pollution are increasing most rapidly in developing countries.

Existing transport systems are therefore not sustainable in the long term, and this is an issue of increasing concern worldwide. It may be several generations before the full impact of the problem is felt, but the time will eventually come when existing transport modes will no longer be available, and it is necessary to begin planning now for this eventuality, and to design transport systems accordingly. In the long term, drastic changes will be necessary in the use of transport. For many this will mean a change in life style and even a reduction in the standard of living: those who make extensive use of private transport, and travel frequently by air will be most affected. Non-essential and leisure travel may have to be restricted. There will have to be much greater reliance on public transport.

Two fundamental requirements are to maximise the efficiency of existing transport modes, and to develop new transport technology which is genuinely sustainable in that it does not deplete non-renewable resources, does not use renewable resources more quickly than they can be regenerated, and does not cause permanent damage to the environment, or to the health of humans, animals or vegetation. With the exception of walking and cycling and some forms of water transport, public transport modes are generally more sustainable and less damaging to the environment than private transport, although animal or human powered modes are the only genuinely sustainable public transport modes at present; obviously these modes can play only a minimal role in meeting future transport requirements. The requirement for sustainable technology, particularly in respect of modes such as air transport for which at present oil-fuelled propulsion is the only option, is likely to take a considerable time to satisfy completely, if it ever can be; therefore in the immediate term every effort must be made to make existing transport systems as efficient as possible.

Even if no positive measures are taken to reduce the consumption of oil, its increasing scarcity will result in price increases which will eventually force a major change. But this will take time, and may not provide the incentive to develop alternatives soon enough. Nor will it necessarily result in a reduction in the rate of production of pollutants to that at which they can be absorbed or dispersed before irreversible damage has been done. A sustainable global transport strategy is required in order to address the issue: although there has been extensive international debate, and various agreements made, these represent little more than an acknowledgement of the problems, and of the need to take action. Little has been achieved in the development of a positive strategy to reduce the level of motorised transport use or the extent to which it depletes resources and damages the environment.

The technical efficiency of all transport modes must be increased by developing more fuel-efficient and less polluting methods of propulsion. Considerable progress has been made in the area of motor vehicle engine technology but in developing countries in particular, technical advances have been partly negated by poor standards of maintenance. More significantly, however, increasing transport use has more than eliminated any benefits from improved technology.

Of greater importance is the need to improve efficiency in the use of transport resources. In general terms this means making maximum use of public transport: in terms of the amount of energy consumed per passenger, conventional buses are approximately three or four times more efficient than minibuses, and twenty times more efficient than cars or taxis. Improvement in the operational efficiency of public transport is also essential, in order to minimise wasted capacity. Improved infrastructure, such as better roads which reduce traffic congestion and operating costs may assist to some extent but in the majority of cases creates more traffic and in fact aggravates the problem. Nevertheless appropriate infrastructure development, including rail systems, road traffic management schemes, and economic measures to control road use, are all useful measures.

Development of sustainable sources of power, including generation of electricity by water, wind, solar or nuclear power, or sustainable chemical alternatives to oil, must be given priority. Some power sources have only limited potential, and the danger must be avoided of putting too much hope in measures which will provide only limited benefits, or which may create other problems. For example, some countries have invested heavily in electricity generation by wind power, which not only has environmental implications, but produces only a very small proportion of total energy requirements; nuclear energy is an efficient means of producing electricity in terms of its use of resources, but presents the risk of catastrophic accident damage.

Government intervention will be necessary in the form of regulatory measures, including land use regulation to optimise transport requirements and to improve co-ordination between the development of transport systems and development generally, as well as between different transport modes. Market forces alone will not achieve this, except perhaps in the very long term, when it will probably be too late. Competition in public transport may in fact be counter-productive, by increasing capacity to a wasteful level; on the other hand, competition will also encourage much-needed innovation, which must not be stifled by regulation. Somehow the right balance must be found between these conflicting requirements.

The question of sustainability and the environmental implications of transport is highly political, and many of the decisions which need to be made are likely to be unpopular with the electorate. There is also a perceived conflict between sustainability and economic growth: for example, the government of the USA has refused to agree to various measures to conserve energy resources and reduce production of pollutants since these may adversely effect the country's economic growth.

All of these factors add to the complexity of providing public transport in developing countries. It is hoped that the following chapters will assist in addressing the issues involved.

2

PUBLIC TRANSPORT VEHICLE TYPES

Road vehicles used for the provision of public transport services range from small animal and pedestrian powered vehicles carrying one or two passengers, to articulated buses built to maximum permitted dimensions and weight, which may carry over 270. Each type of vehicle has a role to play, and to some extent all may be complementary to one another as part of an overall public transport system.

VEHICLE SIZE

An important consideration is the most appropriate size of vehicle to meet a particular transport requirement. Large buses are appropriate in certain circumstances, and small vehicles in others, and it is sometimes difficult to determine whether several small vehicles or one large one would meet the requirements of passengers and operators more efficiently in any given situation. In broad terms, the appropriate vehicle size is influenced by the volume of traffic, in terms of the number of people travelling between the same two points at the same time, the characteristics of the road system, and the type of services which passengers require, and are prepared to pay for.

Passenger flows achievable with different vehicle capacities vary considerably. A service operated exclusively by small buses with about ten seats each can carry up to a maximum of approximately 3,000 passengers per hour in a single lane in one direction; conventional buses, carrying up to 80 passengers each, can carry up to about 12,000 passengers per hour, unless there is severe traffic congestion, and more if there are exclusive bus lanes. Buses operating on busway systems can theoretically carry up to 30,000 per hour in each direction, but this figure will not often be achieved in practice. Trams, operating as single units, can carry similar or slightly greater numbers, but have the advantage of being able to be combined into trains, giving a capacity of at least twice that of a bus service; on exclusive right of way, if stops are not so close together that higher speeds can be achieved, capacity can be much higher. Where traffic volumes are over 30,000 passengers per hour, which is equivalent to one 50-passenger bus every six seconds, heavy rail is usually the only mode which can provide a satisfactory service.

In determining the most suitable mode or vehicle size to meet a specific traffic flow, differences in peak and off-peak traffic flows must be taken into account: if a very high volume occurs over a relatively short peak period, investment in expensive capacity which is required only at such times may not be justifiable, and in practice passengers will always have to tolerate delays and overcrowding at certain times of the day.

Generally, where large numbers of passengers are to be carried so that vehicles can be filled to capacity, as is the case on many urban and inter-urban services in developing countries, the most efficient and economic vehicle is the largest which can be operated legally, safely and practically within the constraints of the prevailing road conditions. The majority of roads in most urban areas lend themselves to the operation of maximum-sized single-deck buses, which with a full load of seated and standing passengers are capable of carrying up to 100 passengers, while articulated single-deck buses can carry 270 or more. A possible constraint is that limitations of the road network may mean that very large buses cannot be diverted from the main routes in the event of road works or accidents.

Full sized buses can, if required, carry a high proportion of standing passengers in greater comfort than small buses, which often have very limited headroom. Larger buses require less road space per passenger, and this can be particularly significant where road space is limited, as well as in depots and at bus stops and stations. Fewer large buses are required to carry the same number of passengers, which will normally result in lower levels of atmospheric pollution, and easier management and control, particularly scheduling, while the number of personnel required to transport a given number of passengers will normally be lower.

In practice, however, much smaller vehicles are used in a number of situations in developing countries, sometimes through necessity, but often inappropriately. Smaller vehicles are necessary on routes where road conditions inhibit the use of larger vehicles: this often applies in the case of routes operating into high-density residential areas with very narrow streets, as is the case in many Indonesian cities, or on steep, narrow and winding roads such as those in the hilly areas around Kingston, Jamaica. Other constraints on the operation of larger vehicles may include low or weak bridges, or terminals and depots with restricted access, as well as legislation in respect of vehicle dimensions.

There are certain advantages in using small vehicles, even on routes where this is not necessitated by road conditions. Smaller buses can provide a higher frequency of service for a given passenger flow, which can improve the convenience of the service, and passengers often prefer small buses because they are faster and take less time to load; this is particularly relevant where services are operated on the principle, common in many developing countries, that buses do not depart from terminals until they are full. Small vehicles also make it possible to offer a greater number of route variations, without seriously affecting service frequency, and this advantage is extensively exploited in some cities, although some of the variations are often so minor that the benefits are insignificant. For some or all of these reasons, the use of small vehicles on conventional bus services, even where there are no constraints on the use of full-sized buses, is becoming more widespread in cities throughout the world, including several European countries.

The development of this concept by the National Bus Company in the United Kingdom during the 1980s makes an interesting case study. During 1984, conventional double deck buses, capable of carrying over 80 passengers each, were replaced on several routes in the city of Exeter by small buses, seating only 16, and with no provision for standing passengers. These vehicles provided a more frequent service, including evening and Sunday services which had previously been reduced or eliminated entirely. The smaller vehicles could penetrate further into housing estates than had been practical with conventional vehicles, and as well as the increased frequency, made possible the concept of "hail and ride", whereby buses would stop and pick up passengers at any safe place, in addition to designated bus stops. The experiment was largely successful: the increased frequency and the "hail and ride" facility were popular with passengers, and the smaller vehicles were regarded as less damaging to the environment on the narrow roads in residential areas. In nearly every case, the number of passengers carried increased substantially. Approximately four small buses were used to replace each full-sized conventional bus, creating additional jobs, although the rates of pay for the drivers were generally lower than for those driving full-sized buses. The scheme was quickly extended to other towns and cities, and within a year there were more than 500 small buses, in fleets of up to sixty, operating in about forty urban areas in the U.K.

The vehicles originally used on these services were not designed specifically for the operation of bus services, for which much more substantial vehicles were normally used, but were standard mass-produced vans adapted for operation as public service vehicles. The life of components such as engines, clutches and gearboxes was relatively short, although this was offset by the low cost of replacement. It was found that these vehicles had a number of limitations, however, and they were progressively replaced by larger vehicles, seating up to 25 passengers with accommodation for up to eight standing, with wider doorways, lower floor height, increased luggage space, and increased internal dimensions. This led to the development by specialist manufacturers of purpose built "minibuses" or "midibuses", and such vehicles have tended to become larger and more sophisticated, as well as much more expensive.

This trend is reflected in many developing countries, where full-sized conventional buses have been largely replaced by smaller vehicles, which are themselves being superseded by types which are becoming progressively larger. In Ghana, for example, the trend in the types of vehicle used by small urban operators appears to be away from small buses (up to twenty seats) and towards purpose-built passenger vehicles in the medium-size (30-35 seats) range. In cities in other countries, mass-produced "midibuses", such as the Toyota Coaster or Nissan Civilian, with about 25 seats, are replacing smaller vehicles. On the other hand there are also many cities where small buses have always been used, and there is no indication that this situation is likely to change; this is the case in many provincial cities in Indonesia.

The size of a vehicle can affect its operating speed in various ways. A small vehicle is likely to have better performance in terms of acceleration and manoeuvrability in traffic than a larger vehicle, while because of its lower capacity and therefore a smaller number of passengers boarding and alighting at each stop, dwell times at stops are shorter. Speed of operation has an effect on system capacity: a vehicle which can achieve a higher average speed over a period will be able to provide more passenger-kilometres than a slower vehicle with the same capacity, although vehicle performance is obviously affected by prevailing traffic speeds. However, where passenger volumes are very high, the advantage of speed enjoyed by smaller vehicles is reduced or even negated by the congestion caused by large numbers of vehicles stopping simultaneously to pick up and set down passengers, and in general, the larger the vehicle used, the greater is the potential capacity of a transport system. When there is a mixture of capacities on one route, the different operating speeds for different vehicle sizes results in irregular services even if buses are despatched from terminals at regular intervals; this was a serious problem on several bus routes in Kingston, Jamaica, in the early 1990s.

Except where by virtue of their numbers they are a direct cause of congestion, small buses can be advantageous in severely congested conditions. They are more manoeuvrable and may cause less congestion per passenger in moving traffic than larger buses if the latter are not full; similarly, where the level of traffic discipline, particularly lane discipline, is poor, smaller and more manoeuvrable vehicles have an advantage. However, a very high service frequency may mean that there are often several vehicles running in convoy, and this can create significant congestion compared with a single large vehicle carrying the same number of passengers in total. When operated at very high frequencies small buses invariably cause more congestion at stops, by requiring more space, while drivers tend to deliberately jostle and obstruct each other, as well as other traffic, through double parking and stopping in the traffic stream. Moreover, a minibus makes wasteful use of road space, occupying nearly three times as much road space per passenger place as a full-sized bus.

Since large numbers of small buses, as opposed to a smaller number of larger buses, can cause increased traffic congestion where road space is restricted, the operation of larger buses is preferable where possible, and where the volume of passenger traffic justifies it, in order to minimise the effect of bus services on traffic congestion. In some cities, small buses have been prohibited in central areas. For example, in Beijing, severe restrictions were imposed in 2002 on the use of minibuses within the area bounded by the Third Ring Road; existing minibuses operating within this area were redeployed on new routes serving outlying residential developments, while the inner route network was augmented with new routes operated by larger buses.

However, if there is severe congestion resulting from high volumes of other road traffic and poor traffic discipline, large vehicles may be at a disadvantage, and the use of smaller vehicles, even though this may cause a further increase in total congestion, may still be advantageous to the individual transport operator. In such cases, the optimum vehicle size, taking into account the interests of all concerned and not only those of bus operators and passengers, may be near the middle of the permitted size range: where congestion is severe, and maximum-sized buses are not practical, buses of nine or ten metres in length, carrying up to fifty passengers, or seventy if a high proportion of standing passengers is carried, are often more suitable than small buses seating up to fifteen passengers, or large buses carrying eighty or more.

Small vehicles are mass produced in greater volume than large buses, and therefore capital costs per seat or passenger-place can be significantly less. Maintenance costs also, principally the cost of spare parts, are often lower for the same reason, and the vehicles are generally easier to maintain, making them attractive to small private sector operators, particularly owner-drivers. The life of a smaller vehicle is usually shorter than that of a larger vehicle, however, so that depreciation costs per passenger may be relatively high. Since each bus requires a driver regardless of its size, labour costs per passenger may be higher for a small bus, but in most developing countries the difference is insignificant since wage rates are generally low. In any case, smaller vehicles require less skill to drive, and therefore recruitment and training of drivers is easier.

Justification for the operation of small vehicles in developing countries is sometimes claimed on the grounds that they create more employment than larger buses, since a greater number of drivers and conductors are required for a given volume of traffic. This may be true when making comparisons with efficiently run fleets of larger buses, but in many cases the operators of large buses, particularly those in the public sector, employ more staff per bus than do private sector minibus operators. Moreover, in an efficient operation, the potentially greater productivity of staff operating larger vehicles usually justifies higher wage levels, with consequent social benefits. The apparent success of small paratransit vehicles compared with larger buses in many developing countries is often not because they are more efficient, but because they tend to concentrate on the on the busiest corridors where large buses would be even more profitable without paratransit competition, and more significantly, because the conventional operators of large buses in many developing countries tend to be excessively inefficient, as discussed elsewhere.

Paratransit is generally far less efficient as a mass mover of people than a service operated with full-sized conventional buses. A typical paratransit vehicle (overloaded) will carry about twenty passengers; a full-sized bus will carry about 100, or five times as many, but will consume approximately three times as much fuel per kilometre; thus the cost per passenger in terms of fuel alone is approximately 70% more by minibus than it is by full-sized bus. In terms of capital cost per passenger place, bearing in mind the longer economic life of a large bus, the minibus may be two or three times as expensive. Differences of the same order apply to costs of tyres and maintenance, and most of these involve foreign exchange and increased drain on the economy for most countries. In order to try to reduce costs, operators of minibuses are often tempted to cut down on essential maintenance, with obvious safety implications.

CONVENTIONAL BUSES

In addition to the wide range of sizes, there are various types of vehicle which may be operated on conventional bus services. Basic choices are between single and double deck vehicles, and between rigid and articulated vehicles. There are many alternative configurations of body and chassis, and mechanical specifications. Different standards of passenger accommodation may be provided, although not normally on the same vehicle, ranging from very basic accommodation, perhaps with the majority of passengers required to stand, to a high level of comfort, with such features as air conditioning, reclining seats, video, toilet and refreshment facilities; as discussed later, it is common, particularly on bus routes with high volumes of passenger traffic, to provide two or more standards of service, using vehicles to different specifications. Detail design considerations are discussed in Chapter 10, but the general characteristics of each vehicle type are described below.

Single deck buses

The vast majority of buses operated throughout the world are single-deckers; often this is the only option. Single deck buses are available in a range of lengths, from approximately five to twelve metres; in some countries even longer buses are permissible, up to a maximum of approximately fifteen metres (normally requiring three axles as opposed to the more usual two), although such lengths are impractical except where operation is exclusively on roads which are relatively wide and straight. If buses longer than twelve metres are required it is normally necessary to use articulated vehicles, as discussed below. The shortest single-deckers, approximately five to six metres long and carrying between ten and twenty passengers, are often referred to as minibuses; the vehicles are usually designed for all passengers to be seated, although in practice standing passengers are often carried, albeit in cramped conditions. Buses of between approximately seven and eight metres, carrying twenty to 35 seated passengers, sometimes with accommodation for additional standing passengers, are often referred to as midibuses, although in some countries these too are known as minibuses. Full sized single deck buses can carry between sixty and 120 passengers including those standing.

Double deck buses

Double deck buses, between approximately nine and twelve metres in length, and even up to fifteen metres in some European countries (again, the longest versions normally require three axles) and seating between sixty and 120 passengers, are operated on urban services in many countries; some are also used for short inter-urban services and even long-distance services, although this is comparatively rare. They are extensively used in the United Kingdom but are less common in Europe. They are also operated in a number of cities in China, including Hong Kong, and several other cities in developing countries, particularly former British colonies, such as India, Bangladesh and Sri Lanka, and in South Africa, and in the past have been operated in Kenya, Uganda, Tanzania, Zambia and Malawi.

Double-deck buses have a number of advantages. They are able to provide a high seating capacity within a limited space, and therefore occupy less road, terminal and depot floor space per seated passenger; in congested traffic conditions and where space is limited this can be a major advantage. However, the saving in space per passenger can be comparatively small, or even negative, depending on the proportion of standing to seated passengers which is acceptable. Where all passengers require seats, as in the case of heavily used premium quality urban services, the double-decker has a greater advantage than where a high proportion of standing passengers is acceptable: a long single-decker, with adequate space for standing passengers, can in fact provide more passenger capacity per unit of road space than a double-decker, which loses space to the staircase and, since standing passengers should not be carried on the upper deck to avoid raising the centre of gravity to a dangerous level, carries a higher proportion of seated passengers.

Disadvantages of double-deckers compared with single-deckers are increased loading and unloading times, and the additional costs arising from the more complex construction, the requirement for a staircase, and also the requirement for greater headroom in depots. Low bridges and other overhead obstructions such as utility cables often restrict the routes on which they can be used, and occasionally result in accidents. There may also be increased risk of buses overturning as a result of the higher centre of gravity, particularly where standards of driving are poor, where loading restrictions are not effectively enforced, or where roads are poorly constructed or maintained.

Articulated buses

Articulated single deck buses, carrying up to 270 passengers and sometimes even more, are efficient movers of large numbers of passengers. As with double deckers, articulated buses are most common for urban services, though a small number are used for long-distance services where road conditions permit. Most articulated buses consist of two, and sometimes three, inter-connected passenger-carrying sections, joined so that the bus can flex, and providing free movement of passengers between one section and another. The engine may be in the front or rear section, and on some vehicles all axles are steerable. Articulated buses are more manoeuvrable than rigid buses of the same length, and therefore in practice can be much longer than rigid buses: up to 25 metres is possible, although the normal maximum permitted length in Europe is 18.75 metres.

Where labour is scarce or expensive, passenger volumes are high, roads are relatively wide and straight, and space is not severely restricted, articulated buses can be very effective. With well-designed bus stop facilities and effective fare collection systems, they can load and unload very quickly despite their size: those used in Curitiba, for example, can load or unload in twenty seconds. However, articulated buses require greater skill to drive, particularly when reversing, while the number of routes on which they may be used is often limited, and specially designed depot facilities may be required. Where congestion is severe and roads are narrow they may be impractical. Their more complex construction makes them more expensive to purchase and maintain than rigid single-deck or double-deck buses (typically,

25% or 30% more than a double-decker), and reliability may be a problem where road conditions are poor. Articulated buses must have good access to bus stops, with all doors accessible from the kerb without obstruction from parked cars or street furniture; it is particularly important to ensure that passenger shelters and safety barriers are positioned so that they do not obstruct any of the doors of buses using the stop.

Articulated buses are still relatively uncommon in developing countries but are becoming more widely used in Asian and South American countries. A small number of articulated buses, using local technology, were introduced in Harare in Zimbabwe during the early 1990s, and imported articulated buses have been operated in a number of other African cities.

A less common form of articulated bus is the semi-trailer combination, with tractor units identical to those used for freight vehicles, towing detachable passenger-carrying trailers. Buses of this type are found in some African countries, in Cuba and in India, where some are built as double-deckers. Some of the Cuban vehicles are approximately 23 metres long, and carry up to 300 passengers. An advantage of this configuration is that mechanically it is much less complex, and therefore easier and cheaper to build, and in the event of a mechanical failure the tractor unit may be replaced rather than the complete combination. If necessary, the tractor unit may also be used for hauling freight trailers, but this capability is unlikely to be required by most public transport operators; it may be more relevant to organisations operating this type of vehicle for transporting their employees. A disadvantage is that communication between the conductor and the driver is difficult, and one-person operation is impossible unless fares are collected off the vehicle or by fully automated means; however, because of the separation of the driver from the passengers, a conductor is normally essential.

Some operators have other unconventional types of articulated bus, often developed in their own workshops. A typical example is a bus from which the engine and drive train has been removed, and which is towed behind another bus, either with some means of operating the original steering mechanism, or with this replaced by a solid axle to convert the towed vehicle to a drawbar trailer. This type of arrangement is often adopted as a last resort to overcome serious shortages of serviceable buses; it was tried in Bangkok in the 1970s, and in some eastern European countries in the 1990s. Some buses are purpose-built to this configuration: they are used in Switzerland and some other European countries, but are otherwise relatively uncommon.

Buses for urban services

Conventional bus services in urban areas may be operated by any of the above vehicle types; in many cities in developed and developing countries all types may be found. The appropriate mix of vehicle types, and indeed the appropriate mix of modes, will vary considerably depending on circumstances.

It is possible to estimate, very approximately, the number of buses required to serve an urban area, based on the size of the population. A more accurate estimate is possible if information is available regarding the proportion of the population which uses buses, and the number of bus trips made per person each day; further refinement will include trip lengths, bus operating speeds, vehicle sizes and operational efficiency. In a typical city, approximately 60% of the population is likely to use a bus service if it is available, and make an average of approximately one journey each day; in a city with a population of one million, this represents 0.6 million bus journeys daily. Assuming that each bus carries 1,200 passengers daily (see Chapter 15), five hundred buses will be required, equating to one full-sized conventional bus per two thousand population This very crude figure is a useful rule-of-thumb guide for a city where conventional buses are the only means of mass public transport; it will be reduced depending on the extent to which other modes are available. In a city served solely by minibuses carrying 240 passengers each per day, the vehicle requirement would be approximately 2.5 minibuses per thousand people.

Buses for long-distance services

For long-distance operation there are various types of conventional bus available to cater for the different types of traffic. In most cases, except where road conditions are unfavourable, the most common vehicle is the full-sized or medium-sized single-deck bus, although small buses and taxis are also often used. There is often considerable variation in the standard of accommodation provided, at different fares, to cater for different sectors of the market. Standards range from basic, enabling the maximum number of passengers to be carried with minimum comfort, to luxurious, with features such as air conditioning, reclining seats, video equipment, on-board toilet and catering facilities. As a minimum, there are usually at least two standards available; in tropical countries the distinction is often between those provided by vehicles with and without air-conditioning, but there are often several more variations.

In the Philippines, for example, some operators provide up to four main standards of service, using air-conditioned buses, to a high standard of comfort; similar buses, but without air-conditioning; buses with more basic seating, and with a higher seating capacity; and older buses, with basic seating, operated at very low fares. In China, there are three principal bus types, namely standard, luxury, and sleeper, available in three basic lengths; the range comprises a 6.7 metre 25 seat standard bus, a 9.2 metre standard bus, with 45 seats, a 9.8 metre vehicle, available as a sleeper or standard bus with forty seats, or up to sixty seats in "three and two" configuration (i.e. with a seat for three passengers on one side of the aisle, and a seat for two on the other), and a twelve-metre luxury bus with forty adjustable reclining seats and air-conditioning as standard. Buses can be supplied in "luxury" form, with fewer seats than the standard types, often adjustable; toilets can be provided as an optional extra. Sleeper buses have reclining bunks, similar to reclining seats, but with a much greater degree of adjustment on the backrest, and with the cushion extended so that the passenger sits with legs outstretched; these are arranged on two levels in various configurations, providing accommodation for 24 to 32 passengers. Usually they operate on inter-provincial long distance routes, providing both day and night services.

Buses for rural services

Conventional buses are less common on rural services in developing countries. Typical vehicles used for rural transport are "truck-buses", trucks modified to carry both passengers and goods, while most buses used on rural routes have roof-mounted luggage racks or freight compartments incorporated in the body. At the lower end of the size range, there is a good deal of interchangeability between passenger and freight vehicles; on rural services in particular, most public transport vehicles carry large amounts of freight as well as passengers, while freight vehicles frequently carry passengers sitting on top of their loads. In many rural areas, especially where road conditions are poor, shared use of private vehicles, particularly pick-ups, is the only form of public transport. Many journeys are made by "hitching" rides on freight transport vehicles. A high proportion of movements are by non-motorised means, by foot, bicycle or animal power. Many movements are by walking, and, particularly in African countries, goods are often carried over long distances to markets as headloads.

Buses for tourists

Because of the varied nature of tourists' requirements, there is a wide range of vehicle types used in the tourism industry. Some tourists have limited funds and require to travel as cheaply as possible and many, especially the younger travellers, are prepared to suffer a certain amount of discomfort to this end. Others, usually the older and more affluent travellers, prefer luxury vehicles. Many tourist resorts are frequented by a range of tourist types, although often a particular resort tends to attract a particular category. The type of vehicle required depends on the number of people in the party, the category of tourist to be carried, the type of journey, and the road conditions. Vehicles used for tourist services include highly-specified air-conditioned luxury buses or coaches, built to maximum dimensions and seating up to 60 passengers or even more; smaller buses, with or without air-conditioning; taxis; and chauffeur-driven and self drive car hire.

Some types of tourist activity, such as game viewing drives, require specialised vehicles. Some tourist vehicles are designed with "novelty" features: for example, some city tour buses are disguised as vintage buses or even as tramcars; or vehicles used for game viewing are designed to look primitive so that tourists are able to imagine that they are "roughing it", although they expect the vehicles to be clean and well maintained, and usually also expect a much greater degree of comfort than the appearance of the vehicle would suggest. Buses used on long journeys are often equipped with toilet and refreshment facilities, especially in countries where such facilities are not readily available en route. Since many tourists carry large quantities of luggage, vehicles normally require ample luggage accommodation.

Double-deck vehicles are becoming increasingly popular as tourist buses, particularly on short-distance tours such as city sightseeing trips, since the upper deck offers much better visibility; where climatic conditions are favourable, many double deck tour buses have no roof to the upper deck. There are also a small number of double-deck touring and long-distance coaches, built to premium specifications; often most of the lower deck is used for luggage accommodation and catering equipment, with limited seating accommodation, permitting the majority of passengers to benefit from the better view from the upper deck.

PARATRANSIT VEHICLE TYPES

There are many local names for paratransit vehicles, such as dala-dala (Tanzania); dolmus (Turkey); emergency taxi or ET (Zimbabwe); jeepney (Philippines); matatu (Kenya); public light bus or PLB (Hong Kong); robot (Jamaica); silor (Thailand); tempo (Bangladesh); and tro-tro (Ghana). In several African countries, minibuses used on paratransit services are also referred to as taxis. In some countries they are known by a variety of names: in Indonesia, for example, they are variously known as angdes, angkot, angkudes, bemo, mikrolet, opelet, pete-pete, taksi, and sometimes by the make or model of the vehicle most commonly used on a particular route, such as Colt, Daihatsu or Kijang. In other countries they are simply known as minibuses or microbuses.

Various types of vehicle are used for paratransit services, although the general worldwide trend is towards the use of purpose built passenger carrying vehicles, usually mass produced. The most typical vehicle types are large cars (usually of the estate car or station wagon type); pick-up trucks or three- to five-ton trucks with a basic box body and bench seating; and mass-produced minibuses or midibuses, usually of either ten- to twelve- or 25-seat configuration, such as the Nissan E23 or Toyota Coaster respectively. The jeepneys, in the Philippines, were originally conversions of the US-manufactured "Jeep"; they have gradually become bigger over the years, with longer wheelbase chassis assembled locally. A common type of vehicle in Indonesia is the mikrolet, similar to the standard mass-produced minibuses, but smaller. Also found in some parts of Indonesia, particularly in Surabaya, is the angguna, which is similar to a mikrolet, but with an open truck body behind a shortened passenger compartment. A typical paratransit vehicle in West Africa is the mammy truck, which is a small to medium-sized truck, fitted with wooden bench seats; the sides are open and protection is provided by a canopy. Total passenger capacity is normally between thirty and 45, but it is common for these vehicles to carry large quantities of freight, which reduces the passenger capacity. Mammy trucks are gradually being replaced by more conventional vehicles, but are still common in rural areas. Full-sized conventional buses are sometimes operated on the same informal basis as the smaller paratransit vehicles, as for example in Sri Lanka, where there are very few public service vehicles with fewer than 25 seats.

Motorcycles and Scooter-based Vehicles

Three-wheeled public transport vehicles based on the motor cycle or scooter are common in several Asian countries, although they are tending to become less common for mass transport, being replaced by slightly larger mikrolets or minibuses. They fall into two categories, the smaller carrying two or three passengers, normally on an individual public transport basis, such as the Bajaj in India and Indonesia, the auto-rickshaw in Bangladesh or the duk-duk in Thailand, and the larger version, normally operated on a fixed-route basis, such as the bemo in Indonesia, the samlor in Thailand, or the tempo in Bangladesh, carrying up to eight (sometimes even ten) passengers on longitudinal bench seats, with an open rear for entry and exit. These vehicles, as well as offering a low standard of comfort, tend to be slow, noisy and often cause severe pollution, with passengers being exposed to excessive exhaust emissions; however, an increasing number of vehicles powered by natural gas are now being operated in some countries, such as Thailand. Although these vehicles are capable of speeds of up to 40 kph, typical average operating speeds are of the order of 8-10 kph, and they are therefore used mainly for short journeys; typical average trip length is approximately four or five kilometres. In some cities, they are now banned from certain roads or areas, both for environmental reasons, and to avoid the obstruction of other traffic.

Motorcycles are becoming increasingly common as a form of individual public transport in many countries, particularly in South-East Asia, such as the ojeks in Indonesia. Capital and operating costs for these vehicles are relatively low; in some cases personal motorcycles are used on a part-time basis to supplement income from other employment. Usually they operate informally or illegally since the regulatory systems in most countries have not been amended to cater for this form of transport. They tend to act as feeders to other forms of public transport, carrying one or sometimes two passengers along narrow residential streets which are not served by other modes; in some cities, where traffic congestion is severe, they are also used as a faster means of travel than taxis.

Human-powered Vehicles

Human-powered vehicles, such as the cycle-rickshaw in Bangladesh, or becak in Indonesia, are common in several Asian countries Most are based on the bicycle: the traditional pedestrian hand-drawn variety is now much less common. In some countries, including Indonesia, conventional bicycles are used for individual public transport, with a saddle provided for the passenger above the rear wheel. Such vehicles are versatile, and although in practical terms their use is limited to relatively smooth and flat roads, they can negotiate very narrow streets which may be inaccessible to other forms of transport. However, the maximum speed for a human-powered vehicle is approximately ten kilometres per hour, although the average operating speed is nearer five; they can cause obstruction to faster traffic, particularly on narrow roads, or where they are used in large numbers, as in Dhaka.

A common problem with non-motorised vehicles is that they tend to take the shortest route between any two points, and this often entails travelling against the flow of traffic, particularly where there are barriers between carriageways, or one-way traffic systems. On busy roads, as well as having serious safety implications, this can also have a significant adverse effect on traffic flow. For this reason, becaks have been banned on many roads and in some entire areas or cities in Indonesia; for a few years they were completely banned in Jakarta, but they are now being used again in some parts of the city. Cycle-rickshaws have also been banned from a number of main roads in Dhaka. On busy streets, where possible, it is desirable to segregate all non-motorised traffic from motorised traffic.

Human-powered vehicles have low capital costs, and apart from labour, almost negligible operating costs: maintenance costs are low, and non-renewable fuel is not required. However, the cycle-rickshaw or equivalent tends to be costly in terms of the fare charged per passenger kilometre, due to the low productivity of the driver and consequently high labour cost per kilometre. Fare levels tend to vary, depending on the availability of alternative employment: when unemployment is high, fares will tend to be lower, and vice versa.

The driving of human-powered vehicles has sometimes been criticised as a degrading occupation, but manual labour of various kinds is a significant employment category in developing countries, and this is not a valid argument against their use. If such vehicles were banned, a very large number of rickshaw-pullers would lose their source of incomes, and most would be forced to resort to begging or even crime for their livelihoods. Some cycle-rickshaws are owner-driven, but most are rented by the driver, usually on a daily basis from fleet owners; there are some quite large fleets in some countries. Licensing procedures are often relatively informal, and poorly enforced, so that entry to this sector of the market is relatively easy.

Animal-powered Vehicles

Animal-powered vehicles, mostly horse-drawn, are used for individual public transport in some countries, but are becoming less common. They are used in many towns and cities as well as rural areas in Indonesia, where there are several types, including the andong or dilman, carrying up to six passengers, the dokar, carrying four passengers, and in parts of Sulawesi, the smaller bendi, which carries only two. These vehicles are slow and cannot negotiate very narrow streets, and cause delay to motorised traffic, particularly where traffic volumes are high. They are therefore most suited to areas where traffic is relatively light, and there is adequate road capacity; they are banned from certain streets or areas, particularly in the larger cities.

CONVENTIONAL TAXIS

The vehicles used for conventional taxi services are usually based on standard production saloon cars, although there are some purpose-built taxis such as the London "black cab". The typical vehicle type used for conventional taxi services varies considerably between one city and another. In some cities, such as Hong Kong, there is a high proportion of taxis based on relatively large saloon cars; in Beijing and other Chinese cities small saloon cars and micro-vans are commonly used as taxis. In other cities, such as Dhaka, there are relatively few conventional taxis, although there are many auto-rickshaws. In Nairobi, a large fleet of London-type taxis was imported in the late 1980s, but purpose-built taxis are relatively uncommon in developing countries.

Where saloon cars are used, the type and standard of vehicles used varies. In some countries, new vehicles are purchased, often as a condition of the licence; in others, very old vehicles are normal. In some other countries, most taxis are purchased new but are operated until they are very old. In several cities there is a tendency for operators to standardise on a particular make or model of car. For example, the most common type of vehicle in use as a taxi in Jamaica in the mid-1990s, and the most preferred by operators, was the medium-sized BMC saloon car manufactured in Britain between 1959 and 1972. There were various models, sharing a common body shell and two standard engine sizes; the most common were the Morris Oxford and Austin Cambridge, but Wolseley, Riley and MG models were also operated. These vehicles could carry up to four passengers, in addition to the driver, in reasonable comfort. Since this type of car was long obsolete, spare parts were difficult and expensive to obtain; nevertheless, operators regarded this as the ideal vehicle for taxi work in Kingston. Virtually all were imported second-hand from the United Kingdom; new cars were generally considered by Jamaican taxi operators to be too expensive, although some of the larger companies bought new vehicles from time to time.

Vehicle standards vary considerably. In many developing countries, the standard of the majority of vehicles used as taxis is poor. Many are over twenty years old and have deteriorated badly through intensive use, frequent minor accidents, abusive driving and poor maintenance. Maintenance facilities available to taxi operators are usually limited, and often maintenance is carried out mainly at the roadside, with minimal equipment. Some fleet operators have rudimentary workshop facilities, although even these carry out much of their work in the street outside their premises. Commercial garages are sometimes used for some maintenance work but this is usually kept to a minimum in order to contain expenditure.

In many cities, legally operated taxis are supplemented by illegal, unlicensed cars. Often these are cars which have failed their roadworthiness inspections; others are private cars used on a part time basis by their owners to supplement their incomes.

RAIL VEHICLES

Passenger vehicles for heavy rail systems vary from locomotive-hauled trains with up to twelve coaches, and sometimes more, to single self-propelled rail cars. Heavy rail coaches can carry up to eighty seated passengers, or 200 including standing passengers in those designed for maximum-capacity urban service. Most common are multiple unit trains, typically with between two and six coaches, powered by diesel or electric motors in one or more of the coaches. These may be coupled together to form longer trains.

Locomotive-hauled trains are more usually used for long-distance services and provide greater flexibility in capacity and composition: the number and types of coaches used can be varied to meet different requirements. Diesel or electric multiple-unit trains are less flexible, but can still provide different types of accommodation in different coaches, or within the same coach. They are most commonly used for urban and medium distance services, but their use on long-distance services is increasing.

The size of vehicle which may be operated is influenced by the track gauge and loading gauge. Most rail systems are built to "standard" track gauge of 1435 millimetres, but a large number are to "narrow" gauge, typically of about one metre. The wider the gauge, the wider the rolling stock which may be operated, but maximum height and width is limited by the loading gauge. Typical rolling stock for standard gauge track is approximately three metres wide, with a maximum height from the track of approximately four metres. Where the loading gauge permits, double-decked trains are sometimes operated, usually on urban services, but in some cases, where there is a requirement for high capacity, also on long-distance services.

Loading gauges for light rail systems are usually more restricted and capacity per car ranges from about eighty to 150 passengers, including those standing. Rolling stock is by definition lighter than that used for heavy rail, and coaches are normally shorter and narrower. LRT trains usually comprise no more than four coaches, or two articulated units, but in some cases single cars are operated.

Rolling stock for street tramway systems is generally similar to that used on LRT systems although where they operate alongside normal traffic this may limit their dimensions. Small-radius curves are often necessary on street systems, and this will restrict the maximum length of cars; it is often necessary to build cars with tapered ends to provide clearance between cars passing on curves. Street trams may, like LRT vehicles, be operated as single cars, articulated units, or trains, but it is unusual for more than two cars to be operated together in a street system. Double deck trams were common in the United Kingdom but less so elsewhere; a small street tramway system using double-deck cars still operates in Hong Kong.

Heavy and light rail locomotives and multiple units must normally be capable of being driven from both ends to avoid the need to turn the locomotive or the complete train at each end of the route. Many street tramway vehicles are similarly configured, although in some systems, turning loops (or in some cases reversing junctions) are provided at the ends of each route, and at intermediate points where trams may turn short, so that only a single cab is required. This requires additional infrastructure in the form of loops and junctions as opposed to simpler cross-over points, but reduces the complexity and cost of the vehicles themselves; capacity is increased since a greater proportion of the internal space is available for passengers, and passenger doorways are required on one side of the vehicle only. Single-cab trams (and even heavy or light rail vehicles) may also be used on circular routes, provided that they are not also required to operate on other routes where there are no turning facilities.

There are also various forms of unconventional light rail vehicle under development. A typical example is the Parry People Mover, being developed in the United Kingdom. This small vehicle, with a capacity of about 35 passengers, requires relatively low-cost track and is driven by a flywheel; at each stop the vehicle makes contact with a third rail which provides low-voltage electric current to power the flywheel sufficiently to take the vehicle to the next stop. Such systems have limited potential but when fully developed may be suitable for public transport in city centre areas.

ALTERNATIVE SOURCES OF POWER

The vast majority of public service vehicles operating throughout the world are powered by diesel engines although several alternative fuels are available. Diesel power is preferred mainly for reasons of economy; the capital cost of a diesel engine is normally higher than that of a petrol engine, but the operating costs are significantly lower. In most countries the retail costs per litre of petrol and diesel, including excise duty, are broadly similar, but fuel consumption achievable from a diesel engine, in terms of litres consumed per kilometre, is at least 30% lower than that of a petrol engine. For the larger engine sizes, diesel is normally the only available option, although a large number of minibuses based on mass-produced designs have petrol engines.

Until comparatively recently the majority of full-sized buses in the former Soviet Union and in China were powered by petrol engines, despite the better fuel consumption obtained from diesel. One reason was that some operators were influenced by the low capital cost of petrol engines despite the fact that over the life of the vehicle operating costs are higher. More significant was the fact that until recently the quality of diesel engines available, particularly in China, was poor; the quality has, however, improved substantially, and the use of diesel is increasing. In Saudi Arabia, petrol engines were preferred by some operators since it was considered that these caused less pollution than diesel powered vehicles.

An increasing number of buses and taxis, particularly in urban areas, are powered by compressed natural gas (CNG) or liquefied petroleum gas (LPG). Compared with diesel engines, gas powered vehicles have cleaner exhaust emission and are generally quieter, but fuel consumption, in terms of litres consumed per kilometre, is higher. In cost terms, depending on relative basic costs and rates of duty, operating costs for gas powered buses may be up to 50% more than for diesel buses. Nevertheless CNG has been made compulsory for buses in several Indian states; the majority of taxis and autorickshaws in several large Asian cities, such as Bangkok and Dhaka, are powered by LPG, resulting in a noticeable improvement in air quality.

Electric power is a viable alternative, particularly for LRT systems. It is also suitable for road-based transport in certain circumstances; the most common form of electric-powered public transport vehicle is the trolleybus, a variant of the conventional bus which draws electric current from overhead cables. Trolleybuses may be rigid or articulated, single or double-decked, and are normally built to near the maximum permitted dimensions, although in some countries trolleybuses of "midibus" size are operated; in some systems in the former Soviet Union trolleybuses are coupled together as multiple-units.

Trolleybuses have certain advantages over motor buses. In particular, they are quieter and do not emit exhaust gases; their contribution to atmospheric and noise pollution is therefore significantly less. It must be remembered, however, that the generating stations which produce the electricity may produce fumes or other forms of pollution including nuclear waste and the risk of nuclear accident, although there are renewable, pollution-free sources of power such as hydro-electricity.

Trolleybuses are particularly advantageous in very hilly conditions, having good acceleration and hill-climbing capabilities. The economic life of a trolleybus is normally longer than that of a motor bus, due partly to the simpler transmission system and the reduced vibration from the electric motor compared with an internal combustion engine, although the effects of wear and tear due to road conditions and corrosion are similar. They are a viable alternative to motor buses on intensive urban routes, and where the cost of electricity is lower than that of fuel oil for a given power output, total costs can be significantly lower.

A disadvantage of electric power compared with liquid fuel is the difficulty of supply to the vehicle. Electricity supplied to trolleybuses through overhead cables has considerable infrastructure implications and restricts the routes on which the vehicles can be used. The provision and maintenance of the power supply equipment is a major item of expenditure, and as with rail-based systems, a high service frequency is necessary to justify the infrastructure investment; at the outer ends of urban routes, and where routes diverge, frequencies may fall below the break-even level, making some portions of route uneconomic. Similarly, if there is competition from diesel buses or minibuses, this may reduce the frequency of the trolleybus service to a level at which the provision of overhead infrastructure is not viable. Electrically powered transport modes are potentially vulnerable to power supply failure, which may be a significant problem in some developing countries. They are also vulnerable to damage to the infrastructure: in Kabul, Afghanistan, for example, a trolleybus system introduced in 1975 ceased operating in 1992 when the power supply was damaged in fighting; there are, however, plans to revive this system.

Other disadvantages of trolleybuses compared with conventional bus systems are inflexibility, including the inability of one trolleybus to overtake another on the same track without retracting the overhead power collectors, and problems with road developments and temporary diversions. Many trolleybus systems have been abandoned in order to avoid the cost of repositioning overhead equipment when major road improvement schemes have been undertaken.

Because of the nature of the power supply system for trolleybuses, it is not normally practical to have a large number of small operators sharing the same system. Trolleybus systems therefore tend to be monopolistic or oligopolistic, and as such are inconsistent with industry structure in most developing countries. There are numerous trolleybus systems in the former Soviet Union and China, and in several South American countries; amongst the world's largest are those in Moscow, Beijing, Sao Paulo (Brazil) and Mexico City. Otherwise, they are relatively uncommon in developing countries. Virtually all trolleybus systems are purely urban, although there are some inter-urban systems, with routes of up to eighty kilometres, mostly in the former Soviet Union.

All trolleybuses are fitted with batteries which, if they are in good condition, will normally enable them to run under their own power for one or two kilometres. This capability is basically for emergency use only, but some transport undertakings operate hybrid vehicles, in the form of trolleybuses fitted with small auxiliary internal combustion engines so that vehicles may operate away from the wires on a regular basis as well as in the event of a power failure.

Other forms of hybrid vehicle currently undergoing development include diesel-electric buses, driven by electric power generated by the vehicle's engine; also under development is a similar system, but which uses a gas turbine in place of the diesel engine. By allowing the engine to operate at optimum speed, these have the advantages of increased engine efficiency, enabling smaller engines to be used than in conventionally powered buses, and hence reduced fuel consumption and exhaust emissions. This arrangement usually incorporates batteries to power the bus in pollution-sensitive areas, such as city centres and covered bus stations; however, as with vehicles powered by batteries only, the batteries impose a considerable weight penalty.

Electricity supplied from batteries carried on the vehicle would be preferable if this were practical but although technology is improving, batteries with sufficient capacity to provide power for a vehicle to operate at reasonable speeds and with a practical range are very heavy and require a good deal of space. There have been numerous experiments with battery-powered vehicles over several decades, including some using trailers to carry the batteries, and systems in which buses are able to charge their batteries at each stop through physical contact or contactless power transfer means; these are still at an early stage of development, and as yet no practical bus has been developed which is powered by batteries alone. Smaller vehicles which operate over short distances are more easily powered by batteries: for example, there are several hundred battery powered three-wheel eleven-seat minibuses operating in Kathmandu, Nepal.

In several European cities, and in some cities in developing countries such as New Delhi, there are small numbers of buses operating experimentally which are powered by fuel cells. Fuel cells are charged with electrical energy produced by mixing hydrogen and oxygen, and power an electric motor which drives the bus. The level of noise from this form of propulsion is low, there is no vibration, and the only emission is water vapour. Disadvantages are the limited range of between 200 and 250 kilometres, potential danger if fuel is not handled with care, and the heavy vehicle weight necessitated by the hydrogen fuel tanks, and associated strengthening of the body and suspension to cater for these. In addition, the cost of the fuel is approximately ten times that of conventional fuel. Nevertheless, future development may overcome these disadvantages and make fuel cell power a viable option.

There have been various experiments with even less conventional forms of propulsion. For example, there have been experiments in Europe from time to time with flywheel-powered buses, usually based on trolleybuses or hybrid vehicles using a diesel engine to power the flywheel, which generates electricity to power the vehicle through an electric motor.

Developments of alternatives to diesel powered bus and rail vehicles, or electric power supplied to vehicles through overhead cables or additional rails at track level, are largely still at the experimental stage. It is essential that alternatives are found, to comply with increasingly stringent controls which are being imposed in many countries on the level of permissible emissions from internal combustion engines, as well as to deal with the longer term problem of depletion of energy resources. In practical terms, however, at present the most appropriate fuel for buses in developing countries is diesel, with petrol as an option for smaller vehicles, while in certain circumstances electric-powered trolleybuses may be feasible in large cities. Similarly, for rail transport, diesel power for long distances and electricity for urban services are the only practical options in the majority of cases.

3

TRANSPORT INFRASTRUCTURE

Transport infrastructure embraces not only the road and rail systems, but also the terminals, depots and workshops, and pedestrian facilities which are complementary to public transport infrastructure as well as being a universal requirement. Inadequacy of infrastructure is a problem in most developing countries: new construction invariably fails to keep pace with population growth and increasing transport requirements, while a substantial proportion of existing infrastructure is in need of refurbishment.

Some elements of transport infrastructure, principally the road system itself, are generally available for use by all public and private transport, while other parts are provided exclusively for public transport services. Provision of the road system is normally a government function; most large transport operators provide their own depot facilities, and sometimes terminals, although the latter are often provided by local authorities. This chapter deals with the road system, its use, and related infrastructure; bus depots and terminals are dealt with in later chapters, but for the sake of convenience, certain items of infrastructure such as tramway tracks or overhead cables for trams or trolleybuses, which form part of the road system but which may be provided by the transport operators, are discussed in this chapter.

The nature and extent of road-based public transport services is influenced by the characteristics of the road system, which is often inadequate in terms of both condition and capacity: where roads are poor, most transport operators will be deterred from providing all but a basic service, while a good road system is likely to encourage development of bus services. If inter-urban roads link towns and cities directly, long-distance buses tend to stop at all major towns, while if most towns are by-passed there tends to be a predominance of non-stop services.

Road capacity in urban areas is normally at a premium, with private transport making increasing demands on scarce road space. Furthermore, most cities in developing countries are continually expanding; ideally, infrastructure development should keep pace with this growth, as should the provision of public transport, but in most cases this is far from being achieved. Although private car ownership will never reach the point where every traveller has access to private transport, growth in car ownership has been such that traffic volumes in many cities are approaching or have already reached saturation levels.

Most city environments are far from ideal, but many infrastructure developments which are designed to cater for increasing volumes of motor traffic result in further environmental degradation. Regardless of considerations of sustainability, even if a completely new city were to be created on a green-field site, it would be impossible to provide the necessary infrastructure for all passenger movements to be made by private transport. Public transport will therefore always be vital, and the urban road infrastructure must be designed or adapted to cater for the requirements of public transport as well as the car. Nor should it be forgotten that streets have purposes in addition to carrying traffic, including pedestrian access to properties, providing light and air for buildings, routes for pipes and cables for services such as water, gas, drainage, sewage, electricity and telephones, accommodation for activities and facilities such as pavement cafes, street markets, and recreation. In countries such as Pakistan and Jamaica, for example, entire streets are occasionally taken over for informal cricket matches, and such activities can have an important place in the life of any city.

It is essential that the provision of transport infrastructure takes into consideration the requirements of public transport and pedestrians as well as other motor traffic, and other urban activities; it should also be appreciated that public transport can play a part in the improvement of the urban environment by reducing the need for expensive road works, which might otherwise be required to accommodate high volumes of private car traffic.

ROAD NETWORK AND CHARACTERISTICS

The nature and extent of the road network is important in determining the type of bus route network which may be provided. A road network may follow a definite pattern. In cities, for example, roads may follow a grid or radial pattern, or a combination of the two. On the other hand there may be no discernible pattern, particularly where the road layout is determined by topographical features; there may be only one route between any two points, or several alternatives. Many otherwise modern cities have an "old" part, with narrow and winding streets which are unsuitable for motor traffic. Some old city centres are not accessible to motor vehicles at all, such as the souks in many Arab cities which may be busy and densely populated commercial and residential areas, but are generally accessible only to pedestrians. Many new city centres and residential areas, particularly in developed countries, incorporate features designed to improve conditions for pedestrians by segregating them from motor traffic, such as pedestrian precincts, shopping malls, or pedestrian decks above street level; the central areas of some cities are divided into zones, between which most traffic other than public transport is not permitted to move directly.

By contrast, the road systems in many cities are designed solely to keep traffic moving, regardless of the requirements of pedestrians and public transport users. Most of the growth of major cities in developing countries has taken place comparatively recently, and the roads have been built to cater for substantial volumes of traffic: they are often very wide, with service roads on either side of the main carriageway, and may also include exclusive bus or cycle lanes. Main highways often present significant impediments to pedestrian movement. Some road networks, particularly those in higher-income residential areas, were designed primarily for private transport, so that public transport routes, if any, are circuitous, and therefore inconvenient, fragmented and expensive to operate. For example a large housing development in which the roads branch out into a series of loops or dead ends will require several bus routes, with lower frequencies than would be provided if a continuous road ran through the centre of the development, requiring fewer bus route variations.

In most cities there is a hierarchy of roads, comprising primary routes, secondary and access or distributor roads. The number of levels in the hierarchy may vary, depending on the size of the town or city: in a large city there may be primary roads, which may be motorways, freeways or expressways; district distributors; local distributors; and access or service roads. The main bus routes will normally follow the primary routes, with deviations and feeder routes using the secondary roads. Few bus routes will follow the access roads, which are mostly relatively narrow streets in the city centres, or residential suburban roads, although smaller paratransit vehicles often serve these areas.

In some cases it may be necessary to operate different types of bus according to the type of road, with larger buses on primary roads and smaller ones on secondary roads. The primary roads should be designed, maintained and controlled to provide a smooth flow of traffic; through traffic should be discouraged or prevented from using access roads. A serious problem in many cities in developing countries is that the total length of access and secondary roads is relatively low compared to the primary roads, so that the primary roads are also used excessively for purposes such as parking and access in addition to their main function. In some cities there is no proper hierarchy of roads, or there is little continuity between roads of a particular class, resulting in inefficient route networks, and problems of traffic control and bus routing.

There are often imbalances in the capacities of different parts of the road system, with for example high capacity multi-lane highways converging on central areas which cannot absorb the traffic, or large multi-storey car parks where the streets approaching them have inadequate capacity for the traffic generated. The problem of road capacity is exacerbated as increasingly tall commercial and residential buildings are constructed in urban centres, housing more people and therefore generating more traffic, while the infrastructure capacity is rarely increased in proportion; even the footpaths are often too narrow to accommodate the additional pedestrians. The desirable traffic capacity of many urban streets from an environmental viewpoint may be much lower than their theoretical capacity, bearing in mind the other functions of city streets. It is easy to say, for example, that street vendors should be removed because they obstruct the traffic, but it can be argued that the converse should apply: it is presumptuous to assume that traffic must always take precedence over all other activities although this is the basis of many traffic plans.

Many urban road systems are adequate for normal traffic flows for most of the day, but not for peak traffic flows. Even if it were possible to construct roads with the capacity to cope with peak traffic flows, they would be under-utilised at off-peak times, representing an under-utilised resource as well as inefficient use of scarce urban land.

Outside the cities, the road systems in most developing countries consist of direct links between towns, with all long-distance traffic having to pass through town centres en route. Main routes should ideally provide reasonably direct links between major towns and cities, within the constraints of geography and topography. Certain towns may be by-passed, but the provision of by-passes is expensive, while the benefits to both local inhabitants and through traffic tend to be greater in smaller towns and cities than in larger ones. Congestion in many smaller towns is largely attributable to through traffic, while in larger towns the proportion of local to through traffic is normally much higher; there may still be sufficient through traffic to justify the provision of a by-pass, but this alone will not solve the urban traffic problems. Alternatively, there may be a national route network of roads designed for high speeds and avoiding most if not all towns and cities; distances on such networks will usually be greater, but total journey times shorter.

On inter-urban roads in particular, factors such as the directness of routes, quality of roads, and provision of by-passes will affect not only the journey times between towns and cities, but also vehicle operating costs. A significant increase in road construction costs may be justified where this results in reduced operating costs. For example the cost of a by-pass, or a route using cuttings or tunnels to reduce distances and gradients may be more than offset by the consequent reduction in the total operating costs of the vehicles using the road, especially where traffic volumes are high; on the other hand, lengthening the route to avoid steep gradients will reduce operating costs per kilometre, but will increase total kilometres operated, and it is therefore necessary to achieve the correct balance in order to minimise total costs. In general terms, the lower the expenditure on road construction, the higher will be the operating costs for vehicles using the road; the higher the volume of traffic, therefore, the greater the justification for increased construction expenditure, since the potential savings will be greater. It is also generally the case that the more spent initially on a road, the less the requirement for subsequent maintenance, and therefore wherever possible, in countries where maintenance standards are poor, roads should be built to the highest affordable standards.

Secondary roads connect smaller settlements with the main routes, while rural access or feeder roads penetrate into the more remote areas. Most access roads are very lightly used, in some cases carrying fewer than twenty vehicles per day, with a high proportion of pedestrian traffic. Expenditure on these roads is often inadequate to maintain them to a standard which provides good year-round access by motor vehicles; tar roads can rarely be justified, and roads are sometimes impassable for considerable periods. This results in increased transport costs and journey times, and transport operators are often reluctant to run services at all: when they do, services are unpredictable, and fares invariably high. The effective isolation of many rural communities by poor roads and transport services affects all aspects of their lives.

Road surface, width and alignment characteristics influence the type and size of vehicle which may be operated. The general condition of the roads, and in particular their state of repair, is also important: experience has shown that improvement of the roads on which buses operate invariably results in improvements in the quality of services provided. Narrow roads and bridges, or small turning radii at intersections, and the positioning of street furniture such as pedestrian refuges, barriers and bollards, may preclude the operation of long or wide buses; this is a problem in many restricted city centre and suburban areas as well as on some rural roads.

The type of road surface, and its quality, can have a profound effect on transport operation. Roads may be surfaced, with tarmac, concrete or other materials such as stone blocks, or may be unsurfaced "dirt" roads, consisting of graded earth, gravel or sand. A surfaced road which is well maintained can permit vehicles to operate at high speeds with relatively little wear and tear; one which is badly maintained, with potholes and broken edges, as well as preventing vehicles from operating at speed, can be dangerous, and result in excessive damage to tyres, suspension systems, chassis and body structures. Dirt roads, if surfaces are well graded, can permit relatively high speeds at comfort and in safety, especially when dry, although the dusty conditions may cause discomfort to passengers, and vehicles may suffer from dust ingress to components unless adequate protective measures are incorporated in their design. If dirt roads are not well graded, however, they can become impassable to many vehicles, particularly during wet seasons.

Vehicle maintenance costs can be significantly increased by poor road surfaces, and safety can be jeopardised, although accident rates on good tarmac roads are often higher, due to vehicles being driven at excessive speeds. There is a natural tendency, particularly where public transport fares are based on distance irrespective of road condition, for operators to prefer the better roads, where operating speeds are higher, and costs lower. This has the effect of reducing transport capacity in areas where conditions are poor; where fares are deregulated, they are invariably higher in these areas, reflecting the higher costs of operation.

Low bridges crossing the road, or tunnels with limited headroom, will restrict the height and sometimes the width of vehicles which may use the road; headroom of less than approximately 4.5 metres will be inadequate for most double deck buses. Overhead power and telephone cables are a prominent feature in many cities. Often these are relatively low, and restrict the height of vehicles which may use the streets; they may present a considerable danger to road users, particularly if damaged by a high vehicle. Where overhead cables are permitted, a minimum height of five metres above the road surface is normally desirable. Weight restrictions on road bridges may limit the laden weight of buses which may be used; this can be a particular problem in rural areas. A restriction at only one point will affect an entire bus route: for example a severe weight restriction on one bridge on a bus route will necessitate the operation of small capacity vehicles throughout the route, unless it is divided into sections, with passengers crossing the restricted bridge on foot to transfer from one vehicle to another.

An important consideration in road design is the level of compliance with weight regulations, in particular axle loads. Where compliance is poor, as is often the case in developing countries, roads must be designed for the maximum possible weight of vehicles which will use the road, rather than the maximum legal weight. Axle loads of up to twelve or fifteen tonnes are normal in many countries, even though this may be double the weight permitted by law. Failure to recognise this reality will inevitably result in premature failure of the road surface.

FACILITIES FOR PEDESTRIANS

Walking is complementary to public transport, since all public transport users are pedestrians at some point during the course of their journeys; therefore infrastructure provided for pedestrians is relevant in any discussion of public transport. In particular, footpaths are used by bus passengers before and after taking their bus journeys, and while waiting for the bus to arrive. In addition many medium distance journeys, as well as journeys to and from bus stops, are made on foot; in developing countries a significant amount of short distance freight is carried by pedestrians, often using handcarts. Many people in developing countries cannot afford to use public transport, and therefore have no choice other than walking; large numbers of schoolchildren in particular have to walk, often for long distances, and may be exposed to unnecessary danger if pedestrian facilities are poor. Improved facilities for pedestrians are therefore of benefit not only to users of public transport, but also to all people with low incomes. Moreover, walking, like cycling, is a sustainable transport mode which should be encouraged and facilitated.

The quality of the footpaths in many cities in developing countries is extremely poor: many are too narrow for the volume of pedestrian traffic using them, or for people queuing for public transport services, and are often badly maintained; in some cities footpaths are shared with cyclists, while some streets have no footpaths at all. Street lighting is often inadequate, poorly maintained or non-existent; lamp posts, as well as street signs, poles carrying power and telephone cables, and other street furniture are often placed without regard for pedestrians, and cause serious obstruction on footpaths. Uncovered drains and other holes in footpaths are common, and are highly dangerous to pedestrians, particularly at night. Footpaths are also often used for car parking, and by street vendors, to the extent that pedestrians are forced to walk in the roadway; as well as being dangerous for the pedestrians, this impedes vehicular traffic. Some city centres are divided by major highways which hinder pedestrian movement.

If walking is difficult or dangerous, people who have access to private transport will tend to use it, even if they might otherwise be prepared to use public transport for some journeys. In very hot or very wet climates, walking can be unpleasant, as is waiting for public transport unless there are adequate shelters; anybody who has the use of a car therefore prefers the door-to-door facility of private transport to walking or less convenient public transport services. Making walking safer, easier or pleasanter, through such measures as the provision of adequate footpaths, and shelters or shade along selected footpaths as well as at bus stops, will improve the quality of public transport, and improve the quality of life for the majority of people. Pedestrian routes must be considered in their entirety: if there is only one part of a route which is impassable for some reason, the entire route may be rendered ineffective.

In areas of heavy pedestrian and vehicular traffic the two should be segregated, for safety reasons as well as to facilitate movement of both. Pedestrian movement is often impeded by streets with several lanes of fast moving traffic which are difficult to cross in safety. Barriers on the footpaths to prevent pedestrians from stepping into the roadway are common in busy city streets, and traffic moving in opposite directions is often separated by barriers intentionally designed to prevent pedestrians from crossing, so that they have to walk long distances to points where the road may be crossed: these barriers are sometimes justified on the grounds of safety, but are often intended merely to reduce the hindrance of traffic by pedestrians. Sometimes communities are effectively divided by roads which cannot easily be crossed.

The provision of adequate pedestrian crossing facilities is particularly important. For safety reasons, there clearly must be some control of pedestrians crossing busy streets, but their requirements should not be ignored and some compromise is necessary between these requirements and the need to keep traffic moving. If crossings are located too close together, they may cause unacceptable traffic delays and congestion; on the other hand, the greater the distance between crossings, the greater the distance which pedestrians must walk in order to cross the road. The best compromise will depend on the relative traffic and pedestrian flows, and traffic speeds, and may vary between approximately 150 and 300 metres. At surface-level pedestrian crossings, vehicular traffic must stop in order to allow pedestrians to cross; these crossings are therefore often controlled by automatic signals, which may be activated by the pedestrians. They may be located between intersections or at signal-controlled intersections, with light phases for pedestrians. In practice, however, in most cities in developed countries, as well as developing countries, there has been a trend away from pedestrian crossings where the pedestrian had priority, such as the "zebra" crossings in the United Kingdom, to those where vehicular traffic takes priority; indeed, at many light-controlled intersections, there are no pedestrian phases, when all vehicular traffic is stationary.

Bridges and subways are safer for pedestrians, and have no adverse effect on traffic flow, but are more expensive to provide than surface crossings. There may be a degree of inconvenience resulting from the steps or ramps, and where bridges or subways are provided it is usually necessary to install barriers to prevent pedestrians from crossing the roadway, which many will otherwise be inclined to do. Subways in particular, and bridges to a lesser extent, may pose a security risk to pedestrians, especially if poorly illuminated, and this can be a serious disadvantage where law enforcement is poor. As with footpaths, if bridges and subways are to fulfil their primary function of providing a means of pedestrian movement, they must be sufficiently wide, properly maintained, and kept clear of obstructions, including informal street traders.

BUS STOPS

In addition to picking up and setting down passengers at off-street terminals and bus stations, which are discussed in detail in Chapter 4, most buses and paratransit vehicles also stop for this purpose at the roadside along the route. In many countries it is normal practice to permit them to stop anywhere on non-urban roads, subject to considerations of safety and traffic regulations, but only at designated stops in urban areas; in some countries, buses or paratransit vehicles stop at any point, even on busy city streets. The need for designated bus stops is determined largely by usage. If there are very few passengers, investment in bus stop infrastructure may be unnecessary, but if there are many passengers, it is not practical to allow them to board or alight from the bus anywhere at their own convenience; this could result in buses stopping every few metres, which would increase journey times to an unacceptable extent and cause serious obstruction to other traffic.

On most urban routes and elsewhere where the volume of traffic is sufficiently high, waiting passengers should therefore be formed into groups at suitable points. These should be indicated by a sign on a pole or passenger shelter, or other item of street furniture such as a lamp standard; the signs should be clearly visible by approaching drivers, and ideally should be illuminated at night. On narrow roads, a single bus stop sign on one side of the road is sometimes used to indicate the stopping place for buses travelling in both directions: where this is the case the sign must be clearly marked to indicate this to intending passengers in order to avoid confusion.

The location of bus stops involves a number of considerations, including those affecting the safety and convenience of bus passengers and other road users, and ideally should be determined through consultation between all parties concerned, including the highway authorities, bus operators, police and possibly representatives of the passengers. Bus stops must obviously be located conveniently to points where passengers wish to board or leave the vehicle, and where it is safe to do so; they should be close to a point where it is safe for pedestrians to cross the road, preferably near to a pedestrian crossing, but they should be located so as to minimise obstruction to other traffic, or danger to other road users, caused by stationary buses or buses stopping or leaving stops.

Bus stops should normally be located not less than thirty metres from a main road junction, in order to minimise obstruction of turning traffic; on the other hand, if passengers are to connect with buses on intersecting routes, it is desirable for buses to stop within easy walking distance of junctions. In residential developments where there are pedestrian routes which are separate from the road system, bus stops should be located where these intersect the roads used by buses.

Unless there is sufficient road width for at least two lanes of traffic in each direction, the bus stops for vehicles travelling in opposite directions should be staggered to minimise the reduction in road width when two buses stop simultaneously. They should normally be positioned such that when two buses are stopped simultaneously, they are facing away from one another, so that when they move away from their respective stops the gap between them is increased rather than reduced, which would be dangerous to overtaking vehicles.

Bus stops in one-way streets should be located on the nearside of the street, unless special facilities are provided for a stop on the offside: this would require a pedestrian island so that passengers would not be required to board or disembark in the roadway, and would not normally be practical except where bus lanes are provided, as discussed below.

Distances between bus stops must also be given careful consideration. If stops are spaced too far apart, walking distances for passengers will be excessive. On the other hand, stops which are too close together may cause unnecessary delay to other traffic, and result in increased bus journey times through additional time lost in decelerating and accelerating; this also increases fuel consumption, wear and tear on vehicles, and therefore operating costs. For city bus services, an appropriate distance between stops is normally between 300 and 600 metres, although the other considerations must also be applied in determining the precise locations; spacing stops at rigidly regular intervals will inevitably result in some being located in inconvenient, unnecessary or dangerous positions.

Where a number of different bus routes serve the same location, providing a high combined frequency, it may be necessary to provide separate stops for different destinations or groups of destinations in order to reduce congestion at stops caused by several buses loading simultaneously. As a general rule, if it is a regular occurrence throughout the day for more than two buses to different destinations to be loading simultaneously at a stop, it will be advantageous to separate them. It is also usually appropriate, particularly at busy points, to segregate stops for standard and premium quality or air-conditioned buses, even if they are operating on the same route, since the two markets are usually quite separate.

It is not normally necessary or desirable to provide a separate bus stop for every route serving a particular location. Routes should be grouped so that where several different routes serve the same intermediate points or operate for a significant distance along a common corridor, all use the same stop: it is unsatisfactory if passengers have a choice of bus routes but cannot know which stop to wait at for the next bus to their destination. A possibility, particularly where segregated bus lanes or busways are in use, is for buses on different routes to be scheduled to operate in convoy, in a predetermined sequence; the stops are separated by a bus length and arranged in the same sequence, so that all buses stop simultaneously, and passengers are waiting at the correct stop. However, such a system requires effective control, and will result in confusion if buses operate out of sequence.

Problems may arise if buses of different configurations, for example buses with entrances in different positions, use the same bus stop. All buses should stop with their entrance doors at the head of the passenger queue; therefore a bus with its entrance at the front should stop with its front at the head of the queue, but one with its entrance at the rear should stop with its front anything up to fifteen metres forward of this position. This obviously has implications for any parking restrictions adjacent to the stop. Similarly, if safety barriers are placed to prevent passengers from entering the road other than at the head of the queue, these may obstruct one of the entrances of a bus which has more than one entrance, or an exit door of a bus which has separate entrance and exit. If a change is made to the standard bus configuration, it may be necessary to make alterations at all bus stops on the routes affected.

Vehicles other than buses should be prohibited from parking at bus stops, for a distance of at least half a bus length on either side of the bus stop sign, to allow buses to pull into and away from the kerb and avoid undue obstruction of other traffic, as well as for passengers' convenience. Bus stop lay-bys are often provided, both on urban and inter-urban roads, to enable buses to stop out of the traffic stream, and eliminate obstruction of other traffic by stationary buses; for a single bus stop, the length of the lay-by should ideally be approximately three bus lengths to allow buses to pull in and out easily. However, on busy roads, particularly where traffic is moving constantly or at high speeds, it is often very difficult for buses to re-enter the traffic stream, and therefore there is a common tendency for drivers not to pull fully into the lay-by. This can cause inconvenience to passengers, particularly during heavy rain when kerbside gutters may be running with water. In recognition of this, some bus stop lay-bys are constructed to only half a bus width, provided that there is sufficient road width for other traffic to pass a stationary bus safely. An advantage of this arrangement is that less of the footpath width is lost, and the length of the lay-by can be reduced to approximately two bus lengths for a single bus stop.

In some cities, the opposite approach has been adopted: instead of lay-bys, kerbs at bus stops are built out by between one and two metres, to discourage illegal parking at bus stops, and to enable buses to stop without leaving the traffic stream. They also provide additional footpath space for passenger queues. This type of bus stop is relatively rare, but can be practical in very heavy and slow moving traffic, and where dwell times at stops are short.

At very busy points, if there is sufficient road and footpath width, it may be feasible to provide double width bus stop lay-bys, so that buses may load simultaneously side by side. This requires the provision of an island between the two buses on which passengers for the buses stopping farthest from the kerb may wait, board and disembark in safety. On inter-city roads, bus stop lay-bys, as well as parking lay-bys provided for other traffic, are often used informally by roadside vendors, selling their wares to bus passengers and other passing travellers. This often prevents vehicles from leaving the traffic stream, and on roads where speeds are high can represent a serious danger. It may therefore be necessary to recognise and cater for this practice by designing lay-bys to be used by vendors as well as the vehicles and customers; the design should be such that the vendors do not encroach on the area required for vehicular traffic. On routes where there is a significant volume of tourist traffic, it may be desirable to provide lay-bys for tourist buses as well as private cars at popular roadside stopping places such as beauty spots and viewpoints.

Where there is no paved footpath, a paved area should be provided adjacent to the bus stop where waiting passengers may stand. In developed countries it is becoming common practice to provide raised kerbs at bus stops to reduce the effective entrance step height. In many developing countries where footpaths are of poor quality, provision of such a facility may be impractical. A potential problem of this arrangement is that the raised kerb may obstruct an outward-opening door, so that buses so equipped must stop some distance away from the kerb, thus negating any benefit.

Where possible, it is desirable to provide shelters for passengers waiting at bus stops. They should be designed to accommodate the maximum number of passengers normally waiting, and to provide adequate protection from the weather; they should be well lit and ventilated, and approaching buses should be visible from inside the shelter. Where waiting times may be long it may be desirable to provide seating. Requirements differ depending on the length and frequency of journeys, and a higher standard of facility is required for long distance services. Shelters at busy stops may incorporate such facilities as kiosks for newsvendors or refreshments, which may provide useful revenue.

If possible, shelters should be illuminated at night. Where a mains electricity supply is not available, solar panels on the roof of the shelter can usually provide adequate power not only for normal lighting but also for passenger information or advertising signs. Smaller solar panels on the bus stop pole itself may be used to illuminate the sign and small information panels.

Shelters in busy streets should normally be positioned close to the kerb, so that boarding passengers do not conflict with other pedestrian movements on the footpath, but must allow sufficient space for other pedestrian traffic; the same considerations apply to space for bus queues, even where shelters are not provided. In some cities, bus shelters have been taken over by informal street vendors, so that passengers are unable to use them; if this cannot be prevented, expenditure on such facilities should be avoided, or alternative accommodation made available for the vendors, providing that this will guarantee availability of the shelters for bus passengers.

Bus stop signs and shelters cost the same regardless of service frequency, and on long routes with low frequencies can represent a high overhead cost. They are usually provided by local authorities and only rarely by bus operators, but it is becoming increasingly common for shelters to be provided and maintained by advertising companies, with the costs being funded from the advertising revenue; similarly, it may also be possible to contract out the provision of bus stop signs to advertising agencies, as is more common with street name signs in some cities.

The stress and friction on road surfaces at bus stops caused by buses braking to stop, and accelerating away, can result in increased wear and distortion of the road surface at stops, and it is therefore desirable for a harder-wearing surface to be provided, particularly at the busier stops. Concrete is often suitable, or special hard-wearing tarmac, with sufficiently deep foundation. A different coloured or textured surface at bus stops is also sometimes helpful in indicating the bus stop area and discouraging illegal parking.

Bus stops are sometimes provided unnecessarily: for example, many new inter-urban road designs incorporate bus stop lay-bys in locations where they will be used by very few passengers, and therefore represent unnecessary expenditure where traffic volumes and bus frequencies are low. Such facilities tend to be used for other purposes, such as short term car parking or informal trading.

As well as bus stop facilities, it is also necessary, particularly in urban areas, to provide taxi ranks or stands, where taxis may park to await passengers. These are sometimes provided only at major hotels and railway stations, but it is usually desirable for ranks also to be located at other convenient points in the main commercial areas. In some cities, taxis are not permitted to pick up passengers except at authorised ranks, but even where it is normal for passengers to hail passing taxis, the provision of ranks reduces unnecessary congestion and pollution caused by cruising taxis at times when demand is low.

Some taxi ranks are very large, accommodating fifty or more taxis, but this can be wasteful of space in central areas, and it is more normal to restrict the number of places to no more than ten. The size and location of ranks should be determined in accordance with passenger requirements, and in consultation with taxi operators and relevant authorities. The ranks which individual taxis are permitted to use may be specified on their licences; alternatively allocation of rank space may be allocated on a "first come first served" basis, or the taxi operators' association or equivalent organisation may take responsibility for allocation.

TRAFFIC MANAGEMENT

(In the following sections, all examples apply to countries where traffic drives on the left side of the road; for countries where traffic drives on the right, therefore, for "left" read "right", and vice versa.)

Traffic management is a specialised branch of highway engineering and as such is largely beyond the scope of this book; however, it is useful to discuss the subject in broad terms in so far as it affects the operation of public transport services. Traffic management provides a means of optimising the use of existing road space, with minimal construction work, and can often produce considerable benefits in terms of improved traffic flows, at very low cost when compared with alternative major road construction. It is normally designed to facilitate traffic flow and reduce accidents, but may also be used to reduce traffic volumes to environmentally desirable levels. Some measures are designed specifically to enable buses to proceed more quickly, sometimes at the expense of other traffic; others, intended to improve traffic flow generally, may be beneficial to bus services, but can sometimes be disadvantageous.

The success of any traffic management scheme is largely dependent on the enforcement of traffic regulations, and this is a problem in many developing countries. It is also common for traffic police to over-ride automatic signals, sometimes because the signals have been poorly phased in relation to traffic flows, but more often in the misguided belief that through manual control they are better able to ensure the maximum traffic flow; this can create further problems. Proper training of traffic police in both the operation of traffic management systems and enforcement can therefore be an important element in the implementation of a traffic management scheme.

Although traffic management projects may be highly cost-effective, and may be particularly appropriate in developing countries where resources are limited, they are often regarded as less prestigious than expensive road construction or improvement projects, and both donors and recipients of aid for transport improvements are often inclined to favour the more capital-intensive schemes.

Traffic Control

Typical measures include traffic control at intersections, co-ordination of traffic signals over a particular area, control of parking, loading and unloading, one-way traffic systems, and the restriction of traffic in certain areas. The most common and basic traffic management measure is the control of traffic at intersections, either manually, by traffic police or their equivalent, or by automatic traffic signals. Measures taken at busy intersections to speed traffic flow often include prohibited right turns, in order to reduce delays and obstruction caused by traffic waiting to turn across oncoming traffic. Traffic which would have made the turn if so permitted must take an alternative route, such as making three consecutive left turns where roads are laid out in a grid pattern. Inevitably the distance travelled by traffic making the turn will be increased, and the journey time for this traffic may also be increased, but there should be a net benefit to all traffic; in some poorly conceived schemes, however, the overall effect is to increase congestion where the additional distance travelled by all traffic is not fully compensated for by reduced delays at intersections.

One-way traffic systems can also help to speed traffic flow by making more effective use of road space and minimising conflicting vehicle movements. However, traffic management measures which result in deviation from the direct route, such as one-way systems or prohibited turns, can be detrimental for buses or passengers: they may enable buses to run at higher speeds but may also result in bus stops, in one direction of travel at least, being located a considerable distance from where passengers wish to board or disembark, thus increasing their journey times. These problems may be reduced by measures such as "bus-only" turns or contra-flow bus lanes, as discussed below.

Traffic Calming Measures

Traffic calming measures are a form of traffic management designed to reduce traffic speeds for safety or environmental reasons, or to reduce traffic volumes on particular streets by encouraging drivers to use alternative routes. They should be largely unnecessary if drivers comply with speed limits, and should be used only if enforcement measures are ineffective. They are often used at accident black spots, near schools, or in residential streets, particularly where drivers regularly drive through residential areas in order to avoid congestion on primary routes. The most common measures, sometimes referred to as "vertical traffic calming measures", are "sleeping policemen", or speed humps, where vehicles must slow down to avoid discomfort to the driver and passengers, or even danger or damage to the vehicle. "Horizontal traffic calming measures" include width restrictions, which prevent large vehicles from using a particular road and slow down other traffic, and chicanes or bottlenecks where vehicles travelling in one direction must stop to give way to vehicles travelling in the other.

Normally the effect of traffic calming measures on bus journey times should not be significant, since even without the measures, buses should be travelling at low speeds at the points in question; however, measures to restrict the width of vehicles using a particular road, often applied in residential areas, may prevent the use of full-sized buses on all routes using that road; this will affect the entire route.

Of greater concern is the physical effect of some traffic calming measures on the vehicles, which because of their greater mass, are much more seriously affected than cars. Continuous operation over speed humps, particularly if these are poorly designed, can cause structural damage to vehicle chassis, suspension, bodywork and sensitive equipment such as electronic ticket machines even if buses are driven at low speeds. Passengers and crews may also suffer severe discomfort as a result of riding over humps, while low-floor buses may ground on excessively high humps. In extreme cases bus services have been withdrawn completely for these reasons.

"Speed tables" are flatter and longer than humps, and are less damaging to vehicles. Some speed humps, or "speed cushions", are designed so that they can be straddled by large buses with a wider track than cars, which are forced to drive over the hump, albeit sometimes with only the wheels on one side of the car. Such measures are often negated, however, by inconsiderate parking of cars, which force buses to drive over the humps instead of straddling them. More complex and often costly measures under development include rumble strips which are more audible within the vehicle than outside it, and inflatable "vehicle-responsive" humps, which are activated only when crossed by a vehicle exceeding the speed limit.

Traffic calming measures are not always fully effective. A common reaction by drivers is to brake and accelerate hard on approaching and leaving speed humps, resulting in increased traffic noise, increased exhaust emission and increased fuel consumption. In Nairobi, Kenya, speed humps were placed in the road on the approach to a large school following several accidents in which children were knocked down by speeding matatus. However, since there was no kerb on either side of the road, the matatus avoided the humps by driving, still at high speed, on the footpath, thus putting the children in even greater danger than before.

There are sometimes restrictions on the number of vehicles which may be used within a particular area, through demand management measures such as road user charging or area licensing. A simple but effective measure used in some cities, such as Manila, makes use of vehicle registration, or licence plate numbers: for example cars with odd-numbered registrations may be permitted to enter a certain area only on odd-numbered calendar days, and even-numbered cars on even days. In practice, such restrictive measures often fall foul of politics, and few schemes are in operation.

Road User Charging

Road user charging, or "congestion charging" as it is known in London, can be an effective measure to reduce traffic volumes, and can raise revenue which may be used to fund road infrastructure maintenance and improvement, or public transport services. The charging of tolls for the use of bridges, tunnels and major highways is widespread; distance-based charging for lorries has been in force for several years in a number of European countries, as well as in New Zealand, and is under consideration elsewhere. However, apart from a scheme which has been operating in Singapore for many years, and smaller schemes in some Scandinavian cities, the concept of road user charging covering all roads in a particular area is still relatively rare, although it is now being seriously considered in several large European and North American cities following its successful introduction in London in 2003.

The London scheme, which applies to the central area including the West End and City, operates between 0700 and 1830 on Mondays to Fridays, although slight changes to the hours are currently under consideration. It applies to all motor vehicles except buses, coaches, taxis, motorcycles, emergency vehicles, and vehicles driven by disabled drivers. The charge is £5 per vehicle per day, although residents within the charging zone pay only £0.50. It is a legal requirement that all surplus revenue is invested in public transport.

Prior to introduction of the scheme, Transport for London (TfL), the authority responsible for all public transport in London as well as the congestion charge, introduced several new bus routes and increased bus services to provide 20% additional peak capacity. After the scheme had been operating for six months, media reports indicated that the number of vehicle movements by private cars and goods vehicles had decreased by approximately 30% and 10% respectively; bus and coach movements had increased by 15% and taxi movements by 20%. Bus patronage had increased by 10%. There were also increases in movements by cycles and motorcycles, by 30% and 20% respectively. A decrease was reported in the total number of people entering the charging zone. Traffic speeds in London increased by 20%, from fifteen to eighteen kph. Average bus speeds increased by 13.6%, from 10.5 to twelve kph, and bus reliability improved, with scheduled kilometres lost falling by 50% from 2.7% to 1.4%.

In London drivers may pay at designated retail outlets, on-line, or through call centres by mobile phone, using credit cards. The scheme is enforced by cameras, located at various points on the boundary and within the zone, which record vehicle registration numbers for comparison with those for which payments have been made; non-payers are traced through vehicle licensing records and penalised. The system in Singapore uses transponders which are carried on every vehicle and transmit signals to overhead electronic gantries; charges are automatically debited to users as cars pass beneath them. This enables charges to be varied by time and place, providing a more effective means of demand management.

Parking Control

Parking control is another important traffic management measure, and if properly enforced can be highly effective in improving traffic flow on busy roads. Uncontrolled parking can lead to obstruction of moving traffic, and hence congestion, and is a serious urban problem in many developing countries. Prohibition of kerbside parking can increase effective road width; where kerbside parking is permitted, keeping bus stops clear of parked cars benefits all traffic since buses can stop at the kerb instead of obstructing other traffic. Prohibition of parking at busy bus stops, or at all bus stops on busy roads, is generally desirable, but is not always effectively applied.

There are various types of parking control, including charging, restrictions of times when parking is permitted, or restrictions on parking duration. Each has its advantages and disadvantages, and may be applicable in particular circumstances; for example restrictions on parking duration may be designed to prevent office workers from parking for the whole day, but to allow sufficient time to enable shoppers to carry out their business. Enforcement is often a problem; clear road markings, and even coloured road surfaces sometimes help to warn motorists of parking restrictions, but will have little effect where such restrictions are generally ignored.

Parking charges, like road user charges, can be used to control the volume of traffic in areas which are destinations for a high proportion of car journeys. High car parking charges may encourage car users to use public transport; the scale of time-based charges may be designed to encourage short-term parking and discourage long-term parking, or vice versa. Parking charges are sometimes used simply to cover the cost of the parking control measures, but may be used to raise revenue for general purposes and sometimes for specific transport expenditure.

Off-street car parks represent an important item of road infrastructure, and while these are intended primarily for private transport, the extent of such facilities does have an effect on traffic congestion and on public transport usage. The question of how much parking should be provided with new developments such as office buildings is a subject for debate, and opinions differ widely. If the amount of parking is restricted, a proportion of travellers will be forced to use public transport, in which case the service provided should ideally be adequate to meet their requirements. If office buildings are provided with parking space for every employee, the road network may be unable to handle the traffic generated, and the resulting congestion will adversely affect bus services.

Building developments in urban areas should ideally incorporate sufficient parking accommodation for all related essential traffic, such as delivery vehicles, but not non-essential traffic such as private cars used by commuters, who should be encouraged to use public transport for all or part of their journeys. In practice, however, in many developing countries, unless there are measures to restrict car use, the majority of car owners are unlikely to use public transport but will park their cars, legally or otherwise, in nearby streets if off-street facilities are not provided. Therefore many new office developments incorporate parking accommodation for large numbers of cars, regardless of the effect that this will have on traffic congestion in the vicinity.

Park and Ride

Public transport services cannot meet the requirements of everybody living in low-density residential areas, and therefore private transport usage by higher-income residents in such areas is invariably high. However, because of road capacity constraints in the downtown areas it is not normally desirable for all commuters to take their cars to their ultimate destinations. In cities with metro or LRT systems, some commuters "Park and Ride", driving their cars to a convenient station, where they park and continue their journeys by rail. In cities without rail systems, Park and Ride facilities may be provided using bus services operating from peripheral car parks into the city centres. Usually such bus services are provided exclusively for Park and Ride users, but in some cases they form part of the regular bus route network. In the latter case, if there are too many stops on the route this may detract from its attractiveness to car users.

Bus or rail services from the Park and Ride site should ideally be frequent and reliable, and there should be good interchange arrangements and sheltered waiting facilities. In the case of very large car parks it may be necessary for buses to stop to pick up or set down passengers at different points within the park.

Car parks at rail stations are often owned by the rail operator, but it is unusual for a private sector bus operator to own a Park and Ride site, which are normally owned by local authorities, or by commercial car park operators. Park and Ride sites require considerable amounts of land, but this is normally less expensive than for city centre car parks. At rail stations in developed countries such as the United Kingdom, where rail freight has been largely lost to road, former freight yards have been converted to car parks. Such land is not usually available adjacent to rail stations in developing countries; multi-storey car parks may be built above stations, but will incur high construction costs.

There is usually a wider choice of location for bus-served Park and Ride sites, although these must still be suitably located at points where sufficient land is available at reasonable cost, and where it is convenient for car users to transfer from their cars to the bus service. The sites should ideally be located near the edge of the built up area, adjacent to main radial roads preferably where these intersect with orbital roads. In developed countries, where commuters tend to travel very long distances, Park and Ride sites are typically situated up to twenty kilometres from city centres. A shorter distance may be appropriate in developing countries, although availability of land may be a problem.

Some Park and Ride schemes are profitable and operated on a commercial basis, but many are subsidised. Park and Ride schemes are usually most successful in conjunction with other measures such as busways, bus lanes or other priority measures to improve the public transport portion of the journey, as discussed later in this chapter, and road user and parking charges. Charges should be such that the total cost of using the Park and Ride service should be lower than the cost of driving into town and parking, but higher than the cost of using public transport for the entire journey. Park and Ride is usually most effective where there is a substantial difference in parking charges between the Park and Ride site and car parks in the city centre.

There is no conclusive evidence that the availability of Park and Ride services results in a significant reduction in car use. Except in large cities where a substantial number of commuters travel by rail, and use their cars to travel from their homes to the stations, Park and Ride normally accounts for only a small proportion of travellers. Moreover, at present the concept is less relevant to developing countries, where car ownership is relatively low, and where car owners tend to be more reluctant to use public transport, than to developed countries where car ownership is high but people are generally more willing to use public transport if the quality of service is considered to be satisfactory. Nevertheless, there is likely to be increasing potential for such services in developing countries as cities grow, and as higher income residential areas develop at considerable distances from city centres.

BUS PRIORITY MEASURES AND BUS LANES

Bus priority measures are designed to optimise the use of available road space through giving priority to vehicles with high occupancy levels, principally buses, over low-occupancy vehicles such as cars, and thereby minimising the aggregate journey times of all road users. In addition to reducing bus journey times, bus priority measures should improve the reliability and convenience of services for passengers, and reduce operating costs through improved bus utilisation. The attractiveness of public transport should be increased, and even if this does not encourage a proportion of car users to transfer to public transport, it may help to slow the tendency of travellers to shift towards private transport. Most important, however, is the potential increase in the capacity of the transport system as a whole, and public transport in particular, which can be achieved through appropriate bus priority measures.

Bus priorities at intersections, with or without signals, are relatively cheap and simple to implement and, if effectively enforced, can bring about significant improvements in bus journey times. Typical examples of such priorities include permitting buses to make turns which are prohibited to other traffic, or giving them preference at traffic signals through the use of devices which automatically activate the signals in favour of the bus, although such measures become less practical where there are high bus service frequencies on all arms of a junction. There is a strong case for exempting buses from all prohibitions on turning movements which apply to ordinary traffic: where the bus service frequency is low, there will be relatively few right-turning buses to delay following traffic; where the frequency is high, the benefits in terms of time savings to passengers will be high, and delays to other traffic may be justified. It may also be desirable to make it compulsory for oncoming traffic to give way to a bus waiting to turn, to minimise delays to other traffic following the bus.

An effective bus priority measure where the road geometry permits it is the reservation of one or more traffic lanes for the exclusive use of buses. There are no hard and fast criteria for justification of a bus lane, but there should be a net saving in total travel time for all road users, including those using private transport. This in effect means a high frequency bus service, when there is severe traffic congestion. In more general terms a bus lane will normally be beneficial if the number of bus passengers exceeds the total number of bus and car passengers who would otherwise be carried in the lane.

"With-flow" bus lanes enable buses to overtake slow-moving or stationary traffic travelling in the same direction; "contra-flow" bus lanes permit buses to travel against the normal flow in one-way traffic systems, enabling them to follow a more direct route than other traffic. In some cities there are streets which are designated as bus-only streets, from which all other traffic except emergency vehicles are excluded, to enable buses to access areas where other traffic is prohibited, or to take more direct routes through traffic management schemes; the traffic flow in bus-only streets may be one-way or two-way. Often they also act as bus stations, with stops and shelters on both sides of the road. This arrangement can give public transport a useful advantage over private transport. However, disadvantages include danger to pedestrians who forget or are unaware that buses may use the street, and fail to take the necessary precautions when crossing; strictly enforced speed limits are usually necessary. In some cases only minibuses, rather than full-sized buses, are permitted in bus-only streets, but this imposes restrictions on the service since passengers must either transfer from a full-sized bus to a smaller bus, or vice versa, during the course of their journeys, or bus routes must be operated in their entirety by minibuses when larger buses would otherwise be more suitable.

The use of bus lanes and other priority measures need not necessarily be confined to buses. Emergency vehicles, and road cleaning and maintenance vehicles, should be permitted to use bus lanes, although the latter, except in emergencies, should be restricted to less busy times. It is sometimes necessary to permit the use of bus lanes by delivery vehicles or other service vehicles requiring access to premises along the bus lane, but wherever possible this should be restricted to times when it will cause the least disruption to traffic flows. Lay-bys for loading might be provided at intervals between the bus lane and the kerb where there is sufficient space, although this is unusual; it is often necessary for loading and unloading to be carried out in side streets, or at the rear of premises where access is provided.

It may also be desirable for pedal cyclists to be permitted to use bus lanes, providing there is adequate width, and the number of cyclists is not so great that there are frequently two or more riding abreast, as is common for example in China. If they are not permitted to use the bus lane, cyclists will be endangered by buses overtaking on the nearside and other vehicles on the off-side. Where the volume of cycle traffic is high, and there is sufficient road width, the provision of segregated cycle lanes, as in many Chinese cities, is generally desirable. In some cities motorcycles are permitted to use bus lanes, but this is not normally practical unless their numbers are relatively low. Bus lanes are also often open to long-distance and tourist buses as well as local buses, although in some cases their use is restricted to the latter. It is, however, normally beneficial for all types of bus to use bus lanes. It may be argued that empty buses should not be permitted to use bus lanes, but since most empty buses are proceeding to or from service, such prohibition would reduce overall bus productivity and therefore increase operating costs, to the detriment of the service as a whole.

It is also often justifiable for bus lanes to be available for use by taxis, on the grounds that enabling taxis to move more quickly makes them more attractive than private cars, thus discouraging use of the latter, while improving the productivity of taxis reduces the number required to meet a given demand. In cities where there are very high volumes of taxi traffic, however, it is normally preferable to exclude them from bus lanes. Allowing taxis to use bus lanes may lead to problems of enforcement, unless taxis are readily distinguishable from private cars; in many cities taxis are painted in a distinctive colour, often yellow, or display prominent signs; in others they have a distinctive shape. Where they are not easily distinguished from cars, they should be excluded from bus lanes. If taxis are not permitted to drive along bus lanes, it may be desirable to allow them to stop briefly in a bus lane in order to pick up and set down passengers, although it may be necessary to impose a strict time limit in order to minimise delays to buses. In some Indian cities bus lanes are also available to slow moving vehicles such as animal-drawn carts; in such cases, unless buses are permitted to leave the bus lane, they may actually be disadvantaged by the bus lane, although other traffic benefits by being segregated from all slow moving vehicles.

Enforcement of the exclusivity of bus lanes can be a major problem but is essential. Poorly enforced bus lanes are often more of a hindrance to bus services than no bus lane at all, as buses are delayed when having to force their way into the main traffic flow to pass illegally parked vehicles obstructing the bus lane. Some car drivers believe that they are not creating any problem by parking briefly in a bus lane to purchase a newspaper or draw cash from an ATM: this opinion was even voiced by a British minister of transport, when addressing a conference on bus priorities! Bus lanes in London are enforced with the aid of cameras, mounted by the roadside and on buses using the lanes. Some bus operators and local authorities in the United Kingdom fund police patrols dedicated to bus lane enforcement.

Bus lanes should normally be positioned at the nearside of the roadway, to enable buses to stop at the kerb to pick up and set down passengers. Where buses are not required to stop, it may be more effective to position the bus lane in the centre of the carriageway, or adjacent to the central reservation; this overcomes the problem of illegal parking in bus lanes. A bus lane in the centre of a single-carriageway, multi-lane road can be made reversible to accommodate peak flows in either direction as appropriate. Contra-flow bus lanes in one-way streets may sometimes be positioned on the "wrong" side of the road if the layout of the road system so requires; if it is necessary to locate bus stops along such bus lanes a suitable island must be provided in the roadway where passengers may wait, board and disembark in safety.

On some urban freeways, the flow of traffic onto the freeway is controlled on the ramps or slip roads in order to keep traffic flowing on the motorway itself when there is congestion on the approach roads. Bus-only lanes on the ramps, permitting buses to by-pass traffic queuing to join the motorway, can be a valuable priority in such situations, where the bus service frequency is sufficient.

In some cities bus lanes are provided only at points where there is severe traffic congestion, resulting in a succession of short lanes at irregular intervals, but a longer, continuous bus lane is usually more effective; although there will inevitably be interruptions at intersections, the flow of both buses and other traffic will usually be improved through reduction of the number of bottlenecks at the approach to each section of bus lane. Bottlenecks at the start of a bus lane can cause traffic queues which delay all traffic, including buses.

In order to maximise road capacity at junctions, and to minimise conflict between buses and other traffic, it is usual for bus lanes to stop some distance short of the junction, so that the full width of the road is available for all traffic at these points. Ideally, the distance should be such that buses can always pass the traffic lights at the first green phase. This will necessitate a "set-back" typically of forty or fifty metres, although the longer the signal cycle time, the longer this distance must be. Where there are several traffic lanes, buses leaving the bus lane on the nearside may have difficulty in crossing all traffic lanes in order to turn right. One means of overcoming this at signal-controlled junctions is to provide two sets of signals, one at the intersection, and the second at the end of the bus lane: buses are permitted to pass the first signal at either red or green, but must stop at the second when this red; all other traffic must obey both sets of signals. When the first signal is red, buses leaving the bus lane will be able to cross all lanes and reach the head of the queue; the second signal should turn green slightly earlier than the first, so that other traffic may reach the second signal before it turns green. The same procedure may be used at bottlenecks where a bus lane ends or is broken, so that buses may enter the bottleneck ahead of other traffic.

Bus lanes require a substantial amount of road space. Where it is necessary to permit pedal cyclists to use bus lanes, the width of the lane should be sufficient to permit buses to overtake cyclists safely without encroaching on the adjoining traffic lane. A minimum width of four metres is desirable, and where space permits, 4.25 or 4.5 metres is preferable; the minimum practical width for full-sized buses, where no cyclists use the bus lane, is three metres, which may be reduced to 2.75 metres for small minibuses. Where there is sufficient road width, a second bus lane, or a single lane wide enough for two buses, can be useful, particularly on busy routes or with contra-flow bus lanes, since this enables a bus to overtake other stationary buses without encroaching on the lanes used by other traffic. A problem with narrow bus lanes, especially when they are physically separated from other lanes, is that since all bus wheels follow the same path, two continuous grooves are created in the road surface; these collect rain water in wet weather, so that pedestrians may be splashed by passing buses. Very hard wearing surfaces, or concrete strips with a central drainage channel, will reduce this tendency.

Bus lane design must take full account of all safety issues. Risk to other traffic, including cyclists, turning across the bus lane, is of particular concern.

Clear road markings, signs and, in some circumstances, barriers, are essential for bus lanes, both for safety reasons and to assist in enforcement. The lane itself should be clearly marked throughout its length, preferably by a continuous solid white or yellow line, up to 400 millimetres wide, separating the bus lane from the adjacent lane; a "ribbed" line, which warns drivers by causing vibration when it is crossed, can be effective. Physical barriers are not normally desirable for demarcation of with-flow bus lanes, unless there is a double bus lane, since these will prevent buses from passing stationary or broken down buses in the bus lane; islands or bollards at intervals may be satisfactory but it is important that buses have sufficient room to overtake pedal cyclists safely where applicable. Separation of bus lanes from other lanes by a raised kerbed strip, at least one metre in width, with ramped shoulders to enable buses to drive over them if necessary to overtake a broken down bus, can also be useful since delivery vehicles may load and unload alongside this strip without obstructing the bus lane, although goods must be carried across the bus lane.

Arrows on the road surface, and lane markings directing traffic away from the bus lane, should be displayed before commencement of the bus lane, together with clearly visible signs, indicating which vehicle types are permitted to use the lane or alternatively those which are prohibited from using it, the hours of operation where necessary, and any other relevant information such as loading restrictions. The signs should also be displayed at the ends of side roads emerging onto the road with the bus lane, and it is usually desirable for repeater signs to be shown every 200 metres or so along long bus lanes. Appropriate road markings, such as the words "BUS LANE" or equivalent, or a recognisable symbol, should be painted at intervals on the road surface, so that they are clearly visible to drivers travelling in the same direction as a with-flow bus lane, and in the opposite direction in the case of a contra-flow lane. A different coloured road surface is also useful for indicating bus lanes.

Buses should be permitted to leave a with-flow bus lane, and mix with other traffic, in order to overtake stationary buses. If there is sufficient footpath width, bus stop laybys may be provided at appropriate points in the bus lane. This may be important where some services are not required to pick up or set down passengers at every bus stop, but it is also important to let one bus pass another even on the same service. Otherwise average times at bus stops will increase, as will congestion at stops, and problems of bunching. In practice, even if buses are permitted to overtake one another, it is often difficult for them to do so if the traffic in the adjacent lane is heavy, so at busy periods buses tend to overtake only if the bus in front is stationary for a long time, for example if it has broken down. The problems caused by buses needing to overtake stationary vehicles in a contra-flow lane of single bus width are greater than in a with-flow lane; when a bus breaks down in a contra-flow bus lane, especially one which is physically separated from the other lanes, often the only possible course of action is to divert the buses round the one-way system with the other traffic until the broken down vehicle has been removed. Where the incidence of bus breakdowns is high, this can be a major disadvantage of contra-flow bus lanes.

Improvements in overall bus speeds resulting from the introduction of a bus lane are sometimes relatively insignificant; indeed, poorly designed bus lane schemes can increase delays rather than reduce them. However, in certain circumstances improvements in journey times of 50% or more have been achieved. Up to 40% savings compared with car travel times have also been achieved, although this is only for the portion of the journey paralleling the bus lane, and total journey times by car will normally still be less than by bus. The capacity of a bus lane in terms of buses per hour varies according to the number of bus stops in the lane, and the regularity of service. Flows of up to 400 buses per hour in a single lane have been achieved in cities such as Bangkok; the capacity of a bus lane in terms of passengers carried per hour may thus be as high as 20,000, or up to ten times the capacity of a lane with mixed traffic. However, flows of 100-150 buses per hour are more typical. The maximum theoretical capacity of a bus lane, without stops, is approximately 700 buses per hour, or one bus every five seconds, giving a passenger volume of approximately 50,000 per hour; such flows are rarely if ever achieved.

The greatest benefit derived from bus lanes is at the busiest times, and in some cases bus lanes are operational at certain times only, for example during peak periods, or during the working day on weekdays. Others are operational for 24 hours per day on every day of the week. Parking should not be permitted in bus lanes except possibly at quiet times, but for ease of enforcement it is preferable for parking to be prohibited at all times.

Bus priority measures may result in increased delays to other traffic, although this is not necessarily so, and in some cases journey times for cars as well as buses have been reduced following the introduction of bus lanes, particularly where the volume of bus traffic is high, and segregation of buses from faster-moving traffic benefits both. Nearby streets may also be adversely affected by a bus lane: for example, displaced parked cars will be parked elsewhere.

Whatever the disadvantages, however, where bus passenger volumes are high, and exceed significantly the number of people travelling by private transport, there will normally be a net benefit from a bus lane or other bus priority measure. Nevertheless, there are often strong objections to bus priority schemes, and in many developing countries the car users represent a vociferous and often influential minority, and bus lanes can become a major political issue. In the United Kingdom, the prime minister made headlines when his official car used a bus lane to avoid a traffic queue: he later expressed his concern at the sight of "frustrated voters" in their stationary cars watching buses speeding past, and was reported to have asked for the bus lane to be abolished. Opposition from the owners of premises along the bus lane, who object to the prohibition of parking outside their premises, either for themselves or their customers, is common; this objection applies to parking restrictions generally, but a properly enforced bus lane reduces the scope for unauthorised parking. It is sometimes possible to overcome opposition to a scheme by introducing it initially on an experimental basis, and making it permanent once the majority have been convinced of its benefits.

Because bus priority measures affect all road users, they must be designed and implemented with full consultation between all parties concerned, including bus operators, regulatory authorities, traffic authorities, police, local authority representatives, and bus user groups. As with other traffic management measures, enforcement is essential if bus priority schemes are to be effective, and unless the drivers of unauthorised vehicles using or parking in bus lanes can be apprehended, and the penalties imposed are an effective deterrent, the benefits of a bus lane will be substantially reduced.

In some cases, rather than bus lanes, lanes are provided for the exclusive use of "high-occupancy vehicles", or "HOVs", which include cars with, usually, three or more occupants, as well as taxis and buses. Enforcement of HOV lanes can be difficult, and unless the general level of discipline is high, it is not normally practical to permit private vehicles to use bus lanes. When HOV lanes were introduced in Leeds, in the United Kingdom, many car drivers simply stopped at bus stops before joining the lane to pick up the required number of passengers to enable them to use the lane. In some cases "non-car" lanes have been introduced, which freight vehicles may also use: these may be appropriate on streets where there is a high proportion of freight vehicles, for example in the vicinity of a market or port.

Another variation of the HOV lane principle is to permit only vehicles carrying a specified minimum number of passengers to use certain streets or sectors of the cities at certain times. In Jakarta, for example, private cars carrying fewer than three people are not permitted to enter the central area during the morning peak period. Like HOV lanes, such schemes can sometimes backfire by creating an informal industry comprising people who will ride in commuters' cars for payment, to make up the requisite number of passengers, so that the desired effect is not achieved. In any case, enforcement of priorities for HOVs may be difficult in tropical countries where many cars have tinted windows which prevent the occupants from being counted: the use of thermal imaging has been proposed to overcome this problem.

BUSWAYS

In some cities segregated rights of way, commonly known as "busways" are provided for conventional buses or trolleybuses. They may be located alongside roads or in the median strips of dual carriageways, or may be independent of the ordinary road system. A busway system consists of a network of such tracks, mostly on radial routes leading into the city centre area; however, the width required for a busway usually means that they must stop short of city centre areas, unless it is possible to provide tunnels or elevated tracks. Short lengths of busway are sometimes constructed to enable buses to provide direct services between areas which do not have direct road connections, for example in city centre areas with restricted access to normal traffic, or between residential areas which do not have direct road links in order to eliminate through car and goods vehicle traffic.

The first fully segregated bus system in Europe was introduced in Runcorn New Town in the United Kingdom, in 1971; plans for other new towns in the UK in the 1970s included busways which were never built, although in some cases the alignments are still available.

There are several examples of busways in South America, some of which have been in operation since the 1970s; these include extensive systems in the Brazilian cities of Curitiba and Sao Paulo, and in Bogota, Colombia. A 13 kilometre busway was opened in Jakarta in 2004, and there are plans for a busway to be incorporated in the new orbital highway encircling Manila, due to be opened in 2005.

Busways have many of the advantages of LRT systems, but at lower cost, and with some additional advantages. Although busways are normally confined to the main traffic corridors, the bus routes themselves are not restricted to a busway but may join or leave it at its ends and at intermediate junctions. This represents a significant advantage over rail, where passengers travelling from points which are not on the rail system must change modes. Busways can be introduced gradually: short lengths of busway can be brought into use as they are constructed, with buses using ordinary roads for the remainder of their journeys; this is not possible with a rail system. Another important advantage is that buses are able to divert from the busway and operate along ordinary roads in the event of an accident or repairs on the busway. A disadvantage of busways is that, like major highways, they may divide communities by inhibiting pedestrian movement.

The exclusivity of busways is much easier to enforce than bus lanes on ordinary roads, and it is possible to incorporate physical means of preventing non-bus traffic from entering the busway if necessary, such as lifting barriers, or bollards which can be retracted into the road surface as a bus approaches, activated by transponders fitted to the vehicles.

A busway system may represent the first stage of development of an LRT system. As demand increases and additional capacity is required the busway can be upgraded for guided buses and finally to an LRT line, although there are few, if any examples of such development. However, apart from the disruption to services which would be caused during conversion to LRT, one of the advantages of a busway system, namely the ability of buses to operate on normal roads after leaving the busway, would be lost: passengers would need to transfer from one mode to another, although with the provision of adequate interchange facilities, and through ticketing, inconvenience to passengers may be minimised. It is also theoretically possible for the same right of way to be shared by a busway and a dedicated LRT track to enable the advantages of both systems to be exploited.

Most busways are designed to a single bus width for each direction of travel, although in exceptional circumstances it may be necessary to permit two lanes of bus traffic. Normally, however, provision for overtaking is restricted to bus stopping places, where lay-bys may be provided; this is essential where traffic volumes are very high, and where some buses operate on a limited-stop basis.

There may also be a requirement for buses to load or unload simultaneously alongside one another at busy stops in order to avoid bottlenecks which would restrict the capacity of the entire busway. If such provision is not made at the time of construction, and if traffic volumes are likely to increase significantly, sufficient space should be reserved where possible for the addition of overtaking facilities in the future. This may not be possible where busways are located in the median strip of a dual carriageway.

Where a busway crosses ordinary roads, the intersections should be controlled by traffic signals, which may be programmed to give priority to bus traffic; for high-capacity busways, grade-separated crossings are desirable if there is sufficient space. There must also be provision for buses to enter and leave the busway safely: this is particularly important where the busway uses the median strip of a dual carriageway. In city centres, where several busways may converge, feeding large volumes of bus traffic into a restricted area, there may be insufficient space for segregated busways. In such cases there must be adequate traffic management and bus priority measures to minimise disruption of the flow of buses along streets shared with other traffic.

Good passenger access to the system is essential. Where passengers must cross busy roads to gain access to bus stops, signal-controlled pedestrian crossings should be provided, with pedestrian bridges or subways on very busy roads. The stops themselves may have built up platforms, level with the bus entrance steps. Where a busway uses the median strip of a dual carriageway, it may be necessary for bus stops to take the form of island platforms between the two tracks, in order to minimise the space requirement. This will require the provision of doors on the offside of each bus, although in practice, doors would normally provided on both sides, so that buses may be used on ordinary roads as well as on the busways. This will restrict the number of seats which may be fitted, and necessitate a high proportion of standing passengers. Busway stations often incorporate facilities for the pre-purchase of tickets in order to minimise boarding times.

The spacing of stops along the busway will affect the average operating speeds of buses using it, and hence its capacity. Stop spacing varies in practice, and may be as little as 300 metres, but approximately one kilometre is normal for a high-capacity busway; other bus services may run in parallel on ordinary roads, together with other traffic, with more frequent stops to cater for shorter-distance passengers or those who do not wish to walk to the nearest busway stop. Such services may or may not provide connections enabling passengers to transfer conveniently to busway services. Whatever the spacing of stops on outer sections of a route, much closer spacing is normally desirable in city centre areas.

Another important design consideration is the size of vehicle using the busway. Bus widths vary, but with a kerb-guided system, as described below, there may be only a limited range within which the width of vehicles using the track may vary, and a busway designed for maximum-width buses may not be usable by smaller buses, and vice versa. Since busways are only viable where traffic volumes are high, it is normally appropriate to construct them for use by buses built to maximum dimensions.

The theoretical maximum capacity of a busway is close to that of LRT, although the maximum achievable in practice is approximately 30,000 passengers per hour in each direction. The actual passenger flow is determined by load factors, as well as the number and design of the stopping places, the type and capacity of buses used, dwell time at stops, and the number and design of intersections with ordinary roads, as well as operating practices as discussed in Chapter 9. A typical actual peak vehicle flow is of the order of 200 buses per hour in each direction, or approximately 12,000 passengers per hour.

A development of the busway concept is the guided bus system. A guided bus is basically a conventional bus which can be driven on ordinary roads in the normal manner but which, when operated along a specially equipped guideway, can be steered by means of guides beside or between the tracks, while the driver controls only its speed. Most guided buses are steered mechanically, typically by means of small wheels fitted horizontally adjacent to the front axle, making contact with the kerbs, and linked to the steering mechanism. Less common is a system employing a flanged wheel attached to a steering arm underneath the bus, which engages in a single track embedded in the roadway, similar to those used for street trams. More sophisticated systems use cables beneath the road surface which emit signals to guide the bus, or markings on the road surface which are detected by optical equipment on the bus; these can be driven over by any vehicle, and can be used in streets shared with other traffic, whereas the kerb-guided system precludes the use of the tracks by any vehicle not so equipped.

The kerb-guided system is most common, and more reliable. The electronic and optical systems are both at an early stage of development, and have suffered from numerous technical problems; an electronic guidance system installed for the Millennium Dome bus service in London in 2000 never operated due to technical difficulties.

Guided buses typically operate along the guideways for part of their routes, reverting to normal operation elsewhere. Guided buses can stop accurately very close to kerbs, using only the nearside guide wheel in the case of kerb-guided buses; if the kerb height is the same as the height of the bus entrance step, it is therefore possible to provide step-free access to the bus, even at stops not on the guideway. In some cities sections of guideway have been installed at congested bottlenecks to facilitate movement of buses, although in most cases properly enforced bus lanes would be just as effective and less expensive, albeit requiring slightly more road width: the cost of equipping all buses used on a route so that they are able to operate through a short section of guideway may not be justifiable.

Guided bus systems allow greater capacity than conventional busway systems: speeds of up to 100 kph can be achieved, at intervals as low as 20 seconds, on a narrower roadway than would be required for a non-guided bus. The roadway need not be fully paved: it is sufficient to provide only two tracks on which the wheels may run. This assists in preventing other traffic from using the guideway: the area between the two running tracks carrying the bus wheels may be loosely surfaced, for example with gravel, or set at a lower level, preventing access by any narrower vehicle.

Vehicle breakdowns on guided busways can cause major delays if buses are unable to pass stationary vehicles. Ideally, vehicle maintenance standards should be such that breakdowns are extremely rare, but it is essential that there are efficient procedures for dealing with breakdowns when they do occur. A problem with a single-width busway, whether guided or not, is access for recovery vehicles required to tow a broken down bus: some systems employ specially built towing vehicles with a driving cab at each end, so that they may be driven towards the defective vehicle from the cab at the "towing" end, and driven from the opposite end once the bus has been attached.

There are several examples of guided bus applications around the world but most are isolated routes within a conventional bus system, and as yet there are no full networks operated by guided buses. A small number of systems have been introduced in the United Kingdom since the mid-1990s, and there are some in Europe and North America. The longest anywhere is a twelve kilometre route in Adelaide, Australia, opened in 1986. The scope for the system in developing countries at present is limited: the technology is still under development and maintenance is likely to be a problem, while in cities where the bus industry is fragmented it may be difficult to ensure that all buses are compatible. In any case, guided busways offer few major advantages and cost more than non-guided busways; the mechanical guiding equipment costs about $7,500 per bus, although the additional infrastructure required for a kerb-guided system is relatively inexpensive.

Despite the many advantages of busways using conventional buses, there are relatively few of them in operation, particularly in developing countries. This is partly due to the fragmented nature of the public transport industry in many countries, and the dominant role of paratransit in some. The authorities would have to play a leading role in providing the infrastructure, and would be dependent on the co-operation of the bus operators to provide the appropriate services; such co-operation would not be guaranteed. Introduction of a guided bus system would be even more difficult. A successful busway needs disciplined operation, and co-ordination between the various authorities involved in its implementation and operation, including highway authorities, bus operators, transport regulatory authorities, police and funding agencies. In some developing countries the necessary standards of discipline and co-operation are lacking.

Another reason may be that where busways require donor funding they may be perceived as less prestigious than high-profile road construction or public transport projects such as LRT systems, which tend to be favoured by both donor agencies and the recipients of aid, even though they may be less beneficial in economic terms. In some cases reallocation of scarce road space to a busway, and priorities for busway traffic at intersections, would result in a reduction in road capacity and delays to other traffic, which may be politically unattractive.

TROLLEYBUS SYSTEMS

The principal infrastructure requirement for a trolleybus system is the electric power supply, delivered via overhead cables, supported by poles at the side or in the centre of the roadway. Two cables, positive and negative, are required for each track. The poles may also serve as street lighting standards, or as supports for other overhead cables such as telephone lines; this requires co-ordination between several different authorities. Overhead power supply cables for street trams and trolleybuses may cause danger to high vehicles unless they are set at a sufficient height, while care must be taken to avoid contact with other overhead cables.

Some large undertakings operating trolleybuses have their own electricity generating capability but this is relatively uncommon, and power is usually purchased from commercial electricity suppliers.

LIGHT RAIL, METRO AND STREET TRAMWAY SYSTEMS

The principal infrastructure component of a rail system is the track, comprising two parallel steel rails; the rolling stock is fitted with flanged wheels which run on these rails. In the case of street tramway systems, the rails are embedded in the road, flush with the surface. As discussed in Chapter 2, rail track may be constructed to different gauges: the most common for heavy rail systems is "standard gauge" of 1435 millimetres, and this is also used for most metro, light rail and street tramway systems. Narrower gauges are also common, with many systems based on metre-gauge track, while a small number of heavy rail systems use gauges wider than standard.

Some metro systems, including some of the lines on the Paris system, are not strictly "rail" systems in that they run on rubber-tyred wheels on concrete tracks, guided in a similar manner to buses on guided busways; otherwise they have all the characteristics of rail systems.

Rail transport makes efficient use of space compared with other surface modes. The minimum corridor width for a single rail track is only slightly greater than the width of the rolling stock used; guided busways require a slightly wider corridor, and non-guided busways at least 50% more than the width of the vehicles used.

On long-distance inter-city routes, availability of land for railway lines is not normally a problem in developing countries, but topographic conditions may necessitate circuitous routes and costly engineering works such as bridges, tunnels, embankments and cuttings. In urban areas land is normally less readily available for new rail lines, and it is often necessary for tracks to be elevated above street level, or in tunnels below it. "Elevated" lines are often built directly above main highways. Most "underground" or "subway" systems are in tunnels not more than ten metres below the surface, and normally follow the alignment of the streets above; they are relatively easy to construct using the "cut and cover" method, although serious disruption to road traffic may occur during construction. Some lines, such as the tube lines in London and in several cities in eastern Europe and the former Soviet Union, are much deeper, so that they are largely unaffected by the location of buildings, streets or underground water and drainage systems; however, the requirement for high-capacity lifts or escalators at stations may increase construction and operating costs substantially.

Some new LRT systems in developed countries have used the alignments of abandoned heavy rail lines, which are no longer required following withdrawal of the suburban services for which they were built, but such opportunities are less likely to arise in developing countries, where existing heavy rail lines are usually required by other traffic. It is possible for an LRT line to share heavy rail track for part of its length, usually on the outer section of a route, where trains may run on a limited-stop basis. Problems can arise, for example with different platform heights for main line and LRT rolling stock, incompatibility of speeds creating scheduling difficulties, and different power supply characteristics, but where these can be overcome, arrangements of this kind can provide useful interchange between main line and LRT services, offering connections to parts of the city centre area not directly served by the heavy rail system.

Provision and maintenance of track and overhead power supply equipment is the major infrastructure cost item for a street tramway system. Where existing streets are used, the cost of land is low or negligible, although the construction of on-street tramway systems may require the costly diversion of underground services such as pipes and cables; this tends to be less relevant in developing countries where such services are often overhead or underneath the footpaths.

Responsibility for maintenance of street tramway track may lie with the roads authority, but more commonly with the tramway operator, who is often also responsible for maintaining the road surface between and immediately alongside the tracks. Many systems suffer from inadequate maintenance to track and overhead equipment, leading to breakdowns and derailments, which usually affect all other road traffic, as well as disrupting the tram service.

Power supply for virtually all electric street tramway systems and most LRT and metro systems is via overhead cables, with similar characteristics to those for trolleybuses as described above, except that only one overhead cable is required for each track, with the rails carrying the return current. An alternative for LRT and metros is a live third rail, at track level; some systems, such as the London underground system, employ two power rails. The live rail system is less costly to construct but requires more frequent sub-stations along the routes; there are also major safety implications in that personal contact with the live rail is usually fatal, so that the entire system must be secure against unauthorised access.

MAINTENANCE OF INFRASTRUCTURE

Like the transport vehicles themselves, transport infrastructure requires maintenance, and as with vehicles, preventive maintenance is more effective and less expensive than deferring repair work until it becomes essential. A common problem in many developing countries is, unfortunately, a lack of maintenance generally, resulting in poor road and track conditions. Damaged road surfaces can cause damage to vehicle suspensions, tyres, body and chassis frames; more seriously, they may also cause accidents. The total increase in vehicle operating costs resulting from a lack of maintenance of roads may easily exceed the short term savings in maintenance costs by four or five times.

In many developing countries, a significant proportion of road expenditure is funded by foreign aid. Often, however, aid finance is provided specifically for road construction or rehabilitation, while subsequent recurrent maintenance expenditure is the responsibility of the recipient country. Recipients of donor aid, and even many donors, tend to favour prestigious road construction or rehabilitation projects, rather than maintenance projects, which have a lower political profile; even less attractive is aid aimed at developing maintenance capability, even though this is often what is needed most.

Far too often, therefore, little or no maintenance is carried out. It is very common for small cracks in the surface of a recently completed tarmac road, which would require minimal cost to repair, to be neglected, so that rainwater enters the crack and begins to erode the subsoil; passing traffic rapidly causes the damage to spread, and very soon the small crack has become a large pot-hole; the rate of deterioration accelerates, and within a matter of months in some cases, the road surface is beyond repair, and total rehabilitation is required. This is often eventually funded by foreign aid, at far greater cost than would have been incurred had proper preventive maintenance been carried out.

In many cases the paint used for road marking is unsuitable for use on road surfaces, and especially where traffic is heavy, wears out in a very short time. As well as the safety implications, where road markings are an essential feature of a traffic management scheme the effectiveness of the scheme is likely to be seriously impaired. Also commonly neglected is the maintenance of road signs and markings. Road signs suffer from the effects of the weather, and in some countries are frequently stolen for their materials. They therefore require regular maintenance, including the clearing of adjacent vegetation which often obscures drivers' view of the signs.

Poor maintenance of infrastructure is a serious problem in most developing countries, and one which receives insufficient attention from governments and foreign aid agencies. However, a recent development in a number of countries, particularly in Africa, has been the establishment of road maintenance funds, funded by contributions from road users, principally through surcharges on fuel.

4

PUBLIC TRANSPORT STATIONS AND TERMINALS

A bus or rail terminal, or terminus, is the point at which a transport route starts or ends, where vehicles or trains stop, turn or reverse, and wait before departing on their return journeys, and where passengers board and alight from vehicles. It also often provides a convenient point from which services can be controlled. The size and nature of a terminal may vary, from a roadside bus stop with no facilities for passengers or bus crews, to a purpose built off-road bus station offering a wide range of facilities, or from a small platform at the end of a rail branch line to a prestigious city-centre structure where dozens of rail lines terminate. In the case of a bus terminal, if the number of vehicles arriving and departing is low, a roadside bus stop, with no facilities, will normally be adequate; with a large number of vehicles arriving and departing, it may be necessary to provide off-road bus station facilities for the convenience of passengers and to reduce traffic congestion.

Although the terms "bus terminal" and "bus station" tend to be used synonymously, the latter is normally more correct since in most cases there are some routes which pass through the station without terminating there. Further, the term "bus station" is normally used to refer to an off-road location with at least basic facilities for passengers, while a terminal may be a fully equipped bus station but might equally be merely a point in the road. To add to the confusion of terminology, a bus station is often referred to in North America as a "depot", a term which in the United Kingdom normally denotes a bus garage; this book uses UK terminology. Railway stations are usually referred to as such whether or not services terminate there. Where a bus station and rail station are on the same site, or on adjacent sites with easy access between them to provide convenient facilities for passengers to transfer from one mode of transport to the other, the complex is sometimes referred to as an "interchange", or "transport interchange".

Because it is usually necessary to provide passenger platforms, trains operating on heavy rail or metro systems require stations wherever they stop for passengers to board or alight; the same normally applies to LRT systems although it is often possible for passengers to board or alight where there are no formal station facilities. Street trams do not normally require special station facilities of any kind except at busy terminals or interchange points.

Bus stations and terminals are a significant element in the operation of both local and long distance bus services. Their design and location affect the efficiency of a transport system, and its impact on other road users; some stations are regarded more as landmarks than as utilities, and as such are often of prestigious rather than practical design, which may detract seriously from their efficiency. In many countries the majority of passengers start and end their journeys at bus stations, and a significant proportion of operators' revenue may be collected at these points. Off-street bus stations are generally desirable for long distance services since these are usually less frequent than urban services, and passengers tend to carry large amounts of luggage; bus and passenger waiting and loading times can therefore be considerable.

Local bus services in many towns and cities are centred on bus stations; often there are large stations in the central area, with smaller ones at the outer ends of the routes. There may also be intermediate stations, especially at points where many passengers interchange between different bus routes, although most intermediate passengers on urban services board and alight at roadside bus stops. The extent to which terminals and stations are used varies considerably. In some cities buses on long distance services are not permitted to pick up or set down passengers other than at bus stations; sometimes buses may set down, but not pick up, at designated roadside bus stops; while in many places they may pick up and set down at roadside bus stops in addition to the bus stations. In a small number of cities even local buses are not permitted to pick up or set down passengers at the roadside on main roads, and must operate non-stop between terminals; this necessitates the provision of many terminals in the city and a route network comprising a large number of short routes, and may require the majority of commuters to change between routes two or three times in the course of a journey.

Different stations are often provided for different types of service such as local and long distance services, for different operators, for different groups of routes or destinations, or for different types of vehicles. It is common for separate stations to be provided for conventional buses and for paratransit vehicles; there are also often separate stations, particularly on long distance services, for different standards of bus, for example air-conditioned and standard buses. To some extent the different types of vehicles cater for different markets, and therefore the provision of separate stations may be appropriate; however, this restricts users' choice since after committing to a particular type of service it is difficult to change.

Bus stations may also be used for parking between journeys for buses which are away from their home bases, but they should not normally be regarded as long-term parking facilities, particularly in locations where land is expensive: when they are not required for loading, buses should be parked elsewhere, preferably at depots where there are facilities for vehicle servicing and cleaning. Buses should not normally be permitted to park in streets adjacent to bus stations. In any case, if buses are utilised efficiently, it should not be necessary for them to spend much more time at bus stations than is required for loading and unloading: the requirement to park large numbers of buses for long periods between trips is often a reflection of inefficiency or excess capacity in the industry, although it may be unavoidable at off-peak times if there is a significant difference between peak and off-peak service levels.

The situation in Kandy, Sri Lanka, typifies the effect of inefficient operating practices. The principal long-distance bus terminal has insufficient capacity for the large number of buses waiting between journeys, and has been supplemented by a large overflow bus park for approximately eighty buses about half a kilometre away; even this is not sufficient, and the surrounding roads are congested with parked buses for up to one kilometre from the terminal.

In practice it is necessary to achieve a realistic compromise with regard to parking at bus stations: while it is expensive to provide parking space at city centre terminals, it can also be expensive and inefficient for buses to be driven for long distances to remote parking areas, particularly if traffic congestion is a serious problem. It may be appropriate for bus operators to be charged for parking on a time basis to discourage them from parking their vehicles for too long; the calculation of such charges should take into account the cost of providing parking facilities, but should not be so high that it encourages operators to park their vehicles elsewhere when this would be uneconomic or undesirable not only to the operator but to the community as a whole.

It is essential that stations are not only constructed to a suitable design and with adequate capacity, but also that they are suitably located. There are a number of considerations in deciding the best location; these are not necessarily the same in respect of urban and long distance services. The location should be where routes should logically connect or terminate, as determined by passenger demand patterns; if the station is used as an intermediate stopping point on routes passing through, it should be conveniently located for passengers joining or leaving vehicles there. Sometimes the location of stations for different classes of vehicles is influenced by the catchment areas of the passengers: for example the majority of those using air conditioned buses may live in a different part of the city from those using standard services.

LOCATION OF BUS STATIONS FOR URBAN SERVICES

An efficient urban bus route network in any city of medium size or larger will inevitably require a large number of terminal points, not only at the ends of each route but at various intermediate points where some vehicles may turn short. It would be both uneconomic and unnecessary to construct large complex terminal facilities at all of these points: in the majority of cases all that is required is the facility for vehicles to turn, without obstructing or endangering other traffic, and sufficient space at the kerb or alongside the road for a reasonable number of vehicles to stand between journeys. It is often appropriate, where the road layout permits, for buses to follow a loop "round the block" at the end of the route, standing between journeys at a roadside stop at some point in the loop, or immediately before or after it.

Similarly, bus stations en route will be required only where demand justifies their provision. As a guide, an off-street bus station may be justifiable if the number of buses standing simultaneously loading, unloading or waiting to depart regularly exceeds ten or twelve, although much will depend on the road layout, and the volume of other traffic: if the road is very wide and there is little traffic, roadside bus stops may cater adequately for up to five buses loading simultaneously on each side of the road. If suitable off-street terminal sites are not available it is usually preferable for routes to terminate on-street, even in central areas, rather than for terminals to be sited at inconvenient locations. As discussed in Chapter 8, efficient routing can minimise the number of routes which must terminate in busy central areas, while efficient scheduling and regulation of departures can minimise vehicle waiting times. Provided there is no excess capacity in the system, no more than two or three vehicles on any one route need be waiting at the central terminal point at any time, so that disruption to traffic can be minimised.

Where bus stations are required, they should be located near to points of high demand for maximum passenger convenience. The location of stations is often determined primarily by the availability of sites, and as a result they are often in inappropriate locations, causing inconvenience to passengers using them, and increasing vehicle operating costs by increasing the distances travelled. Some terminals are so inappropriately located that they are grossly underutilised. For example, in the Indonesian city of Malang, three large terminals have been built in suburban locations purely for urban mikrolet services; two of these are used by only a small minority of operators, while one is not used at all for its intended use, and has been taken over unofficially by local driving schools as a useful training site.

In many cities there are one or more terminal bus stations in the central area. If there is a single central bus terminal, this is convenient for passengers interchanging between routes. However, if there are very many bus movements a single terminal may be impractical, requiring a very large area of land, and creating congestion both within the station itself and on surrounding streets; in large cities, therefore, there are often several terminals, usually located around the periphery of the central area.

Where there are several central terminals, there are normally different terminals serving different groups of routes or destinations; each should ideally be located close to the corridor served by its group of routes. Such an arrangement minimises the number of buses crossing the central area and reduces traffic congestion caused by buses, but may mean that the majority of passengers must walk some distance into the centre to complete their journeys, and passengers interchanging between routes may be seriously inconvenienced by having to walk or use an individual public transport mode to travel from one terminal to another. An alternative is to allocate routes to terminals in such a way that every route crosses the city centre before reaching its terminal. This may increase passenger convenience, but may also increase the level of traffic congestion, and requires a greater number of buses to provide an equivalent service. In some cities the central railway station is a focus for bus routes. This is useful for rail passengers, but unless there is an intensive and heavily used suburban rail network, rail passengers transferring to buses invariably constitute only a small proportion of total bus passengers, and therefore focussing city bus services on the railway station, unless it is centrally situated, will not necessarily be in the best interests of the majority of bus passengers.

Figure 4.1: Location of Terminals for Urban Bus Services

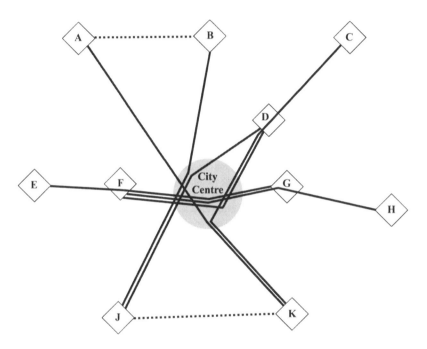

The boxes A to K represent terminals for urban bus services; the solid lines represent bus routes serving the city centre. In this example, there are no terminals in the city centre; all routes terminate in suburban areas. Terminals A, B, C, E, H, J and K are close to the city outskirts; D, F and G are "intermediate" terminals closer to the centre. Some routes (A-K, B-J, C-K) operate from one outer terminal to another; some (D-J, E-G, F-H) operate between an outer terminal and an intermediate terminal; and one (F-D) operates between two intermediate terminals. In many cities there may be routes providing direct connections between outer terminals such as those represented by dotted lines A-B and J-K.

While urban bus services are often severely hampered by traffic congestion, the buses themselves may also contribute to congestion in the city. In particular, city centre bus terminals can cause severe traffic congestion through the concentration of buses arriving and departing. This is particularly so where buses load at the kerbside rather than in off-street bus stations. For example, in Kingston, Jamaica, three out of seven separate downtown terminal points were located at the kerbside on three sides of a square, known as The Parade, which was also an important intersection for other traffic; these three points handled a total of over 4,000 bus departures daily or approximately 250 per hour. Since most buses were required to make a full circuit of The Parade one-way traffic system on each trip, the area suffered from severe traffic congestion throughout the working day; there was little relief at off-peak periods since at these times buses tended to remain on the stands for longer, resulting in double or triple-banked parking.

The congestion caused by buses terminating in central areas can be alleviated by linking bus routes so that the majority operate across the city from one outer suburb to another, stopping in the central area for no longer than is necessary to set down and pick up passengers. All terminal points will be outside the central area, where less disruption is caused to other traffic and there is likely to be more space for buses to stand for long periods, as may be necessary at off-peak times. Additional advantages from this type of operation are that bus utilisation may be improved by reducing the number of times when a bus has to turn, while additional links are provided for passengers whose journeys take them across the city centre. A potential disadvantage is irregularity of services, caused by elimination of the opportunity to compensate for traffic delays by adjustment to layover times at central terminal points, although such delays may be reduced through minimising bus-induced congestion.

Where routes are linked to operate across the city centre, there can be benefit in providing facilities for passengers to interchange between routes. Such facilities may take the form of purpose-built off-road facilities, or roadside bus stops with shelters, perhaps linked by pedestrian bridges or subways. In the former case, the location should be such that buses do not have to deviate significantly from their routes; otherwise much of the benefit of operating through services is lost. However, with appropriate routing, it should be unnecessary for the majority of passengers to transfer between bus routes in the city centre, and extensive interchange facilities should not be required. Off-street bus stations in city centres are, in any case, often a wasteful use of expensive land, although this may be offset by the development of property above the station.

LOCATION OF BUS STATIONS FOR LONG-DISTANCE SERVICES

There are several options for the number and locations of long distance bus stations in a town or city. There may be a single station, catering for all routes, or there may be two or more; the stations may be located either centrally or on the city outskirts. In some cities there is a central station, where all buses call or terminate, supplemented by peripheral stations, where buses call en route. This reduces the concentration of passengers at the central station but the stop at the peripheral station increases journey times for passengers travelling from or to the central station; in many cases, however, there is sufficient demand to justify separate services to each of the stations.

More common is a series of stations, on the outskirts of the city, each serving a different set of destinations, such that all routes terminating at the city do so near the boundary, and do not reach the central area: passengers must continue their journeys into the city by local transport. Many operators prefer such locations since journey times can be reduced considerably by eliminating delays caused by operation through congested roads into the city centre, enabling vehicles to be more effectively utilised; another advantage is that land is normally cheaper, making it more practical to provide long-term parking and maintenance facilities on the same site. A disadvantage is that passengers must transfer to another transport service in order to reach the city centre.

In some cases, services terminate at the station on the far side of the city so that all operate across the city centre, allowing passengers to and from the city centre to board or alight there, at the roadside or at an off-street bus station, without having to change vehicles; this enhances the convenience of the service, but may result in reduced vehicle utilisation through time lost due to traffic congestion, although this may be reflected in the fares charged. Where there are several stations, particularly in the larger cities, all destinations may be served by all stations, enabling passengers to use the station most convenient for them, regardless of their destination; usually there are different services to each station, although, where demand for a particular destination is low, it may be appropriate for routes to be arranged to call at several stations.

In most countries, all major towns have one or more bus stations. In several major cities in China there are twelve or more large stations; in some cities in other countries, such as Manila where several individual operators have their own terminals, there are even more, although most of these tend to be relatively small. The number of bus stations required depends on the total volume of traffic, the size and layout of the city, traffic conditions, availability of land and the quality of service to be provided; in certain circumstances a single station, or two or three large ones, may be most appropriate, while in others several small terminals may be preferable.

If there is only one long distance bus station it should be located where it is easy to access from all parts of the city. If there are several, these are often located on the periphery of the city. Peripheral long-distance bus stations should be located on or near main route corridors where there is a good choice of local bus service; if there is an LRT system, they should be located close to a station, with good facilities for transferring between modes. In many towns and cities, particularly in Africa, bus stations are located adjacent to a market, not only because a large number of the market customers arrive and depart by bus, but also because traders use buses to bring their produce to market.

Sometimes operators have their own exclusive terminals; the locations of these may be scattered over the city, or they may be concentrated in particular areas, as in Manila. In some countries it is normal for the services of small long distance bus operators to commence from the roadside outside their booking offices; often these are poorly located, and there have been cases where operators have had to be forcibly evicted from some roadside departure points because their vehicles were causing serious traffic congestion.

Figure 4.2: Location of Terminals for Long-distance Services

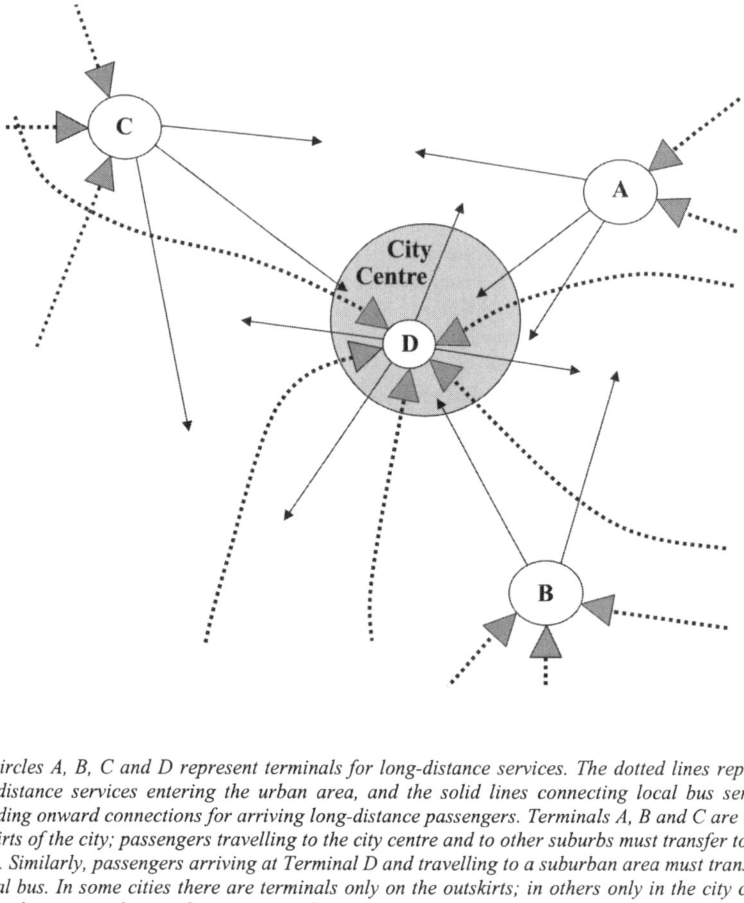

The circles A, B, C and D represent terminals for long-distance services. The dotted lines represent long-distance services entering the urban area, and the solid lines connecting local bus services, providing onward connections for arriving long-distance passengers. Terminals A, B and C are on the outskirts of the city; passengers travelling to the city centre and to other suburbs must transfer to local buses. Similarly, passengers arriving at Terminal D and travelling to a suburban area must transfer to a local bus. In some cities there are terminals only on the outskirts; in others only in the city centre. Where there is a substantial proportion of passengers travelling to the city centre as well as to the suburbs, it may be appropriate to have both peripheral and city centre terminals, with some buses terminating at Terminals A, B or C, and others by-passing these terminals to terminate at Terminal D.

There has been a tendency in recent years in many countries for long-distance bus stations to be relocated from city centre sites to locations on the outskirts of the city; in some cases the stations have been located in open country outside the city boundary. This has been partly due to the high cost of land in city centres, which has made expansion uneconomic or has prompted the sale of the property, and partly in an attempt to reduce traffic congestion in central areas by removing bus traffic from these areas. However, where the majority of long-distance bus passengers are travelling into the city centre, their contribution to traffic congestion may even be increased if, in order to complete their journeys, they must transfer from buses to other forms of public transport, such as taxis, which make less efficient use of road space.

SIZE AND LAYOUT OF BUS STATIONS

A bus station will typically comprise, in addition to the area required for passengers and buildings, a number of departure stands, where buses may wait while passengers board, and a separate bus parking area; there is also usually a separate arrivals area where buses stop to unload passengers. For long distance bus stations there should also be adequate provision for taxis, rickshaws, handcarts and other vehicles carrying passengers and their luggage to and from the station.

Bus stations must be designed to cater for the maximum predicted number of vehicle arrivals and departures, taking into account considerations of safety for passengers and other personnel using the station. The number of departure bays or stands which may be accommodated within a station of a given area will depend on the shape of the site, options for vehicle entry and exit and hence circulation within the station, configuration of the stands and dimensions of vehicles using them, the amount of space required for parking buses other than on the departure stands, and the area required for passenger facilities. The number of arrival and departure stands, and the amount of parking space required, is determined by service characteristics, as discussed below. The amount of space required for passenger facilities and parking of buses will be considerably more for a station catering primarily for long-distance services than one catering for short-distance urban services.

The number of variables makes it impossible to quote the area required for a specific number of departures, or even for a specific number of departure stands. However, in very broad terms, a well laid out terminal of 10,000 square metres, handling short-distance urban services, with minimal passenger facilities and no provision for parking buses other than on the departure stands, will be able to accommodate approximately fifty departure stands; the same number of stands in a terminal for long-distance services will require up to three times the area to accommodate the additional facilities and parking accommodation which will be necessary.

A critical figure is the maximum number of vehicles which will be at a station at any one time, whether they are loading, unloading or parked. Where bus schedules are known, it is relatively easy to plot scheduled arrivals and departures: this will show the number of vehicles in the station at different times during the day. It will be necessary to determine the length of time each bus should spend on the arrival and departure stands; buses spending more time in the station than this should be parked in a separate area, and, again, the number of buses involved and hence the size of the parking area required can be determined from the schedule.

The number of departure stands required will be influenced by the number of routes and destinations, the number of departures for each route or destination, and the length of time vehicles should spend on the stands. Where service frequencies are high it may be necessary to allocate more than one stand to a route or destination.

The service schedules may also affect the flow of vehicles into and out of the station, and the entrances and exits must have adequate capacity for the flow of vehicles in and out. Many long-distance services are scheduled to depart on the hour or half-hour, so that, particularly at the larger stations, there is a large number of vehicles attempting to depart simultaneously, often causing congestion at the exit to the station and in the adjacent streets, and delay to some of the departing vehicles. The practice followed of necessity at busy airports of allocating specific departure slots at regular intervals is rarely followed at bus stations, but at some of the larger stations this can be useful in achieving an even flow of departures. Arrivals tend to be more evenly spread, but are less easy to regulate, and the capacity of arrival areas should be adequate for the maximum number of vehicles expected to be unloading at the same time: the time taken to unload passengers and their luggage must be taken into account in this calculation.

Factors to be taken into account in the layout of a bus station are the shape and size of the plot, options for the positioning of entrances and exits for both vehicles and passengers, which will be influenced by the layout of adjacent streets, and the nature of the operation, in particular the time normally spent by buses in the station, either parked between journeys or unloading and loading passengers. The size of vehicles using the station must be considered, since this determines the space required for manoeuvring, and the area required for each stand; if possible, allowance should be made for future increases in maximum permitted vehicle size. Vehicle configuration, in particular the position of the entrance doors, must also be taken into account in the design of the departure and arrival stands.

It is particularly important to decide how buses should be parked when they are loading. There are various alternatives: each configuration has its advantages and disadvantages, and implications for safety, space requirement, and speed of arrival and departure. Buses may drive through the station, stopping parallel to the passenger stand or shelter to board, or they may park at an angle to the stand, reversing either into or out of the parking space. With a drive-through configuration, a lane wide enough for a single bus will be sufficient if the lane is used by a single route, so that buses may depart in the sequence in which they enter the stand; if the lane is used by several routes loading at separate platforms, the lane must be sufficiently wide for one bus to pass another: the closer the loading platforms, the greater will be the width required for buses to pass. A drive-through configuration with single-width lanes maximises the number of bays for a given area, and is often most appropriate for high-frequency services with minimal layover time.

Where buses park at an angle, this may be at right angles, or an acute angle, typically between thirty and sixty degrees, usually known as "saw-tooth" parking; the less acute the angle, the greater will be the number of bays which may be accommodated in a given platform length, but the amount of space required for buses manoeuvring in and out of the bays will be increased. A saw-tooth layout is most suitable for buses with their entrance doors at the extreme front. It is less suitable for buses with their doors near the centre or at the rear, since this requires passengers to walk in the roadway between the buses; buses with their doors at the extreme rear may reverse into a saw-tooth platform, but this manoeuvre is dangerous since it involves reversing towards waiting passengers. In any case it is impractical to mix front-entrance buses driving forwards into the bays with rear-entrance buses reversing into the bays.

Figure 4.3: Loading arrangement at saw-tooth platforms

Buses drive forwards into the loading bays and park with the front passenger doorway adjacent to the kerb. Passengers board the vehicles directly from the kerb, without having to walk in the roadway, or between buses. In countries where traffic drives on the left, buses have the passenger doorway on the left side, and must park as indicated in the upper diagram; where traffic drives on the right, the passenger doorway is on the opposite side of the bus, and buses must park as indicated in the lower diagram.

It is normally preferable for a bus station, particularly one with drive-through platforms, to have its entrance and exit at opposite ends to minimise turning movements, although this is not always possible. It is important to ensure that platforms are designed so that the bus doors are adjacent to the kerb. With a saw-tooth layout, in countries where traffic drives on the left side of the road, buses must turn to the left to enter the platforms; if buses must circulate through the station they must do so in an anti-clockwise direction. Where traffic drives on the right, the opposite will apply, and buses must circulate in a clockwise direction, and turn to the right to enter the platforms. There are unfortunately many examples of bus stations around the world which have been designed incorrectly so that buses circulate in the wrong direction, and load with their doors on the side away from the kerb.

As well as vehicle circulation through the station, the flow of passengers, including entry to and egress from the station, and movement between the various facilities and departure and arrival stands, must also be allowed for. As far as possible, vehicle and pedestrian movements should be separated. This is sometimes achieved through the provision of pedestrian bridges or subways, with barriers to prevent passengers from walking in the roadways, but the need for these can be minimised by careful planning; where large quantities of luggage are carried, the number of steps or ramps to be negotiated by passengers should be kept to a minimum. Segregation can often be achieved by adopting an "island" layout, where all arrival and departure stands are located around a central island so that once on the island passengers have access to all stands without having to walk in the roadway; this arrangement is particularly suitable with saw-tooth platforms. A very large station may have several islands, which should preferably be connected by pedestrian tunnels or bridges. It is also desirable to separate vehicle arrivals and departures, with vehicles unloading passengers soon after entering the station, before proceeding to the parking or boarding area.

If the size of a site is limited, it may be necessary to restrict the total number of arrivals and departures, and it may therefore not be possible to permit all routes to use it. It is possible to maximize the capacity of a terminal, in terms of the number of departures or passengers handled, in various ways. The most effective is to minimise or eliminate the need for buses to park at the terminal between journeys; if buses are scheduled to spend no more time in the terminal than is required to allow passengers to leave the vehicle, and a new load of passengers to board, there will be no need to provide space for buses to park between journeys. On the other hand, if buses are scheduled to wait for long periods at the terminal, as is often the case, particularly where it is customary for drivers to wait until the bus is fully loaded before departing, the requirement for parking space will be considerable, thus reducing the possible number of departures from the terminal. More flexible allocation of departure stands, so that a bus on any route may use any vacant stand, can also increase capacity significantly, but requires a robust system of control and passenger information. Another means of increasing passenger throughput is to restrict use of the terminal to maximum-sized buses, which make more efficient use of road space.

There is normally a significant demand for local public transport to and from long distance bus and rail terminals: passengers must travel between the terminals and the starting or finishing points of their journeys, often carrying large quantities of luggage. Many urban transport systems do not cater well for this demand, partly because it is relatively low-volume: passengers arrive at irregular intervals by the busload or trainload, and disperse to all areas of the city, so that the provision of bus routes specifically to meet their requirements is rarely justified; the same also applies at many airports. Some bus stations cater for both long distance and local buses, which facilitates transfer between the two types of service, and may also result in certain economies of scale.

Where there are several stations on the outskirts of a city it may be useful to have some urban routes operating from one station to another on the opposite side of the city, providing connections from both stations into the city centre. This is the case in some Indonesian cities, such as Malang, where it is also necessary for some passengers transferring between long-distance services to travel from one station to another using the urban transport service: this is not normally a satisfactory arrangement for the passengers, particularly if large quantities of luggage are carried.

Where local and long-distance services are operated from the same station, it is desirable to allocate separate areas of the station to each type of service, since their operating characteristics differ. Co-ordination may be facilitated where one bus operator provides both city services and long-distance services; this is relatively uncommon, particularly in the larger cities, although in some cases long-distance operators provide exclusive feeder services, often using minibuses, between the terminal and various parts of the city, on a fixed route basis or according to passengers' requirements.

Taxis and other individual public transport modes such as rickshaws or autorickshaws will meet a significant proportion of the demand for connecting local transport, both because of the large volumes of luggage normally carried, and because of the fragmented nature of the demand; in some countries there are large numbers of handcarts operating from terminals to cater for passengers' luggage. There should always be adequate provision at terminals for these complementary forms of transport.

LOCATION AND SIZE OF RAIL STATIONS

In terms of access and convenience, similar considerations apply to the location of rail stations as to bus stations. It is usually more acceptable for rail stations to be located in city centre areas since this does not affect road traffic congestion, other than that caused by road traffic attributable to passengers travelling to and from the station, and the only real criterion is availability and cost of land. The choice of location for a new rail station on an existing line is obviously limited to points along the line; the locations of stations on a new line will be influenced mainly by the options with regard to the alignment of the line itself, as well as availability of land along the route.

The size of a rail station is determined by the number of platforms required and their length, which in turn is determined by the length of the trains stopping at the station. Most intermediate stations will require only one platform for each track. In the case of a double-track line two platforms will be required; on a single-track line a single platform may suffice for a low-frequency service, but it is usual for tracks to bifurcate at stations so that two trains may pass, in which case a single island platform between the tracks, or a separate platform for each track, may be provided.

At busy stations it may be necessary for the tracks to fan out so that several platforms may be provided; this may be necessary at through stations, and more commonly at busy terminals where trains are likely to spend more time at platforms. This increases the space requirement considerably since the divergence of tracks must commence some distance from the station.

In addition to the platforms, space is required for passenger circulation and facilities; as with bus terminals, this requirement will vary according to the types of services using the station, but at most large railway stations, particularly those in developing countries, there will be a high proportion of long-distance traffic, necessitating the provision of extensive facilities.

FACILITIES AT STATIONS

Station layout must take into account the need for facilities such as booking offices, passenger waiting rooms, toilet and refreshment facilities, vendors' kiosks and stands, office accommodation for supervisory staff, and security requirements. The following discussion refers specifically to the requirements for bus stations, but in general is equally applicable to rail stations.

The extent of the facilities required will depend on the number of passengers arriving at and departing from the station, and to a lesser extent on those travelling on buses passing through the station, where they may disembark to use facilities such as toilets or refreshment kiosks. A minimum requirement is the provision of shelters, both for protection from the weather and as a means of controlling queues. For many bus stations catering for urban or short-distance services this will be adequate, but since most passengers using long-distance services may have to wait longer before boarding their buses, bus stations for these services require additional facilities to those required for purely local services.

Particularly important are toilet facilities, ticket sales and luggage handling facilities. Where passengers are likely to be waiting for long periods in the station, as is often the case with those using long-distance services, adequate seating accommodation is essential. Other useful facilities and services which may be provided for the benefit of passengers include waiting rooms, prayer rooms, and rooms for nursing mothers. Also important is information, not only regarding the services using the bus station, but also other relevant matters such as local transport and accommodation; in this respect good and clear signage is essential for basic information, while manned enquiry offices are useful at larger stations. Where security is a problem, closed circuit television cameras for surveillance of critical areas is desirable in addition to the presence of security guards within the station. In most bus stations there are likely to be several small kiosks, selling food, confectionery, magazines, and other items required by travellers; in some cases a much wider range of goods is available for sale. A characteristic of many bus stations in developing countries is a large number of unauthorised traders' stands, which often encroach on the passenger and vehicle circulation areas, and obstruct the flow of both.

Special facilities for disabled passengers are now a legal requirement in most developed countries, and while this may not be the case in many developing countries, the requirements of disabled passengers should be taken into consideration. However, there is a limit to what can be provided, practically and at reasonable cost; the principal requirement is for toilets which are accessible by disabled people, and the elimination of unnecessary obstacles which may create difficulties for disabled people. Other measures include high-visibility barriers and signs and textured surfaces for the benefit of blind or partially sighted people. The proportion of disabled people using wheel chairs is much lower in developing countries than in developed countries, and the need for special facilities to cater for them is correspondingly less.

In European countries, very stringent disability discrimination legislation requires the elimination of all physical barriers to access by disabled people to public transport; a particular requirement is the replacement of all steps with ramps or lifts so that wheelchair users are able to access buses or trains unhindered. While it is relatively easy to design new facilities to meet this requirement, it is often extremely costly, and sometimes impossible, to modify existing facilities to comply. In extreme cases this has led to the closure of rail stations, so that where previously access was denied to the disabled minority, it is now denied to everybody. Certainly the needs of disabled people should be catered for as far as possible, but where resources are limited, as they are in most developing countries, it is important to balance the cost of providing special facilities with their necessity.

Facilities provided for the benefit of the bus operators and their staff may include separate rest rooms and refreshment facilities, and overnight accommodation for long-distance drivers. Vehicle fuelling facilities are provided at many terminals, and there are often facilities for carrying out maintenance and repairs to buses on a formal or informal basis. Maintenance of vehicles at terminals between trips can be an efficient arrangement, and can be a very valuable facility for small operators who do not have their own maintenance capabilities, but this necessitates large areas of land in addition to the public areas, and where terminals are located in city centres on expensive land this may be uneconomic. On the other hand, problems such as reduced vehicle utilisation may arise if buses must travel long distances, possibly through severely congested traffic, from a centrally located terminal to maintenance workshops outside the central area, and a compromise is often necessary.

Where stations are located on the outskirts of a city, it is more feasible to provide maintenance facilities on the same site. In some cities, such as Dhaka, large numbers of buses can be seen parked or undergoing maintenance, including some major repairs, in the streets adjacent to the terminals, exacerbating traffic congestion in the area; provision of suitable facilities within the bus stations can eliminate this problem. Sometimes bus stations are combined with an operator's depot facilities on the same premises; this has certain operational advantages, principally ease of control and elimination of dead kilometres, although there may be security and safety problems.

Not all bus stations have even the most basic of facilities, however, and the standard of those provided varies considerably from one country to another, and even within the same city. For example, most bus stations in China are of a high standard, offering excellent facilities to passengers, and are well organised; some of the stations which are not owned by the state-owned bus companies are, however, very basic in terms of the facilities provided, and some are little more than unsurfaced parking areas. In Ghana, by contrast, most terminals tend to be unsatisfactory in nearly every respect, with limited or non-existent facilities: some have no covered queuing facilities even though at peak times it is necessary for passengers to queue for long periods.

While it is normally essential to provide shelters for waiting passengers, it is relatively unusual for bus stations to be entirely under cover. An exception is where property has been developed above the station; this is becoming more common at city centre stations, where land values are high, and property developments can fund the provision of the station facilities. Where stations are under cover, particularly where there is building development above the station, the supporting columns usually impose severe constraints on the layout: if the columns must be spaced less than ten metres apart, this virtually eliminates turning movements for full-sized buses, and necessitates parallel platforms and entrance and exit at opposite ends of the station. Measures must also be taken to ensure that ventilation is adequate, to maintain temperatures at an acceptable level and to prevent the accumulation of dangerous levels of toxic fumes. Stations can usually be designed so that natural ventilation will be capable of meeting normal requirements in this respect, but in some cases it may be necessary to provide air conditioning or heating in certain parts of the station, or extractor fans to remove vehicle exhaust gases. A satisfactory compromise is often to build above the area used by pedestrians and small vehicles such as taxis, but to leave the area used by buses open; this will normally necessitate a saw-tooth loading arrangement. There is a trend in developed countries towards fully enclosed passenger waiting areas at bus stations, and even at some rail stations, usually with doors activated by vehicles as they arrive and leave. This has safety benefits, and facilitates heating or air conditioning for passenger areas.

It may also be necessary in some cases to provide parking facilities for passengers' cars. This is a comparatively rare requirement at bus stations, but more common at rail stations in developed countries, particularly by commuters travelling by rail. The requirement in developing countries is much less, although in countries where bicycles are a common form of transport, such as China, it may be appropriate to provide secure facilities for the storage of bicycles at bus and rail stations.

Attention to detail is important in the design of station buildings, and failure in this regard can create problems. In addition to fundamental errors such as designing a bus station for vehicles with doors on the wrong side, as mentioned above, minor errors are common. For example, the roofs of some of the passenger shelters in the bus station in Ratnapura, Sri Lanka, are too low and project over the roadway, so that they were constantly being struck by buses, causing damage to both the structure and the vehicles. Instead of altering the shelter roofs, the simpler and less expensive solution which was adopted was to extend the kerb, so that buses stopped farther from the shelters; this reduced the width of the roadways to the extent that buses had difficulty in passing one another. A common error is the incorrect positioning of queue barriers, so that they obstruct the entrances to the buses, and passengers must squeeze between the barrier and the side of the bus in order to board.

The cleaning and maintenance of bus and rail stations is important, but is often neglected in developing countries. This is usually due to insufficient funds, and it is important that station user charges are sufficient to cover these and all other costs, and that the charges are not diverted to other uses, as is often the case with stations owned by government authorities.

REGULATION, OWNERSHIP AND CONTROL OF STATIONS

Bus stations may be owned by individual bus operators, or by operators' associations, local authorities or other organisations. They may be managed by their owners, or under contract or franchise by independent companies or associations of transport operators: for example bus terminals may be owned by a city council, but managed by a bus owners' association, as is typical in Ghana; in other countries, such as Indonesia, bus terminals are both owned and managed by the local authorities. Management systems and procedures for bus stations are discussed in Chapter 9.

In a competitive situation, where a bus station is used by several operators, it is normally desirable that it is owned and managed on a commercial basis by an operators' association, provided that all operators are represented equally, or by an organisation independent of the bus operators, making the station available to all operators on equal terms. It is usually unsatisfactory for a single bus operator to control a bus station which is required for his own and competing services, since this may inhibit competition by giving the station owner an unfair advantage, through imposing excessive charges on other operators or excluding them altogether. Where there is co-operation between bus operators, however, it is common for several operators to share bus station facilities owned by one of them.

Where bus stations are provided and operated by local authorities, provision of these facilities is sometimes regarded more as a means of raising general revenue for the authorities than as a service to travellers. This can lead to the construction of large bus stations in locations where they are not required; such stations are, in effect, extremely expensive and inefficient toll collection facilities, extracting revenue from buses but not from other vehicles. Sometimes, in this situation, in order to avoid payment of charges, buses do not enter stations, but stop at the roadside nearby for passengers to board and alight; this is very common in some parts of Indonesia. To combat this practice, police patrols, or officials of the regulatory authority, may be stationed at strategic points, either to force drivers to use the stations, or to exact payment of fees at other points en route.

In some countries, government regulation of transport services extends to the regulation of bus stations and terminals, often with undesirable results. In Indonesia, for example, there are strict regulations governing the size, location, layout and use of bus stations, and even the distances between them. There are three precisely defined categories of station, designated A, B, and C, each of which must meet certain minimum standards with regard to site area and access. Inter-city services operating between two or more provinces are permitted to use only Category A stations, while inter-city services operating wholly within one province may use only Category A or B stations; local services may use any station. This has resulted in the situation in some cities where different inter-city routes operate into different stations, and passengers transferring from one service to another must often travel between stations by local bus or taxi. Minimum site areas are specified for each category, which vary from one part of Indonesia to another. In Java, these are five hectares for Category A and three hectares for Category B stations, regardless of the volume of traffic which will use them. Also in Java, Category A stations should be 20 kilometres, and Category B stations 15 kilometres apart, regardless of the location of towns along the route, or the need for terminals at such intervals.

As a result, although the regulation regarding the spacing of bus stations is not generally observed, there are several very large stations which are virtually unused. The specification of minimum sizes often results in the unsuitable location of a station even though sufficient land for a station of adequate size to meet actual requirements may be available in a more suitable location. In an extreme hypothetical case, a small town with only one bus passing through it each day, which happens to cross a provincial boundary along its route, would require a station built to Category A specification.

The effects of this policy on the provision of bus stations in Indonesia are exemplified by the station at Kepanjen in East Java, opened in November 2000 at a cost of approximately US$500,000. Because it is used by a small number of inter-provincial services, the station was constructed to Category A specification, even though the number of services using it requires a relatively small space. It has four lanes for buses to unload and five for loading, and five lanes for minibuses, as well as a large parking area for all types of vehicles. Virtually no passengers board or alight at the station, but buses and minibuses are directed through it by enforcement officers stationed at the entrance, and stop only briefly at the toll booth to pay the terminal charge. There are unoccupied administrative, restaurant and toilet facilities and booking offices, and several booths used by the staff of the regulatory authority. The large area of the station necessitated its location in open country, two kilometres from the centre of the town, approximately one kilometre outside the developed area, and far from where passengers wish to go. In theory, bus passengers should transfer at the station to local public transport services for the journey into town, but in practice, they are picked up and set down illegally at various roadside points in the town.

The provision of adequate and appropriate terminal or bus station facilities is important, and despite potential problems from inappropriate or misapplied regulations, some form of regulation is often necessary to ensure that these are constructed to suitable designs, are of adequate size and appropriately located, taking into account all relevant factors in each case; there are so many variables that it is inappropriate to set out rigid design specifications. If facilities are to be provided by local authorities, they will have control over their design; if they are provided by the private sector, government authorities should have power under planning regulations to ensure that the facilities will be suitable. It will normally be appropriate for responsibility for planning control to be given to local authorities, although it may be necessary for central government to determine guidelines to be followed, or to provide expertise to assist in the planning process. As with all transport and planning regulations, it is important that any which apply to bus stations are designed to ensure the provision of appropriate facilities without imposing undue restriction on the services provided or causing undesirable distortion of market forces.

5

DEPOTS AND WORKSHOPS

A depot is a transport undertaking's operating base. It provides parking accommodation, servicing and maintenance facilities for vehicles, an administrative function, and facilities for staff. A fully enclosed depot is sometimes referred to as a "garage". An operator may have one depot or several, depending on its fleet size or geographic coverage; most transport operators have their head offices at one of their depots. Road transport operators with fleets of more than two or three vehicles should have the use of off-street depot facilities. A small operator will normally have facilities for only very basic servicing; the larger the operator, the greater is the scope for carrying out maintenance work in-house.

BUS DEPOTS

The principal operational tasks to be carried out at a bus depot are the allocation of buses and crews to each duty as described in Chapter 8, the despatching of buses in accordance with the relevant schedules, and the processing of cash paid in by conductors or drivers. The various tasks are discussed in more detail in Chapter 9.

Facilities required for these purposes are an office where crews report for duty, often referred to as the "signing-on office", and a cash office, where conductors or drivers pay in the cash collected during their duties, in addition to offices for managerial and supervisory staff. At larger depots it is usually appropriate to provide canteen and medical facilities for staff, and in some cases accommodation for off-duty personnel and standby bus crews, and even overnight accommodation for crews, particularly where long-distance services are operated. Depot management and supervisory staff requiring office accommodation include the depot manager, operations and engineering managers, and administrative, personnel and accounts staff. Adequate and satisfactory storage will be required for operating, engineering, personnel and financial records as well as for equipment such as ticket machines, and tickets and associated documents such as waybills.

The capacity of the signing-on office and cash office must be adequate to handle the maximum number of crews signing on and paying in at peak times. In most operations a large proportion of duties start and finish within a relatively short period, and the signing-on office must be of sufficient size, and be adequately manned, to ensure that all crews can be processed in time for punctual departure from the depot. Sometimes it is possible for the signing on and paying in functions to be handled in a single office; the practicality of this depends to a large extent on the pattern of shifts. For example in an operation where the majority of buses are worked on a two-shift basis, most of the early shift crews will be signing off and paying in at the same time as the late shift crews are signing on, so that it is usually desirable to separate the two. Operating practices also affect the requirement: for example if crews are required to sign off at the end of their shifts this will increase the workload, and hence the space requirement, of the signing-on office. Similarly, time-consuming signing-on procedures will necessitate crews spending more time in the office, and will require more supervisory staff, and therefore more office space, than simple procedures which take less time.

The efficiency of every transport operator is heavily dependent on the quality and adequacy of the vehicle servicing and maintenance facilities available to it: without these it is virtually impossible to maintain vehicles properly. Nevertheless many undertakings are handicapped by the use of maintenance workshops which are poorly planned, inadequate in size or in terms of the facilities provided, are dirty and in poor repair.

Vehicle maintenance facilities fall into three broad categories: own-account, or in-house workshops; main motor dealers, agents and service centres; and roadside garages or workshops. Most large fleet operators have their own workshops; standards vary considerably in developing countries, from very good to very poor. Own-account maintenance workshops may be specialist facilities catering only for vehicle maintenance, but are more commonly an integral part of an operating depot. Exactly what facilities are provided at any depot depends principally on its size, distance from other facilities, and availability of services from outside agents.

It is normal for small private bus operators in developing countries to have no parking or maintenance facilities of their own, with drivers carrying out basic servicing work on their own vehicles, usually at the roadside or at bus stations. Operators of small fleets may have basic parking facilities, or very rudimentary facilities where some maintenance is carried out, and may employ one or two mechanics, but for other work most tend to rely largely on the services provided by commercial workshops, including small informal roadside garages, or "bush mechanics" whose capabilities may vary widely.

The practice of parking buses on public roads when they are not in service, and even worse, servicing and maintaining them at the roadside, is very common, particularly where the industry is dominated by small operators, but can cause congestion and environmental degradation, and should be discouraged. Where there are many individual vehicle owners, maintenance facilities are sometimes provided at terminals, where vehicles may be maintained between spells of duty; many minor maintenance tasks are carried out while vehicles are waiting for their next trips. Some terminals have facilities where such work can be carried out by the drivers themselves; at others there are full-time mechanics who provide maintenance services on a commercial basis. Bus owners' associations can often help in this respect by organising facilities which are available to all operators.

In some developing countries there is a serious shortage of formal commercial vehicle maintenance facilities, particularly away from the larger towns. As the road transport industry develops, and as operating standards improve, the demand for such facilities will increase. At the same time operators should be encouraged, through more rigorous enforcement of roadworthiness requirements and stricter parking controls, to garage their vehicles at proper off-road facilities. If, as a result of more stringent inspection standards, vehicle operators demand a higher standard of maintenance, the commercial workshops will in turn be forced to improve their standards, and facilities will become more widely available. This process can be accelerated by requiring bus operators to demonstrate that they have adequate arrangements for maintaining their vehicles, either on their own premises or at a commercial garage, as a precondition of the issue of operating licences.

BUS DEPOT SIZE AND LOCATION

The size of a bus depot is usually stated in terms of the number of buses which it can accommodate, which may vary from fewer than ten vehicles to several hundreds. The area required for any given number of buses will vary according to the shape and layout of the site: with a good layout the approximate area required for a depot for 100 full-sized buses will be two hectares, or 20,000 square metres, including buildings. The space required per bus will decrease slightly as the number of buses increases since the proportion of the area occupied by buildings will decrease, and there are certain economies of scale: for example the requirement for office accommodation, or fuel issuing equipment does not increase in proportion to the number of vehicles allocated to a depot. The most appropriate size in a particular situation depends on a number of factors, and there is no single optimum size: it is often debatable whether it is better to have one large depot or several smaller ones, and a balance must be achieved between minimising dead mileage between the depot and route starting points, and having depots of an economic and manageable size.

For a large urban undertaking, operating several hundreds of buses in a relatively compact area, the optimum size of a depot is normally between 100 and 175 buses, but up to 300 can be acceptable in some circumstances. Beyond this size control becomes more difficult, although there are examples of depots housing 500 buses or more. With a less intensive operation, the appropriate depot size becomes smaller; otherwise each depot will serve a wide area with increased dead mileage, although this may not apply to a long distance operation in which the majority of routes radiate from a single point. In parts of China there is a deliberate policy to keep depots small, and this is followed to the extent, in some cases, of dividing a site into two completely autonomous depots; in the larger cities it is common for a company to have several small depots in relatively close proximity.

The location of a depot should be chosen for its accessibility and to minimise dead mileage, although there are other considerations, in particular the availability and cost of suitable land. For example, a city centre terminal for a long distance operation may have insufficient space for vehicle parking, servicing and maintenance, since the cost of land in such locations is likely to be high. The associated depot may therefore be situated some distance away, and in normal traffic conditions in many large cities may take over one hour to reach. A practical compromise is to provide facilities at the terminal for basic servicing and minor repairs, and a main depot and workshop elsewhere where land is more readily available and less expensive.

If an urban undertaking has only one depot, a central location is normally desirable, unless the cost of land makes this impossible, in which case a location close to one of the busier routes is preferable; if it has several depots, it is usually better for these to be located in the suburbs, since this will be where most buses start and finish their days' work, and dead mileage will be minimised. If traffic congestion in a city is severe, a number of small depots, each conveniently located near the starting point of a route, may be preferable, in order to minimise the time lost by buses in traffic congestion between their depots and route starting points. In many cases, however, buses start work long before commencement of the normal working day, so that congestion is less of a problem at times when buses are travelling to and from their routes. As an undertaking develops and expands, it may be appropriate to start with one central depot, which would eventually be closed when a number of suburban depots have been established. If there are several operators, each serving a sector of the city, each should have its depot at or near the outer part of the sector.

In the case of some large undertakings, operating depots are supplemented by a separate central workshop where major repairs and overhauls are carried out on behalf of the depots, and where specialist equipment and skills may be centralised. Sometimes these workshops also carry out work for third parties on a significant scale. In undertakings with up to 500 vehicles it is normally more efficient for this facility to be located at one of the operating depots, although it is desirable to separate the central works function from routine maintenance. Sometimes where an operator has a central workshop there is wasteful duplication of facilities: for example major vehicle overhaul work may be carried out at all operating depots as well as at the central works. To benefit fully from potential economies of scale a central workshop is likely to have the capacity to maintain several hundred vehicles, and is therefore appropriate only for very large fleets, unless it is used by more than one operator. For example, the National Bus Company in the United Kingdom achieved significant efficiency improvements and cost reductions in the 1980s by closing the main workshops of its smaller operating companies, and increasing the customer base for those of the larger companies by making them autonomous units providing maintenance services to several operating companies on a commercial basis.

DESIGN CONSIDERATIONS

There are certain basic considerations which should be taken into account in the design of a bus depot or workshop facility, in addition to the relevant local planning and building regulations. The shape of the site is important: ideally the site should be rectangular, with the shorter side, where possible, not less than approximately six bus lengths; an irregularly shaped site can lead to inefficient use of space. Some irregularity in shape may be accommodated by careful positioning of buildings, but a rectangular parking area, or one made up of rectangular blocks, should be regarded as essential. The number of separate buildings should be kept to a minimum, and they should be positioned in such a way that the parking area is not unduly restricted. Access to, and egress from the site is an important consideration: it should be possible for vehicles to enter and leave without causing congestion inside or outside the premises, and conflict between arriving and departing vehicles should be avoided. The dimensions of vehicles using the depot must be taken fully into account: the space required for manoeuvring may be considerable, particularly if articulated buses are operated.

Climate is an important consideration: for instance the prevailing winds will determine the most suitable positions for openings, high temperatures will require good ventilation, while if rainfall is heavy there must be adequate shelter and drainage. If snow is a regular problem in winter there may be a requirement for more covered accommodation for vehicles, and depot roofs must be designed to withstand the weight of the snow. All workshops and pits, and other working areas such as fuel pumps, should be under cover for protection from the weather; it is not normally necessary for pit areas to be fully enclosed, but this may be necessary in cold climates or where there are problems from prevailing winds. Fully enclosed workshops should be adequately ventilated and heated where necessary; where workshops need to be heated in winter, excessive height will unnecessarily increase the cost of heating.

Workshop headroom should be adequate to allow access to the highest vehicles likely to be used; where vehicle lifts or fixed ramps are used there must be additional height to accommodate the height of the ramp. Paint and body shops should be of sufficient height to allow work on the roofs of vehicles: where only single deck buses are operated, headroom of five metres will be adequate, while six metres will be ample for double deck vehicles.

All working areas should be easy to keep clean, to minimise dirt ingress to mechanical parts. Good lighting is essential; adequate electric lighting should be provided in all areas, and building interiors should be painted in a light colour. Maximum use should be made of natural light, with translucent panels in the roof over working areas, although in hot climates this may result in overheating and may therefore not always be practical. Depot yards should be surfaced to minimise problems from dust in dry weather, or mud during wet weather; the most suitable material is concrete; asphalt is less durable, and spilled diesel fuel can cause it to deteriorate. If for reasons of cost it is not possible for the entire depot area to be surfaced, at least those areas at the entrance to the workshop buildings, and at the fuelling and washing areas, should be surfaced.

WORKSHOP REQUIREMENTS

Minimum servicing and maintenance requirements in even the smallest bus depot will normally include facilities for vehicle fuelling, washing and cleaning, inspection pits, tools and equipment for minor routine servicing and mechanical repairs, and facilities for changing and maintaining tyres. All but the smallest depots will require storage accommodation for spare parts, and office accommodation for supervisory staff. Larger depots will require more comprehensive workshop facilities in order to carry out a wider range of work, which would not normally be justifiable on cost grounds in a smaller workshop. Availability of facilities externally will influence the extent of facilities required: for example, if there is a commercial fuelling station close by, the expense of installing dedicated fuel storage and dispensing equipment at a small depot may not be justifiable. Similarly, the requirement for maintenance equipment will be influenced by the availability and quality of manufacturer support and other commercial workshop facilities in the locality.

It is important that the necessary tools and equipment are provided for all maintenance work to be undertaken at a depot, including any specialised tools required for particular vehicle models in the fleet, and that they are kept in good order. Too often, specialist unit shops, machine shops and electrical shops are provided with only basic equipment, while engines, transmissions and other major mechanical units are often dismantled and reassembled on the workshop floor, using equipment which is old and in poor condition, in surroundings which are not kept clean, and in poor lighting. Some quite large depots are equipped to carry out only minor maintenance work, with second-stage maintenance carried out elsewhere. This is an unsatisfactory situation; with the possible exception of major overhauls, every large depot should be capable of carrying out all routine maintenance work on its allocated vehicles.

Fuel storage and dispensing equipment is required at all depots, except at small depots with an allocation of approximately fifteen vehicles or fewer where there are satisfactory alternative facilities. This equipment is often provided by the oil company which supplies the fuel. The number of fuel pumps required can be calculated by taking into account the number of buses to be fuelled, the time taken to fuel each one, and the period over which fuelling is to be carried out. To ensure that buses are always fuelled, it is normally preferable that each bus is fuelled each time it returns to the depot. Fewer pumps will be required if the fuelling of buses is spread evenly over the working day, but it is more common for most buses to be fuelled at the beginning or end of the working day. Two pumps will normally be appropriate for a depot with 100 buses. If there are insufficient pumps, bus availability and punctuality are likely to suffer, and congestion may be caused by buses queuing to refuel.

The total capacity of the fuel storage tanks must be adequate to ensure that fuel is always available. This can be calculated from the number of buses at the depot, daily kilometres operated per bus, fuel consumption of each bus, and the number of days' supply of fuel to be kept. In deciding on the number of days' supply required, it is advisable to allow for possible delays in deliveries; in some land-locked developing countries this can be a major problem, and up to two to three weeks' supply may be required. Where deliveries can be guaranteed, and are made on a regular basis, this can be reduced to as little as two or three days, but the risk of the fleet being grounded through an unforeseen breakdown in the delivery of fuel may be considerable. Two weeks' supply is therefore typical; for 100 buses, this will equate to approximately 150,000 litres.

It is usually convenient to locate the fuelling facilities near to the entrance to the depot, so that buses can be fuelled on arrival. Some operators prefer to fuel buses as they leave the depot, in which case the fuelling facilities should be located near to the exit. In either case, it is important that the layout of the fuelling area is such that if a queue builds up at the fuel pumps this does not result in a tail-back which obstructs other traffic inside or outside the depot. To facilitate maintenance, and to permit fuelling by gravity in the event of a power failure, fuel storage tanks should preferably be above ground unless local safety regulations require underground storage.

Buses should normally be cleaned daily and therefore even the most rudimentary bus depot must have some means of keeping vehicles clean, internally and externally. External washing should be carried out in an area designated for the purpose, with a convenient supply of water, a good surface and adequate drainage which can cope with the volume of mud and road dirt which will be washed off the vehicles. Vehicle washing facilities are often located adjacent to the fuel pumps, so that buses may be washed immediately after being fuelled; an advantage of this arrangement is that any fuel spilled on the bodywork is washed off before it causes damage to paintwork. It normally takes longer to wash a bus than to fuel it, unless high-speed mechanical washing equipment is used, and therefore if there is a constant flow of buses through the fuel pump area it will be necessary to allow space for more buses in the washing area than at the pumps.

Facilities may comprise an automatic bus washing machine or a manual system with hoses and brushes, and there must also be a satisfactory means of disposing of rubbish swept out of vehicles. Where labour is cheap it may be more appropriate to wash buses by hand, but this takes significantly longer, and requires more space than machine washing. Where there is a large fleet a mechanical wash is often justifiable on the basis of savings in time, and hence improved vehicle availability. Interior cleaning is usually carried out manually, with basic equipment such as brooms and mops, but simple mechanical cleaning equipment, such as vacuum cleaners and pressurised water spraying equipment, can often be justified even at comparatively small depots.

The number of wash bays required can be calculated on the basis of the maximum number of buses to be washed in an hour, and the number of buses which may be washed in one hour in a single bay. It is not normally possible to spread the washing process evenly over the working day, since this will require buses to be taken out of revenue-earning service for the purpose, and it is more common for buses to be washed at night, after finishing their work. Where interiors are washed with water, this gives them time to dry before the buses are returned to service. The throughput of the wash bay will therefore vary according to circumstances, but as a rule of thumb, three washing bays should normally be provided for a depot with 100 buses; together with the two fuelling bays, this will require approximately 300 square metres, or 1,000 square metres to allow for access and manoeuvring.

All workshops should have inspection pits or ramps, to enable mechanics to work effectively underneath vehicles, although in many workshops these are not provided and mechanics must work while lying on their backs: this increases the risk of personal injury as well as increasing the time to carry out many tasks, and jeopardising the quality of work.

A pit should be approximately two metres longer than the longest buses which will use it, to permit convenient access at both ends. Most pits are long enough for a single vehicle only; some are constructed to take two or more vehicles in line, but this can lead to problems when one vehicle cannot be moved, and prevents movement of the other. The width of a pit for a full-sized bus should be approximately 1,000 to 1,100 millimetres, and the spacing between pits approximately four metres. The depth of each pit should be such that a mechanic of average height is able to undertake most maintenance tasks underneath a vehicle while standing in an upright position; between 1,100 and 1,300 millimetres is normally appropriate, but with the introduction of buses with very low floor heights some operators may require deeper pits.

Pits may be positioned at an angle to the workshop wall, typically between 45 and 90 degrees; in this case buses are normally driven forwards onto the pit and reversed off afterwards. An alternative is to provide drive-through pits, where buses drive onto the pit at one end and off at the other. This arrangement is safer, and particularly convenient for articulated buses which are difficult to reverse in a confined space. However, in certain climates problems may arise since the workshop building must be open at each end; alternatively, doors must be provided in both openings, which may be excessively costly.

In a large workshop, the pits should be located in groups, according to their purpose, and convenient to related workshop facilities. In some depots, particularly those used for long-distance services, or where buses are regularly away from the depot for several days at a time, inspection pits are placed in the vehicle fuelling and washing area, so that each bus can be inspected for defects on arrival. All pits should be under cover, should be well lit, and equipped with electricity and compressed air for the operation of power tools. Equipment which is used frequently should be readily available at each pit, and work benches should be positioned conveniently adjacent to the pits. The pits should be well drained, so that waste water does not accumulate, and to facilitate cleaning. There should be steps at each end, constructed so that mechanics are able to access the pits while carrying tools or parts. Alternatively, pits may be connected by a sunken workshop below garage floor level, from which mechanics are able to walk directly into the pits. Sunken workshops have several advantages, particularly in terms of safety and ease of access to the pits, but rule out the possibility of drive-through pits.

Pits must be kept clean and in good condition. Often this is not the case, and the pits in many bus depots in developing countries have damaged walls and steps, are poorly lit, and are very dirty. As a result, working conditions are unpleasant and even dangerous; a dirty working environment is usually reflected in a low standard of work. Measures should also be taken to minimise the risk of personnel falling into pits; a useful precaution is for safe walking routes through the workshop to be clearly marked, with white or yellow painted lines or differences in surface colour.

In some workshops, hydraulic or mechanical vehicle lifts are provided. However, these are expensive to purchase and maintain and require additional workshop headroom, and they are not therefore normally justifiable in a heavy vehicle workshop. Where a fleet includes buses with both low and high floor heights, however, it may be desirable to provide vehicle lifts which may be set at different working heights. A cheaper alternative to lifts are fixed ramps, but these require a considerable amount of floor space (approximately one bus length in addition to the working area), and are generally unsatisfactory inside workshop buildings. They are more appropriate in outdoor locations, although it is still preferable that they are roofed, for such "dirty" tasks as chassis washing, where they have an advantage over sunken pits which are liable to drainage problems.

As a general rule, one pit or ramp is required for every ten vehicles allocated to a depot. The exact number can be calculated from the number of buses to be serviced, the frequency of maintenance and repair activity, and the average time spent by each bus over the pit. Where vehicle reliability is poor, and maintenance work slow, a greater number of pits will be required. Many bus depots in developing countries have insufficient pits to meet their requirements, particularly where fleets are in poor condition.

Equipment required for the maintenance of tyres includes a compressor, of sufficient capacity to produce the pressure and volume required for large vehicle tyres; and tools for repairing tyres and tubes, and for removing and replacing wheels and tyres. A safety cage should be provided in which tyres are placed for inflation, to protect personnel in the event of a blow-out caused by defective materials, over-inflation, or failure to follow correct working procedures. For large fleets it will be necessary to provide storage for tyres and tubes; tyre stores are often kept separate from the storage of vehicle spares. Such storage must be secure, both to prevent theft and to minimise the risk of fire.

Specialist contractors are sometimes employed to maintain all tyres on behalf of a fleet operator; in the case of large fleets, such contractors normally work on the operators' own premises; they may provide their own servicing facilities or require the operator to provide them.

A workshop servicing approximately fifty vehicles or more is likely to require a unit shop for the repair and overhaul of major units such as engines, gearboxes and axles. In a very large workshop, or a central workshop, separate shops are normally provided for the different types of unit; typically, there will be an engine overhaul shop, a transmission shop dealing with gearboxes and rear axles, and a shop dealing with smaller units such as steering boxes. A welding shop is also required, with facilities for sheet metal working and related activities. A large workshop will require a machine shop, equipped with lathes, milling machines and drills for the repair and fabrication of components. There may also be a requirement for various specialist shops for the maintenance of ancillary equipment such as ticket machines, air-conditioning units, or communications equipment. The requirement for such specialist shops will depend to a large extent on the amount of work which can be contracted out to commercial workshops.

The fuel pump and injectors are vital components of a diesel engine, and their maintenance is critical in achieving fuel efficiency and controlling exhaust emission. Unless this work is contracted out, a fuel injection shop is required, with equipment for testing, calibrating and overhauling fuel injection systems. This function requires a high level of skill, and the specialist equipment must be maintained in good condition; the fuel injection shop must be kept clean and dust free, and in hot climates will normally require air-conditioning.

An electrical shop is necessary for the repair and overhaul of electrical components; again, it is important that this shop is kept clean and tidy, as many electrical components are easily affected by dirt and moisture. A separate shop will normally be required for the maintenance of batteries.

A large depot should include enclosed workshop space for body repairs and painting, or for carrying out modifications, and a trimming shop may also be required for the repair of seats. Some undertakings carry out only minor body repairs themselves, leaving major repairs to specialists; however, some large operators not only undertake all their own repairs, but also manufacture complete bus bodies, for themselves and for third parties.

An essential part of any workshop is its stores. Suitable shelving, racking and cupboard accommodation should be provided to cater safely and securely for items of varied shapes, sizes and weights. Stores should be kept secure, and well lit, clean and tidy; many items of stock have dangerous characteristics, such as paints and solvents, and appropriate precautions must be taken. An undertaking with several separate workshops and depots is likely to require a central store, from which the depot stores will be replenished as necessary.

Space requirements for workshop accommodation will vary according to circumstances, but will normally be of the order of six square metres per bus in a depot for 100 buses or more, in addition to the space required for inspection pits. The space required for office accommodation and staff facilities, such as rest rooms and canteen, will be approximately 1,500 square metres for a depot with 100 buses; this requirement does not increase in direct proportion to the number of buses, and for a depot with 300 buses, the requirement will be approximately 3,000 square metres.

PARKING ACCOMMODATION

An important function of a bus depot is the accommodation of buses which are not immediately required for operation or maintenance. There must be sufficient space for parking all buses based at the depot, together with any others based elsewhere which require temporary accommodation, and for safe manoeuvring of vehicles in and out of the parking area. In most long-distance bus operations not all buses will be in the depot simultaneously, but in the case of urban bus operations there will normally be a requirement for the entire fleet to be parked overnight, unless a significant number of vehicles are required for all-night operation. If possible, there should be room for future expansion, although this should be limited: beyond a certain point, depending on circumstances, it is preferable to open an additional depot rather than continue to expand existing facilities. Parking will also be required for ancillary vehicles, and employees' cars, motor cycles or bicycles; these should be parked separately from the buses.

Buses may be parked at right-angles to the access aisles or in "saw-tooth" formation at an acute angle (usually 45 degrees) to the aisle. The latter is more common, since it requires a narrower aisle and parking is easier than with right-angle parking. With right-angle parking it is preferable for buses to reverse into the parking spaces, while with saw-tooth parking it is normally easier for buses to drive forwards into parking spaces and reverse out. If buses are parked in such a way that any one may be moved without first moving another bus, approximately twelve full-sized rigid single-deck buses (12.5 metres long) can be accommodated per 1,000 square metres. Alternatively, buses may be parked in block formation, maximising use of space but not permitting access to every bus without moving others; this will increase parking capacity by approximately 50%, to 18 per 1000 square metres. By comparison, in a car park in which all cars accessible, approximately 50 can be accommodated per 1000 square metres.

Block parking makes better use of space, and may be appropriate where space is physically restricted or land is very expensive, but requires care when allocating buses to duties; they must be allocated so that they depart from the depot in the order in which they are parked. Problems can arise if a bus fails to start; this will obstruct the vehicles parked behind it. The parking area should ideally be surfaced, preferably with concrete. It is not normally necessary for the parking area to be covered; if buses are parked under cover, adequate ventilation is necessary for the extraction of exhaust fumes. Some operators allocate permanent parking spaces to each bus; if a bus is always parked in the same position, it is possible to discover oil, water or fuel leaks by inspecting the surface where the bus is parked, and this can be a valuable aid to preventive maintenance.

ENVIRONMENTAL CONSIDERATIONS

The activities of a bus depot and workshop can have a significant impact on the environment, and if adequate measures are not taken, can cause serious damage. The main potential problems are traffic congestion caused by buses entering and leaving the depot, pollution from exhaust fumes and excessive noise from the vehicles themselves and from other workshop activities. Less visible, but often more serious, is environmental damage caused by waste oil or spilled fuel entering the drainage system or polluting nearby rivers; a vehicle workshop generates a considerable quantity of waste oil and if this is not disposed of properly it can cause serious pollution.

These environmental problems can be minimised with good design of the facilities, proper maintenance, and good discipline and housekeeping. Traffic congestion caused by the buses can be minimised through good layout of the depot, in particular the positioning and layout of entrances and exits. Buses should be able to enter the depot without having to stop in the road outside, and fuelling facilities should be positioned so that there is never a queue of buses on the road. If buses have to queue for fuelling or washing, or to enter or leave the depot, there is usually a tendency for the drivers to leave the engines running, causing noise and air pollution; eliminating queues will reduce this, but driver discipline is also important. A major cause of air pollution by buses is poor maintenance of fuel injection equipment, and the workshops have an essential role to play in this respect.

Dealing with waste oil requires special attention; oil drained from vehicles can be stored and disposed of safely, and there should be procedures to ensure that this is done. In addition, however, a significant amount of waste oil and fuel is generated in other ways, such as spillage at the fuel pumps, fuel and oil leaks from vehicles or storage containers, or oil and grease residue washed from the buses during cleaning. All drainage from the depot site, including storm water drainage, therefore, should incorporate adequate oil separation traps, and these should be cleared of oil deposits regularly.

All transport depots are potential sources of pollution, and in most countries there is legislation to control this. However, it is not always effectively enforced, and many developing countries are particularly poor in this respect. Transport operators cannot always be relied upon to take the necessary measures voluntarily: a responsible operator who incurs expense by taking measures to protect the environment may be at a competitive disadvantage relative to less conscientious operators.

6

OWNERSHIP AND STRUCTURE OF THE PUBLIC TRANSPORT INDUSTRY

There are numerous forms of ownership and structure in the public transport industry throughout the developing world. Transport undertakings may be publicly or privately owned, or owned jointly by public and private sectors; they may be structured in various ways, and may vary considerably in size, from one vehicle to many thousands. In any country, city or town, all transport undertakings might be publicly owned or all privately owned, or more commonly, there may be examples of both.

The ownership and structure of the transport industry are important factors in determining the nature and cost of the service provided and the types of vehicles operated. For example, with a predominance of small operators, there is also likely to be a predominance of small buses, since small vehicles are easier for small businesses to buy and operate, while there is less likely to be a co-ordinated network of routes than might be expected if the industry were dominated by large operators. The size and ownership of an individual organisation can have a significant influence on its operating costs: there are both economies and diseconomies of scale, while the operating costs of private sector operators are, for various reasons, invariably lower than those of public sector operators, sometimes by as much as 50%. Each form of ownership and structure has its own characteristics, and is appropriate in different circumstances; there is no ideal form for either which is universally applicable.

To meet the basic requirement for a cohesive transport system there are two basic options. One is for all services to be planned and operated by a single authority, as is common in many cities; a major disadvantage is that it leads to very large organisations which can be difficult to manage efficiently. Alternatively, services can be provided by several independent undertakings, but co-ordinated by a regulatory body; again, there are often practical difficulties with this arrangement. There are many subsidiary options: for example services may be provided by a single undertaking, which is subject to regulation by a separate body; or a state-owned operator may provide a network of co-ordinated services, supplemented by unco-ordinated, and even unregulated, private-sector operators running in competition.

A common arrangement is for a regulatory body to be responsible for the planning and constant updating of the transport system, with particular regard to routes, schedules and fares, while the actual services are operated by independent companies under contract or franchise arrangements.

SIZE OF OPERATING UNIT

Before addressing issues of ownership, it will be useful to consider the implications of the size of a road transport undertaking or operating unit. This is usually measured in terms of the number of vehicles operated, sometimes weighted to take into account variations in vehicle size. Other parameters which may be used in certain circumstances are the number of employees, number of operating depots, total route length in kilometres, or the geographical area served; however, because staff productivity, density of route networks, levels of service operated and the size of depots may vary considerably, these are not normally useful measures, particularly for comparative purposes.

It is necessary to understand the distinction between a transport undertaking and an operating unit; in certain circumstances the sizes of individual operating units is more relevant than the sizes of the undertakings involved. A transport undertaking is a privately or publicly owned organisation or an individual operator, owning or controlling a collection of assets, principally vehicles and related equipment and infrastructure, which are used for the purpose of providing a transport service. It may own only one vehicle, or several thousands; it may operate as a monopoly on a particular route or in a particular area, or it may operate alongside other undertakings, in competition or as part of a co-ordinated system; a large undertaking is likely to have more than one depot. It may be a very large organisation broken down into smaller divisions: the Bangkok Mass Transit Authority, for example, is organised into eight zones, each with several depots, typically four or five. Some undertakings own very few vehicles or none at all, and operate services through sub-contractors or franchisees. In some cases, particularly where the majority of undertakings are small, and have no facilities of their own, infrastructure such as depots, workshops and terminals is owned and operated by separate undertakings from those which operate the vehicles.

A transport undertaking may comprise one or a number of distinct operating units, or conversely may be part of an operating unit which comprises many separate undertakings. An operating unit is an identifiable group of vehicles, which may also include related equipment and infrastructure, under common control but not necessarily common ownership, organised to provide a transport service on a particular route, on a group of related routes, or in a particular area. The unit might be a single company, one individual depot out of several operated by a single undertaking, a co-operative, or an association of individual operators. A typical example of an operating unit comprising a number of different undertakings is an owners' co-operative which co-ordinates its members' activities to provide a service on a particular route or group of related routes.

The operating unit is an important component of a transport system. Most large transport undertakings may be regarded as groups of operating units, each of which may be a separate cost or profit centre. The managers of each unit will normally be familiar with local requirements, characteristics of passenger demand and operating conditions. It is generally appropriate for the majority of decisions to be made at this level, rather than at the headquarters of the undertaking, and for this reason most transport operators in developing countries tend to be locally owned: urban bus services are usually operated by undertakings based within the city where they operate, and many long distance operators are based in provincial towns, and operate into the regional or national capital. In some developed countries, such as the United Kingdom, many transport undertakings have amalgamated into large groups, although these continue to comprise large numbers of locally-based operating units.

There is an important difference between a bus route operated by several small undertakings working together as a single operating unit, and a route operated by a large number of small undertakings working independently as individuals. In the former case, the services will be co-ordinated, possibly with frequencies varied according to variations in demand at different times and on different sections of the route; in the latter case, there will tend to be a free-for-all, with each operator working on the basis of every man for himself, and the service to the public will be less satisfactory.

To facilitate the provision of a service which can be regulated in tune with demand at different times of the day or week, in different directions, and on different sections of route, it is normally desirable for the minimum operating unit to be sufficiently large, in terms of number of buses, to provide the entire service on a single route. The size of a unit operating an urban bus route would typically be of the order of 20-50 buses, including spare vehicles, although this number may be very much higher in the case of a long, high-frequency route in a major city. There may be over 100 buses on a single route; where small paratransit vehicles are operated there may be several hundred vehicles. There is also no reason why larger units, operating several routes, should not be formed. Conversely, on routes requiring a very large number of vehicles it may be practical to have two or more separate units, perhaps based at opposite ends of the route, operating in competition with one another or on a co-ordinated basis. Under a regulatory system where operators require route licences, it is usually more appropriate, where there are several small operators, for the operating unit, rather than individual bus owners, to be the licence holder.

Where an operating unit comprises several small operators, each of these may have its own depot. A larger undertaking, on the other hand, may operate several routes using buses based at a single depot; in this case, the depot would normally be regarded as the operating unit. A suitable size for an operating unit therefore ranges from the number of vehicles required to service one route or group of related routes, to the number which can be easily managed from a single operating depot. The optimum size for an operating unit thus depends on many factors and varies considerably, but in general, larger units, with fleets of fifty vehicles or more, are more appropriate in urban areas, while smaller fleets, of between approximately ten and fifty, tend to be more suitable for rural and long-distance operations. As discussed in Chapter 5, international experience indicates that in an urban transport system a bus depot with an allocation of 100-175 buses is a suitable size in terms of operating costs and manageability, although there are some instances of highly successful operations outside this range.

There are circumstances under which it may be appropriate for single-vehicle fleets to operate independently of one another. For example, there is seldom any need to co-ordinate the operations of taxis, which, by their very nature, operate on an individual basis; it may be necessary to define the areas in which they may operate, but this can be implemented through the regulatory system. An owner-driver form of organisation is therefore appropriate in this case, although large fleets of taxis do exist and there can be advantages for the fleet operator.

SIZE OF TRANSPORT UNDERTAKING

The size of a transport undertaking may be anything between one vehicle and several thousand. The majority in developing countries are small, and there are few with more than 1,000 vehicles, mostly in the public sector; some of the largest are in India, where there are several state-owned bus companies with more than 10,000 buses, while the largest, in Andhra Pradesh, has over 18,000. Some public sector undertakings are also highly diversified, and control a significant part of the transport system. For example in Egypt, the Cairo Transport Authority (CTA) comprises a bus division with a fleet of about 3,000 buses and sixteen depots, a tram system with over 250 two- and three-car sets, a minibus operation, and the Nile Ferries; the CTA does not have a monopoly, however, but is complemented by the Underground Metro, the government-owned Greater Cairo Bus Company, about 30,000 private-sector minibuses, and numerous taxis.

Large and small firms have different characteristics; each has its advantages and disadvantages in different circumstances, and it is difficult to identify an optimum size for any particular situation. Nevertheless, there are certain basic principles, many of which apply in both developed and in developing countries.

Management ability to control and co-ordinate is a constraint which varies from place to place, and from one set of circumstances to another. Many successful small bus or paratransit operations have failed after reaching a certain size, at which the owner is no longer able to control the business effectively and has been unable to make the transition from a small company to a medium-sized one. In general terms, it is normally possible for one manager with average ability to control a bus operation with a fleet of up to ten vehicles, with, in addition to the drivers, some clerical help and some unskilled assistance from one or two labourers, and perhaps a mechanic to carry out basic maintenance tasks.

When a fleet grows beyond this size, it becomes difficult for one person to manage. Employing a second person to assist with the management will add significantly to the cost of the operation, and this additional cost will be justified only if the size of the operation can be increased still further. When the operation grows to a size requiring twenty or thirty vehicles certain specialist skills become desirable within the management team, and a team of three, with operational, engineering and financial management skills may be required. Such a team should then be capable of managing a much larger unit, when it would also become more cost-effective.

Therefore there will tend to be certain sizes of organisation which are relatively efficient, and other sizes which are less efficient: for example, in certain circumstances an operation with between five and ten vehicles, one with forty vehicles, and one with 100 vehicles may all be equally efficient in terms of costs, whereas operations at intermediate sizes may be inefficient. Such a pattern is often discernible, but the size at which operations are efficient and inefficient varies considerably depending on circumstances. Thus in addition to the very wide range of size of undertaking, there may also be a set of "ideal" sizes. However, not all operators are at or even near one of the ideal sizes, and in many cases firms are not able to make the transition from one ideal size to another. It can be very difficult, and sometimes impossible, for a company in one size group to move up to the next, and it is often appropriate for small companies to merge in order to adapt to changing circumstances. Such changes in the structure of the industry should, ideally, occur naturally; the operating environment should be such that it encourages the development of appropriately sized undertakings and operating units, whether they are companies, co-operatives or associations, without the need for intervention by the authorities.

In urban areas, large operating units are usually more appropriate than small ones. Co-ordination and route planning, unless this is the responsibility of a separate planning or regulatory authority, is best carried out by a large operator, while in a regulated situation routes with low demand can be served at a similar quality of service through cross-subsidy as discussed in Chapter 14. On the other hand, the one-man owner-driver is often the optimal type of operator in remote and sparsely populated areas; in such situations they are usually more economical and more flexible than larger operators, with better understanding of local requirements.

The same applies in the case of peri-urban services, generally defined as medium-distance services operating into an urban area from small towns and villages beyond its boundary, mainly carrying commuters to and from work; unless considerable dead mileage is to be incurred, such services, if operated by an undertaking based in the city, require either the provision of small depots near each outer terminal, which are likely to be costly and difficult to supervise, or the scheduling of buses to "sleep out" at the outer terminals. The latter arrangement is often difficult to control: departures may be difficult to regulate, and there is often a risk of theft of fuel or parts from vehicles parked unattended overnight. Such services are therefore usually more effectively provided by small operators based near the outer terminal.

Long distance services tend to be operated by relatively small companies based in provincial towns and cities, offering services between their own town and the main national centres.

In certain respects large organisations have advantages over smaller organisations. These include the ability to provide scheduled and co-ordinated services on a route or group of routes and, beyond a certain size, to provide in-house maintenance facilities. For example, a large transport company which owns its own workshop facilities may enjoy lower maintenance costs per kilometre operated than a small company with only one vehicle, which must have all its maintenance work carried out by a third party.

Certain overhead costs do not increase in proportion to the scale of an operation, so that when these costs are calculated on a per-kilometre basis they will tend to be lower for a larger organisation. Where this is the case the organisation is said to be benefiting from economies of scale. Most large transport undertakings carry out in-house all functions which benefit from scale, including engineering, administration and accounting services, research and development. On the other hand there may be diseconomies of scale. For example, a common salary scale may apply throughout a large organisation, while it might be possible for lower rates to apply to some activities if these were carried out by smaller independent undertakings. A large organisation may require costly management information and control systems in order to ensure that the business is managed effectively, when such systems would be unnecessary in a small organisation where the proprietor is easily able to keep fully informed about the performance of the business.

Some transport professionals suggest that in large bus-operating undertakings the economies of scale outweigh the diseconomies, while others argue the opposite. In fact, international experience strongly suggests that there is little relationship between the size of an undertaking and the average cost per kilometre operated. It is true that large operators have certain advantages by virtue of their size; but small operators have other advantages, and while it would be an over-simplification to suggest that the two cancel out, this is nevertheless true to some extent. In certain circumstances a small operator is likely to have lower overall average costs, and in other circumstances the opposite will be the case. Moreover, the costs per kilometre of certain aspects of an operation may be lowest in a small unit, while others may be lowest in a large unit; for example, average supervisory and administrative costs per kilometre may be lower for a small depot than for a large one, while average maintenance costs per kilometre may be lower with a large, well-equipped workshop than with a small workshop with only basic facilities.

It may be possible for smaller operating units to benefit from economies of scale by appropriate structuring of the industry. For example, if a workshop were to be established of sufficient size to enjoy the economies of scale applicable to such a facility, making its services available to several small operating undertakings, each of these would enjoy the benefits of the larger facility, without suffering diseconomies of scale in other areas. This was achieved by the National Bus Company in the United Kingdom, prior to its privatisation, as mentioned in Chapter 5.

A larger operator has significant advantages in terms of service back-up. In particular, spare buses can be made available to cover for breakdowns; for single-vehicle operators who cannot provide such support, and whose maintenance standards are often poor, breakdowns can be a major problem and have been known to cause riots, with irate passengers demanding their money back from an unwilling bus owner. However, back-up vehicles become feasible at a relatively small fleet size: this could be as low as five buses. The number of spare vehicles required as a proportion of the operational fleet tends to decrease as the fleet increases in size, but stabilises at around fifty vehicles, beyond which the number of spare vehicles required increases in direct proportion to fleet size. The actual proportion will depend on factors such as vehicle reliability and the geographic spread of operation; the spare vehicle requirement becomes greater as operating distances increase. In well maintained fleets in developing countries the proportion of spare vehicles, including those required for preventive maintenance, will be of the order of 15%. There is often a correlation between fleet size and reliability, with vehicles belonging to smaller operators tending to be less reliable than those in larger fleets, although this is less true in the least developed countries, where reliability tends to be poor regardless of fleet size.

An effect of domination of an industry by small operators is that since all operators wish to maximise their incomes, they tend to be unwilling to take their vehicles out of service at times when demand is low, or to operate with less than a full load of passengers. At off-peak times this can lead to excess supply, and to congestion or chaos at terminals since vehicles must wait much longer to assemble a full load. If all buses on one route are run by a single operator, it is much easier to implement schedules which are in line with demand; at off-peak times some buses can be taken out of service, and this can also have the benefit of enabling the operator to schedule preventive maintenance. It is therefore evident that in urban service at least, there is a minimum size of operating unit below which the service becomes erratic, inefficient and unreliable.

On the other hand, in developing countries in particular, there appears to be little advantage in very large size, and there are frequently significant disadvantages; there are comparatively few very large bus operations, with 1,000 vehicles or more, in developing countries which operate efficiently. Most of the largest undertakings are state-owned, and for various reasons these tend to be inefficient, although there are some exceptions. In general, small operators in developing countries tend to have lower costs than the largest ones; therefore combining a large number of small operators into one or two larger ones, which in the past has often been seen as a solution to the problems of an inefficient transport system, does not usually result in expected economies of scale and often results in the opposite, as was the case when the Bangkok Mass Transit Authority was formed in the 1970s. There may, however, be other benefits from larger operating units, such as ease of regulation, better co-ordination of services, and an efficiently run large organisation can often provide the best overall service, albeit at a cost: a great deal depends on the quality of management.

In view of the wide range of variables involved, it is very dangerous to speculate on an ideal size for a bus-operating undertaking. Nevertheless international experience suggests that in a large urban area, or in a semi-urban area in which there are several medium-sized towns in close proximity, where operating conditions are reasonably good and regulations are reasonably well enforced, an efficient undertaking is likely to have between 400 and 1,000 buses, and between four and six depots.

FORMS OF OWNERSHIP

Transport undertakings may be publicly or privately owned although at present in most developing and developed countries there is an increasing trend towards private ownership, with many publicly owned undertakings being transferred to the private sector.

The principal forms of private ownership are ownership by individuals; private companies, such as family businesses or partnerships owned by small numbers of participants; co-operatives; and limited liability companies, owned by large numbers of private shareholders. A typical form of ownership in developing countries is the small fleet owner, often with a single vehicle, who employs drivers under various arrangements as discussed in Chapter 9; also common, particularly in the paratransit and taxi category, is the individual owner-driver, who both owns and drives his own vehicle. In some countries transport co-operatives, comprising large numbers of small operators, are common. The undeveloped nature of the stock markets in many developing countries influences the nature of private sector investment in transport, so that fewer people tend to hold paper shares while more own physical assets than is the case in more developed countries. As a country develops, there is a tendency for more people to invest in shares, putting ownership of the physical assets with companies rather than individuals.

Public ownership may take various forms, but the most common in the transport industry are "parastatals", state- or municipally-owned corporations or transport authorities, which in effect are often departments of central or local government. There is often a mixture of municipal and state ownership, such as in India, where some urban bus undertakings are owned by municipalities and others by the state, or in the United Kingdom before privatisation of the National Bus Company, when a large number of urban bus undertakings were owned by municipalities, while most of the large regional bus companies, many of which operated urban services as well as inter-city and rural services, were owned by the NBC.

Some government-owned companies in developing countries were formed through the nationalisation of private companies following independence from former colonial powers. For example, the major bus companies in Uganda and Zambia were owned by a British holding company, United Transport Overseas (UTO), but were nationalised in the 1970s by direct acquisition by the respective governments. The National Transport Corporation in Tanzania, established as a statutory body in 1969, acquired the UTO-owned Dar es Salaam Motor Transport, which provided urban bus services in Dar es Salaam and long distance bus services throughout the country.

An unfortunate characteristic of many state-owned transport systems throughout the world is that they are inefficient, and tend to have significantly higher costs than private sector systems. There are various reasons for this, such as excessive establishment levels, inappropriate staff selection procedures, lack of management incentive, and government interference; some of these problems may also occur in private sector monopolies.

Publicly owned bus companies in developing countries are often hampered by bureaucracy and national or local politics, often resulting in management decisions being influenced or overruled by politicians. In addition they are typically burdened with top-heavy management structures and excessive overhead costs, often because their fleets have decreased in size without a commensurate reduction in staff or infrastructure. In many cases where foreign-owned bus companies have been nationalised, expatriate management staff were replaced by local staff with inadequate experience, or an insufficient handover period was allowed for local staff to become fully conversant with their responsibilities.

Another common problem for public sector undertakings is that they must abide by government regulations regarding employees' pay and conditions, and are therefore unable to offer high salaries to attract professional management of suitable calibre; on the other hand conditions of employment for junior and unskilled staff are often more generous than those in the private sector, raising operating costs above those of competing operators. There may be government rules which have the effect of inflating the number of employees, or prohibiting dismissal, and which therefore reduce efficiency and standards of discipline, and hence the ability to compete with private sector operators which are not subject to the same rules.

Some transport undertakings are jointly owned by public and private sectors, although this is relatively uncommon in developing countries except in cases where they are jointly owned by the public sector and by an overseas private sector company. There were examples of such joint ventures in Kenya and Malawi, where the foreign investor was the majority shareholder. In Zimbabwe, the government eventually acquired a majority shareholding, and although for several years the foreign partner had responsibility for managing the company, its decisions were frequently overruled by the government, leading to the rapid decline of the undertaking. Some bus companies are jointly owned by a government and a foreign motor vehicle manufacturer, whose vehicles typically predominate in the fleet; this is relatively common in Francophone countries in West Africa. Joint ventures are more common for light rail operations, where the considerable capital investment necessitates some form of public-private partnership.

There are certain advantages in such mixed companies: for example, there are often government restrictions on borrowing by local authorities or their subsidiaries, which do not apply to jointly owned companies; they may also have access to more qualified management, and be less susceptible to political interference.

Some of the larger transport companies in developing countries are owned by foreign groups where foreign ownership is permitted by law; this is relatively common in former colonies, where many transport companies were established by organisations based in the colonising countries. In some countries ownership of transport companies is restricted by law to citizens of the country, although often these laws may be circumvented by the way in which companies are structured.

There are advantages and disadvantages of foreign ownership. Advantages include investment and innovation which might not otherwise have taken place, transfer of technology including management skills, and the development of local expertise. The disadvantages include the repatriation of dividends which would otherwise have remained in the country, assuming that the undertaking would still have earned these dividends under local ownership. Some foreign owners exploit the local economy, for example by procuring spare parts at inflated prices through another of its subsidiaries based in its home country. Sometimes, in practice, there is only limited transfer of skills to local employees, so that if the foreign owner withdraws, it leaves behind little in the way of expertise to enable the company to continue to operate successfully. Disadvantages for foreign owners may include regulations imposing restrictions on the remittance of dividends, or on the employment of foreign staff, and the risks attached to potential political insecurity.

Several transport companies trading separately may be combined under the common ownership of a publicly or privately owned holding company. This form of structure combines the advantages of small operating units with those of larger organisations, without some of the disadvantages of large size. Some holding companies specialise only in operating bus services, but others are very diverse, owning companies in many different industrial sectors, as discussed later in this chapter.

An example of a very large publicly owned holding company was the National Bus Company in the United Kingdom, which was formed in 1969 by combining the bus companies in England and Wales belonging to two existing holding companies, the already nationalised Transport Holding Company and the private-sector British Electric Traction group. NBC's subsidiary companies remained fully autonomous, with the holding company determining policy and providing various specialised services. The NBC was broken up during the 1980s, as the individual companies were privatised. Subsequently many of the privatised ex-NBC companies were regrouped under new, privately owned holding companies, of which the largest are First Bus, Arriva and Stagecoach, which also have bus-operating subsidiaries overseas; more recently they have all formed subsidiaries operating passenger rail services, following privatisation of rail services in the UK.

A large British private sector holding company was the British Electric Traction group, which had numerous subsidiary bus and freight transport companies throughout England and Wales, as well as overseas through in intermediate holding company, United Transport Overseas. As mentioned above, the British bus companies passed into state ownership in 1969, while the overseas companies had all been sold, either to other foreign groups or to local interests, by the mid-1990s.

The paratransit industry is predominantly privately owned; typically, it is dominated by small operators, the majority owning only one vehicle, but there are some relatively large fleets, of up to twenty vehicles and sometimes considerably more. Some major bus operators are involved in paratransit type services in additional to their conventional bus services. For example in Beijing, a large fleet of minibuses, operated in a similar manner to most paratransit services, is owned by the state-owned Beijing Passenger Transport Corporation.

Ownership of taxis and other forms of individual public transport also varies. In some countries individual owner-drivers predominate, while in others virtually all vehicles are owned by large fleet operators. In addition to taxis which are owned by large companies, there are often a significant number operating under the banner of a large company but which are individually owned. Their owners usually pay a fee to the company and in return are allowed to use the company's livery, and benefit from the company's telephone/radio booking system if there is one; the company may also provide the radio equipment for installation in the owner-drivers' cars.

There tends to be a high turnover of businesses in the paratransit industry; the informal nature of the industry makes it difficult to measure the actual rate, which in any case varies considerably from one country to another. A major reason is a generally poor level of business ability; in particular, a lack of awareness of the true costs of operation leads many paratransit operators believe that their businesses are making a profit when in fact this is not the case. Most operators fail to provide for replacement of their vehicles, and are therefore continually reducing their capital.

The typical "life cycle" of a paratransit operator begins with the purchase of a vehicle, either new or second-hand, often financed from savings, or a lump sum payment on retirement from employment. The vehicle may be purchased on credit, in which case interest payments are generally high because of the risks involved in the business. The owner commences operation, usually by hiring out the vehicle to a driver for a fixed fee. The driver is responsible for paying for fuel, and initially the owner's expenses are low, confined to occasional replacement of brake or clutch linings and minor repairs, but little or no preventive maintenance. The vehicle owner usually spends most of the cash generated, either on other business ventures or on a more lavish life style; only rarely will he retain funds for future maintenance expenditure or vehicle replacement.

Eventually the vehicle requires major expenditure, such as a replacement engine, often incurred prematurely due to a lack of basic preventive maintenance such as regular oil and filter changes. However, in many cases the owner has insufficient funds; the vehicle is sold, and the operator goes out of business, to be replaced by a similar operator who will repeat the cycle. Some owners are more prudent, putting money aside for maintenance and replacement; their fleets may grow to a dozen or so vehicles, but often reach a size at which the owners are no longer able to manage them, and again, the businesses go into decline. The cycle may take several years, and there may be at any one time sufficient operators to provide a reasonably adequate service; there may even be an excess of supply.

The development of paratransit services has also caused problems in the conventional bus industry. Although the bus is an efficient mover of large numbers of passengers, there has been a general decline in the number of conventional buses operated in many developing countries, and in some cities paratransit has virtually replaced conventional bus services. For example, in Dar es Salaam, the market share of the state-owned bus operator, which at one time held a virtual monopoly, had declined to below 10% by 1995, and was virtually non-existent by 2000. In Accra, where full sized buses were formerly operated by state-owned transport undertakings, one privately-owned company was the only remaining operator of full-sized conventional buses on urban services by 1995, by which time its operational fleet had declined from around fifty buses to only four, all approximately twenty years old. There are, however, cases where the reverse has happened: for example, minibuses in Kuala Lumpur were replaced by full-sized conventional buses during the 1990s.

It may be useful to follow the typical pattern of development of the road mass transit industry in developing countries. In many cases, the first public transport services were provided by a conventional bus (or tram) operator, running maximum-sized vehicles on a planned network of routes, on a regular scheduled basis. These services were often of a high quality; many were operated by European companies, which set standards similar to those in their home countries. Often such operators were given exclusive franchises to provide the city services. Because of the high, and growing, demand, and minimal competition, these services were usually profitable; many operators practised cross-subsidy, running unprofitable routes in less densely populated parts of the city funded by profits on more lucrative routes.

However, as the pace of urban expansion increased, and with it the demand for passenger transport, many of these operators were unable to expand their services to match. Some were able to generate sufficient revenue to replace their existing vehicles when necessary, but not to purchase additional vehicles for expansion at the rate required. In a large number of cases, the position of the bus operators was made much worse by government action, particularly following independence in the case of former colonies: in most cities, fares were controlled by local or central government, which often refused to allow transport operators to increase their fares, as costs increased, to the extent necessary to maintain existing services, let alone to expand. Faced with declining revenue in real terms, bus operators were unable to maintain their vehicles properly, or to replace ageing vehicles as necessary; average fleet ages tended to increase, which in turn resulted in increased maintenance requirement and reduced vehicle availability. This led to service reductions: many operators, with a misplaced sense of responsibility, reduced services on their busiest (and most profitable) routes so that the less frequent (and unprofitable) routes did not lose their services altogether. Therefore the profitability of the conventional bus operator began to decline, as did the level and quality of service provided, at a time when demand was increasing.

The result was that private individuals purchased small vehicles, often small trucks fitted with rudimentary seating, and introduced services on the busiest bus routes to meet the unsatisfied demand. Usually these services were illegal in that they were not licensed to operate, and the vehicles used did not comply with public service vehicle construction and use regulations: in many cases existing legislation did not provide for the operation of such vehicles. Because they were illegal, the operators could set their own fare levels, which were invariably higher than those charged by the bus operators; but since there was unsatisfied demand, there were sufficient passengers prepared to pay the higher fares necessary to make the businesses viable. Ironically, the fares charged for the inferior services were often higher than the established operators would have charged if the regulatory authorities had permitted them to increase their fares to an economic level. Since most of the new unregulated operators concentrated on the busiest routes, this encouraged the original operators to reduce their services further on these routes, to maintain services on routes not served by the small operators. This further reduced the profitability of the conventional bus services.

As the established bus operators' fleets continued to decline in size, the infrastructure, principally garages, workshops and offices, and other overhead costs, usually did not; the ratio of staff to vehicles increased, as therefore did the cost per vehicle, while the average earnings per vehicle decreased, so that the overall efficiency and profitability of the companies deteriorated steadily. The process of expansion of the small operators, and decline of the large operators, was by now almost irreversible: governments could not restrict the informal sector since this would create a serious shortage of supply; they could not afford to fund expansion of the traditional bus service through subsidies; and the traditional bus operators were unable to invest.

The next development was invariably legalisation of the small operators, sometimes with fares controlled by the government, and sometimes not; in any case, regulating these many small operators was a much more difficult task than regulating one or two large operators, and even if fares were set by government, the official rates were often not observed.

The result of this process is a transport system dominated by low quality, unregulated paratransit operators charging relatively high fares, with many travellers having to rely on high cost individual public transport such as taxis or rickshaws. As the smaller vehicles abstract traffic from the bus services the latter become increasingly unprofitable, resulting in further deterioration of services. The conventional bus operators usually still have valuable but vastly under-utilised infrastructure such as depot and workshop facilities, while the paratransit vehicles are garaged and maintained at the roadside. In some cities conventional bus services are now almost non-existent or have to be heavily subsidised, while the number of paratransit vehicles is increasing rapidly.

OPERATORS' ASSOCIATIONS AND CO-OPERATIVES

In mass passenger transport, the individual vehicle owner or owner-driver is not normally the ideal operating unit, except where demand is low. If a regular service is to be provided which is attuned to passenger requirements, there is a need for co-ordination between services, which normally can be achieved only by relatively large operating units. When the industry is based on small operators, the creation of larger operating units in the form of operators' co-operatives, sometimes also referred to as associations or unions, can enable a better service to be provided than would be possible if all operators worked independently of one another. The majority of paratransit operators belong to associations, of varying degrees of formality, membership of which may be open to all operators on a particular route, area or city.

Most transport co-operatives or associations are formed by a number of vehicle owners, who pool their resources by putting their vehicles into a common fleet, under the control of officers appointed by the co-operative members. The members usually retain direct ownership of their vehicles, and usually continue to employ the crews, typically under "setoran" arrangements as discussed in Chapter 9.

It is necessary to distinguish between an operators' association or co-operative thus defined, and a trade association representing organisations in the public transport industry. A trade association, in any industry, is a body formed to further its members' interests, to provide a forum for the exchange of ideas, and to represent its members' interests to government and other organisations. It should be non-profit-making, and should not engage in businesses of any kind, although it may charge for services provided to its members in order to cover its costs; in particular, a transport operators' association should not be directly involved in the operation of commercial transport services. There are many transport operators' associations which are purely trade associations in this sense, but in some cases there is a degree of overlap between the activities and services provided by the two types of organisation.

The principal role of an operators' co-operative is to provide basic control of the operating unit, whether it is in respect of a single route, a group of routes or an area, and also, usually, control of the terminals connected with the operation. In addition, co-operatives normally carry out various other functions on behalf of their members. Some provide only the most basic services, while others provide an extensive range, such as the dissemination of information, provision of training, operation of maintenance facilities and breakdown recovery services, route planning and scheduling, setting of fares, arranging insurance and finance, purchasing of vehicles and spare parts, providing legal advice and representation, negotiation with regulatory authorities and labour organisations, setting and monitoring standards, allocation of revenue between operators, marketing of members' services, and dealing with publicity and public relations, including passengers' complaints. In Jamaica, the National Transport Co-operative Society provided depot, fuelling and workshop facilities for its members. The depot had previously been owned by Jamaica Omnibus Services, a nationalised operator which had ceased to trade as a result of financial difficulties, unregulated competition and inefficiency; it is relatively unusual for co-operatives to have the use of such facilities.

There are advantages if the co-operatives, rather than individual vehicle owners, are the licence holders for each route. There are fewer licence holders to be regulated, thus substantially reducing the workload of the regulatory authorities, and the co-operative can be held responsible for the behaviour of the individual drivers.

The situation in Ghana is typical. The Ghana Private Road Transport Union (GPRTU) is the major union representing road transport owners and employees in Ghana. Between them, the GPRTU and the much smaller Co-operative Union operate all terminals in Accra. At some terminals, both unions are present: some routes are controlled by one and some by the other. Some union branches are relatively active in organising the operations of their members. For example, they may allocate vehicles to different routes on different days, to share the "good" and "bad" work equitably between operators; much depends on the interest and ability of the local union chairman.

An important role of the GPRTU is to arrange funding for new vehicles for its members through various aid-assisted schemes, supported by the Government. It acquires vehicles, funded by relatively soft loans guaranteed by the Bank of Ghana, and makes the vehicles available to members under a hire-purchase arrangement whereby the operator pays for the vehicle over five years. Another valuable service provided by the GPRTU is to assist its members with loan finance to cover the cost of repairs to vehicles which break down or are involved in accidents.

In some cities there are separate co-operatives for each route, all operating independently. In others there is a single co-operative controlling all routes, while there are situations where there are a number of co-operatives, each controlling several routes. A disadvantage of identifying each route with a separate co-operative is that variations to routes cannot be implemented without affecting the co-operative structure. Increasing or reducing the length of a route is likely to affect the number of vehicles required, and if the requirement is reduced, there may be problems in redeploying vehicles belonging to members who have paid to join the co-operative. Linking of routes would require elimination of one or more co-operatives, or a merger or joint working arrangement between two or more. Elimination of a route would mean elimination of a co-operative.

The influence which the co-operatives often have can be an impediment to the implementation of any major route changes which are desirable in the public interest. It is therefore usually preferable for co-operatives to cover a small group of related routes, to permit flexibility between them, and to enable vehicles to be transferred from one route to another. Such a route group may be based on a specific route corridor, or a distinct sector of a city. Since there will inevitably be some overlapping of routes, such distinctions should not be rigidly drawn, and co-operatives need not necessarily be given a monopoly of any single route corridor or sector.

Sometimes there is an "umbrella" organisation representing the interests of all co-operatives in an area: for example in Malang, Indonesia, all 25 co-operatives are members of FORKOM, or "Forum for Communications", which is the main point of contact between the operators and the regulatory authority.

The services provided by the co-operatives may be funded in various ways, but the simplest and most common is for operators to be charged a fee in respect of each journey operated.

Sometimes there is a combination of a subscription and a journey charge. In Ghana, for example, operators normally register, for a fee, as life members with their local branch of one of the unions. They then pay terminal dues, which are normally charges for each departure, and which vary according to the size of vehicle, the location, and the union branches running the terminals used. The union pays the local authorities for the use of the terminal facilities. Non-members, or "floaters", wishing to use a terminal are charged a higher fee than members; this encourages operators to become members, and floaters are therefore comparatively few. Practice varies between union branches: some charge a monthly lump sum, and pay a portion of this to the terminal at the opposite end of the route; others charge daily. In the case of the National Transport Co-operative in Jamaica, the margin from the sale of fuel to members contributed to the administrative costs of the co-operative.

Some co-operatives control entry to the industry through operating a "closed shop" system whereby only members of the appropriate route co-operative are permitted to operate on a particular route. Membership is often compulsory, with various sanctions, legal or illegal, used against non-members who encroach on the association's territory. Rivalry between operators' associations sometimes becomes violent, as in the so-called "taxi wars" in South Africa, in which gun battles have occurred, and fatalities have included members of the public who were caught in the cross-fire, as well as minibus drivers and owners.

Most co-operatives are concerned only with the interests of their members, which do not always coincide with those of the travelling public. Co-operatives are often inclined to resist any proposed route changes, or the introduction of new routes, even though this would greatly improve the convenience of the service, in case these affect the earnings of their members. Many are opposed to any increase in the number of vehicles licensed on their routes, since this would reduce the earnings of existing members; on the other hand excessive numbers may be encouraged if this provides financial benefit to officials. There is a real danger of restrictive monopolistic practices against the public interest, and there must be provisions within the regulatory system to guard against this, while safeguarding the genuine benefits to the public of co-operation between operators to provide a regular and reliable service.

Some organisations may be described as co-operatives although they are not operators' co-operatives in the true sense. These are companies which are formed as a vehicle for investment by a group of people who are not vehicle owners; for example a large taxi company in Surabaya, Indonesia is owned by a co-operative formed by naval personnel as an investment, and operates in the same way as a normal private company, owning all its vehicles directly, and employing drivers and other staff. Another Indonesian co-operative, Kosabra, in Malang, combines the characteristics of both categories of co-operative. It was formed by the workers on a large construction project, and is involved in a number of businesses, including a department store and supermarkets, as well as a transport co-operative. Kosabra financed all vehicles for a new route in the city, and held the route licences in its own name; the vehicles were then sold to members under a hire purchase arrangement.

In some countries there is conflict between some of the functions of the co-operatives or trade associations and those of government, especially where the government has been instrumental in the establishment of the co-operatives. For example in Ghana, in addition to union dues, the terminal at which the operator is registered collects a daily amount of income tax on behalf of the government, and the union is also expected to ensure that its members comply with all traffic regulations, and to discipline any offenders. Thus while the GPRTU plays an important role in the operation of the transport industry in Ghana, there are serious conflicts of interest between its various activities. As a union, it represents the interests of its members, the operators, for whom it performs a number of valuable services, but as a Government enforcement agency, it is frequently required to take action against its members; its role in enforcing government regulations would be more appropriately undertaken by a Government body.

A similar situation applies in Indonesia, in respect of ORGANDA (ORGanisasi ANgkutan DArat, or Land Transport Organisation). This is nominally a trade association representing all operators in the road transport industry but in some respects is expected to function as a government enforcement agency. Indeed, it was managed by the government until 1998, when management was taken over by officers elected by the membership, although a strong link with government remained, with some government officials holding various posts within ORGANDA.

PRIVATISATION AND COMMERCIALISATION OF PUBLICLY OWNED UNDERTAKINGS

Privatisation, or the transfer of publicly owned undertakings to private ownership, is current government policy in many countries around the world. The popular expectation is that, following privatisation, services will automatically and immediately improve; this is not always the outcome, however, although in several countries, such as the United Kingdom, the efficiency of some public utilities has been transformed through privatisation.

Publicly operated transport services have been privatised in many developing countries, in various ways. In Dhaka, some of the buses owned by the Bangladesh Road Transport Corporation have been leased to private sector operators; buses have been sold by the Bangkok Mass Transit Authority to private owners, who operate them under franchise to the BMTA; in Sri Lanka the operating subsidiaries of the Sri Lanka Central Transport Board were "peoplised" in the 1990s by transferring ownership in the form of shareholdings to their employees, although this process was subsequently reversed.

In some cases, it has been only the ownership of the organisation which has changed: shares have been issued to the public, and existing managers have become major shareholders through preferential share purchase arrangements. Under the same management as before, most of these organisations have become more profitable and more efficient, while their employees enjoy improved conditions and some senior managers have also become extremely wealthy. In other cases, undertakings have been completely restructured under private ownership, and this has often included a broadening of their activities. For example in the United Kingdom, former gas, electricity, water and telephone undertakings, which previously had monopolies of their particular utilities, now provide several or all of these utilities, in competition with one another; similarly, several former bus operating undertakings have diversified into other transport sectors such as rail and air.

An important change which has occurred as a result of privatisation is that some or all of the employees in the business have a greater interest in its success. Many have become shareholders, and therefore have a share of any profit made by the business; this applies in particular to the senior management, who normally have larger shareholdings and therefore are particularly concerned about overall performance, while in some companies all employees have become shareholders. Frequently the organisation will be divided into cost centres, with the manager of each one directly accountable for its performance, and with his financial rewards related to that performance.

As well as an increased financial incentive to perform, employees also realise that their continued employment depends on their contribution to the organisation. An employee who is not contributing will not be tolerated by a manager who, as part owner of the business, is more cost-conscious than before. Finally, the directors of the organisation, to whom management reports (and senior managers are usually also directors as well as major shareholders) are responsible to all shareholders, and if a majority of shareholders are dissatisfied with their performance they may vote them out of office at the company's Annual General Meeting. Thus employees' efforts tend to be more adequately rewarded, while discipline is more effective than is normally the case under Government ownership. There is often a competitive element also: several privatised public utilities have been exposed to competition through the encouragement of other private sector companies to enter the same market, in addition to diversification by former nationalised undertakings as described above. This helps to protect consumers from exploitation through excessive charges or poor performance.

There are a number of ways in which publicly owned systems or undertaking may be privatised; these include management or employee buy-outs, management buy-ins, sale of shares, joint ventures between government and the private sector, and even privatisation of an industry by attrition, for example where paratransit competition results in the demise of the public sector operator. The sale of a transport company to its management, and sometimes also to its employees, through a management buy-out is often the most appropriate option, since it conserves the local knowledge and expertise essential to the business, while the inclusion of the employees in its ownership helps to overcome some of the problems of control. Gradual sale of shares to management and employees through deductions from salary over a period of time is often a practical means of implementing this option, and overcoming the problem of limited financial resources on the part of the purchasers.

Management buy-ins, perhaps in competition with management buy-outs, may be appropriate in the privatisation of a holding company; this option provides the opportunity for the purchase of shares in a particular subsidiary not only to its own management, but to all managers and employees of the holding company, and is more equitable where managers are frequently transferred between companies. An alternative to a management/employee buy-out, which may be appropriate in a situation where services are operated on an informal basis, is to sell the vehicles to their drivers, under some form of hire purchase arrangement, and to dispose of other assets such as properties on the open market.

Sale of shares in a transport company to outside investors depends on the availability of funds at the disposal of individual investors or venture capital institutions; in many developing countries availability of funds for such investment is low, while the absence of a stock exchange may preclude this as an option. Some governments prefer to retain partial ownership, through the establishment of joint ventures between government and private sector, with the government holding a majority share; however, this is not always a practical option, since private sector investors will require a degree of control of the undertaking. Where the government retains only a minority interest this will not be a problem, but the government will then have little control of the organisation; nevertheless there may still be advantages, since the government may be represented on the board of the undertaking, providing a useful means of communication.

When nationalised undertakings are privatised, the sale proceeds are often very low, in some cases less than total asset value, because poor performance under state ownership makes them unattractive to potential investors. Often the share value of a privatised company has increased in value many times over within a relatively short period following its sale, when the new owners are able to demonstrate the potential of the business. There have been cases of asset-stripping where the sale price has been below asset value; in the United Kingdom this happened in the case of some of the first National Bus Company subsidiaries to be privatised, when valuable city centre properties such as bus stations were sold for development, in some cases for more than the purchase price of the entire company.

It is desirable to provide for such contingencies, so that the government is at least able to realise the market value of the physical assets of the undertaking: the sale agreement may include the provision that proceeds from property sales within a specified period after sale may be shared with the vendor on a predetermined basis. Where a nationalised transport undertaking has degenerated irretrievably to a point where it is making substantial losses, the only realistic option may be to dispose of it for its asset value and to allow it to cease trading as a transport operator, while in some circumstances it may be appropriate for a nationalised transport company to be restructured before privatisation if this will improve its viability and increase its sale value.

State owned undertakings may be unattractive to potential purchasers because of non-commercial practices which may be politically difficult to change. A common problem is that many nationalised companies are grossly overstaffed, and the new owners must be confident that they will be able to reduce numbers or redeploy staff without complications. Another is that private sector bus operators are often reluctant to carry passengers entitled to concessionary fares, who were carried by the nationalised undertaking as a matter of course. Sometimes fare levels are too low, and would have to be increased to a level which the majority of passengers might be unable to afford in order to provide an adequate return at existing levels of operation; in any case the new owner must be sure that there will be no impediment to the charging of fares at an economic level.

Privatisation has not always been successful, and some privatised undertakings have failed to perform. Several of the peoplised bus companies in Sri Lanka incurred substantial losses, and the government purchased back majority shareholdings in each. In London, the transport authority established a new publicly owned bus company to operate services where the franchised operators had failed, and control of a private sector rail operator was taken over by the regulatory authority when it failed to meet all of the obligations of its franchise.

While in many cases privatisation has resulted in significant improvements, it need not be necessary to privatise an organisation in order to achieve similar results in terms of profitability and levels and standards of service. "Commercialisation" of a nationalised undertaking or a government organisation can have a similar effect to privatisation without change of ownership. A potential problem with this approach, which may rule it out altogether as an option, is that it may require changes to government regulations for the undertaking concerned, and it may be necessary for it to be treated as a special case within the government organisation. This is often easier with a government-owned company than with a parastatal organisation. If such a commercialisation process is successful, the undertaking will become more efficient with potential to compete profitably in the private sector; the government will benefit from its financial success, instead of selling off an unprofitable asset at a discounted price and allowing private individuals to profit handsomely from its subsequent profitability. If in future the government wishes to dispose of the undertaking to the private sector, it will have become a valuable asset which will realise a significant sale value.

Commercialisation requires similar incentives and disciplines to apply to the management and staff as would apply under privatisation. Management must have a financial incentive which is directly related to the performance of the undertaking, such as a percentage of operating surplus, paid as a bonus each year. Similar incentives may also be applied at lower levels. The management must also be free to make its own decisions, the only constraints being the need to comply with the undertaking's policy and all legal requirements and obligations. It must be allowed to determine its own salary scales and conditions of employment, to recruit its own employees, and to handle its own discipline.

A private sector organisation would have a Memorandum and Articles of Association or equivalent setting out its constitution, principal roles and objectives. A commercialised public organisation should have a similar document, approved by Government, specifying the company's policies in all areas. For full commercialisation, it would be necessary to make provision for the undertaking to operate under its own regulations as opposed to the normal Government procedures, while staff contracts of employment would require amendment, so that terms and conditions were comparable with those applicable to the private sector.

The organisation would require a Board of Directors or its equivalent, with responsibility for formulating policy and appointing and monitoring the performance of its management, and the authority to replace members of senior management giving unsatisfactory performance. It would ensure compliance with policy and all legal and financial requirements, and that its policies were in line with those of Government, although in its day-to-day operation the undertaking would not necessarily be bound by the same Government regulations and procedures applicable to other departments. The Board of Directors would normally include the General Manager and some or all senior managers, as well as directors representing the Government such as the Permanent Secretaries of relevant ministries, including transport; there should also be relevant representatives of the private sector, such as a senior manager of a financial institution, or a senior representative of a large transport undertaking, providing it were not a potential competitor or supplier.

DIVERSIFICATION OF BUSINESSES

Some large transport undertakings are highly diversified, or belong to large diversified groups. Diversification is sometimes regarded as an effective means of improving the profitability of a business, or even supporting unprofitable aspects of a business; in the transport industry, it may be seen as the only means of funding services in areas where demand is low. In a more general sense, diversification may enable surplus capacity, in terms of physical assets or manpower, to be more effectively utilised, thus improving the viability of all parts of the business: in several large state-owned transport undertakings in China, for example, one reason for diversification has been partly to absorb staff who otherwise would be surplus to requirements, and partly to exploit what are perceived to be more profitable business opportunities.

There is considerable variation in the extent of diversification found in transport organisations around the world. There may be diversification in the types of transport service provided: for example, an operator of basic urban bus services may diversify into the operation of premium air-conditioned services, long-distance services, tours or charter services. Further diversification may involve the operation of related transport activities: for example a bus company may run trucks, taxis, or commercial petrol filling stations. Most of the state-owned companies in China undertake maintenance and repair work on behalf of third parties as a means of utilising spare workshop capacity and generating additional revenue; in addition, many have diversified further into other commercial activities, which are almost totally unrelated to the core activity of the undertaking, such as construction, hotels, restaurants, retailing, hospitals, property development, and advertising.

Diversification of activities can be beneficial to the core business if it reduces total costs through spreading fixed costs over a wider operation; this reduction can sometimes be significant, but normally only in the short to medium term. Non-core activities are often unable to compete effectively with specialised organisations in that business, so that their financial contribution to the organisation is, at best, insignificant, while managers are often required to manage activities for which they have little or no expertise. It is debatable, therefore, whether such activities make any significant contribution to the funding of the core business, except through the spreading of overhead costs over a broader range of activities. If these activities are in competition with other businesses, they are unlikely to earn large profits, and therefore in practice will not be in a position to cross-subsidise the core business to any significant extent.

It is may be appropriate and practical for a company to diversify to spread its overheads, particularly where there is limited scope for expansion in the core business. But except in very small organisations, in which management can handle wide diversification of business reasonably well, it is not normally desirable to expect managers to handle widely differing activities, and a relatively high degree of management specialisation is normally required. Transport is a specialised business, and requires scarce specialist skills, particularly in the fields of planning and operation, and vehicle maintenance; these skills should not be dissipated in the management of businesses for which they are not relevant, which will result in both the core transport business, and the subsidiary businesses, suffering from a lack of management expertise.

Such dilution of management resources imposes a severe constraint on the development of many transport enterprises around the world. An organisation engaged in widely differing activities is therefore best structured as a holding company with fully autonomous subsidiaries specialising in individual activities. In a large organisation such specialisation may be quite narrow: for example it is relatively common for urban and long distance services to be operated by separate companies, or for separate companies to be formed to run basic and premium urban bus services. It is often appropriate for the general manager of each subsidiary to serve on the board of directors of the holding company, but with no executive authority over any of the other subsidiaries.

The debate as to the degree of diversification appropriate within a large industrial conglomerate is outside the scope of this book, but in principle there is no reason why a transport undertaking should not be part of a widely diversified group, providing its structure is conducive to effective management.

MARKET SEGMENTATION

Public transport users comprise a large cross-section of the public, with different levels of income, different requirements, and different criteria for their choice of transport mode or service. If only one standard of service is provided, it will meet the requirements of only part of the population, leaving perhaps significant unsatisfied demand. There is thus often scope for more than one standard of service on a route, to cater for passengers with different requirements; substantial benefits can be derived from such segmentation of the market. Many passengers are satisfied with the basic level of service usually provided, and are prepared to suffer overcrowded, uncomfortable and unreliable vehicles; they would not wish, or could not afford, to pay higher fares for a better quality of service. There may be other passengers who are prepared to pay higher fares for a convenient, comfortable, reliable service, with a better quality of vehicle, and a limit to the number of standing passengers carried. There may in fact be scope for several levels of service, ranging from those using the most basic type of vehicle, with a high passenger capacity and minimal comfort, to premium quality services using well-equipped air conditioned vehicles offering a high degree of comfort.

Such market segmentation is common on long-distance services. In China, for example, there are three types of service on most long distance routes: standard, luxury, and sleeper; fares for a luxury bus and for a sleeper bus are respectively approximately 40% and 130% more than the fares charged for a standard bus. It is also widespread in several of the larger cities, particularly in Asia, where basic bus services are supplemented by superior air-conditioned services, for which premium fares are charged, although it is unusual to find more than two standards of conventional urban bus service.

Different standards of service do not necessarily require different standards of vehicles, although it is important that the different services are easily distinguished from one another by the user. Some operators run services on which standing passengers are not permitted, or are strictly limited, sometimes on a limited-stop basis, using standard buses (though often newer ones) at higher fares which are justified by the exclusivity of the service and the reduced earning capacity due to the reduced load factor. In Bangkok, higher fares are charged on "refurbished" buses, which are often buses which have merely been repainted to look slightly smarter than others.

Market segmentation is becoming increasingly common on both urban and long distance bus services in many countries. Where car ownership is low, there is likely to be a range of income levels and preferences amongst the users of public transport. Where a choice of service standards is not available, the fact that in many cases a significant proportion of commuters regularly use taxis, when the next alternative is a much cheaper but basic bus or paratransit service, suggests that there is a market for an intermediate level of service, such as an air-conditioned bus, at a fare between the two. Such a service is likely to attract some passengers from conventional services, who would be prepared to pay more for a better service, but not as much as the taxi fare, and some passengers from taxis, who would prefer to pay less for their transport, but who would not be satisfied with the quality of service provided by the conventional buses.

The provision of different levels or standards of bus services may not necessarily be appropriate on all routes or corridors: a route serving a low-income area may not justify the provision of a superior service, while one serving a middle-income area may require only a premium service. On main route corridors, however, particularly in the larger cities, there is often sufficient demand to justify the provision of both types of service, or even three or four levels. In general, the larger the city, and hence the larger the demand, the greater the number of standards of service likely to be appropriate; market forces will, if allowed, determine the proportional split between the different services. Sometimes the same routes can be followed by the different services, but it is more likely that some variation will be appropriate. For example, standard and premium buses might serve different city centre terminals; at the outer ends of the routes, standard services may terminate in low-income residential areas, and premium services in high-income areas.

The experience in many cities where premium quality services are operated is that these services are often less profitable than ordinary services. The higher fares may be offset by the reduction in vehicle capacity, which may be up to 50%. Load factors are often lower also, particularly off-peak: demand for premium services tends to be more peaked than ordinary services due to a high proportion of commuters carried. Operating costs may be up to 75% more than for standard buses, because of the more expensive buses used: in particular, air conditioning increases operating costs significantly, while in many cases the crews are paid at higher rates than those employed on ordinary services.

Smaller buses, which can provide a higher frequency, are often more appropriate for premium services on many routes. For such services to be successful, therefore, it is important that fare levels, as well as routes, vehicle types and service frequencies, are all appropriate to the service in question. Many urban bus operators in developing countries at present do not have the resources to run premium services: their standard services are overstretched, and diversion of resources to premium services, even if this were to improve profitability, would reduce supply further. Where premium services are available, therefore, these are often provided by different operators from those providing the standard services.

DEDICATED TRANSPORT FOR STUDENTS AND EMPLOYEES

Many large companies, government departments, educational institutions and other organisations operate dedicated passenger transport services for the exclusive use of their own employees or students. While these cannot be regarded as public transport services, they are relevant to this book in the sense that they are substitutes for, or even competitors to, public transport, and may constitute a significant element of the passenger transport system; in some cities the number of buses used solely for the transport of students and employees runs into hundreds.

Normally, dedicated transport is provided because public transport services do not meet the requirements of the organisation concerned; this may be because the place of employment or education is remote from a bus route, or the hours of work are such that normal bus services are unsuitable. No matter how good the system may be, there will nearly always be some institutions for which public transport does not meet the requirements of the personnel involved and a dedicated or "own-account" operation is necessary. However, where a large number of organisations in a town or city provide dedicated transport this is usually a clear indication that public transport services are poor, and a more efficient system might result in overall savings to the economy as a whole by reducing the requirement for dedicated transport operations.

In many developing countries, as in developed countries, the transport of schoolchildren is a major issue, accounting for a significant number of dedicated passenger vehicles. The discussion which follows therefore refers largely to the transport of schoolchildren, but in most respects applies equally to dedicated transport for other categories of passenger.

Subsidised transport to and from schools forms part of the education policy in many countries, and the provision of dedicated transport is often an easier means of achieving this than subsidising the use of public transport services, particularly where a large number of individual operators are involved. In the United Kingdom, for example, following deregulation of bus services, the use of contracted buses increased at the expense of subsidies for public stage services, possibility because of reduced stability in a deregulated situation and the difficulties of dealing with many small operators.

The provision of dedicated transport also has the advantage that vehicles can be made available for other school activities during the day, and if the control of transport is delegated to the schools themselves this enables them to co-ordinate their transport services to suit the timing of the various school activities. Provision of dedicated transport is not a simple solution, however, and is expensive, largely because of the low level of vehicle utilisation, while since students' homes tend to be scattered in all directions, several vehicles may be required to meet the travel needs of each school.

Dedicated school buses may be owned by the government, education authority or even by individual schools, or may be chartered from a transport operator. Chartering is often a more cost-effective option if it is available, since the vehicles may be used for other work when not required for school transport, thus spreading their costs; another advantage is that management and maintenance of the fleet is carried out by professional transport operators. This is feasible where there are good conventional bus operators; however, in many developing countries the availability of buses for charter is limited, particularly at times when they are required for school transport. There are often no operators with the necessary resources in terms of fleet, facilities or even expertise to provide such a service, particularly in remote areas, and the development of such operators is likely to be concentrated in the provision of public transport services rather than specialised services to schools. Moreover, the types of vehicle available for charter are not always suitable for the carriage of schoolchildren, and may be old and in poor or even dangerous condition.

Where vehicles are operated under contract there are various ways of enforcing "quality" control, such as financial penalties for early or late running, failure to provide a suitable vehicle, or other infringements of contract conditions, but in practice these are not always effective, and it is often difficult to ensure that contractors meet their obligations. The charges for such operations will usually be high where vehicles are required at peak periods, because of the low utilisation of the vehicles used. Therefore chartering of buses for the transport of schoolchildren is relatively uncommon in developing countries, and where dedicated transport is provided, the vehicles used are normally owned by the education authorities or by the schools themselves. In the transport of employees, many organisations prefer to own their vehicles rather than rely on a contractor even if the cost is significantly higher; this is particularly common where reliability is essential, as in the airline industry where flights may be delayed due to the late arrival of staff.

In many countries school and employee transport is provided by government-owned vehicles. In some cases a fleet of school buses is operated, either as part of a larger fleet of central or local government vehicles, or as a specialised school transport operation. Sometimes buses are allocated to individual schools or government departments, and operated in isolation, with no central management of the transport fleet; in many cases this is the only option, particularly where schools or offices are many kilometres apart. In urban areas where there are several schools or offices in close proximity there can be substantial benefits in pooling transport resources, under a dedicated professional management. However, the administrative requirement is substantial, and costs and inefficiencies in this area may cancel out any benefits to be derived from pooling.

Many own-account transport operations suffer from poor management and administration. Management is often basic, carried out as part of the general administrative function of the organisation by staff whose expertise lies in unrelated fields. Such complex tasks as vehicle routing may not be performed efficiently, and there are usually few records of costs or activities, so that there is little information on which to base decisions. Staff who are responsible for managing the transport function should ideally be trained in the basic principles of transport management and cost accounting, but in practice this is rare.

The provision of drivers for dedicated buses can also be a problem due to the limited hours of use; except where wage levels are very low this can result in high operating costs. If staff can be deployed who have other duties also, this can make effective use of personnel, but there are often problems in finding staff who are capable of carrying out more than one job. If it is possible to employ part time staff this may be an effective solution, while in some cases school buses are driven by parents of some of the children, for a small payment or on a voluntary basis; this is more common in developed countries at present.

Maintenance of school buses is often a particular problem unless they are chartered from a transport operator. School bus drivers may be trained as mechanics, so that they are also able to carry out routine maintenance work on their vehicles, providing the necessary resources are available: school budgets are normally determined by education authorities, giving a fixed amount of funding per term for all purposes, and headmasters or administrators who control expenditure often give vehicle maintenance low priority in their allocation of limited funds. The result is usually that vehicles are poorly maintained, and availability is low.

Buses operated on own-account are normally very poorly utilised, often operating only two trips per day. In many cases, however, utilisation of vehicles would be equally poor, and therefore equally costly, if the service were provided by a regular transport operator. In Ghana, ownership and operation of some staff buses was taken over by staff welfare associations, some of which now operate the vehicles in revenue-earning public service during working hours to defray expenses; in some cases the buses are operated full-time on public service, to the detriment of the staff they were originally intended to carry.

COMPETITION, COMPLEMENTARITY, AND INTEGRATION

As described in Chapter 1, there are several different modes of public transport, each with different characteristics, and with advantages and disadvantages for different applications; invariably, several different modes will be found operating side by side. For example, public transport in Dhaka is provided by a variety of modes. Most numerous are cycle-rickshaws, followed by three-wheeled auto-rickshaws, while the number of saloon car taxis is increasing; a form of shared-taxi service is provided by three-wheel tempos carrying approximately ten passengers; formal bus services are operated by "minibuses" with approximately thirty seats but with standing capacity for about another thirty, and by some larger single-deck buses with total capacities of up to about eighty passengers; in addition there are double-deck buses, with capacities of up to 100, and on an increasing number of routes there are air-conditioned single-deckers providing premium services. Compared with most other cities, there are relatively few minibuses, which are known in Dhaka as "micro-buses". There is no urban rail system, although there have been proposals for various LRT projects from time to time, but trains on the national rail system are used by commuters, mostly on an informal basis, within Dhaka. There is a similar range of modes in Bangkok, although at the lower end there are no human-powered vehicles, while at the top are newly constructed LRT and metro lines.

In some respects, the different public transport modes operate in competition with one another and with private transport, but in others they complement one another: the distinction between complementarity and competition is not always clear. There are few, if any, countries or cities for which a single public transport mode will suffice: to meet the requirements of all travellers satisfactorily it is necessary to achieve an appropriate mix of several different modes. Although there is a considerable degree of overlap in some cases, each mode has its particular characteristics, and has a different role to play in catering for different market sectors. This is partly reflected in fare levels. Bus services are usually the cheapest alternative, and tend to be used by those at lower income levels; paratransit is often slightly more expensive than conventional bus services; taxis and other forms of individual public transport are normally the most expensive form of public transport, and are used by the higher income groups within the public transport market. Where it exists, LRT tends to be more expensive than bus travel, and is therefore used mainly by commuters who are relatively well off; heavy rail systems usually provide a range of service standards, from basic services which are often considerably cheaper than bus services, to "first class" or its equivalent which may be very expensive.

In a large city there may be a role for all surface transport modes, operating complementary services and catering for different sectors of the market; in a small town, there may be a requirement for only one or two; for longer-distance travel, the choice may include rail, air and water transport. There are also alternatives within each mode: in road transport, for example, there is a range of vehicle types and sizes. The most appropriate public transport mode to meet a particular requirement is influenced by passengers' ability to pay, the length of journey involved, volume of traffic to be carried, and characteristics of the road network.

Public transport modes are complementary to one another when together they provide a linked service between two points, such as a bus service which connects with a rail service, onto which passengers transfer in order to complete their journeys. Taxis, rickshaws and other forms of individual public transport are complementary to long distance bus and train services, for carrying passengers, particularly those with luggage, to and from stations. Minibuses are often effective as a complement to larger conventional buses: the latter are generally a more efficient form of public transport on main corridors, while the smaller vehicles are often more effective where demand is lower, or where the road configuration makes the operation of larger vehicles impractical. In many large cities such as Bangkok and Jakarta, small paratransit vehicles act as feeders to buses, operating from markets or similar focal points on main routes into the narrow streets of the adjacent residential areas.

Different modes may also be complementary in the sense that each caters for a different sector of the market on the same route, for example buses catering for low-income travellers and taxis for the better off; similarly, several different standards of service may be provided on the same route, by one operator or by several. In such cases, however, there is also competition, since a change in the price or quality of one service will result in some marginal passengers transferring from one to another. Moreover if one mode, for example paratransit, is used by some passengers only because of a shortage of capacity on another, such as conventional bus services, it may be regarded as complementary although it also has a competitive advantage. Similarly, public and private transport may be regarded as complementary as well as competitive with one another: both play their part in meeting the overall transport requirement, and there is therefore a role for each, and it is important that a satisfactory balance is achieved between the two. While many travellers use either public or private transport, there are also many who use both, for example commuters using private transport between their homes and a railway station, and public transport into the city centre.

The concept of complementarity is closely linked with that of co-ordination or integration of transport services. Integration should ideally be a natural result of market forces, which should encourage passengers to use the mode or combination of modes which is most suitable in the circumstances. Factors which influence a passenger's choice include not only the costs of using the alternatives, but also the relative convenience of the various services. A typical example of integration is where suburban bus services feed into rail services to the central area, providing an alternative to a journey by bus throughout. For the concept to be acceptable, the physical connection between modes must be as easy for the passenger as possible. This will require buses to be able to stop close to the rail station, with preferably a covered walkway from bus stop to station platform. Passengers making the transfer will incur two spells of waiting time, and these together with the time taken to transfer should be minimised; this will require relatively high frequencies for at least one of the modes. Through ticketing is desirable, so that the passenger has to pay only once, and the total journey cost should be competitive with the alternative of travelling by bus throughout, after taking into account the difference in total journey time, comfort and convenience.

With effective integration of bus and rail services, the number of passengers using rail services is likely to be considerably greater than would otherwise be the case. Savings in total bus operating costs would be achieved by reducing the frequency of bus services between interchange points and city centre; these tend to be the most congested portions of the routes, and therefore the potential savings are considerable. In practice, however, the modal shift which should ideally result from such integration is not always easy to achieve. Passengers are often reluctant to change modes, or even to change vehicles, during the course of a journey. The inconvenience of having to alight from one vehicle, transfer to another and incur additional waiting time may be a serious deterrent, and if there is a choice, many passengers will opt to remain on one vehicle throughout the journey, even if the journey time is slightly longer.

It is sometimes argued that the use of co-ordinated services should be enforced, and that to ensure that passengers use the interchange facility, they should be given no choice. In the United Kingdom, for example, when the Tyneside Metro LRT system was opened in the 1970s, bus services were truncated at interchange points so that bus passengers travelling to the central area had no option but to transfer to the rail service; however, when bus services were deregulated some ten years later, bus operators recommenced operating through journeys to the central area, and abstracted a considerable amount of traffic from the Metro.

It should not be necessary to force passengers to transfer from road to rail during the course of their journeys. Indeed, in the longer term, commuters who feel inconvenienced by an integrated transport service which they are compelled to use may be inclined to switch to taxis or private transport; this tendency may be checked through the introduction of appropriate charges for road use, although in practice this unlikely to be achieved in many developing countries in the foreseeable future. Provided that there is no substantial difference in fares, and convenient intermodal interchange is possible, many passengers will choose rail if the journey time is significantly shorter, and will choose the alternative bus service only if this provides better access to the final destination.

Where there are different LRT systems operating within the same city, co-ordination is often lacking. To be most effective, an LRT system should allow passengers to interchange freely between the different lines, without having to purchase separate tickets for each stage of their journeys. This is invariably the case where all lines are operated by a single undertaking, as in

Beijing or Hong Kong; However, in some cities, this is not the case. In Kuala Lumpur, for example, urban rail services are provided by the national rail system (KTM), and two LRT systems, STAR and PUTRA; the three systems are entirely independent of one another, and changing from one line to another involves walking from one station to another and purchasing separate tickets. Similarly, in Bangkok, there are two separate LRT systems, one elevated and one underground; although passengers may transfer from one system to the other within the same station, there is no through ticketing arrangement.

There is invariably considerable competition between different transport operators, the various modes of public transport, and between public transport and private transport, particularly over shorter distances, where the traveller may have a choice between walking, cycling, using a rickshaw, auto-rickshaw, taxi, bus, minibus or LRT service, or travelling by car. The number of potential alternatives diminishes with distance, so that over the longest distances within the city the choice is basically between a bus, a minibus or a taxi, rail service if available, or private transport. For inter-urban travel over longer distances, there may be a choice between road, rail, air and sometimes water transport. Competition tends to be greater where demand is greater: for example, on main urban traffic corridors there are likely to be not only several road transport operators in competition with one another, but there may also be an LRT system in competition with the road transport services.

On long-distance services between major cities there is often a choice between road and rail. In most African countries buses are usually faster than rail, regardless of distance; rail fares are usually lower, and the service caters for the lower end of the market. In China and several other Asian countries, buses tend to be faster and more convenient for journeys of up to about 200 kilometres; above that distance, rail is normally faster. If rail passenger services were made more attractive, particularly in terms of speed, more inter-city journeys would be undertaken using rail for the greater part of the journey. However, the speed of the rail portion would have to be considerably higher than the road journey in order to compensate for time lost in changing mode, and this will not be achieved with existing infrastructure in most countries. Nevertheless, in order to maximise the convenience of rail travel, and to facilitate complementarity between road and rail it is desirable that wherever practical, railway stations should be conveniently accessible by road transport.

Competition between the various forms of road transport is usually extensive. In addition, there is often competition, some of which is legal and some illegal, between different operators of the same mode. In a city transport system, competition between different modes on the same route is generally preferable to competition between different operators of the same mode, but where several routes operate along a common corridor there is scope for some competition between operators, which is normally sufficient to inhibit blatant exploitation of an operating monopoly.

Competition between different bus or paratransit operators is sometimes limited by the way in which the services are operated. Where services are provided by a large number of small operators, each route is often controlled by an operators' association, co-operative or route committee which enforces a system of operation whereby vehicles leave the terminals in an agreed sequence. Where services are operated by conventional bus operators in a regulated system, two or more operators may wish to co-operate to provide a co-ordinated service: for example, operators serving adjacent territories may operate through routes between their respective territories. Passengers could exercise choice, if they wished, by letting one vehicle go and waiting for another, but in practice it is unlikely that they would do so. Such regulation of services is generally preferable to a free-for-all where vehicles operate irregularly, and race with one another for passengers.

Where car ownership is high, competition between public and private transport may be the most significant form of competition. While competition between operators and modes may improve public transport services generally, and may be encouraged by legislation limiting restrictive practices on the part of operators, public transport often does not compete on equal terms with private transport. Users of private transport, particularly in urban areas, usually pay far less per person for each unit of road space than users of mass transport modes, putting public transport at a severe disadvantage given the superior convenience of private transport to its users.

7

MANAGEMENT STRUCTURE AND STAFF FUNCTIONS

This chapter deals in broad terms with the principles of organisation and management as specifically applied to the operation of public transport, and discusses in more detail those aspects where transport undertakings have special characteristics or requirements. It does not address the more general aspects of management, which are well covered in specialist books on the subject. The discussion is relevant mainly to formal types of organisation, and not to very small units or paratransit operators.

BOARD STRUCTURE

Ultimate responsibility for the operation of a transport undertaking normally rests with a board of directors, or its equivalent, such as a government-appointed commission, authority or executive; the roles of these bodies are broadly similar, and the terms "board", "board member" and "director" are used here as generalisations. The principal functions of the board are to determine policy, and to ensure that management runs the organisation efficiently in accordance with these policies. Directors must have the capability to appraise the organisation's performance, understand the reasons for any changes or trends, and be aware of changes to prevailing conditions and their significance; they must be able to identify opportunities and threats, assess their relevance to the organisation, and decide how the organisation should react to changes in circumstances. The board must also be able to take advice, both from the management within the organisation, and from qualified outside people. It must make appropriate policy and executive decisions, and work with management to ensure that its decisions are implemented. Finally, directors have various statutory obligations, to ensure that the organisation complies with the law, and to protect the interests of its shareholders or owners; the penalties for failing in their legal duties may include heavy fines or imprisonment.

The board plays a vital role in the overall direction of a business, and its composition will therefore have a significant influence on its success. In order to carry out its functions, the members of the board, collectively, should have various skills, including expertise which is specific to the industry, plus general organisational ability. Principal requirements include expertise in transport operational planning, automotive engineering, finance, industrial relations, law, local politics, and marketing. Some directors are appointed specifically to represent the owners of the organisation, while others may represent particular special interest or political groups. The size of the board can vary considerably. Between six and ten directors is fairly typical in the private sector, but much larger boards are also common, particularly in public sector undertakings. The appropriate size is determined to some extent by the number of different interests represented and disciplines required, but as the size increases, the decision-making process becomes more cumbersome, and large boards may therefore be at a disadvantage.

Directorships may be full time or part time: some boards consist entirely of full time, and others entirely of part time members, although most boards include both. Full time directors, or executive directors, are normally senior managers within the organisation. Part time or non-executive directors can be valuable by enabling an organisation to draw on specialist expertise in particular fields which cannot be justified within the organisation on a full time basis. Some directors are appointed because they have connections which are useful to the organisation; often these are people with influential political connections. The holders of certain government positions, such as the permanent secretary of the ministry responsible for transport, may automatically be required to serve on the boards of state-owned transport undertakings. In some countries representatives of the employees are required to serve on the boards of certain organisations, particularly those in the public sector. Retired executives from the organisation, or senior managers of other transport organisations, are sometimes appointed as part-time non-executive directors.

Large organisations may have more than one board. For example there may be a main board, whose principal function is to deal with matters of policy, and an executive board, dealing with management matters. Membership of the executive board may include the Chairman and Chief Executive of the company, some or all of the main board members, and executive directors or senior managers of the company. This arrangement is often appropriate for a holding company, where the main board may be common to several subsidiary companies, while each subsidiary will have a different executive board. It may also apply, for example, in the case of a public sector urban transport authority, where there may be an overall authority comprising mainly political interests (often both local and central government appointees) and an executive board comprising professional transport managers.

The main board directors may also be directors or chairmen of one or more of the subsidiary companies. The majority of the directors of the subsidiaries are, however, unlikely to be main board directors. Main board directors who have specialist skills, such as engineering, operations or finance, may be made responsible for overseeing the relevant functions in the subsidiary companies, even if they are not directors of those companies. In a large group of companies, some functions, such as vehicle selection, purchase of spare parts, or pensions, may be most appropriately handled centrally, and be the responsibility of the main board; local issues should be dealt with by the subsidiary boards. However, the degree of centralisation varies, with some holding companies allowing much greater autonomy to their subsidiaries than others.

Responsibility for appointing directors may be split between different organisations. In a private sector company the shareholders normally elect the directors on a democratic basis; if large blocks of shares are held by single organisations these often appoint one or more directors to represent their interests. Directors of public sector companies may be appointed by central or local government, or both. Care should be taken to ensure that conflicting interests are avoided as far as possible: for example a director who owns a motor dealership may use his influence to obtain business from the transport undertaking on advantageous terms to himself. In some countries board appointments, particularly in public sector organisations, are made for political reasons as "rewards" to people who will make little or no contribution to the organisation; such appointments are invariably detrimental to the effectiveness of the board and to the organisation.

MANAGEMENT STRUCTURE

The principal role of management is the day-to-day running of the undertaking in accordance with the policies determined by the board. The way in which management is structured can influence its effectiveness; there are many alternative forms of management structure, although the same general principles apply to all organisations. In particular, lines of communication should be as clear and direct as possible, and the structure should be such that appropriate delegation of responsibilities is facilitated.

Dangers to be avoided include those of over-bureaucratic organisations, where an unnecessarily large number of individuals are involved in the making of decisions or in taking action. The factors which determine the appropriate management structure for a transport undertaking include its size, geographic spread, ownership, activities, the extent of diversification, and also, to some extent, the qualities and capabilities of the people concerned. A structure which is appropriate for a small organisation will not normally be suitable for a large one. There is a limit to the number of staff and functions which can be managed by one individual, and therefore the larger the organisation, the greater will be the need for division into manageable units. Many organisations have structures which are inappropriate for their size; this is often the case where companies have changed significantly in size, particularly when they have contracted.

A typical bus company structure, which has proved effective in commercial operations throughout the world, is based on functional divisions. There are three main functions in the management of a passenger transport undertaking, each of which, except in a very small operation, normally requires a separate department under its own senior manager. These are the operations function, which is concerned with the deployment of buses on the road; the engineering function, concerned primarily with the maintenance of the vehicle fleet; and the financial and administrative function, which in most respects is similar to that in other commercial organisations. The managers of these departments may typically hold the titles of Operations Manager or Traffic Manager; Engineering Manager, Technical Manager or Chief Engineer; and Financial Manager, Financial Controller or Chief Accountant. All will report to a General Manager or Managing Director, who has overall responsibility for the management of the undertaking.

In a bus company, the engineering and operational functions are complementary; too often, however, the two departments see themselves as rivals, and co-operation between them can be seriously lacking, to the detriment of the organisation as a whole. Often the interests of the operations department appear to conflict with those of the maintenance department, and vice versa; while it is obviously desirable for a bus to be in revenue-earning service for as much of the time as possible, it is also important that it is made available to the engineering department for the necessary maintenance to be carried out.

In broad terms, structures may vary in terms of the steepness of the management "pyramid": a flat pyramid has few levels of management, while a steep pyramid has many. There is no "ideal" form: in some cases a steep pyramid, and in others a flat pyramid is appropriate, but it is important that the number of management levels, or the steepness of the management pyramid, is appropriate to each particular set of circumstances. As a general rule, the number of management levels should be kept to a minimum within existing cultural constraints in order to avoid unnecessary cost and to enhance lines of communication and responsibility.

A flat pyramid will normally be appropriate where it is customary to involve a large number of managers in the decision-making process. Where this is the case, and large numbers of managers regularly attend meetings with the general manager, it is usually more effective if most of them report directly to the general manager; the same will also apply at lower levels. However, there is a limit to the number of staff which can be effectively managed directly by a single individual; the number varies according to the level of management and the tasks involved, the effectiveness of management systems and procedures, and the capabilities of the managers concerned. The smaller the number of people directly managed by any individual, the steeper the pyramid will become, with a greater number of "deputy" or "assistant" positions; however, a very steep pyramid with two-to-one, or even one-to-one, reporting situations is normally wasteful of management resources, and often leads to duplication of effort.

The shape of the pyramid does not necessarily affect the actual number of management staff required: the same number may be employed if there are several layers of management as if there are few layers; but the number of managers at each level will increase as the pyramid becomes flatter, and the number of levels decreases.

The management structure of a transport company becomes more complex when there are several separate operating depots. To some extent, each depot represents a microcosm of the organisation as a whole: its functions are broadly similar, and there needs to be an appropriately qualified junior manager responsible for each. There are two basic alternative structures for the management at depots, geographic and functional, each with its advantages and disadvantages.

With a geographic structure, all staff at each depot report to a depot manager, whose expertise may be in operations, engineering or administration. The depot manager may report directly to the general manager, or to one of the functional managers at headquarters: for example, if he is an engineer, he might report to the engineering manager; or he may report to both the engineering manager and the general manager, in respect of his different responsibilities. The advantage of this approach is that there is a single person responsible for all activities at each location, and especially where distances between the head office and depots are significant, this simplifies the control of each depot. Disadvantages are that the depot manager is required to manage functions for which he has no expertise, and that the functional heads at headquarters have no direct control over staff carrying out duties within their own areas of responsibility; the result is often weak management of most of the functions at the depots.

The alternative is to have functional heads at the depots reporting to the appropriate senior manager at headquarters; this will improve the management of these functions, and allow all managers at the depots to concentrate on their own areas of expertise, but a disadvantage is that there will be no single person at any depot with overall responsibility. A typical compromise is for functional managers to report to their appropriate manager at headquarters, but for one of them to be appointed senior manager at the depot, with day-to-day responsibility for all aspects of the operation; a disadvantage of this arrangement is that there will be several junior managers reporting to more than one senior manager. The most suitable arrangement depends to a large extent on the qualities and abilities of the individual managers concerned.

It is very difficult to identify the most suitable structure. Since the National Bus Company in the United Kingdom was privatised in the 1980s, some of the large groups which acquired most of its subsidiaries have changed their management structures several times, some oscillating between centralised and decentralised structures, and increasing and reducing the number of management levels.

The degree of diversification of an organisation also has a significant influence on its management structure, as well as on its efficiency. A company specialising in a single activity, at one location, requires a relatively simple structure. At the other extreme, organisations which have diversified into a number of unrelated activities require very complex management structures; in practice they often have structures which are cumbersome and inefficient, lacking clear lines of authority, with managers at relatively low levels having responsibility for several different activities. Since the non-core activities may require very different management skills from those required to operate the core transport business, few managers are able to concentrate their energies on tasks for which they have specialist skills or experience, and scarce expertise is not used to its maximum advantage.

STAFF CATEGORIES AND FUNCTIONS

The principal categories of staff within a typical large transport undertaking are listed below. The roles to be filled are much the same in all organisations, although job titles vary; moreover, in some organisations responsibilities are divided between more than one person, while in others several roles may be assigned to a single individual. It is not possible to list every post found in every transport undertaking, since functions may be allocated in many different ways.

Some or all managers may have a number of assistants or deputies; for example, an operations manager may have two or more assistants, separately responsible for different functions such as administrative and operational matters, or alternatively each may have similar roles, but in respect of different geographical areas. Certain specific roles may be assigned to individuals, with appropriate titles: another example from the operations department is that there is often a Planning Manager, responsible for planning matters, a task which in other organisations is merely one of the functions of the Operations Manager or one of his assistants. In a small company, some of the senior management roles may be combined. For example the functions of the operations manager may be divided between the chief engineer and the financial/administration manager, while the general manager, depending on his background and qualifications, may carry out the functions of the operations manager, chief engineer or financial/administration manager in addition to his overall management responsibilities.

Typical senior management positions:

- General Manager
- Operations Manager
- Engineering Manager
- Financial Manager
- Administration Manager

In some organisations, the holders of some or all of these positions may also be members of the board of directors, in which case they may hold titles such as Managing Director, Operations Director, Technical Director and Financial Director.

Typical operations department positions:

- Area Managers
- Inspectors and Controllers
- Cashiers
- Conductors
- Drivers
- Loaders
- Security Personnel

Typical engineering department positions:

- Supervisory
- Mechanics
- Semi-skilled and Unskilled Workshop Staff
- Stores Personnel

Typical finance and administration department positions:

- Personnel Manager
- Information Technology Manager
- Accounts Staff
- Clerical Staff
- Messengers

Each of these categories, other than those whose functions are not specific to the transport industry such as general administrative, accounting and clerical staff, is discussed briefly below, together with the duties involved.

General Manager

The General Manager is the most senior manager in the organisation, reporting directly to the Board of Directors. He has overall responsibility for the management of the organisation, and all other senior managers report directly to him. Qualifications required for the post are primarily good management skills, but an understanding of the main functions of a transport business is also important. In many transport undertakings the general manager has been promoted from the operations, engineering or finance department.

Operations Manager

The holder of this post, often alternatively entitled Traffic Manager, is responsible for the Operations or Traffic Department, the main responsibilities of which normally include the planning, operating and marketing of bus services, collection and control of revenue to the point where the Financial Department assumes responsibility, discipline of crews and monitoring of operations. Qualifications required, as well as good management skills, are a thorough understanding of transport service planning, operating systems and procedures and all relevant legislation.

Engineering Manager

The Engineering Manager, sometimes known as Chief Engineer or Technical Manager, is responsible for the maintenance of all vehicles, equipment, buildings and infrastructure, for managing the workshops and engineering staff, planning and controlling maintenance systems, and monitoring the technical performance of each vehicle. He is often also responsible for controlling the purchase of vehicle spare parts and other inputs such as fuel, and should contribute to all decisions regarding vehicle acquisitions and disposals. A qualification in mechanical or automotive engineering is desirable, as well as practical experience in vehicle maintenance and good general management skills.

Financial Manager

The Financial Manager, Financial Controller or Chief Accountant is responsible for all financial and accounting functions within the organisation; the incumbent is often also the Company Secretary or equivalent, in countries where this post is a statutory requirement. The role is similar to that in most other industries; recognised accountancy qualifications are desirable, and in some countries are required by law. Specialist tasks specific to the transport industry are the revenue accounting procedures, which require individual route or trip revenues to be identifiable, and likewise the costing procedures to enable the financial performance of individual routes and vehicles to be assessed. Sometimes personnel and administrative functions are treated as separate departments but often they are placed under the financial department.

Administration Manager

Where this position exists, the incumbent is responsible for various administrative functions which are not allocated to other managers. These may include personnel functions (if there is a separate personnel manager he may report to the administration manager), and general administration. No special qualifications are normally required other than good administrative ability.

Area Managers

In a large undertaking, or if there is an extensive geographic spread of operations, there may be a number of area managers, each responsible for operations within a specified area, or on specific routes. Area Managers may be responsible for the management of an individual depot, and may hold the title of Depot Manager or Depot Superintendent. In some organisations area managers are responsible for operational matters only; in others, they are also responsible for all engineering, financial and administrative matters within their areas. They may report to the operations manager, or directly to the general manager, depending on the extent of their responsibilities.

Inspectors and Controllers

These are essentially supervisory roles within the operations department, primarily to ensure that bus drivers and conductors operate in accordance with instructions, and comply with the undertaking's rules and regulations as well as any legal requirements. An important role of inspectors is to check that all fares are properly collected from passengers, and that passengers are issued with the correct tickets. Inspectors may be stationary or mobile; the former are based at strategic points and supervise the running of buses passing those points, while mobile inspectors, who may travel on the buses or use cars or motorcycles, move around the system, often checking buses on a "surprise" basis.

In some organisations there is a distinction between revenue inspectors and controllers, or regulators, whose responsibility is principally to ensure that buses depart at the correct times. No special qualifications are required for these positions other than a thorough understanding of the organisation's operating systems and procedures. Inspectors and controllers are often promoted from drivers and conductors, but some undertakings prefer to recruit specifically for these roles to avoid the possibility of collusion with former colleagues.

Cashiers

Large quantities of cash, usually in small denominations, are handled by most transport undertakings, and the role of cashiers in counting and banking cash is essential. In some organisations automatic cash counting equipment is employed, but where labour costs are low this is not normally justified. Cashiers are normally employed in the financial department, but in some undertakings are employed in the operations department.

Conductors

Except where very small vehicles are used, it is normal for a bus to carry one or more conductors, sometimes referred to as "drivers' assistants" in the case of paratransit vehicles. The primary role of a conductor is to travel on a bus in order to collect fares from the passengers, and to ensure their safety while travelling; in some organisations conductors are also responsible for the timekeeping of the bus. Normally there is one conductor on each bus, but where loadings are high, two or even three conductors are sometimes carried. In some cases additional conductors are deployed at peak periods; these may operate on busy sections of routes only, leaving the regular conductor to work the full length of the route.

Not all transport companies employ conductors; in some cases, particularly where labour costs are high, fares are collected by the driver, or tickets are issued automatically by coin-operated machines on or off the vehicle.

Drivers

The primary task of the driver is to drive the vehicle, safely and in accordance with relevant regulations and schedules. Drivers are also usually responsible for carrying out certain basic checks on their vehicles, such as checking fuel and water levels, and the condition of brakes and lights, and they may be given additional tasks such as fuelling or cleaning their vehicles. In some cases drivers may also be required to collect fares from passengers, although one-person operation (normally abbreviated to OPO, or sometimes OMO – one-man-operation) of full-sized buses is less common in developing than in developed countries.

Bus drivers traditionally, although not always, are employed within the operations department. This is appropriate in that the driver is responsible for operating in accordance with the routes and schedules managed by the operations department. However, the driver shares with the maintenance department the responsibility for ensuring that the vehicle is operated safely and without damage; to an extent, therefore, the driver reports to two departments, and this can sometimes lead to problems of accountability.

In addition to bus drivers, most organisations employ drivers for ancillary vehicles such as workshop and breakdown vehicles, and cars used for carrying mobile inspectors.

Loaders

In some organisations, particularly those operating long distance and rural services, there is a requirement for loaders to load and unload passengers' luggage, and unaccompanied freight where this is carried. In some cases loaders travel with the buses as additional crew members, but normally they are based at bus stations and at some other main stops along the route. Loaders who are directly employed by bus operators are normally allocated to the operations department. Many operators do not employ loaders of their own, since this service is provided by loaders employed at bus stations, on a formal or informal basis.

Security Personnel

Security of premises and vehicles is an important function, and many organisations employ security personnel, principally as guards based at the various operating premises. These may report to a security officer within the operations or administrative department, or to the administrative or personnel manager. Often the security function is contracted out to a specialist security company.

Engineering Supervisory Staff

Supervisory staff in the engineering department normally include workshop supervisors, foremen and chargehands. The senior supervisors may be responsible for a number of activities, but those at more junior levels are normally responsible for specific functions or skills, for which they are also qualified themselves. It is normal for most supervisors, particularly those at junior levels, to be "working supervisors", who undertake specific maintenance tasks as well as overseeing others carrying out their tasks. Because of the wide range of workshop skills, it is normal to have a relatively large number of supervisors, responsible for small groups of mechanics with similar or related skills.

Mechanics

As indicated above, there is a wide range of mechanical skills required in the workshops. In a small operating unit, where only a small number of staff can be justified, it will be necessary to employ mechanics who each have a range of skills; in a larger workshop it is normally preferable to employ more specialised mechanics, although some interchangeability is desirable in order to maximise labour productivity in a situation where a significant proportion of the work is unpredictable. The principal skills required cover major units such as engines, gearboxes and axles, fuel systems, electrical systems, welding, bodybuilding and painting.

Mechanics should have relevant qualifications; in many countries there are recognised trade test certificates, while large organisations with apprenticeship schemes may have their own internally recognised qualifications.

Semi-skilled and Unskilled Workshop Staff

In addition to the skilled mechanical staff there is a requirement for various categories of semi-skilled and unskilled staff. These include tyre fitters, cleaners, fuellers, greasers and general labourers. Many mechanics are initially employed in these positions and later qualify for one of the skilled grades.

Stores Personnel

The stores are an important part of the workshop, and stores management is a specialised job. In addition labourers may be required to receive and issue parts, and to handle parts within the stores.

Other Positions

Other positions within a transport undertaking, such as those concerned with financial, administrative and personnel functions, are similar to those in other industries.

DIFFERENCES IN CULTURE AND MANAGEMENT STYLE

Management systems and techniques vary considerably between different organisations and different countries, for a number of reasons. A major factor is cultural differences between countries, which can have a significant effect on management style, and which in turn affect the type of management structure required. For example, in some cultures there is a tendency to evade responsibility and delegate decisions upwards wherever possible: this affects the management structure in that there must be a concentration of capability at the higher management levels. In some countries it is normal and accepted for managers to have their own personal business interests, to which they devote part of their working day: often a significant proportion of their time is spent on activities totally unrelated to their employment. Even where there is an obvious conflict of interest, such as where a bus company manager owns a fleet of paratransit vehicles, this is sometimes considered to be normal and acceptable.

Work ethic also varies considerably from one country to another. This affects the number of hours which a manager is prepared to spend at work, and the level of productivity. The level of productivity in turn influences the number of people required in the organisation, and hence the management structure. In some cultures, also, there is a tendency to involve large numbers of management staff in all decisions, requiring large and time-consuming meetings at which matters are discussed which directly concern only a small number of those present. Again, this requires a different management structure from a system where managers are consulted only on matters which are of direct concern to them; a much flatter pyramid is appropriate in the former case. Attitudes towards the keeping of appointments is a particular problem in some countries, where considerable management time is consumed in waiting for meetings which do not start at the appointed time, or in waiting for officers who do not attend punctually; such problems increase with the size of the management team.

Different managers have different styles, some of which may be compatible with one type or size of organisation, but not with another. For example, the extent to which delegation is practised, or management information is used, may vary considerably, while methods of communication may range from regular formalised meetings to very informal meetings arranged as required, or sometimes very little communication at all. Broad categories of management style include "hands-on" and "seat-of-the-pants"; a manager may have both of these styles. The former implies a small degree of delegation; the latter suggests a lack of use of formal management information or even consultation with colleagues. Both, depending on the abilities of the individuals concerned, can be highly effective in smaller organisations, but generally become less effective as the size of the organisation increases. At the opposite extreme are managers who delegate formally, and make full use of sophisticated management information systems; this more structured approach to management may be stifling to a small organisation, but is necessary in a very large organisation.

A serious problem sometimes arises in public sector companies, where interference from politicians or other government officials can undermine the authority of the management. A similar situation may occur in privately owned companies, particularly family-owned businesses, where even though they do not hold formal management positions, the owners are often tempted to play a major part in the day-to-day management, by-passing the General Manager and giving instructions direct to junior managers.

8

ROUTES AND SCHEDULES

PUBLIC TRANSPORT ROUTE NETWORKS

A public transport system must cater for a very large number of individual movements. Travel patterns are complex and it is not possible to provide direct public transport routes to meet all requirements, although it is possible to go a long way towards this by providing a network of routes, so that passengers can make complex journeys by using a combination of routes. The term "route network" is generally used to refer to the aggregation of transport routes serving a particular area and implies that the individual routes are complementary to one another so that travellers may use one, two or more different routes in the course of their journeys. The most effective network is one in which the number of separate routes used in the course of a journey is minimised, and interchange between routes is made as easy as possible. A network may comprise routes operated by a single transport undertaking or different undertakings within the same mode, or complementary services provided by different modes such as buses, trolleybuses, trams, LRT and metro services.

There may be an element of competition within a network, with different modes, or combinations of modes, offering alternative means of travel. For example passengers may have a choice of making a journey entirely by bus, or by bus and LRT for different parts of the journey; good connecting facilities between modes, and through ticketing so that passengers are required to purchase only one ticket for a journey, are desirable and can be provided even if these are under different ownership. Many systems consist of routes planned in isolation rather than as parts of co-ordinated networks, and as such are often unsatisfactory in meeting the requirements of a significant proportion of travellers; others have been planned to provide convenient links between all points where there is demand. Some have been designed to meet predetermined standards or criteria: for example, a maximum number of interchanges between routes on any journey within a certain area, or a specified level of demand for travel between two points to determine whether a direct service should be provided or an interchange is acceptable.

Basic route networks exist in most cities in developing countries, but many of these need to be refined, in the light of present and future requirements. In nearly every case, route networks which have evolved over the years can be improved; in some cities route revisions are carried out regularly as a matter of routine, but in others there have been virtually no changes for many years despite the city having grown and changed considerably. For example in Kingston, Jamaica, a new central business district, New Kingston, was developed some eight kilometres from the original central area, but for several years there was very little change to the network of bus routes, which was still focussed on the original central area, so that virtually all commuters travelling to New Kingston had to change buses during the course of their journeys.

A deficiency of many route networks is that there are no direct links between some major points, so that a large proportion of travellers must change vehicles during their journeys. A reason often given for a lack of direct connections is that long through services would be badly affected by traffic congestion, but this is often a case of operators' interests taking priority of those of the travelling public, and if there are significant numbers of passengers requiring through services an attempt should be made to overcome the problem in other ways: passengers already suffering from traffic congestion are made to suffer increased inconvenience by having to change buses.

Established operating practices or bureaucratic constraints often result in route networks which cater poorly for passengers' requirements. For example, in Accra, the network comprises a large number of short routes operating non-stop between one terminal and another, so that passengers must transfer between routes, sometimes two or three times or even more, in order to complete their journeys; since most terminals serve a particular route or group of routes, many passengers transferring from one route to another must make their way between terminals: this can sometimes involve a taxi journey. One reason for this type of route structure is to enable operators to charge flat fares which are set at a relatively low level (see the discussion of fare structures in Chapter 14), but from the passengers' point of view the resulting inconvenience is a high price to pay.

Some networks suffer from artificial boundaries which bus routes do not cross. In Beijing, for example, there are several points on the outskirts of the central area where "inner" and "outer" bus routes meet end-on, and all through passengers must transfer between vehicles. In Indonesia the manner in which public transport services are regulated results in a similar situation at city boundaries; although convenient interchanges may be provided, the need to change vehicles increases journey times for passengers, and the additional turn-round times reduce vehicle utilisation. If some of these connecting routes were to be combined operating costs would be reduced, while revenue would almost certainly be increased by making services more attractive to passengers, and thus generating additional traffic.

ALTERNATIVE APPROACHES TO ROUTING

There are many ways of configuring a route network to meet passengers' requirements, all with their advantages and disadvantages: what is appropriate in one city may be unsuitable in another. It is particularly important, when planning a route network, that the fundamental principles and objectives are clear; the structure of the industry, the degree of regulation and the extent to which regulations are complied with, and the extent of competition, will influence the type of route network which is most appropriate, and the way in which services are scheduled. Moreover, a network may be designed to be operated on a fully commercial basis, with every route producing a profit, or there may be social objectives, requiring the provision of some unprofitable services. The principles of bus route planning and scheduling are covered in this chapter: the implications of industry structure, regulation and competition are discussed elsewhere.

In most cities, the majority of passenger movements are radial: most demand is for travel from outlying points to the centre and return. There are also other movements, for example between suburbs, but these are generally less significant. The main public transport corridors therefore tend to radiate outwards from the central area, with branches from these corridors to serve points on either side. The number of these branches will be partly influenced by the nature of the road system, and by policy and market forces: if people are not prepared to walk long distances, public transport routes will need to penetrate further into residential areas than otherwise. Similarly, if there are parallel roads along a corridor, a decision must be made as to whether to concentrate all routes along one road, or to split them between the two roads. The first alternative will give a higher frequency of service, and therefore less passenger waiting time, but a greater average walking distance, and perhaps increased traffic congestion on the route in question; the second will give a lower frequency, longer average waiting times but shorter average walking distances.

The size and layout of a city will affect the route structure. For example, if the central business district lies along a waterfront the scope for cross-city routes is reduced; the number of route corridors may be restricted by rivers or valleys. If roads are laid out in a grid pattern, this will limit the scope for radial routes: unless diagonal roads are superimposed on the grid, some radial routes will involve frequent turns at intersections, leading to delays; the pattern of bus routes may therefore comprise straight routes following the grid, so that many passengers' journeys will involve one change of bus. In a city with a population of approximately one million or more the central area will normally cover a large area so that passengers' destinations are widely dispersed; where the distances between these exceed acceptable walking distances, it is inappropriate for all routes to converge at a single focal point. There may therefore be several points, each constituting the focus of a number of radial routes, and possibly requiring a sub-network of routes connecting them: these routes may be formed by linking two or more radial routes, while several of the routes may be able to serve more than one centre. This will also apply in a conurbation comprising two or more contiguous cities, each with its own distinct centre.

An important choice to be made is whether all routes should terminate in the city centre, or continue across the central area to an outlying point on the opposite side of the city, in effect linking pairs of radial routes to provide diametric cross-city routes. Alternatively, routes may terminate on the periphery of the central area, either on the near side (i.e. on reaching the edge of the central area), to minimise the effects of congestion, but requiring many passengers to walk to complete their journeys, or on the far side (i.e. after crossing the central area), providing a better service to passengers, but with increased problems of traffic congestion. Provision of bus priority measures to enable buses to cross the city centre with minimum delay will reduce the problems, and may make more efficient use of scarce land than providing off-street terminal facilities. A third option is for routes to operate in a loop around the central area, as discussed later. Where virtually all passengers travel to and from the city centre, and rarely travel between one outer suburb and another, the decision as to whether routes should terminate in the city centre or not is a purely operational one. If there are very large numbers of passengers boarding or alighting at the same point an off-road terminal may be desirable to avoid causing obstruction of other traffic.

A disadvantage of routes terminating in city centres is that buses can cause congestion whilst standing between journeys and when making turning movements; often valuable land is occupied with bus terminal facilities; time is wasted by buses turning round, with consequent reduction in bus utilisation and therefore increased costs; and passengers wishing to travel across the city centre will have to change buses or walk for part of their journeys.

Disadvantages of cross-city routes are that schedules are more likely to be disrupted by congestion, since there is no provision for recovery time in the city centre as with buses terminating there; interchange between routes may be less convenient than at a common terminal; scheduling and fare structures are more complicated; crews must take breaks away from the central area; and, depending on the type of fare structure, revenue may be reduced due to a reduction in the number of passengers transferring between routes.

On balance, the advantages of operating routes across the city centre usually outweigh the disadvantages, though each case must be assessed on its own merits. See also the discussion on terminal location in Chapter 4.

Non-radial passenger movements can be catered for in a number of ways. In a large city, it is often appropriate to operate a number of routes linking various suburbs, and not reaching the city centre, perhaps including one or more circular routes linking outer points; often these are operated by smaller vehicles than those used on routes serving the city centre. Sometimes inter-suburban movement can be catered for by extensions or diversions from the main radial routes; this may have advantages in terms of vehicle utilisation, but may mean that longer-distance passengers are crowded out by short distance passengers, while deviations from the direct route add to journey times and cause inconvenience to through passengers. They may also leave portions of the main road corridor without a bus service, or with only a low frequency service.

In certain circumstances, particularly in smaller towns, a "hub and spoke" route system may be appropriate, where all routes meet at a central focal point, and passengers are able to travel between any two points in the city by transferring from one route to another. Such a system may be acceptable where journey times are relatively short, and service frequencies are high so that transfer times are minimised, or all routes are scheduled to connect at the central point, but in general, particularly for regular commuter traffic and where traffic congestion is a problem, a high proportion of indirect journeys will be unacceptable.

A transport network may include a number of "feeder" bus routes, which feed passengers into trunk bus routes and to rail lines. These offer an alternative to operating a large number of different routes along a common corridor, each branching off to serve points off the main route. Through bus services should normally be operated where demand from the outlying points is sufficient to justify them, but where demand is low, it is often more economic to operate feeder services, using smaller vehicles. Also, where road conditions preclude the use of larger vehicles over part of a route, it is usually preferable to operate small vehicles on this section, feeding into a service using larger buses for the main section, thus eliminating the need for small buses operating inefficiently alongside larger buses on main urban routes. Similarly, it may be appropriate for feeder bus services to connect with trams or trolleybuses operating on trunk routes.

Feeder routes may meet a trunk route head on at the terminal point for the latter, or may connect with it at an intermediate point; in some cases the feeder may run parallel with the trunk route for a short distance. A typical example is the routes serving the "hill" areas around Kingston, which because of road system constraints are operated with small or medium-sized buses; instead of operating into downtown Kingston, the majority of these routes operate into focal points where passengers transfer to trunk routes operated by larger buses. In Jakarta, services in many residential areas where streets are too narrow for full-sized buses are operated by twelve-seat mikrolets, and in some cases by even smaller vehicles, which feed into the main routes at junctions with the primary roads.

A trend in major towns and cities in the United Kingdom, based on the premise that frequent, regular services which are easier to understand tend to be more successful, is towards a network of "core routes", a simplification of the route structure to concentrate on main passenger flows, eliminating minor route variants, and increasing frequencies on the remaining routes. In many cities in developing countries, the basic nature of the road system necessitates this form of route structure, but in others route systems are unnecessarily complex and could benefit from rationalisation.

The bus routes themselves may take various forms. The basic and most common type of route is the "end-to-end" route, which operates between two points, following the same roads in both directions, except where one-way street systems necessitate minor deviations. Alternatively, a route may be circular, returning to the point of origin without traversing the same roads twice. Circular routes are often found in suburban areas, sometimes circling an entire city; "inner circle" routes around city centre areas are more common.

Another option is a route combining straight and circular sections, so that at the end of the route the bus, instead of turning and returning by the inward route, operates in a loop, rejoining the inward route after completing the loop, stopping in the central area for no longer than is required to set down and pick up passengers. Such an arrangement can be particularly effective for a central business district as an alternative to operating across the city centre: it can provide better service coverage than a terminal operation since passengers are able both to join and leave the bus throughout the circuit, enabling buses to serve a wider area than would otherwise be the case, and eliminates the need for city-centre terminal or turning facilities. In a medium-sized town it may be possible for all routes to follow the same loop, facilitating interchange between routes. Virtually all routes serving New Kingston operate in this manner. Loops are also common at the suburban ends of routes, where buses operate in a circuit around a residential area to provide maximum coverage.

Another variation of the straight route is one which forks near one or both ends, to serve different terminal points; often these are regarded as separate routes, even though they operate in common for most of their length. Some routes may be "dumb-bell" shaped, with a loop at each end: these are normally found where buses operate across the city centre from one suburb to another, and operate in a loop around the residential areas at the outer ends.

Where buses operate in a loop at one or both ends of the route, all buses may traverse the loop in the same direction, or alternate buses may traverse it in opposite directions; the choice will depend partly on the size of the loop and frequency of service, and on the need for bus priority measures. It is normally more appropriate to operate in both directions; this optimises the service from all points around the loop since no passenger will have to travel more than half way round the loop. However, if the loop is so small that there is little difference in travelling time for any passenger in travelling in one direction instead of the other, it is normally preferable for all buses to operate in the same direction, so that passengers will always know from which direction the first bus will come. Similarly, if the frequency is low, it may be preferable to run all buses in the same direction, since alternating them will result in even lower frequencies. An advantage of one-way operation is that infrastructure such as passenger shelters at bus stops, or any bus priority measures such as bus lanes will be required on one side of the road only. If this option is chosen, buses should preferably operate in the direction with the shorter running time; this will normally be anticlockwise where traffic drives on the left side of the road, and clockwise where it drives on the right, so that the number of turns across oncoming traffic will be minimised.

A route network may comprise routes of several or all of these types; each route may be planned in isolation, as is often the case where there are many different operators, or all may be planned as a co-ordinated network. There are various ways in which bus routes may be combined to form a network. To take a very simple example, the main road system of a small town may consist of two roads, both served by buses, intersecting at right angles at the city centre. The bus routes may be configured in different ways: as two straight, diametric cross-town routes, crossing at the intersection; four radial routes, all terminating at or near the intersection; or up to six cross-town routes, all passing through the intersection, so that most or all pairs of outer terminals are linked, with up to four routes making a right angle turn at the intersection, and two diametric routes crossing at right angles. These alternatives are illustrated in Figure 8.1. The routes need not all be of the same length: in order to provide higher frequencies towards the town centre, some buses may be turned short of the outer terminals. This can be achieved by introducing intermediate turning points on each leg of the cross, and dividing each leg into sections.

Again, there are various ways of arranging the routes to provide tapering frequencies to cater for variations in demand levels on different sections of the route. If, for example, each leg of the cross is divided into three approximately equal sections, and all routes operate across the intersection, each route might comprise four sections, so that none goes right through from one outer terminal to another, and each route would be of similar length, all overlapping on the common sections. Alternatively there could be routes of different lengths, with some routes comprising two sections, some four and some six. This concept is illustrated in respect of a single route in Figure 8.2 (page 180). Further variations in the number of sections in each route could cater for differing levels of demand on each of the four legs of the cross. If all routes terminate at the intersection, some route variants could consist of one section, some of two and some of three. This concept can apply to any number of radial and cross-town routes, of varying lengths and with different demand characteristics.

Thus there are various degrees of complexity for an urban route structure, even for a small and basic public transport system as in the above example. Complex route systems are generally practical only if services are reasonably reliable, and passengers have the confidence to wait for a bus on their particular route variant; if reliability is poor, they will prefer to board the first bus which arrives, and a much simpler route system is therefore desirable. More complex routes and route structures may make scheduling more difficult, and therefore the way in which services are scheduled is also relevant in planning a route network. The types of vehicle to be operated should be taken into account: it is theoretically possible to provide a more comprehensive route network, without the penalty of reduced frequencies, with smaller buses. In a deregulated system, however, this tends not to happen, with paratransit operators, even those operating very small vehicles, congregating on the main corridors where demand is greatest; a more comprehensive and better planned route network is usually achieved where services are operated by a small number of large undertakings, or are subject to government regulation.

Where all-night bus services are provided, it is sometimes appropriate to provide a different route network since travel patterns and traffic conditions at night are often very different from those during the day. In London the night bus route network was originally developed to cater for workers in nocturnal jobs such as employees of the newspapers in Fleet Street or workers in the meat, fish and vegetable markets, and routes were arranged to serve these destinations. Some night buses are staff buses operated by the bus companies which are made available to the general public to generate additional revenue, and as such are not always of much use to many people.

Figure 8.1: Alternative Bus Route Configurations

a: Four separate routes

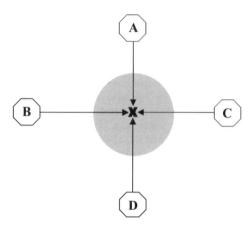

Each route commences at one of the outer terminals (A, B, C or D) and terminates at the Cross in the City Centre.

b: Two routes

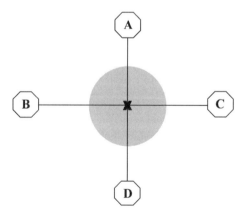

Each route (A-D and B-C) commences at one of the outer terminals, crosses the City Centre and terminates at the outer terminal at the opposite side of the city.

c: Six routes

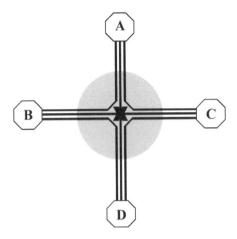

Together with the routes crossing at the City Centre, routes A-B, A-C, B-D and C-D provide through services between all four outer points. If the frequency of service provided by each route is one third of that provided by routes A-D and B-C in the previous example, the combined service frequency along each leg of the cross will remain the same, as will the number of buses required to provide the overall service.

Night bus services are often relatively profitable, even if load factors may be low: the buses used are already available, so that vehicle costs are minimal, while buses can usually operate to much faster running times, resulting in good vehicle productivity. A less significant benefit may be a reduction in depot parking space requirements.

It is sometimes necessary to provide special routes for a limited period to cater for special events, which are not catered for by the normal route systems. Such events may include sporting events such as large football or cricket matches, trade fairs or agricultural shows, or national celebrations, which occur periodically, or "one-off" events such as the Olympic or Asian Games which are held in different venues around the world. The special services may be required for a day or part of a day, or over a period of several weeks. They cater for different passenger movements from regular services, and demand is often very concentrated, with very large numbers of people arriving or leaving a venue within a very short time. Many of the passengers may be visitors to the city, and therefore represent additional traffic, as in the case of international sporting events; on the other hand, for local events, many of the passengers will be local, so that the demand for the services which they would otherwise have used will be reduced.

With an informal, deregulated transport industry it is difficult to cater efficiently for these requirements, and to reallocate buses appropriately from normal services to the special services. If there are a small number of large operators, these will often take buses from other routes, which are reduced in frequency, or may be withdrawn altogether, for the duration of the event. For events which occur on a regular basis, such as football matches or national celebrations, they will often have schedules specifically for use on those days: every route in the system may be affected to some extent. Where there are many individual operators some may move of their own accord onto routes meeting the temporary demand, but this will be on a very disorganised basis. Often, in order to ensure that an adequate service is provided, the organisers of large events hire or even purchase fleets of buses for the occasion, and do not involve local operators at all.

The requirement of the majority of passengers on long-distance services is to travel quickly between their origins and destinations with a minimum of delay en route. Most wish to travel between provincial centres and the main regional centres or the capital, or between provincial centres; the proportion travelling between one small town and another is usually relatively small. Passengers travelling between the main centres do not wish to be delayed by the many intermediate stops required by shorter-distance passengers, and are attracted to services providing direct non-stop connections between the two points. The requirement is therefore often for a series of routes, most of which operate non-stop between two points. Where this is the case, only one fare will normally be applicable for each route, simplifying revenue collection and control, and reducing the opportunities for fraud; because services operate non-stop, vehicle productivity can be good, although a surplus of vehicles on a route often negates this advantage.

There is also normally a requirement for long-distance services which stop at intermediate points, particularly where there are two or more major traffic-generating points close together, and there is insufficient traffic to justify separate services, but in principle the number of intermediate stopping points should be kept to a minimum. Passengers travelling between intermediate points are normally catered for by shorter local stopping services, most of which radiate from the provincial towns to the surrounding villages and to the next large town along the main road, acting as feeders to the long-distance routes as well as linking rural areas with the nearest towns. These services tend to complement rather than compete with those of the long-distance operators, and may be operated by either full sized buses or minibuses, although the latter are generally more common.

Demand-responsive Transport Services

Demand-responsive transport (DRT) services do not normally form part of the regular transport network, but are often an important complementary element of both urban and rural transport systems. The most common form of transport in this category is the conventional taxi, which operates as required by individual passengers, and does not require scheduling. However, some form of scheduling may be required for other forms of DRT, such as route taxis or shared taxis used by several people travelling independently. Demand-responsive services, some using taxis but most using minibuses with up to fifteen seats, and usually equipped to carry passengers in wheelchairs, are becoming increasingly common in many developed countries. Some are organised by local authorities and sub-contracted to operators; most receive a degree of subsidy and in some cases the authority supplies the vehicle. A small number are operated on a commercial basis. They are also found in some developing countries: in Palestine, most inter-city transport is provided by shared taxis, many of which operate on a demand-responsive basis.

There are many applications for DRT services. They may be provided to cater for areas where demand is low and variable, and for passengers with special requirements which are not met by the normal bus service such as for travel to hospitals, or at times when demand is low, such as during the night; they may be operated as feeders to main bus routes and to railway stations, particularly in rural areas; or they may be introduced to serve new developments and be replaced by conventional services as they grow. Problems are sometimes encountered on introduction of DRT systems; in some countries the transport regulatory system does not allow for this type of operation and must be amended if services are to be provided legally. In some cases taxi operators have objected to the introduction of DRT services which they perceive as a threat to their livelihood.

In its simplest form, a DRT service is based on a specified route between two points, calling at recognised stops, with deviations made at the request of passengers who are on board the vehicle; passengers joining the route must go to one of the recognised stops. Scheduling of vehicles on such services normally follows the same procedure as for paratransit vehicles. The more complex DRT services both pick up and set down on request, and may be classified as "many-to-one", in which services pick up at a large number of points, and terminate at a single destination; "one-to many", which is usually the return journey; "many-to-many", where there are multiple destination points as well as picking-up points; and "many-to-few" or "few-to-many" where there is a choice of destination points within a limited area. These require much more complex scheduling procedures.

In the more sophisticated systems, services are controlled from centres using specialised software which produces routes and instructions for drivers, based on requests from passengers received by phone or internet, and sometimes even through communication equipment provided at bus stops. Some are linked to GPS systems which can track and pass on instructions to each vehicle so that passenger requirements may be dealt with at very short notice, while utilisation of drivers and vehicles is optimised. The technology is expensive, but the cost is likely to decrease over time and it may eventually become more relevant to developing countries, particularly as mobile phones becoming increasingly widely used. However, most systems are more basic, with passenger requests processed manually by the control centres.

SCHEDULING PARAMETERS AND CONSIDERATIONS

In general terms, public transport services may be categorised into those which are operated in accordance with a schedule or timetable, and those which are not. The term "scheduling" as applied to the operation of a transport service is used to describe the way in which the deployment of vehicles and crews is planned to provide the service on a route or network of routes. Unscheduled operation can lead to unsatisfied demand, even though capacity may be available within the system, or to wasteful use of resources, with too many vehicles running at off-peak periods or in areas where demand is low, leading to unnecessary cost. A formal scheduling system enables services to be operated in accordance with demand patterns, and better utilisation to be made of vehicles and crews, to the benefit both of the public, by catering more efficiently for the demand, and of the operator, by increasing revenue per kilometre operated.

The three principal scheduling parameters for a bus route are the frequency of service on the route, the running, and the layover time. There is a mathematical relationship between these and the number of vehicles operated, which can be expressed as:

number of buses = $\dfrac{\text{round trip time in minutes}}{\text{frequency, i.e. interval between buses in minutes}}$.

or frequency = $\dfrac{\text{round trip time in minutes}}{\text{number of buses}}$

where the round trip time is the sum of the running times in each direction (or twice the running time if this is the same in both directions) plus the sum of the layover times at each end of the route (or twice the layover time if this is the same at each terminal). These formulae may be used to calculate the effects of changes in one or more of the variables: for example, the reduction in the frequency of the service which will result from an increase in running time on a route due to worsening traffic congestion; or the number of additional vehicles required to maintain the same frequency following an increase in running time.

Frequency

Service frequencies or "headways", expressed in terms of the number of vehicles per hour in each direction, or the interval in minutes between them, should be designed to match the service capacity, in terms of the number of passenger places provided per hour, with the demand. Thus, for a given vehicle size, when demand is higher, frequency should be higher; when demand is lower, frequency should be lower. In theory, the number of departures required per hour can be calculated by dividing the number of passengers wishing to travel per hour in each direction by the average vehicle capacity; in broad terms, the smaller the vehicle, the higher the frequency required to provide the same overall service capacity.

Alternatively, it may be appropriate in certain circumstances to determine an "ideal" or maximum desirable waiting time in the context of local conditions, and then to calculate the required vehicle size according to the level of demand. The length of time which passengers are prepared to wait for transport is an important factor: if they are prepared to wait for only a short time, then a high frequency service is desirable, and if vehicles are not to operate with excessive surplus capacity, relatively small vehicles will be required. On the other hand if passengers are prepared to wait for longer, then the service frequency may be reduced, but since each vehicle will be carrying a greater number of passengers, larger ones will be required.

Costs per passenger are usually lower if larger vehicles are used, provided that these are carrying full loads, although a higher-frequency service operated by smaller vehicles may be justified on economic grounds where the value of passengers' time is high; however, it is unlikely that the value of passengers' time in developing countries is high enough to justify the operation of small vehicles where larger ones would otherwise be more efficient. Operators should, however, beware of the danger of introducing larger buses and reducing frequency where this results in a significant increase in passenger waiting times which, in a competitive situation, may encourage passengers to use competing modes. Indeed, it may be desirable, particularly at off-peak times, to minimise passenger waiting times by providing what might be regarded as an unnecessarily high frequency: this will result in supply exceeding demand due to vehicles operating with less than full loads, but in practice the higher frequency, and therefore reduced waiting time for passengers at stops, often encourages additional travel; conversely, low frequencies tend to discourage passengers, who may choose to walk, particularly for short distances.

Therefore the relationship between vehicle capacity and service frequency is not necessarily linear, and an operator seeking to reduce costs by increasing the size of vehicle operated and reducing the frequency may find that demand is reduced. Conversely, replacing full-sized buses with smaller buses operating to higher frequencies may result in significantly increased patronage, as was experienced in many urban areas in the United Kingdom during the 1980s.

Replacing a large bus with two smaller buses with half the capacity need not result in any change in effective frequency at bus stops if the smaller buses stop at alternate stops, thus reducing journey time instead. Where a large bus is operated, it will normally stop at every bus stop to pick up and set down passengers, except perhaps at peak times, when it may not have capacity to pick up passengers at every stop. Where smaller vehicles are used, they are more likely to carry full loads even at off-peak times, and therefore will tend to stop at fewer bus stops than larger vehicles; this, together with shorter times at stops due to the smaller number of passengers boarding or alighting, will result in a higher operating speed. It will also mean that although the frequency of service, in terms of the number of buses passing a point during a specified period, will increase, the frequency of buses calling at any particular stop may not change.

Problems often arise where there is a range of bus sizes on a particular route. Different sizes of bus operate at different speeds: smaller buses spend less time at stops since they pick up and set down fewer passengers, and usually have better acceleration capability than larger buses. Therefore although departures from the terminal may be at regular intervals, frequencies become irregular with distance from the starting point, while even if it is possible to maintain regular intervals between vehicles along the route, the number of seats provided per period will be erratic. This was a serious problem in Kingston in the mid 1990s, where some routes were served by buses with capacities ranging from ten to over 100 passengers.

Figure 8.2: Tapering Frequencies

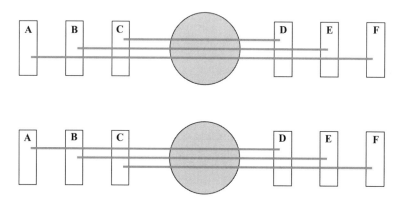

Routes may be divided into sections, which may be combined in various ways to vary the service frequency on each section. In this example, services operate from suburb A, across the city centre, to suburb F; intermediate turning points are provided in suburbs B, C, D and E. In the upper diagram, there are three variants of the main bus route: C-D, B-E, and A-F; in the alternative shown in the lower diagram, the three variants A-D, B-E and C-F are all of similar length, which may have scheduling advantages but there is no through service from A to F . In both cases, if the frequency on each variant is the same, the combined frequency between C and D is three times that between A and B, and between E and F; the combined frequency between B and C, and between D and E, is twice that between A and B, and between E and F.

To maximise passenger loadings and to optimise the service to the public it is necessary to vary service frequencies in line with passenger demand at different times of the day, different days of the week or seasons of the year, and on different sections of a route at any given time. At peak times optimum frequencies are determined by the level of demand and the capacity of vehicles, although in practice actual frequencies are likely to be limited by vehicle availability; at off-peak times it may be more appropriate for frequency to be determined according to the level of demand and the break-even load factor, which is a function of direct operating costs and fare levels.

Since a high proportion of demand on urban services is for travel from outlying points into the central area, the loadings on a typical route increase progressively from the outer terminal to the downtown terminal. Often there is excess capacity at the outer ends of longer urban routes, resulting in unnecessarily high costs, and in addition to the wasted capacity on route sections where demand is low, there is often, at the same time, unnecessary shortage of capacity on sections where demand is high. To minimise excess capacity on the outer portions of routes, and to enable increased capacity to be provided on the inner portions, or alternatively to provide the same effective service capacity with fewer buses, service frequencies should be "tapered", i.e. reduced with distance from the central area.

This can be achieved by scheduling some journeys to operate for only part of the route by turning them short before the outer terminal; a long route may have several turning points along its length. Another means of achieving a tapered frequency, where routes operate across the city centre, is the overlapping of route sections. The options are illustrated in Fig. 8.2. Where several routes converge on a common corridor, the combined frequency will decrease with distance from the city centre, although unless the majority of passengers are travelling for the full length of each route, it will still be necessary to taper the frequencies on individual routes by turning some buses short.

In a less formal situation, where buses are not operated to schedule, tapering of frequencies is less easy to arrange. Indeed, there is a general rule in many countries that buses or paratransit vehicles must not turn short of their licensed destinations, although in such circumstances some operators, in contravention of regulations, turn their vehicles short before completing the route if there are no passengers remaining on board the vehicle. There is even a tendency in some countries for less scrupulous operators to leave passengers stranded by evicting those already on the vehicle and turning short if there is a more profitable load waiting to travel in the opposite direction. Nevertheless, even in a relatively informal operation, tapered frequencies may be implemented on a controlled basis, if somewhat crudely, by dividing a route into overlapping sections of different lengths, and allocating appropriate numbers of vehicles to operate on specific sections.

Tapered frequencies can cause problems, however, particularly on outward journeys from the central area at busy times. A passenger will tend to board the first bus to arrive which will pass his own destination, irrespective of its final destination; if some buses on the route are scheduled to turn short of the final terminus, passengers travelling only short distances will have a greater choice of buses than those travelling longer distances. On those buses operating for most or all of the length of the route, there will be a proportion of short-distance passengers, occupying places which could have been taken by long-distance passengers; the latter may therefore be unable to board a bus which passes their destinations, and may have to wait for several short-journey buses to pass before one arrives which is travelling past their destinations, and which has capacity for them. In addition, when the short-distance passengers have disembarked, there will be surplus capacity on the vehicle, which at peak periods is particularly wasteful.

The problem of short distance passengers crowding out long distance passengers can be addressed in a number of ways. A simple option is through the fare structure. The minimum fare charged on buses travelling to the farther destinations can be set at a level which is higher than the normal fare to some of the nearer destinations; the normal fares would be charged on buses operating for only part of the route, so that short-distance passengers are discouraged from using the longer-distance buses. The type of fare structure used in Hong Kong, described in Chapter 14, will have a similar effect, although to some extent this penalises short-distance intermediate passengers who will pay a high fare in both directions. The system used in Addis Ababa, Ethiopia, in which the flat fare charged for each route varies according to its length, addresses the problem more equitably, although it has disadvantages in other respects. Such measures may be difficult to apply to cross-city routes, however, and are most effective on routes originating in the central area. Imposing minimum fares on certain journeys may be the most effective and equitable method, but may be difficult to apply.

Another possibility is for buses travelling to different final terminal points to pick up passengers at different stops; this is not always practical, however, and may cause problems at off-peak periods, unless short workings are operated at peak periods only. A practice which is sometimes followed on longer routes where frequencies are low, is for one or more duplicate buses to operate at the same time as the scheduled service bus, all carrying passengers for any point along the route; the duplicate buses operate only as far as required, returning to base after transferring passengers to the service bus when the latter has sufficient accommodation after short-distance passengers have disembarked. The duplicate buses are likely to operate to different points each day, according to demand. This arrangement creates complications in scheduling and revenue control, and is not normally satisfactory on high-frequency services.

It is also normally desirable for frequencies to be varied at different times in accordance with fluctuations in demand. This may be achieved by increasing or reducing the number of buses in service, or by increasing or reducing the amount of layover time between journeys. With a bus service provided by a single operator, it is usual for some buses to be taken out of service between the peak periods; this reduces wasteful over-supply, and the same number of passengers are carried as would be the case if all buses remained in service, but at a lower total cost. However, where all buses are operating independently, an operator who takes his bus off the road will earn nothing during this time, and as long as his direct costs can be covered from revenue, he will be inclined to operate throughout the day, thus unnecessarily increasing total capacity and total costs of the operation as a whole. In fact many operators underestimate the direct cost of operation, and operate at a loss at off-peak times.

Running Time

A key parameter in compiling schedules for a route is its running time, defined as the time taken for a vehicle to travel from one terminal to the other; this is a function of the route length and achievable operating speed. It is essential for scheduling purposes that running times are realistically and safely achievable by a competent driver under normal traffic conditions for the time of day, and without exceeding prevailing speed limits. Running times on existing routes can be determined from observations of actual running times; they should be checked periodically and amended if necessary.

The running time for a new route may be synthesised on the basis of running speeds on other routes using the same roads, or on roads not currently served by buses, by using speeds achieved on other roads with similar characteristics. If traffic speeds are known, these may be used, provided that realistic allowances are made for time lost at bus stops. For example, average traffic speeds in the central areas of major cities such as Bangkok, Beijing or Jakarta vary between approximately eight and fifteen kilometres per hour; time lost at bus stops on urban service will reduce the non-stop speeds by between 25% and 50%, depending on passengers loads and operating practices. Making test runs under accurately simulated conditions at different times is the most reliable method; it is relatively time-consuming but is justifiable for high-frequency services where small errors may be compounded to create serious problems.

In practice, running times can vary considerably, and unpredictably, due to variations in traffic and other conditions. On urban routes traffic congestion is the greatest problem, but journey times can also be affected by other factors, such as weather conditions: heavy rain usually slows down traffic, while for example in holiday resorts, traffic levels may increase as a result of good weather. On long-distance and rural routes, running times may vary between wet and dry seasons due to road conditions and demand fluctuations.

Varying levels of congestion on urban routes result in substantial variations in traffic speeds between peak and off-peak periods, and usually between inbound and outbound traffic flows. It is particularly difficult to allow for the effect of traffic congestion on journey times, since congestion tends to be inconsistent and unpredictable. Indeed, some operators have abandoned scheduled operation because of these variations, and the difficulty of predicting them with any accuracy.

Conditions can also vary at different points along a route so a bus may take longer than scheduled over one section but less than scheduled over another, and arrives at its destination on time. If a route were to be scheduled so that every bus was guaranteed to be on time at every timing point it would be necessary to allow the maximum expected running time for every section of the route, even though in reality such a situation would never arise, and therefore the total time allowed for each journey would be excessive under all circumstances. This would not only be very wasteful and inefficient, but would cause inconvenience to passengers.

As far as possible, these variations should be taken into account in the schedules, although it is not possible to schedule for unpredictable delays due to abnormal congestion, unforeseen roadworks or accidents. The most simple approach is to schedule according to actual average journey times, with the same running time allowed for every journey throughout the day. This will result in the late running of journeys at the most congested times, while those at times of least congestion will have more than enough time, and drivers may have to dawdle, and spend time waiting at bus stops, if they are to avoid running early. Generous layover times may be provided at peak times to enable buses to recover lost time, and depart punctually on their next journeys. Some operators allow equal layover times as well as equal running times throughout the day and expect that buses which have lost time during the peak will recover their lost time during the course of their next few journeys.

Both of these methods make scheduling easier, but unless the service frequency is high, may cause problems for passengers since they will not be able to rely on the bus timetable when planning their journeys. Moreover, at off-peak times buses and crews may be under-utilised, although in developing countries where labour costs tend to be relatively low, this is not normally an issue. If the same schedules apply every day, not only will passengers be inconvenienced on those days when traffic is light by being unnecessarily delayed while the bus waits to depart at the scheduled time, but unnecessary costs may be incurred through the scheduling of additional vehicles which are required only on certain days.

A more effective approach is to adjust running times and layover times according to expected traffic conditions at different times of the day, so that the majority of journeys are able to operate on schedule. Passengers should not object to occasionally having to wait for the departure time when the bus arrives at a timing point early because traffic is light. They are more likely to object if their bus usually, but not always, arrives ten minutes late, but they must always be at the bus stop at the scheduled time in case it arrives on time, so that on the majority of days they must wait up to ten minutes for it. These considerations are particularly important in the case of services of relatively low frequency, and even more so in the case of premium services.

A particular characteristic of circular routes and loops is that the running times are usually shorter in one direction than in the other: where traffic drives on the left, right turns normally take longer than left turns; for buses operating in the clockwise direction, most turns will be right turns, and the journey may therefore take considerably longer than buses operating in the anti-clockwise direction, making mostly left turns. The opposite applies in countries where traffic drives on the right. For this reason it may be appropriate for short circular city centre services to operate in one direction only.

Running time is also influenced by operating methods. For example, as discussed in Chapter 9, it is customary in some operations for buses to delay at stops or drive slowly between stops to enable the conductor to collect all fares, while in others fares are collected by the driver, so that buses cannot move until all passengers have paid: these practices result in reduced operating speeds and hence increased running time.

On routes with very high demand, and where there are large numbers of both short-distance and longer-distance passengers, it is often useful to schedule some buses to operate on a "limited-stop" basis, stopping only at certain specified stops. This practice results in reduced running times, as well as reduced journey times for a proportion of the passengers; it may also reduce the problem of long-distance passengers being crowded out by short-distance passengers. There are various ways in which this may be arranged, depending on the pattern of demand. For example, it may be appropriate for certain buses to stop only at all major bus stops along the route, or for some buses to operate non-stop for part of the route, stopping at every bus stop for the remainder. Alternatively, some buses may stop at some stops, with the remaining stops served by other buses. Demand must be sufficient to provide economic loads for all buses on the route, and it is important that the appropriate balance is achieved between the number of limited-stop buses and those stopping at all stops.

In some countries the regulatory authorities have set standards for punctuality, and in such cases it is essential that scheduled times are realistic. It is also essential that the standards set, and the way in which they are applied and enforced, are reasonable. In the United Kingdom, bus operators are penalised if fewer than 95% of journeys operated arrive or depart within a six minute "window of tolerance", in which it is regarded as acceptable for a bus to arrive or depart up to five minutes late or one minute early. Operators have argued, justifiably, that this is unreasonable in view of the unpredictability of many delays, and scheduling to guarantee punctuality when congestion is unpredictable is wasteful of resources. Unreasonable requirements regarding timekeeping standards are often a result of misguided or ill-informed political intervention, and can be counterproductive. Some operators have reduced the number of timing points, sometimes to the terminal points only, in order to reduce the risk of being penalised, or have increased layover times, in some cases to as much as 30% of running time. Others have withdrawn services completely where the risk threatens the viability of the operation; this is a classic example of misguided regulation, intended to protect the public interest, but in practice having the opposite effect.

Layover Time

Layover times, defined as the elapsed time between arriving at and departing from a terminal point, must also be taken into account when compiling schedules. Layover time should be determined to allow a sufficient amount of rest for the driver and conductor, to allow for recovery from any delays, and to minimise congestion at terminal points. On urban services it is normally desirable for most layover to be taken at the outer terminal points; this reduces congestion at the inner terminals, where space is often at a premium. Total layover time, excluding recovery time, in an eight-hour shift should ideally not exceed sixty minutes, or approximately 12.5% of running time, but this will be influenced by factors such as statutory rest periods for drivers, and local industrial agreements. Recovery time should be determined from experience, and should be based on average delays rather than maximum expected delays, unless for some reason a very high degree of service reliability is required, and can be justified on economic grounds, bearing in mind that the more time a bus spends stationary the higher will be the total cost per kilometre operated.

Some route configurations raise special planning and scheduling issues. It is not normally practical to schedule buses to operate continuously on urban services for periods of more than two hours, and it is therefore necessary on circular routes, or routes with loops at both ends, to make provision for layover or recovery time at one or more stopping places; however, passengers travelling across these points will be inconvenienced, and therefore wherever possible layover time should be taken where the number of passengers on board the vehicle is normally lowest, provided that there is a suitable place for the vehicle to stand without obstructing other traffic. On a route with a loop at one end all layover should ideally be taken at the "straight" end, although where the loop is in the city centre there may be a need for control at the inner end also to minimise the bunching of buses. A disadvantage of routes with a loop at the outer end and a terminal in the central area is that it is normally desirable to minimise layover time in central areas, and this may necessitate layover time at some point in the loop, resulting in inconvenience to some passengers. Problems may also arise from the increased effective route length; the longer the route the greater its susceptibility to delays, and effective control is essential.

A route which forks towards the end may cause scheduling problems if the sections beyond the fork are of different lengths, resulting in different running times on each section; unless frequencies are high (with approximately ten minute intervals or less), it may be necessary for the buses on one section to be given excessive layover time at the terminal in order to ensure a regular frequency on the common section of the route. A more complicated solution is to schedule buses to operate both variations of the route on alternate journeys during the course of the day.

DEMAND PATTERNS

Service frequencies should be varied in tune with variations in demand at different times of the day, different days of the week or seasons of the year, and on different sections of each route. These demand fluctuations, which can result in surplus capacity at certain times, and shortage of capacity at others, can seriously affect the finances of transport operators, particularly if frequencies are not adjusted accordingly. There is often a significant variation between the number of buses required to operate services at the peak period (the Peak Vehicle Requirement, or PVR) and the number required at off peak times; in many cases, a large number of buses are operated for only one or two revenue-earning journeys per day.

Variations in demand between peak and off-peak periods are often of particular significance. On weekdays there are normally two peak periods: in the morning when people are travelling to work, and in the evening when they return home. Sometimes there is a smaller third peak around mid-day, when people travel home for lunch or to carry out personal business during their lunch breaks. The length of peak periods also varies; it is influenced by the size of the city, levels of traffic congestion, spread of starting and finishing times at places of employment and education, and behavioural patterns. In some countries, for example, there is considerable activity in the evenings, resulting in this peak continuing until relatively late.

It is also necessary to take into account peak traffic flows. Where there is a clear distinction between residential and commercial areas, the number of passengers travelling to and from work at different times will result in an imbalance of demand: for example in the morning peak, there will be a far greater number of passengers travelling from residential to commercial areas than in the opposite direction; in the evening the opposite will apply. The effect of this imbalance can be reduced to some extent by scheduling some buses to operate non-stop in the direction with lower demand, thus reducing service capacity in one direction, and increasing it in the other; the reduced round trip time will enable the frequency of passenger-carrying journeys in the peak flow direction to be increased. It is also usually appropriate for the first and last journeys operated in the day to commence and finish respectively in residential areas, to minimise the number of empty journeys; this has a bearing on the optimal location for bus depots, as discussed in Chapter 5.

Travel patterns can differ significantly on different days of the week, both in terms of the times at which people travel and the journeys which they take. For example, on weekdays there is significant demand at peak periods for travel to and from the central business district, while at weekends there may be virtually none; on the other hand, people may make journeys at the weekends for leisure purposes to destinations which they would not normally visit during the week. In the case of rural bus services, significant increases in demand are often experienced on market days, typically once per week. Thus it may be appropriate to vary not only the schedules for different days, but also the routes operated.

The demand for transport services in many developing countries is highly cyclical. In addition to normal fluctuations during the working day between peak and off-peak periods, there are usually significant fluctuations during each month, and seasonal fluctuations during the course of the year. Weekly and monthly fluctuations in demand for long distance services are attributable in many countries to the practice of urban workers travelling to their rural homes. Demand for long-distance and rural bus services in many developing countries is highly seasonal, based on agricultural cycles and public holidays. There are, for example, often pronounced peaks at the beginning and end of Ramadan in predominantly Muslim countries, and at Easter and Christmas in Christian countries, while in agricultural countries demand tends to be high following harvesting, when farmers receive a significant proportion of their incomes, and very low during the wet, or growing season.

Peak season activity can be as much as three times off season activity: in Malawi, for example, total passenger revenue on rural and long-distance services run by the national bus operator during the peak month was approximately 2.5 times that for the lowest month. The effects of such seasonal demand variations are often compounded by problems of poor road conditions, particularly in areas where there is a predominance of unsurfaced roads which become impassable for buses during periods of heavy rain. In such circumstances it is normal for operators to have completely different sets of schedules for wet and dry seasons, with a large number of routes operated in the dry season only. In countries with significant tourism industries, fluctuations in tourist activity affect demand patterns for transport services used not only by the tourists themselves, but also, and usually more significantly, by the workers in the tourism industry, such as hotel staff.

Where incomes are low, there is a tendency for people to spend heavily on a wide range of goods and services immediately after receiving their wages, but as money runs short before the next pay day, expenditure becomes limited to absolute essentials such as food, or ceases altogether; where possible, people tend to walk for all or part of their journeys to and from work rather than use public transport. In most developing countries, therefore, there is a distinct pattern in the use of public transport by regular commuters, with demand at its peak following pay-days, and falling steadily until the following pay-day. In some countries it is normal for workers to be paid weekly, in others monthly; in some, workers are paid monthly but receive a mid-month advance. The manner of payment will influence the pattern of demand: where workers are paid weekly, fluctuations in demand tend to be less marked than where monthly payment is normal; in the latter case, demand between pay-days can fall to as little as 25% of peak demand.

There are various ways of assessing the level of demand, ranging from extensive surveys to analysis of available operating statistics; the latter is often the most effective in respect of established routes. Where completely new routes are being planned, it is desirable to carry out origin-destination surveys to estimate probable demand patterns and volumes, but since a new bus route invariably generates additional demand, it is normally necessary after its introduction to make occasional minor adjustments as required as the demand pattern becomes established, and until an optimum position is found; with such a procedure the main requirement is to ensure that the effects of each variation are accurately monitored. A similar "fine-tuning" procedure is normally necessary following the implementation of new schedules on an established route.

Although it is normal to operate more vehicles at peak periods than at off-peak times, public transport services are often insufficient to meet peak demand on many urban routes, and on peak market days on some rural-urban routes, without overcrowding or extended waiting times. The cost of fully meeting peak demand without any lowering in standards of service or comfort would be high. However, in addition to efficient scheduling of buses, there are various measures which can minimise the adverse effects of demand variations. As far as possible, routine maintenance should be carried out during off-peak periods. It is also possible to reduce the effects of seasonal fluctuations through scheduling major maintenance during low seasons, and planning the introduction of new vehicles and disposal of old ones to match fleet capacity more closely to demand. Some operators may be able to hire additional vehicles at peak times, for example from tour operators, whose demand cycle is different, but in practice such possibilities are limited.

DIFFERENT APPROACHES TO SCHEDULING

The forms which schedules may take vary from very basic to highly sophisticated. A basic system may merely specify intervals at which buses should depart from a terminal; a complex system may specify arrival and departure times at both terminals and several points along the route, with specific vehicles and crews assigned to each journey, and sometimes the deployment of vehicles and crews on different routes during the course of the day to maximise their utilisation. The more complex the system, the greater the level of discipline required; some scheduling systems are therefore inappropriate to the less formal type of organisation that is typical of many developing countries.

It is often considered that formal bus scheduling cannot work in many developing countries due not only to the problems created by serious urban traffic congestion, but also to the fragmented nature of the industry; certainly these factors make it more difficult to construct and implement schedules, but the difficulties can be overcome to a considerable extent. An important consideration is that for a scheduled service to operate effectively where there are many small operators on a route, there must be a mechanism to ensure that each individual operator has equal opportunities to earn revenue, and to ensure that each operates in accordance with his allotted schedule.

In the most basic system of operation vehicles are not scheduled at all, but queue at the terminal point until they are fully loaded before departing. This is common in developing countries, due to operators' reluctance to run partly loaded even for short distances; it enables passengers to be allocated reasonably equitably amongst the operators or crews, whose emoluments are often determined by the loads which they carry. There are several variations of the system. In some cases vehicles are permitted to depart empty without waiting for a load, or turn short of the terminal, if the driver believes that there are sufficient passengers to be picked up at the roadside. Alternatively, instead of waiting for full loads, vehicles may leave when a predetermined number of seats have been occupied, or may be despatched in accordance with perceived demand, with more frequent departures at busy times. The decision is sometimes left to the driver as to how to operate, and how many journeys are to be made.

The system of departing only when full ensures that vehicles have good load factors, and guarantees revenue to the operator, and is generally satisfactory for passengers commencing their journeys at the terminals, except at times when demand is low and full loads are slow to accumulate. However, it results in an irregular service and restricts accommodation for passengers wishing to board further along the route, except when space is vacated by passengers leaving the vehicle; it can therefore result in a shortage of supply, even though there may be excess capacity within the system. Passengers may be forced to board vehicles at terminals; in some cities, particularly at peak periods, passengers may be seen boarding inbound vehicles before the terminal so as to be sure of a place on the outbound journey, and vice versa. On some long routes, it is also common at stops where large numbers of passengers disembark, for vehicles to wait again for a full load before continuing the journey; this results in a significant increase in journey time for those passengers who were already on the vehicle.

Another disadvantage of the system is the idle time spent at terminals awaiting loads. Obviously, the larger the vehicle, or the more vehicles there are on a route, the longer each will have to wait for a full load; at peak periods these waits may be relatively short, but at slack times they may amount to several hours. This causes inconvenience to passengers as well as to operators, who are occupied, albeit unproductively, for much of the time; it can cause severe congestion at terminals which may also affect other road users. Few operators wish to stop operating altogether between the peaks for fear of losing revenue, but all would benefit, as would the public, if their activities were co-ordinated to bring the number of buses operating off-peak into line with demand. If a more regulated system were in force to ensure that the work was shared equitably amongst operators, some buses could be withdrawn from service at slack times, which would reduce wasteful operation and congestion, and could provide time for preventive maintenance. If the number of vehicles is inadequate to meet demand, the system of departing only with a full load will result in gaps in the service.

Even in the case of some relatively large operators, buses do not operate to schedule other than to leave their depots at scheduled times for their first journeys; thereafter they are instructed by despatchers at the terminals as to when they should depart, and whether to operate to the opposite terminal or to turn short. This gives flexibility to deal with traffic congestion and fluctuations in demand, but requires terminal despatchers to be fully aware of conditions along the route; in practice, this is difficult to achieve, and provided that levels of congestion and demand are both reasonably predictable a more formally scheduled system is preferable to such an ad-hoc method of operation.

A simple form of scheduled service entails the despatching of buses from terminals according to a predetermined frequency; this may vary through the day, for example every five minutes between 0600 and 0830, every ten minutes until 1500, every five minutes until 1800, and every fifteen minutes until 2200. These frequencies are also likely to vary on different days: for example, weekends may differ from weekdays. With such a system it is important that the number of buses operated on the route is appropriate: if there are too few, there will be inadequate layover time and gaps in the service, while if there are too many, layover times will be excessive.

Slightly more advanced is a system where buses are despatched at specified times, but without scheduled times for arrival at the far terminus, or at any intermediate points. In such cases it is useful to issue despatchers with pre-printed departure sheets, listing the time for every departure, based on the relevant frequencies; where not all journeys are operated for the full length of the route, the destination for each departure must also be shown. A benefit of this procedure is that the sheets can be used to record the identity number of each vehicle as it departs, and possibly additional information such as the number of passengers on departure;

such information can form part of the continuing monitoring procedure. Again, it is necessary to ensure that the appropriate number of buses is allocated to the route.

Full scheduling involves the specification of actual departure times for each journey, with service frequencies at different times and on different sections of the route determined according to passenger demand. Provision must be made for layover times at each end of the route to provide rest for the driver and, within reason, to allow recovery from late arrival due to traffic and other delays. Where two or more routes operate in common along part of their routes, it is desirable, particularly if the average combined interval between buses is more than five minutes, to co-ordinate the schedules of the different routes to provide an even frequency as far as possible. Such co-ordinated scheduling can be very complex and even critical. On busway systems, for example, capacity can be increased by operating buses in convoy, with buses stopping simultaneously and collecting passengers from several points along the bus stop platform; where buses serve several destinations, convoys must be formed to a specified sequence, to coincide with designated queuing points at bus stops, requiring a high degree of precision in scheduling the services involved, and of organisation to ensure that the schedules are strictly observed.

It is normally necessary to issue bus crews with written details of the journeys they must operate: these are variously referred to by terms such as "duty boards", "running cards", "running boards" or "route boards", and usually take the form of a printed card sheet containing full details of all journeys to be operated during the course of the journey.

The schedule or timetable for a journey will normally be based on a number of timing points: these are points on the route for which the times are stipulated when vehicles should arrive, depart, or both. In an extreme case, there would be only one timing point for a route: this would be the starting point, from which the scheduled departure time would be shown; the arrival time at the destination may not be scheduled, for example where traffic conditions are so unpredictable that to give a scheduled arrival time would be unrealistic. There would normally be at least two points, the starting and finishing points: in such a case the respective departure and arrival times would be given. On all but the shortest routes, arrival or departure times would normally also be given for a number of intermediate points. The crews' duty boards would include scheduled arrival and/or departure times at all timing points.

Timing points along a route may be selected according to various criteria. They should be recognisable points and may coincide with some or all fare stages; sometimes only the more important stops, where a large number of passengers are likely to join or leave the bus, may be chosen. Timing points may be close together or far apart. On an urban route it may be desirable for them to be relatively closely spaced; between five and fifteen minutes' running time between points is usually appropriate. On long distance routes they may be several hours apart, depending on the number of important boarding and alighting points.

Timing points are sometimes designated by the regulatory authority. Alternatively, the authority may specify distances or time intervals between timing points; however, this is not normally practical since several of the resulting timing points are likely to be at unidentifiable locations, or at points, for example on freeways, where buses are not permitted to stop. On a rail service it is customary for every station at which a train stops to be shown in the public timetable as a timing point; the working timetable, used only by staff, usually also specifies the times at which trains are scheduled to pass other points. For intermediate points where vehicles normally stop long enough only to enable passengers to board and disembark, it is sufficient to indicate only scheduled departure times on the schedule. For stops where vehicles are required to spend more time, for example to allow connections with other services, or for meal breaks on long distance services, it is appropriate to show both arrival and departure times.

On regular services "clockface scheduling" is sometimes used for simplicity. Under this system buses operate at similar times each hour, making it easier for both passengers and bus crews to remember, but ruling out the possibility of varying frequencies or running times in accordance with demand or traffic conditions. Moreover, any benefits may be substantially reduced if buses are scheduled to wait unnecessarily at terminal points in order to leave at the appropriate time. Clockface schedules are easier to construct, without loss of efficiency, where service frequencies are of the order of five minutes or less; however, at these frequencies passengers do not normally need to be aware of scheduled times. In other cases, the combination of running time and acceptable layover times may or may not permit efficient clockface scheduling, and the cost penalties must be considered against any administrative or marketing advantages.

Having determined the times at which buses should run, it is necessary to allocate vehicles to journeys so that these can be operated using the minimum number of vehicles. The timetable shows the times for every bus operating on each route; from this, schedules for individual buses may be derived, defining precisely all journeys to be operated, and their times, by every operational bus in the system. The schedule for a bus may sometimes involve operation on a number of different routes during the course of the day in order to maximise its utilisation. To ensure that buses are operated in accordance with the schedules, each scheduled bus working or duty should have its own identity. This normally takes the form of a "running number", which relates to the full scheduled day's work for the bus; in some cases, particularly in long-distance operation, a duty may cover more than one day. To facilitate identification of journeys for timekeeping checks and other purposes, supervisory staff should be provided with timetables showing the bus running number against each journey; on intensive services it is useful for the running number to be displayed on each vehicle so that it is visible from the roadside.

Where a schedule comprises a set of bus duties, an important task is the allocation of buses to these duties. Different buses have different characteristics, as do the different duties, and it is therefore important that as far as possible each bus is allocated to the duty for which it is most suited: normally this will mean where it will be most profitable. Where revenue per kilometre does not vary significantly between one route and another, allocation should normally be done in such a way that the highest mileage is operated by the buses with the lowest cost:revenue ratio, and the lowest mileage by those with the highest cost:revenue ratio. In practice this will normally mean that all day duties should be covered by newer, or larger buses and peak-only duties by older, or smaller buses.

There are obviously exceptions to this general rule. In particular, smaller buses should be allocated to routes where demand is very low, where road conditions are unsuitable for larger buses, or, if the fleet includes double-deckers, where low bridges or other height restrictions necessitate the use of single-deckers. As far as possible, buses allocated to a high-frequency route should normally all be of similar capacity in order to minimise bunching. On the other hand, it may be necessary in some cases to schedule buses of different capacities to different duties on the same route: for example a duty which includes journeys with abnormally high loadings may be allocated larger buses. If there is a wide range of vehicle types and sizes in the fleet, depot staff must be given clear instructions regarding the routes to which the various types may be allocated. Allocation of buses must also take into account the requirements of the maintenance programme: buses scheduled for maintenance must be allocated to duties which permit them to be made available to the workshops at the appropriate time and the requirements of the maintenance department should always take priority if maintenance programmes are not to fall behind.

Some operators permanently allocate individual buses to routes, or even to duties. This practice has certain advantages and disadvantages, although normally there are fewer advantages other than simplicity of control. Where there are wide variations in kilometres between one duty and another, it is preferable to rotate buses between duties so that over a period the kilometres operated by each bus are broadly similar. Similarly, operating conditions may vary between one route and another: traffic density may vary, while some routes may be hilly and others flat; if buses are permanently allocated to particular routes some will incur greater wear and tear than others. However, although it is preferable for buses to be flexible in their use, so that each may be used on any route subject to physical constraints, in practice there is often only limited scope for such flexibility. For example, buses may be painted specifically for particular routes, with the destinations and intermediate points sign-written on their bodywork, while in some countries public transport vehicles are required by law to operate on specified routes as a condition of the operator's licence.

It is relatively easy for a large operator to schedule services to provide an efficient and reliable service, and to make effective use of vehicles; where services are operated by a large number of small operators, services cannot be scheduled in the same way, unless they are controlled by operators' associations or similar organisations. Where an association is responsible for several routes, duties may be rotated amongst operators so that each has an equitable share of the best and worst. This arrangement can be complex if there are several operators of different sizes, and if some routes require more buses than others; it will normally be necessary for several different operators to be working on the same route, or for an operator to have vehicles on a number of different routes at any one time. Such a system is also likely to result in increased dead mileage, and will require drivers to be familiar with several routes. In some cases the scope for an operator to increase the efficiency of its scheduling is severely limited by prevailing practices. For example, where the sequence of departure from a terminal is in strict rotation, operators have no control over the utilisation of their vehicles; an operator wishing to improve his vehicle utilisation by reducing idle time at terminals will therefore be unable to do so.

CREW SCHEDULING

Crews must also be scheduled, to ensure that a crew is allocated to every bus duty, and that every journey is covered. Crew duties should be constructed to maximise the productive hours of work in any shift, but must conform to any labour agreements or regulations regarding working practices, in particular hours of work. The simplest method of crew scheduling is to allocate a crew to a bus for the full working day; however, since the working hours for a bus are usually considerably longer than the working day for a driver or conductor, most crew duties will be shorter than bus duties.

The working day for bus crews normally starts significantly earlier, or ends significantly later, than for employees in most other industries, since a primary role of bus crews is to take other employees to and from their work. Most shifts will be "early", from the start of the operating day to about mid-day, or "late", from about mid-day to the end of the operating day. In some circumstances, for example where there is a significant midday peak, there may also be a number of "mid shifts" coinciding approximately with the normal working day for other industries. There may also be a need for a proportion of "spreadover" or "split" shifts, particularly on weekdays: these shifts typically involve working during the morning and evening peak periods only, with a long break, of up to six hours, and sometimes even more, between spells of duty.

Often each crew stays with the bus assigned at the start of the shift until being relieved by a second crew, which operates the bus until its final journey of the day. When the crew has a meal break the bus may remain idle with the crew; alternatively it may be assigned to another crew, with the original crew taking over a different bus (or sometimes the same bus again) at the end of the meal break period. This results in more complex crew schedules. Where the bus remains with the crew, the buses are not being used as intensively as they could be, although the reduction in capacity on the route during break periods can be timed to coincide with reduced passenger demand after the peak. This type of operation is commonplace and efficient where there is a significantly peaked demand; on the other hand there are examples of inefficient scheduling whereby crews are scheduled to take breaks, together with their buses, during peak periods, resulting in an unnecessary increase in the peak vehicle and crew requirement.

In some systems, for example in Bangladesh, it is common practice for bus crews to remain with the same bus for the whole of its working day, which may be up to twenty hours, but to work only on alternate days. This practice can result in severe driver fatigue and consequent safety implications, and is generally undesirable. In many long distance operations, buses are crewed by two drivers. Normally, in theory, one drives while the other rests, but the second driver is often also responsible for collecting fares; if this is the case, on a long journey, both are likely to suffer from fatigue, and this is often a problem with very long routes with journey times of 24 hours or even more. Ideally there should be one or more staging posts along the route where drivers can be relieved but this is relatively uncommon.

Crews and buses are often allocated to duties independently, but some operators allocate the same driver, or the same crew, permanently to a particular bus. This has several advantages, particularly from the point of view of the maintenance department. Any mechanical problem with a vehicle which is due to driver abuse can readily be identified with the driver who caused it, and appropriate action taken, such as training or discipline. Also, a driver will normally take greater care of a bus if he drives it regularly: not only will he probably drive in such a manner as to minimise the likelihood of mechanical failure, he will also be more conscientious in reporting defects as they occur, and in endeavouring to ensure that they are rectified. A disadvantage of such an arrangement is that the number of hours for which a driver may work are limited, and this will restrict the utilisation of the bus. Sometimes this can be justified by the benefits, but not usually in intensive urban operations; a typical compromise is to allocate a regular pair of drivers to each bus.

Where a bus is operated by more than one crew during the course of a duty, the timing of shift changeovers should be arranged to minimise disruption to services, and ideally should take place when demand is low; wherever possible shift changes should be avoided during peak periods. There may be complications where there is a midday peak, as this may coincide with the mid-point of the bus working day, which is normally when shifts would change, unless the bus working day is significantly more or less than two crew working days. The location of crew changeover points is also important. There are advantages if crews can change at one of the terminal points of a route, since this minimises disruption to the journey and potential revenue accounting problems; there are also advantages if crews can change at the depot where they report for duty, since this minimises travelling time required to take up the duty. If the depot is at one of the terminal points, this is an ideal point to change crews. Otherwise some compromise may be necessary; if the route passes the depot, provided that revenue accounting problems can be overcome, it is often most satisfactory for crews to change at the depot. If the route does not pass the depot, it is sometimes possible to arrange for crews to sign on or off at one of the terminals; this will often require crews to sign on at the depot and off at the terminal, or vice versa.

It is often necessary for crews to sign on at their depot and travel to a point on the route where they may join their bus; in such cases the time spent travelling may be included in the payable duty hours, while it may also be necessary to provide transport between the depot and the changeover point: it may be possible for crews to travel as passengers on normal service buses, or if there are sufficient crews travelling simultaneously a dedicated vehicle may be justifiable. In some cases it is normal for the crew finishing their duty to drive the bus back empty to the depot, whence the relieving crew takes it back, empty, to the route. This practice can be very wasteful in terms of dead kilometres, unless the distance involved is very short, in which case the crew might normally be expected to walk.

It is normal to rotate crews to change duties periodically (usually daily or weekly) according to a duty rota, or roster, so that each has a turn on every duty: this arrangement is more equitable than allocating crews permanently to the same duty, since it is impossible for all duties to have the same number of working hours, due to variations in running times and the numbers of journeys operated on each route. However, there may be circumstances in which this is not appropriate, and full rotation of duties should not be regarded as essential. Often, particularly at large depots, the duties are grouped into several separate rotas, which may be based on a particular route or group of routes, or a particular bus type. Crews should remain on the same type of duty (i.e. early, late or spreadover) for at least a week, to avoid unnecessary fatigue due to unreasonably short overnight rests between daily duties.

In compiling the crew duty roster it is necessary to include a number of spare or stand-by crews to cover for lateness or absenteeism; the exact number required will depend on the general level of reliability of staff, but is likely to be of the order of 7.5% of the number of operating duties. Where conductors are employed, it is the policy of some operators to keep the same driver and conductor together, while others prefer to schedule drivers and conductors separately. In the latter case, this is often achieved by cycling conductors through the roster in reverse order to drivers; where more than one conductor is employed per bus, completely different rosters will be required, if the conductors are to be scheduled independently of one another.

Crew rosters may be based on a five-day or six-day week, or sometimes on a 13-day fortnight or other basis, depending on the requirement for rest days as specified by legislation or industrial agreements. Rest days for each crew may change from week to week, and may be on any day of the week, since buses normally operate seven days per week. There are exceptions: for example some operators schedule on the basis of a Monday-to-Friday week, with all weekend work carried out as overtime. In some cases, crews are not rotated, but have regular shifts which they work daily, or regular early and late shifts, alternating between them on a weekly or monthly basis. Where regular shifts are worked, there must be an equitable means of allocating them, since some duties are inevitably more attractive than others. In some undertakings, crews are invited to bid for shifts which become vacant, with allocation being based on seniority; sometimes disciplinary records may also be taken into account.

It is important to consider how drivers and conductors travel to and from work. Unless there is a comprehensive all-night bus service, most of those starting work in the morning will, inevitably, be leaving their homes before the normal bus service commences, with a similar situation at the end of the day. Where buses are parked at depots, bus crews may be expected to make their own way to work, but normally staff buses are provided which collect staff from residential areas early in the morning, and take them home late at night. Staff starting and finishing work during the normal working day are usually expected to use ordinary bus services. Some operators provide sleeping accommodation at the depots for staff starting work early or finishing late as an alternative to providing staff buses, particularly when crews live significant distances away.

Many small operators do not have depots, and the drivers park their buses near to their homes; in some cases this involves a considerable amount of dead mileage where drivers live long distances from the starting point of the route. Minibuses and paratransit vehicles are invariably operated in this way, as are many full-sized buses, particularly those run by small operators.

COMPUTERISED SCHEDULING

Scheduling of buses and crews is a complicated task, and the manual production of efficient schedules requires skill and experience; producing a full set of schedules and rosters for a large depot takes a considerable amount of time. Computer software is available commercially to assist in the compilation of bus and crew schedules, and to produce timetables for internal and public use, and various control documents such as depot run-out sheets and terminal departure sheets. Some of these packages are highly sophisticated and as well as producing schedules which optimise utilisation of vehicles and crews, can also suggest timetable changes which could result in savings in resources. More recent vehicle scheduling systems can also be linked with timetabling, payroll and other software to provide a fully integrated systems. Most large bus operators in developed countries now rely on computers for their scheduling, with significant savings both in terms of improved productivity of scheduling staff, and through the compilation of more efficient schedules than could be achieved manually, resulting in a more efficient operation.

Computerised scheduling is less common in developing countries. The relatively high cost of the software deters many operators, and the direct saving in scheduling cost is minimal where wages are low. Since crew costs are also generally much lower than in developed countries, the potential savings through more efficient utilisation of crews are also low. Moreover, the software requires accurate input of base data including point-to-point running times, vehicle and crew scheduling constraints such as maximum permitted working hours, or restrictions of vehicle types on certain routes, and such accuracy is often difficult to achieve. Where bus services are operated to very high frequencies, and scheduling systems generally are basic, there is also limited benefit from more sophisticated vehicle scheduling techniques. However, in a more complex operation, or where labour costs are high, the potential saving in vehicles, crews and dead mileage are substantial, and can more than justify the cost.

PUBLIC TRANSPORT SYSTEM PLANNING

Transport plans range from short term planning of bus or paratransit routes to comprehensive long-term urban land use and transportation plans covering all transport modes within entire metropolitan regions, and involving a wide range of disciplines in their preparation. Transport planning is a specialised discipline, and as such is outside the scope of this book; the present discussion is confined to the planning of public transport services, and of bus services in particular.

In theory, market forces will eventually lead to an optimal transport system, but in practice such evolution, which effectively is by trial and error, would take considerable time, and since cities are constantly growing and changing, the ideal route pattern will never evolve. Indeed, even with a sophisticated planning capability, development of transport services will always tend to lag behind changes in demand; because of the rapid pace of change, transport planning in cities in developing countries is especially difficult, and plans must be kept under regular review, and revised as necessary.

Planning a public transport system, in terms of the routes to be operated, frequencies of service, and numbers and types of vehicles is a complex task, and it is virtually impossible to determine an optimal system in any particular situation. For a large urban area there is an almost infinite number of possible routes, while the optimal number of public transport vehicles on a route at any time depends on a multitude of factors such as vehicle type and capacity, operating speeds, journey times, operating costs, passenger demand, fare levels, demand elasticity, operators' ability to vary fares, passengers' frequency preference, and whether operators' objectives are to maximise profits or to break even.

Where services are provided by a single operator, it is in its own interest, as well as that of the travelling public, that they are effectively planned and co-ordinated. Where several operators are involved, co-ordination may occur naturally if the operators see the possibility of improving their profits through co-operation, for example by providing complementary rather than competing services, regular frequencies on routes commonly served, or convenient connections between different services; otherwise there may be a case for intervention by the authorities to achieve this through appropriate planning and regulation.

Development of public transport services is a continuous process, and there is a fine distinction between the continuing monitoring and fine-tuning of existing services and the planning of new ones. Operators should be constantly adjusting routes in response to changes in demand and to improve the services offered or improve operational efficiency. Route variations may be diversions or extensions to serve new commercial or residential developments, or curtailment of routes if demand diminishes; routes may be combined to provide new links, or a network of routes may be completely recast to improve the range of direct origin-destination combinations provided. Major public transport route reorganisations will affect passenger flows as passengers become accustomed and adapt to the new system, and this is likely to result in the need for further fine tuning and adjustment, particularly where new routes generate new demand and movement patterns. Plans must therefore be kept under constant review, as the market changes constantly, and a rolling development plan covering five to ten years, updated annually, is often appropriate.

In a situation where bus services are unregulated and are provided by a large number of small operators, planning of bus routes is likely to be rudimentary. Most new operators have very limited knowledge of what services are required, and will tend to follow the routes of established operators, if any; a small number of operators may see opportunities arising as new developments take place, and extend or divert their routes accordingly, but many others will be unwilling to take the initiative, and where all vehicles are individually owned, an owner who sees the opportunity for a new route requiring several vehicles will find it difficult or impossible to establish the new route in isolation. There may be operators' associations which are able to identify a number of potentially profitable routes, but it is unlikely that a route system will evolve which caters satisfactorily for the requirements of the majority of passengers.

Plans by individual operators should take into account, as far as possible, projected developments by competing or complementary operators in the same mode and in other public and private transport modes, including motorcycles and bicycles, and even walking. Developments in other modes may affect not only the demand for bus or paratransit services, but also the operating environment; increased car usage, for example, may have an adverse effect on bus services, not only by abstracting traffic, but also by hindering their operation through increased levels of traffic congestion. If possible, plans for route restructuring should be made in conjunction with any plans for traffic management measures such as one-way traffic systems, bus lanes, bus-only streets and other bus priorities. The provision of parking facilities for cars can also influence the use of public transport: if it is difficult or impossible to park near the destination, travellers are more likely to use public transport; on the other hand, if there are good parking facilities at a railway station or suburban bus terminal, car users may be encouraged to transfer to public transport for the journey into town. Much depends on the prevailing culture, as discussed elsewhere, and this too must be taken into account in the planning process.

Public transport planning may be based on transport demand and supply data, derived from operators' own internal systems, and from surveys carried out specifically for the purpose. Public transport services are rarely planned entirely from scratch; usually there is an existing service, however basic, which, even if unsuitable as the basis of a new system, will provide a source of information on passenger flows. In the case of an informal operation, management information will be minimal, and data must be obtained through surveys of existing operations. A more formal operator is likely to have information on vehicle usage from depot and terminal departure records, and on revenue collected and passengers carried from conductors' waybills or ticket machines; these may be supplemented by reports of observations by inspectors and other operational staff and other forms of market research. These data will indicate trends in demand, and should form the basis for adjusting existing routes and schedules or for planning new routes.

Internally available data may be supplemented by other survey data, such as current and projected origin and destination data indicating flows of traffic on each route at different times, to facilitate identification of the main traffic corridors around which the route network will be planned. Other planning data available to transport operators may include overall transport plans and projections, land use plans, plans for private and public sector developments, traffic demand forecasts, and economic forecasts.

Where there are no established operators, or where the public transport system is very informal, planning must be based on data on potential rather than existing passengers; these may be obtained from surveys, or synthesised on the basis of probable movements between places of residence and places of work, education, commercial and other activities. Surveys carried out on existing operations may include vehicle and passenger counts at bus stations or roadside points, vehicle and occupancy counts at points on all main roads, or counts of passengers boarding and disembarking at each stop, to determine the number of movements at different times; number plate surveys to determine the number of vehicles operated on each route, journey times and the length of time spent waiting at terminals; and passenger interviews to obtain origin-destination information, and other information such as purpose of journey, preferred mode of travel, income levels and social group. Depending on the resources available, surveys may be very basic or highly detailed; for most service planning purposes, relatively simple surveys, recording approximate passenger loads but more accurate vehicle counts, are adequate.

Computer modelling techniques are becoming increasingly widely used in transport planning, particularly in the development of comprehensive transport plans, major infrastructure programmes and traffic management schemes, in the analysis of data such as origin-destination data, and in forecasting demand and traffic flows. In this context, Geographic Information Systems (GIS) are a useful tool, providing useful planning data which can be incorporated in traffic models and other technology. However, although these models can produce valuable input to the planning of bus routes, computerised bus route planning techniques are still relatively undeveloped. Moreover, there are so many variables and unpredictable elements, especially in developing countries, where circumstances can change rapidly, that forecasts and predictions may be wildly inaccurate. Because of the range of variables involved in route planning, and the difficulty in obtaining sufficiently accurate data on each to meet the requirements of a computer model, particularly in a developing country, in practice the most effective method of network planning is still largely manual, while taking full advantage of any available computer-generated data. This is an area of transport operation which still relies heavily on practical experience and local knowledge, and there is no substitute for a proficient public transport planner or operations manager.

Responsibility for planning public transport services may rest with central or local government, through its planning or regulatory authorities or other departments, or with the operators themselves. Certain planning decisions, such as those regarding the location of bus stops and stations, are normally best handled by local authorities, since a number of factors are involved including traffic regulations, safety considerations, effect on traffic flow, passengers' requirements, and the impact on other road users and occupiers of adjacent properties. It may sometimes be appropriate for a government planning body to become involved in planning issues which the operators themselves might be expected to deal with. For example, in planning a transport system it is prudent to take into account the requirements for depots and workshops; depot location is important, and if it is possible as part of an overall transport and land use plan to earmark land in suitable locations for future public transport infrastructure development it may be wise to do so.

In practice, especially where there are large operating units, responsibility for planning is often shared: large operators are likely to plan their own routes within government's overall transport plans which include roads and other infrastructure. Sometimes the bus operator has a wider role: in Dar es Salaam, the state-owned bus operator was given the role of co-ordinating and licensing the paratransit operators' services, and designed a route pattern which was intended to be complementary to its own. However, individual operators within a fragmented industry are less able to contribute to the planning process; they are not in a position to plan routes as part of an overall network, while scheduling refinements such as the tapering of frequencies towards the end of a route, or buses running at regular intervals rather than waiting at terminals for a full load, cannot be achieved by a large number of small operators working independently. In many cases, paratransit operators simply duplicate the main routes of a conventional bus operator, and have often continued to run on the same routes even where the latter has ceased to exist.

A typical arrangement in many urban areas where the public transport industry is highly fragmented, but including some which are served by a single operator or by a small number of large operators, is for a regulatory body, perhaps working in conjunction with operators' associations or co-operatives as appropriate, to be responsible for the planning, and constant updating, of the public transport system, with particular regard to routes and fares. It issues licences, and in some cases franchises, to vehicle owners to operate the routes. Sometimes the authority also produces schedules, and attaches specific schedules to each licence, but this requires a high degree of planning expertise in the authority, which rarely exists. Where routes are planned by a regulatory authority, with potential bus operators being required to apply for licences for specific routes of their own choice, some routes, which are "on the books", often remain without any service because no operator wishes to run them, because of poor demand, difficult road conditions or for other reasons. In some cities, depending on the effectiveness of enforcement, operators ignore licence conditions which require them to operate specific routes, and instead choose other routes which are more attractive. In effect, therefore, while the authorities may plan the route system, the level of service provided is often decided by the operators themselves, with no service at all on some routes. These situations must be addressed if a proper network of bus routes is to be secured.

Where services are provided by a single operator, it is relatively easy to implement plans for a completely new route network by the redeployment of buses between routes, provided that the plans are realistic and the necessary resources are available. Plans developed by an external planning authority requiring compliance by numerous independent operators may be less easy to implement: where every bus is operated by an individual, and is licensed to a particular route, some or all operators may have to be transferred from one route to another, and there may be strong objections. Subsequent fine-tuning also becomes a problem, since this may require further transfers of operators from one route to another.

It is always desirable to involve operators, regulatory authorities and other stakeholders in the planning process as far as possible, and this may be difficult with a fragmented industry, unless there are operators' associations which can represent their members. The effectiveness or otherwise of the regulatory system will be significant in this respect: in a system dominated by the private sector, a stringent regulatory system may enable much of the plan to be implemented. If public transport is provided by the public sector, operators can be directed to comply. Without direct regulation, changes to operators' and transport users' behaviour may be brought about by providing the requisite environment to encourage them to act in the desired manner. It must be established whether or not the existing regulatory framework will facilitate implementation of the plans, and if not, what changes to the regulations will be required, and whether the amended regulations will be effective: a plan will be unrealistic if its success depends on unenforceable regulations.

The structure of the public transport industry and the effectiveness of the regulatory system can therefore have a significant bearing on the ease or otherwise with which plans can be implemented. Successful implementation of a comprehensive bus service plan may require a change in the industry structure, or a change in the composition of the vehicle fleet. If this is the case it is also important to produce a workable plan for bringing about such changes with minimum adverse effect on vehicle owners, taking into account the remaining life of existing vehicles, whether they can be redeployed on other routes, or sold for use elsewhere; it may be necessary, in addition to changes in construction and use regulations or licence conditions, to offer financial incentives to operators to purchase a particular type or configuration of vehicle.

9

OPERATING SYSTEMS AND PROCEDURES

In addition to the operating, administrative and accounting systems and procedures applicable to any business, there are several which are specific to road transport operations. Some are more relevant to conventional buses than to paratransit or individual public transport modes, but others are more generally applicable. While systems vary in detail between one organisation and another, and there are inevitably differences as a result of the different characteristics of each mode, the principles are broadly similar throughout the industry. Unfortunately the efficiency of many transport undertakings in developing countries, and indeed in many developed countries also, is impaired by inefficient or cumbersome procedures, often compounded by poor compliance and poor housekeeping.

DEPOT PROCEDURES

The principal operational tasks carried out at a bus depot revolve around the requirement to provide buses and crews to operate the various services; in order to describe these tasks it may be helpful to follow in sequence the activities of bus crews and their supervisors during the course of a typical working day in a conventional bus operation.

Before commencing work a bus crew must normally report for duty; this activity is often referred to as "signing-on". At all but the smallest depots there is usually an office designated for this purpose; at a large depot the signing-on staff may be employed exclusively for the task, but at smaller depots, or where the majority of crews sign on within a relatively short period, they may have additional duties. Typically, drivers and conductors when signing on will ascertain which duties they are allocated to, usually by consulting a sheet posted on a notice board, or they may be informed verbally by the signing on staff; crews who are on a regular rota will normally know in advance which duties they are to work.

The driver and conductor will then sign the signing-on sheet; this lists each duty in chronological order, with columns indicating the duty number, starting time, and the names and/or staff numbers of the driver and the conductor allocated to the duty. There may be additional information, such as the fleet number of the bus allocated to the duty, the finishing time for the duty, or the route or routes involved. There must be space against each duty number for the driver and conductor to sign their names, or for the supervisor to indicate that they have reported for duty. Sometimes there are separate sheets for drivers and conductors, particularly at larger depots; it is often more practical for conductors to report separately, since they may have to be issued with equipment such as ticket issuing machines, tickets, waybills, and cash bags.

At a large depot, where several signing-on staff are required, it is normally necessary to have separate staff dealing with different rotas, or groups of rotas or duties: each may then be responsible for a separate sheet. The signing-on sheet may be supplemented by other means of reporting, such as a clock card system: this is not normally essential if a signing-on sheet is used, but in some organisations it is used for compatibility with other staff and systems, for example for the calculation of wages.

The signing-on sheet is compiled in advance by signing-on office staff, or by computer, from information from the crew duty roster, namely duty numbers, starting and finishing times; the roster will also normally identify the crews who should operate each duty, but the signing-on staff may be required to make amendments to cater for leave, absenteeism or other contingencies. A number of drivers and conductors are normally scheduled for standby duty, so that they may be deployed if a crew member scheduled for a specific duty fails to report in time. Sometimes if a crew member reports late he is reallocated to standby duty, and may be given work if a subsequent duty requires cover; otherwise, in many organisations, he is sent home without pay.

Sufficient time must be allowed to crews for signing on; typically ten or fifteen minutes are allowed for this process, normally included in the crews' paid hours. There must be sufficient signing-on staff to deal with all crews within the time available; as is often the case in urban operations, if most shifts start within a relatively short period the demands on the signing-on office will be considerable. On completion of their duties crews may be required to sign off, although this is not universal practice. Conductors may be required to return their equipment, and cash must be paid in and checked; a safe is usually essential for depositing cash prior to banking. Drivers may be required to submit defect reports in respect of their vehicles, or statements confirming that there are no defects.

There are various ways of allocating buses to duties. If a bus is permanently allocated to a driver or crew, this will determine its allocation to a particular duty. Where this is not the case, buses are sometimes allocated to specific duties, either on a regular basis or, less commonly, on a rotating basis. More often, however, buses are allocated to duties on a daily basis, either in advance of the crew reporting for duty so that the bus number can be shown on the signing-on sheet or posted separately on a notice board in the signing-on office, or after the crew reports, in which case the crew will typically proceed to the bus parking area after signing on, to be directed to a particular vehicle by the despatcher or officer in charge of the bus parking area, who should keep a record of the bus allocated to each duty.

Where it is practice to allocate buses to duties in advance of the crews signing on, there are several factors to take into consideration. Apart from the need to ensure that the bus allocated to each duty is of the appropriate type, as discussed in Chapter 8, it is necessary to ensure that it is available for service, and is not undergoing repair, or scheduled for routine preventive maintenance; this will require liaison between operating and maintenance staff.

In addition, it may be necessary to determine where buses are parked: as described in Chapter 5, buses may be parked in such a way that all vehicles are accessible, or in blocks so that some buses cannot be moved without first having to move one or more others. The first alternative requires considerably more space than the second, and may not be possible in depots where space is limited. Where they are parked in blocks, it is essential to ensure, when allocating buses to duties, that each is accessible at the time when it must leave the parking area. Since the signing-on sheet should be arranged with the duties shown in chronological order, it is relatively easy, either by means of a physical check or by using a record showing the exact position of each bus in the parking area, to allocate buses in sequence, so that each bus is unobstructed when it is scheduled to depart. If buses are allocated to crews in the parking area after they have signed on, block parking creates less of a problem, provided that different bus types are parked in different blocks, so that at any time it is possible to move a bus of any type; the despatcher can allocate any bus which he can see to be accessible at the time when it is required.

Even where all buses are accessible, it is usually necessary in a depot with more than about 100 vehicles to record the location where each is parked, preferably on a pre-printed sheet with spaces representing each parking space into which bus numbers can be entered by one of the depot staff, so that when a bus is required for service or for maintenance, the driver or mechanic does not have to search for it in the parking area. This may be unnecessary if each bus is allotted a regular parking position, although a plan showing these positions may still be desirable to assist staff who are not familiar with the depot. If a bus is regularly driven by the same driver and nobody else, the driver might be permitted to park in any location, since he should remember where he left it; however, this will not help a mechanic who is looking for the bus, and if the bus has to be moved for maintenance or cleaning, it will not necessarily be returned to the same location before the driver reports for his next spell of duty.

When the crew have located their bus in the parking area, there may be various tasks to carry out before leaving the depot. The conductor may have to check the bus interior and set destination indicators as appropriate, while the driver should carry out basic checks, including a visual check that all tyres are inflated, that basic equipment such as lights and horn are working, and that there is no serious damage to the vehicle which could render it unfit for service; he may also be required to check oil and water levels, and to fuel the vehicle before leaving the depot, but these tasks are often performed by maintenance personnel.

Punctual departure of all buses from the depot is vital if they are to operate to schedule subsequently. Despatching buses from the depot is therefore an important task, which is normally assigned to one or more despatchers; alternatively, crews may be responsible for finding the right bus, and leaving on time, although some form of check will normally be necessary to ensure that all scheduled buses have left the depot. A record should be kept of all departures; this usually takes the form of a pre-prepared run-out sheet, listing in chronological order each duty, with columns showing against each duty the bus number, scheduled departure time and actual departure time. Sometimes the identities of the driver and conductor are recorded also, but this is not normally necessary as these details are recorded in the signing on office: unnecessary duplication of work should be avoided. In certain cases, particularly if the run-out sheet is produced by computer, the numbers of the driver, conductor and bus allocated to each duty may be pre-printed; if this is so, there should be a column in which the despatcher may record the number of a replacement if the scheduled bus or crew was not allocated for any reason.

The run-out sheet is normally completed by the despatcher, but may be the responsibility of a gateman at the exit to the depot; at a large depot where several despatchers are required, or where there are more than one exit, several run-out sheets will be required. Similar sheets should be kept by despatchers at bus terminals, and by regulators controlling bus movements at intermediate points en route, as discussed below. As described in Chapter 15, these data are an important input to the management information system. The sheets should be retained and inspected daily, so that remedial action may be taken where problems are identified; any departures more than five minutes late should be investigated by the operations department.

OPERATING SYSTEMS AT STATIONS AND TERMINALS

Activities at a large bus station or paratransit terminal include the parking of vehicles awaiting departure, control of passengers boarding and alighting from vehicles, despatching of vehicles, booking of tickets, handling of luggage, security, administration and maintenance of the infrastructure. The parking of vehicles before loading, queuing for loading where applicable, and the loading itself, can be chaotic if not properly organised, particularly at larger stations. Some stations are in effect open spaces where vehicles park almost at random, with no designated stands; most, however, have distinct stands, or at least recognised areas permanently allocated for specific routes or destinations. In some cases, vehicles proceed to the departure stands immediately on arrival at the terminal, and remain there until they depart. This can be wasteful of space in the departure area, and more efficient use is made of the departure stands if vehicles park in an area designated specifically for the purpose, and move to the loading area shortly before departure. Whatever arrangements are in force, they should be such that conflicting passenger and vehicle movements are minimised.

The circulation of vehicles through terminals in less formal types of operation is often arranged on the basis that all must queue for passengers, and depart in sequence. In such cases there are normally one or more lanes designated for each route or destination, or for a group of related routes or destinations where frequencies are low. A vehicle will join the appropriate queue on arrival at the terminal, and move forward until it is at the head of the queue, when the passengers are permitted to board; the vehicle will depart when it is full, and the next vehicle in line will move to the head of the queue. In some cases it is permissible for drivers, instead of queuing, to opt to leave the terminal with an empty vehicle as soon as the passengers on the incoming journey have disembarked.

For high frequency services, the queuing arrangement is satisfactory if there is no surplus capacity in the system; vehicles have to wait for only a relatively short time between arriving and departing, and queues are short. There should, however, be provision for vehicles to park away from the queue while the driver takes a longer break. In practice, there is often grossly excessive capacity, resulting in vehicles having to queue for several hours, particularly at off-peak times. A serious disadvantage of the queuing arrangement is that even if a vehicle is waiting for a considerable time, the driver is required to move it forward each time a vehicle departs, and therefore must remain close to his vehicle. It results in increased wear and tear to vehicles, increased fuel consumption and increased pollution, and may prevent drivers from taking adequate rest.

An alternative is to have designated departure bays for each route or destination, where the passengers may wait and board, with buses parked in a separate part of the terminal which passengers do not need to enter. When a bus is due to depart, it moves from the parking area to the departure bay, loads, and leaves. The vehicle does not have to be moved between its arrival and departure, and the driver need not remain with the vehicle unless he is required to do so for some other reason; the vehicle occupies the departure bay only for sufficient time to permit passengers to board. This requires some means of determining the sequence in which buses should depart. It also requires a terminal layout which will permit any bus to be parked, or removed from the parking area, without others having to be moved first. For most long distance services, which are operated to lower frequencies, it is reasonable to expect buses and their drivers to have longer breaks between arriving and departing, and it is usually essential to have separate parking and loading areas.

When, as is usually the case, there are a number of different routes operating from a station, and a number of different operators, departure stands may be grouped by operator or by route. From the operator's point of view the former arrangement may be preferable: it is easier for the operator to control his vehicles if they are all in one place. In order to provide a wider range of options for the passengers, however, it may be preferable for all buses for a particular route or destination to load in the same place.

In certain circumstances it may be more efficient to permit buses to depart from any available stand, instead of allocating stands permanently to particular routes or destinations. This practice, which is common at airports and railway stations, but less so at bus stations, can increase the capacity of a station by maximising the utilisation of available stand space, and is particularly appropriate where some or all routes serving a station operate at low or irregular frequencies, where services do not operate to schedule, or where compliance with schedules is erratic. However, effective control procedures are essential to avoid confusion, and a good passenger information system is required so that all passengers are able to ascertain easily where to board their buses: normally a centrally located departure indicator, operated mechanically or electronically, supplemented by departure indicators at each stand, will be appropriate. In some sophisticated systems departure bays are allocated electronically, sometimes using GPS systems or other signals transmitted by approaching vehicles; as buses enter the station they are directed to the appropriate stand by electronic signs, while passenger information displays are updated automatically.

Passengers boarding and disembarking from vehicles must be properly controlled. In some bus stations passengers are required to disembark at a separate arrivals area, where there may be facilities for unloading luggage and transferring it to hand carts, taxis or other conveyances; this segregates the two flows of passengers, and can be desirable at a large station. In some cases buses unload their passengers outside the station before entering, but this tends to cause congestion in the surrounding streets and should normally be avoided. At most bus stations, particularly those handling local services, there are likely to be queues of passengers; at busy times these may be considerable.

Where there are several routes or operators, there may be several different queues which must be segregated in some way. In some cases passengers may be queuing for a specific bus, especially if they are pre-booked, or may be queuing for the next bus which arrives for their destination; these differences may affect the way in which queues are controlled. Queue discipline and control are often poor, sometimes leading to violence; much depends on the culture of the country concerned. Queue barriers, which segregate queues for different stands, and reduce the scope for queues to encroach on the roadway, are usually necessary but they must be designed to cater adequately for the volume of passengers and their luggage where appropriate, and must not impede access to vehicles.

The departure of vehicles from bus stations may be controlled in a variety of ways. In some operations drivers are required to depart according to instructions from a despatcher. Usually such instructions are issued verbally, but there are some more sophisticated systems; in Beijing, for example, some of the terminals for urban services are equipped with electronic display boards identifying the route number, bus fleet number and departure time, which must be observed by drivers. Where all buses operate to schedule, the drivers themselves may be responsible for leaving at the correct time as shown on their duty boards, but more often it is the responsibility of a despatcher to instruct drivers when to depart.

As described earlier, buses, and particularly paratransit vehicles, often do not operate to schedule but depart from terminals as soon as they are fully loaded, or when the passenger load has reached a predetermined level, in the same sequence as their arrival at the station. Sometimes, where there are only a few different operators, buses of different owners leave in a predetermined sequence: if there are only two of similar size they may alternate. It may be the responsibility of supervisory staff at the bus station to allocate buses to routes; this is more common in urban transport, but may apply to long distance services also.

Sometimes where buses are already allocated to a particular route, the despatcher may have the authority, if he decides it is necessary, to transfer a bus from a route where it is not immediately required to one where there appears to be excessive demand. Where demand is inconsistent, or where operators' knowledge of the demand is inadequate to allocate buses accurately in advance, this practice may be appropriate; however it is not always effective, and is a poor substitute for more formal scheduling methods. Where a despatcher, or a controller along the route, has the authority to over-ride schedules, for example to compensate for traffic delays, or to cater for unexpected demand, such authority must be handled with care, and those exercising it must be properly trained if chaos is to be prevented.

In Harare, Zimbabwe, for example, it was common practice for despatchers to over-ride schedules and divert buses from one route to another whenever one of the passenger queues was considered to have become too long; this required virtually every subsequent bus to be diverted also, with the result that on some days the entire schedule was abandoned after the first few journeys. Where the same changes are frequently made, it may be appropriate to incorporate these permanently in the schedules, and it is therefore important that a record is kept of each occasion on which a despatcher decides to over-ride the schedule, and the reason.

Where services are operated to schedule, problems may arise at bus stations which are used as intermediate stops for buses passing through the town or city. For example, buses on some routes may enter the station already full, but with a few passengers to drop; they then have capacity to pick up the same number of new passengers, but through services are often delayed by having to queue while other buses, some of which may be commencing their journeys at the station, load first. For this reason, in some countries, long-distance buses do not call at all bus stations en route, but stop outside the intermediate bus stations, illegally in some cases, to set down passengers at the roadside. By not entering a bus station, however, a bus is likely to miss passengers who could otherwise be carried; alternatively, the practice may encourage some prospective passengers to wait at the roadside outside the terminal, thus causing problems, principally obstruction of other traffic by buses loading in the road.

Passengers using long distance services often carry large quantities of luggage, and appropriate arrangements are required to deal with this. Sometimes bus loaders are employed by the bus operators, or sometimes by the bus station management. At many stations there are freelance luggage loaders and porters, who may be required to pay for a permit, formal or otherwise, to work at the station. Security is important, especially at long distance stations where passengers may carry considerable amounts of cash in addition to their luggage. Guards are often employed to patrol the area, and to prevent the entry of unauthorised vehicles. The guards may also record bus arrivals and departures, for record and charging purposes. In some bus stations, only passengers are permitted in certain areas, principally the loading areas, and may have to pay a small charge to gain entry.

In some countries, the operations at bus stations are very well organised. At a typical bus station in China, for example, a passenger will first purchase a ticket at one of several ticket windows. Any luggage will then be taken by the passenger to the luggage office where it is weighed, charged for, labelled and despatched to the appropriate departure bay, while the passenger proceeds to a waiting room. When the departure time approaches, passengers queue at the appropriate gate, and when the bus has been brought to the gate they are allowed to board; their tickets are checked by a steward at this point. The luggage is loaded on to the roof of the bus by the bus station staff. Standards vary considerably, however, and in many other countries organisation is poor, and, particularly at busy times, obtaining a place on a bus may be a very unpleasant experience.

Supervisory staff are normally provided by the organisation managing the bus station, although sometimes they are provided by the regulatory body responsible for bus services, or by an operator's association, regardless of ownership of the station. The operators themselves may provide their own staff to supervise their own services, especially if they have many services using the station.

In many developing countries, bus, paratransit and taxi stations are controlled informally, and usually also illicitly, by self-employed despatchers or controllers, such as the "premen" in Indonesia, "runners" in Sri Lanka and "marshals" in Ethiopia. Typically, these people, who in many cases have criminal backgrounds, control the departure of vehicles, ensuring that they leave in the correct sequence; subsidiary roles include touting for passengers, and assisting passengers in boarding. For their services they extort charges from driver, and sometimes also from passengers.

In Malang, Indonesia, for example, there are normally two despatchers for each mikrolet route, operating at the terminals. They are self-employed, and have no connection with the operators or co-operatives, but have their own separate union; their activities are "co-ordinated" by the official terminal officers. An aspiring despatcher must apply to the union and terminal management for permission to operate, and if this is granted he may work on probation for a period; if his work is unsatisfactory, he will be replaced. Once a despatcher has completed the probationary period he has a "job for life" and cannot easily be removed or replaced; often there are restrictions on the number of such positions, which thus acquire a market value, and may be sold by incumbents or passed from father to son. The despatchers collect a fee for each departure from each driver; this normally varies according to the fares charged for the route concerned, or the number of passengers on board. Despatchers make "informal" payments to terminal officials, for example ostensibly as contributions to repairs to the terminal buildings, or for landscaping in the grounds, but in fact as a payment for the right to operate.

They also operate at busy intermediate stops on some routes, directing passengers to vehicles, and extracting money from drivers each time they call at the stop. If a driver refuses to pay, passengers may be prevented from boarding his vehicle, and he may be physically abused or his vehicle damaged. Drivers are often reluctant to report such occurrences to the police, particularly if, as is often the case, they are breaking the law in some way: the stopping point in question may be in an area where vehicles are prohibited from picking up passengers, or the vehicle or driver may lack a valid licence or test certificate; in some cases police officers are in collusion with the controllers' union.

CONTROL OF SERVICES

In addition to controlling the despatch of vehicles from depots and terminals, it is often necessary to regulate services en route. If services are operated in accordance with any form of schedule, there is a need for supervision to ensure that drivers conform; where there are no fixed schedules it is desirable that vehicle frequencies are regulated in accordance with the number of passengers wishing to travel at any time. This includes not only timekeeping and the enforcement of discipline generally; it also requires action in response to irregular fluctuations in demand or traffic conditions which cannot be catered for in the schedules. It should be pointed out that in this context, the terms "regulation" and "control" refer to the day-to-day task of ensuring that bus services are operated in accordance with the schedules, plans and policies determined by management, rather than to the overall regulation of a transport system by an external authority, as discussed in Chapter 19.

Where timetables are published, it is particularly important that these are adhered to. One purpose of a timetable is to indicate to passengers when they may join a bus for their destination; therefore buses should not be permitted to depart before the scheduled time from a stop at which passengers may board. Buses arriving at timing points ahead of their scheduled time should normally be required to wait until the scheduled time before departing, although towards the end of the route, if the bus is scheduled to stop only to let passengers disembark, early arrival and departure may be permitted. Drivers failing to observe schedules may be penalised; where bus services are subject to government regulation, the bus operator may be penalised for failing to adhere to schedules. Where this is the case enforcement should be realistic, and a degree of tolerance applied to allow for unpredictable factors such as traffic congestion, as discussed in Chapter 8.

From a passenger's point of view early departure, which may result in missing the bus, is usually more serious than late departure. From the bus operator's point of view, unnecessarily late operation may disrupt services and reduce productivity. If several operators run in competition, failing to operate to schedule may cause abstraction of traffic, which under some regulatory regimes may be illegal: for example a bus running late, so that it is immediately ahead of the following bus operated by a competitor, will pick up passengers who would otherwise have travelled on the second bus.

Supervision of buses in service is normally the responsibility of regulators, controllers or timekeepers stationed at key traffic points, mainly at principal bus stations but also at other points served by large numbers of buses. These controllers may be employed by the bus operator, an operators' association or by a regulatory body; in some cases, particularly where transport services are operated on an informal basis, they are self-employed, as described above.

The responsibilities of the controllers include ensuring that buses depart at the correct time, sometimes by instructing each driver individually or simply checking that vehicles depart in accordance with schedules, as shown on the drivers' duty boards where applicable. Controllers may instruct drivers to depart earlier or later than schedule, to turn short before the end of the route, or even to operate a different route, to meet unexpected changes in demand or traffic conditions. Such flexibility is desirable in order to meet demand variations, but to work effectively, ideally requires controllers at several points along a route, in contact with one another and with the depot by two-way radio; it is virtually impossible for one man to make the correct decisions in this regard without knowledge of conditions elsewhere along the route.

Radio communication will also enable problems caused by congestion or abnormal traffic patterns to be dealt with effectively, while breakdowns or accidents can be reported and attended to more quickly. Two-way radio between roadside controllers and a central control point is becoming increasingly common, as is radio communication with individual buses. Other more sophisticated forms of control employ television cameras, or electronic or satellite tracking systems. Some of these systems may be linked to real time information systems, and to traffic signals to enable buses to be given priority, and may even able to identify and give greater priority to late-running buses. However, even with such sophisticated systems, many operators still find it necessary to employ supervisors on the road.

Like terminal despatchers, controllers en route should record the registration, fleet or running number of each bus passing their location, together with the time and, ideally, the approximate load carried. Where services are operated to schedule, a sheet should be provided listing the scheduled times for all buses passing the location, with space to record actual times, and the reasons for any variances from schedule. Late running exceeding five minutes should be investigated: if there is no explanation the driver should be disciplined; if it is due to inadequate running times schedules should be amended. Information collected in this way should be incorporated in the management information system.

Where frequencies are low, for example on rural services, it is not usually possible to justify supervisory staff to monitor timekeeping. Problems often arise with vehicles departing early on their return journeys; this can be a particularly serious problem in connection with buses scheduled to sleep out overnight; for example, a bus scheduled to arrive at an outlying point in the evening, and depart at 0330 the following morning, might leave instead at 2230 on the evening of arrival, in order to avoid inspection, or to suit the convenience of the crew. Apart from serious operational implications, such practice sometimes results in accidents due to driver fatigue. In such cases, other means of monitoring may be used, but these may be too expensive or complex for some operators. Tachographs are a useful tool, although they can only show up infringements after the event. More sophisticated systems, such as satellite tracking systems, are becoming increasingly widely used as the equipment becomes more affordable.

A common problem on urban services, particularly those operating at high frequencies, is "bunching", where instead of buses arriving at a stop at regular intervals in accordance with the schedule, two or more buses arrive simultaneously followed by a long interval before another bunch arrives. The main cause of bunching is unavoidable, namely the uneven arrival of passengers at stops. If there is an unusually large number waiting at a particular stop, the first bus to arrive will spend longer at the stop than normal while the passengers board; this will result in its late arrival at the next stop, and it is therefore probable that more passengers than normal will have accumulated at that stop also, and there will be a further delay while the passengers board. Meanwhile the following bus has fewer passengers to pick up, and therefore spends less time than normal at each stop, eventually catching up with the first. The third bus may catch up with the second, but the fourth is likely to be delayed, since the early running of the second and third buses is likely to leave additional passengers for the fourth, thus creating another bunch; in general terms, the higher the frequency of service, the greater the number of buses in each bunch is likely to be.

Other factors can compound the problem: traffic delays may start the bunching process by delaying one bus and allowing queues of passengers to accumulate. When bunching occurs, providing there is sufficient layover time at the terminals, buses can recover lost time, and depart on their next journeys on schedule. However, controlling bunching along the route can be difficult, and requires good discipline on the part of bus crews and judgement on the part of supervisory staff. Where the effect of bunching is slight, the problem will be minimised if buses which begin to run early slow down to keep to schedule. If all buses in a bunch fall behind schedule, the second and subsequent buses in a bunch may be delayed on the instruction of a supervisor to restore the correct service interval, but all will then be running late; the lost time will be recovered at the terminal providing there is adequate layover time. When bunching is serious, it is sometimes appropriate to turn one or more buses round before reaching the terminus, after transferring their passengers to other buses, to fill gaps which have opened up in the service in the opposite direction.

REVENUE CONTROL SYSTEMS

For the majority of public transport operators in developing countries, all income is derived from the fares paid by passengers, and control of revenue is a key requirement of a successful operation. However, transport is susceptible to revenue leakage in various forms, due principally to the fact that vehicle crews are to a large extent unsupervised and usually handle large quantities of cash. Poor revenue integrity is often a major problem, particularly in many of the larger transport undertakings, leading to loss of income and therefore inadequate funds to sustain the operation. Revenue leakage has contributed to the failure of many conventional bus systems, while at best, if an operator is lax in minimising revenue loss fares will be higher than would otherwise be necessary, profits lower, and the service poorer.

Most operators are unaware of the extent of the revenue leakage problem; many attribute the greater proportion of losses to fare evasion by passengers, and underestimate the extent of fraud by their employees. It is difficult to estimate the proportion of revenue lost but a comparison of observed bus loadings with actual revenue received can give an approximate measure. Losses of over 50% have been estimated in some cases, while anything between 10% and 25% is common.

Revenue may be lost through fare evasion on the part of passengers and through malpractices on the part of the operator's own employees; there may also be collusion between passengers and employees to defraud the operator. Passengers may attempt to avoid payment altogether, or pay less than the correct charge for the journey taken. Many passengers travel without paying, by evading the conductor if there is one, or, where buses are one-person-operated, by boarding the bus through the exit door to avoid paying the driver; if passengers are required to purchase tickets from automatic vending machines, they may by-pass the system and travel without tickets.

Revenue integrity is partly a function of the degree of honesty prevailing at all levels in the organisation, as well as the effectiveness of revenue control systems; the extent to which the revenue leakage problem can be resolved will have a bearing on type of service which can be provided, and on methods of operation. Good revenue integrity will enable a much more organised type of service to be provided, while poor revenue integrity necessitates a less formal type of operation. Robust systems and procedures, which are workable within prevailing cultural and ethical characteristics, are usually required if revenue is to be adequately protected.

Except where a flat fare system applies, a common form of evasion is over-riding, or travelling farther than the distance paid for. This is relatively simple: the passenger pays for a ticket on boarding the vehicle, but does not leave the vehicle at the end of the journey covered by the ticket. Detection depends on vigilance by the conductor or by random checks by revenue inspectors; over-riding can be very difficult to control if fares are collected by the driver or by a seated conductor.

However, the most serious problem is usually pilferage by employees, principally those directly responsible for collecting fares, namely the conductors and drivers, but also those in supervisory positions such as revenue inspectors who may be in collusion with crews. Cash handled daily by a conductor can be as much as five times his monthly salary, or even more: the temptation to steal is therefore great. Non-issue of tickets, issue of undervalued tickets, and re-issue of tickets, are all common offences committed by conductors. Collusion between conductors and passengers is common in many countries; typically, a dishonest conductor will charge the passenger less than the correct fare, and issue an undervalued ticket, for an amount less than the amount actually paid or even for zero value, or no ticket at all, so that both parties benefit at the operator's expense. Crews often also defraud passengers by overcharging or giving short change. As well as revenue loss through dishonesty, there may be loss through crew ineffectiveness, or inefficient fare collection systems, resulting in failure to collect all fares.

Most revenue control systems are based on the use of tickets as proof of payment for a particular journey. A ticketing system is usually also a source of management information, providing data on passenger loadings by route and journey, for both accounting and planning purposes. The system should be secure, in that tickets cannot easily be forged, altered or re-used. Tickets should include some means of verifying the journey for which they are valid, and certain information, of which the most important item is a distinctive serial number; usually the fare paid and stage boarded are shown, and also useful are indicators of the route, date of issue, and class of passenger. There may be provision in the system for the numbers of passengers in various categories to be recorded, for example by issuing different types of tickets to different classes of passenger, and for recording the number of passengers carried on individual bus trips. Some systems are more effective than others in terms of security and data generated; in general terms, the more effective the system, the greater its complexity, and the more expensive it is to install and maintain.

Tickets may be issued in respect of a single journey only, two journeys (return or transfer tickets), multiple journeys or unlimited journeys. In some operations, particularly where fares are collected by the driver, passengers are required to pay the exact fare: no change is provided, and a passenger who is unable to tender the correct payment will have to pay more than the requisite fare. This system enables fares to be collected more quickly, and can reduce dwell times at bus stops considerably. Since no change is given, all cash may be deposited directly into a sealed box which cannot be removed from the vehicle, thus providing improved security. However, the exact fare system is not universally accepted: in some cities passengers are willing to comply, appreciating the benefits of reduced journey times; in others, even in the same country, there is strong resistance, and in some cases where the system has been introduced it has subsequently been abandoned.

There are many different ticketing systems, ranging from very simple manual systems using hand-written or pre-printed tickets to sophisticated systems using electronic equipment. A pre-printed ticket system can be relatively simple. Tickets may be printed individually, in rolls or in book form. If a flat fare system is in force, only a single value of ticket is required; otherwise a range of tickets is required, for the various fares and classes of ticket. Sometimes a different set of tickets is printed for each route, with fare stages named on the tickets. A means of cancelling tickets is necessary to prevent them from being issued more than once: usually a hole is punched in the ticket, and often the position of the hole indicates the stage boarded, and in some cases additional holes may indicate the time and date of the journey.

Problems usually experienced with pre-printed tickets include security, forgery and re-issue. On long routes, where there are many different fares, it may not be practical to print tickets for every fare, and therefore a combination of tickets, totalling the correct value, is issued for the higher fares. This is also necessary with some ticket issuing machines which have a limited range of values. Such practice detracts from the value of the ticketing system as a source of passenger information, as the number of tickets issued does not equate to the number of passengers carried. In some systems in which pre-printed tickets are cancelled by punching, the ticket punch is capable of recording the number of punches made, and if multiple tickets issued for one fare are punched together this can provide an accurate record of the number of passengers.

Many systems use ticket issuing machines carried by conductors. These machines print relevant information such as date, fare, and stage boarded onto paper rolls, which may be blank or pre-printed with certain information, such as the operator's name. The value of tickets issued is recorded by the machine, and should agree with the cash paid in by the conductor as indicated on the waybill. As with pre-printed tickets, there may be security problems with ticket machines: many can be tampered with, so that the cash value of tickets issued is under-recorded. Some types of ticket issuing machine have the facility to record all details printed on every ticket issued; earlier machines used a mechanical system, whereby details of each ticket were printed on a separate audit roll retained in the machine; more recent machines record these data electronically. The data can be used as a means of detecting fraud, for example highlighting the issue of zero-value tickets or a suspiciously high proportion of low-value tickets. They are also a useful source of planning data, providing information on passenger loads at each point on a route at different times of the day; this assumes, of course, that tickets are issued correctly, and where there is a high level of abuse the data must be used with caution.

The majority of ticket issuing machines used in developing countries are mechanical; some, which are mounted in the vehicle for operation by the driver or a seated conductor, are electrically powered, but the majority are operated manually. Electronic ticket machines are also available, and their use is now almost universal in developed countries; they are based on micro-computer technology and greatly simplify the fare collection task as well as providing detailed and accurate information on revenue and passenger loadings, while virtually eliminating the need for printed documents such as fare tables and waybills. Information such as fares for each route within the network may be stored within the machine, so that if the appropriate codes for the stage boarded, destination stage, and class of ticket are entered, the machine will display the fare to be paid for the journey, and print a ticket showing the appropriate information.

Data on tickets issued and revenue collected are downloaded from the machine to a computer at the end of the duty or, if required, at various times during the course of the duty. Electronic machines are normally used for driver-only operation or where the conductor is seated at the entrance to the vehicle, since most machines are too heavy and bulky to be carried by a conductor; however, smaller machines are now becoming more widely available which can be carried by conductors. Electronic ticket machines and the hardware and software required for the associated systems are relatively expensive, but the cost may be justifiable if they provide effective revenue security and useful management information.

A further development of the electronic ticket machine is the "smart card", which is still at a relatively early stage of development, but is likely in the near future to facilitate the use of relatively complex charging and information systems. They are already in use in a number of major cities, including Hong Kong and Kuala Lumpur. Smart cards are similar in appearance to credit cards, and carry electronically stored value and data which can be transmitted to a reader on board a vehicle or at a bus stop or station. Card value may be topped up periodically at outlets such as bus or rail station kiosks, shops, banks or post offices; visitors or occasional travellers without smart cards can be catered for with paper cards or smart tokens, available for a limited period or number of journeys. Most cards can be read without contact, and need not even be removed from the user's wallet or handbag. When the card is presented the reader deducts the appropriate value and records any relevant information; it may issue a ticket although in some systems tickets are not used. Some are able to record passengers as they both board and alight, so that the correct fare is charged where a graduated or zonal fare system applies, while useful data may be provided on passenger kilometres and travel patterns. Most cards can be used for other purposes also, typically for taxis, car parking, road tolls, public telephones and sometimes purchases from shops.

As well as eliminating the need for cash transactions on board vehicles, smart cards are particularly advantageous in facilitating accurate allocation of revenue where through ticketing facilities are available on a network provided by several operators. They can automatically give discount, for example for a return journey, or if two consecutive journeys made within a specified time period qualify for a discounted fare. A disadvantage of smart cards is that they require relatively expensive equipment, and the expense may be difficult to justify in many developing countries. However, the costs are likely to decrease as systems become more widely used.

An essential part of most ticketing systems is the waybill, a printed form on which the conductor must record details of tickets issued during the course of his or her duty. Essential information to be recorded on the waybill includes the duty number, date, conductor's name, ticket machine number if applicable, opening ticket numbers, and cash counter numbers in the case of most ticket machines, at the start of each duty and closing numbers at the end of the duty.

From these data, the cash collected and number of passengers carried can be calculated; an essential task is to check that the cash paid in by a conductor agrees with the amount calculated from the waybill. Much more detailed information can be obtained, depending on the complexity of the system used: for example, a conductor is often required to enter certain information such as ticket closing numbers at the completion of every trip, and sometimes at certain intermediate points on each trip, to provide information on passenger loadings by trip or by section of route. Electronic ticket machines record this information automatically.

Mechanical ticket machines are normally stored at the depot and issued to conductors or drivers at the beginning of each shift, and collected at the end; strict control of the issue of ticket machines and associated documentation is necessary in order to prevent misuse, although these controls are not fully effective in some organisations. Ticket machine power units, if applicable, are normally permanently fitted to vehicles, as are most electronic ticket machines; this can sometimes cause problems: for example, when a ticket machine is defective the bus itself cannot be used. Indeed poor reliability can be a problem with electronic ticket issuing equipment, particularly where operating conditions are harsh; in particular, vibration and dust ingress due to poor road conditions, and problems of maintenance, not necessarily of the machine itself but of the vehicle's electrical system, can render it inoperative, although with improvements in design these problems are becoming less serious.

Fares may be collected on the vehicle, or off the vehicle in advance of the journey; in some cases passengers have a choice. On-vehicle fare collection may be by a conductor, who normally moves around the bus but in some systems is seated near the entrance or exit, by the driver, as passengers board or leave, or by automatic ticket vending machines installed in the vehicles. Off-vehicle ticket sales may be by conductors, stationed at bus or tram stops to sell tickets to waiting passengers, by ticket sellers stationed in offices or kiosks at stops, by approved agents or shops, or by automatic machines located at stops. Problems may arise at times when outlets in shops or kiosks are closed; street vending machines overcome most problems but are relatively expensive and may be prone to vandalism. In some systems, pre-purchased tickets must be validated or cancelled on boarding the vehicle by inserting them in a machine adjacent to the entrance.

In most developed countries, unless tickets are purchased before boarding, fares are collected by the driver, principally to minimise labour costs; this practice is rare in developing countries where wage levels are relatively low, and where buses are usually much more heavily loaded. A notable exception was Zimbabwe, where the majority of urban bus services were operated by drivers only; this was facilitated by the type of operation, characterised by a high proportion of end-to-end traffic, which lent itself to pre-collection of fares at the terminals, and required drivers to collect relatively few fares en route. Although one-person-only operation might save labour costs, there is a penalty in terms of additional time spent at bus stops, increasing journey times by as much as 20% if fares are collected by the driver, and therefore normally requiring additional vehicles to operate the service; increased traffic congestion may also result from buses spending more time at stops.

There are several advantages with off-vehicle ticket sales, including revenue security and speed of loading, particularly where buses are operated by the driver only. Off-vehicle ticket sales are relatively common in respect of long distance travel, where tickets may be purchased in advance from agents of the operator: in some cases all tickets are sold in this way, and none are sold on the vehicle. Sometimes tickets are sold by touts standing beside the vehicles, but it is more common in most countries for tickets for long-distance bus services to be sold at booking offices within bus stations. There may be a single booking office which sells tickets for all departures, but more often there are several: sometimes each office will deal with all bookings to certain destinations, or alternatively, and more commonly, each operator may have his own booking office.

A practice followed in respect of long distance services in some parts of China is the sale of all tickets for a particular destination at a common booking office, with each passenger being directed to a specific bus; the driver of each bus collects the appropriate revenue in cash from the booking office before departure. This practice restricts passengers' choice of operator, and constrains competition, since there is little incentive for an operator to try to attract passengers by offering a better service than its competitors; passenger choice should not normally be dictated by bus station management.

There are many cities where tickets for local journeys are purchased before boarding the vehicle. A large proportion of ticket sales on urban services operated by the Harare United Omnibus Company were at kiosks at the bus stations, although this was facilitated by the fact that a high proportion of passengers were travelling from one end of the route to the other. Off-vehicle sales are less practical where there are several operators, although there are some successful examples: For example, in Accra, fares are collected and tickets issued to passengers before they board, by a ticket clerk standing beside the vehicle. When the bus is full, the ticket clerk gives the cash to the traffic office, where union fees and income tax are deducted; the balance is returned to the driver, with a waybill and receipts for dues and tax, so that bus owners have a check on their revenue. In Latvia, the Tram and Trolleybus Board redistributed to the different operators in the capital, Riga, all revenue collected by the operators, and by the kiosks where most tickets were sold, on the basis of estimated numbers of passengers carried.

In some transport systems tokens are used in place of coins. Each token normally has a cash value, and is used in place of a coin of the equivalent value; they might be sold in bulk, often at a discount. Tokens may be used most effectively if they given a value in terms of validity rather than cash: for example a token may permit travel for one zone or fare stage; in a more complex system more or fewer tokens may be required for a particular journey depending on the time of travel. The number of tokens required for a particular journey may remain unchanged, even when fares are increased or reduced: the price of the tokens is varied instead. Universal use of tokens throughout a system would eliminate the need for conductors or drivers to give change, or for cash to be carried on vehicles; however, there would be practical difficulties in implementing such a scheme. Tokens may also be used in ticket vending machines if required.

Some systems operate without tickets of any kind, with passengers handing cash to the conductor or depositing it in a fare box near the vehicle entrance or exit; a fare box may be a simple box with a slot at the top, into which the passenger drops the fare, or it may have an upper compartment with a small window to enable the driver or conductor to visually check the amount deposited by each passenger before releasing it into the main storage compartment. In either case it must be securely attached to the vehicle, and preferably should not be accessible or removable except at the depot by an authorised key holder. Passenger discipline and honesty are important if all passengers are to pay as required. A ticketless system is normally possible only where a flat fare system is in force, otherwise there would be no means of detecting and preventing over-riding; however, there are some exceptions, as in Hong Kong, which has a system whereby only one fare is applicable from any stop, and there is no possibility of over-riding.

Buses may be equipped with turnstiles at the entrance, and sometimes also at the exit, to prevent passengers from entering without paying, or from entering by the exit door. In some cases the turnstiles incorporate coin-operated fare collection facilities, which may be effective with a flat fare system, or they may incorporate counters as a check on the number of passengers carried. They may simply be used in conjunction with a conductor, who would normally be seated near the entrance, to control entry to and exit from the vehicle, and to minimise fare evasion by passengers. Turnstiles have certain disadvantages, however. If they are used for automatic fare collection, passengers travelling at concessionary fares cannot be catered for, unless they are permitted to board through the exit door if no turnstile is fitted there; however, this makes fare evasion by other passengers possible. There have also been problems of reliability, particularly where turnstiles are used for fare collection, and where road conditions are poor, leading to excessive vibration and consequent equipment failure. In practice, their application is relatively limited.

It is essential that the revenue collection system employed is appropriate for the type of operation. On urban services where passenger turnover is high, a rapid means of fare collection is required. Problems can arise if fare collection procedures are too slow to cater for the level of passenger turnover. Where the turnover of passengers on a route is low, for example on long-distance services where passengers travel for several stages, a slower system is adequate. It is the practice in some undertakings, in order to ensure that all fares are collected, for buses to remain stationary at a bus stop until the conductor has collected all fares. In others, drivers drive slowly between stops so that all fares have been collected from passengers who boarded at one stop before the next stop is reached.

These procedures can cause significant delay, not only to buses and their passengers, but also to other traffic; delays to buses reduce utilisation, and increase bus requirements and therefore operating costs. Sometimes additional conductors are carried, for all or part of the day, and sometimes only on the busiest sections of route: this can be effective, but creates complications in revenue control.

As described in Chapter 14, there are various alternative fare structures, and the choice of ticketing system is influenced to a large extent by the type of fare structure employed; the more complex the fare structure, the more sophisticated is the system required. A flat fare system requires only a very simple fare collection system, and does not necessarily require tickets. A zonal system is slightly more complex, while a graduated fare system may require a much more complex ticketing system. The requirements of the system increase further where different classes of fare apply, such as adult and child fares, peak and off-peak differential fares, discounted tickets or concessionary fares.

Any ticketing system requires monitoring to ensure that it is being properly operated, and to minimise abuse of the system. Checks of passengers' tickets are normally carried out by revenue inspectors to detect, or preferably to deter, theft of revenue. These checks should be conducted at random, and inspectors should be trained to detect instances of all types of infringement, by bus crews and passengers. In some cases, independent security companies are engaged from time to time to provide plain-clothes "under-cover" personnel to ride on buses and observe the performance of conductors and inspectors.

On most heavy rail and metro systems, and to a lesser extent LRT, tickets are sold at stations from kiosks or automatic vending machines. They are normally collected, either manually or by automatic barriers at the destination station. Typical systems employ tickets with magnetic strips, which can be read by equipment at the barriers to check the validity of the ticket on entering and leaving the station platform. On presentation of a valid ticket, the barrier will open and permit the passenger to pass; invalid tickets are rejected, and will not open the barrier; tickets with remaining validity, such as monthly season tickets, are returned to the user while expired tickets are retained in the machine. Such systems are more appropriate to rail systems where access to stations is relatively easily controlled; they have limited application for bus services.

If a ticketing system is to work effectively, it is important that all passengers receive the correct tickets. To encourage passengers to ensure that they were issued with a ticket, the national bus company in Malawi ran a promotional scheme, known as the "Wheel of Fortune", whereby passengers entered their tickets in a monthly draw; various prizes were provided. This ran for several years and was considered to be effective. Similar schemes have been operated in other countries from time to time, but in some cases have been prevented by gambling regulations.

The effectiveness of the measures taken depends to a large extent on the integrity of those employed to carry out the various checks, and on strict adherence to procedure. These often leave much to be desired, and even complex, sophisticated, and expensive monitoring systems are not always successful in reducing pilferage to an acceptable level. Some operators deal with the revenue integrity problem by setting daily target revenue figures: bus crews are expected to pay in a minimum amount of revenue, and failure to do so may result in disciplinary action. This reduces the supervisory requirement, but has certain disadvantages, principally a potential reduction in revenue due to the operator. Some operators pay to the conductor, or more commonly to both driver and conductor, a percentage of revenue collected as an incentive to collect all fares and to pay in all revenue. Conductors may be required to pay a guarantee of approximately one day's revenue on commencement of employment, where the risk of conductors absconding with the day's takings is significant.

Incentive schemes are effective in some cases, but not in others, and depend largely on general ethical standards. Where staff tend to be dishonest, and measures to prevent fraud are relatively ineffective, such incentives achieve very little: from the crews' point of view, unless there is a strong likelihood of detection and the penalties are severe, a large percentage of revenue obtained dishonestly is usually preferable to a small percentage obtained honestly. Effective enforcement also requires appropriate sanctions against offenders. The scope for applying sanctions against passengers for fare evasion is determined to a large extent by legislation: in some countries operators have the power to impose on-the-spot fines, while in others offenders must be taken to court. Sanctions against employees are included in the operator's normal disciplinary procedures.

THE VEHICLE RENTAL OR "SETORAN" SYSTEM

A common practice in developing countries throughout the world is the renting of buses, paratransit vehicles, taxis and other forms of individual public transport. It is virtually universal in all forms of public transport throughout Indonesia, where it is known as *setoran*; this is a useful term which has been adopted for use in this book. Variations of the setoran system are practised by many conventional bus undertakings as well as by most operators in the informal sector.

Typically vehicles are rented out, usually on a daily basis but sometimes for longer periods, to their drivers, who are required to pay the owner a specified sum of money at the end of each period. The driver employs one or more conductors if required, and pays for all fuel and route costs such as road tolls and terminal departure fees. The charge is normally calculated to cover the full costs of maintenance of the vehicle, including regular preventive maintenance, unscheduled maintenance, and accident damage, together with replacement costs and a contribution to the owner's overheads, plus an element to provide a satisfactory return on the investment in the vehicle. The charge will also normally reflect the revenue-earning potential of the route operated or area served, and may be varied from period to period to reflect seasonal fluctuations in demand. Drivers are sometimes charged for any excessive or abnormal wear and tear, and are usually responsible for all minor damage to the vehicle. All fare revenue collected, after all costs and charges have been met, is retained by the driver in place of a regular wage.

Mass public transport vehicles are usually rented out to be used on a specified route, and sometimes, in the case of a conventional bus operator, on a specified duty if services are operated to schedule; the charge may vary according to the duty operated. Some undertakings have a fixed charge per bus, regardless of duty; if this is the case, then duties may be rotated to give every driver a fair share of both more and less lucrative duties; alternatively, duties may be "bid" for, or allocated for example on the basis of seniority. In some cases, buses may be used for more than one duty in a day: either the same vehicle is rented out to two separate drivers, or the principal renter sub-lets his vehicle to another driver. Many operators allow drivers to decide how many trips are to be made, and the times of the trips; this is not always satisfactory unless there is some means by which the rental charge varies in proportion to the kilometres operated. Drivers may be allocated a different bus each day, but it is more common for each to drive the same bus regularly; sometimes a replacement bus is provided when the regular vehicle is undergoing maintenance or repair, but it is more usual for drivers to be idle at such times.

The application of the system is sometimes more formal and complex. In a typical arrangement applicable to long distance services in China, for example, the driver has a contract with the operating company to drive the same bus for three years, on a route decided by the company. He pays a rental charge on a per-trip basis, determined according to the type and age of bus, and the route. He also pays for the fuel used, and a maintenance charge calculated by the company; if actual costs incurred in maintenance exceed this charge the driver must pay the difference. In some cases, as an incentive to careful driving, in addition to the fact that it will be in the driver's own interest to ensure that his vehicle downtime is minimised, any unspent funds from the maintenance and accident provision are returned to the driver at the end of each year; this practice is relatively uncommon. Drivers select their own conductors, and pay them at specified company rates. Only one driver is responsible for the bus; if he is on leave or sick, he will find a replacement, and if two drivers are required on long journeys, the second driver is selected by the first, and paid by him in accordance with company rates.

In some applications of the setoran system, more commonly in conventional bus rather than paratransit operation, drivers are paid a salary, or retainer, in addition to their share of the revenue. This should not normally be necessary, although it may be considered justifiable in certain circumstances, for example to compensate for periods when a vehicle is out of service for any reason outside the driver's control. There may also be a requirement for standby drivers, or drivers for special duties which cannot be covered by the setoran system, which may necessitate some salaried drivers on an operator's payroll. Where a salary is paid, the setoran charge is higher than it would otherwise be. In another variation of the system, drivers and conductors are not paid salaries, but receive a percentage, typically around 10%, of revenue collected on their respective buses, to be divided between them; out of this they may have to purchase the fuel, to avoid the problem of theft of fuel from the vehicle owner. However, such a system is not always an effective deterrent against theft of revenue, since it depends on the honesty of conductors to pay in all fare revenue collected, and the temptation remains for conductors to misappropriate some of the money due to the operator.

In effect, under the setoran system the driver becomes a businessman, operating a transport service under an informal franchise arrangement, in accordance with basic requirements stipulated by the bus owner. His rewards are directly related to his efficiency in operating the service, taking care of his vehicle, and controlling his employees, if any. If the revenue is insufficient on some days to cover all costs, the driver must make up the difference; over time, he should earn sufficient to make a reasonable living. The risk of the driver defaulting on a payment can be eliminated by requiring a deposit equivalent to the charge for a rental period, and if a driver fails to make the due payment on any day the owner can refuse to release the vehicle to him on the following day. This sanction can also be applied in the event of any other breach of conditions, such as failing to operate on the correct route.

Since there is much more direct control over revenue, and the vehicle owner is guaranteed a fixed return, the setoran system eliminates the need for all revenue control systems, including revenue inspectors, ticket machine control and waybill processing staff, and a significant part of the personnel function. In the case of large operators, officers may make occasional checks on buses to detect malpractices such as overloading or operating off route, but are not required to check tickets. The system is sometimes regarded as an abdication of management responsibility, but in fact it reallocates part of the management function and responsibilities to the crews themselves. Provided that adequate controls are in place to prevent abuse, this form of management can be highly effective.

There are several disadvantages, however. Although it is effective in ensuring that all fares are collected, and provides drivers with an incentive to work productively, the system encourages various malpractices by crews in an attempt to maximise their incomes. These include racing to pick up passengers, obstructing other vehicles, overloading, overcharging passengers, refusal to carry passengers who are entitled to concessionary fares if a full load of full-fare paying passengers is available, and failing to operate the full route where demand tapers off towards the end. Multiple journey tickets are not normally possible with the setoran system, although other means of discounting tickets may be possible.

There may be a tendency, where the vehicle is hired for a specified number of journeys, for drivers to operate additional journeys: although the driver pays for additional fuel used, the owner must pay for the additional wear and tear to the vehicle. The vehicle owner does not benefit from any increase in demand, but receives broadly the same income per vehicle regardless of the volume of traffic carried: if demand increases, the owner should ideally be in a position to benefit from at least a proportion of the additional revenue, to help compensate for increased wear and tear and, more importantly, to fund fleet expansion to meet the increased demand.

Finally, under the setoran system, there is very little management information regarding passengers carried and revenue earned, as is obtainable under conventional operating systems; thus there is no ready means of monitoring demand, and no sound basis for service planning and development unless comprehensive surveys are undertaken regularly and frequently. In practice it is rare for operators to carry out such work; some transport regulatory authorities do so from time to time, but most planning tends to be undertaken as part of externally funded transport planning studies.

The setoran system is becoming increasingly common in developing countries throughout the world, and is almost universal among private sector operators on local services in both urban and rural areas. It is particularly common in situations where there is minimal regulation, or where regulations are poorly enforced. It can also be applicable in a regulated situation, and indeed some regulation is desirable to minimise the negative aspects of the system. In particular, this requires effective enforcement of the rules governing driver behaviour. Both the traffic police, and the owners and operators' associations or co-operatives where applicable, have important roles to play in this respect: the police should be vigilant in dealing with infringements of traffic regulations, and the operators and co-operatives should enforce rules regarding operational matters such as overcharging passengers or failing to operate the authorised route. It is also essential that there is machinery to ensure that public transport services are constantly monitored and updated in accordance with changes in passenger demand patterns.

INDIVIDUAL PUBLIC TRANSPORT MODES

There are certain operating systems which are applicable only to taxis and other forms of individual public transport which do not operate on fixed routes. Taxis may cruise the streets, to be hailed by prospective passengers from the kerb, or they may wait for passengers to come to them at designated taxi stands or ranks; these are usually found in the central business district, the commercial area, near the main shopping centres and railway stations and airports as well as at the larger hotels. Sometimes there is a distinction between cabs which may cruise and those which can only be booked, for example in London there are "black cabs", which may cruise or wait on ranks, and "minicabs", which may be used only by passengers who book their journeys in advance.

Often the method of operation is determined by law, which varies from country to country. In some countries cruising is not permitted, and taxis must await their passengers at designated ranks. Taxis are sometimes allocated to specific ranks, and may not pick up fares at any other point; after completing each journey they must return direct to their allotted points, although in some cases, if a return passenger is available wishing to go to that precise point he may be carried. Such restrictions can result in high proportion of empty running, and will increase the number of taxis required to meet demand, resulting therefore in increased congestion and reduced income for taxi operators; on the other hand an excessive number of cruising taxis can be equally if not more wasteful.

Taxi firms in some cities operate a radio system, whereby customers may telephone the taxi control centre, which then contacts an available taxi by radio and directs it to where it is required. One firm in Kingston estimated that 80-90% of its business was by telephone. Some taxi firms have a significant number of regular passengers, who may enjoy reduced fares and credit facilities; these include companies which use taxis regularly for transporting their staff, and commuters who have individual arrangements with the operator for their daily travel to and from work.

Virtually all individual public transport modes in developing countries operate under the setoran principle, with drivers meeting all operating expenses and paying a fixed sum to the owner each day.

10

VEHICLE DESIGN AND FLEET PLANNING

The vehicle fleet is the primary tool of any transport operator, and appropriate selection, maintenance and management procedures are therefore vital. The various public transport vehicle types were described in Chapter 2; this chapter discusses the selection of vehicles and planning and management of vehicle fleets; maintenance is dealt with in Chapter 11.

DESIGN CONSIDERATIONS

Selection of the appropriate vehicle from the wide variety of types, makes and models available in the market can make the difference between success and failure of a transport operation. The choice of vehicle will vary according to circumstances, and a number of factors must be taken into account in determining the general configuration required, before drawing up a detailed specification, and selection of make and model. The principal considerations are:

- Purpose
- Size and capacity
- Safety
- Comfort
- Speed of loading
- Reliability
- Maintenance
- Operating conditions and practices
- Regulations
- Requirements for disabled passengers
- Cost

Purpose

Most public transport vehicles are purchased for a particular type of operation and should be specified accordingly. A vehicle which is ideal for one type of operation may be quite unsuitable for another: buses designed specifically for use on urban services, for example, will very have different features from those used on long-distance or rural services or for carrying tourists. Buses for urban services will normally be designed to carry maximum passenger loads, and in many cases a significant proportion of passengers will be required to stand; seats are normally basic, offering minimum comfort since most journeys are relatively short. Little or no luggage accommodation may be required. There may be several entrances and exits to the vehicle, with power-operated doors, to facilitate loading and unloading, and to minimise time spent at bus stops. For the same reason, and also to cater for disabled passengers, an increasing number of city buses are constructed with low floor and step heights. Mechanically, city buses may be fitted with engines giving good acceleration, and other features such as automatic transmission to improve performance and to make the driver's task easier in congested traffic conditions; fare collection and ticket issuing or validating equipment may be installed in the vehicle, particularly if no conductor is carried.

Buses for rural services have different requirements: luggage accommodation is invariably important, since in many countries buses are regularly used for carrying goods to and from market as accompanied freight; most passengers will be travelling for relatively long distances, and while standing passengers are often carried, the majority will require seating. Road conditions in rural areas are often difficult, and vehicles must be sufficiently robust to withstand them. Buses for long distance services normally require seating for all passengers: in this sector of the market standards of service tend to range from very basic to high quality; the latter may require vehicles equipped with air conditioning, adjustable seating, video equipment, toilet and refreshment facilities, particularly where suitable roadside facilities are not available. Buses for tourists normally incorporate most of the features required for high quality long distance services, and may require increased luggage accommodation. Buses used exclusively for the transport of schoolchildren may be specified for the purpose, and need not necessarily be identical to those built for public transport services, but for safety reasons it is normally appropriate for PSV Construction and Use and driver licensing regulations to apply. Many school buses are built to standard bus specifications, although in the case of buses carrying small children, it is usually possible to increase the seating capacity by reducing the spacing between seats.

Vehicle specifications must take all these requirements into account, although it may be necessary to prioritise or compromise in the interests of reducing overall cost. As discussed later in this chapter, a vehicle may be downgraded during its life from one type of operation to another, in which case the specification should allow for this; as far as possible, its original specification should facilitate any modifications necessary for the change of use, without detracting significantly from its suitability in its initial use.

Some vehicles may be used for different types of work at different times. For example it is common practice in some countries for city buses to be used on long distance services at weekends; this improves utilisation of the vehicles, since demand for urban transport normally decreases at weekends, while there is additional demand for long distance services to cater for urban dwellers travelling to the provinces or rural areas. Some operators include a number of "dual purpose" vehicles in their fleets, incorporating features of both urban and long-distance buses; often these are merely city buses with extra seating accommodation, or slightly more comfortable seating.

It is important to bear in mind that any features incorporated in the specification of a vehicle which are not required for its main purpose not only add unnecessarily to the initial cost, but will increase the weight of the vehicle, and therefore its fuel consumption, and will increase maintenance costs over the life of the vehicle.

Size and Capacity

The various considerations regarding vehicle size and capacity are discussed in Chapter 2.

Safety

Safety is an important consideration although, as discussed in Chapter 17, there must be a degree of compromise between safety and operational practicality; there is always an element of risk in any form of travel, and a realistic objective is to minimise this risk without inhibiting the operation of a useful and viable public service. The principal aspects of safety in this context are the safety of passengers when boarding and alighting from the vehicle, and when travelling. Safety when boarding and alighting is maximised by having a single entrance/exit doorway, under the direct supervision of the driver or conductor, if one is carried, with a power-operated door controlled by the driver or conductor, ideally with an interlock mechanism to prevent it from being opened while the vehicle is moving. Positioning of the doorway immediately behind, rather than ahead of the front axle, is sometimes preferable from a safety point of view since it reduces the risk of passengers falling under the front wheels, but can reduce the driver's view of the doorway significantly, and may result in loss of passenger capacity. Many city buses in developing countries do not have doors, or often, if doors are fitted they are not used, sometimes because they are defective due to poor maintenance, or because large numbers of standing passengers on the steps or in the doorways prevent them from being closed. This can result in accidents involving passengers attempting to board or alight while the bus is moving, or falling from the vehicle between stops.

A bus with a lower floor, and therefore with fewer steps for passengers to negotiate when boarding and alighting, is also less susceptible to accidents involving passengers falling.

Safety while travelling is maximised when all passengers are seated, and wearing seat belts. Seat belts are rarely fitted to buses, however, especially those used for short journeys. On some long-distance or tourist buses, belts are fitted to exposed seats such as those at the front or in the centre at the rear; very few have belts fitted to all seats. There has been much debate as to whether this should be compulsory; the fitting of belts, and particularly their maintenance, is costly, and enforcing their use is often difficult. Three-point seat belts are difficult to fit to bus seats, especially seats designed for three passengers, while lap belts are less effective; it is also difficult to maintain seat belts in serviceable condition. The cost-effectiveness of seat belts is questionable, and where funds are limited it is arguable that the considerable cost of fitting and maintaining belts in every seat would be more usefully spent on other safety measures.

Standing passengers, and roving conductors if these are carried, are at risk, especially on buses driven at high speeds. Even on a bus where all passengers can be seated, passengers must normally move about the vehicle while it is moving, when approaching or leaving stops; it is rarely practical, except on long distance services, for a bus to remain stationary at a stop until all passengers are seated, or to allow passengers wishing to leave the vehicle to remain in their seats until it has come to a complete stop. The risk can be reduced by adequate provision of grabrails, straps and padded surfaces where appropriate, and elimination of sharp edges in the vehicle interior.

The arrangement of the staircase on a double decker is important: if the staircase ascends towards the rear of the bus, there is a danger of passengers or conductors using the stairs to be thrown down the stairs under sudden deceleration; a staircase ascending towards the front of the bus is much safer. The way in which a bus is driven obviously has a major bearing on all aspects of safety, and vehicles should be designed to be as easy to drive as possible, although good driver training and discipline will always be essential. Where standing passengers are carried it may be desirable to reduce the maximum governed road speed of the bus, but this may reduce vehicle productivity.

Comfort

Passengers' requirements regarding comfort vary considerably, and are partly determined by journey length. Upholstered seats are generally desirable for journeys of over thirty minutes but for shorter journeys plastic fibreglass or wooden slatted seats are usually adequate. Passengers may be prepared to stand for short journeys but not for long ones; they often object more strongly to having to stand for long periods while a bus is waiting to depart from a terminal than when it is en route, and therefore short turn-round times are generally desirable when a high proportion of passengers must stand.

For longer journeys and premium-quality urban services a higher level of comfort is required. This is sometimes achieved on urban services merely by limiting the number of passengers carried in a standard vehicle, but it is more common for a higher standard of seating, such as seats with adjustable back rests, to be provided, and sometimes additional features such as air conditioning, curtains to reduce glare from the sun, and taped music or video equipment. Many buses used for premium-quality long-distance services include, in addition, on-board toilet and refreshment facilities, and even fully reclining sleeper seats.

Speed of loading

The speed of loading and unloading of vehicles is often an important consideration, particularly on urban services with frequent stops. Where the turnover of passengers is high, journey times, and therefore the number of vehicles required to operate a service, may be reduced through minimising loading and unloading times. These are influenced by vehicle capacity, the proportion of seated to standing accommodation, the number and dimensions of doorways, entrance and exit step heights and the number of steps; these factors have safety and comfort implications, and there are trade-offs between them.

Reliability

The level of reliability required in a vehicle depends to a large extent on its use. For example, a refuse truck need not be as reliable as an ambulance or fire appliance; in the case of a bus service, some passengers will be able or prepared to pay a higher fare for a more reliable service, while others will tolerate lower standards of reliability for a lower fare. Reliability also affects operating costs and total fleet requirement. Although reliability is very much dependent on maintenance standards, the quality of the vehicle is also important: in general terms, the higher the level of reliability required, the higher will be the cost of the vehicle.

Maintenance

Some buses are easier to maintain than others, and as a result are subject to less downtime and lower maintenance costs. The frequency of maintenance interventions, ease of access to components requiring frequent attention, the need for special tools or skills for certain tasks, and the standard of maintenance facilities and skill levels which are available are all significant in this respect.

Operating conditions and practices

Any vehicle must be compatible with prevailing operating conditions and standards, including those of driving and maintenance. For example, a city bus with low floor and rear engine may be inappropriate if there are numerous speed humps or where road conditions are very poor, while a rural bus operated regularly on unsurfaced roads must be specified to minimise problems of dust ingress to the engine. These factors will dictate the type of suspension required, robustness of bodywork, ground clearance, air filtration and other design considerations.

Metal corrosion is a serious problem in some areas, such as humid coastal regions, and if this is the case body components in particular should be treated to minimise the problem. The undertaking's own working practices must be taken into account: for example, if interiors are normally cleaned by hosing them down, the design must incorporate adequate drainage and measures to prevent corrosion of bodywork by wash water. Certain components may be particularly vulnerable to local conditions, and the design should cater for these, through specification of more robust components, or by ensuring that they are easily accessible for repair or replacement.

Regulations

Every country has vehicle construction and use regulations, as discussed in Chapter 19. Vehicle specifications must conform fully with all relevant regulations, and in the case of vehicles operated on international services, with the regulations of all countries concerned.

Requirements for disabled passengers

There is increasing awareness internationally of the transport requirements of disabled people. The issue is becoming an emotive one, with the increasingly widely held view that disabled people should be able to lead as normal a life as possible, and therefore should not be excluded from transport services which are available to the able-bodied. This is having a major impact on the design of public transport vehicles. Certain features to benefit the disabled can be provided relatively easily, such as high-visibility handrails and markings on the edges of steps to assist passengers who are visually handicapped. However, other features are very costly to provide.

Access to conventional transport vehicles is usually difficult, and sometimes impossible, for people with physical disabilities, particularly those requiring wheel chairs for mobility. In developed countries in particular, measures are being introduced to address these problems, including legislation making it compulsory for virtually all new public transport vehicles to be accessible to people using wheelchairs; this often includes taxis as well as buses and trains. In the United Kingdom, for example, all new buses carrying more than 22 passengers on local or scheduled bus services will have to be fully accessible within the next ten years. "Accessibility" generally means that passengers in wheel chairs are able to propel their wheel chairs onto the vehicle without assistance; this requires specially designed vehicles and often infrastructure also. Buses are available with low, flat floors with locations where wheel chairs may be secured, and which have a "kneeling" capability so that the vehicle may be lowered at bus stops to reduce the step height sufficiently for a wheel chair to enter the vehicle. Long distance buses, with higher floors, are available with wheel chair lifts and ramps. "Accessible" buses are of benefit not only to the disabled, but also to other passengers such as mothers carrying young children, and facilitate boarding, alighting and movement within the vehicle for all passengers.

However, vehicles which are fully compliant with these regulations are expensive to purchase, operate and maintain, and unless bus operators are subsidised, the additional cost must be borne by all passengers. Where incomes are low, this may be an intolerable burden, and compliance with such stringent requirements may not be commercially viable. There is a danger that the introduction of similar legislation in developing countries would result in many conventional bus services being abandoned, and replaced illegally with non-compliant vehicles.

Other practical difficulties include reliability problems with special equipment such as lifts and ramps, because of infrequent use, misuse by inadequately trained drivers, and their complexity which may lead to maintenance problems. A further complication in many developing countries is that the roads and footpaths are often incompatible with fully accessible vehicles, while the footpaths themselves may be unsuitable for the use of wheelchairs, so that investment in such vehicles will be largely wasted. Unfortunately, at present universal provision for disabled passengers is an unaffordable luxury in most developing countries.

Cost

The most suitable vehicle for any public transport application is normally the one which adequately carries out the tasks for which it was purchased, to an acceptable standard of safety and reliability, at the lowest whole-life cost per kilometre. To be more precise, the criterion should be whole-life cost per passenger-kilometre, but it is assumed that by this stage in the selection process the most appropriate vehicle capacity will already have been determined. The whole-life cost comprises the initial capital cost plus all operating costs incurred over the life of the vehicle, less the final proceeds from its disposal; vehicle operating costs in this context include the cost of fuel and tyres, and all maintenance, both parts and labour, but not the costs of the crews.

A problem with the application of whole-life costing in the vehicle selection process is that it is difficult to predict the total cost over the life of a vehicle before it is purchased. Good management information is invaluable in this situation: if accurate records of expenditure and vehicle utilisation are available for a specific model, it is possible to estimate with reasonable accuracy what the total cost will be over a vehicle's life, and the time when it should be replaced. In the case of a new model this is not possible, but large fleet operators will know from experience the relevant characteristics of various vehicle makes and types, and major components such as engines, gearboxes and axles. In addition, information in respect of other fleets is often available, and full use should be made of such data, although great care must be taken to allow for differences in operating conditions.

The relative costs and benefits of the various alternatives must be fully considered before a purchasing decision is taken. While some options have little impact on cost, others are expensive: for example a low-floor, rear-engined city bus will cost considerably more to purchase than a bus built on a truck-derived chassis. In many cases, a chassis with a higher initial cost, provided that it is correctly specified for the type of operation and prevailing conditions, will be more reliable, more fuel-efficient and cheaper to maintain, and therefore will have a lower total life cost than one with a lower capital cost. An operation requiring highly sophisticated vehicles will naturally require vehicles with relatively high capital cost.

DESIGN OPTIONS

In the case of conventional buses, there are many different vehicle configuration and design options, each of which is appropriate in different circumstances. The following options must be considered:

- Single or double deck
- Rigid or articulated
- Dimensions
- Proportion of seated to standing passengers
- Door configuration
- Floor height
- Heating and ventilation
- Luggage accommodation
- Number of axles
- Engine type and position
- Alternative fuels
- Transmission
- Suspension
- Other mechanical options
- Body construction
- Detail design features
- Manufacturer and model

Single or double deck, rigid or articulated

The characteristics of single-deck and double-deck, and rigid and articulated single deck buses of various sizes and capacities, and their relative advantages and disadvantages, are discussed in Chapter 2.

Dimensions

Most bus manufacturers offer a range of bus sizes, and the most appropriate dimensions must be selected for the circumstances, as discussed in Chapter 2.

Proportion of seated to standing passengers

On long-distance services and premium urban services, it is normal for all passengers to be seated, but on the majority of urban services it is customary for some passengers to have to stand for all or part of their journeys. Some buses are designed to carry relatively few standing passengers, so that except at peak periods, all passengers are able to sit; others are designed for the majority of passengers to stand, at all times of the day. The principal advantage of carrying a high proportion of standing passengers is that the capacity of a bus is increased substantially; approximately six standing passengers can be accommodated per square metre, compared with fewer than three per square metre seated. In general terms, the shorter the average passenger journey length, the higher the proportion of standing passengers which is acceptable; there is a similar relationship with fare levels: the higher the fare, the greater the number of passengers who expect to be able to sit.

The maximum number of seated passengers is achieved with a 3+2 seating arrangement (i.e. seats for three passengers on one side of the aisle and for two passengers on the other). This configuration is an effective means of maximising the carrying capacity of buses built to a width of 2.5 metres or more, and can provide up to seventy seats in a full sized rigid single-decker and 120 in a double-decker, with in addition up to 25 standing passengers carried in a full-length bus. It results in somewhat cramped accommodation but is usually satisfactory for short to medium length journeys, and in fact is common for "standard" class long distance services in many countries. With 2+2 seating the number of seats in a full-length single-decker will be reduced by about fifteen, but the standing capacity may be doubled, giving a net increase in capacity of approximately ten to fifteen passengers. 2+1 or 1+1 configurations will give a much higher proportion of standing to seated passengers; the latter arrangement will give a capacity of up to 120 passengers in a rigid single-decker.

If only young children are to be carried, as in the case of buses used solely for the carriage of schoolchildren, it may be possible to increase seating capacity by up to 20% by fitting smaller seats and reducing the space between them. In some countries it is permissible by law for three children, up to a specified age, to be carried in each pair of adult seats. The practicality of this rule depends partly on national characteristics, and the age limit for such seating should be set so that the combined average weight of three children does not exceed the combined average weight of two adults. Misuse of the rule can lead to overloading, however, and it is usually more practical to use buses with 3+2 seating.

Door configuration

There are several options regarding the number of entrances and exits, and their sizes and positions. Additional and wider doorways can result in reduced loading and unloading times, and therefore enable operating speeds to be increased, but at the expense of reduced seating capacity, and the provision of additional doorways may have negative safety implications, especially where no conductor is carried. A balance must be struck between these considerations, and this will vary depending on the nature of the operation.

Multiple doorways are relatively common on city buses, although these are not always necessary. In some cities, there is a high turnover of passengers along each bus route due to a high proportion of intermediate traffic; in others, the majority of passengers travel to or from the central area, with little or no intermediate traffic. There may be only a small number of stops where significant numbers of passengers are boarding and alighting simultaneously. Where turnover of passengers is high, and therefore large numbers of passengers both board and disembark simultaneously at most stops, it is usually desirable to use buses with separate entry and exit doorways; but with a low turnover a single doorway will normally suffice. The method of fare collection is also relevant in this context: for example, if all fares are paid before passengers board, several doors may be provided, all of which may be used for both entry and exit.

On long distance or rural services a single doorway is normally appropriate, since stops are relatively infrequent, and boarding times represent a small proportion of total travelling time. In some countries it is a legal requirement for all buses over a certain size, including those used on long-distance services, to have two doorways, resulting in loss of seating capacity, usually unnecessarily. Some large tourist buses used on tours where passengers disembark at several points for sightseeing have more than one doorway, since the time taken for fifty or more passengers to disembark and re-embark through a single doorway can be considerable, especially when a large number of the passengers are elderly, as is often the case.

The doorways may be in various positions. On large modern buses with a single doorway, this is normally located forward of the front axle, alongside the driver. This enables the driver to supervise passengers boarding and disembarking, and operate the doors as required, relieving the conductor of this task; an entrance in this position is virtually essential if the driver is responsible for collecting fares, since passengers must pass the driver when boarding the bus. It also gives the driver a clear view to the nearside when the bus is moving, unless, as is often the case in developing countries, the bus is overloaded to the extent that passengers are carried in the entrance; this is a dangerous practice. A disadvantage with this doorway position is that passengers may fall under the front wheels of the bus when boarding or disembarking, and precautions are necessary to prevent this, although in fact such occurrences are rare. In some countries it is not permitted to have the entrance in this position for safety reasons, but the justification for this precaution is dubious. Where a conductor is carried the entrance door may be positioned elsewhere. A centre doorway has the advantage that no passenger has to walk more than half the length of the bus; if the doorway is at the extreme front or rear, a passenger seated at the opposite end may have difficulty in reaching the exit, particularly if the bus is crowded. Some buses have only a single doorway at the extreme rear, but there are few benefits from this arrangement, other than that a falling passenger can never be run over by the bus unless it is reversing.

If two or more doorways are provided, a further option is whether to permit passengers to both board and disembark through any doorway, or to impose a "flow" system whereby passengers enter the bus by one doorway and leave by another. The former minimises time spent at stops, but is not practical where fares are collected by the driver. If a conductor is carried, he or she must be able to move around the bus quickly enough to collect fares from passengers using all doorways; this is difficult if the bus is crowded. For very busy services, operators often employ two conductors per bus, or sometimes three where three doorways are provided, so that each can be responsible for collecting fares from passengers using a different doorway.

The position of street furniture must also be considered: for example, at some bus stops there are railings at the edge of the kerb to prevent queuing passengers from spilling into the roadway, and a frequent problem where buses with multiple doorways are used is that some of the doorways are obstructed by the railings. Design of buses and bus stops should be compatible.

Where automatic fare collection equipment is fitted, machines may be provided at each entrance for maximum effectiveness, but the cost of the additional equipment must be weighed against the time saved at stops, and the marketing benefit from improved passenger convenience. If passengers are required to flow through the vehicle, and where fares are collected by the driver, they are normally required to enter by the front doorway and leave by a centre or rear exit; if there are only two doorways, a centre exit is preferable, as explained above. The provision of two exits will facilitate passenger movement; one of the most satisfactory flow arrangements is for passengers to enter through a doorway at the centre of the vehicle, with a choice of exits at the extreme front and rear of the bus. A flow system requires a certain amount of discipline, making it impractical in some countries. Where fares are collected by the driver, or by a conductor seated by the entrance, a considerable proportion of revenue may be lost if passengers are able to board by the exit doorway and avoid payment of their fares; for this reason multiple doorways are not used in some cities even though they would enable a faster service to be provided.

The width of the doorway has a significant effect on boarding and alighting times. Doorways wide enough for two passengers to pass through simultaneously are particularly efficient on urban services where there is a high turnover of passengers; time spent at stops may be reduced by up to half if passengers may board two at a time, or if passengers boarding and disembarking are able to pass in the doorway. The chassis design may restrict doorway widths; on many chassis the front overhang is insufficient to allow a double width doorway ahead of the front axle, while with many front-engined chassis the intrusion of the engine restricts the effective doorway width.

Most double deck buses are constructed with sufficient front overhang to allow a double width doorway ahead of the front axle, and there is the option of additional doorways within the wheelbase, or behind the rear axle, although the latter is uncommon. A doorway at the extreme rear of the bus is more common in older front-engined double-deck designs, such as is found in many cities in India and Bangladesh. With this arrangement there is often no door, and the door opening extends across part of the rear of the bus, which enables several passengers to board and disembark simultaneously; this is an advantage on busy urban services, but the open rear platform has adverse safety implications.

There are various types of doors which may be fitted. The two basic options are manual and power operation. Manually-operated doors are normally operated by the conductor, but may be operated by the driver through a linkage to a lever beside his seat. On some buses used for long-distance or tourist services, the driver must leave his seat to open and close the door. Sliding doors are common for minibuses but rare on larger vehicles: they are prone to jamming and heavy to operate manually. Hinged leaf doors are common for buses used on services with infrequent stops: they are invariably operated manually. Inward-opening leaf doors are generally safer since they will not open under pressure from passengers leaning against them, although they enable the bus to be driven with the door open; they may be slightly more complex in their design than outward opening doors since they must clear the internal steps. Doors may be powered by electricity or compressed air. The most common form of power-operated doors are folding, or "jack-knife" doors, in which two or more leaves fold together, or "glider" doors, with two leaves which separate and, when fully open, rest at each side of the doorway, at right-angles to the side of the bus; where the entrance is relatively narrow a single leaf glider door may be practical. Also common, particularly for urban services but becoming increasingly widely used for long-distance buses and coaches, are "plug" doors, with one or two leaves, which open outwards but remain parallel to the side of the bus, so that when fully open they rest flat against the exterior panels. Plug doors increase interior space adjacent to the doorways, and reduce the risk of injury to standing passengers as they are opened and closed, but may strike passengers waiting to board, and may also foul street furniture or kerbs, especially fitted to buses with low step heights, or where the kerbs at bus stops have been built up.

Some buses are fitted with turnstiles at the entry or exit, or both, usually to facilitate fare collection and revenue control as described in Chapter 9; the positioning of these turnstiles can be critical. The entry turnstile should normally be located at a sufficient distance from the entrance door to enable passengers to board the vehicle, and queue to pay their fares to the conductor, or to operate the coin box, after the bus has left the stop: accommodation for approximately twenty passengers on the entrance side of the turnstile will normally be sufficient on a full-sized bus.

In the case of buses operated exclusively for the transport of schoolchildren, speed of loading and unloading is less important than in the case of public service vehicles, and safety is usually of greater significance; a single passenger door is therefore normally appropriate. Unless an attendant is carried at all times to supervise the children, the door should be controlled by the driver, and fully within his view; if the door is positioned ahead of the front axle this will provide optimum visibility for the driver, but measures should be taken to ensure that the vehicle does not move while the door is open, in order to minimise the risk of accidents to children while boarding or disembarking.

Floor height

Bus chassis are available with a range of floor heights. The lower the height of the floor of the passenger compartment, the smaller the number of entrance steps required; this makes access easier, and reduces boarding times, while by elimination of steps in the doorways, more floor space is available for standing passengers, and the capacity penalty of additional doorways is reduced. On the other hand, a lower floor height results in increased intrusion into the passenger compartment by wheel arches and large chassis components such as the engine and gearbox, which reduces passenger capacity, and in particular the number of seats which can be provided.

Low-floor buses are becoming increasingly common in many developed countries, often as a result of legislation setting standards of access to public transport for people with disabilities. A bus with a low floor is generally more complex mechanically, and therefore more expensive, although as they are becoming more widely used their cost is tending to decrease. Of particular relevance to developing countries is the fact that the limited ground clearance can create problems on rough roads.

Where a low floor is not essential, it is becoming increasingly common for bus bodies to be constructed with the floor raised above the chassis frame sufficiently to provide a completely flat floor, with no intrusions. This improves passenger comfort by eliminating legroom restrictions in the area of the wheel arches, and facilitates cleaning of the floor, while the space for luggage accommodation under the floor is increased; a high floor is sometimes specified for buses used on long-distance and tourist services both for this reason and for the improved passenger visibility provided. However, a higher floor increases the height of the entrance steps, while the additional structural framework increases the weight of the vehicle.

Heating and ventilation

Ventilation and heating are important considerations, depending on the nature of the climate; in most developing countries high temperatures are usually the greater problem, so that good ventilation or air conditioning are required, but where both high and low temperatures are experienced, means of both heating and cooling are required. For standard buses in hot climates it is normally sufficient to provide opening windows for ventilation. Horizontally sliding windows are normally the most practical; the sliding portion may be the full depth of the window, so that when it is fully open ventilation is provided through nearly half of the window aperture. Alternatively, part of the window may be fixed, with the upper or lower portion (typically between one third and a half) able to slide.

In very hot climates it is usually necessary for full-depth sliding windows to be provided in all openings along both sides of the vehicle except where it is necessary to provide fixed "push-out" panes for emergency exits. Front windscreens may also feature opening portions although this is uncommon in modern designs; however, it is often possible to provide opening flaps in the panelling above or below the windscreens to provide ventilation. Opening panels in the roof are also very effective in releasing hot air from the interior.

For premium quality services air conditioning is now common; this adds to the capital and operating costs of the vehicle, and increases the maintenance workload. Air conditioning can increase fuel consumption by up to 20%, especially on services with frequent stops, when the constant opening of the doors allows cool air to escape. In difficult operating conditions reliability of the equipment may be a problem, and it is therefore often wise to install opening windows to provide ventilation in the event of failure of the air conditioning system; such windows should be lockable to prevent them from being opened when the air conditioning system is operating. Tinted window glass and a light coloured roof (preferably white) also help to reduce interior heat. Where necessary, heaters which utilise heat from the engine cooling system are adequate for most purposes.

Luggage accommodation

Long distance and rural buses in developing countries require adequate accommodation for the large volumes of luggage and unaccompanied freight which are often carried. Buses with roof-mounted luggage racks are commonly used for long-distance and rural bus services in many developing countries. However, they have disadvantages, particularly on poor road surfaces. Loads carried can be very heavy, sometimes as much as three tons, and this weight must be carried by the body frames; the dynamic loads incurred through operation on uneven road surfaces can cause the frames to fracture, requiring major expenditure, and considerable down-time, for repair.

Two practical alternatives are to carry freight in a separate trailer towed by the bus, or in a specially constructed freight compartment within the vehicle. Freight compartments may be underneath the floor, but the necessary structural framework and resulting high floor are not always suitable for operation on rough roads. It is normally more practical to partition off the rear portion of the passenger saloon as a freight compartment, and provide access through external doors at the side or rear. A disadvantage of this arrangement is a reduction in seating capacity, typically of up to 15%, but this capacity may not be required for all of the time, and experience in a wide range of applications has proved that the benefits of reduced maintenance costs and improved availability from using freight compartments instead of roof racks is greater than the lost revenue due to the reduced passenger capacity. Advantages are load security, protection from dust and rain damage, ease of loading and unloading, and improved vehicle safety due to the lower centre of gravity than is achieved with a roof rack.

Trailers have limited application, and are generally appropriate only where large volumes of unaccompanied freight are carried in addition to passengers' luggage, and on roads which are reasonably good. Tourist buses used on extended tours involving overnight stops will also require substantial luggage accommodation, but those used only for day tours will require space for hand luggage only. Buses used on urban services normally require minimal luggage accommodation.

Number of axles

Rigid buses may be built with two or more axles. A two-axle configuration is more common, but for larger and heavier vehicles it is often necessary to add a third, and in some cases even a fourth axle so that legal axle loading limits are not exceeded. Buses with three axles normally have two axles at the rear; it is becoming increasingly common for one of the rear axles to be steerable, to reduce tyre wear and improve the vehicle's handling characteristics.

Some buses are built with twin steering axles at the front; this provides better weight distribution in the case of front-engined buses, and has a safety advantage in that the vehicle is more stable in the event of a front tyre failure. Articulated buses have three or four axles, with two in the forward section, and one or two in the rear section.

Engine type and position

A wide range of engine options is available. A larger capacity engine may be more expensive to purchase but with the appropriate drive train is often more economical to operate and maintain than one of lower capacity. Many modern bus engines are turbocharged to increase the potential power output of an engine of a given size. As well as enabling smaller and lighter engines to be used, turbochargers are beneficial when operating at high altitudes above sea level by compensating for the lower atmospheric pressure; on the other hand turbocharged engines may create maintenance difficulties where skills are limited. If fuel is expensive, fuel economy is an important consideration when specifying an engine, and this is often achieved through the use of smaller engines as well as by minimising gross vehicle weights.

A front-mounted vertical engine is relatively easy to access for maintenance, and in a hot climate is less susceptible to overheating than one mounted elsewhere; however it will restrict the width of a front entrance and is unsatisfactory in a low floor design. An underfloor engine mounted horizontally amidships or at the rear maximises interior space but may be vulnerable on very rough road surfaces, or if it is necessary to drive through water; it requires a high floor level, although with a rear engine this need only be at the rear. A vertical rear engine, mounted transversely across the chassis, provides good access for maintenance and enables a low floor to be provided throughout the vehicle, but reduces available interior space and requires a complicated driveline, which can cause reliability problems; a longitudinally mounted vertical rear engine, while more simple mechanically, requires considerably more interior space.

Developments in engine technology intended to reduce exhaust emissions have resulted in increased fuel consumption. For example, fuel consumption of engines built to "Euro II" specification is between 10% and 15% more than equivalent "Euro I" engines, while "Euro III" engines are expected to consume even more. This can be offset to some extent by using smaller engines, but at the cost of reduced power and increased maintenance costs.

Alternative fuels

As discussed in Chapter 2, there are various alternative fuels available although diesel power is most common for large buses, and both petrol and diesel are options in smaller vehicles. Electric power is an alternative, but in practice trolleybuses, taking power from overhead cables, is the only practical application for mass public transport at present. Diesel power is generally the most appropriate; trolleybuses have advantages in very intensive urban operation, but operators must consider the potential disadvantages. Mass-produced petrol engines for small vehicles are relatively cheap and easy to maintain, but fuel consumption is higher than for diesel engines.

Transmission

The choice between manual and fully- or semi-automatic transmission must take into account the nature of the traffic conditions, drivers' and mechanics' skills, and relative costs; fuel consumption is invariably higher with automatic transmission, and some more complex transmission systems are difficult to maintain. In an urban environment it is becoming increasingly common to specify automatic transmission for buses in order to make the driver's task easier, but manual transmission is normally more appropriate for rural and long-distance services.

In an urban operation, good acceleration is usually more important than a high maximum speed; therefore vehicles should be relatively low geared; the reverse may apply on long distance services. The number of gear ratios required depends on the operating terrain and type of service; for short-distance operations on flat terrain four or five ratios should normally suffice with most engines, while for long distance services, especially those in hilly areas, six or eight ratios may be required.

Suspension

Some bus chassis are offered with an option of leaf or air suspension; a small number of models are available with independent front suspension. Leaf suspension is simpler and cheaper, although on rough road surfaces, and if overloading is common, leaf breakages may be a problem; if this is the case, it is important that the leaves can be easily and quickly replaced. Air suspension provides a more comfortable ride, and transmits fewer shocks from the road to the vehicle, thus reducing chassis and body damage from rough roads; however, in a dusty environment chafing of the rubber air bags may cause problems. Independent front suspension may be necessary for very low-floored buses, but may cause maintenance problems in a difficult operating environment.

Other mechanical options

Other important mechanical options relate to braking and steering. An option on many chassis is some form of supplementary braking system such as an exhaust brake, electric retarder or integral retarder with an automatic gearbox. These are useful safety features for operations involving constant braking, such as city bus services, or on hilly routes, and can prolong brake lining life so that downtime for replacement of linings is reduced. Most large bus chassis are now equipped with power assisted steering as standard, although it is optional on some. This is particularly desirable on urban and other short-distance services. These features add to the cost of a vehicle, as well as to maintenance requirements.

Body construction

Buses may be constructed as chassis with separate bodies, or in integral or monocoque form with mechanical units mounted directly to the body structure with no separate chassis frame. The principal advantages of integral construction are lower weight and increased strength. However, design and construction are more complex, and since integral buses are normally built to standardised designs, there are fewer options available than there are with separate chassis and bodies; it is therefore not always possible to meet the special requirements of a particular operator.

While the construction of separate bus bodies is possible using basic engineering skills and equipment, and can therefore be carried out on a relatively small scale in virtually any developing country, this is not the case with integral buses, which must normally be imported complete, or with only a small amount of finishing work to be undertaken locally. This invariably results in significantly higher manufacturing and shipping costs. Repair of accident damage to integral vehicles is often more difficult also. For these reasons chassis-on-body construction is far more common in developing countries; it is usual for chassis and body to be built by different manufacturers.

There are various choices of body construction materials. Welded steel angle or tube is generally most suitable for body frames: wooden framed bodies are not normally practical in developing countries due to problems of rot and insect infestation. Appropriately treated plywood or aluminium are suitable flooring materials. Aluminium is normally suitable for external panelling, but steel is necessary for highly stressed panels. Fibreglass is particularly suited to front and rear panels: it is a strong, light material which can be moulded to complex shapes, and can be easily repaired.

Detail design features

In addition to the size, capacity and general configuration of a vehicle, and the type of fuel, the specification must also cover all other aspects of the design, in particular special requirements such as destination indication equipment, special seating, or toilet facilities. Some vehicle manufacturers offer a wide range of options which may meet most operators' special requirements, while in other cases it may be necessary to have the vehicle modified by the supplier, bodybuilder, or specialist equipment supplier. The range of options is greater in respect of the bus body, and careful attention must be given to this aspect of bus design.

Manufacturer and model

Having finalised the vehicle specification and other requirements, it will be necessary to select the make and model of vehicle to be purchased. There will usually be a range of models from several different vehicle manufacturers which will broadly satisfy any given specification, with different characteristics and prices, although operators' choice is sometimes restricted: in some countries only a limited range of vehicles is available locally, and there are often restrictions on imports.

The options may range from inexpensive lightweight to expensive premium quality heavy duty chassis, with significant variations in quality and other characteristics. The principal characteristics of a lightweight chassis are low capital cost, shorter life, higher maintenance cost per kilometre, and lower reliability, especially in later life; those of a premium chassis are higher capital cost, longer life, better reliability, and lower maintenance cost. Fuel consumption for heavier vehicles tends to be higher but this is often offset by the use of fuel-efficient engines, which again are generally more expensive to purchase than less efficient engines.

It is not true that a premium chassis is always preferable to a lightweight chassis: this may be so for intensive operations requiring a high degree of reliability, but in less intensive applications a lighter chassis may be adequate, as for example in the case of vehicles for dedicated school bus operations, which tend to be relatively lightly utilised.

Several bus chassis available in developing countries are "truck-derived" chassis, each of which has much in common with truck chassis built by the same manufacturer. These chassis benefit from high volume production of components, giving relatively low capital cost; spare parts are readily available, the buses are relatively simple to maintain, and are generally durable under harsh operating conditions. Truck-derived bus chassis are therefore often ideal in developing countries.

They should not be confused with standard truck chassis on which bus bodywork may be constructed, either with or without modification to the chassis. While in certain circumstances a standard truck chassis may be suitable for use as a bus, there are usually several disadvantages. In particular, the layout at the front end of the vehicle is often unsatisfactory, giving a poorly positioned entrance or one which is difficult for passengers to negotiate, and an inconvenient driving position. On many truck chassis the engine is positioned over the front axle instead of ahead of it, as is more normal in a purpose-designed bus chassis; as a result, the increased intrusion of the engine into the passenger compartment can cause considerable obstruction at the entrance, and reduces passenger carrying capacity.

An important consideration is the availability of spare parts and service support for a particular make or model of bus. An otherwise ideal vehicle may be rendered unsuitable if its manufacturer has no dealers in the country, so that all spare parts must be imported to order. A large operator with a standardised fleet may be able to purchase vehicles which are not normally available, taking on the responsibility for importing parts direct from the manufacturer or from dealers in other countries, but small operators are dependant on local suppliers.

STANDARDISATION

Vehicle policy should address the question of fleet standardisation. There are substantial potential benefits to be gained from standardisation in larger fleets, including reduced requirement for spares stockholding, and therefore reduced inventory costs, and reduced costs resulting from purchasing power through purchasing in large volume. Mechanics' familiarity with a particular model can result in improved maintenance standards, while the requirement for special tools is reduced. Similarly, drivers are likely to drive more safely and with more sympathy for vehicles if they are required to drive only one type of vehicle with which they are familiar. A standardised fleet can also present a more professional image to the public.

There are, however, real or potential disadvantages to be aware of, particularly if standardisation is taken to extremes. A standard vehicle may not be suitable for every task, and in a highly standardised fleet it may be necessary to compromise with vehicles specified for all types of services operated, without being ideally suited to any of them. Too rigid application of a standardisation policy may also discourage innovation, for example by perpetuating obsolete models. It may put an operator at a disadvantage with its supplier, which in effect has a monopoly position. With a policy of standardisation, therefore, it is important that whenever new vehicles are to be acquired, consideration must be given to the possibility of selecting a new standard model: the advantages of a new model may outweigh the advantages of continuing to purchase the existing standard model.

Some undertakings practice a high degree of standardisation, not only with all vehicles being purchased from the same manufacturer, but also with standardisation of units such as engines and gearboxes. In some fleets, where vehicles are purchased from different manufacturers, standardisation of units is still possible where manufacturers fit components produced by third parties, as is particularly common amongst premium chassis manufacturers. For example engines built by specialist manufacturers such as Cummins, and gearboxes by ZF or Voith, are fitted by several different chassis manufacturers. Standardisation is usually beneficial in fleets of ten or more where all vehicles are required to undertake similar work; it is normally desirable to standardise on no more than two or three models in fleets of up to 100 vehicles, while more than three models may be appropriate in fleets of over 100.

FLEET REPLACEMENT POLICY

Many transport operators have no formal fleet replacement policy, other than to replace vehicles when it is no longer possible to keep them running any longer, or to purchase substantial numbers of new vehicles in years when funds are available, but none for several years in succession; these policies can result in a high average vehicle age and very uneven fleet age profiles. In many countries the average age of the national public transport fleet is very high, and while it is creditable that vehicles can be made to last so long, a high proportion will have exceeded their economic lives by a considerable margin.

An uneven fleet age profile results in fluctuations between very large capital expenditure requirements for vehicle replacement in some years and low requirements in others, and this may create cash flow difficulties. Another significant problem with uneven fleet replacement is the impact on maintenance requirements: if a high proportion of the fleet is of a similar age, when these vehicles are nearing the end of their lives, and demanding a higher level of maintenance input, engineering resources will be severely strained; similarly, if a significant proportion of the fleet simultaneously reaches an age when major expenditure is incurred, for example on unit overhaul or replacement, or body rehabilitation, there will be serious pressure on financial as well as physical resources. Finally, when large numbers of old vehicles have been simultaneously replaced with new ones requiring less maintenance input, there may be significant idle maintenance capacity.

Operation of an old fleet results in excessive operating costs, reduced safety standards and adverse environmental impact, in addition to creating a poor public image. In particular, maintenance costs increase significantly; reliability is reduced, through an increase in the number of breakdowns; availability is reduced, through increased maintenance down-time; and the high maintenance and operating costs, combined with the low level of kilometres operated, result in a very high cost per kilometre compared with younger vehicles, accompanied by reduced revenue. There is also an indirect effect on other vehicles in the fleet: since maintenance resources tend to be concentrated on the older vehicles, the younger ones receive less attention, and therefore deteriorate at a faster rate than they otherwise would. Because of poor vehicle availability, the total fleet size is invariably considerably greater than it would be with an appropriate replacement policy.

There are various criteria for deciding when a vehicle should be replaced, and several options to consider. It may be appropriate to keep the vehicle for a short time and sell it for a relatively high price; to run it until it is only fit to be scrapped; or to sell it at some time in between. Every vehicle has an "economic life", at the end of which it becomes excessively costly to operate, and when purchase of a replacement would be less expensive than continuing to maintain it; it should normally be replaced at this point. The economic life of a bus varies according to the type, operating conditions, standards of maintenance, and the relative costs of spare parts, new vehicles, labour and finance. Costs will vary according to use, and life in years will vary considerably, depending on the level as well as the type of usage.

The life of a vehicle is largely kilometre-related, but not entirely. A vehicle which has very low usage in terms of kilometres operated may become obsolete, and spares may be impossible to obtain, or the bodywork may deteriorate through corrosion, before it is mechanically worn out. In such cases a cheaper, lighter vehicle may be more economic than an expensive premium quality vehicle. In general, the more intensively a vehicle is to be used, the more likely it is that a premium quality vehicle will be more economic overall. It is normally easier to calculate the economic life in kilometres, but in certain circumstances time, measured in months or years, may be more appropriate. It is sometimes more convenient for planning and budgeting purposes, after calculating the economic life in terms of kilometres, to convert this to years on the basis of average kilometres per vehicle per year.

There are two important cost elements to consider when calculating the economic life of a vehicle. The first is the net replacement cost of the vehicle, i.e. the cost of a new vehicle less the proceeds from disposal of the old one; this will increase in absolute terms as the vehicle becomes older, since its disposal value will decrease, but in terms of average cost per kilometre, will decrease over the life of the vehicle. The second is the cumulative maintenance cost, or the total expenditure on maintenance materials and labour over the life of the vehicle; this will increase, at an increasing rate, as the vehicle becomes older, so that average maintenance cost per kilometre, over the life of the vehicle, will increase. The cost of repairing accident damage may be excluded from this calculation, since accidents may happen to any vehicle, irrespective of age. Similarly, tyre costs may be excluded, on the grounds that tyre costs are identical for old and new vehicles, although it may be argued that the tyre cost for an older vehicle may be higher due to wear and tear in steering or suspension units.

For the purpose of determining the point at which a vehicle should be replaced, the following formula may be used to calculate the average cost per kilometre at different points in its life; it should be noted that it need not include all costs, but only those relevant to determining economic life as indicated above:

$$\text{Average per-kilometre cost} = \frac{\text{net replacement cost} + \text{cumulative maintenance cost}}{\text{cumulative kilometres}}$$

If graphed to show the average per-kilometre cost at intervals throughout the life of a vehicle until it can no longer be maintained in serviceable condition, with cost per kilometre on the vertical axis and cumulative kilometres on the horizontal axis, this will normally give a U-shaped curve. Where this figure is a minimum, i.e. at the bottom of the "U", is the optimum point for replacement, in terms of total kilometres operated by the vehicle. The formula may be expressed in terms of months or years instead of kilometres if required, but the results may be less precise. There may be more than one low point on the graph; for example there may be low points at 100,000 and at 1,000,000 kilometres. This might occur if the resale value of the vehicle remains high for the first year or so, and then falls more rapidly, while maintenance costs are very low for the first year and then rise rapidly. This situation is relatively rare, and it is very unlikely that both low points will be equal. The exact shape of the graph will depend on circumstances; if maintenance labour costs are low, for example, the minimum point will occur later than if labour is expensive; the relatively low cost of labour is one reason why vehicles tend to be operated for much longer before being scrapped in developing countries than for example in Europe or North America.

In practice, determining the economic life of a vehicle is far from being an exact science. Few operators have sufficiently large numbers of vehicles of the same type, of a sufficient range of ages to enable the above calculation to be made with any accuracy, and operators must use "best estimates" based on experience of broadly similar vehicles. Nevertheless it is possible to determine with reasonable accuracy when a vehicle is near the end of its economic life, by estimating likely expenditure required to maintain it in roadworthy condition, and comparing this with the anticipated expenditure on a new vehicle to replace it. It is clear that good management information is required in order to determine when vehicles should be replaced. Where this is not available from the operator's own resources, data from other fleets may be available; in such a case, care must be exercised since the characteristics of one transport operation may differ widely from those of another.

Often no detailed analysis is made by operators of the cost of maintaining and operating vehicles of different ages, but general experience with large vehicles shows that these costs increase progressively for the first seven to ten years, and then remain constant at a relatively high level. Typical economic lives under reasonably good operating conditions on surfaced roads are ten to twelve years for premium buses, and seven to ten years for lightweight bus and coach types and small capacity premium buses. On a whole life cost basis, heavyweight buses almost always have economic advantages in the long term, unless the level of utilisation is low. For staff cars and the majority of light service vehicles the economic life is normally around five years, but for some vehicles such as recovery vehicles which in a well maintained fleet should have relatively little use, the economic life may be 25 years or more. Some operators may choose not to take the lowest cost replacement option: for example, for reasons of prestige a tourist coach operator may wish to operate a fleet with a low average age. In effect, revenue earning capability is included in the calculation in such a case.

It is normally desirable to ensure that the age profile of a bus fleet is kept as even as possible: in other words the number of buses in each age band should be broadly similar. With a large fleet, vehicles should therefore be replaced on a regular basis, with, as far as possible, a similar number of new vehicles being purchased each year. The average number of new vehicles required each year for replacement is calculated by dividing the total fleet requirement by the vehicle life in years: thus with a 150-bus fleet and a ten year life, fifteen replacements should be purchased annually. In the case of specialised vehicles which form a small part of the fleet, for example where there is a small fleet of coaches in a fleet consisting mainly of urban buses, the replacement programme for the minority fleet may be less even, but the total annual vehicle replacement expenditure can be maintained at a constant level by varying the proportions of standard and non-standard vehicles from year to year.

The replacement programme should also allow for planned fleet expansion, if necessary: the purchase of abnormal numbers of vehicles in some years should be avoided as far as possible, and this can often be achieved, even where an abnormally large intake of new vehicles is required over a short period for fleet expansion, by deferring the replacement of some of the vehicles for a year or two, or by purchasing a number of second hand vehicles of different ages. In practice, however, small fluctuations in the intake of new vehicles from one year to another will be difficult to avoid altogether.

Cash flow considerations are usually the reason for irregular fleet replacement programmes, with few or no replacements when cash reserves are low, and large numbers of purchases when cash is available. However, it is essential that the replacement policy is able to take into account any fluctuations in the organisation's fortunes: the implications, for example, of delaying the purchase of new vehicles because of a downturn in profits must be clearly understood, and any restriction on vehicle replacements scheduled in accordance with the replacement policy must be regarded as a measure of last resort.

An alternative to purchasing new buses may be to import second-hand buses from overseas. This can often provide good value, since a vehicle which has become uneconomic to maintain and operate in a country with high labour costs may still have several years of profitable life in a country where labour costs are lower. In some cases, buses are withdrawn from service in developed countries because they have been rendered obsolete prematurely, for example through the introduction of legislation to control exhaust emissions which do not apply in other countries, or because there is a requirement for buses which are accessible for wheel chairs; some designs which are obsolete in developed countries are highly suitable for developing countries. The relatively high cost of spare parts to maintain a second hand vehicle must be offset against the saving in labour costs, but there is often a benefit unless import duty on spare parts is high.

Buses available second-hand from other countries are not always suitable for local conditions. For example, suspension systems designed for smooth roads may be difficult to maintain satisfactorily where road conditions are poor; it may be possible for buses designed for operation in cold climates to be modified for use in a hot climate only at great expense; many buses built for developed countries have sophisticated equipment which is difficult to maintain. It is preferable to ensure that buses are imported from countries with the same rule of the road; conversion of a left-hand drive vehicle to right-hand drive or vice versa, is difficult and expensive, although this is done in some countries: for example, a large number of second hand buses have been imported into the Philippines from Japan, and converted from left-hand drive to right-hand drive configuration. There are also examples where buses have been imported but not modified: in Tanzania at one time there were buses imported from Italy with left-hand drive configuration, although traffic in Tanzania drives on the left, and these buses remained with their doors on the right-hand side so that passengers were forced to board and disembark in the middle of the road. In some cases purchasers have compromised by moving the passenger doors from one side of the bus to the other, leaving the driving position unchanged; while this may be reasonably satisfactory from the passenger's point of view, it makes driving the vehicle difficult and less safe, particularly in urban service, and should be avoided wherever possible.

FLEET COMPOSITION AND DEPLOYMENT

Many large transport fleets comprise a mixture of vehicle types, sizes, makes and models, and a wide range of vehicle ages. Such situations may arise for various reasons, including the range of operational requirements, financial constraints, restricted availability of vehicles, obsolescence and changes in the range of models available, mergers or acquisition of operators, changes in the types of services operated, poor fleet planning, or inappropriate purchasing decisions, over a period of up to twenty years: unless vehicles are disposed of before the ends of their useful lives, the results of any purchasing decisions will remain with the operator for the lifetime of the vehicles involved.

Some of the problems arising from the operation of highly diversified fleets have been discussed already; mixing vehicle types on the same route can cause service irregularities, while the operation of vehicles on a service for which they are unsuitable is obviously unsatisfactory. An uneven age profile leads to financial and maintenance problems, while non-standardised fleets require a much wider range of spare parts to be held in stock by operators or dealers if vehicle down-time is to be minimised, and in practice this is not often achieved.

There is therefore a need for fleet planning, to ensure not only that vehicles are purchased to meet current requirements, but also that they deployed over their lifetime to perform a useful and viable role, and that at any time the total vehicle fleet is the most appropriate for the services operated within the relevant constraints including finance, availability of vehicle types, vehicle life and legislation. In a situation where circumstances may change considerably during the lifetime of a vehicle, this is not always easy to achieve, and some compromise will always be necessary; there are very few large fleets whose composition can be described as ideal for all services operated.

It will often be appropriate to vary the way in which a vehicle is used over its lifetime. This may merely involve a gradual reduction in the level of utilisation, or a change in the type of service operated; it may even be necessary to modify the vehicle to meet the requirements of a different type of service. Most buses will remain on the same type of service. A bus designed for urban service, for example, is likely to be used on such services throughout its life. However, when it is new it is likely to be more reliable and less expensive to operate than an older vehicle, and therefore should be used more intensively. Typically a new bus will be used on all-day service on the busiest routes, and as it becomes older it will be transferred to less intensive routes, and towards the end of its life may be used for duties operating at peak periods only.

In a very mixed operation, such as a national operation serving areas with different characteristics, vehicle utilisation may vary considerably between one area and another, it may be necessary to transfer vehicles periodically from one part of the operation to another to spread the kilometres operated more evenly through the fleet, so that each vehicle operates broadly the same number of kilometres over its lifetime. Similarly, it may be appropriate to transfer vehicles between areas with different operating conditions, to even out wear and tear on vehicles. In some large groups of companies, it is customary for vehicles to be transferred between companies as they become older. In an extreme case some companies in the group will purchase only new vehicles, while others will receive only used buses which are transferred to them; companies in the first category will have much lower average fleet ages than those in the second.

Vehicles may be transferred from one type of service to another during their lifetimes, either with the same operator, or through disposal to another operator. For example, for tourist work it is normally necessary to provide modern vehicles which are in good condition; this requires replacement of vehicles after a relatively short time and low mileage. In many cases there is a good second hand market for such vehicles amongst the operators of long distance scheduled services or premium urban services, although former tourist vehicles are not always appropriate for urban operation. Where an operator provides both tourist and scheduled services, it is often appropriate for new vehicles to be used mainly for tourist work, and downgraded for scheduled services after a few years. They may revert to tourist work from time to time to cater for peak tourist demand.

An operator providing a range of tourist services, premium-quality long distance services, standard long-distance services and rural services, may purchase all new vehicles to specifications suitable for tourist services, and progressively downgrade them over their lifetimes. This is likely to require modification at certain stages: on downgrading to standard long-distance services, it may be appropriate to remove the air-conditioning equipment; and on down-grading to rural services the coach type seats may be replaced by more basic seating.

However, the design of many modern buses and coaches limits the scope for such downgrading; most luxury coaches are capable of being used for long-distance services, and may be suitable for premium urban services, but are unsuitable for ordinary urban or rural services, even with extensive modification. A vehicle designed to be downgraded from tourist to basic bus services may be unattractive to tourists. Operators will therefore have to consider all these factors: it may be feasible to purchase all vehicles for specific use only, or to purchase some vehicles which may be used only on one or two types of services, and others which are capable of downgrading; much will depend on the mix of services, and passengers' demands.

In addition to a mixed fleet in terms of make, model, type and age profile, a common problem in developing countries is that fleets are in poor condition, with an excessive number of vehicles out of service at any time, usually awaiting repair. Often many of these are beyond economic repair, although they have not been identified as such, and are retained with a view to being eventually repaired or refurbished; in some cases they are retained merely because they still have book value, and the operator is unwilling to write them off.

In many fleets where vehicle condition and availability are poor, significant improvement would be brought about by eliminating the worst vehicles in the fleet; in general, these will be the oldest vehicles, and those which are awaiting major mechanical or body repairs. Maintenance resources can then be concentrated on the remaining vehicles. Where there are insufficient serviceable vehicles available to operate the full scheduled service, it is advisable to reduce the schedule to reflect the operational fleet strength, and to deploy the serviceable vehicles on the most profitable routes in order to maximise revenue until the position can be rectified through the repair of defective vehicles, or the purchase of replacements. In practice, if the condition of the fleet and availability is poor, reliability will be poor also, so that such a fleet reduction exercise may improve reliability to the extent that the level of service actually provided, and its quality, is improved.

VEHICLE IDENTIFICATION

To manage a bus fleet effectively, accurate and up to date records are essential. Many transport operators keep very poor fleet records, and a surprising number are unable to determine exactly how many vehicles are owned, let alone the number which are serviceable. A primary requirement is a means of identifying each vehicle. Registration or licence plate numbers may be used for this purpose, but this is often unsatisfactory, particularly in a large fleet; it is particularly inappropriate in countries where registration numbers are changed periodically. Sometimes a regulatory authority requires transport operators to display bus identification numbers, either painted on the vehicle or on a separate plate in addition to the registration number plate; this is a relatively common requirement in respect of taxis, but sometimes applies to buses also.

A system of fleet numbering independent of registration numbers is usually the best means of identification. Fleet numbers may be allocated sequentially, but it is often useful, particularly with large fleets, to devise a fleet numbering system which not only enables each vehicle to be identified, but also provides some information about each vehicle. There are many different ways in which this can be achieved, some of which are highly complex. Different operators will have different requirements: some may find it useful for the fleet numbers to convey only very basic information, while others may prefer a system giving a considerable amount of information about each bus.

Examples of the types of system which may be adopted are four-digit numbers in which the first numeral indicates the chassis manufacturer, or vehicle type, such as double or single-decker, city bus or tourist coach, make or model, or any other details considered necessary, with the following three digits allocated sequentially; alternatively alphabetic prefixes or suffixes may be used to indicate these characteristics: for example a fleet number may be prefixed by several letters indicating the type, manufacturer and year of manufacture. The depot allocation may also be included, perhaps as a suffix. Where fleet numbers are used they should be painted on the vehicle exterior in positions where they may be easily seen; normally this will include front and rear panels, and adjacent to the fuel filler to facilitate the accurate recording of fuel issues.

A holding company with several subsidiary companies may find it useful to number the buses in all of its subsidiaries' fleets in a common series. This aids record keeping and facilitates the tracking of vehicles when the transfer of vehicles between fleets is common. However, it can result in a cumbersome numbering system and care should be taken to ensure that the numbering system is as simple as possible so that it is easily understood.

It is also necessary to maintain an accurate, comprehensive, up to date fleet list. This should contain various details of each vehicle, including fleet number, registration number, manufacturer, type, model, passenger capacity, year of purchase or manufacture, and base depot. Summarised lists giving reduced information may be produced for different departments, while there may be a need for a more comprehensive list, including such additional information as purchase price, current book value, and licence expiry date, for more specialised use. Fleet record systems are discussed in more detail in Chapter 15.

11

VEHICLE MAINTENANCE AND MANUFACTURE

MAINTENANCE STANDARDS

Vehicle maintenance is a key activity in the operation of any transport system. The way in which it is managed varies according to the size and nature of the operating units: a large, formal transport undertaking is likely to have extensive workshop facilities, while individually owned vehicles may be maintained at the roadside by their drivers, at commercially operated workshops or at facilities organised by operators' associations or co-operatives. Maintenance standards have a direct bearing on operating costs, vehicle availability and reliability, safety, and the impact of the transport system on the environment: inadequate maintenance expenditure will result in reduced vehicle life and in excessive total operating expenditure. Many bus fleets in developing countries are poorly maintained; this is often attributed to a lack of resources, principally funding, but also to a shortage of suitably qualified commercial motor vehicle mechanics, inadequate workshop facilities, tools and equipment, and difficulties in obtaining spare parts.

Each transport undertaking should have a set of standards for vehicle maintenance; these standards will include those set externally by legislation, such as vehicle exhaust emission standards or minimum tyre tread depths, and standards set internally by the organisation itself, such as bus availability and reliability targets. The quality of maintenance is reflected in records of maintenance costs, vehicle life and fleet availability, reliability and safety. These standards vary considerably between one country and another, and between one organisation and another. The externally imposed standards will be specified in vehicle Construction and Use and other regulations; the transport operator will have to set its own standards for other aspects of maintenance. The higher the standards set, the greater will be the cost and effort necessary to achieve them, and a balance must be struck between what is necessary and desirable and what is affordable and indeed achievable. In most cases there is a trade-off: for example, increased maintenance expenditure to achieve higher vehicle availability and improved reliability will be offset by a reduction in the need for additional spare vehicles to attain a given level of service, in the cost of dealing with breakdowns on the road, and in loss of revenue through lost journeys.

In virtually every country there are regulations designed to ensure that certain safety and environmental standards are met, and these are usually enforced by means of regular compulsory vehicle inspections. In some countries, such as Indonesia, it is a legal requirement for vehicle maintenance to be undertaken at workshops which themselves meet certain requirements and standards specified by government decree. In others, such as China, maintenance policy guidelines are issued by the government, and transport operators are responsible for implementing this policy. In many countries, however, even if the regulations are strict, enforcement is weak, and operators disregard the regulations with impunity. Nevertheless, vehicle maintenance programmes should normally be designed to meet the statutory standards as a minimum. Sometimes, however, government standards are unnecessarily stringent, requiring operators to invest large sums of money in major overhauls on all vehicles, regardless of their condition, repainting them more often than required, and in some cases restoring them to almost new condition in order to meet periodic testing requirements. Transport operators should preferably be permitted to design their own maintenance programmes to meet the needs of individual vehicle types, in the context of prevailing operating conditions and the level of vehicle utilisation, with standards being monitored through government inspections.

In order to monitor the achievement of standards there must be reliable statistics, as discussed in Chapter 15; often, however, these are not available, particularly where bus services are provided by large numbers of small operators. The condition of vehicles operating in many developing countries is generally poor, largely as a result of a lack of preventive maintenance. Private sector operators often appear to be better able to keep old vehicles running, but this is partly due to acceptance of much lower standards of safety and reliability: the incidence of mechanical failure is obviously high in many cases. Maintenance standards can be broadly assessed through observation: obvious indications of poor maintenance standards, in addition to the general appearance of the vehicles, are large numbers of vehicles to be seen broken down at the roadside, vehicles emitting black exhaust smoke or "crabbing", or with tyres which are obviously worn to a dangerous extent.

ROUTINE SERVICING AND CLEANING

An essential part of the maintenance process is the routine servicing and cleaning of vehicles. After completing a day's work, a bus must be prepared for the next day by refuelling and cleaning, and various other tasks should be carried out such as checking coolant and lubricant levels, and tyre and battery condition. In small fleets, particularly single-vehicle operations, these functions are usually the responsibility of the driver; in larger fleets they are normally the responsibility of the engineering or maintenance department. In most operations, the majority of buses are in service for the entire day, returning to the depot during the evening. Much of the servicing work must therefore be undertaken outside normal working hours, so that all buses are ready to recommence operation in the early morning. In some cases it is possible to carry out all servicing work in two or three hours at the beginning or end of each day, but often a full night shift, involving several staff, is required.

The organisation of routine servicing for large fleets can be complex. It is usually most effective for this function to be carried out on a flow-line basis, with buses proceeding through various points where different tasks are performed, by staff specialising on one or two tasks. For example, a bus may arrive at the fuel pump, where one man refuels the bus, and perhaps another checks the engine oil and water, while another checks the tyres; it may then proceed to the washing area, where the exterior is cleaned. Interior cleaning may be carried out simultaneously with external cleaning, at the same location, or may be carried out elsewhere or while buses are parked. The sequence of tasks, and the number of tasks assigned to each person, may vary depending on the number of vehicles to be serviced, the time available, and the depot layout.

Bus exteriors may be washed manually, requiring several labourers equipped with hoses and brushes (or a single labourer, requiring more time), or by mechanical means. Various types of bus washing machines are available, of greater or lesser complexity; some clean the entire exterior, while others require manual washing of vehicle fronts, backs and sometimes wheels. The time taken to wash a bus varies from one type of machine to another. Mechanical washing is common in countries where labour costs are high, but this is not normally the case in developing countries. However, a major advantage of mechanical washing is its speed: it may take as little as one minute to wash a bus by machine, while even with the maximum number of labourers who may be employed to wash one bus without hindering one another (usually not more than eight), it is not normally possible to wash a bus by hand in less than ten minutes. Where a large number of buses must be washed in a short time, or where there is insufficient space in a depot for several buses to be washed by hand simultaneously, mechanical washing may be justifiable by space savings and increased bus availability. Where water is scarce, bus washing machines may incorporate a water filtering and recycling system to minimise water consumption and control the release of pollutants into the drainage system. A problem with mechanical washing in some developing countries is reliability of the equipment; some bus washing machines require specialist skills for their maintenance, which may not always be available, and many installations in developing countries have been idle for several years due to lack of specialist maintenance or non-availability of spare parts.

While cleanliness is a subjective concept, standards can be laid down in terms of the frequency of the various activities; realistic minima, in the context of an urban bus operation are:

- Daily: sweep and mop floor, wipe inside windows and inside and outside front windscreen.
- Every one or two days: wash exterior using water and detergent.
- Every two weeks: full interior clean, including seats, ceiling and side panels, using water and detergent.

- If a bus has seats upholstered in cloth, these should be vacuum cleaned every three months.

In the case of long distance services, or premium urban services, some of these frequencies should be increased.

Maintenance department staff are usually responsible for cleaning buses, although in many long distance operations, and even some urban services, drivers or conductors are responsible for this function. In urban and long-distance operations in China, for example, crews clean their vehicles during layovers: conductors are normally responsible for interior cleanliness, and drivers for the exterior; however, in several undertakings no individual has specific responsibility for ensuring that bus crews carry out these cleaning tasks, which therefore often tend to be neglected.

PREVENTIVE MAINTENANCE

Vehicle maintenance procedures should be designed to ensure minimum vehicle down-time and maximum reliability within budgetary constraints; the most effective means of achieving this is through a planned preventive maintenance system. The primary objective of preventive maintenance is to prevent, or at least to minimise, the occurrence of mechanical failure, through appropriate inspection, lubrication, and replacement of components before they fail; it can extend the economic life of a fleet, improve vehicle reliability and availability, and reduce maintenance expenditure by identifying defects before they develop into major, and expensive, problems. The alternative, which unfortunately is all too common in developing countries, is to attend to a vehicle only when a defect occurs; this results in increased expenditure, since failures generally cost more to rectify than to prevent, while service reliability, and hence revenue, will suffer since breakdowns usually occur while vehicles are in service.

Preventive maintenance requires a programme of regular inspections, undertaken at frequencies determined by the nature of the operation and the level of vehicle utilisation, supplemented by defect reports submitted by drivers and analysis of records of engine oil and fuel consumption. Inspections should cover basic mechanical and safety items, including lights, brakes, steering and suspension, and fluid levels, while bodywork should be checked externally and internally for damage. There should ideally be a pre-printed checklist for each vehicle, which should be used by inspection staff and retained for a period for record purposes. It is also important that drivers carry out basic vehicle checks, and report any defects found in the course of their duties; rectification should be carried out as necessary before a vehicle is returned to service.

The frequency of routine inspections may be defined in terms of kilometres operated, time, or even the quantity of fuel issued since the last inspection; each of these measures has its merits and applications in different circumstances. For many operations it is sufficient to undertake the inspections at the same frequency as the minor routine services as discussed below, but where buses are subjected to arduous operating conditions, such as long-distance services on dirt roads, more frequent inspection may be necessary. A time-based inspection and maintenance schedule is normally easiest to control and plan for, but has disadvantages where the utilisation of vehicles varies significantly, or where vehicles operate under a variety of conditions. In an urban bus operation, there is often a significant difference in the level of operation at peak and off-peak times; this results in part of the fleet being required for relatively few kilometres per day. Unless vehicles are rotated between all-day and part-day work, some buses will operate considerably more kilometres per period than others, and therefore a kilometre-based maintenance schedule may be more appropriate. On the other hand, it is normal practice for the oldest buses to be used for peak-only work, and since these tend to be less reliable than newer vehicles, they may benefit from more frequent inspection in terms of kilometres. In a typical urban bus operation this inspection would be carried out weekly or approximately every 1,500-2,000 kilometres. Some operators, usually those running long distance services, require every vehicle to be checked each time it returns to the depot: in some African countries this is known as a "Safari Check".

The regular inspections are supplemented by routine services or "minor docks", carried out at intervals of perhaps two to four weeks, depending on the types of vehicle and operation. These will normally entail the regular routine inspection, plus greasing, a change of engine oil and filter (not necessarily at every service), and the replacement of components as necessary, either as a result of inspection or as a matter of routine in the case of components which should be changed at predetermined intervals. Most maintenance programmes also include an annual service or major dock, which in addition to the work undertaken at the minor docks, may include replacement of certain units, and other repairs not carried out during previous services. Annual services should normally be scheduled to coincide with preparation of the vehicle for the statutory vehicle inspection where this applies.

Finally, there may be more comprehensive maintenance interventions every three or four years, which may include routine replacement of major units such as engine or gearbox, reupholstering of seats and a complete body repaint. A planned maintenance programme can include the overhaul of major units before they are likely to fail. The appropriate intervals for these unit overhauls can be determined from the management information system; their cost is substantially less than the cost of repair after a major failure.

Many operators carry out major rehabiliation of the chassis and body during the lifetime of a vehicle to prolong its life; rebodying may even be appropriate in some cases. Rehabilitation and rebodying of buses is common in some countries, especially with large operators but sometimes with small operators. In Ghana, for example, full-sized buses which were considered to be uneconomic for further operation by large state-owned operators were refurbished and used by private sector operators, in some cases for longer than they had been with their original owners. Such work should form part of the preventive maintenance programme, and should not be carried out to compensate for a lack of maintenance previously: periodic major rehabilitation or overhauls are not an effective or economic alternative to proper maintenance.

In some cases, however, where maintenance has been neglected, rehabilitation may be worthwhile, provided that proper preventive maintenance is carried out afterwards. Much depends on the original quality of the vehicle, and rehabilitation may not be viable with vehicles which are less substantially built: it is not always possible to extend their lives sufficiently to justify the investment. Some long distance operators in the Philippines have a policy of keeping buses for ten years, and rehabilitating them with new bodies after six years, on the grounds that while chassis last for ten years, bodies deteriorate so that after six years they are no longer attractive to passengers. However, such a policy is not always cost-effective and can result in unnecessarily increased cost; during the life of the second body, the chassis will be less reliable due to its age, so that the effective life of the new body is reduced further. The costs and benefits should be carefully evaluated before embarking upon a rehabilitation or overhaul programme.

Tyres represent a significant item of expenditure, and as a major safety-related item must be included in the preventive maintenance programme. Tyre life is influenced by the quality of the tyres themselves, operating conditions, and driving standards; however, maintenance is possibly the most critical factor, yet standards in this respect often leave much to be desired. An essential aspect of tyre maintenance is ensuring that correct pressures are maintained at all times; it is also important to ensure that the vehicle wheel alignment, steering and suspension are maintained in good condition.

In some countries, such as Ghana, there is widespread use of second-hand imported tyres, mostly from Europe. These are tyres which are worn to the extent where the tread depth is no longer adequate to meet legal requirements in the countries from which they are imported but which still have a limited life remaining; the dangers are that the tyres will be used for much longer than is safe, and that some of the tyres may have defects other than low tread depth when they are imported.

Remoulds or retreads can be used successfully and safely to extend the life of a tyre casing significantly; up to five, and sometimes even more, retreads may be possible, extending the life of the casing perhaps by four times. It is sometimes claimed that retreaded tyres are dangerous, but provided that the process is properly carried out, the tyre casings to be retreaded are in good condition, and they are used properly by operators, there are no safety risks: in fact in countries where the safety of retreads is questioned, tyre standards generally are often appalling. There are sometimes problems of poor quality but some of these are because operators run their tyres beyond the point where retreading is possible. Careful control is necessary to ensure that tyres are removed for retreading at the most appropriate time: removing them too soon is wasteful; on the other hand, retreading is not possible beyond a certain level of wear, and a common failing is to run tyres beyond this point, again resulting in unnecessary waste of carcases or failure of the retreads if the process is carried out.

Retreads of mediocre quality may extend the life of the tyre insufficiently to justify the cost. With good driving and maintenance standards and using retreads as appropriate, a total tyre life of up to 150,000 kilometres can be achieved with a large commercial vehicle tyre, but 100,000 to 120,000 is more common. Maintenance of tyres is often contracted out to specialists, usually tyre suppliers and sometimes manufacturers. There may be a fixed charge per kilometre for the supply and maintenance of tyres; in such cases the tyres may be owned by the contractor rather than by the bus operator.

Maintenance programmes should be fully documented, and records should be kept of all maintenance carried out, for analysis purposes; sometimes there is a statutory requirement to keep maintenance records for periodic inspection by the transport regulatory authority. The following should be recorded in respect of each vehicle every time it is attended to in the workshops:

- Date of inspection or service
- Type of inspection or service (eg 2-week, 4-week, annual, etc)
- Confirmation that programmed work has been carried out
- Work carried out other than programmed
- Name of foreman or supervisor responsible for work

Preventive maintenance programmes should be reviewed from time to time and modified if necessary in the light of experience, using data provided by the management information system.

RECTIFICATION OF DEFECTS AND ACCIDENT DAMAGE

Even with the best preventive maintenance programme, there will always be some unexpected defects and failures requiring unscheduled rectification. In an ideal situation where the preventive maintenance programme is so effective that there is no requirement for unscheduled work, the percentages of time or money spent on preventive and unscheduled maintenance would be 100 and 0 respectively. In practice this is not achievable, and, except where maximum reliability is essential, as in the case of emergency vehicles such as fire-fighting appliances or ambulances, would indicate that in fact maintenance expenditure was excessive. An acceptable ratio of expenditure on scheduled and unscheduled maintenance for a typical bus operation is in the region of 70:30.

Vehicle defects normally occur on the road. If these result in the vehicle becoming immobile or unsafe to be driven, there must be a procedure whereby maintenance staff are notified and mobilised to rectify the fault. Other defects may permit the vehicle to continue to operate, but require rectification as soon as possible and there should be procedures for this to be done either at a terminal point or suitable point en route. Minor defects may be left until the bus returns to the depot on completion of its duty, and there must be effective procedures whereby drivers report mechanical defects, and for these to be dealt with promptly.

A daily record should be kept of all defects attended to, giving the following information:

- Bus identification (fleet number or registration number)
- Driver's name
- Route
- Location
- Time
- Nature of defect
- Action taken
- Name of responsible mechanic

Breakdown records should be analysed to identify any particular problems, in general or with any particular vehicle type, on a particular route, or even involving a particular driver, so that action may be taken to reduce the incidence of mechanical failure.

A separate category of maintenance is the repair of accident damage. Most minor accident damage should be repairable at the operator's own workshops where applicable but except in the case of large operators with fully equipped body shops it is normal for major repairs to be contracted out to specialists in such work.

Each operator must have appropriate arrangements for dealing with vehicles which break down or become involved in accidents in service, and for dealing with their passengers. These procedures will vary according to the type of operator, and the type of service operated. An owner-driver will normally be solely responsible for arranging for the necessary work to be carried out; a large bus operator will require set procedures to be followed by its crews. In an urban operation, where buses are never very far from their depots, all breakdowns might be dealt with by the operator; with long distance services, the arrangements may have to involve commercial garages or other bus operators in the locality of the breakdown. However, even an owner driver should have a predetermined routine to follow in the event of a breakdown in order to minimise loss of earnings.

There must be effective and clearly understood procedures for the crew to communicate with the depot. This would normally be via the nearest control point where there is an inspector or timekeeper in radio or telephone communication; if necessary a message can be sent with the conductor of the next bus heading in that direction. Many operators in developed countries, and an increasing number in developing countries, equip their vehicles with two-way radios so that drivers may communicate with their depots; a cheaper alternative, which may be particularly appropriate for long-distance services, is to provide drivers with mobile telephones. In the event of an accident involving injury to passengers or others the emergency services should be notified.

Details should be given of the location of the bus, its route, running number, and the nature of the failure or accident. In the event of an accident, details of its severity, and the approximate number of passengers or others requiring medical attention, should also be given. The depot should send a replacement bus as soon as possible; the crew will need to be instructed properly so that they regain their appropriate schedule after allowing for time lost. Any passengers on the bus must be transferred as quickly as possible to a following bus on the appropriate route; at peak periods it may not be possible to accommodate all passengers on the first bus, and in an extreme case it may be necessary to await the arrival of the replacement bus. In the event of an accident the operator must co-operate fully with the police and other emergency services as appropriate.

A large bus operator should normally have one or more suitable recovery vehicles to tow buses back to the depot if they cannot be repaired at the roadside. Otherwise it is necessary to rely on facilities provided by third parties; it is often useful to have contracts with selected garages or other operators to carry out breakdown recovery and repairs. Bus owners' associations can assist by providing breakdown recovery services for their members, but in practice this is comparatively rare.

SPARE PARTS

For any maintenance programme to be fully effective, and to minimise vehicle downtime, essential spare parts must be readily available, and it is invariably necessary to keep an adequate stock of spare parts within the workshop premises. Control of the purchase, issuing and storage of spare parts is a skilled task. There are also security implications, since the total value of stocks held is likely to be high; many parts are relatively easy to remove from stores without detection, and are readily saleable in the open market. Optimum stockholdings of each part depend on a number of factors, but mainly on the rate of consumption and delivery lead time. A figure of 10-15% of vehicle purchase value is often quoted as the approximate value of spare parts which should be held, but such figures relate only to value and not the selection of parts, and must be treated with considerable caution. The rate of usage of parts is dependent on the level of operation in terms of kilometres run; the operating conditions, namely the type of terrain, road conditions, and climatic factors; driving standards; and quality of maintenance. Also, the greater the scope of the workshop, and the number of maintenance activities which are undertaken in-house, the higher will be the level of stock holding required. The degree of standardisation in the fleet is also relevant, as discussed below.

Manufacturers are often able to advise on spare parts consumption under specified conditions, but their advice invariably needs to be amended in the light of experience; a good management information system is essential for this purpose. The availability of parts from suppliers is an important factor. Where parts are easily obtainable locally at a reasonable price, stock-holdings may be relatively low, and only fast-moving spares need to be held in stock; very slow-moving parts should not be stocked at all, particularly if they are of high value. On the other hand, if parts are difficult to obtain, and delivery lead times are long or unpredictable, stock levels will need to be much higher in order to avoid stock-out situations.

A common problem is the holding of excessive stocks of certain parts, and insufficient stocks of others, due to inefficient purchasing. Many large operators have substantial amounts of capital tied up in excess stock, including large quantities of unusable obsolete spare parts, while at the same time suffering shortages of essential fast-moving spares. There is also the possibility of corruption on the part of those responsible for purchasing: suppliers may offer incentives to persuade purchasing officers to buy inappropriate parts or excessive quantities.

An operator with more than one depot will need to keep stocks in several locations, and this may compound the problem: in such circumstances it is normally appropriate to maintain a central stores, in which the bulk of the stocks are held, and to keep smaller stores of fast-moving parts at each depot which are replenished regularly from the central stores.

In some developing countries, serious problems are created by long lead times for imported goods; the time from initiating an order to receipt of the goods may sometimes exceed a year, due to bureaucracy, transport difficulties, or both. The procedure for importing items such as spare parts can be cumbersome and slow. A typical sequence of events is first for the importer to obtain proforma invoices from potential suppliers, which then form the basis of an application for an import licence; this may require approval from the central bank and other government departments. Once the application has been approved, it may be necessary to await allocation of foreign exchange before the order may be placed with the supplier, and sometimes, if the price has increased during the time it has taken to reach the ordering stage, it may be necessary to obtain approval for the increase. On arrival of the goods, there may be further delays while the goods are cleared at the port of entry. For landlocked countries in particular, these delays may be compounded by long transit times.

The effect of long lead times is to increase stockholding requirements significantly, resulting in a much higher proportion of capital tied up in spare parts than would otherwise be the case. If the operator purchases from local suppliers, rather than importing direct, the supplier will bear the inventory cost, which will be reflected in the price to the operator. Alternatively, operators or suppliers may maintain low stocks, with the result that vehicles are out of service for considerable periods awaiting spare parts; this situation is typical of transport undertakings in many developing countries.

Standardisation of vehicle types in a fleet can have significant benefits in terms of stockholding requirements for a given fleet size, since a smaller number of stock lines will be required, and therefore the levels of stock required, particularly of slower-moving parts, will be significantly reduced. Another advantage of standardisation is that when there is a shortage of spare parts there is the option of cannibalising other vehicles as discussed below. A large operator, with several different models in its fleet, and vehicles based at a number of depots, should minimise the number of different types allocated to each depot, in order to reduce the stockholding requirement at each depot.

It is important to recognise the difference between "genuine" and non-genuine, or "spurious", parts. The former are parts produced by the same manufacturer which supplied the parts fitted to the vehicle when it was assembled, and should therefore be identical in every respect to those originally fitted unless approved modifications have been made in the meantime. Spurious parts are substitutes for the genuine parts, produced by different manufacturers: usually they are cheaper than genuine parts; they may be of equivalent quality, but often they are inferior. Sometimes spurious parts are fraudulently marketed as genuine parts, and purchasers must endeavour to verify the authenticity of all parts purchased; this is not always easy, and requires considerable expertise. While they may be cheaper, spurious parts are often less reliable and have shorter lives; in some cases the disadvantages will outweigh the advantages, but in other cases they will not, and purchasing decisions should be made accordingly.

Good management information systems, or effective monitoring procedures, will enable operators to evaluate the relative cost-effectiveness of genuine and non-genuine parts. It is possible to make considerable cost savings by using non-genuine parts if this is done in a controlled manner. On the other hand, indiscriminate use of non-genuine parts may result not only in increased expenditure, but also in reduced reliability, and may even be dangerous. Where there is any doubt, spare parts used should be purchased only from the manufacturer of the original vehicle equipment, or from a reliable manufacturer who is prepared to guarantee that the part is suitable for the specific application, even though the cost may appear high. This applies particularly in the case of parts which have a significant influence on safety, principally steering, brake and suspension components, and for items such as filters whose performance directly affects the life of much more costly units.

Stock-out situations, both in an operator's own spare parts store and at local suppliers, tend to occur frequently in most developing countries, for various reasons. In such circumstances, it is a common practice to "cannibalise", by removing a part from another vehicle which is out of service for some reason, usually because it is awaiting repair of accident damage, or is awaiting a different replacement part. If several vehicles are out of service because they are awaiting different parts, it is logical to transfer parts between vehicles so that at least some of them can be returned to service; however, this often leads to complete stripping of vehicles which are then almost impossible to restore to serviceable condition. A common sight in many bus depots in developing countries is large numbers of buses, some of which may be relatively new, which lack engines, gearboxes, axles, windows, seats, and other parts; part of the depot becomes, in effect, a scrap yard, and the buses are treated as a source of parts rather than as serviceable vehicles. A considerable amount of capital may be tied up in these vehicles.

Cannibalisation of buses for spares is therefore potentially a dangerous practice, and should not normally be permitted except as a last resort if spares are genuinely unobtainable: it is essential that if it does occur, sufficient quantities of the parts in question are ordered to return all vehicles to service as soon as possible, and to restore stock holdings to the required level. The only circumstance where cannibalisation is acceptable is when a batch of similar vehicles is becoming due for disposal by scrapping: as units fail, the vehicles concerned can be taken out of service, and the parts which are still serviceable can be removed for use in similar vehicles which are still operational; this process can continue until none of the vehicles is complete, when any parts which are still useable, and which are suitable for other vehicles in the fleet, may be retained for future use.

MAINTENANCE MANAGEMENT

Maintenance is a key function and its quality is heavily dependent not only on the physical resources available but also on the effectiveness of management and staff, their specialist qualifications and experience, standards of training and discipline, the management structure and work procedures. If maintenance is delegated to an outside contractor, there must be adequate procedures for ensuring that work is carried out in accordance with requirements and to the proper standard. For effective control of maintenance, as with management generally, a good management information system is essential; the key performance indicators applicable to the engineering function, as discussed in Chapter 15, are those measuring bus availability, reliability, materials usage and expenditure, fuel consumption, tyre life and labour productivity, and full use should be made of this information. Unfortunately, engineering management is often weak; good engineers and technicians do not always make good managers, and sometimes become so involved in practical matters that their supervisory or managerial responsibilities are neglected; on the other hand, there is also a danger that engineering is regarded as an end in itself, and the pursuit of excellence in this function may not always be fully consistent with commercial considerations.

The operating pattern has a major influence on the management of the engineering department. In a typical urban operation, with peaks in the morning and afternoon, and most if not all buses returning to the depot each night, servicing or minor maintenance can normally be carried out between the two peak periods or overnight, although a proportion of the fleet requiring major servicing or repair will need to be available for maintenance during peak periods.

To maximise fleet availability it is generally desirable for as much servicing and maintenance as possible to be carried out overnight. In practice, however, there are usually limitations on the extent of overnight working; these limitations vary from place to place, and depend to a large extent on local circumstances. Typical problems with night work, particularly in overcrowded or poorly laid out depots, are that supervision is more difficult, and it can be difficult to access pits and workshops when large numbers of vehicles are parked in the depot, while unless stores are also open at night vehicles it may not be possible to carry out all necessary work due to non-availability of parts. Night work often involves premium payments to staff, although the cost difference is normally outweighed by the improvement in vehicle utilisation, and this is not normally a significant factor in developing countries.

On balance it is normally more satisfactory for most maintenance work to be carried out during the day, and most routine servicing and cleaning to be done at night. In a long distance operation the pattern may be different: for example, if there is a predominance of overnight operation, buses can be serviced and maintained during the day.

The engineering and operations departments must co-ordinate their activities so that buses are available for maintenance when required: this may mean that specific buses must be allocated to specific duties on the days when they require maintenance. By the same token, it may be necessary at times of exceptional demand, for example at holiday times in the case of a long-distance operation, for some maintenance work to be rescheduled in order to make the maximum number of buses available for operation.

In practice, no matter how well maintenance and operational schedules are co-ordinated, there will always be some buses undergoing repair or maintenance at any particular time, and the vehicle fleet should include a number of standby vehicles or "engineering spares" in addition to the peak vehicle requirement. In an urban operation with typical morning and evening peaks, engineering spares will account for between 10% and 15% of the fleet; this may increase to as much as 25% in an operation without peaks, and in which all maintenance must be carried out during the working day. Benefits from increased vehicle productivity, if this is achieved by increasing the number of hours worked by each bus, may therefore be negated by an increased spare requirement, and a balance must be found between maximum vehicle utilisation and minimum engineering spares requirement.

There are trade-offs between operational productivity and maintenance requirements in other areas also. For example, a trend in some countries is towards the use of one-person-operated buses; these tend to be of more complex configuration to facilitate the driver's work, typically with rear engines and automatic transmission instead of front engines and manual transmission, and often have sophisticated electronic fare collection and ticket issuing equipment. The productivity of traffic personnel may be increased but the increased technical complexity of the vehicles required, and consequently the additional requirement for spare vehicles, can result in increased vehicle capital and maintenance costs by up to 50%.

Many large bus operators outsource their maintenance, typically through contracts with vehicle manufacturers or their dealers. Maintenance may be carried out on the operator's own premises or at the contractor's workshops. Outsourcing relieves the operator of management of the specialised maintenance function, and sometimes of the need to provide the necessary infrastructure and equipment. This is particularly advantageous when establishing a new operation; in the case of an existing in-house maintenance operation it may be necessary to transfer staff and facilities to the contractor. In theory, if contracts are subject to competitive tender, the maintenance service will be provided at minimum cost. In practice, although some commercial workshops provide a high quality service, this is not always the case. Independent organisations are often unable to meet the requirements of the operators; a contractor may commit himself to an unrealistically low price in order to obtain the business, and the quality of work inevitably suffers. There is also a real danger that the operator will lose control over quality and service: it may be difficult to monitor the contractor's performance since relevant management information may not be readily available. If a contractor is found to be unsatisfactory it may be difficult for the operator to make alternative arrangements if he has relinquished his own maintenance capability, and there are no alternative contractors to take over the work. A disadvantage of outsourcing maintenance to a vehicle manufacturer or supplier is that it may restrict the operator's future choice of vehicles.

Drivers play an important part in the maintenance process, in taking care of their vehicles when in service, and in carrying out basic checks. At its most basic, their role is to drive vehicles in a sympathetic manner so that wear and tear is minimised, but an important complementary role is to identify vehicle defects, and to report them so that the necessary action can be taken. Training and discipline of drivers, to ensure that they understand the basic principles and act accordingly, has a bearing on the overall condition of the fleet, its reliability and operating costs.

Many companies have a policy of permanently allocating one driver to a particular bus, as discussed in Chapter 8; this normally increases the driver's interest in caring for the vehicle. However, it is possible for the driver's involvement to be taken too far. In the case of several long distance operations in China, for example, the extent to which drivers are able to determine the level of maintenance carried out on their vehicles is of particular concern. The system of remuneration, whereby maintenance costs are deducted from drivers' emoluments, gives them an incentive to minimise maintenance costs: this is commendable if it is achieved through careful driving and proper preventive maintenance, but many drivers either arrange for maintenance work to be carried out cheaply, and invariably to a low standard, by private garages, or fail to ensure that proper preventive maintenance is carried out. Engineering staff have difficulty in controlling this situation, and some companies acknowledge that they have forfeited the right to control their fleet maintenance.

Good housekeeping is essential in any workshop for reasons of work quality and hygiene, but is an area which tends to be badly neglected by many undertakings, and poor housekeeping in workshops is a major reason for low maintenance standards in many transport undertakings in developing countries. It is far too common to find workshops and depots littered with scrap vehicle parts, including complete vehicles or their shells, worn tyres, drums of used oil, garbage swept from vehicle interiors, and other debris; buildings and equipment are frequently dirty, damaged and unpainted; and the surfaces of parking areas badly rutted, muddy in wet weather and dusty in dry. The floors of inspection pits are often littered with discarded small parts; usually waste oil has soaked into porous surfaces in both workshops and parking areas, and pits and their surrounding areas are often covered with a thick layer of compacted dust and grease. Dirt ingress to mechanical parts when they are repaired in dirty conditions increases the rate of wear, and hence operating costs and the likelihood of subsequent mechanical failure, while the health and safety of employees can be adversely affected by working in a dirty environment.

This problem is not confined to the workshops; poor housekeeping is often found in all parts of an organisation. Typical examples in administrative offices are notice boards with notices several years out of date, so that new notices are often not seen; old files kept for years longer than necessary, increasing storage requirements and making it difficult to locate material which is required, and untidy and disorganised desks and offices, reducing staff productivity.

Experience has shown that while this is an area of management culture which is often difficult to change, any improvements in housekeeping which can be achieved, including routine repair and maintenance to buildings and equipment, and repainting at appropriate intervals, has a marked effect on staff morale, the quality of their work, and their productivity. In turn this improves the profitability of the undertaking, and users benefit from reduced costs and improved service quality.

BUS MANUFACTURE AND ASSEMBLY IN DEVELOPING COUNTRIES

Manufacture of vehicle parts, bodies and chassis is becoming increasingly common in developing countries, both for the local market and for export. In some countries the industry is rudimentary, and is restricted to the manufacture of bus and truck bodies for the local market; in others there are flourishing motor vehicle manufacturing industries which compete in the international market with European, North American and Japanese manufacturers.

India, for example, has two large bus and truck manufacturers in addition to car manufacturers and a number of large commercial vehicle body manufacturers. Most of these vehicle manufacturers were originally established by overseas manufacturers, and often continue to produce vehicles based on those manufacturers' designs. For example, the two large chassis manufacturers in India, Ashok and Tata, were formed by the erstwhile Leyland company of the United Kingdom and Daimler-Benz of Germany respectively. For many years both Ashok and Tata models resembled those produced by their European progenitors, albeit often obsolete. However, the perpetuation of these designs is not necessarily a disadvantage, since technology which is obsolete in Europe or North America is often still more appropriate in developing countries, where complex and sophisticated vehicles are unsuitable for local road conditions, and the skills required to maintain them may not always be available.

A smaller manufacturer is Dahmer, in Zimbabwe, which produces complete buses and trucks using mainly DAF components imported from Holland, together with some parts which are manufactured locally. Dahmer vehicles are widely used in Zimbabwe, and are exported to neighbouring African countries.

A fully developed motor manufacturing industry embraces the manufacture of all vehicle component parts and the assembly of complete vehicles. There are few countries in the world, including developed countries, where every process involved in motor vehicle manufacture is carried out: virtually every country must import some of its raw materials, component parts, or even complete units such as engines, gearboxes or axles, and as the industry becomes more specialised, the imported content of most motor vehicles is tending to increase. Less developed vehicle manufacturing industries, which are more typical of developing countries, are based on the manufacture of vehicles using a relatively high proportion of imported components, while some units are manufactured using superseded production equipment purchased from manufacturers in other countries.

Some bus chassis which are manufactured in developing countries are significantly cheaper than others of similar specification manufactured elsewhere. However, although standards are gradually improving as manufacturers respond to international competition, quality standards are often low, making these vehicles unreliable and costly to maintain; their life expectancy is generally much lower than for similar vehicles manufactured in Europe, Japan or North America. The main reasons for the lower prices and quality are lower labour costs in the countries of manufacture, low skill levels, poor supervision, inferior quality of materials used, poor processes such as protection against corrosion, inadequate equipment, ineffective quality control procedures, and broader engineering tolerances, while some vehicles are built to obsolete designs. A "cheap" vehicle is therefore likely to be more expensive to run, less reliable and have a shorter life. In some circumstances such vehicles are suitable; in others they are inappropriate, as discussed in Chapter 10. Many purchasers are influenced by the low initial cost, and this is natural when funds are scarce and credit facilities are difficult to obtain. However, in the long run it is generally preferable, if possible, to invest more in a better quality vehicle which has a lower whole-life cost.

Chassis manufacture involves the design of complete chassis, including the specification of all units, and the final assembly of these chassis. Some chassis manufacturers produce their own mechanical units, such as engines, gearboxes and axles, but to an increasing extent these are sourced from specialist manufacturers. Therefore identical engines, gearboxes and axles may be found in chassis marketed by several completely independent manufacturers, and the chassis frame itself is often the only major part of the vehicle which is unique to a particular manufacturer. Often even the frame components are not manufactured in-house, but are fabricated by sub-contractors to the appropriate design. Therefore it is possible to manufacture vehicle chassis on a relatively small scale, and there are several very small manufacturers operating on this basis, with the main activities being the design itself, and the assembly of bought-in components. There are, however, relatively few such manufacturers in developing countries, even though with the right resources they would be relatively easy to establish.

A notable exception is the manufacture of jeepneys in the Philippines; some of these are modified Japanese light truck chassis with locally manufactured bodies, but many of the chassis are manufactured in the Philippines, using new or second-hand imported parts. A disadvantage of these small chassis manufacturers is that because of the small volumes produced, they are unable to offer a wide range of models; on the other hand some produce a variety of models in very small numbers, leading to problems of standardisation and poor spare parts availability. Their low volume production also limits their purchasing power, so that bought-in components are often expensive, resulting in turn in relatively expensive chassis.

Further down the manufacturing scale is vehicle assembly, where local plants assemble chassis or complete vehicles from kits of parts supplied by overseas manufacturers: often the assembly plants are fully or partly owned subsidiaries of the overseas company, but the majority have a high level of local investment: some are joint ventures with local companies or government. Most of these plants use a proportion of locally manufactured parts, and as a country's industry develops, the local content increases.

Advantages of the local assembly plant include low labour costs, and reduced transport costs since vehicle parts imported in containers require less space than fully assembled vehicles, and are less susceptible to damage. Some locally manufactured parts incur minimal transport costs. Assembly plants can also form the basis for the eventual development of a local motor vehicle manufacturing industry if circumstances are appropriate. Disadvantages of local assembly can include limited choice of models available, poor assembly quality due to low skill levels or poor supervision, poor quality of locally-produced components, and delays in supply due to non-availability of parts. Since there is much in common between the processes, skills and equipment required for the assembly of all types of motor vehicle, most plants assemble a range of vehicle types, including full-sized buses and minibuses, heavy and light trucks, and cars. Some assembly plants, even those wholly or partly owned by a single foreign manufacturer, assemble vehicles of other manufacturers by agreement. Not all have been successful, and some ventures have ceased trading for various reasons, including political instability, inappropriate regulation, problems of enforcing discipline, corruption, and bad debts.

Most of the least developed countries have no chassis assembly plants, but several have successful commercial vehicle body building industries. Bodies for buses and trucks are less complex to build than chassis and require relatively simple equipment. Design can be consistent with appropriate technology for developing countries, incorporating relatively basic techniques for ease of manufacture and maintenance. Some modern construction techniques are inappropriate in developing countries: for example, bonded glazing and stretched one-piece body panels are difficult and costly for small transport operators to maintain. Many modern buses and coaches manufactured in developed countries are of integral, or monocoque, construction, in which the mechanical units are mounted directly to the body structure, with no separate chassis frame; specialised equipment is required for manufacture, putting it beyond the capabilities of most small body-builders. There are therefore few examples of integral construction in developing countries, other than at assembly plants controlled by foreign manufacturers.

Several large European bus bodybuilding companies have established plants in developing countries, with varying degrees of success. Some manufacturers produce bus bodies in "completely knocked down" (CKD), or kit, form for assembly in various overseas countries, on the customers' own premises, by their own staff under the body manufacturer's supervision, or in purpose-built factories. However, commercial vehicle body-building is a sector of the industry which is usually wholly locally-owned, and while there are several large, well-organised and relatively sophisticated bus and truck body manufacturers in developing countries, bodies are also manufactured by many very small enterprises. Nevertheless, with generally improving standards of vehicle, and the phasing out of the more basic types of passenger vehicles, the number of new bus bodies built by the smaller manufacturers is declining in many countries, and the industry is tending to become more organised. Standards of manufacture and materials used vary considerably: in some countries standards are poor, while in others, bodies are produced to standards which would be acceptable in many developed countries. Marco Polo is one of the world's largest bus body manufacturers; it produces high quality bodies in Brazil, where the company is based, and has plants in South Africa and Portugal, as well as joint ventures in China, India, Colombia and Mexico.

The manufacture of vehicle parts in developing countries has a number of potential benefits, particularly in terms of foreign exchange conservation. In countries where skill levels are low, it is usually feasible to manufacture only basic parts such as springs, batteries, filters and brake and clutch linings, but as skills develop more complex parts can be successfully produced such as certain electrical components. In many developing countries, particularly in South-East Asia, manufacturing industry has developed dramatically in recent years, and many European manufacturers of high-technology equipment of various kinds now sub-contract a considerable proportion of their work to manufacturers in these countries; the manufacture of most types of vehicle parts is therefore well within their capability. In countries where chassis are assembled, this can provide an opportunity for local parts manufacturers provided that they can meet the appropriate quality standards.

The limited local market in many of the less developed countries does not justify investment in the manufacture of complex vehicle parts but the production of simple items such as filters may be viable. However, in such cases high quality is essential: poor quality locally manufactured springs and filters, fitted as original equipment to locally assembled vehicles or as replacements for genuine parts on imported vehicles, frequently result in premature failure, or failure of other more expensive units such as engines and gearboxes in the case of filters. Moreover, where locally produced replacement parts are used in place of original equipment the vehicle warranty may be invalidated. However, as with spurious parts generally, there are applications where the fitting of locally produced parts can be cost-effective. In some countries, in order to assist local industry or to conserve foreign exchange, or both, there is a legal requirement for commercial vehicles assembled in the country to incorporate a minimum local content. This can create problems, particularly if the required level of local content is set too high, so that relatively critical components must be produced locally. Quality, and hence vehicle operating costs and reliability, and sometimes safety, may suffer.

Tyres are manufactured in several countries, sometimes by purely local manufacturers, but often by subsidiaries of international tyre manufacturers. The production process necessitates high volume production, thus requiring a large market. Countries such as Kenya or Tanzania are able to sustain at least one manufacturer, particularly if there are opportunities for exporting to neighbouring countries, and larger countries can support several, but in smaller countries, a tyre manufacturer must rely heavily on exports to maintain a viable volume.

Associated with tyre manufacture is the retreading of used tyres; this is a relatively low-technology operation which can be carried out at low volume and if performed to appropriate standards can result in substantial cost savings for operators. There are retreading plants in many countries, although it is not always fully appreciated that retreading can result in substantial savings to transport operators in terms of cost, and can also save foreign exchange, particularly where tyres are imported.

As countries develop, problems of quality are being overcome, but in the meantime local industry is at a disadvantage. Domestic manufacturers of poor quality products cannot compete with imports unless there is a substantial price difference, and often this is achieved only through prohibitive import duties, and poor quality exports from developing countries are very uncompetitive in the international market. The users of such products suffer from increased operating costs and reduced reliability as discussed above.

Local manufacturers can be encouraged to improve quality through exposure to competition from imports, and through effective enforcement of vehicle roadworthiness regulations; most countries also have bureaux of standards which, if properly organised and managed, can help to raise the quality standards of local industry. An input from foreign manufacturers in the form of a joint venture or shareholding, can also bring benefits. In the longer term, as skill levels improve, this can encourage the development of purely local industry.

While there are various arguments in favour of manufacture of vehicles or parts in developing countries, there are also a number of pitfalls, and in some cases the development of domestic industry has created more problems than it has solved. Potential savings in foreign exchange through a reduction in imports, and earnings of foreign exchange through exports, are often seen as major benefits; in reality, these benefits are seldom realised. Another argument sometimes put forward for local manufacture is that a vehicle can be produced which is designed specifically for local conditions. This again is usually a spurious argument, since the international manufacturers are able to design vehicles to meet all conditions, and usually have greater design expertise available. National pride is often a factor, but in this context is an indulgence which few developing countries can afford.

Global trends in motor vehicle manufacture are towards consolidation and the formation of large international groups, which have a strong competitive advantage over smaller manufacturers, including those in developing countries. In the manufacture of vehicle chassis and major units there is a critical mass in order to justify the type of equipment necessary for manufacture. This requires a market larger than is available in many countries and unless it is possible to export to other countries the domestic industry will not be viable. If the local market is limited, there is often scope for development of the industry to compete in the regional market; however, by the same token, there is potential for increased competition from manufacturers and suppliers in neighbouring countries.

Governments in some developing countries have actively attempted to promote the establishment of motor vehicle manufacturing industries where there has been little chance of success; various artificial measures, such as restrictive duties on imported vehicles and parts, have been introduced in an attempt to encourage the growth of local industry, but in virtually every case this has the effect of increasing domestic transport costs while the local manufacturing industry, with little competition, has no incentive to operate efficiently. An industry will develop naturally in the right circumstances, and governments can assist in this respect by creating an environment where the returns are adequate. The nature of the international motor manufacturing industry is such that, except in very large countries, the most likely entrant to the chassis manufacturing sector of the industry will be one of the established international companies, usually in the form of an assembly plant. Governments can assist through favourable policy with regard to such operations.

Vehicle body manufacture is a relatively simple process which is within the capability of virtually all developing countries, and has developed naturally; again, participation and competition from foreign manufacturers can help to improve the quality. A vehicle parts manufacturing industry will develop where demand is sufficient; where there is a vehicle assembly industry, the market for locally manufactured parts will potentially include the assembly plants, provided that the quality is acceptable as original equipment. Increasing demand, and a requirement for improved quality, will gradually encourage local entrepreneurs to invest in businesses such as the manufacture of spare parts, and it is to be hoped that governments will take any measures necessary, such as facilitating the availability of credit, to encourage such business to grow naturally.

It is particularly important that a country's strengths and limitations are taken into account. Countries with raw material such as iron and steel or rubber are often better placed to manufacture vehicles or parts than those which must import all raw materials. In the latter case, often the only cost saving is on labour, and such savings may be offset by poor quality. Availability of skills at all levels will determine, for example, whether it is possible to establish an industry which is wholly domestically owned, or whether some form of foreign participation is necessary, at least at the early stages.

12

PERSONNEL MANAGEMENT AND TRAINING

Transport is a labour intensive activity. It requires staff with a wide range of skills, many of which are specific to the industry; therefore there tends to be less mobility of labour between transport and other industries than applies generally. Many senior managers in the transport industry have progressed upwards through a single organisation during the course of their careers, sometimes from very junior levels.

Most transport organisations which employ large numbers of people have personnel or human resources departments, although in some organisations each operating department is responsible for handling its own personnel matters. The main roles for a personnel department in a transport company are administrative, principally concerning the recruitment and termination of staff, the maintenance of personnel records, organisation of training, enforcement of disciplinary procedures, and relevant legislative issues.

Training is an important requirement, and management of training is a key function within any large organisation; training requirements are diverse, as is the availability of training, and an officer who is fully conversant with the issues involved is essential to any large organisation. The administrative function alone is a major task which normally justifies a separate training department, particularly where staff turnover is high, and there are benefits in maintaining all staff records centrally, especially where employees may be transferred from one department to another. There is an increasing amount of labour legislation requiring special expertise, and it is normally preferable to employ specialist staff who are conversant with such matters, rather than to require all management staff to be conversant with all relevant regulations: this can detract from their efficiency in their main jobs.

STAFFING LEVELS

Numbers of staff, relative to the size of the operation or level of activity, vary considerably from one undertaking to another, and from one country to another. The size of an undertaking can be defined in various ways, but most relevant in this context are the number of buses operated, and the number of kilometres run. In making comparisons between one operation and another, it is therefore useful to compare ratios, such as the number of staff per bus, or kilometres per employee per year. For some activities more specific measures are appropriate: for example, for staff employed at bus stations, a useful measure is the number of bus departures per employee per day. Other personnel indicators are discussed in Chapter 15.

These ratios must be used with care, however, and the possible reasons for variations must be clearly understood. For example the optimum staff-per-bus ratio can vary for any of a number of reasons. In the case of bus crews, the number of staff per bus will be significantly influenced by the level of one-person operation; if conductors are employed, the requirement will be approximately twice as great as where vehicles are operated by drivers only. Bus productivity, and the length of the working day, will also have an impact on staff numbers; increased bus productivity or longer working hours may require a greater number of crews. The type of operation has a major bearing on vehicle and staff productivity ratios: kilometres per bus or per employee for an express long-distance service will be much higher than for an urban operation where operating speeds are lower.

The number of staff per bus owned will invariably be lower than the number per bus operated, since a proportion of the fleet will normally be out of service for maintenance at any time. Often the number of buses out of service is excessive. It is often the case, therefore, that although the ratio of staff to buses owned may appear to be reasonable, the number of staff is excessive in relation to the number of buses operated, due to a high proportion of unserviceable vehicles; productivity in terms of kilometres per crew member will be low, and if statistics are kept of hours paid but not worked, these will be found to be significant.

Ratios depend on levels of utilisation and working practices: for example, if each bus is operated regularly by the same driver, the ratio of drivers to buses will be 1:1; if all buses are operated on a two-shift basis, seven days a week, the number of drivers per bus may be three or more, including those required to cover for days off, holidays and absenteeism. Where conductors are employed the number will be similar to that for drivers, where one conductor is employed per bus; in some busy urban operations more than one conductor is employed on some or all buses, so that the figure for conductors will be higher than that for drivers. Typical ratios of staff per bus owned in developing countries range from around five to ten, but much higher figures are found in some cases, especially where operations have contracted and staff have not been reduced proportionately. Ratios of staff per bus operated cover a much wider range, from around five to as high as thirty, and even more in extreme cases, where the proportion of unserviceable vehicles is very high.

The ratio of staff to departures at bus stations varies considerably, depending on the type of facilities provided, and whether these are staffed by employees of the bus station operators, the bus operators using the station, or by franchisees or contractors. If booking offices are provided, these are often staffed by the bus operators, but in some cases they are manned by bus station employees. Other facilities, such as restaurants, are usually managed by third parties. In China, amongst a sample of bus stations examined in 1995, the lowest ratio was at the Zhengzhou North

Long Distance Bus Station, run by an operators' association, with 120 staff handling 360 departures daily, or three departures per employee; the worst was Xinxiang, with only 1.5 departures per employee. In each of these cases booking office staff were employed by the bus station operators, while refreshment facilities were run by third parties.

Staff-per-bus ratios for three African bus companies

	Nairobi		Harare		Malawi	
	Total staff	Staff/ bus	Total staff	Staff/ bus	Total staff	Staff/ bus
Number of licensed buses	*268*		*665*		*259*	
Senior Management	4	0.01	5	0.01	4	0.02
Drivers	636	2.37	964	1.45	441	1.70
Conductors/ ticket sellers	630	2.35	163	0.25	420	1.62
Inspectors	162	0.60	95	0.14	162	0.63
Mechanics etc	452	1.69	550	0.83	499	1.93
Administrative and clerical	255	0.95	302	0.45	293	1.13
Trainees and apprentices	62	0.23	0	0.00	93	0.36
Other	86	0.32	132	0.20	280	1.08
Total	2287	8.53	2211	3.32	2192	8.46

The above table shows the total number of staff, and numbers of staff per bus, broken down by main category, for three African bus companies (Kenya Bus Services, Nairobi; Harare United Omnibus Company, Zimbabwe; and United Transport Malawi) in 1988-1991. Because of differences in the way in which certain categories were broken down in the three companies' accounts, a more detailed comparison is not possible, but the figures nevertheless provide a useful guide. It is clear that there are significant variations, even though the three companies were part of the same international group (United Transport Overseas), and management principles were broadly similar.

The relatively large number of drivers per bus in Nairobi reflects a longer working day on urban services, while many of the services operated in Malawi were long-distance rural services, requiring only one driver per day on each vehicle. All buses in Harare were operated without conductors, although ticket sellers were employed at bus stations to sell tickets to passengers prior to boarding the vehicles. Differences in the numbers of inspectors reflect not only the intensity of operation and geographical spread of services, but also the revenue integrity characteristics in different places. The lower number of engineering staff per bus in Harare is partly because higher labour costs encouraged economy in the number of ancillary staff, and partly because of the lower level of vehicle utilisation; labour productivity was higher also. The large number of "other" staff in Malawi was due partly to the geographic spread of the company's operating area, requiring a large number of small depots and increased security requirement; the company also had a large building maintenance section.

Many transport undertakings are overstaffed in relation to the number of buses operated. A typical example of overstaffing was the situation with the principal bus operator in Malawi (formerly United Transport Malawi) in September 1999 after some years of neglect. Total staff was 1,808, or 6.5 per bus owned. This figure would not have been unreasonable under local conditions if all buses were operational; however, in terms of buses actually operated, which averaged 122, the figure became excessive at 14.8. In terms of the operational fleet, a reasonable total staff figure would be of the order of 750: in other words, the company was overstaffed by approximately 1,050 staff, or 140%, with excess staff in all departments. To put the staff-per-bus ratio into perspective, it would be unimaginable for the operator of, say, two buses to employ a total staff of thirty people. The breakdown by department was as shown in the following table:

Staffing Levels, Malawi, 1999

	Total staff	per bus owned	per bus operated
Drivers and conductors	790	2.8	6.5
Management/admin/ supervisory	350	1.3	2.9
Engineering	574	2.1	4.7
Other	94	0.3	0.8
Total	1808	6.5	14.8

Wage rates in developing countries are generally low in comparison with developed countries, so that more labour-intensive methods may be viable; for example manual rather than mechanised bus washing is more economic in many developing countries, while in most developed countries high labour costs justify expenditure on expensive automatic bus washing equipment. However, low labour costs provide little incentive to keep staffing levels to a minimum, and often result in a tendency to over-staffing. Although the effect on costs is less severe than in a country where labour costs are high, excessive staff does increase costs to some extent, and also results in increased accommodation, administration, management and security requirements. Over-staffing should therefore be avoided as far as possible.

Excess staff is a particularly common problem amongst transport enterprises in the public sector. This is often due to government employment policy intended to minimise unemployment; some governments have decreed from time to time that parastatal organisations (and even private sector organisations in some cases) should recruit additional staff, even though these staff may not be required. While this may help to achieve government employment objectives in the short term, it reduces the efficiency and competitiveness of the transport undertaking, particularly if the operator is competing with private sector operators not subject to this ruling, and in the long term may contribute to the collapse of the public sector organisation.

Such a requirement to employ excessive numbers of staff was given as one reason for diversification by transport operators in China into totally unrelated businesses, but such diversification to utilise surplus staff can only be effective if there is a shortage of supply in the sector chosen for diversification. Otherwise the market will become over-supplied and the new activities will be unprofitable. In some cases, however, better use could be made of some of the excess staff, and the performance of some tasks which may be neglected, such as effective preventive maintenance of vehicles or cleaning of workshops, could be improved. Where demand for public transport services is increasing it is possible to improve the staff/bus ratio by restricting expansion in staff numbers as the level of operation increases, and increasing staff productivity by introducing more efficient working practices. Where there is excessive staff, therefore, it is important that any expansion in activity to meet increased demand is not accompanied by an increase in staff, until all existing staff are fully employed on productive work.

As well as considering staff levels in overall terms, it is important to examine the various categories separately. There are often imbalances in the allocation of staff to functions: in many organisations there are surplus administrative staff, while there are insufficient drivers to meet schedule requirements, or insufficient mechanics and cleaning staff to maintain vehicles and premises in good condition. There is also often inefficiency through the deployment of skilled staff in unskilled work. For example, even where there is a shortage of skilled mechanics, these employees may be required to clean their working areas, when the employment of more readily available and less expensive unskilled labour for these tasks would release the mechanics for skilled work. In some cases, where there has been an imbalance, staff have been transferred between jobs; this is not always successful, however, and may result in staff being required to carry out tasks for which they are unqualified. It is usually more effective in such circumstances to replace such staff with more suitable people, and therefore retrenchment or redundancies may be necessary even when staff are being recruited for other posts.

In some countries it is customary for public sector organisations to retain employees on the payroll as pensioners after they have retired; this normally applies in countries such as China where employees tend to remain with one organisation for most of their working lives. Where pensioners are included in staff establishment figures, appropriate adjustments should be made when calculating staff ratios. A disadvantage of the practice is that it restricts mobility of labour, and can create problems if there is a move towards privatisation.

High staff turnover is a problem experienced in transport undertakings in many countries, particularly amongst drivers and conductors, although in some countries, such as China, turnover is virtually at the minimum level resulting from staff retirements and recruitment of replacements. The problem is particularly acute where labour mobility is high, and tends to be worst in the private sector. It is not uncommon in some countries for turnover of drivers and conductors to exceed 100% per annum, particularly where there are several operators in an area providing alternative employment. A high rate of turnover results in increased costs, and can create problems through a general lack of experience in the organisation, leading to poor safety standards, inefficiency and increased supervisory requirements. The higher the rate of turnover, the higher will be the administrative and training costs associated with recruitment; as discussed in Chapter 13, training costs for some categories of staff, particularly drivers and mechanics, can be very high, and therefore a high rate of turnover is particularly undesirable in these categories.

There are several reasons for high staff turnover. A significant factor, particularly in the case of conductors, or drivers when they are also responsible for collecting fares, is discipline: theft of fare money is a common problem in many areas and a high proportion of staff are dismissed for such offences, or, alternatively, abscond with the day's takings. A high rate of dismissal of drivers for poor driving is often the main reason for high driver turnover. The nature of the job also has a bearing on the problem. A factor which tends to be more relevant in developed than in developing countries, is the unsocial hours associated with driving and conducting work; this has proved a serious impediment to staff recruitment and retention, particularly at times of full employment. Assaults on staff are an additional problem in some countries.

STAFF SELECTION, RECRUITMENT AND TRAINING

Selection of suitable staff, as well as subsequent training and motivation, is essential at all levels of an organisation. Minimum standards, including where appropriate age, health and educational requirements, must be established for the recruitment of all staff; this is particularly important in respect of driving, conducting and mechanical staff, who are responsible for the safety of passengers and other road users, the care of valuable equipment, and the handling of large quantities of cash. Operators should set their own standards but the regulatory authorities also have a role, particularly with regard to standards for public service vehicle drivers.

In some countries, despite the fact that it is usually illegal, tribalism is a significant factor in recruitment. There is often prejudice against some tribes and preference for others, either for employment in any capacity, or in respect of different levels in the organisation. The owner or chief executive of an undertaking may be responsible for such discrimination; sometimes the officers responsible for recruitment exercise their own prejudices. This is largely a cultural factor, which is rife in some countries but non-existent in others.

The quality of management has a major influence on the efficient running of any organisation, but many transport organisations in developing countries, especially those in the public sector, suffer from poor quality management. This may be due to managers being appointed with inappropriate qualifications, inadequate experience, or lack of ability or integrity. Selection of suitable management personnel for a transport undertaking is often a problem. Some functions, such as those of the traffic manager or chief engineer, are specialist and specific to the road transport industry, making recruitment more difficult, especially if the industry is at an early stage of development. Other positions, such as that of chief accountant, are not specific to the industry, but there may be strong competition in the market generally for managers of good quality. The candidate for any management position should have appropriate qualifications, experience, and ability, and where relevant be able to prove a good track record in the industry.

In some countries there is a serious shortage of transport management expertise due to the small number of large conventional transport operators. If no suitable candidates are available locally, it is often preferable to recruit suitably qualified expatriates on a short to medium term basis in order to safeguard an operation; however, where this is found to be necessary, steps should also be taken to ensure that local personnel are developed to take over such positions as soon as possible. Indeed, a key role of expatriate management in many cases is to train local management, or give them support while they gain experience. This usually applies at relatively senior levels although there are exceptions. Expatriate staff are sometimes also recruited at junior levels for skills which are not available locally, while in certain countries, such as Saudi Arabia expatriate staff, or "third country nationals" are employed for unskilled work.

Similarly, there is a shortage of expertise in the transport planning field, and overseas consultants are frequently employed to carry out planning tasks, usually as discrete projects, but also often on a continuing basis to undertake routine planning tasks. An advantage of employing consultants is that different consultants, with different areas of expertise, may be employed for specific tasks as appropriate.

Because of the skilled nature of many of the tasks involved in transport operation, adequate training is an essential requirement. Many transport operators are not fully aware of their training needs, while individual employees' perception of training requirements is often distorted by a tendency to regard training more as a means of enhancement of their prospects for employment elsewhere than as a means of improving performance in their present positions.

A significant problem is that training budgets in many organisations are severely limited; several use only those external management training courses and seminars which are provided free of charge. Many organisations do not budget for training at all, while in others there is often a danger that training budgets could be cut further, or even eliminated entirely, to reduce costs. Training is a more important issue than is sometimes appreciated, both for new entrants to an organisation, and for those already employed. Most positions within a transport undertaking require certain basic skills, such as driving, mechanical and management skills, but many people in the industry, especially small operators and owner-drivers, learn largely by experience, with little or no formal training. The resulting lack of basic skills, or awareness of general and specific transport management techniques, causes many of the problems facing transport operators in developing countries.

There is also a requirement for training within local and central government, particularly within agencies involved in the development and application of regulations regarding both private transport and public transport services; in addition to general principles of transport operation and management, their requirements include a broader range of subjects, depending on their particular roles, such as economics, law, and civil engineering, as they are applied to transport.

Training can take various forms, ranging from on-the-job training to full-time courses of study; each is appropriate in particular circumstances. On-the-job training is effective in many cases, but requires high quality supervisors or managers as mentors; if these are not available the temporary employment of expatriates may be appropriate, particularly for the training of senior managers. Short and long courses, workshops and seminars, both in-house and at external institutions, are a valuable means of enhancing employees' skills. It is important, however, that such training is appropriate to the individual's role in the organisation, and to his or her ability; very often people are sent on unsuitable courses as a reward or incentive rather than because the training will be beneficial to the organisation, or to the individuals in the performance of their duties.

Courses of study in transport subjects organised by professional bodies can be useful. Normally these are part-time courses which can be taken at evening classes or through correspondence, and the latter facility is particularly useful in countries where the size of the formal transport industry cannot support the provision of courses in transport subjects. Full time study can be a valuable means of providing in-depth knowledge of particular subjects. Some people study transport, at universities or other full-time educational institutions, before embarking upon a career in transport, either in a government agency or in the transport industry; an increasing number of universities, both in developed and in developing countries, are offering specialised courses in transport subjects. Sometimes employees, particularly those in the public sector in some countries, are given paid or unpaid leave of absence for a year or more to pursue a full-time course of study; as with short courses, such opportunities are often given to inappropriate people, so that the investment may be of little or no benefit to the organisation.

There are various national and international professional organisations associated with the transport industry. They perform various functions, but primarily they provide a means for the establishment of best practices within the industry, disseminating information on developments in technology or management techniques through media such as professional trade journals, and a means of training. They fall into two broad categories, namely professional associations, such as the international Chartered Institute of Logistics and Transport (CILT) based in the United Kingdom, which provides individual members with internationally recognised professional qualifications, and operators' associations, such as the International Union of Public Transport (UITP), based in Brussels, which provides a forum for operators to meet and exchange views, knowledge and experiences, and discuss particular aspects of their operations, usually at periodic international conferences. There are national, regional and local operators' associations in most developing countries, but many lack resources and their contribution to the development and organisation of the industry in their respective countries is generally limited.

Professional organisations can play a very important part in the education process. Some organisations such as the CILT hold professional examinations based on courses of tuition which follow the Institute's syllabus; it is possible for candidates to study at approved educational centres in a large number of countries, or through distance learning programmes, sitting their exams at designated centres in their own countries. The resulting qualification indicates that an individual has met the Institute's standards, and has satisfactorily completed an approved course of study in particular transport subjects. Professional qualifications in transport can therefore be valuable as an indicator of an individual's suitability for a position with a transport undertaking. Some organisations insist on such qualifications as a requirement for eligibility. However, this can be unduly restrictive, and there may be people who by virtue of their experience are better suited to a particular position than somebody who has paper qualifications but inadequate experience. A serious problem in developing countries is that many junior staff are unable to afford the fees charged by overseas professional bodies.

On-the-job training is particularly valuable in transport, since many aspects of its operation are highly practical and can best be learned through experience. Many successful senior managers have worked their way up through their organisations, becoming thoroughly familiar with the tasks at each level before promotion to the next. However, such a career progression may take many years, and the path will embrace only a limited number of the activities of the organisation. Where there is a shortage of skilled managers, it is particularly important that the process should be as rapid as possible, while allowing sufficient time in each position to provide a thorough grounding, and also that all vital areas are covered. This requires a structured training programme, involving a logical progression through all key departments, supplemented by appropriate external courses in various subjects from time to time, and culminating in a junior management position; thereafter, the career should follow a path determined largely by the individual's particular aptitudes.

Some large transport organisations have established their own colleges for transport training, many meeting all requirements from the basic training of drivers and mechanics to advanced courses for senior management. In the United Kingdom, a number of large public and private sector transport groups, representing all modes, collaborated to establish the British Transport Staff College, which for many years provided specialist transport management training for candidates both from the UK and overseas; unfortunately this was a casualty of the privatisation of the public sector transport undertakings during the 1980s.

It is normally desirable within an organisation, whether it is a single operating unit or a holding company with a large number of subsidiaries within the passenger transport industry, to encourage the progression of employees upwards through the organisation, while taking measures where appropriate to develop their skills in relevant fields. Where there are several companies within the industry, it is common for personnel to move between companies in order to gain broader experience and more rapid promotion; in the case of large groups of companies, transfer between one company and another is often actively encouraged. Employee development in a large organisation should be linked to succession planning, so that, as far as possible, suitable people are always available to succeed employees who are promoted or retire.

Both central and local government authorities can facilitate training in transport; it is in their interest to do so, since improved standards of safety, reliability and efficiency in transport are beneficial to the economy generally. Indeed, funding for training may be a suitable subject for external aid finance where real benefits are likely to be achieved. Governments may assist indirectly by setting and enforcing standards of operation, which in turn require transport operators to employ appropriately trained staff; for example, in some countries there is a requirement for licensed transport managers to hold a recognised certificate of professional competence, which requires a specific programme of training to obtain. Many governments provide grants to organisations which provide approved training programmes for their employees.

A more direct approach is to facilitate the establishment of training institutions which can offer training in transport subjects, such as the Egyptian National Institute of Transport, and the National Institute of Transport in Tanzania; there are large transport research and training institutions in several cities in China. Such institutions can often justify government subsidy, and it may be desirable to provide certain operators, such as those in the informal transport sector, with free training, and possibly a small grant to compensate for loss of income during training. However, there is often a general lack of availability of suitable training, even in some developed countries, due partly to insufficient demand from operators who are not fully aware of their training requirements, and partly to a shortage of suitably qualified trainers. It is sometimes necessary to bring in experts such as external consultants to organise on-the-job training; this is not always viable except for very large operators.

A limiting factor in most developing countries is education, and while great progress as been made, and in general the present younger generation is receiving a far higher standard of education than previous generations, those with qualifications and experience are still too few in many cases to meet all the demands of a developing country. Standards vary considerably between countries, but levels of literacy are often low and there may be serious deficiencies in skills, both technical and administrative. In some cases, where qualified people are available, industry has not developed to a point where it can absorb them all, while many people with good qualifications have no practical experience in the industry. In many countries, great strides are being made in training future managers: but existing senior management is often faced with the medium-term problem of maintaining and improving standards, in an environment of increasing demand, and in the face of competition from other industries and from government for what is still a limited pool of expertise. This affects the transport industry both directly and indirectly: not only is the requirement increasing for skilled and qualified staff for the operating undertakings, but the organisations supporting the industry, their suppliers, and the local and national authorities, are all in a similar position and their resources are often stretched to the limit.

For an efficiently run, formal public transport system, it is therefore essential to address the requirement for training in transport management, and to facilitate the acquisition of practical experience. Principal areas to be covered in management training for senior and middle-level executives should include operating systems and procedures, the use of management information systems to provide the necessary data for planning, monitoring and control of operations, and methods of operational costing to enable appropriate rates and charges to be set and to calculate the viability of individual services. Senior managers should also have a broad awareness of the tasks to be carried out at lower levels, such as operational control systems, route planning and scheduling, marketing of transport services, vehicle maintenance and its management, and PSV driving and conducting; obviously, more thorough training will be required in these areas for those engaged in these activities.

Training for junior and middle management in operational control systems should cover the use of management information systems and the control of fuel, tyres, kilometres, revenue, stores, hours worked and other controllable cost items. Route planning and scheduling is a specialised skill, and training in this subject should be aimed principally at junior operations management; it should cover collection of data including traffic statistics from existing operations, market surveys, origin-and-destination surveys and demand forecasts, development of route networks, calculation of service frequencies, scheduling of buses and crews and production of timetables. There is a requirement at middle and senior management levels for training in marketing techniques as applied to transport operations to enable companies to compete in a commercial environment; this should cover the basic principles of marketing, including market research techniques, together with transport-specific aspects such as passenger information systems, customer relations and fleet presentation.

There is a specific requirement for training in management of fleet maintenance, in addition to regular technical training. This training should ideally be given at three levels: senior management will require short courses or seminars covering general management principles, but in particular stressing the need for adequate management of the maintenance function; training for middle management should cover in more detail the main issues such as planning of preventive maintenance, control systems and procedures; and for junior management and supervisory grades there will be a requirement for a series of courses, covering each maintenance topic separately and in much greater detail. Vehicle mechanics may be trained through formal apprenticeship schemes, sometimes supplemented by appropriate courses at technical colleges or similar institutions. In most countries there are recognised certification schemes for vehicle mechanics.

Driver training is vital, both for reasons of safety and for efficient operation. There are two principal aspects: driving skills, and matters specific to the operation such as route learning and operating practices. Some operators, particularly smaller ones, recruit only drivers who already hold licences to drive public service vehicles, and give them little or no additional training before they commence work. It is more common for large bus operators to train drivers in-house, with qualified instructors. Standards of driver training vary considerably; many operators provide very basic training, but some have highly developed programmes which involve extensive classroom instruction in addition to road training, provision of vehicles with simulated loads, and even the use of driving simulators.

Route training is an important aspect of driver training in a large undertaking with an extensive network; newly recruited drivers cannot be expected to know the routes, and should be given appropriate instructions. For regular bus services, even in the case of operators who restrict drivers to a single route, initial familiarisation with the route is necessary, although this is a relatively simple exercise. Ideally a new driver should be accompanied by an experienced driver, until he has completed the route at least once, and preferably several times. If he can be accompanied by a driving instructor for the initial journeys, this is even more beneficial; however, this is rarely practical, especially where turnover of drivers is high and training resources are limited. Where conductors are employed, it may be feasible for a new driver to be teamed with an experienced conductor who is able to show him the route. In some organisations it is normal practice for all drivers to be recruited from conducting staff, so that they should already know the routes; there are both advantages and disadvantages with such a policy. A more common alternative is for the new driver to travel as a passenger on all routes. A recent development has been the introduction of bespoke computerised route learning software, which incorporates maps and visual simulation to enable drivers to become familiar with any route without leaving the classroom.

In some countries it is normal for aspiring bus drivers to arrange and fund their own training, through independent driving schools, before applying for employment with a transport operator; however, this requires an investment by the individual which many cannot afford, although loans may be available. Some operators put trainee drivers on the payroll at the commencement of their training, while others do not employ them until they have satisfactorily completed their training. Some require trainee drivers to pay for their training subsequently through deductions from their salaries, and may require drivers to work for them for a minimum period so that the investment in training is recovered. It is common for small operators to recruit drivers who have been trained by larger undertakings.

DISCIPLINE AND INCENTIVES

Safety, service standards, timekeeping, revenue collection and passenger relations depend very much on standards of discipline and levels of motivation amongst bus crews and other staff. Discipline is difficult to enforce in most transport organisations since many of the staff, particularly drivers and conductors, work largely unsupervised: unless an officer such as an inspector is travelling on a bus the activities of the crew can be monitored only at points along the route where supervisors are stationed; the problem is particularly acute in long distance operations.

Common examples of indiscipline are failure to operate in accordance with schedule or to follow the correct route, dangerous or aggressive driving, theft of fare revenue or failure to ensure that all fares are collected, discourtesy to passengers, and overloading of buses.

Motivation of staff also presents problems, particularly in public sector undertakings. Low salaries and weak supervision in many organisations have contributed to a situation of low morale and poor discipline, corruption or dishonesty amongst employees at all levels, and to problems of recruiting and retaining good staff. A common problem in some countries, particularly in public sector undertakings, is that it is difficult to impose appropriate sanctions in order to maintain discipline; the scope for dismissal, and even redundancy, is often restricted by government policy. Similarly, staff motivation may be difficult where public sector employees are subject to standard government conditions of employment; in many cases a complete overhaul of government pay and conditions is desirable, and while there is a trend towards reform in this area in many countries, there are still many where the efficiency of all public sector undertakings is seriously affected. Private sector organisations are normally less constrained, although labour legislation sometimes militates against effective discipline.

Driver discipline is particularly important where earnings are related in some way to the revenue earned by the vehicle, for example where the setoran system applies; an incentive to maximise revenue often leads to aggressive and dangerous driving. Drivers with bad accident records should be dismissed or transferred to non-driving duties if suitable and appropriate vacancies exist. However, drivers should be given a chance to improve after their first accident, unless this was due to blatant disregard for safety or regulations; inexperienced drivers are likely to have accidents, and should learn from them. Moreover, the dismissal of one inexperienced driver will usually result in his replacement by a driver with even less experience, who is more likely to have an accident than his predecessor.

A sanction which is sometimes applied to drivers is to require them to pay for accident damage for which they are responsible. However, this is rarely practical, since the cost of many accidents is more than a driver can afford to pay; the cost is often recovered by regular deductions from the driver's salary, and this may take several years. Many drivers accumulate massive debts, as they continue to have accidents while working to pay for previous ones; they are not dismissed, since this will make further recovery impossible. A safe driving incentive scheme is usually more effective, as discussed below. Bad driving is a problem in almost every transport organisation, and while the consequent costs can be minimised by effective discipline and training, these can never be eliminated entirely and must be recognised as a normal operating expense.

Discipline is also important in respect of staff responsible for handling money or valuable items such as spare parts or fuel. Effective revenue control procures, and adequate measures to ensure that they are followed, are essential to discipline in fare collection; this issue is discussed in Chapter 9. Some operators which do not practise setoran deal with the problem of theft of fuel from vehicles by requiring drivers to purchase their own fuel from salaries which include an element for the purpose; this may also have the effect of encouraging drivers to drive in a more economical manner, and therefore more safely and with more sympathy towards the vehicle.

Incentive schemes can be a valuable disciplinary tool, as well as being a means of motivation and increasing staff productivity. Some operators provide incentive schemes to crews to encourage them to collect and pay in all revenue, by paying bonuses based directly on revenue; however, the effectiveness of such schemes is usually limited except where standards of honesty are generally high. Bonuses based on other performance measures, such as attendance or punctuality, may be effective, provided that the incentives are attractive to the staff concerned, and the measures are readily defined and measured. Above all, the benefits to the undertaking from any bonus scheme must exceed the cost of the scheme, including its administration.

Safe driving award schemes for drivers have been adopted by many transport undertakings and can, if effectively implemented, be very cost-effective through reducing the number and severity of accidents. Most involve cash payments based on the length of time a driver has worked without a blameworthy accident, and are typically awarded each year; for each additional year of accident-free driving, the amount of the award is normally increased. A potential problem with such schemes is the apportionment of blame for an accident, which can often lead to disputes, while it is difficult to cater for blameworthy accidents of varying severity: it may be considered unfair for a driver with several years of accident-free driving to lose his bonus due to a minor, but blameworthy accident. Some safe driving bonus schemes include reports of dangerous driving as a reason for loss of bonus; this may be even more subjective. Accidents are expensive, and high bonus payments can be justified if it can be proved that they result in an even greater reduction in accident costs, but such proof may be very elusive.

Long service award schemes are sometimes used in an attempt to reduce staff turnover where this is a problem. Like safe driving schemes, they usually involve cash payments for each year of continuous service, often with the amount increasing each year. In some cases bonuses are also related to discipline, with loss of bonus as a penalty for certain misdemeanours. As an alternative, pay scales may include an automatic increase in basic rate for each year of continuous service.

Such schemes are only commercially justifiable where they are instrumental in reducing staff turnover, and hence in reducing the related costs of recruitment and training by a greater amount than the total sum paid out in bonuses. This may apply in respect of staff with high training costs, such as drivers, but not for unskilled labour, or for skills which are readily available; similarly, it would not apply to staff categories with low turnover rates. However, industrial relations problems may arise where some categories of staff are eligible for long service payments while others are not.

The effectiveness of discipline and incentive schemes is heavily dependent on adherence to supervisory procedures. Crews must accept instructions from, and be fully co-operative with, the operator's supervisory staff and, where applicable, the staff of the regulatory authorities in the performance of their duties. Inspectors play a key role in the disciplinary system, by detecting offences committed by crews and receiving complaints from passengers. In most instances offences should be reported to the operations department, for the necessary action to be taken: the operations manager or one of his assistants (preferably not a personnel manager) should decide on such action and ensure that it is carried out.

Operators must keep disciplinary records in respect of every employee: all offences must be recorded, together with the disciplinary action taken in each case. The role of a personnel department in the maintenance of discipline must be carefully considered: while staff in the personnel department should be more conversant with all relevant legislation than those in other departments, discipline is very much part of the management function, and as such should be the responsibility of individual departmental managers. For example, a workshop manager is responsible for maintenance standards within his department, and is aware of the consequences of failure to follow correct procedures; he will be in a better position to discipline his staff than a personnel manager who is less conversant with maintenance procedures. In many organisations disciplinary cases are dealt with by a panel comprising members of the individual's departmental management and the personnel department. This is normally effective although the common tendency for the panel to become excessively large should be avoided.

Many transport organisations, particularly the larger ones, issue uniforms to various categories of staff, principally drivers, conductors and inspectors, while workshop staff are normally issued with protective clothing to a standard pattern. In addition to projecting a good public image, uniforms may represent a significant benefit to the staff involved. By making staff readily identifiable, they are also useful in assisting enforcement officers in carrying out their duties, and enabling members of the public to report misdemeanours on the part of bus crews. For this reason it is useful for operators to provide all road staff with individual numbers which should be clearly displayed on their uniforms. Inspectors' uniforms should be clearly distinguishable from those of drivers and conductors. In some countries it is a statutory requirement that uniforms should be worn by all road staff, with badges which clearly indicate the organisations by whom they are employed, and their functions.

13

OPERATING COSTS

COST CATEGORIES

The cost structure of a public transport service is complex: some costs are fixed in the medium term, regardless of the level of activity; some vary with the number of buses, and some with the number of kilometres operated. It is important to understand the characteristics of the various cost elements in order to be able to establish with reasonable accuracy the cost of any activity, such as the cost of operating the full service on a particular route, or the cost of an individual journey in the bus timetable.

Fixed costs, commonly referred to as overhead costs, are those costs which remain constant, regardless of the number of buses, kilometres or routes operated. They include the costs of providing and maintaining depots, workshops, offices and terminals, the salaries and wages of most management, administrative and maintenance personnel, the cost of training, of ancillary vehicles and other such expenses. They also include certain interest charges and taxes which are not affected by the level of activity, and which have to be paid.

The time period over which costs are fixed varies depending on the item concerned. None are fixed in the very long term: all assets require replacement eventually, and their size or number can be varied at that time, while staff numbers can be increased or decreased within the relevant terms of employment. The level of fixed costs as a proportion of total costs depends on the nature of the organisation concerned. An operator with only one vehicle which is garaged at the roadside has negligible overhead costs other than those incurred in respect of his vehicle. At the opposite extreme, a large fleet operator may have a head office complex, several bus stations and operating depots and a large workshop facility; rail-based systems also have considerable track costs which must be covered. The proportion of fixed to variable costs can have a significant bearing on the basis of charging for transport services.

Costs which vary directly according to the number of vehicles operated include the cost of owning each vehicle, principally interest on the purchase cost, insurance, licence fees, roadworthiness inspection fees, and an element of depreciation; other costs which vary closely with the number of buses are crew wages, washing and cleaning of buses, and sometimes garaging.

Costs which vary directly with the number of kilometres operated include the costs of fuel, lubricants, tyres and maintenance materials; it is also realistic, when calculating actual costs of operation, to include depreciation in this category, since in practice the life of a vehicle is determined more by the extent to which it is used than by time, even though depreciation is usually treated as a time-based cost for accounting purposes. Some labour costs also very with kilometres operated, but it is normally more practical to regard most labour costs, other than those of crews, as an overhead.

Costs which vary directly with the number of kilometres operated should be quoted as a cost per kilometre, for example fuel costs at x cents per kilometre. They may be calculated by dividing the expenditure over a period by the number of kilometres operated over that period. Those which vary with the number of buses operated may be quoted as costs per bus per day, per week, month or accounting period, for example bus cleaning at y dollars per bus per day. They may be calculated by dividing the expenditure over a period by the number of buses owned or operated during that period, and then dividing by the period for which the parameter is to be expressed if this is shorter. For example, to calculate the expenditure per bus per day on cleaning, where expenditure is accounted for monthly, it will be necessary to divide monthly expenditure on cleaning by the number of days in the month, and then by the number of buses operated. Where the number of buses varies over the month, an average daily figure for the number of buses must be calculated; if the variation is small, it is sometimes sufficient to use the month-end fleet figure.

Some costs vary according to other parameters. For example, terminal departure charges or road tolls may vary with the number of journeys operated. In some cases it is possible to identify certain costs which are fixed for each route, varying according to the number of routes operated and in some cases the length of the route. They include such items as terminal and bus stop costs, where these are specific to individual routes, and the cost of supervision and inspection, again, where such activities are specific to particular routes. In some countries each route requires a separate licence, in which case the cost of a route licence will be a route-related cost, but this will normally be insignificant.

Some costs which are fixed for one undertaking may be variable for another. For example, if an undertaking owns its own terminal facilities the cost of providing these will be a fixed cost; but if it uses terminal facilities provided by a third party, and pays a charge for each bus departure, this becomes a variable cost. Similarly, if maintenance is contracted out and charged for at a fixed rate per kilometre, all maintenance costs including the cost of workshop equipment and labour become kilometre-related rather than fixed or bus-related. Some costs may be directly related to revenue: for example, in some large groups of companies, subsidiaries are charged a percentage of revenue as fees for technical and advisory services provided by the head office; for route costing purposes, such costs are best dealt with by reducing revenue by the relevant percentage.

The relationship between these various cost categories is important for costing purposes, and to some extent in the calculation of fare rates. The provision of an additional journey on a route might be accomplished without increasing the number of buses required, by scheduling an existing bus to operate additional kilometres during the course of the day; this will incur only additional kilometre-variable costs. If, however, a number of additional journeys are provided which require an extra bus, the additional costs incurred will be the kilometre-variable costs plus the vehicle-variable costs. In neither case will fixed costs be affected.

The daily cost of operating a bus route may therefore be calculated by multiplying the number of buses required to operate the route by the daily bus-variable cost; multiplying the total daily kilometres operated on the route by the total cost per kilometre of all kilometre-variable costs; and summing the two figures, together with any route-related costs. A bus route is viable if it earns sufficient revenue from the fares collected to cover these variable costs. Equally, a single bus trip is viable if it earns sufficient revenue to cover only the kilometre-variable costs incurred, provided that it does not require an additional bus to operate it. However, over the operation as a whole the total revenue from all routes must cover not only the variable costs, but the total fixed costs also. This means that there will have to be some routes which earn considerably more than their variable costs to compensate for those whose contributions are much smaller, or which break even.

Increasing the number of kilometres operated on a route without increasing the number of kilometres will reduce the overall cost per kilometre for the route, since the per-bus costs will be spread over more kilometres; conversely, reducing the number of kilometres without reducing the number of buses will increase average total costs per kilometre. Similarly, operating speeds can have a significant effect on total cost: more buses will be required to operate a given number of kilometres on an urban route, where speed is restricted due to congested conditions, than on an inter-city route where speeds are higher, so that per-bus costs for the urban route are spread over fewer kilometres, and costs per kilometre will therefore be lower.

It is also useful to analyse costs by the nature of the input, particularly for the purpose of cost control, and to be able to assess the impact on total costs of a change in the cost of an input, such as a rise in the cost of fuel or a general salary increase. The principal inputs are labour, fuel, maintenance materials and the vehicles. The relative significance of the various cost elements varies considerably between transport undertakings in developed countries and those in developing countries, due largely to differences in the relative costs of inputs. For example, labour costs in developed countries may account for up to 70% of total costs, while in developing countries, where wage levels tend to be very much lower, it is usually less than 50%, and may be as low as 10%. On the other hand, fuel costs are often more significant in developing countries, but the actual percentage varies considerably, due largely to different rates of excise duty. Vehicle capital and maintenance material costs are also often much higher in developing countries, since many of these items are imported, and may be subject to high rates of duty, while their costs may suffer from continuing inflation due to falling exchange rates.

For management accounting purposes it is customary to categorise costs according to the nature of the activity or function. This enables the managers of the departments responsible for each major activity to be held accountable for those costs. In a typical transport undertaking the three main cost headings are Operation, Maintenance, and Management and Administration. Each of these can be broken down into numerous sub-headings, each of which, in a large organisation, may have its own manager who is accountable for all costs under that heading; the larger the organisation, the greater the number of sub-headings which is likely to be appropriate for accounting and cost control purposes. The following shows a typical breakdown of costs; not all headings will be applicable to all operators, while some operators will require headings which are not included:

Vehicle Operating Costs:

- Manpower
- Fuel, lubricants and grease
- Depreciation or fleet replacement provision
- Vehicle insurance
- Licences and permits
- Bus station charges
- Other vehicle operating expenses

Vehicle Maintenance Costs:

- Manpower
- Maintenance materials
- Tyres and tubes
- Consumables
- Outside maintenance
- Ancillary vehicles
- Other maintenance expenses

Management and Administrative Costs:

- Manpower
- Stationery
- Telephones and postage
- Ancillary vehicles
- Advertising
- Claims and bad debts
- Agents' commissions

- Other insurance
- Training
- Interest
- Taxation
- Other management and administrative expenses

These cost headings are discussed below.

Manpower

Manpower costs are normally a significant item, and appear under all three main cost headings as shown above. To monitor and control manpower costs it is normally necessary to break these down in two ways: by staff category, and by the various elements, such as basic salary, overtime, etc. (Other cost categories which may appear under more than one main heading include the costs of ancillary vehicles, buildings, utilities, and communications; depending on their overall significance in relation to other costs, it may or may not be appropriate to consolidate and analyse these in a similar way.) Staff categories are discussed in detail in Chapter 7, but typical categorisation of staff for accounting and costing purposes may be:

Operating staff:

- Inspectors
- Drivers
- Conductors
- Ticket sellers or booking clerks
- Bus loaders
- Trainees

and/or by service category, for example:

- Urban services
- Rural services
- Long-distance services
- Charter, tours and excursions

Maintenance staff:

- Management
- Foremen
- Chargehands
- Skilled
- Semi-skilled
- Unskilled

- Trainees and apprentices

and/or by activity, for example:

- Running repairs
- Unit shop
- Minor docks
- Major docks
- Body shop
- Tyres
- Ancillary vehicle drivers
- Cleaning
- Stores
- Other

Management and Administration staff:

- Senior management
- Middle management
- Supervisory
- Clerical
- Secretarial
- Cashiers
- Office cleaners
- Security staff
- Ancillary vehicle drivers
- Trainees
- Other

and/or:

- Operations management
- Operations planning
- Advertising and public relations
- Personnel
- Computers/IT
- Internal audit
- Finance department
- Insurance and claims
- Security
- Other

Manpower costs, whether or not they are broken down by category, may also be broken down into their elements, which may include the following:

- Basic salary
- Overtime payments
- Premium rate payments such as enhanced payments for working spreadover or night shifts
- Bonus and other incentive payments
- Social security and other statutory payments by employer
- Accommodation and subsistence allowances (often applicable to long-distance operations)
- Housing allowances
- Medical insurance
- Pension contributions by employer
- Long service and other awards
- Uniforms and protective clothing

Vehicle operating manpower costs are variable partly with the number of vehicles and partly with the number of kilometres operated. In actual fact, they are variable more with time than with kilometres, but for most costing purposes it is usually more practical to convert time to kilometres. The number of drivers, and conductors if these are employed, is usually closely related to the number of buses operated. The actual proportion will vary, depend on levels of utilisation and working practices. The basic salaries of these crews will be directly related to the number of buses, but certain payments such as overtime will vary to a large extent with kilometres operated.

Certain operating manpower cost elements vary with other parameters; for instance if crews operating long distance services are paid overnight accommodation and subsistence allowances on duties which involve one or more nights away from base, this cost will vary according to the number of such journeys operated. A refined costing model will take these other types of variation into account, but for most costing purposes it is sufficiently accurate to assume that all crew costs are variable with the number of buses only. An important exception is in the calculation of marginal costs, or the costing of individual bus trips or parts of trips, where a variation in the number of kilometres operated may result in an increase or decrease in hourly basic and overtime payments. Where crew emoluments are paid directly out of fare revenue, as is the case where the setoran system is in force, these should not be regarded as an operating cost; in some cases, however, the operator pays a small amount in basic salary or benefits to crews, which is augmented by the revenue collected under the setoran arrangement, and such payments should be treated as bus-variable costs.

Where labour costs are high, as in most developed countries, it is common for buses to be operated by the driver only, as discussed in Chapter 9. The driver may be responsible for collecting fares; sometimes fares are collected before travel. Although one-person-operation (OPO) may save labour costs, the savings are normally significantly less than might be expected, while there are other disadvantages also. OPO drivers are normally paid at a higher rate, typically up to 25% more than drivers working with conductors, to recognise the additional responsibility. Where the driver is responsible for collecting fares, dwell times at bus stops are increased, and this increases overall journey times so that additional buses (and drivers) are required to maintain a given frequency; unless labour costs are very high, the cost of the additional vehicles may offset any savings in labour costs.

Maintenance manpower is sometimes regarded as a fixed cost, although the workshop labour requirement is actually a function of the workload, which in turn is determined by the number of kilometres operated and also by the age and condition of the fleet, and operating conditions generally. It is normally possible to vary the number of staff employed for this function, although there is likely to be some delay, particularly when staff numbers must be reduced. Taking these factors into account, it is normally more appropriate to regard this as primarily a bus-variable cost.

Management and administration manpower costs are only indirectly influenced by the fleet size and level of activity, and are more appropriately treated as a fixed cost. The degree to which manpower costs are fixed is to some extent affected by labour regulations, and terms and conditions of employment. Where employment can be terminated easily at short notice, or where casual labour is readily available so that the staff complement can be increased or reduced at very short notice, a higher proportion of manpower costs becomes variable, either with the number of buses or with kilometres. This will normally apply more in the case of unskilled jobs; those requiring special training or experience will be less easy to treat in this way.

Other labour costs such as uniform costs, housing benefit, and medical insurance are usually directly related to the number of employees, and unlike salaries and wages do not vary directly with the level of activity. Pension costs may be based on basic salaries but may vary with total pay. If pensioners are paid from current revenue rather than from a pension fund, as in countries such as China where it is customary for public sector organisations to retain employees on the payroll as pensioners after they have retired, the cost of supporting pensioners replaces the cost of making pension contributions in respect of existing employees. In an undertaking which is expanding, revenue is likely to be more than sufficient to support the pensioners; however, if it is contracting, this can become a major problem. Unless full provision is made for future pension payments, and charged to current operations, this is a fixed cost which is not affected in any way by the current size of the undertaking or level of activity.

Fuel, lubricants and grease

For accounting purposes, fuel costs may be recorded as total expenditure on fuel, including fuel purchased in bulk and delivered to the company's own storage tanks, and any fuel purchased from other sources such as roadside filling stations or drawn at other operators' depots or terminals. Where drivers are required to pay for their own fuel out of revenue, as is the case in some undertakings such as those which operate on the setoran principle, fuel cost need not be regarded as an operating cost for accounting purposes.

As discussed in Chapter 15, detailed records should be kept of all fuel issues so that the fuel consumption of each individual vehicle can be calculated for monitoring purposes, and overall fleet fuel consumption figures, and consumption figures for different vehicle categories or different categories of operation, can be calculated for costing purposes. Fuel costs per kilometre may be synthesised for costing purposes from the price of fuel and the vehicle fuel consumption. Where buses of different types are operated, with significantly different fuel consumption figures, each type should be costed separately.

The cost of lubricating oils and greases is similarly related directly to kilometres operated. It is normally of the order of 5% of fuel cost, and while it is useful to record expenditure on these items separately for monitoring and accounting purposes, for most costing purposes, it is convenient to include lubricants and greases with fuel.

Depreciation or fleet replacement provision

If a bus service is to continue on a viable basis, it is necessary that it generates sufficient revenue not only to cover its direct operating costs, but also to fund replacement of the vehicles used when this becomes due. When analysing bus operating costs it is important to distinguish between the depreciation charges shown in the accounts, and the true cost of replacing the vehicle. It is the latter which is relevant in the present context, and may be very different from the cost of depreciation, which is usually based on the purchase cost of the vehicles: the true cost of replacing the vehicles will be the actual cost of the new vehicles at the time they are purchased.

Where current cost depreciation is practised, the difference should be insignificant, but when depreciation is based on historic cost, and where there is significant inflation in the economy, there is likely to be a very large difference between the two. Moreover, depreciation is usually calculated on a time basis, although the life of a bus is more realistically measured in kilometres. Some deterioration takes place over time regardless of the degree of use, such as corrosion, which is largely time-related rather than distance-related; however, most wear and tear is more directly related to kilometres operated.

For the purpose of calculating operating costs, therefore, it is more realistic to divide the current replacement cost for a vehicle by the number of kilometres it is expected to operate over its lifetime to give a replacement cost per kilometre. It may be necessary to deduct the expected residual value, but again, this must be based on actual value, such as the resale value at current market prices, or the scrap value including the value of any components which may be put to further use, rather than a notional residual value which may be used for accounting purposes.

Vehicle insurance

Vehicle insurance, at least for third party liability, is normally a legal requirement, and may be a significant item of expenditure. Motor insurance premium rates have risen substantially in recent years, for a number of reasons. Increasing traffic levels in cities, and higher speeds on inter-city highways have resulted in an increase in the number and severity of accidents, while the increasing complexity of modern vehicles tends to increase the cost of accident repairs. The "litigation culture", which is now widespread in developed countries and spreading to developing countries, is resulting in increasing numbers of claims being filed and increasingly generous court awards. Many claims are spurious or fraudulent, but even if these are eventually rejected, the administrative costs involved may be significant.

Premiums are normally charged on the basis of the number of vehicles operated, but often a blanket premium is charged based on the operator's claims record, which in turn is related more closely to the level of operation than to the number of vehicles. Therefore, although insurance is often regarded as an overhead or vehicle-related cost, for medium-term operational costing purposes it is usually more realistic to base it on kilometres operated.

Substantial savings, in both insurance and accident repair costs, can often be made through greater attention to accident prevention and control, as well as by selecting the most cost-effective form of insurance. Most operators purchase third-party motor vehicle insurance. This does not cover accident damage to the operator's own vehicles, which must also be taken into account in calculating operating costs; usually such costs are included in maintenance expenditure, although it is desirable that they are identifiable separately so that the total cost of accidents including insurance can be monitored.

Some large operators opt to self-insure, where this is permitted by law. In this case it is essential to make adequate provision for all accident costs and any other claims which would otherwise be covered by insurance; again, this provision is primarily a kilometre-variable cost. It is also usually prudent, when self-insuring for normal accidents, to insure against catastrophic claims, although by definition the likelihood of such claims is small and therefore the premiums should not be a major expenditure item; these premiums are normally best treated as an overhead expense. Self insurance often requires the deposit, with a government agency, of a sum of money as a form of security; although this usually earns interest it is a cash payment, but is a one-off payment and is often substantially less than the premium which would otherwise have been paid. There can be significant cash flow advantages from self insurance, since while premiums are normally paid in advance, settlement of claims is made in arrears.

Owners of taxis and paratransit vehicles often have difficulty in obtaining suitable insurance cover. Some insurance companies are not prepared to insure these vehicles, or charge what are regarded as excessive premiums. One reason sometimes given for operating taxis without the proper licences is so that the owners can insure the vehicles as private cars, although the insurance is likely to be invalidated in the event of accidents incurred whilst vehicles so insured are in use as taxis.

Licences and permits

Operators of public transport services, like all road users, are invariably subject to a series of fees and charges, including vehicle licences and fees for vehicle safety inspections; these are directly related to the number of vehicles. Other licences may relate to routes, or to the operation as a whole; such costs are usually minimal and not considered to be significant. The subject of licensing is discussed in Chapter 19.

Bus station charges

Unless a bus station is owned by the operator who uses it, bus operators are normally charged for its use. Charges are usually based on departures; there may be a flat fee per departure, but sometimes the fee varies according to the capacity of the vehicle, or its type: for example, the fee for a luxury bus may be higher than for a standard bus. Sometimes the charge is based on the number of passengers carried, on a proportion of revenue collected, or on a combination of these elements. Operators may also be charged for parking their vehicles at bus stations; although this is relatively uncommon, the economic cost of long-term parking at stations, particularly those in city centres, can be considerable, and may justify high parking charges.

Because of the monopoly or near-monopoly positions which many bus stations hold, some form of control may be necessary over the charges made to bus operators. Control may be exercised by an operators' association whose membership includes the majority of transport operators, or by a statutory regulatory body. Rates should be set so that the full ownership, maintenance and management costs of the bus stations are covered, with a reasonable profit margin if appropriate; however, it will be necessary to ensure that the stations are efficiently managed, to prevent the "cost plus" charging approach from resulting in wasteful expenditure.

Other vehicle operating expenses

There are numerous other vehicle operating costs, which are difficult to allocate to specific vehicles or routes, although in a large undertaking it may be desirable to include each as a separate heading in the accounts; they are generally small, and for convenience are normally regarded as fixed costs. They may include such items as depot and bus station rent, rates, utilities and maintenance, provision and maintenance of facilities at bus stops and terminals, stationery, ticket printing, maintenance of equipment such as ticket machines, radios, bus stop maintenance, staff cars and training vehicles. Commissions paid to agents in respect of ticket sales are sometimes included under this heading; however, these can normally be allocated to individual services, and the most appropriate way of treating them for route costing purposes is to deduct them from revenue.

Maintenance materials

This is a major item of expenditure, and includes all parts and materials used in the maintenance of the vehicle fleet; normally tyres and consumables are accounted for separately. For the purpose of monitoring vehicle maintenance expenditure, it is important that materials used for the maintenance of vehicles are accounted for separately from materials used for other maintenance, for example buildings, workshop equipment, or ticket machines.

Usage of virtually all materials is directly related to the level of vehicle usage, and therefore should be treated as a kilometre-related cost. Where there are significant differences in the type of operation, there may also be significant differences in costs: for example buses used on poorly surfaced roads will require replacement of suspension parts much more frequently than those operated only on smooth tarmac roads. For the purposes of the management information system, all maintenance materials used should be allocated to individual vehicles.

In most developing countries a large proportion of spare parts is imported, and as with other imported inputs their costs will be sensitive to exchange rate fluctuations.

Tyres and tubes

The cost of tyres, and tubes where these are used, is a significant item. Tyre expenditure can vary considerably, depending on the nature of the operation and maintenance standards. For costing purposes, an average tyre cost per kilometre is calculated by dividing total expenditure on tyres, including purchase of new tyres and any retreading, by the total number of kilometres operated by the fleet over a specified period.

If there are wide variations in the nature of the operation, and where specific vehicles can be identified with each type of operation, it is useful to calculate tyre costs separately. For example, in an operation with urban services running on good tarmac roads, and also rural services operating on unsurfaced roads, tyre costs should be calculated separately for the two types of service for more accurate route costing.

Consumables

Some maintenance materials are used in small quantities or are difficult to measure or allocate, such as nuts, bolts, screws, rivets, hydraulic fluids, or electrical cables for minor repairs. These normally represent an insignificant proportion of total costs and are therefore treated as a single item in the accounts; for costing purposes they can be included with maintenance materials costs as a kilometre-related cost.

Outside maintenance

Where all vehicles are maintained by outside contractors all maintenance expenditure can be included under this heading. It will include materials, labour, and overheads of the maintenance contractor. Where some maintenance is done in-house and some outside, for costing purposes outside maintenance costs can be added to maintenance materials costs, since both are kilometre-related.

Ancillary vehicles

Most undertakings operate a fleet of ancillary vehicles such as breakdown recovery trucks or vehicles used to carry supervisory staff while on duty. In addition, there are usually a number of official cars provided for senior management as part of their employment terms. The number of ancillary vehicles required is not normally directly related to the level of operation, and this cost is best regarded as fixed. This cost heading may appear in the accounts under all three main cost headings.

Other maintenance expenses

Other items of maintenance expenditure may include workshop rent, rates and utilities, repairs to plant and equipment, and cleaning. Bus cleaning is often treated as a maintenance cost, and is not normally allocated to individual vehicles. The number of cleaning staff is related to the number of buses, although the amount of cleaning required will be related to the level of activity, and therefore cleaning costs are partly kilometre-related; in practice this is a relatively small cost item and for convenience may be treated as a bus-related cost or even as a fixed cost. In some cases cleaning is the responsibility of drivers and conductors, and does not require a separate cost heading.

Management and administrative costs

By far the greatest portion of management and administrative costs is attributable to manpower. There are various other costs, which in a large undertaking are normally accounted for separately; several of these apply also to operations and maintenance, and in large organisations may be allocated to those departments as appropriate. The main items are stationery, telephones, and postage, advertising and public relations, claims and bad debts, and insurance (other than vehicle insurance). All of these costs may be regarded as fixed. Other administrative expenses which may be too insignificant to account for separately, except in a very large undertaking, include travel and entertainment, office equipment maintenance or rental, security, subscriptions, donations, bank charges and legal and professional fees.

Training

Training may be a major cost item, particularly in respect of bus crews: it can cost approximately 25% of a driver's annual salary to train a driver who has no previous experience of driving large passenger vehicles. If staff turnover is high, training costs will therefore be significant: for example with a 50% annual turnover of bus drivers, training costs will equate to approximately 12.5% of the annual drivers' salary costs.

It is common for only the larger undertakings to train drivers, with the smaller operators recruiting drivers who have already been trained. Where training is provided by driver training institutions, employers normally pay for the training of their drivers; it is unusual for drivers to pay directly for their own training.

Training in other areas, particularly maintenance, may also be a significant cost. Some employers deduct training costs from employees' salaries, particularly if they leave within a specified period. Training costs are normally regarded as an overhead, but in the case of drivers are in fact directly related to the number of drivers employed, and therefore to the level of service provided. Unless staff turnover is low, the number of drivers employed can be varied relatively easily, and it may therefore be argued that it would be more realistic to regard driver training as a bus-related cost.

Interest

Many transport undertakings have substantial borrowings for various reasons. Interest payments may therefore be a significant expenditure item, but their treatment for costing or accounting purposes is not always straightforward. Some interest charges are directly attributable to specific areas, such as interest on loans to finance the purchase of vehicles; for costing purposes these charges may be treated as bus-related costs. Interest on loans for the purchase of workshop equipment would, on the other hand, be treated as a fixed cost. Many loans, however, are not attributable to any specific item, as in the case of a loan or overdraft used to provide working capital. Many transport undertakings rely on such funding and are constantly in debt, although the extent may fluctuate considerably, as will interest payments.

It is misleading to regard these interest payments as an operating cost; rather, they are a consequence of the undertaking incurring deficits as a result of expenditure exceeding revenue at certain times. A common accounting practice is to quote profits before interest and tax, thus eliminating all interest payments from the calculation.

The financial structure of the organisation also has a bearing on the way in which interest charges are treated. A private sector company paying dividends to its shareholders, in return for the provision of capital, pays these dividends out of profits; if profits are low, or a loss is incurred, the undertaking has the option of paying a reduced dividend, or none at all. A state-owned company, on the other hand, whose capital is provided in the form of a loan from government, must usually pay the interest on the loan regardless of the profitability of the undertaking. This interest is equivalent to a dividend to shareholders, but unlike a dividend may not be varied to reflect the company's ability to pay it; it may also be subject to fluctuations in interest rates, which can impose additional financial burdens on the organisation. In effect it is an overhead cost which must be met regardless of the level of operation or financial performance.

In some cases, when financial performance has been poor, transport undertakings have paid interest on their loans by means of further borrowing; this exacerbates the financial problems of the organisation, usually with disastrous consequences.

Taxation

In addition to taxes which apply to all businesses, transport undertakings often have to pay various other taxes, some of which may be regarded as operating costs. Taxes vary considerably between one country and another, but in most countries there are excise duties payable on fuel, while licence fees, dealt with elsewhere, are also a form of tax. Transport operators are also often affected by import duties on vehicles and spare parts. Some taxes are fixed costs; others, such as fuel tax, are variable. Other than taxation of profits, which cannot be regarded as an operating cost, virtually all taxes are included in the costs of the respective inputs, and need not be accounted for separately.

BREAKDOWN OF COSTS

Because of widely differing circumstances, differences in the nature of the operations, different accounting practices and major fluctuations in currency values, it is not possible to give examples of typical costs for any input or activity, or to make accurate comparisons between operating costs in different countries. Comparison of percentages is reasonably useful, but it should be borne in mind that if one cost item is significantly higher in real terms in one country than in another, and also in percentage terms, other cost items will appear lower in percentage terms, even though in real terms some may be the same in both countries. Caution must therefore be used in making such comparisons.

The following table shows the costs of the same three African bus companies as were used in the example of staff ratios in Chapter 12, broken down into the major components by percentage, using the three different criteria discussed earlier. Although the figures are for three different years, and relate to periods more than a decade ago, they are nevertheless representative and provide a useful example which is still relevant today.

Breakdown of costs for three African bus operators

	Nairobi 1990-91	Harare 1988-89	Malawi 1987-88
Number of buses operated	*268*	*665*	*259*
by Input	%	%	%
Salaries and Wages	29	33	13
Fuel and Oil	20	22	37
Maintenance Materials	22	23	17
Tyres	5	4	8
Depreciation	6	5	9
Other	18	13	16
by Activity	%	%	%
Vehicle Operating	60	49	61
Maintenance	31	39	25
Management/Admin	9	12	14
by Cost Category	%	%	%
Fixed	9	7	10
Bus-related	42	41	27
Kilometre-related	49	52	63

The companies concerned (Kenya Bus Services, Nairobi; Harare United Omnibus Company, Zimbabwe; and United Transport Malawi) were at the time all subsidiaries of the United Transport International group, and the figures, which represent the financial years indicated at the top of each column, are taken from the companies' management reports. The companies in Kenya and Zimbabwe operated only urban services, in Nairobi and Harare respectively, while the company in Malawi operated urban, inter-urban and rural services throughout the country. The three companies were managed on broadly similar principles, and operating standards, reporting procedures and cost allocation principles were reasonably consistent. Nevertheless, as the table shows, there are some substantial differences in the breakdown of costs.

Salaries and wages were significantly lower in percentage terms in Malawi than in the other two countries; this was largely because that at that time wage rates in Malawi were particularly low, even by African standards, while those in Zimbabwe, particularly in the cities, were above average for Africa; the effect of high wages on bus operating costs in Zimbabwe was lessened by the fact that all buses in Harare were operated by the driver only, while in Kenya and Malawi all buses carried conductors. The high percentage of Malawi's costs which were attributable to fuel reflects the high cost of fuel in that country. The relatively high proportion of expenditure on tyres in Malawi was due largely to the high proportion of kilometres operated on unsurfaced rural roads, while the low tyre expenditure in

Harare reflects the good condition of the roads in the city at the time. The higher depreciation and lower maintenance costs in Malawi reflects a much younger fleet than in the other two countries.

In the analysis of costs by activity, there are marked differences in the split between operating and maintenance expenditure. The low percentage of expenditure on maintenance in Malawi is due partly to the relatively young fleet, but also to the fact that the high cost of fuel has a major effect on operating costs; low wage rates also helped to reduce maintenance costs compared with the other countries. The low percentage of vehicle operating costs in Harare were due partly to the relatively high cost of maintenance, which resulted from a relatively old fleet, and to the fact that buses were all one-man-operated. Again, the high proportion of kilometre-related costs in Malawi were due largely to high fuel costs. It is interesting to note that fixed costs account for only 10% or less of all costs in all three companies, with those in Harare lowest at 7%. To some extent this may indicate small economies of scale, although the differences are not significant.

ROUTE COSTING AND PROFITABILITY

It is sometimes difficult to determine whether a bus route is profitable or not. It is normally relatively easy to ascertain its revenue, particularly where each vehicle remains on the same route throughout the day, but it is much more difficult to calculate the cost of operating it. A very crude method of estimating route profitability used by some operators is to calculate the average cost per kilometre operated for the undertaking as a whole, and to compare this with the revenue per kilometre for individual routes; alternatively, some include an apportionment of overheads in the cost of operating a bus route, and compare the result with revenue. If cost exceeds revenue on either of these bases, the route concerned is regarded as unprofitable.

However, neither of these methods take into account the difference between fixed and variable costs, and can be highly misleading: a route may appear to be unprofitable, when in fact it is earning sufficient revenue to cover all its variable costs even though its contribution to fixed costs may be small. The converse may also apply: a route with a very high revenue per kilometre may appear to be profitable, but if kilometres operated on the route are low, for example in the case of a route operated during peak periods only, revenue may be insufficient to cover the bus-related costs.

If the total number of kilometres operated by an undertaking is reduced, because of schedule changes or due to a deterioration in vehicle availability or utilisation, fixed costs will be spread over fewer kilometres, and average costs per kilometre will therefore increase; if revenue from the remainder of the operation is unchanged, some routes which previously appeared to be profitable may now appear to be unprofitable, although in fact their viability remains unchanged. However, some operators have been misled into the belief that the profitability of these routes has decreased, and have reduced the level of service to compensate, thus increasing average fixed costs per kilometre even more. This is a trap which must be avoided.

Proper route costing requires the identification of all costs associated with the operation of a route; some costs are relatively easy to identify and calculate, while others are more obscure, and in some cases estimates or apportionment on a somewhat arbitrary basis may be unavoidable. For accurate cost calculation, it is essential to know the cost characteristics of the organisation, in particular which costs are fixed, and the parameters against which costs vary as discussed earlier.

For a transport operation as a whole to be viable, all costs, including its overhead costs, must be covered in full. Ideally, the revenue from every route, and every journey operated, should cover the variable costs incurred in its operation, and also make at least a small contribution towards fixed costs, such that in aggregate the contributions from all routes cover fixed costs in full, as well as providing a reasonable profit where this is required. The contribution is likely to vary considerably from route to route, so that an operator running several routes will need some means of determining the profitability of each: it is highly improbable that each will have similar cost and revenue characteristics.

The levels of service and demand on a route may vary between different days: for, example, weekend travel patterns are invariably different from those on weekdays, and services should be adjusted accordingly. It is therefore useful to determine the viability of the route on these different days. It is also useful to be able to calculate the cost, and hence the profitability, of an individual bus journey, or even part of a journey; for example, it will be helpful to be able to calculate the financial effect of removing a journey from the schedule, turning a journey short, operating an additional journey, or extending a route. This will necessitate establishing the revenue generated on the particular journey or part of journey, as well as calculating the cost of operating it.

A service which covers its variable costs in full but does not make a contribution to fixed costs is not unprofitable to operate even though its revenue per kilometre is lower than the average total costs per kilometre for the undertaking as a whole. In many cases, services which are claimed to be unprofitable fall into this category, but their withdrawal would reduce the total surplus of the undertaking.

To calculate the cost of an additional journey which would not require an additional bus to operate it, or the cost of an existing journey which, if removed from the schedule, would not enable the bus requirement to be reduced, the kilometres operated should be multiplied by the rate per kilometre for all kilometre-related costs, principally fuel, tyres, maintenance materials and, if appropriate, crew overtime costs and other trip-variable costs such as terminal charges or road tolls. The resulting figure should be compared with revenue, anticipated or actual, to determine the viability or otherwise of the journey. Where the journeys involve an additional bus, or the potential saving of a bus, the bus-related costs per day should be added to the daily kilometre-related costs to give a total daily cost, again to be compared with anticipated or actual daily revenue.

Route costing is further complicated by differences in the level of service between peak and off-peak periods. Some buses are required for only part of the day, and operate relatively few kilometres; some operate only one revenue-earning trip in each peak period, with minimal revenue in the direction of travel against the peak flow. Since all bus-related costs must be covered by the surplus of revenue over direct costs if the service is to be viable, such operations are likely to incur losses, and detract from the viability of the route as a whole. It is therefore important to be able to calculate the costs of each journey operated, and each bus working, and to compare these with the revenue earned by each.

As well as identifying loss-making trips, this calculation will provide the basis for assessing the effect of different levels of service provided at peak and off-peak times, and of fare policies such as peak/off-peak differentials. The calculation must take into account the number of buses which may be required between peak periods for maintenance, and which would be required in any case: peak services operated using these buses will not be required to cover their bus-related costs. In many undertakings some of the buses used for peak-only operation are buses which are nearing the ends of their economic lives; their depreciation costs may therefore be relatively low, or zero if the buses are fully written down, but on the other hand it is likely that, because of their age, their maintenance costs per kilometre will be significantly higher than the fleet average. Crew costs may also be affected: where spreadover shifts are operated to cater for peak schedules, these may involve substantial penalty or overtime payments.

The effect on revenue of adding or deleting journeys can also be complex. Some bus routes, or parts of routes, may appear to be uneconomic, but may generate demand for other routes. The same may apply within a single journey. If for the last few kilometres there are very few passengers travelling on the bus, so that the revenue earned does not cover the variable costs for that part of the journey, it is not necessarily true that reducing the length of the route would improve its profitability: shortening the trip or route would lose passengers on the busier portion of the route if these passengers boarded in the busy section to travel to the "unprofitable" section or vice versa. Some journeys on a route may be uneconomic, but their operation contributes to the revenue on other journeys on the same route at different times of the day. For example, most passenger journeys are paired, in that an outward journey is normally followed later by a return journey; a passenger using a lightly-loaded journey will also contribute to the viability of another journey for his opposite journey, and withdrawing one because it is unprofitable may mean that this passenger is lost to the other also. Similarly, the last bus of the day may be lightly loaded, but its existence gives confidence to passengers to use the preceding trip, whose patronage may be reduced if the last journey is withdrawn; conversely, sometimes adding a later bus results in an increase in demand for what was previously the last bus but is now the penultimate bus of the day.

It is possible to have a situation in which all services are viable, in that they make a contribution to overheads, but the undertaking as a whole is not: this will arise if the total of all contributions is inadequate to cover total overheads. This is relatively common with rail-based public transport systems, in which the proportion of fixed costs is very high, but can also apply to bus operations. It is not necessarily the case in such circumstances that the services could be operated more economically by smaller operators with lower overheads, since these operators may have higher direct costs, for example because they do not have workshop facilities their fuel, tyre and maintenance costs may be higher.

Where a company is unprofitable simply because its overheads are too high, and the deficit cannot be eliminated by increasing fares, it may be possible to rectify this by increasing the level of operation to spread the overheads further; it is vital, though, that any additional services operated make a contribution to overheads, and that the overheads themselves are not increased. In some cases, particularly with rail based systems, such measures are not possible, and some form of subsidy may be justifiable in order to preserve the service. It is sometimes possible to reduce costs through "efficiency" measures such as improved systems and procedures, staff reduction, closure of some depots, or rationalisation of workshops.

14

PUBLIC TRANSPORT REVENUE AND FUNDING

The potential revenue from a public transport operation depends largely on the purchasing power of the community which it serves. Total revenue received must be sufficient to cover all costs and in addition, in a commercial undertaking, to provide a reasonable return on capital. However, the road transport industry in many developing countries is barely viable, in that the majority of operators, while managing to remain in business, are unable to earn sufficient revenue to maintain their vehicles to a reasonable standard of roadworthiness and reliability, and to provide adequately for their replacement. The result is usually a poor standard of service with insufficient capacity to meet demand, and the operation of old, unsafe, unreliable and uneconomic vehicles.

SOURCES OF REVENUE

The principal sources of revenue for a public transport undertaking are:

- Regular public transport services
- Private hire or charter operations
- Excursions and tours
- Accompanied luggage
- Carriage of unaccompanied freight or parcels
- Advertising
- Depot and station charges
- Rental of properties
- Concessions
- Commissions
- Subsidy

Revenue from fares, and in some cases external subsidy, normally accounts for almost all revenue received. A transport operator must be able to distinguish in its management accounts between revenue from the different sources. It is particularly important to be able to identify revenue which is directly attributable to the services operated such as fares or charter revenue, indirect revenue such as advertising income, and revenue which is totally unrelated to the operation, such as dividends from subsidiary companies and proceeds from the disposal of assets.

Fares from regular public transport services constitute the principal source of revenue for all operators: for many this accounts for 100% of all income. Fare systems are discussed in detail later in this chapter.

Private hire or charter operations are often useful sources of additional revenue where these are not core activities. The potential for these activities varies: where there is a substantial tourism industry there may be considerable scope for charter arrangements with tour operators; elsewhere there may be very little. While such activities may be regarded as a form of diversification, they have much in common with ordinary bus services and as such enable fixed costs to be spread over a broader base. Some bus operators earn substantial sums from private hire for special events. In Malawi, for example, thousands of participants in national celebrations at the stadium in Blantyre were carried from all parts of the country on buses hired by the government from the national bus operator, providing a significant proportion of its revenue in several months of the year.

Similarly, the direct operation of excursions and tours where there is a viable market can be a useful source of revenue, but tourism is a specialised business, and unless there is sufficient volume to justify a dedicated management team, there is a danger that management time and effort may be diverted to these activities to the detriment of the core business.

Many rural and long-distance operators charge passengers for the carriage of accompanied luggage and freight, although it is normal for small amounts to be carried free of charge. Where passengers regularly carry large volumes of luggage this can be a significant source of revenue, while charges may be imposed partly as a constraint on the carriage of excessive loads. However, unless all passengers board at bus stations or offices where there are facilities for luggage to be weighed, there can be problems in ensuring that all passengers are correctly charged.

The carriage of unaccompanied freight and parcels on normal service buses can also be a profitable business on long-distance and rural services, but normally requires a well developed network of offices or agents. Where the volume of business is high, it is sometimes justifiable to provide additional luggage accommodation on vehicles, or even to attach trailers to buses. Some bus operators run freight vehicles in addition to their buses on routes where the volume of freight is very high.

Revenue may be generated, particularly in urban areas, through the sale of space on vehicles and buildings for advertising; this often includes advertising on tickets and through recorded advertising material broadcast over public address systems on vehicles. As much as 10% of total revenue may be earned from advertising, but there are often significant costs; in particular, the cost and downtime involved in repairing accident-damaged buses carrying advertisements can be high if expensive signwriting is required, and most advertisers are unwilling to pay for buses carrying damaged advertisements.

Some operators make their stations or depot facilities available on a commercial basis to other operators. Bus station charges are normally based on the number of departures, as discussed in Chapter 13. There may be a scale of charges for various depot services, such as parking, cleaning, or repairs; where fuel is provided, this is often sold with an element of profit. In some countries it is common for passengers to be charged for access to bus stations, or for the use of certain facilities such as rest rooms or waiting rooms. Charges are also usually levied on individuals providing services such as loading or porterage, and on taxi, rickshaw and baggage cart operators entering the station.

Revenue may also be earned through renting out space on the operator's premises for various purposes, such as booking offices used by other operators using a bus station, or shops and refreshment facilities for passengers and employees. Retail outlets may be particularly lucrative; they are relatively common at the larger bus and rail stations, while duty-free shops raise a substantial amount of revenue for most international airports. Surplus office or depot accommodation may be let to third parties; this may be particularly relevant to operators whose levels of activity have declined. Property development on sites belonging to the undertaking may provide a valuable source of revenue: for example, almost 50% of the revenue of the Kowloon-Canton Railway in Hong Kong is attributable to property developments adjoining its stations.

Instead of renting out facilities, an operator may award concessions to third parties to provide services such as refreshment facilities at bus stations and terminals or staff canteens at depots. Concessionaires may be charged at a fixed monthly rate, or on a percentage of revenue or turnover; the latter is more difficult to administer but enables the operator to benefit from the success of a concession although conversely, if the concession's business is poor, the operator's income will suffer.

An operator may take bookings on behalf of other operators, and earn commission on tickets sold. This is relatively common in the case of long-distance operations, and can be a useful source of additional income if the operators' own booking staff are not fully occupied, but, unless the business is significant, may be unprofitable if it necessitates the employment of additional staff.

Some transport undertakings receive subsidies from central or local government: the subject of subsidies is discussed later in this chapter.

Various other sources of revenue may also be available. Some undertakings diversify into other fields of business, largely unrelated to transport, in order to increase the revenue base, as discussed in Chapter 6; some have subsidiary companies, or substantial shareholdings in other businesses, the dividends from which may be a significant source of revenue. The interest earned from a positive cash balance may also be significant; as discussed in Chapter 16, public transport is a cash business and with good financial management it may be possible to earn substantial sums from time to time in this manner. In some circumstances it may be appropriate for temporary cash surpluses to be invested, rather than banked, but such practice should normally be avoided because of the risks involved. From time to time income may be generated from the sale of assets, such as time-expired or surplus vehicles, equipment or buildings.

A transport operator must not permit secondary revenue-raising activities to undermine the core activity; dissipation of management effort is a particular risk. Different activities may interfere with one another: for example, the provision of too many kiosks in a bus station may reduce its capacity to the detriment of the services using it.

FARE LEVELS

In general terms, the level of fares, rates and charges should be such that total revenue earned by a public transport service is sufficient to cover the total cost of providing it. For the profitable operation of a transport business, the optimal level of fares and service will be such that marginal cost and marginal revenue are equal; this will occur when the operation of one additional journey, or one journey fewer, or an increase or decrease in the rate charged, would reduce the total surplus of revenue over direct costs. If there is free competition on a route, such equilibrium between fares and service levels will, in theory, be determined by market forces. However, as discussed in Chapter 13, the cost structure of a transport operation is complex, and the cost of providing a service will vary from place to place, route to route, or time to time, as will its demand. Similarly, transport users have different characteristics and some are prepared to pay more than others for a similar service, while the existence of competition or potential competition also has a bearing on the fares which may be charged.

Optimisation of revenue, therefore, necessitates a complex structure of charges. The principle used in many transport operations of "charging what the traffic will bear" evolved from this requirement; in extreme cases, particularly with individual public transport modes, fares are subject to negotiation. In practice, however, while there is scope for some variation in the fares charged, it is impossible to calculate an optimum fare for every journey; for this to be achieved, fares would need to vary constantly throughout the day, and from day to day, and even between one passenger and another.

Bus fares in many countries are subject to government control. There is a common tendency for governments to delay fares increases, and to authorise smaller increases than are required to compensate for cost increases, in an attempt to avoid adverse public reaction. However, this has invariably had undesirable results. Very long delays in the implementation of a fares increase can cause serious shortages of cash, and eventually result in an operator becoming insolvent: this has been a contributory cause of the collapse of many bus companies, such as the Jamaica Omnibus Services in the 1980s. Moreover, if regulated bus operators are unable to cover their costs by charging the authorised fares there is a tendency on the part of the less formal operators to overcharge illegally. When a fares increase is finally granted it normally has to be so large that adverse reaction from the public is stronger than would have been the case if there had been regular but small fares increases in line with inflation. If any public transport system is to operate on a stable basis, therefore, it is important that a satisfactory fares policy is put in place. Fare regulation is discussed in more detail in Chapter 19.

Affordability of bus fares is a major issue which is often raised by politicians when the subject of fares increases is under discussion: a common argument is that bus fares must be limited to a level which is universally affordable. Many users of public transport in developing countries are very poor, and some households spend up to 30% of their incomes on fares. On the other hand, there are often segments of the market which are able, and prepared, to pay higher fares. The existence of alternative means of transport such as route taxis charging higher fares than the regular services is frequently an indication that there is scope for a superior standard of bus service in addition to the basic service, for which higher fares may be charged.

Making services affordable to the poorest users often means that fare revenue is inadequate to sustain them at existing standards; by the same token, while services in many instances may be considered to be poor, and demands are made for their improvement, passengers may not be prepared, or able, to pay the fares necessary to cover the cost of a better service. Indeed, lower income groups are often unable to afford to pay public transport fares which will support even the most basic of services; they certainly cannot afford the fares required for the type of service demanded by people who are better off.

For a reasonable standard of public transport services which is universally affordable, therefore, there must be separate fares for different classes of passenger, different standards of service at appropriate fares, and perhaps also some form of subsidy. In a free market economy, salary levels, costs, and levels of service provision should, in theory, all find their correct level; the problem of affordability will be resolved, often with a wide range of different service standards and different fare scales. While in practice this will never be fully achieved, with an appropriate policy towards public transport fares and services it is possible to make considerable progress towards it.

Related to the concept of affordability is that of price-elasticity of demand, which is a measure of the extent to which demand changes as the result of a change in price, or fares. It is determined principally by passengers' ability to pay, their need to use the services, and the cost and availability of alternative means of transport. Where price elasticity is equal to 0, a change in fare levels will have no effect on demand; where elasticity is equal to -1, a fare increase will result in a fall in demand, but total revenue will remain unchanged; if elasticity is between 0 and -1, then total revenue will increase if fares are increased; if it exceeds -1, the fall in demand as a result of an increase in fare levels will be so great that total revenue will decrease.

The number of variables makes it difficult to calculate elasticity accurately even when detailed operating statistics are available. In developing countries there are other factors which distort the picture: for example, where there is shortage of capacity, a fares increase may simply reduce the amount of unsatisfied demand without affecting ridership; in a city where population is increasing at a high rate, a loss of patronage following a fares increase may be hidden by normal traffic growth.

Elasticity will vary between different times of the day: most passengers travelling at peak times have no option but to travel, so that their demand is less elastic than those travelling at off-peak times, whose journeys may be less essential. Elasticities also vary from place to place and over time. The number of alternative transport services may vary considerably between one place and another, as will other factors such as income. Over the long term, when passengers have time to adjust to an increase in fare levels, for example by changing their places of residence or work, or acquiring some means of private transport, demand is likely to be more elastic than in the short term. Elasticities may also differ depending on whether fares are increased or decreased: former passengers who have made alternative arrangements following a fares increase may not revert to their former travel patterns if fares are later reduced.

In practice, while demand invariably falls following a fares increase, part of the lost demand is often restored after a short time as some of the passengers who found alternative means, or reduced the extent of their travel, do revert to their former travel habits; others are lost permanently.

The negative effect on revenue of a fares increase is commonly known as "fares resistance"; in some countries more aggressive reaction to fares increases is common, such as stoning or even burning buses. To minimise resistance, it is preferable to make small fares increases relatively frequently, rather than large increases infrequently. The latter approach, as well as incurring the displeasure of users, also has an adverse effect on the finances of the organisation. An annual fares increase is normally most appropriate, except in cases of extreme inflation.

Demand for one mode of public transport is also affected by a change in the price of another. For example, if bus fares are increased, some bus users may use taxi services instead, while if bus fares are reduced the reverse may occur. This is known as cross-elasticity; where it is high, a small change in the price of one service will result in a large change in demand for the other. Cross-elasticity of demand between two competing services is likely to be higher if the difference between their prices is relatively small.

FARE STRUCTURES

There are three basic types of fare structure for public transport services: flat fares, zonal fares, and graduated fares.

Flat Fare Systems

The simplest is a flat fare system, in which all passengers using a route network are charged identical fares regardless of route, distance travelled, or type of passenger. Alternatively, flat fares may be applied to individual routes within a particular area, with different fares charged on different routes, or to a particular class of passenger; in some transport systems, graduated fares apply to the majority of passengers, while certain categories, such as schoolchildren or pensioners, are charged a flat fare. The fare may also be varied between times of day. In essence, however, under a flat fare system all passengers, or all passengers in a particular category, on a particular bus journey will be charged the same fare.

Flat fare systems are relatively common in urban transport, particularly in smaller towns and cities, and in larger cities where services are subsidised so that short distance passengers not deterred by high fares; they are less common on rural and long-distance services. An important advantage of the flat fare system is its simplicity. The fare required to cover costs or to meet a specified revenue target can be easily calculated if the total number of passengers is known, although passengers' ability to pay and elasticity of demand must be taken into consideration. Passengers are unable to over-ride by travelling greater distances than they have paid for. The conductor's task simplified and boarding times are reduced if passengers pay on entry. The system can even preclude the need for a ticketing system and its attendant costs.

If all or a majority of passengers travel approximately the same distance, the fare can be set to reflect the cost of the journey, and will be similar to what would be charged under a graduated fare system; this situation may arise where all passengers travel the full distance from one end of the route to the other, or where all travel short distances, with a high turnover of passengers along the route. However, where individual journey lengths vary widely, as is more usual, passengers travelling short distances will pay more per kilometre travelled than those travelling longer distances, and the disparity becomes greater as the route length increases. On long routes in particular, therefore, flat fares may be considered inequitable. Flat fares would be more equitable in a city in which the richer passengers lived nearer the city centre and poorer people farther out, since the former would pay a higher rate per kilometre than the latter. On the other hand, in a city where the poorer people lived farther from the centre, the reverse would be the case, and a flat fare system would be highly inequitable.

In a competitive market other operators charging lower fares may abstract the shorter-distance traffic, leaving only the longer-distance traffic to the operator charging a flat fare. In certain circumstances this may be intentional on the part of the longer-distance operator, with flat fares set at a level designed to discourage short distance riders. Very long routes, where the average distance travelled by passengers is long, can become uneconomic to serve with a flat fare system unless fares are set at a high level, which may deter short-distance passengers; some operators overcome this problem by inserting an artificial break into the longest routes, requiring the payment of a second fare by passengers travelling across the break. A very busy route might be divided into sections of varying length, with some buses operating the entire length of the route and others operating over the shorter sections; different flat fares would be charged on buses operating the different sections so that the fares paid would be more closely related to the length of the journey taken, provided that each passenger travelled on the appropriate bus. Another possibility is to vary the fare according to the length of the route, so that the flat fare for a short route is lower than that for a longer route. Where several routes operate along the same road, therefore, passengers will pay different fares for the same journey depending on which route the bus they board is operating on.

Some flat fare systems work successfully when they are first introduced because the fare is set at a convenient amount, typically the value of a single coin, so that it is easy for passengers to tender the exact fare and the need for giving change is minimised. However, there may be problems when it becomes necessary to increase the fare by a small amount, if this results in the need for more coins to make up each fare and an increase in the need to give change. The alternative would be to impose much higher fares increases less frequently, to the next denomination of coin, but this may result in strong passenger resistance and financial problems for the operator. The problem may be overcome to some extent by the pre-purchase of tickets or by the use of tokens instead of coins, as discussed in Chapter 9.

Graduated Fare Systems

The most common type of fare structure, particularly for long-distance and rural services, is the graduated fare system, with fares based on the distances travelled by individual passengers.

A graduated fare system requires each route to be divided into fare stages, with the boundary point of each stage clearly identifiable; in practice, the boundary point itself is normally referred to as the stage. Sometimes fares are based strictly on distance, so that the fares charged for each stage will vary according to the length of the stage, but in many systems, where the distance between stages is reasonably consistent, the fare for a journey is based on the number of stages travelled, with the fare increasing directly with the number of stages. Fare scales may be "tapered", so that the rate charged per kilometre decreases with distance, while in some cases a minimum fare applies, for example, for the first two or three stages or a specified distance, with distance-based graduated fares thereafter. Stages may be close together, with small increments in the fare at each stage, or they may be widely spaced, with larger increments; the resulting fare scales are referred to as "fine" and "coarse" respectively.

The spacing of the fare stages may be varied to reflect differences in operating costs or different demand characteristics, on different sections of a route. For example in Kingston, Jamaica, several routes operated into the hills surrounding the city; the higher costs of operating in this difficult terrain were compensated for by closer spacing of fare stages on the hilly sections of each route. Similarly, a longer journey using an expressway may cost less to operate than a shorter one using ordinary roads, and the fares charged for a given distance may therefore be lower through the wider spacing of stages. Sometimes the only stages on inter-city or rural routes are in towns or villages, so that the distance between them can vary considerably, as will the increments in fares if these are calculated on a per-stage basis; this can result in short-distance passengers within certain stages paying abnormally high fares. Where several routes operate along a common stretch of road, it is normally appropriate for the same fare stages to apply to each route, although this is not always the case.

A graduated fare system may be considered to be reasonably equitable, since the fare for each journey is related to the distance travelled and hence the cost of providing the service; the finer the fare scale, the more equitable it becomes, provided that the distances between fare stages are consistent. In certain circumstances, however, it may be argued that a graduated system is less equitable than a flat fare system, for example where low-income residential areas are located on the outskirts of a city, so that the poorest passengers pay more to travel to work or school in the city centre than more affluent residents of areas closer to the centre.

Problems can also arise with fares on circuitous or indirect routes. Bus services do not necessarily follow the most direct route between two points, but may deviate to serve areas off the direct line of route; this increases the distance travelled, and if fares are based purely on distance, the fares will be increased accordingly. Thus passengers must pay more, even though they are inconvenienced by having to travel farther than necessary. Sometimes there are alternative routes between two points, where there are different deviations along the route; the resulting route variations may be of different lengths, with different fares for what, to the passenger, is virtually the same journey. In such circumstances some operators adjust fares so that the same fare is charged between two points regardless of the route taken; this can sometimes result in anomalies where the fare for a shorter distance is greater than for a longer distance on the same route.

A common problem with a graduated fare system is over-riding by passengers, which can be difficult to detect, and can result in serious revenue loss. Calculation of fares is complex, and if fares are increased regularly it can be a time-consuming task to alter all the fares; this problem is reduced if fare table production is computerised.

A system which combines some of the characteristics of flat and graduated systems is found in Hong Kong, where different fares are charged for journeys in different directions. All passengers boarding at a particular stop must pay the same fare, based on the distance from that stop to the terminal point, regardless of the length of their journeys, but as the bus arrives at each stage the fare is reduced. A sign, which is changed at each stage, is displayed at the entrance of the bus indicating the fare payable, and no tickets are issued to passengers. Most passengers making a return journey between any two points will therefore pay two different fares according to the direction of travel, but the average of the two is normally reasonably equitable. Over-riding is not possible with this system. Another advantage is that it reduces the problem of short distance passengers crowding out long distance passengers on routes with tapered frequencies, since the fare charged on buses turning short is lower than the fare charged on buses operating for the full length of the route. A disadvantage is that passengers travelling short distances between intermediate points will pay a relatively high fare in both directions.

Zonal Fare Systems

A zonal fare system is, in some respects, a combination of flat and graduated systems, and is most common in urban areas. Typically, an area is divided into concentric zones, usually centred on the central business district. For a journey wholly within one zone, there is only one fare, in effect a flat fare; for a journey crossing into the adjoining zone, a higher fare will apply, and the fare will increase with each crossing of a zone boundary. Zones may be small or large, the equivalent of short or long stages with a graduated system. Like the flat fare system, a zonal system is relatively simple to administer. However, problems can arise with some routes, for example fares charged on routes running parallel with a zone boundary for a significant distance will be abnormally low in relation to the distance travelled; this can be particularly relevant in the case of circular routes. Care will be necessary in setting the zone boundaries in order to avoid anomalies, for example where a road doubles back and recrosses a zone boundary. As with graduated fares, over-riding by passengers can be a problem.

It is necessary to consider carefully the alternative fare structures to determine the most appropriate basis for charging in a given situation, for example whether a graduated, zonal or flat-fare system should be applied, and, unless a flat-fare system is adopted, the most appropriate lengths of stages or widths of zones. There should be consistency across the system although special requirements of particular routes, such as the hill routes in Kingston, must be catered for in the most realistic and practical manner. In practice, there is not always consistency, and where there are competing operators they will not necessarily use the same system of charging: for example in Kuala Lumpur, there was inconsistency between the fare structures of the two principal bus operators, even on common sections of route, with one operating a flat fare system and the other a graduated system.

FARE DIFFERENTIALS AND PROTECTIVE FARES

Sometimes different fares are charged for what would appear to be the same journey taken under different circumstances; the fare may vary according to time of day or season, or may reflect a different standard of service. If properly applied, fare differentials can produce significant benefits both to operators and to the travelling public, by increasing total revenue and enabling better services to be provided.

A common differential is between fares at peak and off-peak times. Passenger loadings at off-peak periods, which are normally significantly lower than at peak times, can be increased through the adoption of fares differentials, charging lower fares for travel at such times. The charging of higher fares at peak periods may also be intended to reduce the volume of traffic carried at these times, with the overall effect of smoothing out the volume of traffic through the day, although if this results in a switch of some demand to private transport during the peak, rather than to public transport services at less busy times of the day, this could be disadvantageous, and the consequences must be carefully considered. Experience generally has shown that because the demand for off-peak travel is generally much more elastic than for peak travel, reduced off-peak fares can result in substantially increased patronage, and sometimes in a significant increase in revenue despite the lower fares. Because of their different proportion of fixed to variable costs, with a greater proportion of their costs varying directly with kilometres operated, paratransit operators often find it difficult to match the off-peak fares which a large conventional operator may charge.

Higher fares are often charged for all-night bus services: these may be as much as twice the normal fare, and in some cases are even higher. The higher fares are partly to reflect the fact that load factors are generally much lower at night; elasticity of demand tends to be much lower at these times, and passengers are therefore prepared to pay the higher fares.

Different fares may be charged for travelling on different types of vehicle. The justification is obvious in some cases: for example higher fares are usually charged for travelling on air-conditioned buses than on ordinary buses operating on the same route. In other cases there is less justification: when midibuses were first introduced in Zimbabwe, higher fares were approved to reflect the higher operating cost per passenger resulting from the lower capacity, although standards of comfort and service were virtually identical.

There is often scope for the provision of better quality services, in addition to the basic services, at higher fares, as discussed in more detail in Chapter 6. Where fares are regulated, legislation should permit this, rather than stipulating one fare scale for all services regardless of quality, as is sometimes the case. It is important that the better quality services are recognisable as such, to deter operators of basic services from increasing their fares to the same level.

Fares and charges for tourist services in particular reflect the wide range of standards of service which are usually offered, and the seasonal nature of the business. There may be different scales for different standards, for different types of tourist, from the wealthy to the back-packer. Usually there are higher rates for the high season, and low rates in the off-season, and a range of rates in between. Lower rates are often charged for residents of the country, to reflect the substantial differences in local and foreign spending power. This applies particularly to hotel accommodation, but is less common with public transport fares since it is less easy to enforce; however, tariffs for tourist transport services are often several times higher than local bus fares for equivalent journeys. The differences may be reflected in the quality of vehicles provided, but this is not always the case.

Some fare structures incorporate protective fares of various kinds; these are fares which are higher than those normally charged, in order to discourage certain passengers from using a particular service. Typically, a minimum fare equivalent to the fare for several stages is imposed on all or part of a route. The main reason for charging protective fares is to give priority to the passengers for whom the service is primarily intended: for example, to discourage short-distance passengers from using a long-distance service so that they do not crowd out the long-distance passengers, or to reduce delays at stops caused by a high passenger turnover. Such protection is often applied to long routes which are paralleled by shorter, more frequent services. It may be necessary to charge protective fares in one direction only, for example on outward journeys from a city centre area in the case of long-distance routes running in parallel with routes terminating within the city boundary.

Another reason for imposing protective fares is to protect a particular operator, by discouraging passengers from using the buses of another; for example fares charged for journeys wholly within an urban area may be higher on buses operated on routes to and from outlying towns than on buses operated by a local undertaking on shorter routes within the city. Prior to deregulation of bus services, this practice was common in the United Kingdom to protect municipal bus operators from abstraction of revenue by longer-distance operators running into the towns.

Protective fares are often applied informally, where passengers travelling short distances are charged significantly more than the approved fare by conductors who favour longer-distance travellers; at times of peak demand, passengers may be allowed to travel only by paying the fare for a much longer journey. This is particularly common amongst paratransit operators, and with the setoran system of operation.

MULTIPLE-JOURNEY AND TRANSFER TICKETS

Many transport undertakings offer multiple-journey tickets of various kinds. There are broadly two categories of multiple-journey ticket: those which entitle the holder to a specified number of journeys, and those which permit unlimited travel, either between two specified points or throughout a network or part of a network, for a specified period. A common type of multiple-journey ticket is the return ticket, which may or may not offer a discount compared with the purchase of two separate tickets for outward and return journeys respectively. Multiple-journey tickets often relate to a specific number of journeys between two points, for example a ten-journey or "weekly" ticket may allow a commuter to make five journeys in each direction between home and work.

Some operators offer transfer tickets, enabling a passenger to transfer from one route to another during the course of a journey; there is usually a time limit, typically one hour or ninety minutes after the initial purchase or validation, within which the second journey must commence. Such arrangements are common on urban transport systems in developed countries, and are particularly appropriate where the route network is based on the "hub-and-spoke" principle, or follows a grid pattern. They may also facilitate intermodal connections, by enabling a passenger to make a journey comprising, for example, bus and metro elements, using only one ticket.

There is a strong case for transfer tickets where the route network necessitates transferring between routes on a high proportion of journeys. They may also be more equitable with a flat fare system, or a sharply tapered graduated system, in which passengers who must travel on more than one route to make a journey will pay a higher fare than a passenger travelling the same distance but who does not have to change. With a flat fare system the transfer ticket should cost the same as a single journey ticket if it is to be fully equitable: for simplicity it makes sense in such cases for every ticket issued to be valid as a transfer ticket; however, in systems where every ticket permits one transfer, disembarking passengers who are not intending to transfer may be inclined to hand their tickets to others waiting to board, perhaps depriving the operator of a significant proportion of revenue.

On many transport systems, mostly in urban areas, tickets are available which provide unlimited travel throughout a network, for a specified period, usually one day. They may be valid on the services provided by a single operator, or several operators; sometimes they are valid on several modes, such as bus, tram, LRT and metro systems. They cannot relate cost or fare to the journeys made, but are very convenient for the user and as such are a simple means of selling public transport services. Such tickets are often referred to by such names as "Travelcard", which now tends to be used as a generic term in countries such as the United Kingdom.

Also very common are weekly, monthly or annual season tickets. They may relate to specific journeys between two points, but permit an unlimited number of journeys. Others permit unlimited travel throughout the system, in some cases on several modes, and in effect are long-term travelcards.

Multiple-journey tickets are usually sold at a significant discount, to encourage regular or more frequent use of public transport services. There are several advantages: in many cases the availability of multiple-journey tickets increases demand to the extent that the operator's revenue is increased, even allowing for the discount; they have cash flow advantages for the operator, in that passengers pay in advance of their journeys, by up to twelve months; and they significantly reduce the number of cash transactions. As described in Chapter 8, there are often considerable fluctuations in demand, with peaks immediately following pay-days, followed by a decline in demand until the next pay-day. With the option of purchasing a ticket on pay-day, which will cover all journeys to and from work until the following pay-day, many commuters will do so, even if this means that their total expenditure on transport over the period will actually increase.

It may be argued that offering lower fares to commuters through the sale of discounted multiple journey tickets encourages increased use at times of greatest demand, and that instead, fares should be higher at peak periods. It is, however, possible to provide season tickets for commuters within a pricing policy which takes into account the differences in both demand and cost at different times of the day, through differential peak and off-peak fares as discussed above.

Where there are several operators in competition with one another on a particular route, the scope for selling multiple-journey tickets may be limited. Unless operators are able to agree on a revenue-sharing system, tickets will be restricted to the services of a single operator, and many passengers are unwilling to commit themselves in this way, preferring to retain the option of boarding any bus which comes along. Sometimes co-operation between operators to accept one another's multiple-journey tickets is regarded as anti-competitive, and is prohibited by law; in any case, it is normally practical only where there are relatively few operators, or where an operators' association is able to organise an equitable revenue-sharing arrangement amongst its members. There are, however, examples where several transport undertakings, often in more than one mode, have co-operated to provide travelcards which are valid on all their services within an area.

A potential problem with multiple-journey tickets is security: they are of relatively high value and are therefore more susceptible to forgery than single-journey tickets. Unless effective security measures can be taken the potential revenue loss may be significant. A multiple-journey ticket is not normally transferable from one passenger to another, although an increasing number of operators permit this for certain types of tickets. Security measures are often taken to deter unauthorised transfer, such as a requirement for a photograph of the authorised user of the ticket.

A disadvantage of certain types of multiple-journey tickets, particularly those permitting unlimited travel, is that it is very difficult for the operator to obtain detailed passenger statistics, which are required for control and planning purposes. It is usually necessary to calculate conversion factors based on surveys, to enable the total number of passengers carried to be estimated from the number of passengers purchasing single journey tickets, on a route by route or journey by journey basis. The higher the proportion of multiple-journey ticket users, the greater the likely inaccuracy of the figures. Similarly, where several operators are involved in a joint travelcard scheme, accurate apportionment of revenue can be very difficult. However, all of these problems can be overcome, albeit at a cost, with smartcard technology, as described in Chapter 9.

CONCESSIONARY FARES

In many countries it is customary, and often a legal requirement, to offer concessionary fares, providing cheaper, or sometimes free, travel for certain "deserving" or disadvantaged classes of passenger who may not otherwise be able to afford to travel. Such fares must not be confused with discounted fares offered commercially. The justification for non-commercial concessionary fares on social grounds is debatable: essential commodities such as food normally cost the same for everybody, and there is no logical reason why public transport fares should be treated any differently. It may be argued that government funds spent on concessionary fares would be more effectively spent on subsidies to improve services for all users: these are social policy issues which are outside the scope of this book.

The most common beneficiaries of concessionary fares include schoolchildren, pensioners and disabled people, although the number and categories of eligible passengers varies considerably from one country to another: in some, there are no concessions at all, while in others only schoolchildren are entitled to concessions. An extreme example was in Latvia, where in 1994 out of a population of only 2.7 million, 24 categories of passengers, totalling more than one million were entitled to concessionary fares or even to travel free of charge. These included about 660,000 old age pensioners, for whom there were local arrangements varying from city to city; over 100,000 students, paying about 50% of the regular fare; over 150,000 schoolchildren, travelling free of charge in rural areas and enjoying substantial discounts in the cities; and nearly 100,000 disabled persons travelling free of charge. The smaller categories included police, military personnel, security services, court representatives, orphans and formerly politically repressed persons. Proposals were accepted to reduce the number of categories to six: children between one and seven years of age, travelling free of charge; and children between seven and ten years of age, students, disabled, politically repressed, and orphans travelling at half fare.

Some concessionary fare schemes are relatively simple. In some cities, although a zonal or graduated fare system may apply generally, schoolchildren and pensioners are subject to a flat fare, set at a relatively low level. Often there are restrictions on the times when concessionary fares are available: for example, pensioners may not be eligible for the concessionary fare at peak times.

Concessions for children vary between countries, and even within the same country. Ages at which they apply are influenced partly by the ages at which children normally commence and complete their education, and when they may commence in formal employment. Typically, children travel free of charge up to the age of three, four or five years, and are eligible for concessionary fares up to the ages of between fourteen and eighteen years. The amount of the concession also varies, but is typically half, and sometimes two-thirds, of the standard adult fare.

As with other differential fares, concessionary fares can be justified commercially only where they result in an increase in total revenue without an offsetting increase in costs. This may apply to reduced off-peak fares for pensioners, which encourage them to travel at times when there is spare capacity, when they would otherwise not travel at all. Many concessionary fares, however, such as those for students, have the opposite effect since they apply at peak periods, and reduce the proportion of full fare-paying passengers which may be carried; if additional buses are operated to carry the students, additional cost will be incurred. Another effect of concessionary students' fares is that they may encourage parents to send their children to more distant schools, compounding the peak problem through increasing the demand for public transport.

Responsibility for funding non-commercial concessionary fares sometimes lies with central or local government through various forms of subsidy, and sometimes with the transport operators themselves; in some cases the responsibility is shared. Operators in many developing countries are required by law to carry certain categories of passenger at concessionary fares, with no compensation of any kind; in some cases, for example in Tanzania, minibus operators are legally required to carry a specified number of children per vehicle if there is demand. Operators rarely comply with such regulations, which prevent them from maximising revenue.

Where the operator is required to bear some or all of the cost, this in reality is borne by those passengers who pay full fares. If government policy requires operators to provide non-commercial concessionary fares, there should ideally be compensation by subsidy; otherwise market forces will be distorted and service standards will suffer. The most equitable and effective means of providing such a subsidy is normally to subsidise the beneficiaries directly, for example through the issue of season tickets, or tokens which can be used in payment of fares, and exchanged by the operator for cash.

The effectiveness of concessionary fares depends to some extent on the degree of regulation, and the structure of the transport industry. Where there are many small unregulated operators, concessions are difficult to enforce, and in practice concessions are not fully applied by many operators, with a tendency for priority to be given to passengers paying full fares. Large operators, particularly those which are publicly owned, are usually expected to apply concessions, while the smaller operators fail to do so, thus putting the larger operator at a disadvantage. There are often problems of identifying passengers who are entitled to concessions, and preventing abuse by those who are not entitled. Some form of identity card is often required, in the case of children or pensioners to show proof of age. Child concessions may be based on height rather than on age, making it easier to settle disputes without the need for an identity document: in China, for example, children below one metre in height travel at half fare.

Strictly speaking, concessionary fares funded by government should not be regarded as subsidies to the transport operator, but rather to the individual; nevertheless, they may have the effect of increasing the operator's revenue if they result in increased ridership.

FARES FOR INDIVIDUAL PUBLIC TRANSPORT MODES

Fares for taxis and other forms of individual public transport tend to be much more flexible than for mass transit modes. In the case of the more informal modes, such as human-powered or scooter-based vehicles, it is common for fares to be negotiated between driver and passenger; in the case of taxis, it is more common for fares to be based, albeit often somewhat loosely, on a predetermined scale. Except where fares are negotiated, there are two basic alternative bases of charging, namely a distance-based system and a zonal fare system, in which an area is divided into zones, and the fare is determined by the number of zones traversed. The zonal system often includes a number of standard fares for journeys which are frequently made, such as journeys between specific downtown hotels and airports.

The distance-based system is by far the more common, and lends itself to metering. Where meters are used, it is normal for charges to comprise up to five elements: a fixed "flagfall" charge, which is incurred as soon as the passenger enters the taxi; a constant charge per kilometre; a time-based charge which is only incurred when the taxi is stationary or operating at a very low speed, to compensate the operator for the effects of traffic congestion, or to cater for occasions when the passenger requires the taxi to wait; "extras" which may be charged, for example, for additional passengers or heavy items of luggage; and a fixed surcharge which may be imposed, for example, for journeys late at night, on public holidays, or for other special reasons. Sometimes time and distance based fares are varied by time or day in lieu of such a surcharge. Modern electronic taximeters can cater for all such variables, which enables fare structures to be designed to take into account all the factors involved.

In many countries all vehicles to be used as taxis are required by law to be fitted with taximeters, the operation and calibration of which should be in accordance with approved fare scales. In some cases this rule is not enforced, particularly where meters can no longer be used since they have become outdated, and cannot be adjusted to current fare values. This is often a problem with old mechanical meters under conditions of inflation, but electronic meters can overcome this problem. If meter legislation is to be effective, there must be a realistic fares policy, while the meters themselves must be capable of adjustment within a very large range.

Where meters are not used it is necessary for taxi operators to devise alternative means of calculating fares. The most common is a fixed charge per kilometre, but very often the vehicle odometer is inoperative and therefore the passenger must rely on the driver to know and use the correct distance when calculating the fare. Often the methods used by operators and drivers to calculate fares are too imprecise and can lead to overcharging. In some cases, where meters are not required, a table showing the scale of charges, either by distance or for specific journeys, must be displayed inside the vehicle. Many taxi drivers are opposed to the use of meters and prefer the flexibility of being able to negotiate fares; this may be satisfactory where regular passengers are involved, but visitors to a city are frequently exploited by unscrupulous drivers.

Taxi fares are usually subject to central, or more commonly local, government control and operators are required by law to charge the fares which have been officially approved. However, regulation is not always effective, or properly administered. In some cities, often because of bureaucratic inefficiency, there has been no increase in the approved fares for several years, even where costs have risen substantially during that time.

Where fares are regulated it is important that they are set at realistic levels to enable operators to cover the costs of operating vehicles safely and maintaining them in roadworthy condition. In addition a procedure is necessary whereby fares are increased periodically to compensate for cost increases, to prevent the situation arising where operators are forced to charge inadequate fares, or, as is sometimes the case, completely ignore the approved rates and charge whatever they feel is reasonable or what the traffic will bear. An appropriate fares policy is essential if the taxi industry is to provide an acceptable standard of service, and maintain or improve this standard; operators will not invest in vehicles or in maintenance of their fleets if they are unable to earn a satisfactory return.

SUBSIDY

Public transport services may be subsidised by local or central government, often to a substantial extent: this is more common in developed countries, but is practised in some developing countries, principally in urban areas. There are many valid reasons for subsidising public transport, but there are also strong arguments against it: direct subsidy to operators, to make good any losses incurred, often leads to inefficiency and even abuse, and in any case is normally practical only with a formal industry structure; if inappropriately applied, subsidies can distort the price mechanism so that the service provided is less efficient than it would be if operators had to cover their costs in full.

For costing purposes, some subsidies are more appropriately treated not as revenue items, but as negative costs, by deducting them from the costs of the relevant items on the expenditure side of the accounts. These include automatic rebates of duty on certain inputs, for example fuel or parts, which in effect reduce their costs. Others, such as payments to compensate for losses incurred on certain services, or payments in respect of concessionary fares, should be treated as revenue items.

Justification for Subsidy

In many developing countries, the official justification for subsidising public transport is to make fares affordable to the majority of passengers. In reality, they often do more to support inefficient public sector operators, and the benefit to the public of lower fares is limited. In Sri Lanka, for example, the public sector bus operators received government subsidies, and were required to charge lower fares than the private sector; however, several of the public sector operators were able to provide only very limited services, so that the majority of passengers had no choice other than to use the more expensive private sector services.

Subsidies may be targeted at specific services or passengers. In most public transport networks there are routes, or sections of routes, for which demand is low for part or all of the day; as a result, if market forces prevail, service frequencies will be low, or no service operated at all. It may be considered desirable to provide certain unprofitable services to facilitate mobility, and to enable a city or rural area to function more efficiently.

Subsidies may be justifiable to cover an undertaking's fixed costs, in a situation where every service operated generates sufficient revenue to cover its direct costs, but not to cover the fixed costs in full. Virtually all rail-based urban public transport systems are subsidised to some extent; some receive subsidies to cover operating deficits, but many, which are said to be viable, in fact cover only their variable costs, making little or no contribution to their infrastructure costs, or the interest on the capital invested in infrastructure. This to an extent is a legitimate claim where substantial sunk costs are involved: the overall economic benefit of continuing to operate in these circumstances is invariably greater than if the operation were to cease. However, the dangers of encouraging inefficiency on the part of the operator must be recognised.

A subsidy may be provided to enable bus services to compete on equal terms with other public and private transport modes, particularly where infrastructure and external transport costs are not equitably shared between the various modes.

Subsidies for additional public transport capacity may be preferable to spending considerably more on additional road capacity to cope with an increasing volume of private transport. As discussed in Chapter 3, many urban road systems are inadequate for peak traffic flows. Even if it were possible to construct roads with the capacity to cope with peak traffic flows, they would be under-utilised at off-peak times, representing inefficient use of scarce urban land. A public transport system which can cope fully with peak demand similarly suffers from the problem of surplus off-peak capacity, but much of this surplus capacity takes the form of vehicles and personnel and need not occupy valuable city-centre space. While the surplus capacity is costly to the transport operator, it is normally far less costly to the community as a whole than surplus road capacity.

As an alternative to massive expenditure on road construction there is therefore a strong argument in favour of subsidy for public transport operators to meet the cost of peak public transport capacity, principally additional buses, trams or trains and personnel. However, this presupposes that an improved public transport service will result in a sufficient reduction in the use of private transport to render the alternative road construction unnecessary; in practice this is not usually so without other measures, such as road pricing, to discourage private transport use, and possibly to generate revenue to contribute towards the subsidy. While this proposition may be attractive in theory, in practice it may be very difficult to implement: car owners represent a strong political lobby in most developing countries, and they are not easily persuaded to use public transport, even where traffic congestion is severe.

Where new urban development is taking place, there may be a case for subsidising public transport as a form of "pump priming", to fund provision of a service for the first users before demand builds up to make the service profitable, when the subsidy would no longer be required. This would help to accelerate development, and discourage the first users from finding alternative and less efficient means of transport where this is an option. It could be argued that the transport operator should be prepared to incur losses until the traffic increases to a viable level, but this would require effective regulation to protect an operator, who has invested in building up patronage in this way, from others entering the market once it has been developed. Similarly, subsidy may be justifiable to fund expansion of services or experimental operations in their early stages.

A major problem in many developing countries is slow or even negative development in rural areas, even though the economic survival of these countries may depend on a strong agricultural base. Measures must therefore be taken to encourage rural development, including the channelling of resources into rural areas; however, market forces will often tend to encourage development in urban areas at the expense of the rural areas, and it may therefore be necessary for market forces to be over-ruled in order to improve the availability of goods and services to rural dwellers. This may be achieved through central or local government subsidies to various rural industries, including public transport operators incurring losses on rural routes.

Subsidised transport for schoolchildren and students is relatively common in developed countries, but less so in developing countries. In some countries, education authorities have a statutory obligation to ensure that adequate and affordable transport is provided for schoolchildren and students; sometimes this transport must be provided free of charge. If a government chooses to subsidise education, as many do, it may be argued that logically it should also subsidise transport for schoolchildren to ensure that all are able to benefit equally from the subsidised education, regardless of where they live or their parents' ability to pay for transport. Expenditure on transport for educational purposes tends to increase with higher levels of education: children travelling to secondary schools normally have to travel farther on average, while university students not resident on campus must travel farther still.

For subsidies to be effective, the providers of subsidies must be capable of administering them efficiently, while the transport operators must be prevented from wasting them through inefficient practices or abuse; a degree of regulation will be necessary to ensure that operators meet their obligations. In many developing countries administration and enforcement are poor, and large sums are spent on subsidies which in reality provide very little benefit to the users.

Forms of Subsidy

There are various forms of subsidy, which may be broadly categorised as general operator support, revenue enhancement, cost reduction, and the provision of services under contract.

General operator support is normally the most simple to administer, and is often applied to public corporations, with the government making good any losses incurred, or to private sector undertakings where a specified level of profit or return on capital is guaranteed, with government funding any shortfall. A major disadvantage of this form of subsidy is that it provides no incentive to the operator to manage the business efficiently, and very often results in gross inefficiency: many public sector transport undertakings in developing countries are in this situation. Close supervision by the regulatory authorities is required to ensure that operators do not abuse the provision of the subsidy.

Direct revenue enhancement may be appropriate where the objective of a subsidy is merely to keep fares at a low level. It may apply to all routes in a system, or selected routes, and the level of support may vary from route to route. It may be based on the level of activity, such as a kilometre-based subsidy, or on the volume of business, such as a per-passenger subsidy: for example, the state-owned bus operator in Addis Ababa receives a fixed amount of subsidy in respect of every ticket sold. A subsidy based on the number of passengers carried may be appropriate if all fares are to be kept artificially low as a matter of policy, but there is a danger that operators will concentrate resources on the routes with highest demand, and neglect those where patronage is low. There may also be a risk, especially where there is a flat rate of subsidy per passenger, that unscrupulous operators will inflate the number of passengers, for example by splitting routes so that more passengers must transfer, or increase the number of short-distance passengers by offering very low short-distance fares. Similarly, a subsidy based on the number of kilometres operated may encourage operators to run more kilometres than are necessary. Such systems require a high level of supervision, and are difficult to administer unless the operator has good ticketing and record systems.

Alternatively the passengers, rather than the transport operator, may be subsidised, with the fares for their journeys paid for by government. This may apply in the case of concessionary fare schemes for particular classes of passenger such as schoolchildren or pensioners. Such schemes may require the funding authority to purchase multiple journey or season tickets from the operator, for issuing to the concessionees, or making some form of payment direct to the concessionees who would then pay the standard fares. The latter approach has some advantages, particularly where the industry is fragmented, but direct subsidy of the user in this way is particularly difficult to administer, and may be susceptible to serious abuse. It is more common for the authorities to make blanket payments to transport operators for all concessionary travel, usually based on a sample to determine the extent of such travel.

Other forms of subsidy, which are not targeted towards specific services or routes, or classes of passenger, are measures to reduce operating costs. The subsidy might take the form of grants for the purchase of vehicles, tax concessions on inputs such as fuel or spare parts, or even the provision of subsidised infrastructure such as workshop or depot facilities. Other possibilities include the provision of favourable finance terms for the purchase of equipment: for example the state-owned transport companies in Ghana were able to purchase vehicles at low rates of interest. Where a rail operator is not required to make any interest payments in respect of its infrastructure, the foregone interest on the capital is equivalent to a cash subsidy.

Such cost-reduction subsidies have been applied in the United Kingdom, where bus operators receive a fuel duty rebate in respect of all stage bus services, but not long-distance services, tours or contract operations. The rate of rebate is currently 80% (but airlines and rail operators receive 100%). A subsidy which no longer applies was the New Bus Grant, which provided substantial grants towards the cost of purchasing new buses for stage carriage services.

These types of subsidy do not detract from any incentive for the operator to manage the business efficiently, but they may cause some distortions. For example, a subsidy for new buses may result in a waste of resources through vehicles being replaced before their economic lives have expired; a fuel duty rebate does not encourage operators to minimise fuel consumption.

With these forms of subsidy operators' usage of the relevant inputs must be accurately assessed, while there needs to be some means of ensuring that subsidised buses or equipment are not used for other types of service which are not eligible for subsidy. Payment to transport operators is normally only practical where the authorities are dealing with a small number of relatively large transport operators, or where there is a well administered operators' association which can deal satisfactorily with such matters on behalf of its members. Where the industry is fragmented, administration of a subsidy scheme can be difficult, and highly susceptible to abuse and fraud on the part of the users and the operators.

Another means of subsidising operators running unprofitable routes, or special services such as those for schoolchildren, is for the local authority to appoint operators to run them under contract; the operator is paid the full cost of providing the service, perhaps with some or all revenue being paid to the funding agency. In the case of some contracted bus services, the authorities may purchase the buses and lease them to the operators, for a nominal charge. It is essential that contract bids are evaluated carefully; it is not usually sufficient merely to accept the lowest-cost bid, since the service quality may be poor, and there must be effective sanctions against operators failing to satisfy the terms of the contract.

In many developed countries, unprofitable transport services are provided under contract or franchise arrangements with local or central government authorities; the various alternatives are discussed in Chapter 19. Often such contracts cover entire networks, they may apply to individual routes, and sometimes only to specific journeys on some routes. In the United Kingdom, for example, there are many routes which are operated for most of the day on a commercial basis; however, the operators of these services are not normally prepared to fund journeys at times when demand is insufficient to cover costs, such as in the evenings or at weekends, and the authorities may secure the operation of journeys at these times by contracting with an operator to provide them under contract. Often the contract is awarded to the operator of the commercial journeys, but this is not always the case.

An alternative is to contract out complete networks, including profitable and unprofitable services, to a single operator who would take responsibility for all services, facilitating efficient use of resources. The profitable routes would operate on a commercial basis, while the unprofitable routes, or journeys, would be subsidised. Accurate route costing is essential in such cases.

For contract arrangements to provide best value there must be several eligible and competent operators to bid competitively for the contracts. In developing countries there is often little or no competition in the tendering process, in which case there must be an effective means of ensuring that the successful operator does not exploit the situation.

Funding of Subsidies

Subsidies for public transport are normally funded by central or local government out of taxation, but increasingly, particularly in developed countries, through hypothecation of receipts from road user or parking charges, fines for infringements of traffic regulations, or fuel duty; this may be justified on the grounds that the resulting improvement in public transport services will reduce the need for additional investment in road and parking space. Sometimes local authorities have the power to impose local taxes, for instance on fuel, parts or vehicle registration; these can be effectively hypothecated.

Development levies are another potential source of revenue for subsidising public transport. These are charges imposed by government authorities on the developers of commercial or residential properties, sometimes as a condition of the granting of planning permission; planning legislation may include formal provision for such charges. Where a portion of this revenue is allocated to subsidising public transport, the development can benefit in various ways: if car ownership is low, good and more reliable public transport can broaden an employer's labour catchment area, thus enhancing the value of a commercial development; a residential development will be more attractive to potential residents if a good public transport service is provided from the start, even when demand is low. In the United Kingdom some developers have undertaken to support bus services, to a specified level and for a specified period, to serve new housing developments.

Employee taxes, levied on employers, may take the form of a local charge per employee, part of which may be directed towards improving public transport provision, which again will benefit employers by increasing the employee catchment area.

Where major transport infrastructure developments are to be funded, such as LRT schemes or busways, property owners may be charged a levy on the increase in the value of their properties as a result of the new transport project. But it is extremely difficult to assess such increased value, and with some developments, there has been no positive evidence of increased property values attributable to the scheme. An alternative approach, which was used to fund the construction of metro lines in Hong Kong, is for government to compulsorily purchase at existing values all property within a specified distance of the project, and to resell it at its new value once the effects of the project have materialised.

Security of a subsidy is often a major concern: a change of government, a change in policy or spending priorities, or a shortage of funds, may result in substantial cuts in subsidy, or even complete withdrawal. There may be concern that government will divert funds obtained through hypothecation to other areas of government spending; sometimes governments commit only to a limited term for hypothecation, and this may not be long enough to pay back private finance loans for large public transport infrastructure projects. In London, following introduction of congestion charging, which generated funds for the purpose of increasing the subsidy for public transport, central government reduced its contribution by a similar amount. Such lack of continuity, or the threat of it, can destabilise the provision of subsidised public transport services.

CROSS-SUBSIDY

While government policy, such as the requirement for affordable public transport fares, may call for subsidies, in reality funds are invariably limited, particularly in developing countries. Cross-subsidy is sometimes seen as a practical and viable alternative to government funding. This is the subsidy of an unprofitable activity from the surplus generated by a profitable activity. It may involve one trip subsidising another; one route subsidising another; one group of services, such as those operated by a particular depot or serving a particular area, subsidising another; or one company subsidising another under the same ownership.

For example, unprofitable bus services in rural areas may be subsidised by profitable urban services, while urban services with low demand may be subsidised by others where demand is much higher. Where a flat fare system is in operation, there is also an element of cross-subsidy between long and short distance passengers. A premium service may subsidise a regular service operating on the same route, so that in effect one class of passenger subsidises another. Some transport businesses are subsidised by profits from entirely different businesses under the same ownership: for example in Mumbai, public transport services operated by B.E.S.T. are subsidised from profits earned by electricity generating stations which are owned by the same undertaking.

Cross-subsidy occurs only when activities which earn insufficient revenue to cover their variable costs are funded from the surpluses of other activities. Operators sometimes claim that bus services are unprofitable, and are being subsidised by more profitable services, when their revenue per kilometre is lower than the average total costs per kilometre for the undertaking as a whole. However, this is not necessarily true: such services are not unprofitable to operate provided that they cover their variable costs in full, even if they make only a small contribution, or none at all, to fixed costs, as explained in Chapter 13. When bus services were deregulated in the United Kingdom, it was feared that many services, which operators claimed were being cross-subsidised, would disappear. In fact the number of services withdrawn completely was lower than expected, indicating that, while less profitable than some routes, many were in fact still viable.

The principal rationale for cross-subsidy in public transport is that while demand in some parts of an operator's territory may be sufficient to enable services to be operated profitably, there is insufficient demand at the prevailing fare levels in other areas to support a service; residents of these areas will therefore suffer from a lack of good transport facilities, and it is argued that profits from the former should subsidise the latter.

In Malawi, what was known as the "Prime Route Policy" was designed to guard against the problem of inadequate transport services in rural areas. Under this policy, which applied until bus services were deregulated in the 1990s, all bus operators were expected to operate unprofitable routes in addition to providing services on the "prime" or profitable routes; they were in fact expected to run at least 40% of their total kilometres on unprofitable routes, although these were not clearly defined. Fares were also controlled so that, in theory at least, there was no possibility of one operator undercutting another on prime routes. Malawi was untypical of developing countries in that most of its bus services until the late 1990s were provided by a single operator, which practised cross-subsidy to a considerable extent. As a result, the network of rural bus services in Malawi was much more extensive, and of better quality, than in most developing countries.

Potential problems with a policy such as this are that the distinction between profitable and unprofitable routes will vary depending on the efficiency of the operator, while small operators, particularly those with only one vehicle, cannot practice cross-subsidy unless they operate on routes with both profitable and unprofitable sections. In practice, effective implementation and enforcement are very difficult.

A criticism of cross-subsidy in transport is that passengers on profitable services who, by definition, are normally the majority of users, have to pay more for their travel, and receive a lower standard of service, than they would if the route did not have to generate revenue for the financing of other routes to benefit the minority. In a regulated or non-competitive situation, in order to practise cross-subsidy, the operator will use its monopoly position on profitable routes to charge higher fares than would apply under competition, in order to inflate returns to a level sufficient to cross-subsidise as well as to pay an adequate dividend; the higher fares result in reduced demand, and the level of service provided is correspondingly lower.

Cross-subsidy in transport, as well as in other fields, can normally be effective only if there are relatively large operators with a spread of activities, while regulation is required in order to control competition on the profitable routes; competition will tend to eliminate the surplus required for cross-subsidy. Moreover, cross-subsidy should be practised consistently by all operators. In a situation where only some operators practise cross-subsidy, but where all operators are required to charge the same fares, those which do not practise cross-subsidy will make excessive profits, since none of their revenue is diverted to support unprofitable routes.

Thus although passengers will be paying inflated fares, most of the benefit will be enjoyed by the bus operators, rather than by the people living in rural areas and elsewhere where services are unprofitable. On the other hand, if fares are not controlled, operators with no loss-making routes will be able to undercut those which have to finance unprofitable services; the profits of these operators will be reduced to the point where the loss-making services can no longer be supported. This occurs in many countries, with the result that in practice cross-subsidy is rarely effective. Even where there are controls designed to facilitate cross-subsidy, the enforcement authorities often lack the resources to ensure that the controls are properly applied.

Cross-subsidy is more easily applied by an operator which is not required to produce a surplus, such as a public-sector transport undertaking, than by an operator which is required to provide a return on investment; any return will be reduced or even eliminated by cross-subsidy, depending on the extent to which unprofitable services are operated. If the undertaking were privately owned, its owners would forego part of their dividend income to enable unprofitable services to be provided to the public. In a truly commercial situation, this would reduce the attractiveness of the undertaking to investors, who would transfer their funds elsewhere, with the result that the undertaking would eventually die.

15

MANAGEMENT INFORMATION AND RECORD SYSTEMS

Information is essential for the effective management of any business: the better the availability of information, and the greater its accuracy, the easier it will be for management, and also the regulatory authorities where applicable, to make appropriate decisions and take appropriate action. A management information system (MIS) involves the collection and analysis of information which is generated in the course of the operation of the business, and the use of this information for monitoring, control and planning purposes. It is particularly useful as a means of identifying problems or trends, such as increasing or declining demand or increases in costs. Some of the data may also be used by regulatory authorities to enable them to monitor and compare the performance of different operators, or to compare the results of an operator with target or benchmark figures. Every business, whatever its size, requires management information, but the volume, and the complexity of the appropriate information system, will increase with the scale of the operation.

Comparatively few transport undertakings in developing countries produce adequate management information. In many organisations vast volumes of data are generated daily, which however are not effectively used, partly because they are not available in a readily usable form, but often because managers lack the expertise required to interpret management information correctly, or do not fully appreciate the uses to which it may be put.

In addition to the basic management information required by any business, essential categories of information required by a transport operator are those which quantify demand patterns and volumes, and operational performance, such as statistics relating to kilometres operated, revenue collected, and expenditure. These statistics may be obtained from the various operational control systems and records, and should be used in conjunction with base data such as vehicle inventory, route details and staff establishment records to produce key performance indicators (KPIs) and exception reports.

BASE DATA

A transport business, like any other, should maintain certain base data and records regarding its assets and operations: of primary importance are inventories of vehicles, stocks of spare parts, fuel and tyres, staff records, details of properties owned or leased, and details of the services operated. These base data are required for a number of purposes: to manage assets effectively it is necessary to have details of those assets, while most base data are used in conjunction with operating statistics in the derivation of key performance indicators.

Base data may be maintained to a very high level of detail: this is generally desirable even though some of the details will be required relatively infrequently, and the management information system should be designed to use details only when they are required. For example, while vehicle records may include very specific details such as chassis and engine number, type of seating, or advertisements carried, such detail will not be required in an analysis of vehicle utilisation, although it will be required for other purposes. Some operators, however, record only basic information, and often there is no accurate record of vehicle makes or models in a fleet; in extreme cases, even the number of vehicles owned is not accurately known. Regardless of the level of detail, such records must be accurate, and regularly updated; with a computerised system base data can be updated constantly if necessary.

The types of information which may be recorded under the various headings are indicated below: not all will be applicable or relevant to every operator, and the appropriate level of detail will depend on the nature of the operation, the operating environment, regulatory regime and other factors. In addition, the information should be available in various forms to meet the requirements of different departments or individuals within the organisation, and with an effective computerised system it is relatively easy for data to be presented in the most appropriate form to meet these different requirements. For example, if an undertaking has several depots, it is usually desirable, in addition to the master fleet list, for separate lists of vehicles to be produced for each depot, detailing only the vehicles allocated to that depot; the operations department may require a list of buses, by identification number, allocated to each route; the department dealing with advertisements carried on buses may require a list of all buses showing the advertisements carried by each; or the department dealing with bus charter services may require a complete list of vehicles showing seating types and capacities. It is unlikely that a full list of vehicles, showing all details contained in the database, will ever need to be printed.

Fleet Details: information to be recorded in respect of each vehicle:

- Registration or licence plate number
- Fleet number (if applicable)
- Manufacturer
- Model

- Type (e.g. single-deck, double-deck, articulated)
- Seating capacity
- Total passenger capacity (i.e. including standing passengers if applicable)
- Year of manufacture
- Year of purchase or entry into service (e.g. if vehicle was acquired second-hand)

It may also be useful to include additional information against each vehicle, for example:

- Chassis number
- Engine number
- Body number (if applicable)
- Depot to which allocated
- Route(s) to which allocated (if applicable)
- Livery or colour
- Advertisements carried, externally and internally
- Door configuration
- Whether roof luggage rack or freight compartment is fitted
- Type of seating (e.g. bus/coach, with/without head rests, fixed/reclining)
- Rehabilitation date (if applicable)
- Original purchase price
- Current book value
- Planned disposal date

Staff: information to be recorded in respect of each employee:

- Name
- Staff number
- Home address
- Date of birth
- Sex
- Educational and other relevant qualifications
- Licence numbers and expiry dates (for drivers)
- Position
- Salary or grade
- Date engaged
- Date appointed to present position
- Previous positions held and transfer/promotion dates
- Record of training provided during employment
- Disciplinary record, showing offences committed with dates and any penalties imposed

Other information may be relevant in certain circumstances, for example:

- Whether employed full-time or part-time
- Nationality
- Place or country of birth
- Ethnic group or tribe
- Whether physically disabled and nature of disability

Stocks: Stock control is a specialised discipline outside the scope of this book, but in addition to detailed information on stockholdings of each individual line required for stock control purposes, the following are useful for general management information:

- Total stock value
- Total value of obsolete stock
- Total value of surplus stock
- Total value of stock on order
- Total value of stock shortfall (stock required but not available)
- Litres of fuel in stock

Routes: details to be recorded in respect of each route operated:

- Route number or other means of identification
- Terminal points
- Principal intermediate points
- Roads traversed
- Route length (inwards and outwards - these may differ e.g. because of one-way systems, etc)
- Sequential list of fare stages with distances from starting point
- Number of daily scheduled kilometres to be operated (weekdays, weekends)
- Running times - inwards and outwards, and at different times or on different days if applicable
- Basic frequencies at inner end of route (weekdays, weekends, peak/off-peak)
- First/last bus times (weekdays, weekends, peak/off-peak)
- Number of buses required (weekdays, weekends, peak/off-peak)
- Timetable (if applicable)
- Fare table (if applicable)
- Route licence number (if applicable)
- Route licence expiry date (if applicable)

Properties and Infrastructure: recorded details in respect of each property owned or leased may include the following:

- Location or address
- Type of property (e.g. depot, bus station, office, staff accommodation, etc)
- Area of plot
- Floor area of buildings and number of storeys
- Whether owned or leased

- Date purchased
- Lease commencement and expiry dates
- Purchase price
- Current value
- Monthly or annual rental

Financial Data: Financial data requirements in transport undertakings are similar to those applicable in any commercial organisation, and are outside the scope of this book; aspects of financial management which are specific to transport operation are discussed in Chapter 16.

RECORDS AND OPERATING STATISTICS

As with all organisations, it is necessary to keep accurate records of various aspects of the operation. The most obvious requirements, which apply to all businesses, are the keeping of financial records, principally accounts and balance sheets, and personnel records. Essential records which are specific to a transport operation are operating statistics, vehicle maintenance and accident records.

Of vital importance is information on revenue, and this is obtained through revenue control systems, as described in Chapter 9. The information generated enables sources of revenue to be identified, and revenue to be analysed by bus route, time of day, or day of week; this is invaluable in the identification of profitable and unprofitable activities. It is useful to be able to apportion revenue to individual journeys, although normally this is only relevant on an occasional basis when examining the performance of a bus route in detail. Some operators identify revenue collected by individual vehicles, but this is rarely relevant. An additional, and important, use of the data is to facilitate the detection of fraud.

Operating statistics record the level of activity, or the output and consumption, of the operation. The simplest and most commonly used measure of output for a road passenger transport undertaking is the number of kilometres (or miles) operated. This may be calculated by recording the odometer or tachograph reading for each vehicle at the end of each day, or other appropriate period; however, these instruments may be unreliable, particularly where road conditions or maintenance standards are poor; an odometer attached to one of the wheel hubs on a vehicle, known as a "hubodometer", is generally more reliable, and these are becoming more commonly used by large fleet operators. Many operators have tachographs installed in their vehicles: in some countries this is a legal requirement. A tachograph is an instrument similar to a speedometer, but with the capability of recording hours of operation, kilometres and vehicle speed in graphic form, and in some cases other data such as engine speed. This will provide information on kilometres operated, as well as other valuable data: tachographs can indicate adherence or otherwise to schedules, speed limits, and permitted hours of working or driving, the operation of unauthorised journeys, engine idling for excessive periods, and other instances of bad driving. They can be invaluable in the investigation of accidents.

Other methods of calculating kilometres may also be used. A common method in a scheduled operation is to calculate "standard kilometres" for every bus duty, and on the basis of records of duties carried out by each bus, together with records of additional kilometres and scheduled kilometres not operated, the daily, weekly or monthly kilometres can be determined for each bus. This system requires accuracy in the initial calculation of standard kilometres, as well as updating each time schedules are changed, and in keeping and analysing records. In this respect it may not be practical for many operators in developing countries.

Sometimes kilometres operated are estimated on the basis of fuel consumed. This is acceptable as a guide, for example daily fuel issues may be used as an initial indicator of kilometres operated before more accurate figures become available, but should not be the sole means of calculating kilometres. If this is the only measure, it will be difficult, if not impossible, for example, to check on fuel consumption rates, or to detect fuel theft.

In some organisations there is a tendency for operations management to understate kilometres, since this makes the revenue per kilometre figures, for which they are responsible, appear better; while engineering management tends to overstate kilometres, since this makes most engineering performance indicators appear better. The accuracy of records of kilometres operated provided by either of these departments may therefore sometimes be suspect if there is no effective means of verification.

The most commonly used measure of consumption for a passenger transport operation is the number of passengers carried. It is not always possible to ascertain this figure accurately: often the figure quoted is in fact the number of tickets issued, but in many cases, because of a limited number of ticket denominations available, it is necessary to issue two or more tickets for certain fares, so that the number of tickets issued exceeds the number of passengers carried. Sometimes this fact is ignored; sometimes the figure is adjusted on the basis of a sample. Where tickets are not issued, as is normally the case in less formal public transport services, this information may be obtained by means of censuses or sample surveys. Mechanical and electronic passenger counters are available, which detect and record passenger movements on and off a vehicle, but these tend to be unreliable, particularly in a difficult operating environment. In practice, informal operators are interested only in revenue earned, rather than numbers of passengers carried. However, even if the number of passengers carried can be measured accurately, a fundamental defect of this measure is that it does not reflect distance travelled, and therefore revenue from fares often provides a more useful measure of patronage.

Kilometres operated and passengers carried, as measures of output and consumption respectively, cannot easily be compared with one another, and therefore do not provide a ready means of assessing how closely supply and demand are matched. In this respect a more useful unit of output would be seat-kilometres, or where there is significant standing capacity on buses, "passenger-place-kilometres", or "potential passenger-kilometres". The equivalent measure of consumption is "passenger-kilometres", which represent the actual usage of the transport service, and is the sum of the number of kilometres travelled by each passenger carried in a period. It can be difficult to measure, however, particularly where the turnover of passengers is high, and is most easily estimated from the revenue collected unless a flat fare system applies. In practice, therefore, these figures are seldom used as a means of comparing supply and demand for transport services, and the principal measures used are kilometres operated, passengers carried, revenue collected, and expenditure. These should be recorded so that they may be identified with specific vehicles, routes or other aspects of the operation as appropriate; for example, it should be possible to ascertain the number of kilometres operated by a particular vehicle or group of vehicles, or on a particular route or type of service, and to allocate revenue to particular routes or trips.

A transport vehicle is a valuable asset and if it is standing idle it is not earning its keep. It is therefore important to be able to measure the utilisation of vehicles, in terms productive and unproductive time, as well as kilometres operated. This requires records to be kept of the work done by each vehicle. Where services are operated to schedule it is normal to keep a record of the duties worked by each bus; otherwise a record of the time at which each bus leaves the depot, and when it returns after completing its day's work, will be useful, but will not show any idle time at terminals. Terminal departure sheets are a valuable record in this respect.

It is often necessary to keep detailed records for drivers, in respect of hours worked, discipline and accidents. In many countries, as discussed in Chapter 19, there is legislation which restricts the number of hours which a driver may work in a day or week, as a safety measure; in some countries (although in relatively few developing countries) operators are required to keep records of hours worked by drivers, for inspection if required by enforcement agencies. Driver discipline is important, and compliance with national regulations and the operators' own rules and regulations must be monitored, to safeguard standards of safety and operational reliability. A driver with a poor accident record, or who frequently fails to operate in accordance with schedules, is a liability to the operator, and it is essential that such drivers are identifiable so that appropriate action may be taken.

Vehicle maintenance records are also important; again, in some countries transport operators are required by law to keep maintenance records for each vehicle, so that compliance with statutory maintenance standards, set for safety reasons, may be checked. Even where such regulations do not apply, however, it is in the operators' interests to keep accurate maintenance records, to ensure that vehicles are maintained in accordance with their own standards. Such records may be based on maintenance job cards or equivalent documents, which should provide a record of all maintenance work carried out on each vehicle.

Expenditure records are essential for financial control and accounting purposes, but are also an important element of a management information system. Expenditure should be broken down not only by activity such as route or service type, but by category such as fuel, materials and labour; some items of expenditure, such as fuel and spare parts costs, should be allocated to specific vehicles.

These are the most important items of information required to monitor the operation of a transport service, and should be recorded as accurately as possible. There are likely to be a large number of other statistics which are required by particular operators for specific purposes, as discussed later. Operating statistics should be collected monthly, weekly, daily or even hourly as appropriate, while the frequency of updating base data should be consistent with that of the management reports. Most of the information will be most appropriately collated on a daily basis: except in the case of long-distance operations where buses may be away from base for more than one day, revenue will be paid in daily, and fuel issues, particularly where the operator has its own fuelling facilities, are also normally made daily, and should be summarised at the end of each day. Some items, such as expenditure, may not be available on a daily basis if these are processed less frequently; expenditure figures are often available only on a weekly, or even monthly basis.

Information which should normally be recorded daily includes the following, although not all of these data will be applicable or available in every operation:

- Fare revenue (by route)
- Passengers carried (by route, and by category: adult, child, etc)
- Total kilometres operated
- Scheduled kilometres operated (by route and by vehicle)
- Unscheduled kilometres operated
- Scheduled kilometres not operated (by reason, e.g. vehicle breakdown, vehicle non-availability, staff non-availability, road/weather conditions, industrial action)
- Litres of fuel issued (in total and by vehicle)
- Litres of engine oil issued (in total and by vehicle)
- Number of vehicles available at peak periods
- Number of vehicles operated at peak periods
- Number of accidents, including number of fatalities
- Number of mechanical breakdowns
- Number of tyre failures
- Total number of hours worked by drivers
- Total number of hours worked by conductors

In addition to monthly totals of these daily figures (or totals for each accounting period, if appropriate), the following should be recorded monthly or for each accounting period:

- Wages and salaries (by staff category: drivers, conductors, etc)
- Expenditure on spare parts
- Expenditure on fuel
- Expenditure on tyres
- Other expenditure
- Total expenditure
- Operating surplus or deficit before interest and tax

KEY PERFORMANCE INDICATORS

Key performance indicators (KPIs) are calculated from the operating statistics and base data to provide figures (usually ratios) which give an immediate indication of how the operation is performing; normally they must be compared with a base figure or a target. Some indicators may be calculated in respect of the entire operation, or parts of the operation, for example by route, by vehicle type, or by time. KPIs can show trends, or warn of problems, and will influence immediate action or longer-term plans. For example, if the revenue per kilometre is showing a steady increase over time, this will influence the organisation's plans for expansion; if there is a sudden fall or increase, this could indicate an unexpected occurrence, which must be investigated. Therefore as well as establishing systems to produce these indicators there needs to be a procedure for monitoring them and for initiating appropriate action.

KPIs must be used with care. They must be clearly and unambiguously defined, and based on accurate information, as well as produced in time to be put to good use. It is essential that their meaning is fully understood by all concerned, particularly if they are to be used for comparative purposes: differences in circumstances may influence the indicators so that comparisons may be misleading. Care must be exercised when setting targets for KPIs: not only must these be realistically achievable, but they must not encourage managers to perversely manipulate other parameters in order to meet the targets. For example, a targeted increase in the recorded number of passengers carried per bus per day, intended to ensure that conductors collect fares from a greater proportion of passengers, might instead be achieved by shortening routes so that more passengers must interchange and therefore make more journeys, by reducing the number of buses operated, or by increasing the length of the operating day, any of which might be detrimental to the operation as a whole.

The following key performance indicators are commonly used:

Operational Indicators

- Kilometres per vehicle per day (KPVPD)
- Fare revenue per vehicle per day (RPVPD)
- Fare revenue per kilometre
- Passengers carried per vehicle per day (PPVPD)
- Average fare paid per passenger
- Load factor
- Vehicle utilisation
- Percentage of scheduled kilometres operated
- Percentage of "dead" kilometres
- Kilometres per accident
- Punctuality

Engineering Indicators

- Expenditure per kilometre on fuel, tyres, and maintenance materials
- Vehicle availability at peak periods
- Fuel consumption
- Engine oil consumption
- Kilometres per mechanical breakdown
- Kilometres per tyre carcase
- Ratio of expenditure on preventive maintenance to total maintenance expenditure
- Average age of fleet

Personnel Indicators

- Number of staff per vehicle
- Expenditure per kilometre on salaries and wages
- Kilometres per employee per period
- Kilometres per driver per day
- Kilometres per man hour
- Staff turnover

Financial Indicators

- Total expenditure per kilometre
- Operating surplus or deficit
- Return on capital employed

The financial performance indicators applicable to any business also apply to public transport businesses, and are not discussed in detail in this chapter, except to highlight particular considerations applicable to public transport operations.

This list of KPIs is not exhaustive, although it includes all of those which are likely to be of most value to the majority of operators. Some operators will require additional indicators to meet their specific requirements or to enable them to monitor particular problem areas. For example, some might find it useful to record minutes of lateness of each departure from a depot or terminal, if there are regular problems of punctuality; passengers left at stops due to insufficient service capacity; the number of minutes of lateness of crews reporting for duty, the number of crews absent each day, or crew availability as a percentage of requirement or of the number on the payroll, where there are labour shortage or disciplinary problems; the number of scheduled duties not operated, where there are problems of labour and/or vehicle shortages; the number of unfinished duties, where buses frequently lose time during the day due to severe traffic congestion; the number of vehicles off the road for seven days or more, where there are problems of maintenance control or shortage of spare parts; or the number of buses washed or swept daily if cleanliness is an issue.

It is important to ensure that definitions are understood and are used consistently. The definitions used for some KPIs vary between one undertaking and another. For example, utilisation of buses may be measured as the number of buses owned as a percentage of those available, or of the licensed fleet, or of the fleet owned. Similarly, staff per bus may be measured as the number of staff per bus owned, or per bus licensed, or per operational bus or of the number of buses operated at peak periods. Care must therefore be exercised when comparing KPIs for different undertakings.

As described in Chapter 2, there are wide international variations in geographic, climatic, demographic, political, institutional, economic, environmental and cultural factors which influence the operation of a transport undertaking. It can therefore be very misleading to quote typical figures for any of the key performance indicators, while any attempt at benchmarking must be made with extreme caution, and allow for these differences. However, as a general guide, the following paragraphs give an indication of ranges of values found under different conditions. There will be many cases where figures fall outside the ranges quoted, for good reasons; but once acceptable ranges have been determined for a particular set of circumstances, all indicators falling outside these ranges should be examined to determine the reason.

Kilometres per vehicle per day (KPVPD)

This indicator provides a measure of vehicle productivity. A vehicle should be used as intensively as possible, provided that sufficient traffic is available to cover the direct costs of operation. A high KPVPD figure indicates intensive use, but does not give any indication of the viability of the kilometres operated, and therefore does not necessarily imply optimum usage of a vehicle in economic terms. Wasteful or unnecessary use, even though it increases utilisation, should obviously be kept to a minimum.

Vehicles are not used every day, and therefore it is important to distinguish between kilometres operated by a bus in the course of a day's work, and average daily kilometres over a year; the latter is more easily calculated, and therefore is the figure which is most commonly used. If, for example, vehicles are available for only 85% of the time, the average daily kilometre figure, if calculated from the annual figure, must be divided by 0.85 to give the actual daily kilometres operated by each vehicle when it is used. It is also important to be clear as to whether the calculation is based on the number of vehicles owned, licensed or operational. Normally the most appropriate measure in this context is the number of kilometres operated daily per licensed vehicle. When calculating this indicator, it is essential that the definition is clear, and applied consistently.

Kilometres per vehicle are influenced by operating speeds, proportion of idle to running time, and hours of operation each day. In an urban operation where speeds are low due to frequent stops, time taken by passengers boarding and alighting, and delays due to traffic congestion, and a proportion of buses are used at peak periods only, kilometres per vehicle per day will be low. Urban buses on all day service will normally operate between 150 and 300 kilometres per day, but where a proportion of the fleet is operated at peak periods only the average kilometres per vehicle will be lower than this. Typical figures will be between 100 and 200 per day; substantially higher figures are achieved in some cities, while in others much lower figures are achieved. At the other extreme, buses operating on long distance services, running at high speeds on inter-urban main roads, with infrequent stops and long hours of operation, may achieve over 750 kilometres per day. Buses on inter-urban stage services will normally operate between 200 and 400 kilometres per day. Kilometres per licensed bus will be lower than these figures, depending on the proportion of licensed buses which are actually operated.

Where several different categories of service are operated, it will normally be useful to calculate this indicator for each category separately; similarly, it may be useful to calculate it for different depots or divisions within a single organisation.

The productivity of paratransit vehicles varies considerably, depending in particular on the proportion of running to idle time as well as the length of the working day. A minibus may operate between seventy and 360 kilometres per day; a taxi may make between ten and fifty trips in a day, covering between eighty and 200 kilometres; a scooter-based vehicle such as a Bajaj or duk-duk will make between fifteen and thirty trips in a day, covering between fifty and 100 kilometres; and a human-powered vehicle such as a cycle-rickshaw will typically make between ten and fifteen trips and cover between eight and twenty kilometres per day.

Calculation: Total kilometres operated during a period, divided by total number of buses licensed in that period, and then divided by the number of days in the period. It is normally most convenient to use the number of buses licensed on a particular day, such as the last day of the period; the figure might be distorted if a significant number of buses is licensed or delicensed during the course of the period, but this is not normally a serious problem.

Fare revenue per vehicle per day (RPVPD)

This is a useful, ready indicator of viability: the direct costs of owning and operating a vehicle are reasonably easy to calculate, and if RPVPD exceeds this figure then the operation is making a contribution to overhead costs. The figure is influenced by vehicle load factors and utilisation, fare levels, and revenue integrity. It is important to distinguish between fare revenue (i.e. money paid by passengers in order to travel) and other revenue such as that received in respect of advertising on buses, rental of company property to third parties, or subsidies. Except in the case of some subsidies, which are directly related to particular routes, such revenue is not normally related to the level of service provided and it would be misleading to allocate it on a per-bus or per-kilometre basis.

It is useful to calculate this indicator as an average for the operation as a whole, and for individual routes or groups of routes, and it is equally important to ensure that any comparison between revenue and expenditure per vehicle is on an appropriate basis. Again it is important to be clear as to the exact definition; revenue per licensed vehicle is normally most useful in this case, but some operators calculate revenue per operational vehicle, or per vehicle used.

Calculation: Total fare revenue collected (for the organisation as a whole, or part of the organisation such as all services operated by a particular depot, or for a particular route) during a period, divided by total number of vehicles licensed (for the operation as a whole, part of the operation, or route, as appropriate) in that period, and then divided by the number of days in the period.

Fare revenue per kilometre

This is another useful operational and financial indicator. It is influenced by vehicle load factors, fare levels, and revenue integrity. If, overall, fare revenue per kilometre exceeds expenditure per kilometre, the operation is profitable; if fare revenue per kilometre exceeds direct costs per kilometre, but not total costs per kilometre, the operation is contributing to overheads but is not earning a profit. As with revenue per bus, it is useful to calculate this indicator as an average for the operation as a whole, for different categories of service, and for individual routes or groups of routes. Where an undertaking operates different types of services, for example urban, rural and long-distance, it is useful to be able to compare the financial performance of each. It may be found that one or more types of service is not viable, even if the undertaking as a whole is profitable; alternatively, if one type of service is found to be particularly profitable, the undertaking may decide to concentrate more of its resources in this type of service.

Revenue per kilometre for individual routes is a good indicator of route viability: if revenue per kilometre for a route exceeds the *variable* costs per kilometre, the route is making a contribution to the undertaking's overheads, and is therefore viable. Uninformed use of this measure can be dangerous, however. A route may show a high revenue per kilometre figure, but if the level of kilometres operated is low, for example because of a highly peaked operation or inefficient scheduling, the route may be less profitable then the figure might suggest since bus-variable costs may not be fully covered. It is also important to note that a group of routes, an individual route, or individual trip, whose revenue per kilometre falls below average expenditure per kilometre for the undertaking as a whole, is not necessary unprofitable: this will be the case only if revenue per kilometre falls below direct expenditure per kilometre. Some operators have misguidedly compared revenue per kilometre with average *total* costs (i.e. including overheads) per kilometre, and assumed that routes earning below this figure are unprofitable. Withdrawal of such routes, if they in fact are making a contribution to overheads, however small, will worsen the undertaking's financial position, rather than improve it.

Calculation: Total fare revenue collected (for the operation as a whole, or part of the operation such as all services operated by a particular depot, or a particular route) during a period, divided by total number of kilometres operated (for the operation as a whole, part of the operation, or route, as appropriate) in that period.

Passengers carried per vehicle per day (PPVPD)

This is an indicator of the level of patronage of a bus service. It is influenced by vehicle capacity, length of operating day, length of route, average distance travelled per passenger, total demand and the extent to which demand varies between peak and off-peak periods, and the kilometres operated per bus per day. The route structure has a significant influence: for example, a route network comprising a large number of very short routes requiring passengers to interchange several times during the course of a journey will result in a much higher PPVPD figure than a more complex route structure providing a greater number of direct links. Similarly, the average passenger's journey will tend to be longer in a large city than in a small town, so the PPVPD figure will be lower in the former than in the latter.

Therefore very wide variations are possible, and the reasons for these must be understood. Buses on long distance services may carry full loads of passengers from one end of the route to the other, with no intermediate traffic; if only one trip is made per day, PPVPD will be approximately fifty for full-sized buses. Buses on city services, making several trips, with a high turnover of short distance passengers, may carry up to 3,000 PPVPD. Passenger-kilometres, however, could be the same in each case: if, for example, the average distance travelled by long distance and short distance passengers were 120 kilometres and two kilometres respectively, the number of passenger-kilometres would be 6,000 in both cases.

As with other indicators, it is normally most appropriate to base this calculation on the number of buses licensed. On this basis, and assuming that approximately 85% of the fleet is operational, the normal range for buses with a capacity of 80-100 passengers on city services is between 1,000 and 2,000 PPVPD. For articulated buses with a capacity of between 150 and 175 passengers a normal range would be between 1,800 and 3,000 PPVPD. There are particularly large variations in the daily numbers of passengers carried by paratransit vehicles, as a result of the wide variations in daily kilometres as discussed above. A minibus may carry between 100 and 500 passengers per day, a taxi between fifteen and fifty, a scooter-based vehicle between fifteen and thirty, and a human-powered vehicle up to fifteen. In some cases higher figures may be achieved, but in many cases the figures are substantially lower, particularly where there is significant surplus capacity in the industry.

Calculation: Total number of passengers carried (for the operation as a whole, part of the operation such as all services operated by a particular depot, or a particular route) during a period, divided by total number of vehicles licensed (for the operation as a whole, part of the operation, or route) in that period, and then divided by the number of days in the period.

Average fare paid per passenger

This indicator, which is not normally relevant with a flat fare system, gives a guide to the average distance travelled by passengers. The average will also be influenced by the number of passengers in different fare categories, such as students and other passengers paying fares at concessionary rates. The shorter the average distance travelled, the lower the average fare will be; a very low average fare may also indicate that there is a problem of pilferage or fare evasion, principally through over-riding, or the issue of undervalued or zero-value tickets, which should be investigated. It is useful to calculate this figure in respect of the operation as a whole, and for individual routes.

Calculation: Total fare revenue for a period, divided by the total number of passengers carried during that period.

Load factor

This indicator shows the average load on a bus as a percentage of its capacity. The higher the load factor, the more profitable the operation. The theoretical maximum of 100% is rarely achieved; buses are rarely full for an entire journey, and usually there are directional imbalances in demand at different times, resulting in buses operating with heavier loads in one direction than in the other. High load factors may mean that not all demand is being met, with full loads at times of low demand, and insufficient capacity at times of high demand. Where all demand is being met, this often means that at certain times of the day buses are running with very few passengers, and the load factor is correspondingly low. The break-even load factor will depend on the level of fares charged, and the standard of revenue integrity, but in practice will normally be between 65% and 75%; this is achievable on most services in developing countries, but many services in developed countries where car ownership is high operate with much lower load factors, and are not commercially viable. Where overloading is common, load factors in excess of 100% will be recorded for some journeys, but it is unlikely that this will apply to a whole operation.

Calculation: Load factors can be difficult to calculate, especially where there is a high turnover of passengers, and bus occupancy and distance travelled by individual passengers varies significantly. Where fare rates are directly related to kilometres, it is possible to calculate reasonably accurately the average number of passengers on a bus at any time by dividing the average revenue per kilometre by the fare rate per kilometre, although the figure will be distorted by concessionary and other special fares. In most cases, however, the figure must be estimated, or based on surveys or detailed analysis of tickets or bookings where applicable. Certain types of electronic ticket machines, as well as smart cards, provide data to enable load factors to be calculated accurately, provided that tickets are correctly issued.

Vehicle utilisation

This indicator shows the extent to which vehicles are used, and must not be confused with availability, which is discussed below. There are various measures of utilisation; these include mileage or hours (kilometres per vehicle per period or operational hours/days per vehicle per period); analysis of days or hours of operation as a percentage of total available time; or the number of vehicles operated in a day as a percentage of the number available.

The most useful indicator is the number of vehicles used on revenue-earning service at a particular time (usually peak periods) as a percentage of the number of buses which are available for service at that time (i.e. excluding those undergoing maintenance or repair or not available for other reasons). In most city operations the morning peak is more concentrated, and therefore it is normally most useful to use this as the basis for calculation. Where there is no discernible peak, the maximum number of buses in service at any time during the day may be used. Utilisation is sometimes expressed as a percentage of the total licensed or owned fleet, but this may give a false impression since a low level of utilisation may be because insufficient buses are available, due for example to a large number of vehicles off the road for repairs, and not because the operations department is unable to find profitable work for the whole fleet.

Utilisation normally varies between different times of the day (i.e. between peak and off-peak periods), different days of the week, and different times of the year. At peak times utilisation on urban bus services should normally be between 95% and 100%. A small number of vehicles may be kept as spares in case of breakdown, but some operators schedule all available buses at peak periods, risking the need to cancel some journeys in the event of a breakdown. On a long-distance operation utilisation is normally lower, and an acceptable figure is around 90%. Poor utilisation (as opposed to poor availability) may be due to a surplus of vehicles, inefficient scheduling, shortage of driving and/or conducting staff, or road or weather conditions which prevent the operation of some services.

A high level of utilisation does not necessarily mean a high degree of efficiency or profitability. A fleet may be well utilised, but on services for which there is little demand and which consequently lose money. In addition, some buses may be used for very short periods during only one of the peaks, so that their revenue-earning capability is severely limited.

Calculation: Number of buses operated during the busiest peak period of the day, expressed as a percentage of the number of buses available for use; this figure should be calculated each weekday. The average for a period should be calculated by taking the average number of buses operated during each weekday morning peak, expressed as a percentage of the average number of buses available during the relevant peak on each weekday in the period.

Percentage of scheduled kilometres operated

This is an indicator of overall service reliability in an operation in which buses are run to schedule. Ideally the figure should be 100% but this is rarely achieved. A reasonable figure for urban services in ideal operating conditions would be between 97.5% and 99.5%; a figure below 95% should give cause for concern. In many developing countries, however, the figure is much lower than this, often between 70% and 80% or even lower, due not only to poor mechanical reliability and organisational weaknesses, but also to problems of unpredictable traffic congestion which cannot be provided for in the schedules.

Alternatively, some operators use lost kilometres as a percentage of scheduled kilometres as an indicator; "lost kilometres" are scheduled kilometres which are not operated for any reason. A reasonable figure would be between 0.5% and 2.5%; a figure over 5% should give cause for concern. Another measure is to calculate lost kilometres as a percentage of total kilometres operated, but this may be misleading, particularly where a high proportion of unscheduled kilometres is operated. It is not always easy to record lost kilometres accurately: sometimes it is easier to record lost trips rather than lost kilometres, but this figure is distorted by vehicles which break down during the course of a trip, and there will normally be wide variations in trip lengths between one route and another. It is useful if the figures for lost kilometres can be analysed by reason, such as vehicle breakdown, non-availability of vehicle, or non-availability of crew.

Calculation: Number of kilometres operated in a period *on scheduled services*, as a percentage of the total number of kilometres scheduled to be operated over that period.

Percentage of "dead" kilometres

Unproductive, non-revenue-earning or "dead" kilometres are kilometres operated out of service, for example between the depot and the terminal at the beginning and end of the working day, and often contribute significantly to poor utilisation. Some operators disguise dead kilometres by allowing passengers to be carried on such journeys, but unless there are significant numbers of passengers these journeys should still be classified as dead. Approximately 5% of all kilometres is a typical figure for dead kilometres although much higher figures may be recorded; 15% is not uncommon. It is partly dependent on the location of depots in relation to the terminal points, and the level of dead kilometres will tend to be greater as the number of depots decreases. Inefficient scheduling is a common cause of excessive dead kilometres, for example where buses make empty journeys between terminals and depots for crew changes, instead of scheduling these to take place at the terminals.

Calculation: Total dead kilometres operated during a period, as a percentage of all scheduled and unscheduled kilometres operated during that period.

Kilometres per accident

This is an indicator of safety, reflecting both standards of driving and maintenance within the organisation, and driving standards generally. Ideally the type of accident should be taken into account, with each weighted according to its severity, but this introduces a large element of subjectivity, although some operators calculate repair costs as a guide. In practical terms, the number of accidents in total, and the number of fatalities, are the most useful measures. The definition of an accident may vary: some undertakings record only "reportable" accidents, in other words those which by law must be reported to the police; this definition may exclude relatively serious accidents where only accidents involving injury are reportable. Others record only those involving personal injury. It is normally appropriate to record all accidents involving damage to vehicles and injury to passengers, employees or third parties. Details of all fatal accidents should be recorded, including the number of fatalities in each case. If possible, it is useful to distinguish between accidents for which the transport operator or driver is blameworthy, and those attributable to a third party, although it is not always possible to make this distinction impartially or accurately.

The number of kilometres per accident will vary considerably, depending largely on the type of operation, and driving standards generally. Accidents will occur more frequently on urban services, due to greater traffic volumes, although their severity is likely to be less, due to lower speeds. Where all accidents involving injury and damage are recorded, a typical figure for urban services in developing countries may lie between 10,000 and 60,000 kilometres per accident; on long distance services the figures will normally be higher. Alternatively, this indicator may be expressed in terms of the number of accidents per 100,000 kilometres.

Calculation: Total number of kilometres operated over a period (scheduled and unscheduled) divided by the total number of accidents incurred during that period.

Punctuality

Another measure of service reliability, in an operation in which buses are run to schedule, is punctuality; however, this is more difficult to measure than lost kilometres. It is normally practical to record bus departures at selected points only, such as terminals or depots, and report total minutes of lateness, or average minutes of lateness at each point per departure per period; the average figure is usually more useful. Since it is not normally desirable for buses to depart early, early departures should be reported separately from late departures, and under no circumstances should early departures be offset against late departures: this could give rise to a situation where the average figure showed all buses leaving on time, when in reality there is very poor adherence to schedule. In certain circumstances it may be appropriate to record separately both early and late departures, particularly where early running is a problem: buses leaving before their scheduled departure times may result in even more inconvenience to passengers than those running late if it results in passengers missing their journeys. It may also be useful to record details of all delays over a predetermined figure, for example fifteen minutes on an urban service or one hour on a long-distance service, so that these may be investigated.

An acceptable standard for punctuality is difficult to prescribe, and to an extent what is acceptable will vary according to service frequency. It will also depend on what is achievable: for example, in a very congested city a greater variance from schedule may be tolerated than in a city where traffic congestion is not a problem. A reasonable target in most operations is for 90% of journeys to operate "on time", where this may be defined as up to five minutes late for services with frequencies of up to fifteen minutes, up to ten minutes late for services with frequencies between fifteen minutes and two hours, and up to thirty minutes late for services with frequencies of more than two hours. A bus departing more than one minute early should not be regarded as an "on-time" departure, unless it is already full and would not be able to carry additional passengers.

Calculation: The number of minutes of lateness should be recorded each time a bus departs after the scheduled departure time. For a period (normally one day, although it is also useful to make the calculation in respect of a week and/or a month), calculate the total number of minutes late, and divide this by the total number of departures in the period (i.e. including those which were on time or early). The resulting figure will give average lateness per departure in minutes. Where it is considered necessary to record early departures also, it is preferable to present three separate figures: the number of late departures; the number of early departures; and the number of departures on time. For early and late departures, the average is calculated by summing the number of minutes late, and the number of minutes early (as a separate calculation), and dividing by the total number of late and early departures respectively. The figures are expressed separately as the average number of minutes late and the average number of minutes early per departure.

Expenditure per kilometre on fuel, tyres, and maintenance materials

Expenditure figures are more useful as an item of management information when related to units of output; in the road passenger transport industry these are normally kilometres operated, as discussed earlier. This is particularly relevant in the case of those items of expenditure which are directly related to kilometres operated, such as fuel or tyres. It is possible to determine reasonable benchmark figures by applying local costs for the various inputs to appropriate measures such as fuel consumption or tyre life; where direct ratios are not available, such as use of maintenance materials, reasonable figures are less easy to estimate.

Calculation: Expenditure per period under each heading, divided by the number of kilometres operated during the period.

Vehicle availability at peak periods

This indicator shows the extent to which the vehicle fleet is available for revenue-earning work, and to a large extent reflects the effectiveness of the maintenance arrangements. It may be expressed as a percentage of the owned or licensed fleet which is available over a period; the two definitions are usually different since all vehicles owned are not necessarily licensed; sometimes vehicles are classified as "owned" if they remain on the company's books, when in fact they have been delicensed for a considerable time and have been cannibalised to the extent that there is virtually nothing left. It is therefore usually more useful to base this ratio on the number of buses licensed rather than owned. Availability may also be expressed in terms of average days available per year, but this is less usual.

Because vehicles spend varying times undergoing maintenance or repair, the number available will tend to vary constantly throughout the day. The most relevant time for calculating vehicle availability is at the time of peak vehicle requirement, and it is appropriate to record the number of vehicles available at this time each day, and to calculate the average over a period, such as a week or a month.

There will rarely be 100% availability except possibly for short periods, since every vehicle requires time out of service for routine maintenance, and there will always be an element of unscheduled maintenance and accident repairs. Some operators regard vehicles as available when they are undergoing scheduled routine maintenance, but this is incorrect, since they are not available for revenue-earning service at these times. If availability is calculated on a daily basis, there may be days on which 100% is achieved: for example, on weekends or public holidays when no routine maintenance is carried out and there are no vehicles out of service for unscheduled repairs or accident damage. Some operators may achieve 100% availability during peaks if routine maintenance can be co-ordinated with operational requirements so that all maintenance is undertaken between peak periods, although this is unlikely to be achieved on a regular basis. With effective preventive maintenance it should be possible to obtain average availability figures of 90% of licensed fleet; 85% is a reasonably good figure in most circumstances, although 75% is more typical in developing countries. However, in many countries, particularly in Africa, extremely low availability figures are recorded, where large numbers of vehicles are unserviceable for various reasons, but principally due to shortage of spare parts: availability figures of 10% or less are not unknown.

Calculation: Average number of vehicles available for service during the peak period (morning or evening, whichever has the greater vehicle requirement), expressed as a percentage of the total number of vehicles licensed. This may be calculated daily, and for a period such as a month. In the latter case, the average number of vehicles available each day during the period should be expressed as a percentage of the licensed fleet at the end of the period.

Fuel consumption

This is normally measured as litres of fuel consumed per 100 kilometres (ltrs/100 kms) or as kilometres per litre. The former tends to be more commonly used by transport operators. This indicator should be calculated in respect of each vehicle, as an average for all vehicles of a particular type, allocated to a particular route, or based at a particular depot, and as an average for the entire fleet: each basis of calculation is useful in different ways. Fuel consumption is influenced by the type of vehicle used, vehicle condition, operating speeds, traffic conditions, the frequency of stops, road conditions, and driving standards. A high recorded fuel consumption may also be a result of fuel theft, which is a serious problem in many organisations. Some fuel consumption figures are rendered inaccurate by inaccurate kilometre figures: this is a common problem, especially as many operators use calculated kilometre figures where vehicle odometers are unreliable.

For most single-deck buses of maximum capacity used on urban service fuel consumption would typically be between 35 and 45 ltrs/100 kms. On long-distance services it could be between 25 and 35 ltrs/100 kms. Smaller buses naturally consume less fuel: minibuses will consume between 15 and 25 ltrs/100 kms on urban service, and midibuses between 20 and 30 ltrs/100 kms.

Calculation: Total number of litres of fuel issued during a period, divided by the total number of kilometres operated over that period, and the result multiplied by 100, or total kilometres operated divided by the number of litres of fuel consumed for a kilometres-per-litre figure.

Engine oil consumption

As with fuel, this may be measured as litres of fuel consumed per 100 kilometres (ltrs/100 kms) or as kilometres per litre. This is a useful indicator of engine condition: the higher the rate of consumption the poorer the condition of the engine. Oil consumption is affected not only by the engine condition and standard of maintenance, but also by operating conditions: as with fuel, oil consumption will be higher under more difficult operating conditions.

Some operators exclude oil issued for routine oil changes, basing their calculation of consumption on oil issued for topping-up only; however, if oil consumption is high, a significant proportion of oil used for changes will be equivalent to topping-up oil, and the true consumption will be understated. Therefore it is generally more appropriate, as well as easier to record, if all oil issued is taken into account in the calculation. On this basis, average consumption figures for a fleet of full-sized buses should normally be between 0.15 and 0.30 for long-distance services operated under favourable conditions, and between 0.25 and 0.45 for urban services.

Calculation: Total number of litres of oil issued during a period, divided by the total number of kilometres operated over that period, and the result multiplied by 100, or total kilometres operated divided by the number of litres of oil issued for a kilometres-per-litre figure.

Kilometres per mechanical breakdown

This indicator is a measure of the mechanical reliability of a fleet. Overall, it will give an indication of the standard of maintenance as well as of general fleet condition. The older and less well maintained a fleet, the lower the number of kilometres per breakdown is likely to be. It is useful to calculate this indicator separately for different groups of vehicle; this will enable reliability to be compared between different makes or models of vehicles, vehicles of different ages, or operated on different routes or in different areas. In a large undertaking it is useful to record breakdowns by category, such as engine, power train, steering, suspension, brakes and electrical. It is particularly desirable to record tyre failures separately, since these are not directly related to mechanical condition; they reflect not only the standard of tyre maintenance, but may also highlight problems directly related to operating conditions, or to different types or makes of tyre.

The definition of a mechanical breakdown may vary. The most appropriate definition is any mechanical defect on a vehicle which causes or requires it to stop, and which makes it impossible or unsafe for it to continue with the journey without remedial action of some kind. Defects which prevent a vehicle from commencing a journey, for example if a vehicle fails to start, should not normally be included in this calculation; the effect of these defects will be reflected in the figures for availability. Whatever definition is used, it is important that it is used consistently within an organisation so that valid comparisons may be made. Accidents should be recorded separately, since these indicate safety standards rather than mechanical reliability.

Some operators calculate the number of kilometres per "involuntary stop", which includes such causes as accidents and running out of fuel in addition to mechanical faults. As an example, involuntary stops were analysed under the following headings by United Transport Malawi:

- Accident
- Road conditions
- Tyre failure
- Fuel shortage
- Fuel system
- Engine
- Gearbox
- Clutch
- Prop shaft
- Suspension
- Brakes
- Steering
- Electrical
- Miscellaneous

Achievable figures vary considerably, depending on factors such as maintenance standards, types of service, operating conditions, fleet age, and driving standards. A well-maintained fleet of buses operated on long distance services on good roads and with good driving standards should achieve over 50,000 kilometres per breakdown; at the other extreme, poorly maintained buses operating on city services in conditions typical of a developing country may achieve as little as 2,500 kilometres per breakdown, or even less, although a typical urban fleet will achieve between 5,000 and 10,000 kilometres per breakdown. A typical inter-city or rural operation will achieve between 8,000 and 15,000 kilometres per breakdown. Within a fleet there will be wide variations between the best and the worst groups of vehicles: for example, in a fleet averaging 7,000 kilometres per breakdown, the newer vehicles may achieve over 30,000 kilometres per breakdown, while the older ones may achieve fewer than 2,000.

Alternatively, this indicator may be expressed in terms of the number of breakdowns per 10,000 kilometres. Another alternative measure which is sometimes used is the number of breakdowns per day, expressed as a percentage of the number of buses in service. This is less specific since it does not reflect the level of activity, but has the advantage of being much easier to calculate, particularly where accurate kilometre figures are not available. On this basis, with a fleet averaging 200 kilometres per bus per day and 2,500 kilometres per breakdown, the figure for daily breakdowns in service would be 8%. For a long distance operation, with buses averaging 500 kilometres per day and 50,000 kilometres per breakdown, the figure would be 1%.

Calculation: total number of kilometres operated over a period (scheduled and unscheduled), divided by the number of breakdowns incurred in that period.

Kilometres per tyre carcase

This figure gives an indication of the standard of tyre maintenance as well as the quality of the tyres used. It requires accurate records of the number of kilometres operated by each tyre, from the first time it is fitted to a vehicle to the time when it is scrapped; where a carcase is retreaded, the kilometres operated between retreads must be recorded. If a tyre is used on more than one vehicle, care must be taken to ensure that the correct kilometre details are recorded each time the tyre is fitted to or removed from a vehicle. It is also useful to calculate the average number of retreads per carcase. Tyre life is affected by the standard of driving, and by operating conditions, including the nature of the road surface, ambient temperatures, frequency of stops and starts, and road alignment. Where tyres are retreaded at the appropriate times, a total carcase life of 100,000 kilometres is typical, with between two and four retreads during the life of the tyre. Without retreading, a life of up to 40,000 kilometres is more typical.

Calculation: The total kilometres run by all tyres scrapped during a period, divided by the number of tyres scrapped. The sum of the number of times each of the tyres scrapped in a period was retreaded, divided by the number of tyres scrapped, will give the average number of retreads per carcase.

Ratio of expenditure on preventive maintenance to total maintenance expenditure

As discussed in Chapter 11, preventive maintenance is normally more cost-effective than reactive maintenance; ideally, therefore, 100% of maintenance expenditure should be on preventive rather than reactive maintenance, although obviously this will be virtually impossible to achieve in practice. An acceptable percentage figure in most circumstances in developing countries would be approximately 70%, although typical figures vary between

20% and 60%. Some operators carry out no preventive maintenance at all, in which case the figure is 0%.

Average age of fleet

Although strictly not an indicator of performance, this is a useful indicator of the status of the fleet and is worth calculating on a regular basis. If the fleet has an even age profile, the average age of the fleet will be approximately half the age of the oldest vehicle. An acceptable average age depends on factors such as the types of vehicles operated, levels of utilisation and operating conditions, and is sometimes influenced by legislation: in some countries the operation of buses over a certain age is not permitted. A high average age may be because high standards of maintenance enable vehicles to be successfully operated over a long life, but more often is because insufficient funds are available for fleet replacement. A very low average age may be because vehicles are replaced when they are relatively young but may indicate that poor maintenance has resulted in a short vehicle life. In practice, where the latter is the case, it is not usually reflected in the average age because younger vehicles tend to remain on the "book" fleet strength even when they are no longer fit for further use. For a reasonably well maintained fleet of premium quality vehicles operating on urban services in a developing country, the average fleet age would typically be between five and eight years.

Calculation: The sum of the ages of all vehicles in the fleet (preferably in months) divided by the number of vehicles in the fleet. The resulting figure may then be expressed in months, although it is more commonly expressed in years, to one decimal place.

Number of staff per vehicle

The staff-per-vehicle ratio is a useful measure of the effective use of staff, but must be treated with care, particularly when making comparisons between different operators. It will be influenced not only by levels of productivity and efficiency, but also by the length of the operating day, and by the extent to which work is carried out in-house or is contracted out. In some operations, particularly on intensive urban services, three shifts per day are required by bus crews, while on others, such as long-distance services, buses are normally worked by only one crew in a day, albeit often with very long shifts. The number of staff will be substantially lower if buses do not carry conductors. The figure will also be affected if a significant amount of work, such as maintenance, is contracted out, although this is not common in the case of large operators in developing countries.

In an efficiently run urban undertaking in a developed country, a typical staff/bus ratio will be of the order of three staff per bus where all buses are operated by the driver only, and all maintenance work undertaken in-house; if all buses carry conductors this figure would increase to about five or six. In a developing country where wage levels are low and therefore many tasks may be undertaken using more labour-intensive methods, a reasonable figure, with conductors, would be between five and nine. Often, particularly in state-owned undertakings, the figures are very much higher than this. Excessive numbers of staff per bus not only result in unnecessarily high costs, but increase the problems of management and control.

Calculation: Total number of staff employed on a particular date (usually at the end of each accounting period), divided by the total number of vehicles licensed on that date. The calculation may also be made in respect of the principal categories of staff: crews, maintenance staff, traffic supervisory staff, and management.

Expenditure per kilometre on salaries and wages

This indicator may be useful in addition to the staff-per-bus ratio where labour costs are considered to be high; in this context, expenditure should include all salary and wage costs, including overtime and bonus payments, holiday and sick pay, terminal benefits paid to staff leaving (but not normally redundancy payments), and statutory deductions or employers' contributions to national insurance, pension or health care schemes. In developed countries labour costs tend to account for a very high proportion of the total costs of a road transport undertaking, usually substantially in excess of 50%. In developing countries, where wage levels are normally much lower, the proportion is correspondingly low, although it may be adversely affected by excessive staff numbers, especially at senior levels where salaries may be very high: it will generally be between 10% and 40%. As well as calculating this figure for the organisation as a whole, it is also very useful to calculate it for the principal categories of staff.

Calculation: Total expenditure on salaries and wages during a period, for all staff and for the principal categories, divided by total kilometres operated during that period.

Kilometres per employee per period

This indicator is used by some organisations as a measure of employee productivity. In effect it combines the vehicle productivity and staff per bus indicators, and is influenced by the same factors. It may be useful to present these figures by category such as crews, mechanical staff, administrative staff and others. Kilometres per employee per year may be as low as 2,000 in an urban operation in a developing country, where bus speeds are very low due to congestion, with drivers and conductors on each bus, and where staff levels in general are disproportionately high. At the other extreme, for an efficiently run long distance operation the figure could be as high as 30,000; in exceptional cases, there may be figures outside this range. However, more typical figures for an urban operation in a developing country would be between 5,000 and 12,000, while for a mixed urban, rural and long distance operation the range would be between 5,000 and 15,000.

Calculation: Total number of kilometres operated during a period, divided by the number of employees. For absolute accuracy this should be the average number of staff employed over the period; in practice, the number of employees at a particular time, such as at the period end, will normally be an expedient measure.

Kilometres per driver per day

This is a measure of driver productivity. Like kilometres per bus, it is influenced by the type of operation, with drivers on long-distance services achieving much higher figures than those on urban services. Typical figures are between thirty and 100 kilometres per day for urban services, and up to 250 on long distance services.

Calculation: Total number of kilometres operated during a period, divided by the number of days in the period, and by the number of drivers employed at a particular point during the period, such as at the period end.

Kilometres per man hour

This is a refinement of the above indicators, taking into account the number of hours worked by each employee. For the majority of operators it is unnecessary to make this detailed calculation, and in many cases the work involved will not be justifiable. The figure will vary considerably, depending on kilometres operated per bus and the ratio of staff to buses. The range in developing countries may be between 0.5 and 4.0, but typical figures are between 2.5 and 3.5. It may sometimes be useful to calculate this figure in respect of drivers only: typical figures for an urban operation would be between 3.0 and 5.0.

Calculation: Total number of kilometres operated during the period, divided by total man hours worked by all staff during the period.

Staff turnover

In some countries a high rate of staff turnover is a characteristic of public transport undertakings, although in others turnover is low. Where turnover is high, and is recognised as a problem, measures should be taken to minimise it, and the rate of turnover for the principal staff categories should be calculated regularly so that the effectiveness of such measures can be monitored. Turnover is usually expressed as an annualised figure.

Calculation: Number of staff recruited, or number of staff leaving employment, during a period, as a percentage of total staff on the payroll at the end of the period, multiplied by the number of periods in a year. The resulting figure is likely to be in excess of 100% for many operators.

Total expenditure per kilometre

Expenditure per kilometre on items such as fuel, tyres, maintenance materials, salaries and wages has already been discussed. It is also useful to calculate total expenditure on a per-kilometre basis as an overall indicator of the financial performance of the undertaking, and for comparison with total revenue per kilometre.

Calculation: Total expenditure on all items during a period, divided by the total number of kilometres operated during the period.

Operating surplus or deficit

This is the difference between total revenue from operations and total variable costs, including depreciation of vehicles based on current replacement cost. An operating surplus will mean that the operation as a whole is contributing to the undertaking's overhead costs, but may not mean that these are covered in full; if they are not, the undertaking will incur a loss. In such a situation, reduction in the level of operation will not necessarily improve the situation: it may however be possible to reduce overhead costs, or make savings in operating costs. It may also be possible to identify some activities, such as routes or groups of routes, which do not cover their variable costs, and withdrawal of these services would improve the financial position. If all services are contributing to overheads, but not sufficiently to cover these in total, and if there is no scope for reduction in either variable or fixed costs, it may be possible to improve the position by an increase in the level of activity, providing that this does not necessitate an increase in fixed, or overhead costs.

It is important to distinguish between depreciation of vehicles at current and historic costs. Current (or replacement) cost is more useful in determining the viability of an operation, since the revenue generated must be sufficient to cover all costs, including replacement of the vehicles required to operate the services when necessary.

Return on capital employed

This is a standard financial measure, and depends on the viability of the undertaking as well as the amount of capital invested in it. Rates vary considerably, and will be negative where undertakings are incurring losses, although some undertakings, particularly those operating long distance services, may enjoy high rates of return. A high rate of return in monetary terms is particularly necessary for sustainability where the rate of inflation is high, as is the case in many developing countries. The return on capital employed for a successful public transport business should be consistent with returns obtainable on low-risk investments in the local financial market. Care should be taken when using this measure, particularly in connection with public corporations which are funded by loans, the interest on which is treated in their accounts as a cost rather than as profit.

EXCEPTION REPORTS

Managers need to be informed of exceptional circumstances, or when performance deviates from normal or from expectations; exception reports are therefore an essential management tool. An exception report should show all indicators which fall outside predetermined ranges. For example, if fuel consumption for a particular bus type should normally be between 25 and 35 litres per 100 kilometres, a report should be produced listing all buses of that type whose fuel consumption fell below 25 or exceeded 35 litres per 100 kilometres, so that the reasons for the variations may be investigated, and appropriate action taken. Similarly, a range may be specified for revenue per kilometre, with exceptionally low figures for a route indicating problems such as poor demand or revenue leakage, and high figures indicating the possible need for additional capacity. In some cases, it is necessary to specify only one figure: for example, in the case of departure delays, it will normally be necessary only to report delays in excess of a predetermined figure.

Useful subjects for exception reports include the following:

- Fuel consumption by vehicle
- Maintenance expenditure by vehicle
- Passengers per bus per day by route
- Revenue per bus per day by route
- Revenue per kilometre by route
- Revenue by route, duty or conductor
- Departure delays for specific points

MANAGEMENT REPORTS

It is normally useful for management information to be presented in the form of regular reports. In many organisations no regular reports are produced, and management receives raw information on an ad hoc basis. There is often no analysis of data. For example, while revenue by route, and total operating costs may be reported, there is often no analysis of route profitability nor any detailed analysis of costs by area of operation or vehicle category. Other statistics, such as vehicle availability, utilisation or breakdowns, may be collected but not analysed at all. Conversely, there is often a tendency for too much information to be passed to senior levels of management. Production and distribution of large volumes of information in the form of computer printouts is common, but is generally wasteful of paper, and also of management time if the documents are used at all. In practice, many print-outs are never even looked at, and occupy scarce storage space when they are filed instead of being disposed of promptly. A high level of detail is required only at lower levels of management, and then only in respect of each individual's area of responsibility; at senior levels, only key information should normally be provided, in summarised form as regular management reports, of which KPIs and exception reports should form the basis. A senior manager may request more detail on a particular matter which may be drawn to his attention by one of these indicators.

Management reports should be presented in a form which can most easily be assimilated by their users. Data may be presented as numerical tables, key performance indicators or exception reports as appropriate. Depending on the nature and requirements of the undertaking it may be appropriate to produce a single report on a regular basis, perhaps monthly, or a range of reports, of different frequencies and with different levels of detail, covering different aspects of the operation, and to be used by different levels of management.

A range of reports is usually preferable, since some information should be presented daily, some weekly, and some monthly, while different individuals or departments require information on different subjects. Reports comprising extensive tables of numerical data, such as details of expenditure for each individual vehicle, or actual against scheduled departure time for every bus leaving a terminal, may be useful for record purposes but not as part of a management report: it takes considerable time to read through all the figures and identify those which provide significant information, and management cannot afford to spend this time. These reports will normally be used only when the summarised management information shows the need for further investigation into a particular area. The management report should include some narrative where appropriate to explain any significant variances, and to record other relevant information, such as major road works, industrial action or civil unrest which may cause problems in the operation of services. Such text should be kept to a minimum: there is often a tendency for much of the text in a report to put into words what is already evident from the tables of figures, which is wasteful of time in both the compilation and perusal of the report.

A key management report in most passenger transport operations is the periodic (normally monthly) Traffic Report. The principal item is the Traffic Return, which provides, in respect of each route, data such as the number of passengers carried, revenue earned, and kilometres operated during the period. These figures may be compared with the previous period, the same period for the previous year, or with forecast or budget, as a means of monitoring the performance of each route, so that services can be adjusted as necessary in accordance with changes in circumstances. Some operators' traffic returns include calculations of operating costs for each route, and the net financial contribution of each. The Traffic Report should also indicate the number of routes operated and vehicle requirement at period end, and give details of any significant route or service changes implemented during the period.

Another vital report concerns vehicle maintenance, particularly its cost. The monthly Engineering Report should include a summary of engineering activities carried out during the period (by depot or division if relevant), broken down into main activities, such as engine changes, engine overhauls, statutory roadworthiness inspections (divided, if appropriate, into inspections for newly delivered buses and inspection of buses undergoing routine periodic inspection), minor and major routine services, oil changes, and the number of defects reported. Vehicle maintenance costing is based on an analysis of expenditure on materials and labour used in the maintenance of each vehicle. It may be collated to provide information on the costs of maintaining different vehicles or types of vehicle, and may be broken down to cover the cost of maintaining and replacing components such as engines, gearboxes and axles.

This enables detailed comparisons to be made between different vehicle types, makes and models, and can provide data on the effectiveness or otherwise of changes to vehicle specifications. It provides valuable information for use in determining vehicle purchasing and replacement policies.

The appropriate frequency of reports may be determined in the light of experience, and will depend largely on the potential for change in a parameter, and the significance of a change. For example, management may wish to know immediately of a sudden change in the level of revenue, and would therefore need to receive this information daily so that appropriate changes to vehicle deployment could be made immediately. An exception report of excessive fuel or oil consumption by a particular vehicle may indicate imminent engine failure, which could be prevented by immediate action; such reports should therefore also be produced daily. Information on the incidence of mechanical breakdowns, on the other hand, may be required only weekly or monthly, since sudden changes in this indicator are less likely, and trends will become evident only over a period. There will normally be a reduction in the level of detail presented as the reporting time period increases.

The following reporting frequencies will be appropriate for most operators:

Daily (in respect of previous day)

- Total revenue
- Kilometres operated (not always available immediately)
- Fuel issued (as a guide to kilometres operated)
- Exceptional fuel and oil consumption by vehicle (if available)
- Exceptional revenue per kilometre by route (if available)
- Number of breakdowns
- Delays

Weekly (in respect of previous complete week)

- Weekly total of daily figures
- Kilometres per vehicle per day (KPVPD)
- Revenue per vehicle per day (RPVPD)
- Revenue per kilometre
- Passengers carried per vehicle per day (PPVPD)
- Vehicle utilisation
- Percentage of scheduled kilometres operated
- Punctuality
- Vehicle availability at peak periods

Monthly, or at end of each accounting period (in respect of previous month or period)

- All KPIs

The management report at the end of each period should also include some or all of the following information:

- Number of vehicles owned at period end (if appropriate, by type, service category and depot)
- New or additional vehicles acquired during period
- Number of vehicles owned but not licensed at period end
- Vehicles withdrawn from service or disposed of during period
- Number of ancillary vehicles at period end (if appropriate, broken down by category, e.g. cars, pick-ups, recovery vehicles, training buses)
- Staff employed at period end (broken down into drivers, conductors, mechanics, other, total)
- Number of staff engaged during period
- Number of staff having left employment during period, broken down by reasons for leaving (e.g. dismissal, retirement, death, etc)

It is usually convenient for management reporting periods to coincide with accounting periods. The choice of periods should be given careful consideration, as this can affect the usefulness of management information. Typically, calendar months are used; although this may be convenient in many respects, there are a number of disadvantages. Because the number of days varies from month to month, as does the number of weekends, this can make it difficult to make comparisons of certain parameters between one month and another. It also makes it difficult to identify trends, since variations between one month and another may be caused by, or hidden by, the different characteristics of the different accounting periods. For example, revenue usually varies between one part of the month and another, with peaks at month ends, and between different days of the week, with significant differences between weekdays and weekends; a substantial difference in revenue between one calendar month and the next may therefore be due entirely to differences in the number of weekdays and weekend days, and may not indicate any change in actual demand. On the other hand, a significant change in demand may be totally obscured.

Some operators choose to have thirteen four-weekly periods in each year: this has the advantage that all periods are of the same length and have the same number of weekdays and weekends, but comparison between periods will be distorted since each period will cover a slightly different portion of the month, and some periods will have no month end. Payments made by the undertaking at the same time each month, such as payment of salaries to its employees, will not occur in certain periods, further distorting the picture. Some operators use a combination of four-week and five-week periods which equate approximately to the calendar months; again, this has the advantage of having complete weeks, but occasionally a period will include two month ends, or no month end, again making comparison between periods difficult. These differences highlight the need for great care in interpreting management information.

For most operational analysis purposes, calendar months are usually the most appropriate, but for some purposes it is more useful to convert all figures to daily averages over each accounting period; however, if calendar months are used the averages may still be distorted by variations in the number of weekdays and weekends. Some figures are best presented in the form of moving averages, which reduce the effects of fluctuations and enable trends to be more easily discerned. For example, recording daily revenue as a seven-day moving average eliminates the effect of demand differences between weekdays and weekends, and can show revenue trends over a month; recording monthly revenue and expenditure as twelve-month moving averages removes the effects of monthly fluctuations caused by seasonal changes, and can show the rate of cost increases over time.

Timeliness in the preparation of management information is essential, as is the accuracy of the data. Very often, management information is received too late to be of any real value, even where data processing is computerised. A common cause is delay in the inputting of data. Sometimes management information reports are so exhaustive that they are inevitably submitted late: it is far more useful to have a smaller volume of information, but which is accurate and received in time to take the necessary action. Computerisation helps in speeding up data processing, increasing the amount of information which can be analysed, and improving accuracy; the temptation must be avoided, however, of producing an unnecessarily large volume of information. In a large organisation, where reports are produced by separate divisions, it is important that the reporting format is standardised throughout the organisation, to enable comparisons to be made, and for standardised reporting procedures to be adopted: this is particularly relevant where systems are computerised.

16

FINANCIAL MANAGEMENT AND CONTROL

In transport, as in any commercial undertaking, control of revenue and expenditure is vital. The principles of financial control in transport undertakings are broadly similar to those in any other business, but financial constraints on public transport services are often aggravated by poor financial management, due partly to a lack of understanding of these principles. An important objective of financial control is ensuring that the level and standard of services provided are sustainable by the revenue which can be generated, taking into account the full current and expected future costs of the operation.

In order to remain in business, a public transport service must generate sufficient revenue to cover all its operating costs, maintain and replace its assets, and provide a rate of return consistent with rates obtainable elsewhere in the market, and commensurate with the risks involved. The rate of return from a public transport business is influenced not only by the market and the operator's efficiency, but also by the degree of regulation and the effectiveness of enforcement. There may be regulatory constraints which limit potential revenue, while many developing countries suffer from high rates of inflation, steady depreciation of their currencies in relation to others, and foreign exchange restrictions; the effects of these problems on operating costs may be significant due to the high proportion of imported inputs such as fuel, vehicles and spare parts. Currency valuation is a reflection of a country's ability to pay; devaluation of currency may necessitate a reduction in public transport services when existing levels of service are no longer affordable.

CASH FLOW

Public transport is basically a "cash business"; effective control of cash flow can have a significant positive impact on the viability of an operation, while poor control can, and often does, lead to serious problems. In most developing countries all public transport journeys are paid for in cash at the time of travel, although in some more sophisticated operations an increasing number of journeys are paid for in advance through the purchase of multiple-journey tickets. If, as is normally the case with formal transport operators, payment for fuel, spare parts, staff salaries, and other inputs is made in arrears, the operator has the use of the cash between its collection and disbursement; in certain circumstances it is possible to maintain a positive bank balance at all times.

This characteristic of public transport operation is advantageous to the operator and contrasts with many other types of business where payments for their products or services are made in arrears. The advantage is less significant in the case of informal operators who must normally pay cash for inputs such as fuel or spare parts, but even here certain items of expenditure, such as maintenance, are incurred after the receipt of the revenue to which they relate.

Not all payments can be made in arrears, however, and cash is required to meet those payments which must be made in advance, such as the cost of new vehicles and equipment where these are not purchased through borrowing, or insurance premiums. Similarly, some revenue, such as payment for charter or contract services, advertising, or subsidies, is often received in arrears, and sometimes there are significant delays in payment. Poor debtor control will lead to serious cash flow problems. Many long distance operators employ agents to sell tickets for their services, and late remittance of receipts is a common problem which has an adverse effect on cash flow. For many undertakings one of the worst offenders for late payment, or even non-payment, are government agencies, which in some countries conduct a substantial amount of business with the larger transport operators in respect of travel warrants for civil servants, police, and members of the armed forces travelling to or from leave or on official business. Public sector operators are particularly susceptible to this problem, but in many cases the private sector is equally vulnerable since it is often impossible, for legal or merely practical reasons, to take any form of action against the government for non-payment of debts.

A common reason for cash flow problems where fares are regulated is fare levels, in real terms, falling too low in times of inflation to cover costs, when approval for fares increases is delayed. These problems are largely outside the control of the transport operator, although measures can, and must, be taken to reduce their impact. A significant factor affecting cash flow in many undertakings, which is within their control, is poor vehicle maintenance, which not only increases operating costs but results in reduced fleet availability and therefore reduced revenue. If an operator has insufficient funds to purchase fuel or essential spares, some vehicles will have to be taken out of service, reducing revenue further; it is easy for such a vicious circle to develop, and very difficult to break out of it.

The basic principles of cash flow control are to maximise the proportion of revenue collected in advance or at the time of travel, and minimise the proportion of revenue collected in arrears; and to maximise expenditure incurred in arrears, and minimise advance payments. Good credit control is normally essential to minimise the incidence of late payment or non-payment by creditors. The controlled use of an overdraft facility to compensate for cash flow fluctuations is good business practice, provided that the overdraft is not in constant use: ideally, the average overdraft over a full financial year should be close to zero. Some transport undertakings, particularly in the public sector, maintain working capital by deferring payments to creditors, often withholding salary deductions such as national insurance contributions due to the government, and even the salaries themselves; however, such practice is unethical and cannot be condoned in normal circumstances.

BORROWING

A transport undertaking may borrow money for various reasons. Borrowing for investment in a new business, new equipment, fleet replacement or rehabilitation or for expansion or development of the business is justifiable provided that the return on the investment will be adequate to cover the cost of the loan. A common reason for borrowing is to provide working capital when cash flow is poor, but apart from the use of overdraft facilities this should not normally be necessary with good financial management, unless there are reasons outside the control of the undertaking; extreme care must be exercised in such circumstances to ensure that the situation remains under control, and that it will be possible to repay any loan within a reasonable time. Many small operators in particular fall into the trap where what is perceived to be surplus cash is spent outside the business, so that it is not available when required, for example for major maintenance work or vehicle replacement; this expenditure must then be funded by borrowing.

The principal sources of finance for setting up a potentially viable private sector transport business are loan finance from financial institutions or share capital from private investors. Loan finance may take the form of fixed or variable term loans, at fixed or variable interest, while share capital will entail the payment of dividends. An advantage of the latter is that if the business performs poorly, dividend payments may be reduced or waived, whereas interest and loan repayments must normally be made regardless of the financial performance of the business. Funds for the establishment of new public sector operations will normally be provided from government sources, and in most cases will take the form of loans; it is less common for public corporations to be financed through share capital. Partnerships between public sector and private sector investors are becoming more common, particularly for infrastructure-intensive projects such as LRT systems, to broaden the range of sources of finance.

A major expenditure item for any transport operator is the replacement of assets, principally the vehicles themselves, but a common failing, particularly amongst smaller operators, is to make inadequate provision for this. Where loan finance is readily available on reasonable terms, this should not be a problem provided that all loan servicing costs can be adequately covered from revenue. However, a common problem is that because of inflation, a new vehicle will cost considerably more than the one it is replacing, as will the cost of servicing a loan for the new vehicle, resulting in a sharp increase in costs following replacement. In a fleet with an even age profile and regular replacement requirement the cost increase will be relatively smooth; but if the replacement requirement is uneven, in years when there are an unusually large number of vehicles requiring replacement there will be significant step increases in costs. Where interest rates are stable at a reasonable level, borrowing is often a viable option but must be carefully evaluated against the alternatives, such as leasing vehicles rather than purchasing them; there are usually tax implications, which vary from country to country, and which may influence the operator's decision.

Some public sector undertakings set funds aside purely for replacement purposes. These are often based on formulae which do not provide adequately for full replacement costs, particularly in an inflationary situation; where this is so, it often results in deferral of replacement, with consequent increases in operating costs and reduced reliability, and ultimately in a decline in the size of the operation.

Depreciation as shown in an undertaking's accounts is rarely adequate to cover true replacement costs: because of inflation and depreciating currency the cost of new vehicles is usually escalating rapidly and depreciation on a historic cost basis will not provide sufficient funds for replacement. As a rule of thumb, the actual average annual replacement cost equates approximately to the total cost, at current prices, of the average number of vehicles required as replacements each year; this is the sum for replacement which must be generated by the operation during the year, and should be incorporated in the budget. It may be necessary for a proportion of profits to be retained for this purpose rather than being paid out in the form of dividends.

Many undertakings in developing countries are badly run down through a lack of proper maintenance and as a result are unable to generate sufficient revenue for sustainability, but could become viable if arrears of maintenance could be made good through appropriate rehabilitation programmes. This normally requires an injection of funds, since its necessity stems from the fact that funds were not available to carry out proper maintenance when it was required; the number of buses in revenue-earning service is often far less than the number requiring rehabilitation, and it is impossible for the serviceable buses to generate sufficient revenue to cover, in addition to the cost of their own maintenance, the cost of rehabilitating the remainder of the fleet. Expenditure on rehabilitation represents an investment requiring a return, and in some respects can be treated similarly to investment in new vehicles: if it is viable, funds should be obtainable. In developing countries such funding is often provided by overseas aid agencies either as grants or as loans. Once a rehabilitation project has been undertaken it is important that the fleet is subsequently maintained to a satisfactory standard.

In a situation where demand for public transport is increasing, as in most developing countries, the industry must be constantly expanding, through an increase in the size of existing operators, an increase in the number of operators, or both. It is often appropriate for expansion to be funded through borrowing; the strong positive cash flow from a well managed transport company may be sufficient to provide adequate security for a loan for this purpose, while it should be possible to raise capital for a new enterprise on the basis of a realistic business plan. However, in practice increases in supply tend to lag behind increases in demand, and therefore services are almost always inadequate. In a competitive situation, this should result in higher fares, providing operators with increased profits, which will encourage them to expand their services, and will attract new entrants to the industry.

It may be argued that passengers should not be expected to contribute towards the cost of services which other passengers will be receiving in the future, through having to pay excessive fares for services which continue to be inadequate and unacceptable. On the other hand, if fares are restricted by government regulation, the operators will be unable to expand without reducing service standards, unless an alternative source of funds for expansion is made available. It may be justifiable in such circumstances for a form of subsidy, such as the availability of finance at artificially low rates of interest, to be provided for expansion, possibly through external aid funding; such assistance should be tied to a programme to ensure the efficiency and viability of the undertaking.

The availability and cost of loan finance depends to a large extent on an operator's creditworthiness, which in turn is based largely on his past record for payment, and ultimately on the quality of his financial management. If there is a good positive cash flow, there will normally be little difficulty in obtaining finance at a reasonable rate of interest for an investment which will yield an adequate return. If cash flow is poor, indicating poor performance, the risk attached to any borrowing will be greater, and this is likely to be reflected in a higher rate of interest. Operators with poor credit ratings are often required to pay in advance for items such as fuel or spare parts.

In many developing countries credit facilities for the purchase of new buses, particularly for the private sector, are difficult to obtain, and require guarantees, such as a mortgage on the borrower's property, in addition to the security represented by the bus itself, reflecting the perceived risk involved. Often the risk is overestimated, making investment in transport services unreasonably difficult and expensive, and easier access to funds for the purchase of new buses would provide a valuable boost to the development of bus services in many developing countries.

Borrowing may be in local or foreign currency. Borrowing for imports, such as new vehicles, is often in a foreign currency, but because of exchange rate fluctuations, exchange losses resulting from depreciation of the local currency may cause severe cash flow problems, and to minimise exposure to the risk of a loss on exchange, the financing of imported vehicles with foreign currency loans is often inadvisable. Local borrowing is usually preferable even though this may incur very high rates of interest.

Whatever the reason for a loan, the borrower must be able to afford to pay the interest charges, as well as make the necessary repayments as these become due. In extreme cases operators have increased their borrowings merely to pay interest on existing debts, thus increasing the level of interest payments even further: it is almost impossible to recover from such a situation, which is relatively common in public sector transport undertakings in developing countries. In several cases governments have written off the debts of public sector undertakings in order to help to keep them afloat; such a measure can be justified only if it will ensure the future viability of the operation, but in practice this is rarely achieved and in the case of some undertakings the rescue process has been repeated several times.

BUDGETING AND BUDGET CONTROL

Budgeting is an essential element of financial control. It involves forecasting the amounts and timing of revenue received and expenditure incurred, and facilitates reaction to unexpected changes in the fortunes of a business.

Neither income nor expenditure flows are constant; they fluctuate, often quite considerably, from period to period, with heavy outflows of cash at month ends when salaries and creditors become due for payment, and revenue following a fluctuating seasonal pattern. Some of these fluctuations are predictable; others are not. Without effective budgeting and budget control there is a risk that financial resources may be overstretched, or major items of expenditure may become due at a time when funds are not available to cover them; alternatively, funds may become available but are not put to effective use. Budgeting is normally carried out on an annual basis, but it is also useful for planning purposes to budget further ahead, typically up to five years, albeit in somewhat less detail. Annual budgets should be broken down into periods, which should coincide with accounting periods.

All anticipated revenue and expenditure must be included in the budget, in as much detail as possible, so that variances from budget can be easily identified later. The budget headings must be selected to provide the information required in a readily understandable form. Costs should be broken down into the main headings as discussed in Chapter 13; it is particularly important to ensure that capital expenditure is clearly separated from recurrent expenditure in the budget. In a large undertaking the budget should be broken down into logical accountable divisions, even if these are not formally treated as cost centres, as described below; depending on the nature and structure of the undertaking these divisions might be operating areas or depots, types of service, or both. If different types of service are operated such as urban, rural, long distance, private hire or charter, or if there are different brands, it is usually appropriate for revenue and expenditure to be broken down within each division between the different types of services or brands. Other sources of revenue as described in Chapter 14 should also be shown separately under individual headings. It is important that every cost and revenue heading can be identified with members of the management team, who are responsible for controlling the items concerned, and who should be able to explain the causes of any variations between budgeted and actual performance figures.

Before commencing the preparation of a budget, it is necessary to make certain assumptions, which must be as realistic as possible, with regard to all relevant internal and external factors. Internal factors include such items as fleet replacement requirements, plans for expansion, and staff salary reviews as well as overall levels of activity in each area of operation; they also include performance ratios or indicators, such as fuel consumption for different vehicle types. Principal external factors include the economic situation, such as rates of inflation, exchange rates and economic growth, changes in the operating environment, for example whether competition from other operators will increase or decrease, whether or not there are likely to be any legislative changes which will affect the operation of the industry, changes in road conditions, or climatic considerations.

It is particularly important that allowance is made for inflation in both cost and revenue forecasts. Inflation can be a particular problem where fares are controlled, since there may be no guarantee that the operator will be permitted to increase fares to compensate for increased costs, and even if this is permitted, the approved fares increases may be lower than required and there may be considerable delays before the increase may be implemented. The budget should therefore reflect the most probable outcome of fares increase applications, and the likely effects of fares resistance. In practice, even if fares are not controlled and may be adjusted whenever required, it is not possible to adjust fares exactly in line with changes in the value of money, while in some cases passengers will be unable to afford fares increases in line with inflation. Inflation is not easy to predict, particularly where it is at a high rate, and it is sometimes necessary to adjust the budget during the year if the prediction turns out to be very inaccurate; this should, however, only be done as a last resort.

Using these assumptions, the next task is to make an initial estimate of the revenue and expenditure under each heading for each period during the budget year. This task should be broken down and allocated to the staff who are responsible for the activities related to each heading; some of these may be at relatively junior levels. On completion of the first draft of the budget, it should be examined critically by the members of management responsible for each cost and revenue heading to ensure that the forecast revenue, expenditure and results in terms of operating surpluses or deficits for each activity are reasonable, and consistent with one another. It will probably be necessary at this stage to make adjustments to the budgeted levels of activity, or fares, if this is possible, in order to ensure that cash flow will be adequate to cover expenditure, and that the overall result is satisfactory.

Budgets must be as realistic as possible to be of any use as a control. Sometimes there is a tendency to distort the budget: for example an operator wishing to justify a fares increase under a regulated system may present a pessimistic budget to the regulatory authorities, while one attempting to impress a potential investor may present an optimistic one; sometimes management are rewarded according to their performance against budget, and they may present a "soft" budget, which they know can easily be achieved or improved upon, in the hope that this will be accepted as the base. If a budget is to fulfil its purpose as a management tool such practices should be strictly avoided.

The final budget should be used throughout its term as a base against which the performance of the undertaking is measured, through the comparison of actual revenue and expenditure figures for each period with those shown in the budget. The main causes of expenditure variances are differences in price between those assumed in the budget and those actually charged; variations in the rate of usage or consumption; variations in the level of activity or output; or theft or fraud. For example, if actual expenditure on fuel is higher than budgeted it may be due to an unexpected increase in the cost of fuel, a deterioration in vehicle fuel consumption, an increase in the number of kilometres operated, theft of fuel from vehicles or storage tanks, or a combination of these. Revenue variances may be due to changes in fare levels, in patronage, in the level of operation or loss of revenue through fare evasion or fraud. The performance indicators and financial figures included in the management accounts are important to this appraisal process.

The management accounts, as distinct from statutory accounts prepared for tax purposes, form an essential component of the management information and budget control systems; they should record all revenue and expenditure in a form which enables management to see at a glance where the money is coming from, and where it is being spent. Each set of accounts should immediately be compared with the budget for the same period; the reasons for any significant variations between budget and actual figures should be investigated, and appropriate action taken where necessary.

The accounts should be consistent with the budget, and presented under identical headings, using the same accounting periods, so that variances from budget may be easily identified. It is therefore important that the accounts are not only accurate, but are produced quickly and coincide with the presentation of management reports: with effective computerised systems it should be possible for the accounts to be completed within two weeks of the period end at most. Some organisations produce their accounts quarterly, but in an operation where changes may occur frequently this is generally unsatisfactory, since trends may take several months to detect, and any necessary action will therefore be delayed. As discussed in Chapter 15, the use of calendar months and four-weekly accounting periods both have their advantages and disadvantages, and one or the other will be more appropriate depending on circumstances; on balance, calendar months are more convenient for the majority of operators, provided that allowance is made for the different numbers of days and weekends in each month when preparing budgets and interpreting the figures contained in the accounts.

COST CENTRES

It is often useful for budgeting and control purposes to divide a business into "cost centres" or "profit centres". In effect each centre operates as if it were a separate business division, with its own budget and management accounts, and dealing with the other centres in the organisation on a quasi-commercial basis, buying and selling products and services at notional prices.

For example, the engineering function within a bus company may be designated as a cost centre, whose charges and services can be compared with those of third party workshops offering similar services; the operating depots, which would also be separate cost centres, would make notional payments to the engineering centre for all maintenance work carried out, while the engineering centre would pay an operating centre for services such as the provision of vehicles for the transport of workshop staff. The notional payments are recorded in the respective management accounts as payments or receipts, although no actual cash transfer is made. The financial performance of each centre is assessed according to the notional profit or loss made in each period.

Taken one stage further, each centre may be required to obtain the best value for money, which may involve dealing with outside organisations: thus each cost centre must be able to compete with other organisations outside the business offering similar services. This approach is particularly useful in large organisations; it shows the relative viability of each part of the organisation, while helping to ensure that the undertaking is not incurring unnecessarily high costs in any area.

17

SERVICE STANDARDS

Service quality, embracing reliability, punctuality, safety, convenience, comfort and security, should be the first responsibility of a transport undertaking to its customers. Standards are often difficult to define and measure; they vary considerably from one country to another, as well as over time, as do opinions as to what is satisfactory and what is not. It is therefore impossible to specify standards which are universally acceptable. Achievable standards are constrained by what users can afford or are willing to pay for, and as discussed in previous chapters, different standards are demanded by users at different income levels. However, it is clear from comments in the media and elsewhere that there is general public dissatisfaction in many developing countries with the quality of public transport services. Another indication of the perceived quality of service is the often considerable extent to which organisations find it necessary to operate personnel transport on their own account, suggesting that many users regard public services as inadequate for their requirements.

RELIABILITY AND PUNCTUALITY

Reliability is an important element of service quality, and where users have a choice, has a strong influence on demand; when services become unreliable, some passengers are lost who are never regained. There are several aspects of reliability: most fundamental is whether a particular scheduled service operates at all, and if it does, whether it operates according to scheduled departure and arrival times. Also important is reliability on the road; frequent vehicle breakdowns detract considerably from service quality.

Where services are operated to a timetable, passengers' expectations with regard to punctuality vary considerably; some expect to have to wait a considerable time for a bus, regarding this as normal, and may not even be aware of scheduled departure times or understand the concept of scheduling. In some countries it is usual for long distance passengers, particularly those living in rural areas who travel infrequently, when they wish to travel, merely to go to the nearest point where they may join the bus, and wait until one arrives; this may be several hours later. However, most passengers, particularly those using urban services, are becoming increasingly conscious of waiting times, and are dissatisfied when buses fail to arrive on time or operate at the appropriate frequency. It is also very much in the operator's interest to ensure that buses run in accordance with their schedules, in order to achieve satisfactory passenger loadings and vehicle utilisation.

Standards of reliability in developing countries, particularly on long distance services at the lower end of the market, are often very low, due partly to road conditions, but also to poor management control. Many services do not operate to schedule, but even where schedules apply, timekeeping is often poor. A primary determinant of service reliability is the reliability of the vehicle itself, which can be measured in terms of average kilometres per breakdown; an excessive number of mechanical failures is a common problem. Accidents also affect service reliability but primarily are a safety issue, as discussed below. The effects of breakdowns are often compounded by long recovery times, particularly in the case of long distance bus services, when vehicles may break down many hundreds of kilometres away from base; broken down buses may have to wait several days before being recovered, and when reliability within an operation is poor and several breakdowns occur each day, this has a seriously adverse effect on vehicle availability, affecting all services.

Reliability may be measured in terms of the percentage of scheduled kilometres or journeys operated, the percentage of journeys operating on time or less than a specified number of minutes late, and in terms of the number of involuntary stops due to mechanical failure or other reasons, as discussed in Chapter 15.

In theory, 100% reliability is achievable, but the cost in terms of preventive maintenance and standby vehicles would be prohibitive, and it must be decided what is an acceptable level. This will vary: passengers paying a high fare for a premium-quality bus service will expect a higher standard of reliability than passengers paying a much lower fare for a service operated by very basic vehicles; the cost of reliability will be reflected in the fare. There is, however, a minimum level of reliability, below which a service will not be viable at any fare commensurate with the quality of service provided: the cost of recovering and rectifying broken down vehicles, and the reduced vehicle utilisation resulting from frequent mechanical failure will, if the incidence of breakdowns is very high, increase operating costs to the point where they cannot be covered by revenue. The exact point at which this occurs will depend on fare levels, patronage and the costs and time involved in dealing with breakdowns, but in general terms if fewer than 3000 kilometres are operated per breakdown, the viability of the services or vehicles concerned will be doubtful.

SAFETY

It is generally recognised that high standards of safety are a desirable objective. However, it is estimated that between 75% and 85% of fatalities in road accidents worldwide occur in developing countries, despite low levels of car ownership; moreover, while the number of road accident fatalities has been falling in developed countries during the past two decades, it has been increasing in developing countries, where a significant proportion of road accidents involve public transport vehicles.

Public transport safety does not only impact on its users: other road users may also be involved in accidents with public transport vehicles, while every accident has external costs which affect the economy generally. However, while a reduction in the number of accidents is beneficial in both economic and social terms, there are costs associated with increased safety standards, including the cost of safety-related vehicle design features such as anti-skid braking, maintenance of safety-critical components, driver training and enforcement of driving standards, as well as the cost of providing a safe transport infrastructure. There is a point at which the cost of an increase in safety outweighs the economic benefits, and where certain measures to improve safety, such as very low speed limits, become unacceptable to the general public: the decision to improve standards beyond this point becomes largely political.

In many cases the fares which passengers can afford will pay for a relatively low standard of safety, in terms of vehicle specification or condition. Some bus operators are able to remain in business only at the expense of standards of maintenance and fleet replacement, and therefore safety. Furthermore, what is regarded as an acceptable standard of safety varies considerably, and is related to perceptions of other values, including even the value of human life. For example, in most countries, street lighting poles are designed to collapse when struck by a vehicle, in order to minimise injury to the vehicle occupants; in some countries, however, concrete blocks are positioned adjacent to street lighting poles to protect them from damage from vehicles, at the expense, sometimes, of the safety of vehicle occupants, implicitly placing a higher value on the lighting poles than on human life.

There is often inconsistency between the safety standards demanded from different modes of transport, with a far higher rate of fatalities accepted for road than for rail. For example, following a number of fatal rail accidents in the United Kingdom during the past decade, rail operators were expected to introduce safety measures which were far more costly in terms of the number of fatalities likely to be prevented than equivalent measures required for road transport, despite the fact that statistically travel by rail in the UK was already six times safer than by car.

The principal causes of accidents are poor driving standards and poor vehicle condition. A serious problem in many developing countries is the very poor safety record of long distance buses: reports of disastrous bus accidents, where buses have left the road and overturned, killing many passengers, are all too frequent. This arises principally from a tendency for drivers to drive at dangerously high speeds, often compounded by overloading and poor vehicle maintenance. Road conditions are not normally a major cause by themselves, although failure of drivers to regulate their speed in accordance with road conditions is a common cause of accidents; ironically, improvements to roads often lead to an increase in the severity of accidents, since vehicles are able to operate at higher speeds. Most passengers prefer a shorter journey time, and where there is a choice, opt to travel with an operator offering a faster journey, often unaware of or oblivious to the dangers of excessive speed. Many operators deliberately schedule buses to operate at speeds well in excess of prevailing speed limits, and often pay speeding fines incurred by drivers, treating these as a normal operating cost. Speed becomes a competitive factor: operators try to be faster than their competitors, and drivers try to be faster than their colleagues as a matter of personal pride; this invariably results in dangerous driving, including dangerously high speeds and overtaking on blind brows and bends, and taking advantage of the size of their vehicles to intimidate the drivers of smaller vehicles. Because of the competitive nature of the market, an operator who tries to restrict his vehicles to safe speeds will lose business to his faster competitors; therefore the services of all operators tend to be equally dangerous, and passengers have little choice in this respect.

In many developing countries there is a high incidence of accidents at night. Vehicle lighting is often poor, as a result of poor maintenance, and in some countries it is common for vehicles to be driven at night, even on unlit roads, with no lighting at all: other common nocturnal hazards are broken down vehicles, with no lights, left in dangerous positions, and animals straying onto the road. Vehicles are frequently driven at excessive speeds so that stopping distances exceed the range of the headlights. In Tanzania, long distance buses were prohibited from operating at night for reasons of safety. This seriously affected the viability of bus services by reducing bus utilisation and was a particular problem on the longer routes, several of which exceeded 1,000 kilometres in length and could not therefore be completed within daylight hours at normal driving speeds, resulting in a tendency for buses to be driven even faster than before: accurate statistics are not available to indicate whether the accident rate increased or decreased as a result of this measure. A significant proportion of long-distance passengers prefer to travel at night, and it is questionable whether a ban on overnight travel is preferable to improving safety through other means; unfortunately, in many cases standards of enforcement are so poor that this is not a practical option, and the ruling in Tanzania reflects the reality of the situation.

Poor maintenance is a frequent cause of accidents, and the importance of adequate maintenance, as discussed in Chapter 11, cannot be overemphasised. A factor which contributes significantly to accidents in many countries is poor tyre condition, due largely to inadequate regulations in this respect, but more often to poor enforcement of those regulations which do exist. Safety is also an important consideration in the design and specification of vehicles, as discussed in Chapter 10.

Following serious accidents there are often calls by politicians and the news media for safety measures which would be unduly onerous. These may include the compulsory fitting of seat belts to all seats in buses, and even air bags for passenger protection. Apart from the additional capital cost and maintenance requirements, if the wearing of seat belts on buses were made compulsory, this would preclude the carriage of standing passengers and mobile conductors; it would also mean that disembarking passengers would have to remain in their seats until the bus had stopped, while the bus would not be allowed to leave a stop until all passengers were seated with their belts fastened. Thus journey times would be increased and vehicle capacities reduced, with consequent increases in operating costs. Much safety legislation, although less extreme than this theoretical example, is misguided or unbalanced. The "compensation culture" of the developed world, which has resulted in many counter-productive safety measures, should be avoided as far as possible: taken to the extreme, complete safety can be achieved only by prohibiting all travel. Safety measures specified in legislation must be realistic and practical, and the benefits of safety must be strictly weighed against their costs.

CONVENIENCE

Aspects of convenience include accessibility, frequency of service, extent and comprehensiveness of the route network, interchangeability between services, speed of service, and comprehensibility. Accessibility to bus services is a function of the density of the route network and the distance between bus stops. It can be expressed as the average distance users must walk between the starting point of their journey (normally their homes) and the bus stop, and the distance between the destination bus stop and the ultimate destination. Targets or standards may be set for average and maximum walking distances: for an urban bus service in a city with low car ownership an average walking distance of half a kilometre with a maximum of one kilometre may be regarded as satisfactory, but in many cities in developing countries these distances are greatly exceeded.

Accessibility for long-distance services varies considerably. Average access distances are greater, and it may be necessary to use a local transport service in order to gain access to the longer distance service. Even in some large cities, there is only one long-distance bus terminal, often inconveniently located; in others, passengers using long distance services have a wide choice as to where they may board buses, with readily accessible bus stops and stations in different parts of the city.

Another measure of the effectiveness of a route network is the number of route kilometres per 1,000 head of population, where total route kilometres are defined as the total length of road over which buses are operated (i.e. a road used by several routes is only counted once); the higher the figure, the better the accessibility of the network: typical figures for cities in both developed and developing countries are between 0.5 and 1.5 route kilometres per 1,000 population.

Average waiting time is an important element of convenience: the shorter the waiting time, the greater the level of convenience. Waiting time is a function of both service frequency and the capacity of the service: even with a high frequency the waiting time may be excessive if inadequate capacity results in users having to wait for several full buses to pass before one arrives which has accommodation. As discussed in Chapter 8, frequency is determined partly by demand, but where demand is low a higher frequency may be provided by using smaller vehicles. Frequency is also influenced by the route network density: a higher frequency can be provided, but at the expense of increased walking distances and hence accessibility, if the density of the network is reduced.

A network which enables the majority of passengers to complete their journeys without having to transfer from one vehicle to another is, other things being equal, more convenient than one which necessitates several changes of vehicle during the course of a journey. However, each route in a network offering a large number of direct links will, of necessity, offer a less frequent service than if there is are fewer routes, and therefore there is an optimum combination of direct routes and good service frequency which maximises total convenience for all passengers. It is not always easy to identify this optimum. Where it is necessary for passengers to use more than one service in the course of a journey, convenience of interchange is important. The walking distance between one service and another should be minimised: ideally, if a passenger must change buses, both routes should stop at the same stop so that there is no walking involved, but this is not always possible. If it is necessary to change between a bus and a rail service, buses should be able to pick up and set down passengers as close to the rail station as possible.

Speed, or journey time, is an important factor, especially over longer distances, and the majority of passengers prefer minimum journey times. On urban services achievable speed is normally determined by the level of traffic congestion, and can be very low. It is also influenced by operating practices such as the method of fare collection. In good conditions, average operating speeds of up to twenty kilometres per hour can be achieved, but speeds of ten kilometres per hour or less are common. On long distance services, speed is largely dictated by road conditions, and speed limits where these are observed. Operating speeds and journey times are also influenced by routing and scheduling practices: a direct, non-stop service will obviously have a shorter journey time than one following a circuitous route with frequent stops. The scope for the faster service is determined largely by the level of demand, but in many cases, due to poor routing and scheduling, the potential is not fully realised.

Ease of payment is another element of service convenience. Some fare collection systems are much more "user-friendly" than others. For example, a system which requires passengers to have the exact fare ready when boarding the bus may detract from the convenience of the service if the majority of passengers prefer the facility to be given change; in another situation, the majority of passengers may prefer an exact fare system if this reduces time spent at bus stops. Similarly, advance purchase of tickets from roadside vending machines is acceptable in some countries but not in others. Much depends on passenger preferences, which can vary from one place to another, even within the same country. Familiarity with fare systems and collection procedures is important, and some relatively complex systems may be successful with appropriate marketing.

No matter how good a service is, if the prospective passenger cannot understand it, or is unable to discover where bus or rail services run, the convenience is greatly reduced. Regular passengers will be familiar with the services which they use, but prospective passengers may be deterred from travelling or, if they have the means, they may use taxis or private transport. As discussed in Chapter 18, availability and accuracy of information is therefore vital, as is ease of identification of the vehicle on a particular service, or to a particular destination; this is an area of weakness in many developing countries.

COMFORT

Comfort is an element of service quality which is difficult to quantify, and where standards, and passengers' expectations, differ widely. The main determinants of comfort are vehicle design and construction, standards of maintenance, load factors, and driving standards. Relevant vehicle design features include the type of seating, in particular its pitch, or spacing, design, and materials used; the proportion of seated to standing passengers; gangway widths; step heights; heating and ventilation systems; and luggage accommodation where this is required. Standards vary considerably in these respects, mainly for monetary reasons. Of obvious significance is seat pitch: increased pitch will offer greater comfort, but at the expense of seating capacity, and hence the revenue-earning capacity of a vehicle. In many western countries there are now regulations setting stringent standards such as very low step heights to facilitate access by disabled passengers, but these increase the cost of vehicles, as well as reducing capacity, and detract from the viability of a service.

The type of vehicle typically operated on basic services in many developing countries offers a relatively low standard of comfort, often compounded by poor maintenance standards, so that on older buses the interiors are in a poor state of repair. Poor standards of cleanliness also detract from passenger comfort. On the other hand, some vehicles used on premium quality urban and long-distance services in developing countries offer very high standards of comfort, in some cases superior to those found in many developed countries.

Load factors have an important bearing on comfort, and where buses are frequently overloaded, passengers may suffer severe discomfort. Where overcrowding occurs only at peak periods, the reduced comfort at these times may be regarded as the equivalent of a peak surcharge and a degree of overcrowding for short periods should be acceptable, but where overloading occurs throughout the day, this is largely a result of fares being inadequate to fund the required service capacity.

Overcrowding may be defined in different ways, and standards and expectations vary. A bus which is overloaded in the sense that its design capacity or gross weight is exceeded may be regarded as overcrowded, while a service may be regarded as overcrowded if passengers must wait for significant periods, letting several full buses pass, before one arrives which has accommodation available. In many cases, particularly where it is customary for buses to leave terminal points only when they are full, passengers regard crowded vehicles as normal, and consider a vehicle to be overcrowded only when it is physically impossible for an additional passenger to board.

Driving standards affect passenger comfort as well as safety. A passenger will be more comfortable on a bus which is smoothly driven than on one which is driven roughly, particularly where standing passengers are carried. There is a tendency for buses carrying conductors to be better driven than those operated by the driver only, since the conductor will object if the driver makes his job difficult or dangerous by driving badly; on the other hand, some conductors enjoy the bravado of exposing themselves to unnecessary risk, and even encourage drivers to drive dangerously.

Apart from the comfort of the vehicles themselves, it is important to consider the passengers' comfort before boarding the vehicle. Where weather conditions may be severe, some protection for waiting passengers is desirable, especially at busy stops, as discussed in Chapter 3. Poor discipline at bus stops and on boarding the vehicle, with passengers being jostled or losing their places in a queue, can also detract seriously from the quality of a service, and passengers may be deterred from using it if they have a choice, although in some countries a degree of jostling is regarded as normal and acceptable.

SECURITY

Many transport systems have poor reputations in respect of passenger security, with pickpockets a particularly serious problem, both on buses and at bus stops and stations; in some cases violent robbery is common. The pedestrian components of public transport journeys are also often relatively unsafe. On long-distance services in some countries, particularly where buses with roof luggage racks are used, theft of passengers' luggage en route is a regular occurrence. Theft from operators can also be a serious problem. Theft of vehicle parts and diesel fuel, both from workshops and from the vehicles themselves, is common in some countries. Most theft is for resale but some items are stolen for other purposes: for example, bus seat cushions are often stolen for use as mattresses; sometimes only the foam rubber stuffing is taken.

Security is partly a reflection of standards of law and order in the country generally, but can be influenced by the way in which transport is operated. In particular, overcrowding of vehicles and poor discipline at stops and terminals increases passengers' vulnerability to pickpockets, while the presence of staff such as conductors or inspectors on the vehicles reduces the opportunities for crime. Good lighting on buses and at bus stops also has a beneficial effect. As with other aspects of service quality, the degree of security is partly a reflection of affordability.

Security is difficult to quantify: the number of reported incidents, related to kilometres operated, is a useful measure, although this does not take into account the severity of each case, while few operators maintain adequate records and many incidents tend to go unreported.

ENVIRONMENTAL STANDARDS

Public transport standards in respect of environmental issues are receiving greater attention throughout the world, particularly in developed countries. Exhaust emissions are a major cause of pollution, and increasingly stringent standards are being imposed in an attempt to reduce this. Noise is another area where many governments are attempting to control levels, and maximum standards have been established in most developed countries. As yet, the governments in many developing countries have not set standards for emission and noise levels, and those which have are not always able to enforce them effectively; as a result, levels of pollution attributable to motor vehicles of all kinds are generally high in developing countries.

As discussed in Chapter 5, transport depots are a potential source of pollution, principally through the improper disposal of such substances as waste oil, or spillages of fuel. Again, standards in this respect are difficult to quantify; the number of pollution offences committed by an operator or at a particular site during a period would provide a crude guide, but where legislation and, more importantly, detection and enforcement, are weak, there will be little useful information on which to base such measures.

The appearance, or visual intrusion of public transport vehicles and related infrastructure such as passenger shelters or overhead wires for trolleybuses and trams is also sometimes an issue. Standards of appearance are highly subjective, and therefore difficult to define. In some countries, such as Pakistan, buses are highly decorated and individual, and this is accepted; in other countries such buses are regarded as unsightly, and while they might do their jobs satisfactorily, they are at a disadvantage from the point of view of marketing and general acceptability. This is highly subjective, and tends to be less of an issue in developing countries than in developed countries where the environmentalist lobby tends to be much stronger, and more concerned with visual pollution.

It is unusual for legislation to cover vehicle cleanliness specifically, although in some cases, especially where bus services are franchised, operators are required to clean buses in accordance with specified schedules: for example, buses to be washed externally at least every two days, and swept internally daily. Standards of cleanliness vary substantially, and much depends on culture, and attitudes with regard to cleanliness: for example, large quantities of litter in the streets may be regarded as normal in some countries, but incur severe penalties in others.

RAISING STANDARDS

Where standards are considered to be unsatisfactory, various remedial measures can be taken by transport operators and local or central government; many of these are already in place. There are certain international standards, set by organisations such as the International Standards Organisation, while most countries have bureaux of standards whose role is to set standards in various fields, and to monitor adherence to these standards. These can be effective in some areas, although a bureau of standards cannot cover all transport operating standards.

It is important to ensure that where operators are required to meet certain standards these are realistic and achievable, and reviewed from time to time as circumstances change. Some standards, such as housekeeping, which is particularly poor in many transport undertakings in developing countries, cannot be directly measured, but may be partly covered by other standards, such as those relating to health and safety on industrial premises. Others, such as those relating to the keeping of vehicle maintenance records, can be defined, and can be made a legal requirement, with penalties for failing to meet them. Some must be largely voluntary. Operators can often improve standards through better management, improved systems and procedures, and the use of appropriate equipment, while governments can contribute to an improvement in standards through regulation, and, more importantly, enforcement of those regulations. Where transport services are operated under contract or franchise, compliance with certain standards may be made a condition.

Reliability standards can normally be improved by better control of maintenance, and in particular through planned preventive maintenance programmes. Also relevant is the quality of vehicles purchased, and of spare parts used: genuine parts are often more reliable than cheaper spurious parts. Prompt attendance to breakdowns when they occur can also help to improve the quality of service. Reliability of service can be achieved in various ways: maintaining a fleet of buses to a high standard of reliability; keeping a number of standby buses to cover for breakdowns; hiring in vehicles from private operators to cover for breakdowns; or all three as required. The first will require the operation of good quality buses, maintained to a high standard and replaced before they become unreliable and costly to maintain; 95% availability can be reasonably expected under these conditions, so that one bus for every twenty will be required for standby if service reliability approaching 100% is to be achieved. If greater reliance is to be place on standby vehicles than on reliability of the fleet, the number of standby buses required will depend on the overall standard of the fleet: with a fleet of poor quality, including overage vehicles and with poor maintenance standards, a high percentage of standby vehicles will be required to provide a reliable service. The practicality of relying on hired vehicles depends on the availability of vehicles for hire, and the lead time in obtaining them: it is unlikely that this will ever be a substitute for standby vehicles altogether, although it may always be necessary to have the facility to hire in emergency situations. Where reliability is of less concern than cost, buses of lower quality may be specified, although maintenance standards should never be allowed to slip.

Punctuality can be badly affected by traffic congestion, which is outside the control of the operator, who however can minimise its effect through allowing adequate running and recovery time in schedules. More effective control procedures, including control of the despatch of buses from terminals and periodic roadside checks, can assist in improving and maintaining standards of punctuality. Traffic management measures and bus priority schemes can result in significant improvement.

Safety standards are partly within the control of transport operators, who can take steps to improve the driving standards of their own employees, and to maintain their own vehicles to a higher standard of safety. The behaviour of other road users is often a major problem which can be reduced to some extent by training in defensive driving techniques. Enforcement of vehicle safety and driving standards by the authorities is essential to ensure that transport operators and other road users comply with the relevant regulations, carry out appropriate training and enforce driver discipline. Maintenance standards in many cases will improve only if roadworthiness regulations are enforced. Better enforcement of existing regulations would often be sufficient, but in some cases this needs to be followed by a progressive tightening of regulations. Driver training and examination standards are often poor, and this must be remedied. Improved driver behaviour, as well as improving road safety, would also increase road capacity in urban areas; traffic congestion is aggravated by bad driving practices such as poor lane discipline, failure to give way when necessary and non-observance of traffic signals. Road improvements can have a major impact on safety, and often relatively low cost measures can be highly effective: for example, reflective road marking paint can help to reduce night-time accidents but in many countries this is not used.

Convenience of public transport services can be improved in various ways. Improved routing and scheduling can bring about significant improvements, often with no increase in the cost of operation: indeed such improvements often result in reduced costs, and increased revenue. Journey times can sometimes be reduced by eliminating unnecessarily long waits at stops, but operators should not encourage the use of excessive speed. Good passenger information is another means of improving convenience: this may be relatively cheap although comprehensive information systems can be costly to set up and keep up to date. Regulatory or transport planning authorities can often assist by producing information and in the provision of bus stop, terminal and interchange facilities.

Comfort standards should be appropriate to the type of service provided, and can be raised where necessary through the provision of well-designed vehicles. Maintenance and cleanliness are also important in this context; in particular, seats should be clean and well maintained, for comfort and safety, and to avoid soiling or damaging passengers' clothing. Enforcement of driving standards will improve comfort as well as safety, and both operators and authorities have roles to play in this regard.

Security can be improved through the control of passengers at busy stops, the provision of adequate facilities including lighting, and sufficient personnel to ensure that passengers are safe. Governments can assist through adequate policing where required, and appropriate penalties to deter criminals. At busy stations closed circuit television systems are sometimes used for security, as a deterrent to potential criminals and to facilitate the deployment of security personnel when required; CCTV footage is also often permissible as evidence in court. Some transport operators employ security staff to ride on vehicles and patrol stations, often in co-operation with the police, or permit police officers, on and off duty, to travel free of charge, in return for their assistance when required, but this concession may be abused. However, in practice few transport operators in developing countries are pro-active in providing for the security of their passengers.

Pollution caused by public transport services can be reduced through better maintenance, including vehicle cleaning, improved driving standards, and by using the most appropriate types of vehicle: for example one large bus will cause less pollution than several minibuses.

Excessive noise and exhaust emissions are almost entirely due to poor maintenance, and this is within the control of the operators, although governments can make a significant contribution by setting and enforcing standards. Facilities at depots, workshops and stations to prevent pollutants from entering the drainage system are also necessary.

Quality control is not so easy to achieve in transport as in manufacturing industry, due partly to the problem of supervision resulting from the nature of the operation. Nevertheless some form of quality control is desirable, and feasible. A quality assurance programme for a transport undertaking would include the setting of realistic targets or standards of performance, covering all aspects of service quality as discussed above; it would include effective procedures to indicate when standards are not being achieved, and for remedial action in cases of non-achievement. It would also require the provision of the facilities, equipment, staff training and supervision necessary to achieve the standards. Some operators employ managers with these specific responsibilities, often combined with the task of dealing with complaints from the public. Passenger feedback is important; this may take the form of complaints, received in writing or orally via supervisory staff, or through surveys or questionnaires conducted by operators themselves or by regulatory authorities. As discussed in Chapter 18, an effective procedure for dealing with such comments and complaints is essential.

18

MARKETING, PUBLICITY AND PASSENGER INFORMATION

The use of public transport, like any other product or service, can be profoundly influenced by the way in which it is marketed, although the marketing of public transport services tends to be relatively unsophisticated even in some developed countries. "Marketing" in this context refers not only to the promotional advertising of public transport services, aimed at influencing users' choice in order to persuade them to use a particular public transport mode or operator, or to use public transport in preference to private transport; it also includes informative publicity, principally the dissemination of information to enable potential users to determine what services are available, and to choose those which best meet their requirements. The provision of informative publicity is arguably the most important function of transport marketing, although promotional advertising is significant where there is choice between modes or operators.

Since regular passengers are normally fully aware of the services available to meet their immediate requirements, it may be argued that there is little need for anything more than basic information to enable them to recognise the routes on which vehicles are operated, and that the expense of additional expenditure on marketing, which will attract few additional casual travellers, cannot be justified. It is true that in broad terms advertising is worthwhile only if its cost is at least covered by the additional revenue generated; this may be difficult to verify, but there is little doubt that there is considerable merit in good information on public transport services, in order to encourage and facilitate maximum use. A significant number of potential public transport users, particularly visitors to an area, may be deterred by difficulty in obtaining information, and in the long term good publicity is generally effective in increasing demand; it is, of course, important that the transport services are able to meet this additional demand, and in many developing countries there is already a shortage of capacity.

Promotional advertising may be targeted at all potential users as a means of promoting public transport in general, or may relate to a specific mode, operator, or service. It is particularly relevant where users have a choice: the greater the degree of choice, the greater is the potential benefit from advertising, although if services are inadequate, it may be counter-productive. In most developing countries, promotional advertising for public transport services is relatively limited; much of the advertising takes the form of slogans displayed on the vehicles themselves. Otherwise newspapers and radio are normally appropriate media for promotional advertising of bus services; television has a relatively limited use for advertising public transport in most countries except for targeting higher-income users, and therefore may be applicable only to premium quality services. Cinema advertising may be effective where this is a popular form of entertainment, but it is important to ensure that the types of services advertised are relevant to the audiences who will be targeted.

As well as advertising, special promotional schemes can be successful in increasing ridership. Discounted fares or even free travel are relatively simple methods of promoting public transport. The "Wheel of Fortune" promotion in Malawi, mentioned in Chapter 9, was another form of promotion, which was primarily intended to encourage passengers to obtain tickets after paying their fares, but also attracted some passengers from competing services.

Informative publicity may be disseminated through various channels, including the distribution of printed leaflets, display of information on the vehicles and at appropriate points at the roadside, particularly at bus stops, and through agencies such as enquiry offices or tourist information centres. Newspaper and radio announcements are appropriate in certain circumstances, particularly to notify users of changes to transport services; web sites and even mobile phones are also becoming increasingly widely used for this purpose. All types of publicity material, and all media for their dissemination, are largely complementary to one another, and their application should be carefully co-ordinated as a structured marketing and publicity programme.

In many developing countries, standards of literacy are low, limiting the effectiveness of written advertising and publicity material. This applies in particular to the majority of public transport users, although most users in urban areas are sufficiently literate to recognise basic route information provided on vehicles and roadside signs. Colour codes are sometimes used to identify bus routes, and can be effective in assisting not only the illiterate but all passengers. In countries where the Roman alphabet is not used, it may be appropriate for information relating to bus routes, particularly place names, to be displayed in more than one script, including Roman, to cater for foreign users; for the same reason, it may be useful to provide some information in English as well as in the local language. This may not necessarily apply to all services, but will be particularly relevant in respect of premium or air-conditioned urban and long-distance bus services which are likely to be used by foreign visitors. This practice is already relatively common in rail and metro systems, but much less so for buses.

There are various agencies which may take responsibility for marketing, and the provision of information on public transport services. These include the transport operators themselves, operators' associations, regulatory authorities, and local authorities. Most countries or cities which attract a significant number of tourists have tourism departments, which often include the publication of public transport information amongst their activities.

Large operators should be aware of the value of marketing, and should have marketing programmes with appropriate budgets; this is still relatively uncommon in developing countries. Small operators, particularly owner-drivers or single-vehicle owners, are unlikely to carry out any marketing of their own; an operators' association may provide marketing on behalf of its members, but again this is relatively uncommon. It is often in the interests of the local authorities to publicise transport services, in order to maximise the use of public transport, and discourage increasing use of private transport. The operators themselves will obviously benefit from increased traffic resulting from any marketing initiative and should be expected to contribute towards its cost; where licensing fees are levied, it may therefore be appropriate to include an element for marketing.

ROUTE INFORMATION

It is important that potential passengers are made aware of the services which are available to enable them to plan their journeys. Essential information includes details of the routes operated, points at which vehicles may be boarded, and the places served along each route, as well as their final destinations; it is also useful to know the times at which services operate, the fares for the journeys to be made, types of tickets available, and arrival times at destinations. The extent to which such information is available, and the manner of its presentation, varies considerably. In many developing countries the only means of finding out what services are available is to ask: this may entail locating the appropriate terminal, and enquiring of bus crews, touts or other passengers.

Where transport services are operated to schedule, operators may publish timetables, based on the working schedules used internally, as a means of providing potential passengers with relevant travel information. These timetables may take various forms, such as departure time summaries displayed at major bus stops and terminals for each route, or printed leaflets for each route or zone. The most detailed timetables show the times at which every journey should operate, including departure times from terminals, times at major intermediate stops, and arrival times at the destination.

Such information is of most benefit if there are relatively few operators, however; if there are many small operators serving a particular route or area, each producing its own timetable information, the result is likely to be confusing to potential passengers, and some means is required of collating the information from the various sources. Where public transport services are subject to licensing, the licensing authority may have access to the information required for dissemination to the public, and may collate individual schedules shown on route licences to produce comprehensive timetables for each route; this facilitates the monitoring of individual operators' adherence to schedule as well as enabling the authority to provide useful service information to the public. Even where services are not regulated, and operators may decide for themselves which services they provide, there is often a requirement for operators' licences; if this is the case, it may be appropriate for transport operators to be required, as a condition of their licences, to provide the licensing authority with details of their schedules, and to notify it in advance of any planned changes to services. The authority should maintain up-to-date records of all services operating in their areas, and these can provide the basis for a public information system. Unfortunately, this rarely happens in practice.

Information displayed at bus stops is effective, but cannot easily provide full system details except in very small towns. The amount of passenger information displayed at on-street stops can vary, from a simple sign identifying route numbers of services using the stop, to detailed information on routes, fares and times of operation; in many cities no roadside information is provided at all, and the only information available is that displayed on the vehicles. Sometimes information is displayed on signs and notice boards at terminals, but not along the route.

In some cities published information, for example in the form of route maps and schedule information, is made available, either free of charge or at a price, by transport operators or agencies of central or local government, while it may be possible for members of the public to obtain information by telephone. Some operators and agencies provide service information in the press, or on radio or television, but the effectiveness and coverage of such advertising is limited, and it is not always cost-effective, except when targeted at specific services or market sectors. In many developed countries, public transport information is now available on the internet and it is claimed that it has resulted in significant increases in ridership; this is rapidly becoming more practical as an option in developing countries, although access to this source of information will be restricted to only a small proportion of potential travellers.

It is essential that whatever information is provided is accurate and kept up to date; the form in which it is presented should therefore take this requirement into account, since updating can be a costly process, especially if services change frequently as may be the case in fast-growing cities. Publicity material displayed at the roadside, while most effective in that it is accessible to the majority of potential passengers, is often the most costly and difficult to update, because of the large number of locations. The continued display of outdated information can be detrimental to service quality, and every effort must be made to ensure that this does not happen. Where bus stops are maintained by advertising contractors, the contractors may be required to update the service information if this is incorporated in the advertising panels.

It is possible, using the latest technology, to provide "real time" information at bus stops or railway stations: information is displayed on dot matrix or similar indicators, controlled electronically, typically giving the actual expected arrival time, route and destination of the next buses or trains to arrive. Such systems are usually linked to automatic vehicle location systems. The information displayed at bus stops and stations is reassuring, but since passengers must be at the stop in order to see it, it does not reduce their waiting time, although it may encourage them to wait rather than walk or take a taxi. However, real time information can also be transmitted as text messages to mobile phones, or via the internet and accessed by WAP mobile phones as well as computers. A typical text system requires a user to dial a number which is unique to a specific bus stop or rail station; the display will then show the expected arrival times of all buses or trains in the next few minutes.

There is no doubt that real time information increases user satisfaction, and may encourage additional patronage, although there is little conclusive evidence in the latter respect. However, it is not normally necessary where services operate at high frequencies; the costs involved in providing such information are high, and where the public transport system is highly fragmented it is unlikely that the full participation of all operators will be easily achieved.

ROUTE IDENTIFICATION SYSTEMS

Where a network of routes is provided it is essential that prospective passengers are able to identify the route on which a vehicle is operating. Many operators, particularly those in the informal sector, do not display any service information on their vehicles, but rely on the conductor calling out details of the route at each stop, while at main stops and terminals there may be touts who perform a similar role. Sometimes no information is given at all, but regular passengers know that vehicles departing from a particular point are all operating to the same destination; the only way for a stranger to find out is to "ask around". In most cases, however, the vehicles themselves carry signs which inform passengers of their route and destination. There are several means of providing this information, such as route details painted on the vehicle or a route numbering system accompanied by textual destination information; the route is often identified simply by the colour of the vehicle.

The most commonly used means of indicating the route on which a bus is operating is a system of route numbers, or sometimes letters, and often a combination of numbers and letters, with each number or letter code uniquely signifying a particular route. There are many systems of route numbering: some simply involve the sequential allocation of numbers to routes as they are introduced, while others follow a logical pattern; some have evolved over many years and have become over-complicated as a means of route identification. There is no "best" system: much depends on the nature of the operation and the equipment available, but the primary requirement is that it is easily understood by users of the service.

It is generally preferable for each route to have its own distinct number, and to have separate numbers for all but the most minor variations in the route; these are often indicated by a suffix letter: for example route 12A may be identical to route 12 apart from a minor deviation along the way or at the end of the route. In some systems, route numbers give an indication of the area, type of route or service (for example whether it is a standard service stopping at all stops, express, premium, or a variation of a main route), and this may be helpful to passengers using a complicated route network.

Routes serving a common corridor may be given consecutive numbers (or numbers ending in the same figure, such as 53, 63, 73 and 83), while variations such as loops or forks may be identified by means of suffix letters. In the route numbering system for Kingston, Jamaica, where routes serving New Kingston operate in a loop around the Central Business District, the use of a system of suffix letters was adopted to indicate the direction of travel round the loop, using the suffixes A and B to signify clockwise and anticlockwise travel respectively.

Short workings, i.e. journeys which are not operated for the full length of the route, should normally have the same number as the base route, provided that there is some other means of indicating that the bus will be stopping short of the ultimate destination. The use of different route numbers for short workings is not normally necessary or appropriate, and can lead to an unwieldy proliferation of numbers. It may, however, be appropriate in some circumstances to indicate that a bus is turning short by means of a prefix or suffix letter, which can eliminate the need for the destination itself to be shown on the vehicle.

Letters may also be used to indicate the type of service operated; in this application prefixes are most commonly used. For example an "X" prefix may signify an express service: sometimes such services may be numbered in a series independent of ordinary routes, or a prefix may be used to signify an express variant of a regular route, so that a bus on route X12 follows the same route as one on route 12, but stops less frequently. Another use of prefixes is sometimes to identify the area in which a route is operating: for example A12 may be a local route in Arusha, and D12 a local route in Dodoma; this allows an operator to use the same numerical series in different locations. For most practical purposes, it is preferable to restrict route numbers to not more than three characters, or at most four, including any prefix or suffix letters. This helps to keep the numbering system simple, and easily remembered by passengers, and is particularly relevant where route numbers are displayed on changeable indicators, to minimise the cost of the equipment.

As an example of the way in which route numbers can be used to indicate the type of service operated, the following shows the numbering series used by United Transport Malawi (not all numbers in each series were used):

101-199	Southern Region country stage services
201-299	Central Region country stage services
301-399	Northern Region country stage services
401-499	Lilongwe city services
501-599	Blantyre city services
601-699	Express services (all regions)

Some route identification systems use only letters instead of numbers, although this practice is less common. An advantage of using letters is that a greater number of codes may be obtained from the same number of characters displayed; for example, only 100 combinations will be available from a two-character display using the numerals 0-10, compared with 676 using all letters of the Roman alphabet. Where letters are used, it may also be possible to incorporate the initial letters of main points on the route in the route identification code, to facilitate recognition by passengers; all routes in Malang, Indonesia, are coded in this way, as indicated by the following examples:

AG	Arjosari – Gadang
GA	Gadang – Arjosari (by a different route from AG)
ABG	Arjosari – Borobodur – Gadang
AJG	Arjosari – Janti – Gadang
AMG	Arjosari – Mergosono – Gadang
MK	Madyapura – Karang
MKS	Mulyorejo – Klayatan – Sukun

Where there is a single operator or a small number of relatively large operators serving a particular area, it is common for the operators themselves, or an operators' association, to decide on the route numbering system to be used, and to allocate their own route numbers. Sometimes the larger operator allocates the numbers, which are used by others running on the same route, whether in competition or on a co-ordinated basis. Where conventional bus services are operated alongside paratransit services, the latter sometimes adopt the route numbers used by the conventional bus operator.

It is generally unsatisfactory where several operators serving similar routes allocate their own numbers or letter codes without reference to those used by others. In some cities, for example, it is possible to find two or more different route numbers used for the same route, where it is served by several competing operators, while the same route numbers may apply to several totally different routes run by different operators. There have also been instances where an operator has claimed the sole right to a particular number for a particular route, as his own "brand", while competition legislation may actually prevent different operators from using the same route number for identical routes. Situations of this kind can lead to confusion and detract considerably from the quality of the service as a whole. It is often preferable, therefore, where a large number of operators provide services in the same area, for a regulatory authority to take responsibility for the allocation of route numbers, and for the use of these numbers to be a condition of an operator's licence. Where this is the case, however, it is desirable that the practical considerations mentioned above are taken into account in the design of the system.

For a route numbering system to be fully effective there must be sufficient information available to enable users to know where each route operates. This information should be provided at the bus stops served by the routes in question, but as discussed above information should also be available to the public giving details of all routes in a network. Such information should preferably be in the form of a route map on which the route numbers are clearly marked, accompanied by a list of routes in numerical order, giving for each route details of the terminals and major intermediate points. Ideally, there should also be information on service frequencies, departure times of first and last buses, and fares.

However, route information displayed on the exteriors of the vehicles is often the only information available to intending passengers, and is therefore particularly important. It should be possible for any prospective passenger to know by looking at a vehicle, perhaps assisted by information provided at the bus stop, exactly where it is heading, and which points it will serve en route. Where route numbers or letter codes are used, these alone will not normally indicate the direction of travel, and will not indicate the final destination of the vehicle where the same route number is used for short workings. Route numbers must therefore usually be accompanied by a further indicator on the vehicle giving details of the current journey; it is common to indicate the ultimate destination, and often the main intermediate points also. Sometimes the terminal points at both ends of the route are shown, with no indication of the direction of the current journey, and this can be confusing to infrequent travellers.

In some cases the buses carry only the route identification number, sometimes backed up with information displayed at bus stops advising passengers what each number signifies. The state-owned bus operator in Addis Ababa uses this system. The concept may be taken even further, with numbers being used to indicate a particular destination, as well as the route taken; in such cases buses travelling in opposite directions on the same route will display different numbers. Such a system obviates the need for the display of any other route or destination information on the vehicle itself, thus saving expenditure on equipping buses with complex destination indication equipment, provided that detailed information is displayed at bus stops to enable specific numbers to be identified with specific route and destination variations. This requirement is however often difficult to meet, with maintenance of information displays at bus stops being a particular problem, and is therefore not normally a practical arrangement, particularly where changes to routes are frequent.

Some buses have route information permanently painted on their bodywork, sometimes supplemented by the use of colours to indicate specific routes or route groups. This restricts the use of the bus, and while it is suitable for a small operator who operates on only one route, it is less satisfactory for a large operator requiring flexibility in the allocation of buses to routes. Many vehicles, particularly those used on urban services, therefore have destination indicators which can be altered to show details of the route being operated, and the destination of the current journey. These may take various forms, including simple paper labels or removable signwritten boards displayed in the windscreen or in a glazed panel provided for the purpose, roller blinds, and electronic dot-matrix displays. Whatever system is used, the sign must be legible from a distance sufficient to enable a prospective passenger to read it in time to signal to the driver of an approaching bus to stop, except in a system where all buses stop at every bus stop; the sign should be illuminated so that it is visible at night.

The most suitable type of destination indicator for most purposes in developing countries is the roller-blind type, using "negative" printing on light-coloured or white linen or thin plastic film, with light letters on a dark background, so that the lettering can be illuminated from behind. Such blinds are more legible than the alternatives but require relatively expensive equipment on the vehicle, can tear or crease and may be difficult to update for route changes.

Signwritten removable boards may be suitable provided that these are properly housed and illuminated, and that there is adequate stowage on the vehicle for signs for all routes or journeys to be operated by the bus during the course of its duty. Where signs are displayed in bus windscreens, it is important to ensure that they are not positioned in such a way that the driver's vision is dangerously restricted. Electronic dot-matrix destination indicators have the advantage that they can be programmed to show any destination or other message, but are very expensive, are liable to malfunction when used under harsh climatic or operating conditions, and can be difficult to maintain, although as the technology improves their suitability for use in developing countries will increase.

BRANDING AND PRODUCT DIFFERENTIATION

Some operators use branding as part of their marketing strategies. Branding, in this context, is the presentation of basically similar types of service as though they were different services, targeting different sectors of the market. Branding should not be confused with the provision of genuinely different standards of service, such as basic and premium services, as discussed elsewhere. In a typical example, buses which are otherwise identical and operating on the same route are painted in different liveries and marketed as different brands, at different fares; most passengers will opt for the lower-priced brand, which as a result tends to carry larger loads, but those who are prepared to pay the higher fare for the "superior" brand are able to travel on less crowded vehicles. This has been practised successfully on several routes in Bangkok. The use of different vehicle liveries obviates the need for different route numbers, although some operators may choose to use different numbers as a means of emphasising the difference between the brands.

A variation of the branding theme is to provide ostensibly different service standards, but at normal fares, using standard buses on selected routes but presenting them as a different brand using a special livery; this can be effective on routes where the level of competition is particularly high. An example of this was the "Bluebird" services operated by Kenya Bus Services in Nairobi, whereby standard buses in a special livery, crewed by selected staff given special training in customer care, were operated on the principal route corridors in an attempt to combat paratransit competition.

FLEET IDENTITY

Many bus fleet operators have their vehicles painted in distinctive corporate styles, which can distinguish them from those of other operators, and provide an opportunity for effective marketing, branding and product differentiation. An identifiable fleet may also provide an incentive to an operator to maintain standards. In addition to marketing considerations, it is also desirable, particularly for enforcement purposes, for the owner of a vehicle to be readily identifiable without the need to consult vehicle licensing records: in most countries it is therefore a legal requirement for the owner's legal name and address to be displayed, typically in letters between approximately 2.5 and 6 centimetres in height in a consistent position, such as on the lower side panels immediately to the rear of the front nearside wheel. Apart from such legal requirements, and except when buses carry "all-over" advertisements, it is relatively uncommon for operators to rely solely on textual or graphic signs displayed on each vehicle to indicate its ownership or to distinguish between different types of service.

The livery, or colour scheme in which buses are painted, is the most commonly used means of identification of ownership. Alternatively, a livery may be used to identify not an operator, but a route, or group of routes, even where these are provided by several different operators: in some cities, even where all vehicles are separately owned by individuals, regulations require that they are all painted in a common livery; this is particularly common in some parts of Indonesia. Franchised operations may require franchisees to adopt a specified livery: a typical example is the National Express long-distance bus system in the United Kingdom, which is operated by a large number of contracted independent companies, whose vehicles are all painted in a common corporate livery. A livery may be varied within a common theme to indicate the type of service for which the vehicle is normally used: for example, a common practice followed for many years by operators in the United Kingdom was to transpose the dominant and subsidiary colours in their liveries to distinguish local buses from long-distance coaches.

Where several companies are associated, as in the case of a group of companies belonging to the same holding company, a standard livery may be considered desirable in order to present a corporate image, and to facilitate transfer of vehicles between companies, but there are also advantages in retaining a local identity for each company. Some operators consider it an effective form of marketing to use different liveries for different parts of their territories, to give a "local" image; opinions differ in this regard, but it is possible to compromise, by using different liveries with a common theme, such as different colours applied in a consistent pattern. The use of a corporate livery is not always possible; in China, for example, many buses, particularly those used by smaller operators on long distance services, are delivered in the manufacturers' colour schemes, and since legislation makes it difficult for owners to change the colour of their vehicles, there is little scope for the corporate identity of an operator to be displayed on the vehicles.

Liveries may vary from the application of a single colour to the use of several colours applied in a highly complex pattern. There are two, often conflicting, considerations in the design of a livery: the need for an attractive livery to satisfy marketing requirements, and ease and cost of application and maintenance. As a general rule, a livery should be kept as simple as possible without detracting from its passenger appeal, in order to minimise painting costs and maintenance; this is particularly relevant for operation in congested urban conditions, where the need to repair minor accident damage may be frequent. In countries where labour costs are low, the direct cost of repairing a complex livery after an accident may be correspondingly low, but the vehicle downtime may be considerable and therefore costly.

A further practical consideration is the effect of colour on passenger comfort: dark colours absorb heat, while light colours reflect it, so that the use of dark colours will increase the internal temperature of a vehicle. It is therefore preferable for buses operating in tropical conditions to have white or light-coloured roofs in order to minimise interior temperature. Even where buses are air-conditioned, a white roof will increase the effectiveness of the equipment and reduce the power requirement.

In addition to bus liveries which play a major part in presenting an identifiable corporate image, corporate logos and lettering styles are also important; a classic example is the familiar London Transport roundel motif, which is displayed on vehicles, bus stops, tube stations, depots, offices, and publicity material, and which has been plagiarised, with varying degrees of modification, by other transport operators in many parts of the world. As well as being an effective marketing tool, it enables users to identify easily the services they are seeking: a bus or LRT station, for example, can be recognised from a considerable distance. Where there are many operators, it is usually desirable to have a common symbol for bus stops, for example, to assist in distinguishing these from other street signs, and to assist in the promotion of public transport services.

Advertisements displayed on bus exteriors should not obscure legal lettering, fleet numbers, and other necessary signage. Advertisements often obscure the fleet livery; "all-over" advertisements, in particular, although often a valuable source of income, may be disadvantageous in a situation where there are several competing operators, by making it difficult for intending passengers to distinguish between different operators or services. An operator may compromise by retaining the fleet livery for the front of a vehicle, so that it may be recognised by waiting passengers as it approaches bus stops, leaving the remainder of the vehicle available for advertisements.

ENQUIRIES AND COMPLAINTS

An important element of marketing is the facility for members of the public to enquire about public transport services, and to register complaints when necessary; in the latter case there must be a mechanism for complaints to be effectively dealt with. It is in the operator's interest to ensure that this function is carried out as effectively as possible, but procedures will vary depending on the structure of the industry.

In an industry comprising very small operators, enquiries and complaints must be handled on their behalf by an organisation such as an operators' association; sometimes a regulatory authority has this responsibility. Larger operators should have the capability for answering travel enquiries from the public, and for dealing with passengers' complaints, and may be able to justify full time employees for these tasks; they should have at least one member of staff nominated to deal with public enquiries and complaints received by telephone, by post or in person. In addition, on-road supervisors and inspectors should be instructed and trained to answer queries wherever possible and to receive complaints from members of the public, which, unless they can be dealt with satisfactorily by the inspector on the spot, should be passed to the appropriate member of staff for attention.

All complaints should be investigated, provided that sufficient information is provided by the complainant, and a record should be kept of the result of the investigation and any disciplinary or other action taken. The complainant should be informed that the matter has been dealt with but the operator or authority should be allowed to decide whether or not to disclose the action taken.

19

REGULATION OF PUBLIC TRANSPORT SERVICES

Public transport services throughout the world are subject to a degree of regulation, in addition to the more general government regulations which apply to all businesses. The principal objectives of transport regulation are normally to ensure that services are operated in accordance with government policy, that demand for public transport is satisfied as far as possible, that standards of quality and safety are maintained, and that fares are controlled at "affordable" levels. Regulation may also be deemed necessary to prevent operators from abusing any monopoly position which they may hold, or, in a competitive situation, to control undesirable or potentially dangerous aspects of competition between operators. Stringent regulations, directed primarily at safety, apply to rail transport services in most countries; however, the nature of rail transport is such that regulation of its services is less of an issue than it is with road transport. This chapter therefore deals principally with the regulation of road transport services.

The extent of regulation varies considerably from one country to another. At its most basic, it covers the licensing of vehicles only, usually with certain provisions designed to promote safety. At the other extreme, it may cover almost every aspect of the transport operation, including licensing of vehicles, operators, drivers and conductors, construction and use of vehicles, the supply of services, fares, safety standards, conduct of drivers, conductors and passengers, administration of route franchising or tendering, and allocation of subsidies. There is considerable debate regarding the extent to which market forces should be allowed to determine the nature of the transport system provided, and the extent to which regulation should over-ride market forces; this issue is discussed later in this chapter. While it may be acknowledged that market forces often fail to achieve the desired results, and transport operators lack the capability of developing efficient systems without external intervention, it must also be recognised that regulatory failure can create even greater problems. Government intervention in transport operation is often misguided or irrational, and can do more harm than good. Regulation might stifle enterprise on the part of the operators, who often have a better idea of what services are required than many bureaucrats. It is debatable whether or not poor regulation is preferable to no regulation at all.

The most appropriate regulatory regime in any particular situation is determined largely by the structure of the passenger transport industry. As discussed in Chapter 6, the industry can take various forms. Each form of ownership and structure has its own characteristics, advantages and disadvantages; the disadvantages should be minimised through appropriate regulation. Conversely, the regulatory regime has a strong influence on the nature of the industry, and the way in which it operates. A change in the structure or nature of the industry might be engineered by modifying regulations to encourage the industry to develop in the desired way. Ideally, the regulatory system should create an environment in which efficient transport operators, whether in the private sector or state-owned, can develop naturally in the form which is most appropriate in the circumstances, in terms of fleet size and composition, routes, and fares charged, and can co-operate or compete with one another on an equal basis as appropriate to provide the best possible service to the users.

A monopoly operator, whether state owned or private, may provide a cohesive network of services, but may abuse its position by restricting supply and charging higher fares than would apply under competition. It is quite likely to be inefficient, particularly if it is in the public sector. In this situation regulations will be needed to prevent the abuse of monopoly, and to ensure that reasonable standards of service are met, at reasonable fare levels. A monopoly may leave gaps in its services which, if enforcement of regulations is weak, will be filled by illegal operators, providing an inferior standard of service. If there are a small number of large operators serving an area, the regulations should prevent them from colluding to exploit users as a monopoly might; on the other hand, they should not be prevented from co-operating in a responsible manner to provide a co-ordinated network of services.

Where the industry comprises both public and private sector operators, regulations must ensure that neither sector has an unfair advantage over the other. If the public sector operator enjoys advantages such as tax exemptions, the regulations must counter this, for example by demanding a higher level of service. On the other hand the public sector operators may be at a disadvantage, for example by being required to charge lower fares, or to operate unprofitable services; again, the regulations should take this into account as far as possible.

If in addition to the larger, formal bus operators there are many small informal operators, the regulations must protect the formal operators from malpractices on the part of the informal operators; the small operators must likewise be protected from predatory tactics on the part of the larger operators. The small operators may provide essential services in some areas, filling gaps left by the larger operators, and should not be hindered in this role. Regulations must ensure that competition is fair, and encourage all operators, large and small, formal and informal, to provide the services for which each is most suited.

Where services are provided by a large number of small informal operators, an essential regulatory function will be to prevent dangerous competitive practices such as racing between drivers; the regulatory task is also likely to include a certain amount of planning to ensure that there is an appropriate route system, and that each route is adequately served. The regulatory workload increases with the number of operators to be regulated; in this situation, therefore, the task may be extremely difficult, and in practice regulation is often weak, with a significant part of the task being left to informal "regulators".

Regulations which prevent efficient deployment of vehicles and stifle innovation should be minimised, and where there is competition, operators should be allowed to compete on both price and service in an orderly manner. It is normally inappropriate to impose regulations which restrict entry to the transport industry: there should be free access provided that certain essential conditions are met. Regulation of fares, if inappropriately applied, can result in serious problems, and must be handled with care. It is particularly important to establish how much regulation can realistically be applied and enforced in practice, and in many cases it is expedient to limit regulations to the minimum necessary to meet the requirements of safety and service.

The three broad thrusts of public transport regulation are the quality and quantity of the services provided, and the fares charged.

QUALITY REGULATION

Quality regulation in road transport is generally accepted as essential, irrespective of the existence or otherwise of regulations governing the level of service provided, or the fares charged. It includes the general area of regulation, applicable to all forms of road transport, public or private, passenger or freight, which governs vehicle construction and use, and is primarily intended to ensure the safety of road users and to protect the road system and other infrastructure from damage. It is concerned with the setting and enforcement of standards and does not impose any significant barriers to entry to the industry for transport operators who meet these standards. In this context, "quality" embraces a number of attributes, including safety and "environmental" factors such as exhaust emissions; virtually all countries have regulations specifying vehicle design parameters, vehicle inspection requirements, and safety-related rules in respect of maximum speeds and drivers' hours of work.

It is normal for the standards for construction and use of all types of road vehicle to be specified in road traffic legislation; there are usually additional regulations which apply specifically to passenger transport, dealing particularly with standards of safety and also, to some extent, convenience and comfort. Vehicle construction regulations specify design parameters such as maximum permitted dimensions, weights, and axle loads. Some are highly specific: for example, in the case of public service vehicles, they may specify details such as minimum spacing between seats, maximum entrance step heights, and minimum door and aisle widths. It is desirable, when formulating vehicle construction regulations, to take into account relevant international standards as far as possible, so that mass-produced vehicles available on the international market may be purchased and used without unnecessary or expensive modification.

Regulations must be appropriate to local conditions and circumstances: in particular, they must have regard for operating conditions and cost. There is sometimes a temptation for legislators to specify vehicles which are too sophisticated. For example, operators may be required to provide easy access for disabled passengers by the use of low-floor buses, or even buses with a "kneeling" capability, when these are too expensive to be funded by the level of fares which passengers can afford, and where the road infrastructure may not be compatible with the use of such vehicles.

It is desirable that, as far as possible, each public transport service is operated by the most appropriate type of vehicle. Choice of suitable vehicle types can be encouraged by various means, including appropriate construction and use regulations. In some cases this has been achieved by the provision of grants for the purchase of buses to approved designs: for example, the New Bus Grant which was effective in the United Kingdom during the 1970s was designed to encourage the introduction of new buses specifically designed for one person operation, by subsidising the purchasers of buses which met certain design requirements. Such a policy can be harmful if not properly implemented, however, and whatever measures are taken, great care must be taken to avoid the imposition of unreasonable restrictions: if the design parameters are inappropriately specified, the industry will be burdened with an unsuitable design of vehicle; even if the specification is suitable when first drawn up, it can become outdated and restrict innovation in the industry if it is not kept under constant review. In Kenya, two design features, which are almost universal on buses throughout the world, were not permitted for several years, ostensibly on the grounds of safety: these were the use of fibreglass for front bodywork panels and an entrance or exit door ahead of the front axle; although dispensations were granted in some instances, these regulations resulted in the widespread use of vehicles of unsuitable or inefficient design. Even vehicle appearance is sometimes subject to regulation, such as where bus, minibus or taxi operators are required to adopt a common livery. In China, each public service vehicle licence carries a photograph of the vehicle, and indicates its colour, which may not be changed by the vehicle owner.

Regulations must be realistic and practical. For example, regulations dealing with passenger capacity on buses should permit a realistic number of standing passengers, based on relevant criteria such as the gangway floor area which is available for standing passengers, and take into account vehicle size, configuration and maximum permitted gross weight. However, it is not uncommon for the licensed standing passenger capacity of a bus to be crudely calculated as a percentage of the number of seats; on this basis, buses designed with relatively few seats to permit a large number of standing passengers to be carried will not be licensed to carry their full design loads, while buses with high seating capacities will be licensed to carry more standing passengers than can be accommodated. In Jamaica, as a result of such ill-conceived regulation, there were large buses designed to carry up to sixty standing passengers, but licensed to carry only twenty; needless to say, this restriction was ignored.

It is important to ensure that regulations do not prevent operators from providing non-standard services designed to meet specific requirements. For example, "truck-buses", carrying broadly similar proportions of passengers and freight, may be the most appropriate type of vehicle for serving some rural areas; but often regulations do not provide for this, requiring vehicles to be licensed either as passenger vehicles, which may carry only limited quantities of freight, or freight vehicles, which may not carry passengers. As a result, such vehicles are often operated illegally.

Quality standards should reflect a country's culture, its level of development, and in particular its wealth: what is appropriate in one situation may not necessarily be appropriate in another, and there is no point in imposing high standards in a country which cannot afford them. Ideally, the standards set should be the highest which are affordable or achievable, and these should be reviewed periodically in the light of changes in the prevailing circumstances. Regulations should be consistent within a country, and where bus services are operated between one country and another, it is obviously desirable for regulations to be consistent throughout the region.

Safety and maintenance standards are invariably covered by legislation, which normally requires regular examination of vehicles, carried out at an approved test station, generally once or twice per year. Sometimes the requirement is excessive. In some provinces of China, for example, tests were required to be carried out three times per year at testing stations approved by the licensing authority, and a further four times per year by the police, although in practice the tests were normally carried out once per year on each vehicle by both authorities. Such a high frequency of routine testing should be unnecessary, although random roadside vehicle safety checks should be carried out on a continuous basis.

In some countries there is a limit to the age of vehicles which may be licensed for operation on public services. However, it is possible for a very old vehicle to be maintained in better condition than a newer one, and as a general rule such a policy is unnecessarily restrictive. Strict enforcement of regulations relating to vehicle roadworthiness is normally preferable; this has the effect of improving the condition of vehicles generally, but also tends to result in the elimination of the least suitable vehicles from the fleet. Owners of buses which fail their roadworthiness inspections are faced with the choice of scrapping them or spending money to restore them to an acceptable standard, and such expense is justified only in respect of vehicles which will subsequently be able to earn sufficient revenue to cover this expense. Such measures may be perceived to increase the cost of operation, where a bus owner is faced with expenditure which otherwise would not have been incurred. However, in the longer term the preventive maintenance measures which operators will have to adopt in order to satisfy roadworthiness requirements will normally result in lower operating costs.

Regulations often stipulate minimum standards for vehicle maintenance facilities; an applicant for an operator's licence may be required to provide proof that he has adequate premises for garaging and maintaining his fleet, or alternatively a contract with a commercial garage to provide these services. On-street garaging of vehicles over a certain size may be prohibited.

The principal regulations concerning the use of vehicles normally relate to loading and speed of operation, and are designed to ensure safety of operation. Regulations to prevent overloading of buses are intended to ensure that passengers are not subjected to unacceptable overcrowding, and that the safety of the vehicle is not jeopardised by carrying a weight in excess of its design capabilities; overloaded vehicles can also cause damage to road surfaces and infrastructure, and another objective of the regulations is to minimise such damage. Similarly, excess speed increases the risk of accidents both to passengers and to other road users, and restrictions are imposed to reduce this risk. Regulations may impose certain conditions with regard to routes and bus stops, in order to minimise the congestion or danger caused by buses being operated along roads or stopping in places which are unsuitable. Other regulations designed to improve safety may prohibit operation in certain circumstances or at certain times. For example in Tanzania, in response to an apparently excessive rate of accidents involving long distance buses occurring at night, the government introduced a ban on overnight bus operation outside the towns, in the belief that this would reduce the number of accidents.

Licensing of bus crews is a means of protecting the safety and security of passengers and other road users. It is a requirement in most countries for bus drivers to hold specific public service vehicle (PSV) driver's licences in addition to the ordinary car drivers' licences. The stringency of licensing requirements varies. PSV drivers' licences are issued in some countries to drivers who can merely show that they have held an ordinary licence for a specified period, regardless of actual driving experience; in others, a special driving test is required prior to the issue of a PSV driver's licence. There may also be a requirement for a medical examination to ensure that the driver is physically fit for the job, while police records are often checked to avoid the employment of drivers with unsatisfactory criminal records.

Where conductors are employed, they are sometimes required to hold conductors' licences to ensure that certain standards of integrity and competence are met. These might be issued on completion of an appropriate training programme, and there may also be checks on physical fitness and any police or criminal record. Requirements in respect of bus conductors are usually less stringent than for drivers, and in most countries conductors do not require licences at all.

A taxi driver must also usually hold a special licence in addition to the ordinary driver's licence. This is normally issued subject to the licensing authority being satisfied that the applicant is of good character and is fit to act as a taxi driver; in addition, the driver may be required to pass a written examination covering driving techniques and mechanical knowledge, and in some cases knowledge of the area in which he intends to work.

There are usually other regulations regarding the safety aspects of driving; for example, drivers might not be permitted to talk, smoke or eat while driving, or to drive after consuming alcohol or drugs, or if suffering from an illness which could impair driving ability. There are often restrictions on the hours which a driver is permitted to work in a day or week. Typical drivers' hours regulations, as specified under the 1968 Transport Act in the United Kingdom, were broadly that drivers may not drive for more than five and a half hours without a thirty minute break; or drive for more than a total of ten hours in a 24 hour period, with a maximum duty spreadover of fourteen hours, or drive for more than sixty hours in a week. At least eleven consecutive hours of rest were required in any 24 hour period, and a rest day of at least 24 consecutive hours once per week. Subsequent changes to legislation added further restrictions. Similar conditions apply in most developed countries and in many developing countries, although in the latter the regulations tend to be less stringent and less strictly enforced.

Drivers' hours regulations, while intended to improve safety, can often cause other problems: by reducing driver productivity they normally result in increased staff requirement and hence increased costs, while any staff shortages will be aggravated, with a detrimental effect on the standard of service provided. If drivers' salaries are increased to compensate for the loss of earnings due to a restriction on working hours, and to ease the problem of staff recruitment and retention, operating costs will increase. While such regulations are desirable, therefore, they should not be unreasonably restrictive, and the benefits should be weighed against the costs.

Sometimes there are also limits to the distances which drivers may drive in a day, although these are rarely practical While it may be an easier parameter to control, the distance which may be covered within a given time will vary considerably depending on conditions. Long distance operation is often less tiring than slow driving in urban traffic, and the operation of several hundred kilometres in a day on an open road may be less tiring than one hundred under difficult urban conditions.

Third party insurance, which includes cover for death or injury to passengers, is normally compulsory in respect of all buses and taxis, and proof of insurance cover may be required before an operator's or vehicle licence is issued; comprehensive insurance is rarely a legal requirement although some vehicle owners may wish to purchase such cover. In some countries it is not a requirement for state owned undertakings to insure their vehicles on the basis that any compensation arising from accident claims will be paid out of government funds.

Regulations may apply not only to the quality of the vehicle and the way in which it is used, maintained and driven. The quality of management of the undertaking operating the vehicle has a significant influence on standard of service and therefore some form of operator licensing may be appropriate, to ensure that operators of public transport services meet specified standards of competence and integrity. In some countries, in order to hold a licence to operate buses, it is necessary to demonstrate the basic ability to manage a transport operation. In the United Kingdom this is provided by the Certificate of Professional Competence (CPC), issued when the applicant passes an examination on matters relating to the operation and management of a transport undertaking. Licence applicants may also be required to provide evidence of financial standing and a satisfactory police record.

QUANTITY REGULATION

Quantity regulation in passenger transport has been widely practised for many decades, but its validity is now being increasingly challenged. It concerns the extent of the services provided, and relates principally to the control of public transport routes, numbers of vehicles operated and frequency of journeys run. It was originally devised principally to engender co-ordination or integration of transport services, to address a situation where there were seen to be too many buses on busy routes and too few on less profitable routes, and to curb what was regarded as wasteful competition. In many cases operators were given protection from competition on "good" routes to enable them to earn sufficient profits to provide "adequate" services on unprofitable routes: this principle of cross-subsidy, at one time regarded by many in the transport industry as sacrosanct, is now condemned as undesirable by protagonists of market forces.

Under the traditional system of quantity regulation, protection of established operators makes it difficult for new operators to enter the market. The argument in favour of this type of regulation is that passengers benefit from a more consistent service throughout an area, with good route coverage even where demand is low. Counter-arguments are that protected operators are likely to abuse their position to the disadvantage of the passengers, and that where the regulations encourage cross-subsidy, passengers on busy routes suffer from an inferior service so that a minority can benefit from a standard of service for which they are not prepared to pay the full cost.

The basis of quantity regulation is normally a licensing system which controls the number of vehicles operated on a particular route, the number of journeys run, and often the number of transport undertakings permitted to operate in a given area; even where there is no quantity regulation, operators may still be required to hold route licences for administrative reasons and as a means of checking service reliability as part of a quality regulation procedure. The licensing system used in the United Kingdom between 1930 and 1985 was typical. Every bus operator required a licence for each route operated; the conditions attached to the licence included the exact times at which each journey was to run, the fares to be charged, and sometimes the type or capacity of vehicle to be used. Applications for new licences and for renewals or amendments to existing licences were considered at public hearings by the Traffic Commissioners, who were responsible for administration of the system; other bus operators, the railway operators, police, local authorities and members of the public were all entitled to object to any application. The Traffic Commissioners' decisions took into account the current and potential demand for the service, the current level of supply, and the public interest generally. In theory, excess capacity was not permitted on any route, although on cross-subsidised routes with low demand this was clearly not so. Variations on this system of regulation are still found in many parts of the world, particularly in former British colonies.

A route licence may specify very little, for example the two terminal points of the route only; on the other hand it may include such details as the route number, the exact route, naming each road to be traversed, the timetable to be followed, fares to be charged between stages, and the type of vehicle to be operated. Some licences are highly specific, to the extent that they restrict the operator's ability to use vehicles efficiently. In most cases, it is sufficient for the route licence to specify, in addition to the geographic details of the route, the maximum number (excluding standbys or maintenance spares) and type (in general terms) of vehicles to be operated, without identifying specific vehicles; a condition of the route licence should be that every vehicle operated should hold a valid vehicle licence. Only one route licence should normally be required for each route, with minor variations included in this licence rather than treated as separate routes. Fares should not normally be specified on the licence, although where fares are controlled the licence should require the operator to comply with the relevant regulations. It may be appropriate for timetables to be included; alternatively, service capacity or frequencies might be specified. It need not be a requirement that every journey operates for the full length of the route, although it may be necessary to specify a minimum number, or percentage, of journeys which do. Licences for demand-responsive services must allow operators more flexibility although routes and schedules may be specified in general terms.

The route licensing system often includes measures designed to protect one operator from competition from another operating on the same route, or part of it. For example, buses on long-distance services may not be permitted to carry passengers whose journeys both commence and end within a particular urban area, in order to protect the operators of local bus services in that area. This was a common feature of the licensing system in the United Kingdom, where urban bus operators, many of which were municipally owned, were protected from competition from longer-distance services operating into the towns, by conditions attached to the licences for the latter. These conditions either prohibited the carriage of passengers on journeys wholly within the municipal area, or required the longer-distance operator to charge higher fares for this traffic, thus discouraging short-distance passengers within the urban area. Protection may take other forms: in Kuala Lumpur, for example, operators are allocated specific route corridors; an operator will not be given a licence to operate on another's corridor without the consent of the incumbent.

Conditions attached to route licences often include restrictions on the operator's right to withdraw the service, in order to protect the public from unexpected loss of a service: for example, bus operators may be permitted to withdraw from any route but only after giving thirty days notice to the licensing authority and to the public. A route licence is normally issued in respect of the operator, although if it applies to a specific vehicle it might be automatically transferable to the new owner if the bus is sold.

The licensing system can also be used to encourage operators to purchase buses of appropriate size and configuration for the routes on which they are to be used; while it is unduly restrictive, and often impractical to impose specific seating capacities as a licence condition, it may be appropriate for a licence for a route to specify a range of capacities within which the buses operated on the route should fall. Three ranges are normally sufficient; for example, these might be classified as "small bus" or "mini-bus", seating between eight and twenty; "medium-sized bus" or "midibus", 21 to 35 seats; and "full-sized bus" with more than 35 seats. It may also be appropriate to specify whether single or double-deck, or articulated buses, may be operated on a particular route, or impose length or height restrictions according to road conditions on the route. The issue of vehicle size is discussed in Chapter 2; the licensing authority should consider each case within predetermined guidelines.

A feature of the road service licensing system in many countries is the restriction of each bus to a particular route, or even to a particular schedule. This however can lead to inefficiency, and hence increased cost, and is therefore generally undesirable. It is normally preferable for an operator running several routes to have the flexibility to operate any bus on any route for which a licence is held, and to be permitted to transfer buses between routes to suit different levels of demand at different times and in different areas, provided that the buses are suitable for the routes concerned. Even with a small fleet of vehicles, utilisation can be significantly improved by the facility to interchange vehicles between routes: an obvious example is the need to be able to reallocate a bus from one route where it is not immediately required to another to fill a gap left by a breakdown, or to keep a pool of vehicles which can be allocated to any route for which the operator holds a licence to replace vehicles which are out of service for maintenance. The idle time of a bus with several hours between journeys on one route could be used to operate a journey on another route, thus reducing total vehicle requirements. Licensing regulations should therefore permit buses to be operated on more than one route or schedule: specific vehicles should not be identified on the licence for a route, and no specific route should be identified on the licence for a bus.

Under some regulatory systems an operator may change the route on which he operates by surrendering his route permit and applying for a new one for another route; in other cases this is not permitted. Some licensing authorities have the power, if they wish to instigate route changes, to order operators to accept changes to their licensed routes, but where this is not applicable the regulations might provide for the change to be made compulsorily on renewal of the permit; the licensing authority might be given the power to reallocate buses from one route to another, regardless of the operator's wishes. However, such close involvement on the part of a licensing authority in the deployment of buses is relatively rare.

In parts of China, when applying for a licence for a bus, the owner must specify the route on which he wishes to operate it. The licensing authority may accept or reject the application after reviewing the passenger volume and the existing licences for that route, or may suggest an alternative route. Licences for the most profitable routes are sometimes auctioned, in order to allocate buses more evenly amongst the available routes, to raise money for new and improved bus station facilities, and to limit the possibility of preferential treatment in the granting of licences; licences are awarded to the highest bidders, in monetary terms, with no allowance for differences in service quality. Existing licence holders are given no preference other than automatic qualification to bid, while others are subjected to a screening process. Imbalances between demand and supply can be rectified by withdrawing licences or issuing additional licences; however, operators cannot always be forced to operate uneconomic routes and a shortage of supply on a route which is uneconomic may necessitate the provision of a subsidy if a service is to be provided.

In Sri Lanka, where the private sector of the bus industry comprises a large number of individual owners, most with only one bus, the transport authorities in some provinces prepare the timetables for each route, allocating each departure on the basis of an auction system; the most popular departures command the highest values. This system has a number of disadvantages. It makes it very difficult for the authority to make any changes to timetables, since an operator who has paid for a specific departure will object if the time is changed, or if an additional journey is added to the timetable close to his own. It results in inefficient use of buses, often with long layover periods between journeys, as evidenced by long queues of buses at the terminals. It makes it difficult, or impossible, for an efficient operator to provide a better or more economical service through efficient scheduling and utilisation of buses.

In a similar category to route licences in some licensing systems are contract licences, issued in respect of vehicles to be used on contract services such as the carriage of parties of tourists or the provision of staff transport for a third party, and excursions and tours licences, permitting an operator to provide services for tourists. Like route licences, tour licences may be very specific, detailing the routes to be followed by each tour, and sometimes limiting the number of occasions on which it may be operated, or they may give the operator complete flexibility to provide such services wherever and whenever he sees fit.

Quantity licensing for individual public transport modes normally involves limiting the number of licences issued in a particular area. There are often territorial restrictions to control competition, as well as to give each area authority the means of controlling service quality within its own area: as a typical example, taxis licensed to operate in the Kingston Metropolitan Region in Jamaica are not permitted to pick up passengers outside the KMR; they may however pick up passengers within the KMR and take them to points outside. In some Indonesian cities, taxis are not permitted to operate outside their licensed areas, even to drop passengers who were picked up within the licensed area; this is unduly restrictive, and results in a considerable amount of illegal operation. In some cities airport and rail operators and large hotels charge taxi operators for operating from their premises; some give exclusive access to some operators, and restrict the number of taxi permits issued. Such restrictions sometimes result in a shortage of supply and consequently a tendency for excessive fares to be charged; in such cases the value of a licence may be high if it can be sold by one operator to another, and may even exceed the value of the vehicle itself.

Sharing of private cars by commuters is a common practice in some countries but in many it is illegal for the owner or driver of the car to charge passengers for the journey. However, such practice makes efficient use of transport resources and should not necessarily be discouraged. If it is to be permitted, however, some provision should be included in the legislation to ensure that private car owners do not operate as unlicensed taxis, and in practice this is likely to be difficult to enforce.

It is often argued that quantity licensing is unnecessary, since market forces will eventually ensure that the optimum number of vehicles are owned and operated. In practice, this rarely happens, and excess capacity in both mass and individual public transport modes is found in many cities throughout the world, sometimes on a massive scale. Fleet over-capacity does not necessarily result in service over-capacity: service capacity may still be inadequate, such as where vehicles wait for full loads before leaving terminals, usually resulting in unsatisfied demand along the route.

The regulatory authorities are not always effective in preventing such over-capacity, even with a quantity licensing system, and the criteria for assessing service capacity are often inappropriate. In some cities in Indonesia licences are normally granted for additional vehicles on a route on the basis of an assessment of the load factors on existing vehicles on the route. However, since the majority of vehicles do not leave the terminals until they have a full load, load factor surveys carried out along a route will inevitably suggest that there is justification for additional vehicles, even though there may be long queues of empty vehicles waiting at the terminals for loads. The problem is often compounded where excessive numbers of licences are issued corruptly. For a quantity licensing system to be effective in matching supply to demand, therefore, the licensing authority should regularly monitor the demand for and supply of services on each route, based on surveys designed to reflect the true position.

Excess capacity in the taxi industry has less serious consequences than in the bus industry: the lower capital cost of a taxi compared with that of a bus, and the fact that in most cases the vehicles used are standard saloon car models, makes entry to and exit from the industry relatively easy, if the licensing system so allows. It might therefore be argued that it should not be necessary to limit the number of taxi licences issued: if there is demand, operators should be allowed to meet it; if demand for taxis declines, through increased car ownership or through improved bus services, market forces will bring about a reduction in the number of taxis. Quality standards should be strictly enforced, however.

In some countries, public sector bus companies do not require licences or permits to operate, even though private sector operators may be subject to regulation. Unless the public sector undertaking has a monopoly, this concession is not usually appropriate, particularly in terms of the regulation and co-ordination of the services provided by different operators. The same rules should apply to all operators if the legitimate objectives of a licensing system are to be achieved.

REGULATION OF FARES

Public transport fares are regulated in most developing countries, and enforcement is often more stringent than in the case of any other aspect of regulation. The regulations may specify actual fares to be charged, a maximum permitted charge, or a charge for a basic service which operators are permitted to exceed at their own discretion for premium services; different fare levels may be authorised to reflect different standards of service. As discussed in Chapter 14, fares are usually specified in terms of a rate per passenger-kilometre, and sometimes per zone or fare stage; in the latter case, care must be taken to avoid wide variations in the length of fare stages, unless this is to reflect differences in operating costs on different sections of a route.

Several reasons may be given to justify the regulation of bus fares. Sometimes the motives are purely political, and there have been several instances where governments have restricted the level of bus fares in order to gain popularity with the electorate. The stated objective is often to ensure that fares are "affordable" by the travelling public. Where an operator has a monopoly, the objective may be to prevent the abuse of monopoly powers; if there are many operators on one route it is usually desirable to ensure that fares are consistent, and to prevent the formation of cartels in which the stronger operators force the weaker ones out of the market by charging uneconomically low fares and then exploit their resulting position of oligopoly.

However, there is considerable disagreement as to whether regulation of fares is necessary to protect passengers from exploitation by unscrupulous operators, or whether it distorts the market to the passengers' disadvantage. In fact, fare regulation, while designed to protect passengers' interests by preventing operators from charging fares which they cannot afford, often has the opposite effect; inappropriate control of bus fares has caused numerous problems, and has brought about the demise of bus companies in many parts of the world, as described in Chapter 6. Where a government, probably with the best of intentions, has prevented bus operators from increasing fares to a level sufficient to sustain the services provided, passengers have often found themselves ultimately paying more than would have been the case if the bus operator had not been so restricted, for an inferior standard of paratransit service.

Another common effect of fares regulation is that due to the cumbersome administrative procedures which are often involved, operators have to wait a considerable time before a fare increase is approved. The effect of the time lag between cost increases, such as an increase in the cost of fuel or wages, and implementation of a fares increase, can be serious, particularly where the rate of inflation is high. Another problem is that the increase, when it is finally approved, is often significantly less than was requested; for this reason there is a tendency for operators to apply for larger fare increases than are necessary, which can damage their credibility. Ideally fare increases should be authorised at regular intervals, preferably on a similar date each year, and be based on a formula which links bus fares to an appropriate price index. Relatively frequent, but small, fares increases are preferable to infrequent and large increases, which usually cause adverse passenger reaction in addition to the financial difficulties created for the operator.

It is important that operators are able to predict with reasonable accuracy how fare levels will change, so that they may budget accordingly, but the uncertainty often inherent in fare regulation can discourage investment. If operators cannot be confident that they will be able to adjust fares to compensate for changes in the cost of inputs, investment in a bus becomes risky and unattractive.

Regulation of bus fares can therefore create serious problems if not administered sensibly. It is recognised that there may be political obstacles in some countries to deregulating bus fares, but in most situations this would be beneficial in the longer term. Operators are aware that there is a limit to what passengers can afford or are prepared to pay, and in a competitive situation this will prevent them from attempting to impose unreasonably high charges; those who do will lose business to those charging less. Allowing operators more scope to determine their charges will give them the opportunity to explore different markets, and adjust charges in line with variations in demand. In a monopoly situation, there must be measures to ensure that the fares charged are reasonable, but it is still preferable for the fares to be set by the operator rather than by the regulatory authority.

If bus fares are to be regulated, however, it is important that the regulations allow operators a degree of flexibility in their charging policies. For example, an operator might wish to charge different fares at different times of the day to reflect variations in demand, offering cheaper travel to many users, or to introduce a higher quality service in addition to the basic service, at a higher fare level. In some cases such services have been proposed but have not been permitted since the authorities would not agree to fares being charged above the approved level, even though the basic service would still be available to those who could not afford to pay the premium fare, and there might even be people who would transfer from taxis to the premium bus service, and therefore pay less than before. Operators should be permitted to make such pricing policy decisions within the overall policy framework set by the government. If superior services are offered at higher fares, there should be a mechanism to ensure that these fares are not charged on ordinary services, and that operators do not restrict the level of operation on ordinary services in an attempt to force passengers to use the superior services. This may be achieved by attaching appropriate conditions to the licences for the services concerned.

An appropriate fares policy is essential to sustain the operation of services which meet demand and which are affordable by the travelling public, whilst providing the operator with an adequate return on investment. There may be a need for a degree of control to ensure that passengers are able to ascertain in advance of their journeys how much they will have to pay, to avoid the confusion which might arise if several operators were to charge different fares for the same journey. This can be resolved by a requirement for operators to notify the authority of their fare scales, and to observe a specified period of notice before any changes are implemented. It may be considered necessary to introduce legislation to prevent operators from colluding to fix rates at an unreasonable level: however, as mentioned above, such fares will not be sustainable in a competitive situation, and it is important that ill-conceived anti-trust legislation does not stifle co-operation between operators which is in the public interest, such as the provision of a regular bus service by several operators who agree on a joint timetable, and who charge the same fares.

DEREGULATION AND COMPETITION

Some forms of regulation are designed to restrict competition between operators, on the premise that uncontrolled competition in public transport is undesirable. However, the view is becoming more widely held that public transport can be more efficient and less costly when there is an element of competition, and that market forces, if given free reign, will result in the development of an optimal transport service; it is frequently argued that regulation of transport services should be confined to safety issues, leaving market forces to determine the nature and extent of the services provided, and their price. Current thinking and policies are therefore generally in favour of reducing the extent to which transport services are regulated, on the grounds that the consequent increase in competition will result in improved services; what is commonly termed "deregulation" is usually, in effect, a relaxation of quantity controls while retaining control of quality.

It is true that there are potential disadvantages in a fully regulated system. An operator protected from competition may exploit the users of the service, for example by providing a lower frequency or lower quality service at higher fares than would apply under competitive conditions; without the threat of competition the operator may become complacent and inefficient. Probably more serious is that, as with any form of external control, those responsible for regulation must have adequate knowledge of what they are controlling to enable them to make the appropriate decisions: in practice this is difficult to achieve, and the result is often a transport system which is poorly planned, has not adapted to changes in demand, and which consequently provides an inferior service. However, an adequate and orderly public transport system does not normally develop through market forces alone. While in theory competition encourages operators to respond to passengers' requirements, the operators rarely know precisely what these requirements are, particularly where the industry is dominated by informal operators. Moreover, in a rapidly changing situation, as is typical in developing countries, the capacity of a system driven by market forces alone will tend to lag seriously behind demand.

The theoretical advantages of deregulation and competition between operators are lower costs, improved services, and innovation; if bus operators are free to determine the routes on which they operate, and the number of journeys they run, market forces will, over time, ensure that supply on each route equates to demand. Cross-subsidy will be reduced or eliminated; this may or may not be regarded as a benefit. Operators will have the flexibility to react quickly to changes in the market, and will have the freedom to experiment with innovative services. The result will be a general increase in the level of service, improvement in service quality, and an overall reduction in cost. This in turn will stimulate growth in the number of passengers carried; some of these may be attracted from private transport, and some will be newly generated traffic.

Although in theory market forces will eventually bring about the optimum level of transport service, this does not normally occur in practice. The theory of perfect competition assumes that all producers and consumers have "perfect knowledge" of the market. In reality, this is never the case, and in developing countries in particular, knowledge of the market, by any of the parties concerned, is far from perfect: indeed, operators' market knowledge is often extremely limited, resulting in a general failure to respond to market conditions. Moreover, it takes considerable time for market forces to bring about the equilibrium position, and in a rapidly changing situation, equilibrium will never even be approached.

Private sector operators in an unregulated, competitive situation are seldom able to provide networks of routes, making the availability of public transport uncertain, and travel inconvenient and unattractive. Therefore there is usually a need for external intervention, in addition to basic safety regulation, if a satisfactory transport system is to be created; there must be adequate controls to ensure that the service provided meets the requirements of the users on all routes, and not only on those which are most attractive to the operators, and to control some of the less desirable aspects of competition without preventing transport operators from running their businesses on sound commercial principles.

Another major problem in developing countries is that competition is not always fair. The true benefits of competition will only be realised if all operators compete on exactly equal terms; where some fail to maintain their vehicles adequately, or drive dangerously in order to be the first at a bus stop where passengers are waiting, they have an unfair advantage over those who act in a more responsible manner. An operator may be forced to break the law in order to compete on equal terms with the less scrupulous element, and in this context, the degree to which regulations are enforced is highly relevant. The benefits of competition in transport are therefore often outweighed by the disadvantages.

Deregulation of bus services, if not properly managed, can destroy much that is good as well as eliminating the deficiencies of a regulated system. Co-ordination and route planning, which is best carried out by a large operator or by a regulatory authority, may suffer, and established bus companies can be destroyed, to be replaced by a disorganised service provided by a large number of very small operating units. Complete deregulation of services may lead to over-concentration on prime route corridors, removal of services from poorer routes or at quiet times of the day, and problems arising from aggressive, competitive driving, although it must be acknowledged that due to poor enforcement these problems may exist under regulated systems. Quality regulation must be rigorously enforced in order to curb unacceptable operating practices which may lead to unreliable services and reduced safety standards; this may be achieved through operator licensing, which provides the means to prevent irresponsible operators from operating at all.

Some lessons can be learned from the deregulation of bus services in the United Kingdom during the 1980s. There was a common tendency for additional buses to be deployed by newcomers on profitable routes which were already adequately served, to compete with the incumbent operator: this resulted in increased total vehicle-kilometres, but with a smaller proportionate increase in passenger-kilometres. The profits of the incumbent operator were reduced, while those of the newcomer, whose buses had often been transferred from less profitable routes, were increased, but usually by a smaller amount; in the majority of cases, therefore, the overall result was a net disbenefit for both bus operators and users. The removal of regulations which had protected the established operators from competition from others, led to a number of cases where existing operators were driven to insolvency by those engaging in such predatory tactics as swamping routes with buses, deliberate obstruction of buses at stops, the provision of services at unsustainable fares or even free of charge until the existing operator was forced to withdraw, and incentives for staff to transfer from the incumbent to the predator. Although such activities were subsequently ruled illegal by the Office of Fair Trading, the damage in most cases was already done, and the penalties imposed upon the new operator were largely ineffective.

Deregulation in the United Kingdom led to instability and fragmentation of route networks, and the withdrawal of services at unprofitable times or on unprofitable routes, particularly in rural areas, and significant variations in service quality. On the positive side, it led to a number of innovations, increased levels of service on busy routes, and better quality services on some. In some parts of the country it was felt that there were overall benefits while in others deregulation was considered to have been detrimental to service quality.

Monopolies or cartels may exploit consumers through such tactics as restricting the supply of a product or service, so that it can be sold at a higher price than would otherwise be the case; they may protect their positions by preventing others from entering the market through various means. Such practices are clearly undesirable, and in many countries there is anti-trust legislation to prevent them, but there is a real danger that prevention of monopoly behaviour or the promotion of competition becomes an end in itself, rather than protection of consumers' interests.

In the case of public transport, where several different operators provide services on the same route, it is normally in the interests of passengers for the operators to co-ordinate their timetables to provide a regular frequency, rather than for all their buses to run at irregular intervals in bunches, competing for passengers at every stop. Where this occurs there may be higher capacity in terms of seat-kilometres, but much of the capacity is wasted, and the effective service capacity is lower than it would be if a regular frequency were provided, even with fewer buses. Similarly, a co-ordinated service provided by two operators based at opposite ends of a route is more beneficial to all concerned than one where the two are forced to compete, running an irregular frequency. Therefore agreements between operators as to which serves particular areas or routes, to operate to co-ordinated timetables providing regular frequencies, to charge consistent fares, or to accept one another's return tickets, can all result in better services, often at lower cost to the user. Where several operators serve a common area, there is often genuine merit in their agreeing to divide it so that each part of the area is served exclusively by one operator, enabling the provision of a more cohesive network of services.

However, in some countries such co-operation is not permitted under anti-trust legislation. Following deregulation of bus services in the United Kingdom in 1985, many such agreements between bus operators ceased to be exempt from Restrictive Trade Practice legislation, and were discontinued; more recently, with a subsequent government's policy of integration of transport services, conflict has arisen between the role of the Office of Fair Trading to prevent "anti-competitive" practices, and the policy of the Department of Transport to improve "integration" of transport. UK competition law does not permit operators to agree on co-ordinated timetables; there are limited concessions permitting them to agree on charges for travelcards, but not to sell tickets which are valid on different operators' buses. Some operators have been prosecuted and penalised for co-operation such as agreements to withdraw from one another's territories or routes, while some co-ordination schemes which had operated for many years were withdrawn due to fear of prosecution.

It is true that transport services operated by monopolies may be inefficient, and introducing an element of competition often provides a spur to greater efficiency. However, the experience of the United Kingdom shows that predatory competition must be controlled, while certain supposedly anti-competitive practices such as co-operation between operators to provide a better service, should be permitted. There should be suitable provision within the anti-trust legislation for genuinely beneficial agreements, together with a mechanism for preventing abuse. Public transport has certain special characteristics which do not apply in other industries, and anti-trust legislation must take these differences into account; it should also be remembered that, even if there are monopolies within the industry, there is invariably competition between different public transport modes, as well as between public and private transport.

In conclusion, it is clear that public transport needs a degree of regulation, to secure the provision of an adequate service to reasonable standards, without dangerous competitive practices or monopoly exploitation; however, the regulatory system must be appropriate to the circumstances.

REGULATORY BODIES

A wide range of central and local government, statutory and non-governmental bodies have roles to play in the regulation and control of road passenger transport, even in a free-market situation. Central government ministries such as Transport and Communications, Works, Finance and others may be directly involved in various ways. Local authorities, including regional, district or city councils, are also usually involved, while there may be different authorities responsible, for example, for the planning and licensing of transport services and traffic management strategy. Some government bodies, such as those dealing with issues of health and safety, or competition, will have a regulatory role with regard to all industries, including transport. In some countries, regulation is devolved to a very local level: in Latvia, for example, licences for rural transport operators are issued by parish administrations. There are sometimes separate authorities at various levels responsible for buses and paratransit, taxis and non-motorised transport. The police may also have certain responsibilities, in addition to the enforcement of traffic regulations, such as the issuing of vehicle and drivers' licences.

Various non-governmental agencies may also be involved. Operators' associations often have some regulatory roles, including enforcement. State-owned bus operators are sometimes responsible for regulating the services of other operators within their territory. There may also be a role in the regulatory process for pressure groups, such as Friends of the Earth and Transport 2000 in the United Kingdom, and users' representatives such as consumers' associations or more specifically focussed commuters' associations; where the licensing procedure involves public consultation such groups should be given the opportunity to present their views in order to discourage them from resorting to less formal tactics.

Some regulations are most appropriately determined at national level, others locally. For example, vehicle construction and use regulations should be determined nationally, since vehicles may be operated in any part of the country, while if fares are regulated it is often more appropriate for rates to be determined locally, to take into account regional variations in spending power. Knowledge of local conditions is obviously valuable. Regulation at local level may, however, be particularly susceptible to politics: for example route licensing may be handled by local politicians who may be inclined to favour their own constituencies. Another potential problem of local regulation, particularly in developing countries, is a lack of understanding of the broad principles involved, and in practice some guidance from central government is often desirable. Central government should be responsible for national transport policy on matters such as the extent to which transport is regulated, the level of state ownership in the industry, and fiscal policy regarding transport. If the policy is one of regulation, the regulatory system must be designed to achieve the objectives of the overall policy; if it is one of deregulation, or minimal regulation, central and local government should provide the environment in which the transport industry can develop and operate efficiently.

Various aspects of transport regulation often come under different government departments. For example, vehicle roadworthiness certification and driver licensing may be the responsibility of the Ministry of Home Affairs or its equivalent, while the licensing of bus routes may be under the Ministry of Transport; the Ministry of Finance may have a role in fares regulation. The licensing aspects of regulation are usually administered by a central statutory licensing authority; this is often separate from the vehicle licensing department, although both are usually under the same government ministry. Except in smaller countries, responsibility for licensing is often divided amongst a number of regional subsidiary offices, which in some cases are virtually autonomous.

As a general principle, the number of authorities involved should be kept to a minimum, in order to minimise problems of liaison, and, even worse, conflicting policies, and it may be preferable for most, if not all, transport regulatory functions to be brought under the administration of a single Government institution.

A typical example of a transport regulatory authority is the Transport Authority in Jamaica, which is responsible for regulating and monitoring the island's public transport system, including the issue of all licences in respect of road vehicles, and ensuring that the requirements of the Public Passenger Vehicle (PPV) licensing system are met; it is directly responsible to the transport ministry. The principal road transport regulatory bodies in China are the Ministry of Communications, with national authority, the Provincial Communications Department in the Provinces and the Communications Bureau in the counties; at each level there is a Transport Management Division (TMD) which is concerned mainly with the implementation of laws and regulations. In Tanzania, the body responsible for regulation of urban passenger transport is the Central Transport Licensing Authority (CTLA); following legalisation of the paratransit operators in 1983, the state-owned bus operator, which had held an exclusive franchise to operate bus services in Dar es Salaam, was given responsibility for regulating passenger transport within the city, including planning and allocating routes to the paratransit operators, although this responsibility subsequently passed to the CTLA. Motorised road transport operation in Bangladesh is regulated by the Bangladesh Road Transport Authority (BRTA), under the Roads and Road Transport Division of the Ministry of Communications; bus and paratransit routes in Dhaka, the capital, are determined by a Road Transport Committee, chaired by the Police Commissioner, and including representatives of the BRTA, Dhaka City Council, Roads and Highways Department, bus owners and unions; at the local level, certain regulatory functions, including licensing of autorickshaws and non-motorised transport, are carried out by the municipalities and district transport committees.

Where some or all transport regulation is handled by local authorities, there can be problems with routes which cross boundaries from one area to another. In some countries, routes crossing boundaries are regulated by a national authority, while those operating wholly within a single area are dealt with locally. In Indonesia, the categories of bus routes are AKAP (inter-city services crossing provincial boundaries), controlled by a central government authority, AKDP (inter-city services wholly within one province), controlled by provincial authorities, angkot (city services) and angkudes (rural services), controlled by city and rural authorities respectively. In Sri Lanka, bus services are regulated at provincial level by Provincial Road Passenger Transport Authorities, while services crossing provincial boundaries are regulated separately by the National Transport Commission. This division of responsibility can lead to problems of co-ordination of services, and in some cases results in services being curtailed at boundaries. The approach adopted in the United Kingdom when bus services were regulated was for routes which crossed boundaries between Traffic Areas to be given "primary licences", usually issued in the Traffic Area where the operator had its head office, supplemented by "backing licences", issued by the Traffic Commissioners for the other areas served by the routes in question; this system worked well.

Local or regional transport authorities with overall responsibility for the regulation of all public transport in large urban areas are common in both developed and developing countries; sometimes they are also responsible for roads and the control of road traffic. In some cases, the authorities own the transport undertakings directly; these may enjoy monopoly status or may be supplemented by private sector operators. There are many different models, and such authorities tend to be continuously evolving. The Passenger Transport Authorities (PTAs) and Executives (PTEs), formed following the 1968 Transport Act in the United Kingdom, are a good example. The PTAs were local government bodies responsible for planning, co-ordinating and regulating all public transport within their areas; the PTEs were responsible for the provision of services, either directly through wholly-owned undertakings, or through third-party operators, which they regulated; they also set fares and service levels for local rail services. When the PTEs were formed, they acquired all municipally owned and some state-owned and private sector bus operators in their areas. The PTAs' responsibility for bus services was abolished in 1986, but they retain a statutory responsibility to secure provision of properly integrated and efficient public transport systems; with bus service deregulation and privatisation this became more difficult, but several projects have been initiated such as major infrastructure developments, including bus stations, busways, and LRT systems and travelcard schemes. There have recently been proposals for the PTEs to become rail franchising authorities for their areas.

Operators' associations and co-operatives, trade associations, and professional organisations are sometimes involved in the regulation of transport services, in addition to their more usual role of representing their members' interests. The road passenger transport industry in Ghana is self-regulated to a significant extent, with responsibility for regulation being shared between the government and a number of trade associations. Government intervention has been greatly reduced in recent years, and passenger fares are no longer controlled by legislation; nor is there any system of operator or route licensing. Government regulation is, in effect, limited to the licensing of new vehicles, roadworthiness inspections, and basic construction and use regulations. The principal Government agency responsible for enforcement of vehicle use and safety regulations is the Police Motor Transport Traffic Unit (MTTU), whose functions consist mainly of checking vehicle licences, roadworthiness inspection certificates, and compliance with vehicle weight and axle loading regulations. The principal operators' association, the Ghana Private Road Transport Union (GPRTU), and other associations to a lesser extent, are largely responsible for regulating transport operations through management of the bus terminals. In this respect the activities of the operators' associations represent a substitute for an operator licensing system. There is no formal quantity control, although the unions could impose this through restricting membership. Passenger fares are set by the GPRTU, whose members are expected to adhere to them: operators who do not do so are barred from using the union's terminal facilities. However, the GPRTU rates are generally applied, and the degree of competition within the transport industry is such that there is relatively little departure from these levels. The GPRTU has also been appointed by Government as an agent for the collection of income tax from road transport operators, and employs enforcement officers to check vehicles on the road for compliance; GPRTU officers have authority to arrest any person driving a commercial vehicle carelessly or while under the influence of drink or drugs.

In Bangladesh, route committees established by the operators' associations are involved in the allocation of route permits, and in controlling the number of buses operated on each route: where an excessive number of buses is licensed on a particular route, the route committee may exclude certain buses on certain days, normally on a rotating basis, to reduce the proportion of idle time for those buses which are operating.

The body responsible for setting fares and ensuring that they are correctly applied is usually, nominally at least, the transport licensing authority. However, because bus fares can be a highly political issue, the responsibility for setting fares is often assumed by senior members of government. In many countries, the Ministry of Finance or its equivalent is involved in this process, although the licensing authority is often required to advise on what would be a reasonable level of fares. In China, the Provincial Price Bureau is responsible for the administration of charges for commercial goods and services, including bus fares which are jointly regulated and implemented by the Price Bureau and Communications Departments at each level, while the City level Bureau and Department administer charges for ancillary services such as bus terminal facilities. In Indonesia, where there are "economy" and "non-economy" bus services, fares for economy-class inter-provincial (AKAP) services are regulated nationally by the Director General of Land Communications; intra-provincial long-distance (AKDP) economy fares are regulated by the Provincial Governor, and fares for local transport services (angkot and angkudes) are regulated by the district authorities. The regulations specify maximum fares for economy services, but operators are permitted to charge higher fares for non-economy services.

ADMINISTRATION

Transport regulation, as discussed earlier in this chapter, is typically based on a series of licences, covering operators, vehicles, personnel, and routes, and the principal tasks involved in the administration of the system are the processing of applications for new licences, ensuring that licences are renewed when required, and monitoring compliance with regulations and licence conditions. Licences may serve several purposes, but in principle they constitute a means of ensuring that specified standards are met, controlling service levels if required, and providing certain statistical data on transport operations. Suspension or revocation of a licence can be an effective sanction against an operator for unsatisfactory performance.

Where licences are required in respect of the operators themselves, these are normally intended to ensure that the holder is suitably qualified. A system is required to screen applicants, and, when a licence has been issued, to ensure that licence holders continue to meet the requirements. In some countries all businesses are required to be licensed: where this is the case it is important to distinguish between business licensing generally and licensing specific to road transport operators, and to avoid unnecessary duplication of administrative requirements.

Vehicle licensing is necessary to facilitate the enforcement of regulations relating to vehicles, and to control the number of vehicles operated where quantity regulation applies. Public transport vehicles usually require licences to permit them to be used as such, in addition to the general licensing requirements applicable to all road vehicles. A licence should be issued in respect of each vehicle, and should be conditional on compliance with relevant regulations, such as those regarding dimensions, weight, and engine emission standards; renewals are normally subject to a certificate of roadworthiness issued following an inspection of the vehicle.

A vehicle "licence" may, in fact, comprise several documents. There is usually one containing basic information, such as the vehicle registration number, manufacturer, type, capacity and licence expiry date, for display on the vehicle, to facilitate roadside inspection by police or others. In addition, there is usually a more comprehensive document, sometimes referred to as the registration document, which is retained by the owner or operator separate from the vehicle, containing additional information including the owner's name and address, the vehicle's date of manufacture, chassis number, unladen weight, and maximum permitted load in terms of seated plus standing passengers. Other information may be included but it is desirable that only essential details are recorded, to avoid unnecessary administrative work in updating the document in the event of a change in the particulars of the vehicle; there are no significant benefits, and several disadvantages, in requiring details such as engine or body number, or vehicle colour, to be specified on the licence, and these should therefore normally be omitted. Vehicle owners should be permitted to alter the colour of the vehicle, or change the engine or even the body without having to notify the licensing authorities, unless the change affects an item specified on the licence, such as the vehicle weight or carrying capacity. In some countries a photograph of the vehicle must be attached to the licence, but this should not normally be necessary.

A third document, sometimes referred to as a PSV licence, may be required to authorise use of the vehicle as a public service vehicle. Unless the regulations require that individual vehicles are restricted to particular routes, which is inappropriate in most cases, there should be no reference to routes on the vehicle licence, which should ideally permit the vehicle to be operated on any route for which a route licence has been issued. In addition, it is often desirable that a vehicle licensed to one operator may be used on a route licensed to another under a mutual agreement between the operators concerned. Duplication on the PSV licence of details included in the normal vehicle licence should be avoided as far as possible, in order to minimise administrative work; ideally, both licences should be combined, unless this will create problems of liaison between different government departments.

Every motor vehicle for use on public roads is normally identified by a unique registration number. Systems vary in their complexity: letters, numerals, or colours may be used to indicate, for example, the category of vehicle, the area in which the vehicle was registered or is used, and the year of manufacture or first registration. In Jamaica, different coloured plates are used, together with letter codes, to identify six different categories of vehicle, namely public passenger vehicles; vehicles for private use; vehicles for commercial use, such as goods vehicles; rental vehicles; government owned vehicles; and vehicles used by diplomats. This number of categories is unusual, but it is quite common for different coloured plates to be issued for private and commercial vehicles: in Indonesia, buses, trucks and taxis carry yellow plates, private vehicles black plates, and government vehicles red plates. There may be a requirement for some other means of indicating that a vehicle is licensed as a public service vehicle: in some countries, such as Kenya, every bus is required to carry a "PSV" identification plate adjacent to the rear number plate, which obviates the need for a separate registration number series for this category of vehicle. In some systems there is no distinction between vehicle categories.

A vehicle normally retains the same registration number throughout its life, although in some systems new numbers are issued periodically; in others, registration numbers are allocated to the vehicle owners, who will transfer them from one vehicle to another on replacement. This can make it difficult for the authority to keep track of vehicles when they change ownership, and unless records are accurately kept, it is possible for a vehicle to appear more than once in the system, with different registration numbers.

Licences for bus and taxi drivers, and conductors where applicable, are intended to ensure that they are suitably qualified for their positions; in the case of drivers, licences are usually conditional on passing a test on the type of vehicle to be driven. It is important that all licence requirements are adequately checked in respect of new applicants, and also at each licence renewal.

Route licensing may be very complex, particularly in respect of a quantity-regulated system in which licensing is a means of influencing the pattern of operations and levels of service. Administrative requirements are therefore often substantial; if transport licensing is localised, for example if it is administered by city authorities or area administrations, long distance routes may require separate licences from several authorities. Under a regulated system, operators normally select routes and apply for licences to run on them; routes might be planned by the regulatory authority, or by the operators themselves. An applicant for a new route licence or amendment to an existing licence may have to justify the application, and answer objections from other operators or interested parties at a public hearing; renewal of licences, even without amendment, may be subject to the same procedure. A route licence might incorporate attachments specifying, in addition to the route, the schedule to be followed and the fares to be charged.

Where fares are regulated, there is a need to consider and approve operators' applications for amendments, usually increases, in fares; this can be a cumbersome and politically charged procedure, and may involve senior government officials. In order to regulate fares properly the authority should always have current operating cost information; ideally it should construct an appropriate inflation index to apply to fare levels, with appropriate weighting given to each of the main cost elements, such as cost of fuel, spare parts, wages and salaries. It would be necessary to review the formula from time to time, since the weighting of inputs may change; for example, a change in working practices to reduce manpower, such as the introduction of one-man operation, would reduce the weighting to be applied to wage costs. Even where fares are not regulated, operators may be required to advise the authority of the fares they propose to charge. Under both quality and quantity regulation, the licensing authority may need to keep a record of the fares applicable to each route, to enable it to ensure that operators charge the advertised fares. Under a system of quality regulation only, route licensing provides a useful sanction against operators to ensure compliance with regulations, and can be a means of ensuring stability and continuity of operation.

Licence fees are sometimes nominal charges, representing an insignificant proportion of total operating costs; they may be intended to cover only the administrative costs involved in processing licences, but they may sometimes be used as a means of raising revenue. Typical of the fees and charges which transport operators must pay, in addition to taxes paid by all businesses, are licence fees in respect of the operator, vehicles, routes and bus crews; fuel tax; road tolls; terminal charges; testing or examination fees for vehicles and drivers; and registration number plate charges. In some countries the structure of charges is complex. For example, in some provinces of China, charges include a Road Maintenance Fee, payable to the Highway Administration Bureau, a Bus Fare Tax and a Transport Management Fee, both payable to the regulatory authorities; however, the charges are not always applied equally to all operators, and some loss-making enterprises are able to negotiate with the authorities for exemptions. Fees may be fixed, regardless of vehicle size or the level of operation, or may be based on parameters such as the number of seats, total passenger capacity, vehicle length, weight or engine capacity in the case of a vehicle licence, or revenue, the number of vehicles or kilometres operated in the case of a route licence. Such refinement is unusual and largely unnecessary, and increases the administrative workload. A simple system of charging is easier to administer, but a more complex system may be more equitable, and can enable the authorities to use the pricing mechanism to control the market; however, it presupposes that the scales of charges are accurately determined to meet the relevant objectives, and this is not always easy to achieve.

All licences should be issued for a specific duration, since refusal to renew a licence is a useful sanction, whether against an operator for poor performance, against a driver for a poor record of accidents or driving offences, in respect of a route which has not been operated in accordance with relevant regulations, or a vehicle which has been poorly maintained. The period of validity of all licences should be carefully considered. Too frequent renewals result in unnecessary administrative work; with too infrequent renewals some of the benefits of licensing are lost. Since personal attributes, particularly health, may change over a relatively short period, the period of licence validity for personnel should reflect this, and may vary according to the age of the licence holder. Similarly, the condition of a vehicle may deteriorate quickly. Typical periods are one year for a vehicle and three to five years for routes, crews and operators. Renewal dates should be staggered: all taxi licences in Jamaica expired on the same date each year, causing long delays in renewal due to the upsurge in the volume of work; staggering of dates could have spread the workload evenly through the year.

Some means is required of monitoring the performance of operators in order to ensure compliance with the conditions attached to their licences, and to facilitate the enforcement of regulations. One of the administrative functions of the licensing authority should therefore be to maintain a database incorporating details of all licensed operators, routes, vehicles and drivers; a mechanism for keeping this up-dated is essential. In addition to the recording of basic data there is a need to collect information on route and operator performance; if fares are regulated, data on passenger loadings, revenues and costs may be required also to facilitate consideration of fares applications. Operators can sometimes be relied upon to submit accurate returns of passenger carryings, which can be analysed to identify any surpluses or deficiencies. In practice, this is uncommon in developing countries, and reliance must be placed on roadside observation, which must be carefully organised to provide the data required accurately and in a form which can be readily analysed. The regulatory authority will therefore require a monitoring unit to carry out these tasks; the size of this unit will depend on the size of the operation to be monitored, the structure of the industry, the extent of regulation and the level of supervision and enforcement considered to be necessary.

Some administrative systems are unnecessarily bureaucratic and transport operators expend a considerable amount of time and energy in complying with their requirements. They often involve a large number of separate authorities, and with many separate licences and fees, and unnecessary duplication of roles amongst several authorities. This can result in delays in processing licence applications, and in some cases operators having purchased vehicles may have to wait several months before they can legally operate them. Regulations must be designed so that the administrative system can cope; as a general rule, the simpler the system, the easier it is to make it work efficiently. There may be a requirement for checks and double-checks to ensure that procedures are being followed, but this can result in duplication of procedures, excessive cost, and delay; a balance must be found, but ideally systems should be sufficiently robust to require a minimum of checking.

ENFORCEMENT

A primary requirement of any regulatory system is that it is enforceable, and this depends largely on ensuring that regulations are appropriate to the circumstances as well as on effective administrative and enforcement procedures. Poor enforcement of regulations generally, not only those applicable to transport, is a common problem in developing countries, because of lack of resources, unsatisfactory systems, or general inefficiency or inability on the part of the staff responsible. Ethical standards have an important influence, while standards of enforcement of law and order generally will be reflected in the effectiveness of enforcement of transport regulations. What can be achieved varies considerably between one country and another: in some countries there is general respect for the law, while in others it is almost universally disregarded. In the latter case, it is practical to enforce only the most basic regulations, and the transport regulatory system should be designed accordingly.

The ownership and structure of the transport industry is of particular relevance. Public sector operators are often easier to regulate than private sector operators, while the regulatory task is substantially greater in respect of an industry comprising a large number of individual owners than one dominated by larger units, whether these are companies or owners' co-operatives. The extent of the enforcement task is also influenced by the number of operating parameters which are subject to regulation, and where enforcement is difficult these should be kept to a minimum. Many regulatory systems are unnecessarily complex, and are difficult or impossible to enforce with the limited resources which are often available.

Responsibility for enforcement of transport regulations may lie with a number of bodies, including the police, regulatory authorities, central and local government departments such as the licensing authority, road transport department, environment department, and treasury, operators' associations, the operators themselves and even, to some extent, the passengers. The different enforcement agencies have different roles to play, and it is important that these are not confused. An operators' association, for example, can have a role in enforcing those regulations which are clearly in the interests of its members; but some regulations, which it might be in members' interests to infringe, should be enforced by a separate body. There is no reason why there should not be an element of self-regulation in the industry with operators' associations playing a key role. For example, the association might set standards for driver behaviour and vehicle condition, with its own sanctions against members for failure to comply, as in Ghana, where in some cases, operators who do not comply with the requisite standards are not permitted to use union-controlled terminal facilities. However, careful thought needs to go into any scheme of this kind to ensure fair play; compulsory membership of a union should not be a feature of the system.

ORGANDA, the Indonesian road transport operators' association, is in many respects regarded by government as its enforcement agency, and in the past this has led to problems of conflict of interest. Tourist operators' associations can play a useful role in preventing the unlawful exploitation of tourists by individuals and organisations taking advantage of visitors' ignorance by charging excessive rates for services. In some instances the operators themselves can play a role in enforcement. Several bus owners operating a service as a co-operative can be made jointly responsible for compliance with regulations, provided that the penalties are a sufficient deterrent; one owner who fails to comply may be dealt with by the others, for example by being temporarily or permanently excluded from the service. Similarly, if passengers as well as the operator are penalised for overloading a bus they are less likely to board buses which are already full.

Enforcement, and therefore compliance by transport operators, is often inconsistent: some regulations may be stringently enforced while others are neglected. The easiest regulations to enforce are usually those which can be dealt with as they occur: the most obvious are driving offences such as speeding or illegal parking, which once detected can usually be dealt with immediately by enforcement officers. Police forces equipped with radar speed measuring devices may therefore concentrate heavily on infringement of speed limits, while ignoring other offences such as non-compliance with vehicle roadworthiness requirements; others, without such equipment, may disregard the most flagrant speeding offences. Overloading of buses, which is easily detectable, may also be the subject of regular police attention; while such offences, if limits are exceeded substantially, are serious, operators are often penalised for only minor excesses. On the other hand buses operating off their licensed routes or outside their authorised areas of operation may be less easy to detect, and this type of offence may be committed blatantly.

Some transport operators are more conscientious than others in their observance of the rules; often public sector operators conform while private sector operators do not, thus giving the latter an unfair advantage. In some countries police tend to discriminate against certain classes of road user; bus or taxi drivers may be given more attention than car drivers, some of whom may be citizens of standing whom the police are reluctant to apprehend. Certain offences committed by car drivers, such as illegal parking, are frequently ignored, even though by increasing the level of congestion this can have a seriously detrimental effect on all traffic, including public transport services.

Enforcement of regulations regarding vehicle roadworthiness is often very weak, with many buses, as well as other vehicles of all types, being operated in an obviously dangerous condition. In Ghana, for example, all motor vehicles are required to be inspected every six months for roadworthiness; however, in the late 1980s evasion of inspection was estimated to be as high as 65% for trucks and 80% for motorcycles, although less significant for buses and cars. Compliance was higher in respect of vehicles operated in urban areas or on main inter-city routes, where the likelihood of detection was greater, while evasion was correspondingly higher in remote rural areas. As a result, standards of roadworthiness were extremely low.

Traffic regulations are poorly observed in many developing countries, and a common problem for most bus operators is driver discipline. Even if an operator wishes drivers to comply with regulations, the fact that they are unsupervised makes it difficult to ensure that they always do so. Much of the enforcement of driver discipline, in practice, is therefore left to the police and other authorities. A serious problem in many developing countries is the high incidence of road accidents which are attributable to excessive speed, particularly on inter-city and rural roads where traffic is relatively light. Accidents involving buses, in which large numbers of passengers are killed, are unfortunately a common occurrence, and while careless driving, poor mechanical condition of vehicles and road or weather conditions are often blamed, excessive speed is the primary cause in the majority of cases.

There are various measures for controlling vehicle speeds and enforcing speed limits, and these are used with varying degrees of success. Compulsory fitting to buses and trucks of road speed governors, which limit vehicle maximum speeds, has been successful in some countries but has failed in others due to poor enforcement. The fitting of tachographs, which provide a permanent record of the speed at which a vehicle is driven, and which can enable examiners to determine the speed at any point on a journey, is compulsory in many countries, but the resources of the enforcement agencies are often inadequate to make this an effective tool. The cost of fitting tachographs or speed governors is seen by many operators as unreasonable, while their maintenance is given low priority, and often such equipment is deliberately put out of action. Simple measures such as police checks at regular intervals along a long-distance route are inexpensive to implement and can be highly effective, provided that the penalties are adequate. If all buses must operate in accordance with timetables, drivers may be penalised for failing to comply. However, there are practical problems which would make this difficult to use as an enforcement tool, and in some cases bus operators produce timetables which actually require drivers to exceed speed limits if they are to run to time.

An effective form of timing check for busy routes uses a number of selected points at which all long-distance buses are checked, by police or transport regulatory authority officers. Each driver is given a ticket showing the time arriving at and departing from the point; there is space on the ticket for subsequent timing points. The officer at each point, having recorded the arrival time of the bus, should be able to determine from the departure time at the previous point whether the bus had been driven at an excessive speed between the two points. Some form of pre-prepared table may be used, indicating the earliest acceptable arrival time at the timing point against each departure time at the previous timing point; the driver or operator of any bus arriving earlier than the acceptable time would be penalised. Timing points should be selected so that there are no major stopping places between them where buses could lose time; popular refreshment stops make good timing points, provided that buses are checked both when they arrive and when they depart. Origin and destination should also be timing points. At busy points the checks could be mechanised. At less busy points, such as the outer terminals of routes with low frequencies, only occasional checks may be possible, but the possibility of a check should act as a deterrent.

Measures such as this can be implemented relatively easily and quickly, but it is desirable to give operators sufficient notice, in general terms, to enable them to adjust their operating patterns to one which is compliant with the regulations: for example a significant reduction in operating speeds, and hence in productivity, in response to more stringent enforcement may result in a requirement for additional vehicles and drivers.

Compliance is often particularly poor in respect of adherence to route and timetable requirements where these apply. Many operators, particularly the less formal ones, operate in accordance with their perception of demand at the time, with complete disregard for the conditions attached to their licences. Therefore the number of vehicles actually operating on a route at any given time may differ substantially from the number licensed; of those which are operating, it is common for several to be operating illegally, either because they are unlicensed, or are licensed for a different route.

Kuala Lumpur provides a typical example of how regulation of services may fail to work in practice. Minibuses were introduced to the city in 1975 to supplement conventional bus services, which were not expanding fast enough to keep pace with increasing demand. Each minibus operator was given a franchise entitling him to operate one bus on a specified route; most routes operated across the city centre. A flat fare was to be charged, regardless of the length of journey taken. After a while operators started to change the routes. Most cross-city routes were truncated to terminate in the city centre, so that passengers had to pay two fares instead of one for a cross-city journey, thus increasing operators' revenue, as well as the cost to the passenger; operators continuing to operate across the city centre charged two fares instead of one for cross-centre journeys.

Illegal taxi operation is a similar problem. In Kingston, for example, despite the fact that there are no restrictions on the number of licences issued, and therefore entry to the industry is not difficult for anybody with a car in roadworthy condition, there are reported to be large numbers of cars operating illegally as taxis without the requisite licences. Most operate on a full time basis, but some are private cars owned and driven by commuters who offer lifts on a fare-paying basis to others travelling along the same route; some are cars which have failed to pass the roadworthiness inspection and are therefore not eligible for taxi licences. Illegal operators often use the same livery, and have radios in their cars tuned to the same frequency, as one of the large taxi operators, enabling them to abstract passengers from them.

Another common offence by all types of transport operator is failure to charge authorised fares: this may take the form of undercutting to abstract traffic from other operators, or overcharging of passengers. This is particularly common amongst the smaller bus operators and paratransit operators, who may charge exorbitant fares when demand is high, but undercut other operators with very low fares at other times.

Vehicle and driver licence offences are very common in many developing countries. In some countries a significant proportion of drivers and vehicles do not hold valid licences or roadworthiness certificates, or carry licences which have been forged, stolen or obtained through corruption. If this type of offence cannot be controlled, withdrawal or suspension of a licence is ineffective as a sanction against drivers or operators.

Roadside checks by police or other enforcement agencies, are an essential element of enforcement of regulations. They are particularly effective for checking the validity of vehicle and crew licences, and in detecting infringements of regulations such as speeding, driving under the influence of drugs or alcohol, non-adherence to route or schedule or failure to complete journeys which passengers have paid for, charging incorrect fares, and illegal discrimination against certain classes of passenger such as those entitled to concessionary fares. Such checks can be carried out relatively quickly, without causing serious inconvenience to passengers; it is also useful to carry out more thorough checks on a small number of vehicles, such as mechanical inspections to verify a vehicle's roadworthiness. To facilitate roadside inspection, it may be necessary to require certain documents to be carried on buses. These may include relevant licensing documentation, and roadworthiness test certificate if applicable, timetable for the journey being operated, fare tables, and a waybill giving details of the journey, passengers carried, and revenue collected. It is also important to monitor driver discipline generally, in terms of "competitive" driving, deliberately obstructing other operators, and causing unnecessary traffic congestion.

Compliance with vehicle construction regulations as well as safety and maintenance standards may be verified by means of regular routine inspection of vehicles at designated testing centres. Spot checks of vehicles on the road, examination of maintenance facilities used by operators, and checking of maintenance records in addition to regular vehicle inspections are an essential task: often the vehicle inspectorate or traffic police have this responsibility but for public transport vehicles it may be appropriate for some inspections to be carried out by the licensing authority.

Examination of operators' records is a means of monitoring their performance and verification of compliance with operator licensing requirements, maintenance, safety and service standards and other regulations. Enforcement of drivers' hours regulations in particular requires accurate record keeping, which is difficult to ensure without great expense: records may take the form of tachograph charts, log sheets, time sheets, manual clock cards, pay records, or data recorded electronically from swipe cards. However, much of the information required for monitoring is not available through routine statistical returns and can be obtained only through inspections or surveys. This may require a large number of staff whose principal task is to observe operation on the road and report on operators' activities.

Service standards can be measured in terms of passenger waiting times, service punctuality and reliability, whether or not services are operated at all, and the degree of overloading. Safety standards can be monitored in various ways: accident statistics, if these are accurately recorded, are a valuable source of data, but usually need to be supplemented with more subjective data from observations of driving standards on the road.

Effective enforcement requires a system of realistic penalties for all infringements, and a major problem in many countries is that penalties are often inadequate to act as a deterrent. Financial penalties are widely used but are often ineffective and can be counter-productive: in the case of a vehicle being operated in unroadworthy condition, for example, a financial penalty will reduce the owner's ability to pay for repairs, and he is likely to be tempted to continue to operate his vehicle in defective condition. Fines for offences such as excessive speed, licence infringements or operation of unroadworthy vehicles are often regarded as normal operating expenses.

Financial penalties must be sufficiently severe to deter operators from offending, and must be regularly adjusted in line with inflation to prevent them from becoming ineffective over time; in many countries, where fines have not been increased and the rate of inflation is high, penalties have become wholly ineffective. One possibility is to set penalties as a multiple of the licence fee, which may be adjusted each year. It is difficult to make monetary penalties reasonable where there are wide variations in income levels, as is often the case in developing countries: a fine may be insignificant to a car driver with a high income, but unaffordable by a bus or taxi driver on a low income. Moreover, too wide a gap between an offenders' ability to pay and the fine may lead to corruption. There is therefore often a case for different levels of penalty for different classes of vehicle, to reflect offenders' ability to pay, although if the system becomes too complicated other problems may arise.

An effective non-financial sanction for most offences committed by a driver or transport operator is suspension or revocation of licences, provided that there are effective deterrents against unlicensed operation: quite often the penalties for this offence are meaningless. Where enforcement generally is poor, therefore, a good starting point may be to introduce measures to ensure that any driver or vehicle operating without a valid licence is effectively penalised; the initial penalty may be temporary impounding, followed by confiscation and perhaps destruction of the vehicle, with imprisonment as the ultimate penalty for persistent offending.

Sanctions against vehicle operators who fail to meet the required standards of roadworthiness should include prohibition of the use of defective vehicles until they have been rectified and inspected; when there is a surplus of vehicles in the system, as is often the case, this will cause no inconvenience to passengers, and will help to reduce surplus capacity.

Other non-financial penalties could include preventing a bus from proceeding until its scheduled time, if the driver has been found speeding or driving dangerously; if other safety regulations such as a requirement for a speed limiter or tachograph are not complied with, or in certain cases, if a vehicle is found to be unroadworthy, it could be prevented from moving altogether, requiring a relief vehicle to take the passengers on their way. These measures would cause great inconvenience to the passengers, but would give them an incentive to discourage operators from infringing regulations. Enforcement should always be reasonable: there should be a small margin of tolerance, so that drivers and operators are penalised only for genuinely serious offences or repeated minor offences; it is important that the system is fair, and is not abused by those enforcing it.

Whatever action is taken against offenders, it should be quick in order to be effective. Enforcement through the courts can be a slow process, and it is often appropriate for certain offences to be dealt with by other agencies such as the transport regulatory authority, subject to the right of appeal to the courts. Offenders should be taken to court only as a last resort, as in the event of defaulting on a fine.

Ability to enforce varies widely from one country to another, and depends on factors such as the general honesty of the population, the level of resources available to the enforcement agencies, the integrity of the police force, levels of corruption, the severity or otherwise of penalties, and general respect for the law. Poor liaison or lack of consistency between different enforcement agencies sometimes leads to problems. For example a bus operator may be penalised for infringements of parking regulations, with buses being moved on from stops, particularly in busy areas, before their scheduled departure times, resulting in an infringement of licence conditions instead. Sometimes the objectives of the regulations are seen to be different by the different authorities concerned; the transport regulatory authority will regard the regulations as a means of achieving a transport system with certain standards and meeting certain requirements, while the police may regard their enforcement as a means of raising revenue; their priorities may well therefore be different.

Corruption on the part of the enforcement agencies is common in some countries. It is sometimes argued that this is less of a problem, from the point of view of enforcement, than may at first appear: if an offender is penalised by having to bribe a policeman, this still represents a disincentive to offend provided that the "unofficial" penalty is severe enough. However, the motive of corrupt enforcement officers is not to prevent offences from being committed, but to increase their incomes; therefore the "unofficial" penalties will tend towards the maximum level at which the majority of offenders are prepared to risk having to pay, without actually being deterred from committing the offence. In any case, corruption in the long term will undermine the enforcement of regulations and cannot be condoned.

Regulation of informal bus or paratransit services is made particularly difficult by the fact that the authorities must usually deal with many individuals, who may be constantly breaking the law in various ways, instead of a few, normally reasonably responsible, large operators; the regulatory mechanism must therefore be very robust to be effective under these circumstances. In many countries, there is little or no formal regulation of paratransit operations; instead, this function is carried out by informal regulators, of dubious legality and in some cases with criminal connections, often in collusion with the police, many of whom are themselves directly involved in the paratransit business. The low salaries of most of the enforcement officers also renders them susceptible to corruption. Sometimes operators have sufficient collective power to enable them to defeat any attempt to enforce regulations. In several instances, paratransit operators have threatened to withdraw all services when the authorities have announced their intention to enforce regulations; the authorities, knowing that the resulting chaos will have political repercussions, have usually backed down.

The solution to many transport problems, and indeed many other problems facing developing countries, lies not in a change in regulations, but in their enforcement; effective enforcement is therefore crucial. In an ideal situation where there is total compliance, the authorities will be able to ensure provision of the appropriate transport system simply by introducing the appropriate legislation. If compliance is poor but can be improved through more effective enforcement, there may be a range of options; otherwise, there may be little prospect of any improvement, and indeed every likelihood that the situation will deteriorate further. In practice, total compliance is never achieved, and it is therefore necessary to establish what can realistically be expected: little will be achieved by retaining or introducing legislation which is unenforceable. Often the only practical solution, in addition to strengthening the capability of the enforcement agencies through improved organisation and training, is to reduce their workload through simplifying the regulatory system, focussing on the most essential areas and those where enforcement can be most effective.

Improvements in enforcement of regulations may be difficult, but can often be effected gradually. A suitable area for initial targeting is safety: appropriate standards can be set for vehicle mechanical condition, which can be enforced through inspection and appropriate penalties. When strengthening enforcement of safety regulations, or introducing new regulations, it is usually necessary to implement these measures progressively in order to avoid a situation where a substantial proportion of the national transport fleet is put off the road at the same time for failing to comply with required standards. Items to be examined should be arranged in order of priority, commencing with the most basic safety-related features such as tyres, braking systems, lights and steering; the inspection programme should be well publicised, giving dates by which operators would be expected to satisfy each requirement, so that all operators may take steps to ensure that their vehicles comply with requirements in accordance with the programme.

Vehicles should be examined not only at their regular statutory inspections but also at roadside spot checks or inspections carried out at operators' own premises. Operators would be encouraged to invest in new vehicles to replace those which are no longer economic to maintain in roadworthy condition, unless they decide to withdraw from the industry altogether, leaving it to the more professional operators who are better able to maintain vehicles to the required standard. Enforceability may improve over time: once compliance with existing regulations has reached a satisfactory level, it should be possible to achieve compliance with additional regulations, provided that these are introduced at a manageable rate.

FRANCHISING

Public transport services in many developed and developing countries are provided under various forms of franchise. A franchise or concession in this context is the granting to an appointed organisation of the right to operate a specified public transport service. Normally the right is exclusive, and the transport operator is required to comply with certain terms and conditions. Franchising enables central or local government to control the provision of services, while delegating the task of operating them to selected private sector operators, co-operatives, or consortia of operators. The benefits of competition, and the efficiency of private sector management, are combined with government control over the types of services operated, routes, service levels and standards. Competition between operators is largely at the bidding stage, when they are competing with one another for the award of a franchise; any competition within the market once the franchise has been awarded is limited largely to situations where, for example, several routes operated by different franchisees follow the same roads for part of their length.

The majority of franchising arrangements apply to urban bus services but there are several examples of franchises for rail services, long distance bus services, tourist and taxi operations. The franchising concept may also be applied to other components of a transport system such as terminal facilities. In many cases, franchising has replaced public ownership following privatisation of public sector transport undertakings, enabling the authority to retain a measure of control. It is becoming increasingly common in Europe, where it is generally recognised that the most successful public transport systems are operated under franchise arrangements. Outside Europe, there are numerous examples of franchised bus operations. Bus services in Hong Kong and Bangkok have been operated under franchises for many years; more recent examples include Dhaka and Lahore. Subsidiaries of United Transport Overseas operated urban bus services in several African countries between the 1950s and 1990s. A well known example of franchising of tourist transport services is the US tour operator Gray Line, which has franchisees in many developed and developing countries throughout the world.

There are several alternative franchising models. A franchise may give one operator the exclusive right to provide all bus services within a specified area, as was the case with the franchise held by Kenya Bus Services in Nairobi and Mombasa, and Harare United Omnibus Company in Harare, or it may apply to a sector of an urban area, as for example in Kingston, Jamaica, where there were five franchise zones, each allocated to a different operator. It may apply to individual bus routes, as in London. In some instances, as in case of long distance services in the Philippines, a separate franchise is issued in respect of each vehicle, permitting the operation of one bus on a specified route. It is even possible for a franchise to apply to a specific journey or journeys within a schedule on a route served by several different operators. A franchisee may be given a monopoly in an area, but with the condition that it operates a network of routes, including some which are unprofitable, which may be specified by the franchising authority. There may be separate franchises for different types of vehicle or service, such as minibuses, standard buses, and premium services, on the same route or within the same zone. The cost and complexity of administering the system will increase with the number of separate franchises, and ease of administration and enforcement must be a major consideration.

Enforcement of franchise exclusivity is obviously an important issue; in many cases in developing countries, however, this exclusivity has been breached by the uncontrolled incursion of paratransit operators due to poor enforcement of regulations.

In the case of a sector-based bus franchise system, each franchisee is responsible for all services within a particular sector. Ideally its depot should be located to serve the sector with minimum dead mileage. An advantage of a sector or area franchise is that the operator is able to identify transport needs within the area and, if the terms of the franchise permit, develop routes and schedules accordingly: unless the operator is responsible for a network rather than a set of unrelated routes there will be little incentive to be innovative in this respect. An area or sector franchise, if appropriately framed, may also ensure the operation of a number of unprofitable routes if this is considered to be necessary. A perceived disadvantage of a sector-based system is that some sectors may be more profitable than others, so that few operators are prepared to bid for the less attractive sectors. This is sometimes true, but in a densely populated urban area with relatively low car ownership as is typical in developing cities, the differences will not normally be great; the level of service on all routes can be adjusted to optimise operating margins, and provided fare levels are realistically set all routes should show a positive return. The idea sometimes advocated that routes can be put into groups or packages for franchising purposes so that each package has the same proportions of "good" and "bad" routes assumes a detailed and accurate knowledge of the characteristics of each route, that these characteristics will not change, and that the operators themselves are unable to influence the profitability of a route by their own actions. These assumptions are invariably unrealistic.

The most satisfactory geographical shape for each bus franchise sector to meet the requirements of commuters in most cities is likely to be a "wedge" shape with the central business district at its apex. However, except where all routes are strictly radial, and converge at a terminal or terminals in the central area, it is not usually possible to divide an urban area between operators into absolutely distinct areas, because this inhibits cross-city operation unless joint operation of bus services is permitted. There must usually be a central common zone served by all franchised operators. In Kingston, Jamaica, which has two major destinations for bus passengers (New Kingston and the Downtown area), there was a relatively large common area where the routes of all franchise holders overlapped. This was not a disadvantage: there was a certain amount of competition between operators for traffic which was wholly within the common area, and all passengers were able, by observation, to make general comparisons between the service standards provided by the different operators.

The sector boundaries must take into account the possible need for the linking of routes to provide cross-city connections and other links between major centres; there is likely to be a degree of overlapping of sectors as dictated by travel requirements. It is argued in Chapter 8 that it is normally preferable for urban bus routes to operate across the central area of a city rather than to terminate within it. Where a city is divided into different sectors for franchise purposes, such a routing arrangement could result in routes being operated by more than one franchisee. However, if the routes are linked on an overlapping basis, with all routes crossing it to terminals on the far side of the central common zone, the encroachment into other operators' sectors could be minimised. It is essential that the setting of sector boundaries does not inhibit the effective provision of services which meet the requirements of the travelling public, and there must be provision for routes which cross sector boundaries.

Where a route network is very complex it may be impractical to identify distinct sectors; in such cases it may be more appropriate to offer franchises on an individual route basis, although each operator may be permitted to hold several franchises. If franchises are based on individual routes, there may however be considerable dead mileage operated by buses between depots and distant route termini.

There are significant differences in the way in which a franchise may be structured financially. In many cases, particularly in developing countries, franchisees must operate services without subsidy, and are permitted to retain all profits earned. This is a satisfactory arrangement where, given an appropriate regulatory regime, there is sufficient demand for public transport to enable an efficient operator to earn an adequate return. Involvement by the franchising authority may be minimal, and the operator will have a commercial incentive to perform efficiently. There may be a charge for the franchise, but in most cases there are no charges other than those intended to cover the administrative costs incurred by the authority in awarding and managing franchises. If non-subsidised franchises are subject to financial bids, the danger must be avoided of awarding the franchise to the highest bidder regardless of the quality of the bid: it is important that the franchise is awarded to an operator with the resources and capability of providing services to the specified standards.

Where franchised services are more directly controlled by the authority so that the operators have less control over their nature and extent, the financial arrangements tend to be more complex, particularly if franchised services are subsidised, as in most developed countries. In broad terms, franchise agreements or contracts may be on either a "net cost" or "gross cost" basis. With a net cost contract, if the service is unprofitable, the operator retains all fare revenue, and the authority pays a subsidy to the operator, on a predetermined basis, to cover the shortfall between cost and revenue. On the other hand, if the service is profitable, the authority receives a proportion of the revenue, or all revenue above a predetermined level: this may contribute towards administrative costs, or be used to subsidise other services. With a gross cost contract, the authority reimburses the operator in full for the cost of providing the service; all revenue is passed to the franchising authority. If the service is profitable, the authority will receive a surplus; otherwise it must fund the shortfall. In each case, the basis on which costs are calculated and reimbursed must be written into the contract; in the case of a net cost contract, the basis on which revenue from profitable services is apportioned between the operator and the authority must also be written into the agreement.

A net cost contract may be structured to provide an incentive to the operator to minimise cost and maximise revenue. Gross cost contracts provide a guaranteed return so that there is less incentive, although the franchisee may be able to benefit from efficiency savings in operating costs: however, there is a danger that operators may be tempted to perform below standard to cut costs. There is no direct incentive for the operator to perform well, or to increase patronage through service quality, since any additional revenue due to quality improvement, or investment in new vehicles, will be passed on to the authority.

The terms of a franchise may vary considerably, but should be consistent with all relevant legislation and regulations, although there may be additional provisions. They should also be such that an operator is encouraged to maximise efficiency and maintain a certain standard of service for the duration of the franchise. The franchisee may be given a free hand to decide on the routes to be operated, frequencies and types of vehicle; at the other extreme, routes, fares and schedules, and vehicle types may be specified in detail by the franchising authority, as may operating practices, fare collection methods, bus liveries, or crew uniforms. The franchisee may be required to provide equipment or infrastructure such as bus stop signs, shelters or terminal facilities, or the franchising authority may undertake to provide these; the authority may also control functions such as publicity and ticketing, particularly where there are several separate franchises making up a single system. In some cases the franchisees own few of the assets. Vehicles may be provided by the franchising authority, or may be leased rather than owned by the operator, giving greater flexibility to vary service levels during duration of contract or franchise, and reducing the operator's risk when committing to a contract or franchise. For example, most rail rolling stock in the United Kingdom is not owned by the train operating franchisees, but by rolling stock leasing companies.

The franchising authority should specify which items should be included in franchise bids; in some cases bidders are authorised to include additional items, but this can lead to problems. For example, in the case of the first rail franchises to be negotiated in the United Kingdom, bidders were given considerable latitude in proposing how the franchises would operate, and what innovations or investments they would make. This made comparison of competing bids very difficult, and when the franchises became due for renewal, the requests for bids were much more specific.

A franchise generally has a defined duration, which should be sufficiently long to justify any necessary investment in vehicles or equipment. In the case of a bus franchise this is normally between five and ten years, although in exceptional cases much longer franchises have been granted: in the 1950s and 1960s, the British holding company United Transport Overseas negotiated franchises for thirty years for some of its African operations. For rail services, a term of between fifteen and twenty years is normally appropriate. Often there is provision for reviews during the term of the franchise. For example, in a fifteen year franchise, there may be reviews after four and nine years, with twelve months notice of termination if the outcome of the review is unsatisfactory.

There may be provision in the franchise agreement for an extension to be granted for a specified period. Some agreements provide for the franchise to be extended automatically if the service has been operated satisfactorily; this reduces the cost of the re-tendering process, and gives operators an incentive to perform well. Notification of renewal may be given in advance of the scheduled expiry date, to enable the operator to make appropriate investment decisions. For example, if the delivery lead time for new buses is twelve months, it is helpful if the operator knows at least twelve months in advance whether or not the franchise will be renewed, so that the process of fleet renewal is not interrupted. This requirement will not apply if buses are leased or provided by the franchising authority, or if there is provision for buses to be transferred between a franchisee and its successor.

The franchise agreement must itemise penalties for non-compliance with the specified requirements and standards. Penalties may range from permitting additional competition from other operators, a reduction in the franchise area or route length or in the length of the franchise, to termination of the franchise. Imposition of financial penalties for non-compliance with franchise terms may be counter-productive, however, since this may reduce the funds available for the operation of the business, and may lead to deterioration in the service. As a general principle, financial penalties are appropriate only in respect of infringements which give the operator a financial advantage. There also should be provision in the franchise agreement for renegotiating some of the franchise conditions, such as fare levels, service standards or vehicle specifications, during the term of the franchise.

Franchising enables the authority to determine what services are provided, and to control standards: this is particularly beneficial if the operators involved lack planning capability. It may assist in the implementation of broader transport policy. For example, introduction of congestion charging in London was facilitated by the fact that buses were operated under a franchising arrangement: the authorities were able to ensure that additional buses and routes were introduced prior to implementation. Where subsidies are provided, franchising is a useful means of ensuring that operators provide value for money, and gives better control over the use of funds. However, it is essential that the franchising authority has the requisite expertise to monitor operators' performance.

It is important to ensure that franchises are appropriately framed, and there should not be unduly onerous penalties for operators who fail to perform because their bids were unrealistic: the franchising authority should make every endeavour to ensure that bids are realistic before any awards are made. Problems arise if franchises are poorly framed. For example in the United Kingdom, compensation was paid to several rail franchisees for poor trading performance for reasons deemed to be outside their control, but which should have been foreseen; within the first five years of rail franchising, every single franchise had been renegotiated to some extent, highlighting the problems of the learning process, as well as reflecting the government's desire to hasten the privatisation process as a general election approached.

BUS QUALITY PARTNERSHIPS

A recent development in the United Kingdom has been the "bus quality partnership", an agreement between local authorities and transport operators to implement measures to improve the quality of transport services on particular routes or in particular areas. A quality partnership could form the basis of a franchise agreement and the concept is sometimes regarded as an alternative to regulation.

The development of quality partnerships was partly a consequence of changes in transport legislation. Urban bus services in most major British cities were operated by municipalities, which were also responsible for infrastructure and traffic management, but following deregulation of bus services under the 1985 Transport Act, most disposed of their transport undertakings to the private sector. In order to maintain co-ordination between provision of infrastructure and public transport services, some entered into agreements, of varying degrees of formality, which became known as quality partnerships. Current British government policy is to encourage quality partnerships, and some have received government funding. However, they are not a substitute for regulation, and in fact a degree of quantity regulation is required if the terms of an agreement are to be effectively enforced.

The transport operators involved in a quality partnership normally undertake to provide specified standards of service quality and frequency. This may involve investment in new or refurbished vehicles, usually to a higher specification than those previously used; they might be fitted with special equipment such as transponders for the activation of bus-priority traffic signal phasing, or as part of a real-time passenger information or automatic vehicle location system, or equipment for a guided bus system.

Commitments by the authorities may include bus priority and other traffic management measures and physical improvements to roads and other infrastructure, such as improved kerbs, passenger shelters, or busways. They might even include pedestrian facilities to provide "quality" door to door travel. Enforcement of traffic management measures is usually an essential part of a scheme. Fares and service frequencies need not be specified, but operators may agree to limit fare increases or provide services at agreed minimum frequencies. It is not always necessary for all operators on a route to be included in the agreement but if this can be achieved the benefits from the partnership are likely to be maximised.

Quality partnerships must be cost-effective for all parties involved. The benefits in terms of increased numbers of passengers should justify the investment by the bus operator, while spending by the authorities must be justifiable in terms of net benefit to the community. It may be appropriate for any additional revenue resulting from a partnership to be distributed between operator and authority partners in proportion to the investment made by each. The operators might bear some of the infrastructure cost, in which case they would require some exclusivity or recompense from other operators who did not contribute, but who benefit from the scheme; without such measures, the contributing operators would be at a disadvantage, and would be discouraged from further participation. As with a franchise agreement, the duration of a quality partnership agreement should be sufficient to allow time for a substantial part of the investment costs to be recovered, but should not be so long that standards may degenerate; a term of between five and ten years would normally be desirable, but it may be appropriate to provide for extensions under specified circumstances.

Certain features of quality partnership schemes, such as co-ordination between the services provided by different operators, or the inter-availability of multiple journey tickets on services provided by different operators, may contravene legislation designed to promote competition. The requirement in the United Kingdom for competitive tendering for bus journeys which are subsidised by the local authorities, and the policy of some authorities to accept the lowest tender, can also detract from the benefits: some services may be operated below the required standard as a result of being awarded to operators who are not involved in the partnership.

Some partnerships have been criticised for being biased in favour of one of the parties. For example, an authority may make a major commitment in terms of provision of costly infrastructure and other measures, while the transport operator makes little or none, other than investment which would have been undertaken without the agreement. Enforceability of partnerships is not always guaranteed, and failure by one party to comply with the terms of an agreement may have serious consequences for the other; sanctions against an operator or authority for non-compliance may be inadequate. The question of enforcement has been addressed to some extent through the concept of Statutory Quality Bus Partnerships, the terms of which are enforced by the Traffic Commissioners. However, not one such partnership had become effective in the United Kingdom by late 2004.

Nevertheless, quality partnerships are generally considered to have been successful in the United Kingdom, although in fact there are far fewer than had originally been anticipated. Experience has been varied, but there have been some substantial increases in the number of passengers carried: up to 40% has been claimed in some cases, with some passengers transferring from private transport, and existing bus passengers making more journeys.

The quality partnership concept may be relevant in some developing countries, where the structure of the transport industry is suitable, and standards of enforcement are adequate, perhaps in conjunction with the introduction of busways or premium bus services. Partnerships could include other public transport modes in addition to buses. The concept will not be appropriate in every case, however. Most private sector bus operators in developing countries are small and numerous: the more parties involved, the more difficult it will be to agree and enforce the terms of a partnership, unless an operators' association or equivalent organisation has the authority to act on behalf of all operators, and is able to ensure that all operators comply with the terms of an agreement. Competition from unregulated paratransit operators is likely to undermine a quality partnership scheme, unless it is possible to enforce the necessary regulations to prevent this; poor enforcement standards will, however, be a major obstacle in many cases. Inadequate local authority financial resources, and limited funding capability on the part of the operators, will be another problem: unless all parties are able to make the necessary financial commitments the partnership will be ineffective.

20

IMPROVING PUBLIC TRANSPORT SERVICES

Problems of inadequacy and inefficiency in public transport occur throughout the world, in both developed and developing countries, although there are substantial differences in degree. They tend to be most severe in developing countries where the demand for transport is increasing rapidly with population growth, and where operators are hampered by serious shortages of resources. The principal problems are manifested in inadequate and low quality services which give poor value for money, and low standards of safety and efficiency; urban traffic congestion, which contributes to atmospheric pollution, is partly a cause and partly an effect of poor public transport. The causes and effects of these problems, and alternative measures to deal with them, have been discussed in detail in the earlier chapters of this book.

Although the problems are becoming progressively worse in many countries, most could be addressed effectively and at relatively little financial cost. Some of the remedial measures may be taken by government, and some by the operators themselves, although intervention by government will often be necessary to motivate operators to take the appropriate action. Few of the measures require substantial government expenditure: most investment can be made by the private sector. Circumstances vary widely, but it should always be possible to take steps to encourage the development of the type of public transport system which is most appropriate in any particular case. Direct government intervention should be kept to a minimum; an essential requirement, however, is government commitment to implementing and enforcing the measures necessary to create an operating environment which is conducive to the provision of a good public transport system, within the constraints of underlying cultural, economic, demographic, geographic and climatic factors.

There is a broad range of possible scenarios, from a highly organised formal public transport system to a completely unregulated informal paratransit system. It is particularly important to encourage the development of a transport industry in which the structure and ownership, the types and sizes of vehicles operated, types of service, operating systems, and regulatory framework, are appropriate in the prevailing circumstances. Fundamental requirements are that services should be safe, reliable and predictable, with sufficient capacity to meet demand at all times. The industry must also be capable of adapting to changing circumstances, particularly in developing countries where the pace of change may be very rapid indeed. However, what can be achieved, and what standards are acceptable, will vary from place to place, and over time. What may be best practice in one situation may be unworkable in another; what is acceptable in one country may be unacceptable in another, while what was acceptable a generation ago may be unacceptable now, and it is to be hoped that future generations will aspire to even higher standards.

THE MAIN PROBLEMS: CAUSES, EFFECTS AND REMEDIAL MEASURES

The causes of many of the problems of public transport in developing countries can be influenced, at least to some extent, by government or by the transport operators themselves, although the ease with which they may be changed, and the time scale over which this may be possible, will vary considerably. These include the provision of infrastructure, allocation of funds, availability of skills, enforcement of laws and regulations, the institutional and regulatory framework, and industry structure. Some problems are due to factors which cannot be changed, such as climate or geography; other causes, such as economic factors, may be partially within the control of government, but are outside the control of individual transport operators. Nevertheless, measures can often be taken to minimise their effects: for example, climatic factors should be taken into account in the specification of vehicles, and standards of service must be tailored to economic constraints.

Inadequate infrastructure, in terms of the design, capacity and condition of the road system, and facilities such as workshops, depots and bus stations, is a serious problem for many transport operators. Bus services in many urban areas suffer from severe traffic congestion due to inadequate road system capacity, compounded by poor traffic management and discipline; this affects service capacity and reliability, and results in increased operating costs. Long-distance and rural bus services may be affected by poorly constructed or badly maintained roads, resulting in delays to services, increased wear and tear to vehicles, and increased costs. Inadequate depot and workshop facilities contribute to poor maintenance standards, and in many cases a total lack of such facilities necessitates on-street garaging which compounds traffic congestion and environmental problems. Many bus stations and terminals are too small, poorly laid out, inappropriately located, and inefficiently managed, detracting from overall service quality, and again resulting in unnecessarily high operating costs.

The provision of new infrastructure, or the rehabilitation of existing infrastructure, can result in considerable improvement to transport services; for example road improvements are usually followed by an improvement in public transport services using them, and well designed and located bus stations can bring about substantial improvements in convenience to passengers and enable services to be more effectively controlled. Compared with other measures, development of transport infrastructure is likely to be costly, although much investment will have relatively long-term benefits. Infrastructure projects must be sustainable, and it is essential that allowance is made for subsequent maintenance; this may include the provision of maintenance equipment and training in its use, and the establishment of appropriate and adequately funded maintenance programmes. Where operators are charged for the use of infrastructure, the charges should be such that public transport is not at a disadvantage when compared with private transport.

In most situations, the only viable public transport mode is road transport. Rail-based systems may be cost-effective where traffic volumes on a route corridor are very high for most of the day, but in practice this occurs only rarely except in very large cities. There are few existing rail systems which can operate without subsidy of any kind, whereas in a suitable operating environment bus-based systems are capable of carrying high volumes of traffic on a fully commercial basis. Exclusive bus lanes, and busways where traffic volumes are very high, are usually more economically justifiable alternatives to rail lines, and offer much greater operational flexibility. However, where rail or street tramway systems already exist, it is often economic to retain them, particularly in large cities, even if this requires expenditure on rehabilitation of track and rolling stock.

As a more cost-effective alternative to heavy investment in urban road infrastructure, traffic control and demand management schemes or bus priority measures can often bring about considerable improvement, although the full potential of traffic management, including restraint on traffic volumes through such measures as road user charging, has not been achieved anywhere. Major schemes are often politically difficult to introduce and enforce, but together with appropriate public transport provision, can potentially resolve many urban traffic problems. As the need for sustainable transport becomes more widely accepted, such measures must become more commonplace.

Many public transport vehicle fleets, particularly in urban areas, are inadequate or inappropriate in terms of their composition, capacity and condition. Externally initiated fleet development projects may therefore be appropriate in certain circumstances, particularly where there is inadequate system capacity, or existing vehicles are unsuitable to meet requirements. These may involve the provision of new fleets of buses, or the rehabilitation of existing fleets, and may require considerable expenditure, although it is often possible for most of this to be borne by the private sector, perhaps with some assistance from government or from foreign aid donors. Governments may make available, to suitable transport operators, loans on favourable terms for the purchase of specific vehicles or equipment; importation of the vehicles may be arranged by the government or aid donors, or by approved vehicle dealers, possibly in collaboration with the funding agencies. It is essential that the vehicles meet local requirements, and it will normally be necessary for detailed specifications to be provided. As with infrastructure projects, it is important that any such project is sustainable, and caters for the subsequent maintenance of the fleet; this may include the provision of workshop facilities and equipment, training of maintenance staff, and the establishment of appropriate maintenance systems, including parts purchasing and control.

Service levels and quality are constrained by the availability of funds, which in turn is determined principally by users' ability to pay, and the level of demand. Although incomes are low in most developing countries, demand for public transport is generally substantially higher than in developed countries due to low car ownership; nevertheless total revenue from passengers' fares is often sufficient to fund only very basic services. Fare levels are sometimes restricted by government regulation, often compounded by inefficient operation, poor revenue integrity and poor financial control. Other sources of revenue may be available, such as advertising on vehicles, but these too are limited by purchasing power within the market generally, and do not normally represent a significant proportion of total revenue. Therefore the majority of services in developing countries are provided using vehicles of basic design, often in poor condition, and with inadequate capacity at peak periods; on the other hand services used by more affluent passengers, such as premium quality urban or long distance services, may be to very high standards. In summary, any public transport service must be designed to be viable within prevailing financial constraints, and this normally means that relatively low standards must be accepted by the majority of passengers. Nevertheless, in most cases, with more efficient management and control, including effective revenue control procedures, existing standards are capable of considerable improvement.

Subsidy of public transport is another means of securing a more effective service, although limited government financial resources often rule this out as an option in most developing countries. In certain circumstances, however, subsidies can be cost-effective, and should be given serious consideration: for example, there may be overall financial savings if subsidising urban public transport reduces the need for road expenditure. Pump-priming subsidies may be justified to fund the introduction of new services which will become self-financing once they have become established: this often applies in the case of bus services serving new residential or commercial developments, and it may be possible for such subsidies to be funded through levies imposed on developers.

Also significant are shortages of skills at all levels, due largely to poor educational standards and limited training facilities; the situation is improving in many developing countries but in some it is deteriorating, particularly where populations are growing at a high rate and expansion of the education system cannot keep pace. Even basic driving and mechanical skills are often lacking, leading to poor safety standards, mistreatment of vehicles and poor maintenance, and hence reduced reliability and increased operating costs. At more senior levels, lack of management skills, in general terms and specifically with regard to transport management, is often a serious problem, leading to inefficient operating practices and hence poor service standards, poor utilisation of resources and excessive costs. Poor maintenance standards are partly a result of poor management, as well as limited technical skills, adversely affecting safety, reliability and costs. Poor standards of housekeeping, another symptom of ineffective management, adversely affect virtually all aspects of a transport operation. All public transport operators, including operators' associations and co-operatives, should have suitably qualified management, and staff at lower levels such as drivers and mechanics should have the necessary technical skills; the same applies to the regulatory authorities.

Training is therefore an essential ingredient of any programme to improve public transport services, not only for people employed at all levels in the transport industry, but also for central and local government officers involved in the planning or regulation of transport services, and advisers and consultants in transport. This normally requires improved education generally, but in particular the provision of specialised management and technical training facilities, which should be readily available to all concerned. In addition to appropriate training programmes, it is desirable that relevant personnel should be given the opportunity to gain practical experience of transport operations in other developing and developed countries, through temporary employment with transport organisations or as members of consultancy or advisory teams engaged in specific projects.

The structure of the transport industry is an important determinant of the nature of the services provided. A formal transport industry makes possible the provision of a comprehensive network of scheduled bus services; if the schedules are effective, and properly in tune with demand, the standard of service and resource utilisation should be reasonably good. Services provided by an industry dominated by informal operators, on the other hand, will be much less organised; the route network will be more basic, standards are likely to be lower, and capacity less effectively utilised. What is an appropriate structure will depend on circumstances, but in many cases there is potential for improvement through a change in structure, usually from a less formal to a more formal one. Much depends on the ability to enforce the necessary regulations.

The extent to which regulation of public transport services is necessary varies according to circumstances, and is the subject of considerable debate. Regulations governing transport operations are often inappropriate, and the demise of several large transport undertakings has been due to misguided government intervention, such as regulations which keep bus fares artificially low; also common are regulations imposing unreasonable constraints on vehicle types, or restricting the types of services which may be operated, and territorial restrictions which prevent the operation of through services, resulting in poor vehicle utilisation and inconvenience to passengers. Regulations which were appropriate at the time when they were drawn up have often been rendered obsolete by changes in circumstances, so that they inhibit the development of public transport services in line with changing requirements. A review of the regulatory system should be carried out on a regular basis: approximately every ten years will probably be appropriate in most countries; amendments should be made as appropriate, taking all relevant factors into account, but in particular the objective that the resulting regulatory system will be effective in securing a public transport system which satisfactorily meets the requirements of the community as a whole.

Quality regulation is necessary to establish and maintain basic standards; as a minimum it should ensure that transport services are operated safely and with minimal adverse environmental impact; it can also influence the industry structure, vehicle types and sizes, and operating systems. Maintenance has a significant effect on reliability, safety and cost, and appropriate standards should be set and monitored; annual vehicle inspections can play an important part, but it is also useful to stipulate standards for keeping maintenance records, so that these may be checked from time to time.

The justification for quantity regulation, which controls route networks and the level of service provided, is less clear. It is the policy of some governments to place heavy reliance on market forces rather than regulation to bring about a suitable transport system. It is true that the transport operators themselves can do a great deal in this respect; by improving the services they provide, they benefit not only themselves but also the public. However, their effectiveness and profitability will be limited by their knowledge of the market in which they are operating, as well as their general management and entrepreneurial skills. Although in theory market forces will eventually result in the optimum service, in practice this will not happen since the circumstances and requirements are constantly changing as countries develop and cities grow. Some quantity regulation is therefore usually required, but it is essential that this is appropriate to the circumstances, and is properly administered and enforced.

Regulations controlling competition and fare levels can also create problems if inappropriately applied. Anti-trust legislation, designed to encourage competition, can be detrimental to public transport services where it prevents operators from co-ordinating their services when this is in the public interest. Fare regulation, which determines the fares charged, must also be carefully administered if it is not to cause harm by starving operators of funds.

The institutional frameworks within which transport systems must operate are often unnecessarily complicated, involving several different agencies with overlapping responsibilities, at different levels of government. At best, such a situation causes a lack of co-ordination and conflicting measures, and time wasted in liaison between the various agencies; sometimes there is open rivalry between them, which can lead to one undermining the work of another, or deliberate duplication of effort with competing schemes or projects. In many cases transport regulatory institutions lack resources, in terms not only of funds but also of adequate numbers of skilled, trained and experienced personnel, and are unable to cope with the continually increasing problems of administering the public transport system as cities grow. Where the planning, administrative and enforcement capabilities of the authorities are weak, the transport system must be such that it can function with a minimum of intervention, and should be self-regulating as far as possible: it will therefore of necessity be a relatively unsophisticated service, although this will usually be preferable to a system which is badly regulated.

Some of these problems may be resolved through institutional reform. The number of agencies involved in the provision and regulation of transport services should be kept to a minimum. This will minimise the scope for bureaucratic delays, unnecessary duplication of effort, and inconsistent policies. A secondary advantage is that fewer personnel will be required, and the likelihood of recruiting sufficient qualified and competent staff will therefore be increased.

A major contributor to the problems of public transport in developing countries is poor enforcement of law and order generally, and of transport regulations in particular, leading to a lack of discipline on the part of operating staff, passengers and other road users, low safety standards, illegal competition and non-compliance with licence conditions. Safety standards, which are particularly important, are determined to a large extent by the effectiveness of enforcement of traffic regulations, construction and use regulations, and standards of maintenance and driving. Many transport systems would be able to operate far more effectively if only existing regulations could be effectively enforced, while the scope for improvement in transport provision through legislative change is seriously limited by poor enforcement. Therefore one of the first measures which must be taken in introducing improvements to a transport system is to improve enforcement of all regulations: this usually applies not only to transport regulations, but to law and order in the wider sense. Where standards of enforcement and compliance are generally poor, it may only be possible to rectify this by stages, commencing with those measures which are easiest to enforce, and preferably those which will also have a significant impact. The most practical first step in many cases will be to introduce effective sanctions against operating without valid driver or vehicle licences, and then to use revocation or suspension of licences as a penalty for other offences.

In many countries this is such a serious issue that there is little point in attempting to tackle transport problems unless enforcement can be dealt with first. Institutional strengthening, training and appropriate incentives, and in particular measures to deal with corruption, are often prerequisites for any improvement in transport, and in many other areas also, but tend to receive insufficient attention. There may be very broad implications: for example a common reason for corruption is poor conditions of employment within the enforcement agencies, and indeed in the entire public sector. It is no exaggeration that in many countries radical public sector reform is an essential prerequisite to implementation of improvements in a number of fields.

Finally, political instability is a problem in several developing countries. The greater the degree of instability, the less attractive is investment in any industry; public transport is particularly vulnerable, and in an unstable situation, only informal transport operations tend to be successful. Transport is a political issue in many countries, and frequent changes in government, and consequent changes in transport policy, cause disruption in the transport industry which can seriously impair its performance and retard its development. When much transport investment is of longer duration than the life of a government, this may discourage investment within the industry. However, it may be argued that political instability is largely a result of people's dissatisfaction with the way in which their country is run. Improved services in all areas, including public transport, can play a major role in improving the standing of a government, and therefore its stability.

The problems involved in the provision of a public transport service are many and complex, as are the means of dealing with them. However, the most critical requirements are simple and basic, and these must be met if a system is to function effectively, to develop in line with demand, and to be sustainable in the long term. These are:

- Route planning
- Vehicle maintenance
- Vehicle utilisation
- Revenue control

It is self-evident that the routes operated should be designed to satisfy as far as possible the requirements of the users. In broad terms, a network of services is required which enables all users to make affordable journeys between any two points with relative ease. This is often not the case, however, for various reasons, such as failure to respond to changes in travel requirements as cities grow, or inappropriate legislative constraints, but should be achievable relatively easily through effective planning based on data derived from analysis of existing operating statistics and appropriate surveys. There should also be effective procedures to monitor changes in travel requirements, and to ensure that changes to the route system are implemented as required.

Good standards of maintenance are crucial, for maximum vehicle availability and reliability, minimum cost, and safety, and to prolong vehicle life: many transport operations have failed due to inadequate maintenance. Appropriate preventive maintenance procedures and suitable workshop facilities are therefore an essential requirement for a successful transport operation.

Public transport vehicles are expensive, and their revenue earning potential should therefore be maximised. This can be achieved through maximising the proportion of time each vehicle spends in revenue-earning service, and minimising idle time. In many developing countries vehicles are very inefficiently utilised, with a high proportion of time spent idle at terminals. This is often due to inefficient operating systems, such as the practice of waiting for a full load before departing, or to excessive numbers of vehicles on some routes. Vehicle utilisation can be improved through more efficient scheduling systems, but in many cases external intervention is required in order to make better use of resources, and in extreme cases to eliminate excess capacity in the system.

For sustainability the total cost of providing a service must be fully covered by revenue; this requires an adequate level of fares, and also that all revenue due to the vehicle owner or operator is duly received. Poor revenue integrity has caused the demise of many large bus operators, and a robust revenue control system is therefore essential.

ADAPTING TO CHANGING CIRCUMSTANCES

By definition, constant change is a characteristic of a developing country, and it is necessary for the transport industry to be able to adapt accordingly, in terms of its structure, types of vehicles used and operating practices. A medium sized town may be adequately served by an informal public transport system dominated by individual paratransit operators, but as it grows in size this system may no be longer appropriate; a change to a more formal system, comprising larger units operating full-sized conventional buses on a regular scheduled basis, may be required. Such a transition may not occur naturally, at least in the short to medium term, and will probably require government intervention; the most suitable strategy will depend on local circumstances.

For transition from a system dominated by paratransit operators to a more formalised system, probably using larger vehicles on at least some routes, it will be necessary to reduce, or phase out completely, the fleet of small vehicles currently operating. There may be several alternative strategies, but first it will be necessary to establish whether the existing type of operator will continue to have a role, albeit probably a smaller, complementary one, within the new system, and if so, the extent of this role. Having estimated the eventual number of existing vehicles which will continue to be required, it will be possible to determine a practical fleet reduction programme. Alternatives to be considered would include a ban on paratransit vehicles in certain areas or on certain routes, and progressively extending the area of the ban; a ban on the licensing of new paratransit vehicles; or a ban on replacement of existing ones, so that they would gradually disappear from the scene.

An immediate outright prohibition of paratransit vehicles may be effective in certain circumstances, but normally would not be acceptable; the livelihood of hundreds or thousands of people is involved, and in any case it is not practical to introduce large fleets of vehicles other than on a gradual basis, and a phased transition programme is normally necessary. It may be possible to introduce an effective route or area licensing system, then to identify bus and paratransit routes, and gradually withdraw paratransit licences as conventional buses are introduced. If the rate at which the existing vehicles become due for replacement is compatible with the rate at which the larger vehicles are to be put into service, the transition will be relatively straightforward in terms of the vehicle fleet, although the question of how the displaced owners are to be dealt with must be resolved. If the existing vehicles need to be withdrawn at a faster rate, it may be possible for them to be sold for use elsewhere. Enforcement of all relevant regulations and legislation is essential; otherwise the transition is unlikely to take place.

Paratransit operators may be encouraged, through changes in the operating and regulatory environment, to combine into more formalised groups, and to pool their resources to invest fewer, but larger, vehicles to operate a conventional bus service more in line with the requirements of the city. They might delegate the management of their vehicles to a co-operative, or form larger operating units through merging or by acquisition. The government might assist, for example through the provision of soft loans to purchase vehicles, or training in operating procedures where appropriate. Alternatively, existing owners might become shareholders in a limited liability company by exchanging their vehicles for shares to the market value of their vehicles. Owners could be given the choice of becoming employees of the new company, or investors taking no active part in its operations, but in either case would receive a share of the company's profit in the form of a dividend proportionate to the value of their shares. Even when vehicles are sold or scrapped, shareholdings would remain intact and the former owners would continue to receive dividends. It should also be possible to encourage the development of larger operating units by making it attractive for individuals or organisations to invest substantial sums in fleets of buses, either through buying out existing owners, investing in new buses, or both. This would require long term security in terms of revenue and other conditions; in other words a stable regulatory system and a fares policy which would enable an adequate return to be earned on the investment.

With a conducive operating environment, and appropriate regulations properly enforced, an industry structure will tend to emerge to suit the requirements of each individual case. In the larger towns and cities the outcome is likely to be an industry comprising a number of medium sized operators. Large, inefficient operators and numerous individual operators will gradually be replaced by fleet operators of varying degrees of efficiency; the more successful of the smaller operators will tend to grow until they reach the optimal size, and the less efficient ones will contract, die out or be absorbed by others. Where appropriate, different types of service will emerge to cater for different sectors of the market, providing a range of quality levels at commensurate fares; these different types of service may be provided by a single operator, or there may be several operators, each providing a different standard of service. Whatever changes are required, the future of the existing owners and their vehicles must be taken into account, and whatever steps are recommended must be acceptable to the owners themselves, as well as to the authorities and the travelling public. Otherwise, disgruntled paratransit vehicle owners are likely to take action to sabotage the introduction and operation of the new bus services in order to protect their livelihoods. Owners should not suffer any undue financial loss as a result of the changes, but neither should the authorities incur unnecessary costs, such as substantial compensation awards.

Such changes will be strongly influenced by cultural characteristics, which must always be taken into consideration: for example the concept of holding shares in an organisation rather than owning physical assets is alien to many small entrepreneurs, particularly in developing countries, and a change in attitudes cannot easily be forced.

In many developing countries there are state-owned public transport undertakings which are in very run-down condition, both physically and financially, typically with only a small proportion of vehicles available for service. However, these organisations often have valuable assets in terms of depot, workshop and station facilities, as well as transport management expertise. These resources are usually worth preserving or restoring as the basis of a formal transport operator which in the right circumstances can play a much greater role in the provision of services. Transfer to the private sector is often the most practical option but this must be implemented carefully in order not to destroy the good features of the system, while avoiding burdening the new owner with inefficient practices. There are various commercialisation and privatisation models, and the most appropriate must be selected in order to realise these objectives.

FOREIGN AID AND TECHNICAL ASSISTANCE

As has been propounded several times in this book, it is unlikely that a satisfactory public transport system will develop without some form of intervention. As circumstances change, an established system may be slow to adapt without external influence, particularly where this requires major changes in operating practices or in the structure of the industry; in the meantime travellers must accept an inferior service. If it is accepted that intervention is necessary, it is important that this achieves the desired results. In particular, it is necessary to identify the most appropriate industry structure, operating systems, route network, vehicle types and institutional framework, while the ability to implement is crucial. Considerable skill, specialist knowledge and experience are required, and these must often be imported in the form of technical assistance from foreign countries; many transport projects in developing countries have been facilitated in this way.

Public transport studies or projects aimed at improving services while involving minimum expenditure on infrastructure can be highly cost-effective if their recommendations are properly implemented. However, not all aid projects have been successful in bringing about the most appropriate transport system, and many have incurred unnecessarily high levels of expenditure. Prestige often takes precedence over necessity, and instead of relatively inexpensive but less prestigious schemes such as bus priority measures, both donors and recipients frequently demand expensive and inappropriate, but politically conspicuous projects such as major road construction schemes or metro systems. These often benefit only a small percentage of travellers, while consuming funds which could have been used for more widely beneficial transport projects; funds allocated to bus services are likely to be more equitably spent since a much greater number of public transport users will benefit. Otherwise expenditure could have been allocated to other essential services such as policing, health or education.

Some projects reflect what donors or recipients believe is required on the basis of inadequate information, or may be biased to boost the donor country's exports of equipment such as vehicles or road building machinery. Prioritisation of projects is also often influenced by corrupt officials seeking financial gain. Projects involving the award of costly construction contracts are particularly attractive in this respect, while those which yield little potential gain to such individuals, such as public transport projects with minimal investment, may be rejected unless the officials concerned are bribed to approve them; even where studies are carried out or plans developed, the recommendations are often not implemented. In many countries where corruption is rife, aid projects funded by foreign agencies are regarded primarily as a source of income for corrupt government officials, and any benefit to the country is purely incidental.

Several donors may be involved in providing aid to the transport sector, with different, sometimes conflicting, objectives, interests and policies; projects are not always co-ordinated, leading to fragmentation and inconsistency. The need for a sector wide approach, whereby all aid to a particular sector is co-ordinated by the donors and recipients, is becoming more widely recognised, however.

When aid is provided for public transport it is important that projects are sustainable. There have been many projects involving the establishment of transport undertakings, including the provision of vehicles, or the rehabilitation of existing fleets, as well as major infrastructure projects, which have failed due to poor management or lack of maintenance. A common reason is that management has been given inadequate support and training, and sometimes because a restrictive regulatory framework has resulted in failure to generate sufficient revenue to sustain the operation. In some cases, the process has been repeated some years later, even where the original project included the provision of maintenance workshops and equipment. This is particularly common in the case of road construction projects, and is very wasteful of resources; a project should not be embarked upon unless its sustainability can be guaranteed.

A comprehensive technical assistance programme aimed at improving public transport services should include the following components:

- Assessment of operating environment
- Assessment of users' requirements
- Evaluation of existing services
- Determination of appropriate industry structure
- Determination of appropriate operating systems
- Determination of appropriate route network
- Determination of appropriate vehicle types and numbers
- Determination of infrastructure requirements
- Determination of appropriate regulatory and institutional framework
- Economic and financial appraisal
- Development of short-term and long-term strategies
- Training
- Implementation

It would require expertise in the following specialist areas:

- Transport planning
- Automotive engineering and maintenance
- Operations management
- Traffic engineering
- Transport legislation
- Transport economics

Selection of suitably qualified and experienced advisers and consultants is essential; many projects have been unsuccessful, and inappropriate advice has been given, because of the appointment of unsuitable personnel. Public transport planning, operation and regulation are complex and specialist subjects, requiring considerable practical experience in addition to formal training. As has been emphasised throughout this book, operating conditions vary considerably from place to place, and there are many potential solutions to the various problems. Identifying the most appropriate strategy for a given situation requires practical knowledge and experience of the alternatives; there have been numerous cases where totally inappropriate solutions have been imposed, with disastrous consequences.

An important indirect benefit of foreign technical assistance is the transfer of skills and knowledge to the recipient country, so that over time the need for external assistance will be substantially reduced, if not eliminated entirely. Similarly, financial assistance should be temporary: projects should be self-financing and sustainable so that the benefits enable any loans to be repaid, and cover the subsequent maintenance and management costs where applicable. In practice, unfortunately, this does not always happen, and some countries are heavily dependent on continuing technical assistance and financial aid, with little motivation to become self-sufficient, either financially or in terms of human resources. On the other hand, some developing countries have developed high levels of expertise which they are able to offer to assist other countries.

THE ROLE OF GOVERNMENT

Certain functions can be carried out satisfactorily only by central or local government; even where the provision of public transport is left entirely to the private sector, the government has an important role to play, if only to ensure through appropriate policy measures that the operating environment is conducive to the development of a suitable transport industry. A fundamental requirement is full government commitment to the success of the transport system even if this requires difficult political decisions.

The types of solution which may be applied to the transport problems of a country will depend to a large extent on government policy, both in overall terms and with specific regard to transport. Transport policy objectives vary according to the type of government, and transport policies have often been influenced by political motives rather than by what is best in order to achieve the optimum transport system. Socialist governments tend to favour greater government intervention in both the regulation and operation of transport services, and rationalisation, co-ordination or integration often feature prominently in their policy statements; in the broader context they tend to emphasise the need to protect the rights of employees, and may encourage trade union participation in both government and industry affairs. Capitalist governments, on the other hand, tend to favour a laissez-faire approach, with minimal regulation and maximum private sector participation. Some governments attach great importance to the democratic right to freedom of choice, and actively encourage and protect competition in the market place in order to secure this right. Individual politicians may have different personal views as to the objectives of transport policy: for example some may favour public transport while others may wish to encourage private transport. Policy may also be influenced by aid donors, who often have their own agendas which are not necessarily in the best interests of the recipient country.

In general terms, regardless of political differences, government transport policy should recognise the role of transport in contributing to economic growth and national prosperity, and should be aimed at achieving the optimum balance between cost and quality of service, efficiency and safety, in the context of the resources available. It should define clearly the respective roles of the public and private sectors in the provision and funding of services, and indicate expenditure priorities for both public and private sectors, as well as for donor funds. The principal public transport policy objectives should include minimising travel requirements; maximising personal mobility, in particular for the majority who are dependent on public transport; optimising allocation and use of financial, physical and human resources; minimising the adverse effects of transport on public health and the environment, with particular attention to traffic congestion and pollution; maximising safety standards within the relevant constraints; and sustainability in every sense. An appropriate regulatory framework is particularly essential, but its nature will depend on government policy generally. Whatever the ingredients of the transport policy, however, it is essential that it can be implemented within the resources available.

An essential government role is to set appropriate laws, rules, regulations and fiscal arrangements and to ensure their effective and consistent enforcement. Regulations must motivate transport operators to provide a suitable network of routes, with a reasonable quality of service, without being unduly restrictive. Enforcement of regulations is of vital importance; this is an area of considerable weakness in many developing countries and its importance cannot be overemphasised. The effectiveness of enforcement measures will have a substantial influence on the nature and quality of the transport system, as well as on many other aspects of daily life; the design of the transport system must take this into account.

Other optional functions which government might perform in order to facilitate the development of a good transport system include the provision, directly or indirectly, of services for which small operators may not have the necessary resources, such as training. There must be institutional capacity and capability to manage the transport system; if the operators are lacking in this respect the government must assist in making good the deficiency. A large transport operator should be capable of planning its own route network, but where the transport industry consists of very small operating units there will be little or no planning capability within the industry itself. In these circumstances planning becomes a central, or more usually, a local government role. It is essential, however, that planning is properly carried out, and poor planning may be worse than no planning at all.

Provision and maintenance of infrastructure is another area in which Government must play an active role; even if it does not directly control or finance the provision of infrastructure, it should oversee private sector investment in this area to ensure that no inappropriate investment is made which may hinder the provision of efficient public transport services. As well as infrastructure for all transport modes, principally roads, governments may provide bus or rail station facilities at suitable locations, and possibly depots and workshops for use by public transport operators, who may be charged for their use. They may also instigate measures to facilitate public transport, such as traffic management and bus priority schemes, where these are necessary.

Governments can also influence the behaviour of transport operators and the nature of the public transport system through fiscal measures. A policy of high taxation will make possible substantial government investment in infrastructure, and a subsidised public transport system may be an option. On the other hand, with a policy of low taxation, the scope for public expenditure will be limited; there may be little investment in infrastructure unless the private sector is permitted to take on this responsibility, while the provision of subsidies will be unlikely. In reality, low income levels, and in many instances widespread tax evasion, invariably rule out high levels of taxation in developing countries. Fiscal measures must be rational in order to avoid the danger of inefficient allocation of resources: for example some governments impose higher rates of duty on imported spares than on new vehicles, to the extent that this discourages maintenance and encourages premature and therefore wasteful vehicle replacement. Taxation of transport should be seen not as a means of raising general revenue, but should be designed to promote the development of the most appropriate modes; however, as with other forms of regulation, the system must be enforceable, with minimal opportunities for evasion.

Fuel tax is possibly the easiest tax to administer and enforce, but does not differentiate between public and private transport; fuel tax rebates for public transport operators have been used in some countries to give public transport an advantage over private car users, but these can be difficult to administer and liable to abuse. An alternative to a fuel tax rebate which would be relatively simple to administer is to plough back a proportion of fuel tax revenue into subsidised facilities for public transport, such as terminals, workshop infrastructure, shelters, pedestrian bridges or footpath improvements. Varying the licence fees or road tax rates for public transport vehicles can influence operators' choice of vehicles: for example larger vehicles could be given a tax advantage if this type of vehicle is to be encouraged. Reduced rates of duty on imported buses and spares may be beneficial, but many components used in bus manufacture are also used for other commercial vehicles and even private cars, and this fact must be taken into account. Where foreign exchange is scarce, and controlled by government, it will often be advantageous to give priority in the allocation of foreign currency for purchase of vehicles and spares for public transport, which requires less currency input per passenger than private transport.

If it is necessary to restructure the transport industry in order to improve the services provided, government will almost certainly have to play an active part, particularly when leaving the process to natural forces would take too long. Where all organisations involved are in the private sector, legislation is likely to be necessary, and probably government assistance in implementation. Implementation of plans for improved public transport systems can be difficult, and in many cases recommendations by expert advisers have been ignored or inappropriate solutions have been adopted. The reasons are often political, with governments not wishing to be seen to make unpopular decisions. Implementation may involve large-scale redundancy which may be politically undesirable; for example, there have been cases where governments have refused to make any employees redundant, resulting eventually in the total failure, and the loss of employment for the entire work force, of organisations which could otherwise have been saved. Influential groups such as car users, even though they may be in the minority, often put pressure on governments to block measures which may be to their disadvantage; for example the recent introduction of congestion charging in central London, while actively promoted by local government, was opposed by central government fearing strong reaction from the powerful motoring lobby.

The roles of central and local government institutions are vital and it is therefore essential that they should function effectively, and be provided with the necessary resources, in particular adequate numbers of suitably qualified personnel. The number of government departments and organisations dealing with transport should be as few as possible, although there should normally be at least one body at local level in addition to those at central government level. Conflict between them must be avoided through clear definition of responsibilities. The agency at national level would normally be part of the ministry responsible for transport, of which there should normally be only one, and should be responsible mainly for policy and legislation. It might also provide assistance as appropriate to local agencies. Local responsibilities, under the municipal or equivalent authority, should include planning and implementation of local traffic management schemes, enforcement of local traffic regulations and parking controls, usually carried out in liaison with the traffic police. Local authorities may also be responsible for regulation of buses and taxis, and possibly the planning of bus routes. It is usually appropriate for local authorities, with accountability to local taxpayers, rather than central government to have responsibility for road maintenance and the provision of public transport infrastructure, especially if this is wholly or partly funded from local taxes.

CONCLUSION

Public transport services in most developing countries are inadequate and unsatisfactory, hindering development and detracting from the quality of life. In many cases the situation is deteriorating. However, most of the problems can be resolved. The main requirement is full government commitment to making the necessary institutional, legislative and regulatory changes, and to effective enforcement of regulations. Some of the measures required may be politically challenging, but the potential benefits are considerable.

GLOSSARY OF TERMS

The terminology of the passenger transport industry can be confusing: some terms may have different meanings when used by different organisations, while several different terms may have the same meaning; there are also differences in terminology between one English-speaking country and another. The following glossary gives the definitions used in this book, together with (in parenthesis) some commonly used alternatives.

Availability The proportion of a vehicle fleet which is available to be used in service at a particular time.

Breakdown Immobilisation of a vehicle by a mechanical defect. See also *Involuntary stop.*

Bunching Buses on the same route catching up with one another so that several run together, followed by a long interval before the next bus.

Bus A road vehicle carrying passengers at separate fares, usually on a fixed route. See also *Minibus, Midibus and Coach.*

Bus duty See *Duty.*

Bus lane A traffic lane on a public highway, reserved for the exclusive use of buses.

Bus route The roads followed by a bus between the starting and finishing points of its journey. The term is also used to refer to the bus service provided between two points, by a particular route.

Bus service See *Service.*

Bus station See *Station.*

Bus stop A designated point at which buses may stop to pick up and set down passengers.

Bus stop lay-by A lay-by at a bus stop for the exclusive use of buses using the stop.

Bus terminal See *Terminal.*

Busway A track, alongside or separate from the public highway, reserved for the exclusive use of buses.

Cannibalisation The removal of parts from one vehicle to be fitted to another.

Clockface timetable A timetable in which regular journeys depart at the same minutes past every hour.

Coach A bus which is usually built to a more luxurious specification, for use on long-distance or premium-quality services. Sometimes referred to simply as a "bus". Alternatively, a rail vehicle, which may be coupled to others to form a train.

Concessionary fare A reduced fare applicable to specified eligible passengers such as schoolchildren or pensioners.

CNG Compressed natural gas.

Conductor A person employed to travel on a bus, in addition to the driver, primarily to collect fares from passengers.

Crew Bus driver and conductor.

Crew duty See *Duty.*

Cross-subsidy Subsidising an unprofitable activity from the surplus generated by a profitable activity.

Dead mileage or dead kilometres Mileage or kilometres operated by a bus which is not in revenue-earning service, most commonly between the depot and the point at which the bus takes up its route.

Demand-responsive transport A public transport service operated in accordance with the requirements of the users; typically using small buses on a basic route, from which deviations are made to demand.

Depot A transport operating base, where vehicles are garaged and maintained (in North America this term is often used to refer to a bus station or terminal).

Despatch Control of departures of vehicles from a depot, station or terminal.

Despatcher A person responsible for despatching vehicles from a depot, station or terminal.

Destination The point at which a journey or trip ends.

Downtime Time when a bus is not available for service due to maintenance or repair.

Duplicate bus A bus operated to the same schedule as another, to provide additional capacity when this is required.

Duty The scheduled work carried out by a bus or crew during the course of a day; in some long-distance operations a duty may cover more than one day. Crew duties are sometimes referred to as "shifts" or "turns".

Duty roster See *Roster*

Dwell time Actual time spent by a vehicle at a stop or station, in picking up and setting down passengers.

Early shift A crew duty starting in the early morning and finishing around mid-day.

Express service A service on which all buses operate without stopping, or with few stops, between terminal points.

Fare The charge for a journey made by a passenger.

Fare revenue Revenue obtained from passengers in the form of fares.

Fare stage In a graduated fare system, each route is divided into sections, or stages, which determine the fare for any journey. In practice, the point at which one fare stage ends and the next begins is normally referred to as the "fare stage".

Feeder route A route from which all passengers transfer to another route at a specified connection point.

Flagfall charge The element of a taxi fare payable by a passenger immediately on entering the taxi.

Flat fare A system in which the same fare is charged for any journey, irrespective of journey length.

Fleet number A unique identification number allocated to a vehicle by its owner.

Freeway A highway designed for fast-moving traffic, with limited access and usually with grade-separated junctions; slow-moving and non-motorised traffic and pedestrians are normally excluded, and parking on the carriageway is prohibited. (Sometimes referred to as a "motorway".)

Frequency The interval in minutes or hours between vehicles operating on a route in one direction, sometimes expressed as the number of vehicles per hour. See also *Headway.*

Garage A facility where vehicles may be parked or stored, usually under cover. The term "bus garage" usually refers to a bus depot which is under cover.

GPS Geographic positioning system, using satellite tracking to indicate the exact location of a vehicle at any time.

Graduated fares A system in which the fare charged varies according to the length of the journey taken.

Headway The interval in minutes or hours between vehicles operating on the same route. See also *Frequency.*

Heavy rail A rail transport system employing rolling stock constructed to maximum weight and dimensions.

Individual public transport Public transport modes used by individuals or small groups of passengers travelling together, who select the destination and pay one collective fare. See also *Taxi.*

Informal passenger transport See *Paratransit.*

Inspector In general, an official responsible for checking compliance with regulations. Specifically, in passenger transport, an official responsible for checking that passengers have paid the correct fares and have been issued with the correct tickets. Sometimes known as "ticket inspectors" or "revenue inspectors".

Interchange A facility where passengers may transfer from one transport service to another; the term is often used specifically to refer to transfer between different modes.

Intermediate passenger transport See *Paratransit.*

Involuntary stop Stoppage of a bus caused by a mechanical breakdown, tyre failure, accident or road conditions.

Journey A single movement of a bus or other vehicle from one end of its route to the other, or to an intermediate point being used as the terminus for that particular journey. Alternatively, a single passenger movement between two points. Also referred to as a "trip".

Late shift A crew duty starting in the afternoon and finishing in the evening.

Lay-by A short section of roadway provided at the side of the main carriageway to enable a vehicle to stop out of the traffic stream.

Layover Non-driving time spent by a bus or train crew at the terminus between journeys.

Light rail A rail transport system employing rolling stock constructed to less than maximum weight and dimensions.

Light rail transit A public transport system based on light rail.

Limited-stop service A service which is scheduled not to stop at all stops on a route, and which normally operates to a reduced running time.

Livery The colour scheme and insignia applied to a vehicle.

LPG Liquefied petroleum gas.

Maintenance The process of keeping a vehicle in working condition.

Mass public transport A public transport mode which is available to multiple passengers travelling independently of one another.

Metro A self-contained urban rail passenger system, typically to light rail specification, often underground or elevated.

Minibus A small bus, typically with seats for 8-20 passengers. There is normally no accommodation for standing passengers. (Larger buses, with up to 35 seats in some cases, are sometimes described as minibuses).

Midibus A medium-sized bus, usually with seats for 20-35 passengers. There may be accommodation for some standing passengers.

Motorway see *Freeway*.

Nearside The side of a vehicle nearest to the kerb, i.e. the left hand side of the vehicle where traffic drives on the left side of the road, and the right hand side of the vehicle where traffic drives on the right side of the road. See also *Offside*.

Network see *Route network*.

Non-issue of tickets Failure by a conductor to issue a ticket to a passenger after collecting the fare, with the intention of defrauding the operator.

Offside The side of a vehicle farthest from the kerb, i.e. the right hand side of the vehicle where traffic drives on the left side of the road, and the left hand side of the vehicle where traffic drives on the right side of the road. See also *Nearside*.

Omnibus Bus (a somewhat old-fashioned term which is no longer normally used).

OMO One-man operation: see *OPO*.

Operating unit An identifiable group of vehicles, which may also include related equipment and infrastructure, under common control but not necessarily common ownership, organised to provide a transport service on a particular route, group of routes, or in a particular area.

Operator An individual or organisation providing a transport service. (The driver of a bus or train is sometimes referred to as the operator.)

OPO One-person operation, i.e. the operation of a bus, tram or train by the driver only. A bus or tram driver may be responsible for collecting fares from passengers, but in some systems passengers must pay their fares before boarding the vehicle, or purchase tickets from automatic machines on the vehicle.

Overhaul Major maintenance work carried out on a vehicle, or on a unit such as an engine or gearbox, normally involving the removal and replacement of a large number of parts.

Over-riding Travelling, by a passenger, farther than the distance paid for.

Paratransit Public transport operated in an informal and largely disorganised manner, typically using small vehicles, owned by individuals. (Also known as "informal" or "intermediate passenger transport".)

Peak period The time during which passenger demand is at its greatest. There are normally two peak periods in a day, i.e. in the morning when people are travelling from home to work or school, and in the evening when they return to their homes. There may also be seasonal peaks, for example at holiday times when large numbers of people travel.

Peak vehicle requirement The maximum number of vehicles required to operate a transport service at peak periods.

Peri-urban Transport movements between urban centres and points outside the city boundary, but within normal commuting distance, typically up to 50 kilometres from the centre.

Personalised mass transit A vehicle used by several individuals, travelling independently, travelling between the same two points, or along the same route; the vehicle will deviate from the direct route to meet the requirements of individual passengers. See also *Demand-responsive transport* and *Shared taxis*.

Premium service A high-quality public transport service, catering for passengers who can afford higher fares and competing with modes such as taxis and even private transport.

Preventive maintenance Maintenance of vehicles to minimise the occurrence of mechanical failure, rather than only rectifying defects as they occur.

Programmed maintenance A maintenance programme based on preventive maintenance principles and including planned maintenance activities such as periodic repainting, chassis and body overhaul.

Public service vehicle A vehicle licensed to carry passengers for hire or reward. (The term is normally used to refer to buses only but in some countries includes taxis.)

Rail service See *Service.*

Rapid transit A means of mass transport offering a faster service than the alternatives, typically with average operating speeds of 50 kph or more, often on exclusive right of way. It may employ buses or light rail.

Rebodying Replacing a bus body with an entirely new body.

Recovery time Additional layover time allowed to enable departure from a terminal to be made on time following late arrival from the previous trip.

Reissue of tickets Issue to a passenger of a ticket which has already been used with the intention of defrauding the operator.

Road staff Drivers, Conductors and Inspectors.

Roster A list showing the allocation of crews to duties.

Rota The cycle of duties to be worked by crews over a period, typically several weeks.

Round trip time The total time taken by a bus or train to complete a return journey on a route: the sum of the running times for the outward and return journeys, and the layover times at both ends of the route.

Route See *Bus route.*

Route network An aggregation of transport routes serving a particular area, with individual routes complementary to one another so that travellers may use one or more routes during the course of their journeys.

Route number An identification number given to a bus or tram route. (Sometimes referred to as "service number").

Route taxi See *Shared taxi*

Running number An identification number given to a bus duty.

Running time The time taken by a bus to travel from one point on a route to another; normally, if no points are specified, used to refer to the time taken for the whole route.

Run-out The departure of buses from the depot at the start of the operating day.

Service number See *Route Number.*

Setoran A useful Indonesian term, which has been adopted in this book, for the widespread practice by owners of hiring out vehicles to drivers for a fixed charge, typically by the day but sometimes for longer periods. Drivers are responsible for meeting all vehicle running costs, including payment to conductors where these are carried, and retain all fare revenue collected after these expenses, and the setoran charge, have been met, in lieu of a salary.

Schedule The times at which a journey or set of journeys is operated, or a working timetable giving details of bus or crew duties. See also *Timetables.*

Service The aggregation of bus or train movements on a route or in a particular area. ("Service" is sometimes used synonymously with "route", and sometimes, more commonly in rail systems, it refers to a particular timetabled journey.)

Shared taxi A taxi, usually operated on a fixed route, used simultaneously by several people travelling independently; and paying separate fares; deviations are sometimes made from the direct route to meet the requirements of individual passengers. Also known as "route taxis". See also *Demand-responsive transport.*

Shift See *Duty.*

Short working A journey which is scheduled to turn short before reaching the terminus of the route.

Spreadover A crew duty in two parts separated by a break of several hours, to cover both peak periods. (Sometimes termed "split" or "broken shift")

Stage service or **stage carriage service** A regular bus service, stopping frequently to pick up and set down passengers. See also *Express service.*

Station A stopping place on a railway line or bus route, usually with buildings housing facilities for passengers. A bus station is located off the public highway.

Taxi A small motor vehicle used for individual public transport. (The term is sometimes used, particularly in several African countries, to include minibuses as well as conventional taxis.)

Terminal A station at the end of a route. (The term "bus terminal" is often used synonymously with "bus station".)

Terminus The point at the end of a route. This may be at a terminal or station but may be at a roadside point where there are no facilities of any kind.

Timetable The times at which all journeys on a route are operated, or the document showing these times. See also *Schedule.*

Timing point A point on a route for which the times are stipulated when vehicles should arrive, depart, or both.

Tram A large passenger carrying vehicle running on rails, usually along the public highway which it shares with other traffic, but sometimes on dedicated track. Usually powered by electricity, collected from overhead cables.

Transport service See *Service.*

Trip See *Journey.*

Trolleybus A bus powered by electricity, collecting current from overhead cables.

Truck-bus A freight vehicle, with basic modification to carry passengers as well as freight, typically with longitudinal bench seats at each side, and a canopy. Used for rural transport in some developing countries.

Turn See *Duty.*

Undervalued ticket A ticket issued for a value less than that paid by the passenger, with the intention of defrauding the operator.

Utilisation The extent to which available vehicles are used in service.

Waybill The document on which the conductor records details of tickets issued.

Zonal fare structure A system in which an area is divided into zones, usually approximately concentric; the fares charged vary according to the number of zones traversed during the course of a journey.

BIBLIOGRAPHY

Armstrong-Wright, A. (1986). *Urban Transit Systems - Guidelines for Examining Options.* World Bank Technical Paper no 52, Washington.

Armstrong-Wright, A. et al. (1986). *Urban Transport - A World Bank Policy Study.* World Bank, Washington.

Armstrong-Wright, A. and S Thiriez (1987). *Bus Services - Reducing Costs, Raising Standards.* World Bank Technical Paper no 68, Washington.

Barrett, R. (1988). *Urban Transport in West Africa.* World Bank Technical Paper no 81, Washington.

Birks, J.A., Y. Brittan, K.A.S. Dickie and T. Beetham (1990). *National Bus Company 1968-1989.* Transport Publishing Co., Glossop.

Blakey, G. (Ed.) (1995). *New World Transport 95.* Sterling, London.

Bonavia, M.R. (1963). *The Economics of Transport.* Cambridge University Press, Cambridge.

Carbajo, Jose (Ed.) (1993). *Regulatory Reform in Transport: Some Recent Experiences.* World Bank, Washington.

Cole, S. (1987). *Applied Transport Economics.* Kogan Page, London.

Department of Environment, Transport and Regions (1997). *Keeping Buses Moving: a Guide to Traffic Management to Assist Buses in Urban Areas.* HMSO, London.

Department of Transport (1984). *Buses White Paper.* HMSO, London.

Faulks, R.W. (1969). *Elements of Transport.* Ian Allan. London.

Fawcett, P. (1989). *Get Coached to Competence.* Croner, London.

Fawcett, P. (1989). *Minibus Services.* Croner, London.

Gubbins, E.J. (1996). *Managing Transport Operations* Kogan Page, London.

Heraty, M.J. (Ed.) (1987). *Developing World Land Transport.* Grosvenor Press International, Hong Kong.

Heraty, M.J. (Ed.) (1989). *Developing World Transport.* Grosvenor Press International, Hong Kong.

Heraty, M.J. (Ed.) (1991). *Urban Transport in Developing Countries.* PTRC, London.

Hibbs, J. (1963). *Transport for Passengers.* Institute of Economic Affairs, London.

Huntley, P.G. (1989). *Tendering and Local Bus Operation.* Croner, London.

Lambden, W.T. (1969). *Bus and Coach Operation.* Iliffe, London.

Munby, D.L. (Ed.) (1968). *Transport.* Penguin, London.

Pattison, T. (Ed.) (2002). *Jane's Urban Transport Systems.* Jane's Information Group, London.

Ponsonby, G.J. (1969). *Transport Policy: Coordination through Competition.* Institute of Economic Affairs, London.

Rallis, T. (1988). *City Transport in Developed and Developing Countries.* MacMillan, London.

TAS Partnership Ltd. (1997). *Quality Partnerships in the Bus Industry: A Survey and Review.* TAS Partnership, Preston.

Thornthwaite, S. (1994). *School Transport: the Comprehensive Guide.* TAS Partnership, Preston.

Walters, A.A. (1979). *Cost and Scale of Bus Services.* World Bank Staff Working Paper no 325, Washington.

White, P.R. (2002). *Public Transport - Its Planning, Management and Operation.* Spon Press, London.

Whitelegg, J. and G. Haq (Ed.) (2003). *World Transport Policy and Practice.* Earthscan, London 2003.

INDEX